EUROPEAN COMMUNITY LAW

TEXT, CASES & MATERIALS

John Tillotson BA(Nottm) LLM(Exeter)
Lecturer and Course Director for EC Law
University of Manchester

Cavendish
Publishing
Limited

First published in Great Britain 1993 by Cavendish Publishing Limited,
The Glass House, Wharton Street, London WC1X 9PX.
Telephone: 071-278 8000 Facsimile: 071-278 8080

British Library Cataloguing in Publication Data

Tillotson, John
European Community Law
Text, Cases & Materials
I Title
341.2422

ISBN 1-874241-14-7

Printed and bound in Great Britain

PREFACE

The basic purpose of this book is to provide students with a clear guide to the main constitutional, institutional and substantive features of European Community law. The importance of this subject is undeniable; it will soon become a compulsory, foundation subject for undergraduate students on full-time qualifying law degrees. It is a subject of a diverse and dynamic character embracing political, economic and social issues and aspirations of which we all - as individuals and lawyers - are a part.

In this country we have played and continue to play a part in the development of Community law which, in turn, continues to flow back, permeate and change not only the operation of our political and legal institutions but also the way we engage in business and other affairs as, amongst other things, employers, employees and consumers.

No book, no course, in European Community law could hope or wish to cover all aspects of this wide-ranging and rapidly evolving subject. The treatment is therefore selective, whilst falling within the guidelines outlined by the Law Society and the Council for Legal Education in July 1993.

The book falls into four overlapping parts: (1) The European Community and Community Law, (2) The Nature and Effect of Community Law, (3) Aspects of Community Economic and Social Law, and (4) Remedies and the Enforcement of Community Law. Efforts have been made throughout to set the law in its political, economic and social context, particularly by the use of appropriate materials from a wide variety of sources including the writings of specialist academic and other commentators.

The main provisions of the EEC Treaty, which form the basis of the case law to date, are reproduced and major decisions of the Court of Justice are dealt with in some depth. It has been assumed that the Maastricht Treaty on European Union will shortly come into force, and the main changes it brings, as it converts the EEC Treaty into the EC Treaty, have been brought to the reader's attention - similarly the programme for the completion of the Internal Market and the increasingly important question of Community rights for individuals.

At the end of each chapter is a list of references and further reading and at the end of the book can be found an appendix on 'How to Find Community Law'.

My thanks go to Jo Steiner for the many discussions we have had on a variety of issues, and to the following who have kindly agreed to allow the use of materials in this book: the Court of Justice of the European Communities, the Office for Official Publications of the European Communities, Times Newspapers Ltd., Guardian Newspapers Ltd., Lord Mackenzie Stuart and Mr. Gavin Smith.

John Tillotson

CONTENTS

PART ONE:
THE EUROPEAN COMMUNITY AND COMMUNITY LAW

CONTENTS

PART TWO: THE NATURE AND EFECT OF COMMUNITY LAW

CONTENTS

PART THREE: ASPECTS OF COMMUNITY ECONOMIC AND SOCIAL LAW

CONTENTS

CONTENTS

TABLE OF CASES (Chronological)

EUROPEAN COURT OF JUSTICE

TABLE OF CASES (Chronological)

TABLE OF CASES (Chronological)

TABLE OF CASES (Chronological)

TABLE OF CASES (Chronological)

TABLE OF CASES (Chronological)

TABLE OF CASES (Chronological)

TABLE OF CASES (Chronological)

TABLE OF CASES (Chronological)

EUROPEAN COURT OF FIRST INSTANCE

TABLE OF CASES (Alphabetical)

EUROPEAN COURT OF JUSTICE

TABLE OF CASES (Alphabetical)

TABLE OF CASES (Alphabetical)

TABLE OF CASES (Alphabetical)

TABLE OF CASES (Alphabetical)

TABLE OF CASES (Alphabetical)

TABLE OF CASES (Alphabetical)

TABLE OF CASES (Alphabetical)

TABLE OF CASES (Alphabetical)

TABLE OF CASES (Alphabetical)

TABLE OF CASES (Alphabetical)

EUROPEAN COURT OF FIRST INSTANCE

NATIONAL COURTS

NATIONAL COURTS

UNITED STATES COURTS

EC COMMISSION DECISIONS

TREATIES AND CONVENTIONS

UK LEGISLATION

ABBREVIATIONS

AC	Appeal Cases
ACP States	African, Caribbean and Pacific States
AG	Advocate General
All ER	*All England Law Reports*
BYIL	*British Yearbook of International Law*
CA	Court of Appeal
CAP	Common Agricultural Policy
CFI	Court of First Instance
Ch	Chancery
CLP	*Current Legal Problems*
CMLR	*Common Market Law Reports*
CML Rev.	*Common Market Law Review*
COREPER	Committee of Permanent Representatives
DC	Divisional Court
DG	Directorate General
EAT	Employment Appeal Tribunal
EC	Economic Community
ECB	European Central Bank
ECJ	European Court of Justice
ECLR	*European Competition Law Review*
ECR	*European Court Reports*
ECSC	European Coal and Steel Community
ECU	European Currency Unit (formerly unit of account)
EEA	European Economic Area
EEC	European Economic Community
EFTA	European Free Trade Association
EIPR	*European Intellectual Property Review*
EL Rev.	*European Law Review*
EMS	European Monetary System
EMU	Economic and Monetary Union
EPC	European Political Co-operation
ERM	Exchange Rate Mechanism
ESCB	European System of Central Banks
EURATOM	European Atomic Energy Community
GATT	General Agreement on Tariffs and Trade
HL	House of Lords
ICLQ	*International and Comparative Law Quarterly*
ICR	*Industrial Court Reports*
ILJ	*Industrial Law Journal*
ILO	International Labour Organisation
IRLR	*Industrial Relations Law Reports*
JALT	*Journal of the Association of Law Teachers (The Law Teacher)*
JBL	*Journal of Business Law*
JCMS	*Journal of Common Market Studies*
JLS	*Journal of Law and Society*
LIEI	*Legal Issues of European Integration*
LQR	*Law Quarterly Review*
MEP	Member of the European Parliament
MLR	*Modern Law Review*
NLJ	*New Law Journal*

ABBREVIATIONS

OEEC	Organisation for European Economic Cooperation
OJ	*Official Journal*
OxJLS	*Oxford Journal of Legal Studies*
PL	*Public Law*
QBD	Queens Bench Division
SAD	Single Administrative Document
SEA	Single European Act
TEU	Treaty on European Union
YEL	*Yearbook of European Law*

PART ONE

THE EUROPEAN COMMUNITY

AND

COMMUNITY LAW

CHAPTER ONE

THE EMERGENCE AND DEVELOPMENT OF THE EUROPEAN COMMUNITY

INTRODUCTION

In March 1957 six sovereign Western European states signed a legal document binding themselves to the creation of an economic community. The signing in Rome of the Treaty Establishing the European Economic Community by its six original Member States (France, West Germany, Italy, Belgium, the Netherlands and Luxembourg) was an act which represents a unique and practical conjunction of the political, the legal and economic. The aims of 'the Six' in coming together in this way are outlined in the Preamble to the Treaty:

Determined to lay the foundations of an ever closer union among the peoples of Europe,

Resolved to ensure the economic and social progress of their countries by common action to eliminate the barriers which divide Europe,

Affirming as the essential objective of their efforts the constant improvement of the living and working conditions of their peoples,

Recognising that the removal of existing obstacles calls for concerned action in order to guarantee steady expansion, balanced trade and fair competition,

Anxious to strengthen the unity of their economies and to ensure their harmonious development by reducing the differences existing between the various regions and the backwardness of the less favoured regions,

Desiring to contribute, by means of a common commercial policy, to the progressive abolition of restrictions on international trade,

Intending to confirm the solidarity which binds Europe and the overseas countries and desiring to ensure the development of their prosperity, in accordance with the principles of the Charter of the United Nations,

Resolved by thus pooling their resources to preserve and strengthen peace and liberty, and calling upon the other peoples of Europe who share their ideal to join in their efforts,

Have decided to create a European Economic Community...

The main, most clearly defined objective in this preliminary statement is that of the maintenance of 'economic and social progress'. Such progress is to be achieved by 'common action to eliminate the barriers which divide

Europe'. This process of economic integration must however be seen in the context of the first stated aim: 'an ever closer union among the peoples of Europe'. As such, it can be argued that the drafters of the Treaty of Rome can be taken as envisaging, at some future date, a Community in which economic solidarity has merged with political solidarity.

It is clear from the Preamble that the Community is open to new members (there are now twelve, and more countries waiting to join) and that it takes its place within the world economic (and political) order as an upholder of peace, liberty and a free market economy.

The Treaty of Rome therefore indicates that European integration has many dimensions. To be understood properly, it should be appreciated that it may, or must, be viewed from a variety of perspectives: the global, the supranational, the Member State and last, but certainly not least, from the viewpoint of the individual.

The EEC Treaty, although of tremendous significance, is but one of several treaties relating to the process of European integration. At the present time (August 1993), the existing European Community Treaties are on the verge of being incorporated into the new overall framework of the Treaty on European Union (TEU). This Treaty was agreed in Maastricht in the Netherlands in December 1991 and signed by the twelve Member States in February 1992. After some difficulty, particularly in Denmark and the UK, eleven Member States have now ratified the Treaty and Germany is expected to ratify shortly. [In effect 1 November 1993.]

In any event it is clear that the Treaties (and the new Treaty) are not to be regarded merely as international agreements but, in the words of the European Court of Justice, as 'the constitutional charter of a Community based on the rule of law'.

DEVELOPMENTS: 1945 TO THE PRESENT DAY

As already indicated, no study of European Community law[1] can be pursued in an effective manner without taking account of the political, social and economic forces with which it is inextricably intertwined. This is the case whether one is dealing with the relationship between the EC and the Member States, with trade regulation within a Single European Market, with environmental issues, or with questions of equal pay or pension rights.

---

[1] It is accepted practice to speak of the European Community although there are three Communities: the European Economic Community (EEC), the European Coal and Steel Community (ECSC), the European Atomic Energy Community (Euratom). We will concentrate almost entirely on the EEC, but see also below on the Maastricht Treaty.

Any account of the establishment and continuing development of the EC must be approached along the same interrelated lines. The history of European integration, as one might expect with such an immense undertaking, is one of considerable complexity and neither the theory nor the practice is free from controversy. This opening chapter merely serves to draw attention to the more significant milestones and signposts along the way:

> The European Economic Community is an outgrowth of the European movement, a complex composite of political, social and economic forces which have come to the fore in strength since World War II. By the end of the war, national government structures in Continental Europe were weakened to the point of collapse. Europe, devastated and enfeebled by war and the loss of colonies, faced the two emergent giants, the United States and the Soviet Union. Its division by trade barriers underlined its weakness. Determined to build on pre-war ideas of a united Europe, on the feeling of the people that there must be no more internecine European wars, and on a variety of special national interests favouring such a movement, a small group of individuals pressed for new institutions to advance unification of Europe. The process of institution-building was marked from the beginning by a pervasive ambiguity. Should new institutions be built so as to preserve the nation state with all its trappings of national loyalties and rivalries, or should there be new transnational institutions which would dilute or supersede the nation state and provide a constitutional foundation for a unified Europe? Today the ambiguity is still with us: Stein, Hay and Waelbroeck, *European Community Law in Perspective*, 1976.

At the present time, that 'pervasive ambiguity' remains, not least in the shape of a recent British Prime Minister. In 1946 another Conservative leader, Winston Churchill, in his famous 'United States of Europe' speech in Zurich, spoke of a unified and democratic 'greater Europe'. However, according to his Private Secretary:

> He never for one moment during or after the war contemplated Britain submerging her sovereignty in that of a United States of Europe or losing her national identity ... In January 1941, at Ditchley, he went so far as to say that there must be a United States of Europe and that it should be built by the English: if the Russians built it there would be communism and squalor; if the Germans built it there would be tyranny and brute force. On the other hand, I knew he felt that while Britain might be the builder and Britain might live in the house, she would always preserve her liberty of choice and would be the natural, undisputed link with the Americans and the Commonwealth: John Colville, *The Fringes of Power*, 1985.

In 1947 in order to assist in the reconstruction of post-war Europe amid fears of Soviet expansion westwards in Europe beyond what became known as the Iron Curtain, the then US Secretary of State, George Marshall, initiated a 13 billion dollar *Economic Recovery Programme*. However, in the words of a State Department memorandum of the time, it was imperative that the recovery of Europe be tied to:

> ... a European plan which the principal European nations ... should work out. Such a plan should be based on a European economic federation on the order of the Belgian–Netherlands-Luxembourg Customs Union. Europe cannot recover from this war and again become independent if her economy continues to be divided into many small watertight compartments as it is today.

The result was the establishment in 1948 of the inter-governmental *Organisation for European Economic Co-operation* (OEEC) consisting of eighteen European (but not Eastern bloc) countries. In the required spirit of 'continuous and effective self-help and mutual aid', the OEEC worked with considerable success in the field of trade liberalisation through the gradual removal of quota restrictions, and, through its European Payments Union, it provided a clearing mechanism for multilateral settlement of trading accounts. However, by 1949 speedier progress towards 'an integration of the Western European economy' was being urged at an OEEC meeting:

> The substance of such integration would be the formation of a single large market within which quantitative restrictions on the movement of goods, monetary barriers to the flow of payments and, eventually, all tariffs are permanently swept aside.

Within a matter of months, these aspirations began to take practical shape. The Schuman Declaration of 9 May 1950 was based on a plan devised by another Frenchman, Jean Monnet. In part it read:

> Europe will not be made all at once, or according to a single plan. It will be built through concrete achievements which first create a de facto solidarity. The coming together of the nations of Europe requires the elimination of the age-old opposition of France and Germany. Any action taken must in the first place concern these two countries.
>
> With this aim in view, the French Government proposes to take action immediately on one limited but decisive point. It proposes to place Franco-German production of coal and steel as a whole under a

common higher authority, within the framework of an organisation open to the participation of the other countries of Europe.

The pooling of coal and steel production should immediately provide for the setting up of common foundations for economic development as a first step in the federation of Europe, and will change the destinies of those regions which have long been devoted to the manufacture of munitions of war, of which they have been the most constant victims.

The solidarity in production thus established will make it plain that any war between France and Germany becomes not merely unthinkable, but materially impossible. The setting up of this powerful productive unit, open to all countries willing to take part and bound ultimately to provide all the member countries with the basic elements of industrial production on the same terms, will lay a true foundation for their economic unification.

In 1951 the EUROPEAN COAL AND STEEL COMMUNITY was established under the terms of the Treaty of Paris. Six countries subscribed to the principles of the Schuman Plan: France, West Germany, Italy and the three Benelux countries. It is important to appreciate the following points regarding the ECSC:

1   The primary motive underlying this integrative initiative was *political* rather than economic.

2   It was seen merely as a first step in the integrative process – a *sectoral* scheme providing guidelines for a more general form of economic union later.

3   Great weight was attached to the creation of new, European institutions, in particular a *supranational* High Authority, under the executive control of which the coal and steel production of the Member States was placed.

4   The *independence* of the non-elected High Authority was balanced by a Council of Ministers (from the Member States), and a Common Assembly (later, Parliament) with the power to dismiss the High Authority.

5   The Community was firmly set in a *legal* framework with a Court of Justice charged with the duty of ensuring the observance of the law in the interpretation and application of the Treaty.

Represented though they were in the Council of Ministers, the Member States nevertheless relinquished and transferred a large measure of their national sovereignty and control in the coal and steel sectors when they signed the Treaty, in as much as the supranational High Authority possessed the power to take decisions binding on national enterprises without the intervention of the Member States.

This direct linking of the institutional control of the High Authority to economic sectors located in different countries involved jettisoning the traditional inter-governmental approach to international co-operation. The basis of this novel strategy is to be found in what was called the *functionalist* approach to integration: a method which has been described as one 'which would ... overlay political divisions with a spreading web of international activities and agencies, in which and through which the interests and life of all nations would be gradually integrated': David Mitrany, 1933.

The integrative cornerstone of the Coal and Steel Community was a Common Market which combined elements of the concept of free movement of goods and a competitive market system with a minimum of institutional intervention in the market:

ECSC TREATY

Article 1

By this Treaty, the High Contracting Parties establish among themselves a EUROPEAN COAL AND STEEL COMMUNITY, founded upon a Common Market, common objectives and common institutions.

Article 2

The European Coal and Steel Community shall have as its task to contribute, in harmony with the general economy of the Member States and through the establishment of a Common Market as provided in Article 4, to economic expansion, growth of employment and a rising standard of living in the Member States.

The Community shall progressively bring about conditions which will of themselves ensure the most rational distribution of production at the highest possible level of productivity, while safeguarding continuity of employment and taking care not to provoke fundamental and persistent disturbances in the economies of Member States ...

Article 4

The following are recognised as incompatible with the Common Market for coal and steel and shall accordingly be abolished and prohibited within the Community, as provided in this Treaty:

a   import and export duties, or charges having equivalent effect, and quantitative restrictions on the movement of products;

b   measures or practices which discriminate between producers, between purchasers or between consumers, especially in prices and delivery terms or transport rates and conditions, and measures or practices which interfere with the purchaser's free choice of supplier;

c   subsidies or aids granted by states, or special charges imposed by states, in any form whatsoever;

d   restrictive practices which tend towards the sharing or exploiting of markets.

Article 5

The Community shall carry out its task in accordance with this Treaty, with a limited measure of intervention.

To this end the Community shall:

— provide guidance and assistance for the parties concerned, by obtaining information, organising consultations and laying down general objectives;

— place financial resources at the disposal of undertakings for their investment and bear part of the cost of re-adaptation;

— ensure the establishment, maintenance and observance of normal competitive conditions and exert direct influence upon production or upon the market only when circumstances so require;

— publish the reasons for its actions and take the necessary measures to ensure the observance of the rules laid down in this Treaty.

The institutions of the Community shall carry out these activities with a minimum of administrative machinery and in close co-operation with the parties concerned.

Regarding the outcome of this amalgam of free market and *dirigisme,* it has been said that:

The High Authority emerged from the negotiations presiding over a highly imperfect single market in raw materials and manufactures, with powers to interfere in transport, with the capacity to make some decisions of its own about capital investment, and presiding over a common labour market which existed only in theory. Where the economic distortions of the nation state were replaced, it was less by the neutral, anonymous efficiency of the free market, or of an expert technocratic decision-making body, than by a set of complex regulations arising from the careful balancing and adjustment of the interests of the various nation states to allow them to achieve particular national objectives. The future political economy of the Treaty of Rome, the analysis of which by any neo-classical formulations is likely to reduce the analyst only to a state of bewildered despair, had already taken shape.

Yet in many respects this was a big improvement on what had gone before. It not only made a set of economic issues which had been closely intermingled with the causes of war and peace the subject of permanent government regulation but it provided a permanent international governmental organisation, with some public appearance of neutrality, to regulate them: Alan Milward, 1984.

Later in the 1950s, following the failure of attempts to establish a European Defence Community (and European Army containing West German elements) and a European Political Community possessing institutions with supranational authority, it became increasingly evident that economic integration would have to precede political integration. Planning moved away from the idea of progressive integration of the European economy by sectors towards the creation of a wide-ranging economic union. In 1955, the Foreign Ministers of the six members of the ECSC declared their intention to:

... pursue the establishment of a United Europe through the development of common institutions, a progressive fusion of national economies, the creation of a Common Market and harmonisation of social policies.

Over a nine-month period beginning in June 1955, an Inter-governmental Committee presided over by the Belgian Foreign Minister, Paul-Henri Spaak, worked on the preparation of treaties which would lay down the legal basis of such goals. Britain was invited to participate in this planning but her contribution was minimal and short-lived. Her ties with the Commonwealth and the USA, together with a preference for traditional inter-governmental co-operation and a less advanced form of integration based on a free trade area, all militated at this time against joining the 'relance européene'.

The Spaak Report was adopted by the Foreign Ministers of 'the Six' in May 1956 and became the basis for the treaties establishing the EUROPEAN ECONOMIC COMMUNITY (EEC) and the EUROPEAN ATOMIC ENERGY COMMUNITY (EURATOM) signed in Rome in March 1957 (effective 1 January 1958).

The aims and principal features of the report are to be found in Part One: Principles, Articles 1–8 of the EEC Treaty:

EEC TREATY

Article 1

By this Treaty, the High Contracting Parties establish among themselves a EUROPEAN ECONOMIC COMMUNITY.

Article 2

The Community shall have as its task, by establishing a Common Market and progressively approximating the economic policies of Member States, to promote throughout the Community a harmonious development of economic activities, a continuous and balanced expansion, an increase in stability, an accelerated raising of the standard of living and closer relations between the States belonging to it.

Article 3

For the purposes set out in Article 2, the activities of the Community shall include, as provided in this Treaty and in accordance with the timetable set out therein:

a the elimination, as between Member States, of customs duties and of quantitative restrictions on the import and export of goods, and of all other measures having equivalent effect;

b the establishment of a common customs tariff and of a common commercial policy towards third countries;

c the abolition, as between Member States, of obstacles to freedom of movement for persons, services and capital;

d the adoption of a common policy in the sphere of agriculture;

e the adoption of a common policy in the sphere of transport;

f the institution of a system ensuring that competition in the Common Market is not distorted;

g the application of procedures by which the economic policies of Member States can be co-ordinated and disequilibria in their balances of payments remedied;

h the approximation of the laws of Member States to the extent required for the proper functioning of the Common Market;

i the creation of a European Social Fund in order to improve employment opportunities for workers and to contribute to the raising of their standard of living;

j the establishment of a European Investment Bank to facilitate the economic expansion of the Community by opening up fresh resources;

k the association of the overseas countries and territories in order to increase trade and to promote jointly economic and social development.

11

Article 4

1 The tasks entrusted to the Community shall be carried out by the following institutions:

an ASSEMBLY [later, the PARLIAMENT],

a COUNCIL,

a COMMISSION,

a COURT OF JUSTICE,

Each institution shall act within the limits of the powers conferred upon it by this Treaty.

2 The Council and the Commission shall be assisted by an Economic and Social Committee acting in an advisory capacity.

Article 5

Member States shall take all appropriate measures, whether general or particular, to ensure fulfilment of the obligations arising out of this Treaty or resulting from action taken by the institutions of the Community. They shall facilitate the achievement of the Community's tasks.

They shall abstain from any measure which could jeopardise the attainment of the objectives of this Treaty.

Article 6

1 Member States shall, in close co-operation with the institutions of the Community, co-ordinate their respective economic policies to the extent necessary to attain, the objectives of this Treaty.

2 The institutions of the Community shall take care not to prejudice the internal and external financial stability of the Member States.

Article 7

Within the scope of this Treaty, and without prejudice to any special provisions contained therein, any discrimination on grounds of nationality shall be prohibited.

The Council may, on a proposal from the Commission and in co-operation with the European Parliament, adopt, by a qualified majority, rules designed to prohibit such discrimination.

Article 8

1   The Common Market shall be progressively established during a transitional period of twelve years.

This transitional period shall be divided into three stages of four years each; the length of each stage may be altered in accordance with the provisions set out below.

2   To each stage there shall be assigned a set of actions to be initiated and carried out concurrently ...

At the time of the signing of the Rome Treaties, a Convention was concluded which provided for a single Court of Justice and a single Parliamentary Assembly for all three Communities. By 1965 it was also found necessary by means of the so-called Merger Treaty to establish a single Commission of the European Communities (replacing the ECSC High Authority and the EEC and Euratom Commissions) and a single Council.

Even before the entry into force of the EEC Treaty, an attempt (initiated by the UK) was made to create an OEEC free trade area including the EEC as an economic unit. When this was strongly rejected by France as constituting a potential dilution of the integrative process, seven OEEC countries (the UK, Denmark, Norway, Sweden, Austria, Switzerland and Portugal) signed a treaty in Stockholm in 1960 establishing the EUROPEAN FREE TRADE ASSOCIATION to be run on an intergovernmental basis.

Britain's eventual accession to the European Community (together with Ireland and Denmark) on 1 January 1973 came about after two French-inspired rejections of applications made by the Macmillan government in 1961 and the Wilson government in 1967. In the intervening years the UK had come to realise that its economic future lay in Europe. However, then as now, the true extent of her commitment to the progress of economic and political integration in Europe remains somewhat an open question.

Treaty of Accession

Article 1

1   The Kingdom of Denmark, Ireland, the Kingdom of Norway* and the United Kingdom of Great Britain and Northern Ireland hereby become members of the European Economic Community and of the European Atomic Energy Community and Parties to the Treaties establishing these Communities as amended or supplemented.†

---

* (Following a national referendum, Norway did not accede.)

† (The other three new Member States acceded to the ECSC Treaty at the same time.)

2   The conditions of admission and the adjustments to the Treaties establishing the European Economic Community and the European Atomic Energy Community necessitated thereby are set out in the Act annexed to this Treaty. The provisions of that Act concerning the European Economic Community and the European Atomic Energy Community shall form an integral part of this Treaty.

3   The provisions concerning the rights and obligations of the Member States and the powers and jurisdiction of the institutions of the Communities as set out in the Treaties referred to in paragraph 1 shall apply in respect of this Treaty ...

Act of Accession

...

Article 2

From the date of accession, the provisions of the original Treaties and the acts adopted by the institutions of the Communities shall be binding on the new Member States and shall apply in those States under the conditions laid down in those Treaties and in this Act.

Prior to the 1973 enlargement, the Community had in 1965 experienced severe crisis when, mainly in protest against Commission proposals concerning the financing of the Common Agricultural Policy, France withdrew from the Community's decision-making process for a period of six months. This impasse was only broken after the Council of Ministers adopted the so-called 'Luxembourg Accords', which redefined and reduced the Commission's role and extended the unanimity requirement in the Council beyond the Treaty provisions:

The Luxembourg Accords

(b) Majority voting procedure

I   Where, in the case or decisions which may be taken by majority vote on a proposal of the Commission, very important interests of one or more partners are at stake, the Members of the Council will endeavour, within a reasonable time, to reach solutions which can be adopted by all the Members of the Council while respecting their mutual interests and those of the Community, in accordance with Article 2 of the Treaty.

II   With regard to the preceding paragraph, the French delegation considers that where very important interests are at stake the discussion must be continued until unanimous agreement is reached.

III The six delegations note that there is a divergence of views on what should be done in the event of a failure to reach complete agreement.

IV   The six delegations nevertheless consider that this divergence does not prevent the Community's work being resumed in accordance with the normal procedure.

The effect of this compromise was to slow down the pace of decision-making until a new impetus was found in the mid-1980s for the completion of the *Internal Market* in 1992. Further internal and external, political and economic difficulties from the late 1960s to the early 1980s (eg the energy crises, inflation, world recession and prolonged differences over the UK contribution to the Community budget) were all instrumental in that period to a weakening of the political resolve of the Member States in finding Community-based solutions and implementing new common policies.

Nevertheless tentative first steps were taken in this period in several fields including *economic and monetary union* (1969-71) and *European Political Co-operation* (1970). Some of the advances as were forthcoming did however have a profound effect on the concept of supranationality and the aims of European federalists. For example the basis for European Political Co-operation was laid by means of regular *intergovernmental* meetings of the Foreign Ministers of the Member States plus the President of the Commission. Similarly it was decided in 1974 to institutionalise the Summit Conferences of Heads of State or Government which had been held since 1969. In this way the *European Council* was established; a development which elicited this comment from Jean Monnet:

> We were wrong in 1952 to think that Europe would be built with the High Authority of the Coal and Steel Community as a supranational government. What matters now is that the Heads of national governments meet together regularly in the European Council. That's where the authority is. It's a very big change.

In its *Solemn Declaration on European Union* 1983, the European Council outlined its role in the following terms:

15

2.1   The European Council

2.1.1   The European Council brings together the Heads of State or Government and the President of the Commission assisted by the Foreign Ministers of the Member States and a member of the Commission.

2.1.2   In the perspective of European Union, the European Council

provides a general political impetus to the construction of Europe;

defines approaches to further the construction of Europe and issues general political guidelines for the European Communities and European Political Co-operation;

deliberates upon matters concerning European Union in its different aspects with due regard to consistency among them;

initiates co-operation in new areas of activity;

solemnly expresses the common position in questions of external relations.

2.1.3   When the European Council acts in matters within the scope of the European Communities, it does so in its capacity as the Council within the meaning of the Treaties.

It should be noted that both the European Council and European Political Co-operation (EPC) in the field of foreign policy were later provided with a legal basis by the Single European Act 1986.

Other major developments in the 1970s were the establishment in 1977 of the *exchange rate mechanism* (ERM) for the stabilisation of currencies within the Community (the UK did not join until 1990 and suspended membership in 1992 following turbulence in the international money markets), and the first *direct elections* to the European Parliament in 1979 – an event of great significance for European federalists, not many of whom were to be found in the UK, where voter turnout was only 32.6% (the lowest in the Community). MEPs are no longer merely delegates from national legislatures but the elected representatives of 'Euro-constituencies' and political parties from within the Member States. The legal basis for direct elections in the EEC Treaty was Article 138(3) as replaced by Council Decision and Act of 20 September 1976 on Direct Elections.

Also in the 1970s, on the basis of the Budgetary Treaties of 1970 and 1975, the EEC (and Euratom) moved from a system whereby revenue was raised by direct financial contributions from the Member States to one based on the fiscal federalist concept of the Communities' *'own resources'* (ie its own tax revenue). Since 1988, 'true' own resources have been made up of customs duties levied under the Common Customs Tariff on imports from non-member countries and agricultural levies and duties charged on imports and on some internal CAP over-production. These sources are supplemented by the application of a 1.4 per cent contribution from Member States' value-added tax (VAT) assessments and further, variable contributions from Member States depending on Community needs and Member States' ability to pay. An important feature of the Budgetary Treaty 1970 was the measure of control over the EC budget that was granted to the Parliament. This was necessary to the extent that own resources no longer passed through Member States' budgets subject to control by their Parliaments.

Enlargement of the Community to its present twelve Member States came about through the accession of Greece in 1981 and Spain and Portugal joined in 1986. However, the most significant development of the 1980s was the Commission's proposal in 1985 of a programme for a *Single European (OR INTERNAL) Market* to be achieved by the end of 1992. Not that considerable progress had not already been made in this direction. The Commission had announced the creation of a customs union between the original Six in 1968 and between 'the Nine' in 1977. However many non-tariff barriers and national tax differentials remained to hinder the free movement of goods and uneven progress had been made as regards removing obstacles to the achievement of the other freedoms essential to the establishment of the Common Market to be found in Article 3(c) of the Treaty of Rome, ie the free movement of persons (including the right of establishment for firms), of services and of capital.

In February 1986 the twelve Member States signed the SINGLE EUROPEAN ACT (amending the EEC Treaty) so giving legal effect to the Commission's proposals. A new Article 8A of the Treaty of Rome stated in part that:

> The Community shall adopt measures with the aim of progressively establishing the internal market over a period expiring on 31 December 1992 ... The internal market shall comprise an area without internal frontiers in which the free movement of goods, persons, services and capital is ensured within the provisions of the Treaty.

However the Single European Act was not important merely in terms of '1992'. The Preamble noted 'the results achieved in the fields of economic integration and political co-operation and *the need for new developments*' (emphasis added). In this light the Preamble went on to express the will of the Member States 'to transform relations as a whole among their States into a European Union, in accordance with the solemn Declaration of Stuttgart of 19 June 1983' (see above). Further, the Preamble drew attention to the

'Conference in Paris from 19 to 21 October 1972 [at which] the Heads of State or of Government approved the objective of the progressive realisation of Economic and Monetary Union'.

In the result, and in a renewed drive towards an as yet undefined 'European Union', the 1986 Act amended the Treaty to introduce new, or rather to develop existing but unrealised, policies in the fields of, for example, economic and monetary 'convergence' (Article 102A), social policy (Article 118B etc.) and the environment (Article 130R). It also, as will be seen, improved the Parliament's position as regards the Community's law-making process by means of a new 'co-operation procedure' between the Council and the Parliament, and it extended the permitted range of majority voting in the decision-making process of the Council.

In the early 1990s, with the completion of the Internal Market arguably on course, the main focus of attention and debate switched away from the first of the Community's 'tasks' in Article 2 of the 1957 Treaty – 'the completion of a Common Market' to the second – the progressive approximation (or beyond?) of the economic policies of the Member States. The next 'Great Debate' began in Rome in December 1990 at the Intergovernmental Conferences on Economic and Monetary Union and on Political Union.

At the conclusion of these conferences in the Dutch city of Maastricht in December 1991, the European Council adopted a Treaty on Political Union and a Treaty on Economic and Monetary Union, the whole making up the TREATY ON EUROPEAN UNION (TEU). The Treaty was signed in February 1992 and it was intended that it would enter into force on 1st January 1993 following ratification by all twelve Member States in accordance with their respective constitutional requirements. However a negative vote in the Danish referendum on the Treaty in June 1992 cast serious doubts as to its future. Following concessions to the Danes, a second referendum in May 1993 resulted in a 'Yes' vote and at the present time only Germany has yet to ratify the Treaty. Various reservations however have been expressed in a number of Member States regarding the further steps towards 'an ever closer union' (particularly monetary union) that the new Treaty represents. With this uncertainty and delay in mind, only the following issues covered by the Treaty are noted at this stage. (Other amendments to the institutional arrangements and the law-making process of the Community will be incorporated into later chapters as appropriate.)

EUROPEAN UNION AND EUROPEAN COMMUNITY

The three existing Treaties (subject to various amendments) are incorporated into the structure of the TEU. By this Treaty, the Member States establish among themselves a European Union: Title I Common Provisions, Article A, para. 1. Throughout the Treaty, the term 'European Economic Community' is replaced by the term 'European Community': Title II (Amending the EEC Treaty), Article G (1).

The Three 'Pillars'

Article A, para. 3 TEU states that: 'The Union shall be founded on the European Communities, supplemented by the policies and forms of co-operation established by this Treaty.' The provisions on economic and monetary union (and Union citizenship) are incorporated into the EEC Treaty as amended by the TEU but those on two further areas, co-operation on Common Foreign and Security Policy (European Political Co-operation under the Single European Act) and Justice and Home Affairs are not. Although it was agreed that further steps be taken towards more intensive co-operation and, if necessary, joint action in these fields, it was also decided that such co-operation should proceed on an inter-governmental and not on a Community basis (although Community institutions, particularly the Council, will be used). These provisions of the TEU remain therefore outside the amended EEC Treaty – hence references to the three 'pillars' of the TEU within the structure of the new European Union (but see also the remarks at the end of Chapter Two). 'European' policy has been neither common nor effective in connection with the Gulf War or the crisis in the former Yugoslavia.

The areas of activity listed in the TEU as being of 'common interest' in terms of 'co-operation in the fields of justice and home affairs' include asylum and immigration policy, the combating of drug addiction and international fraud, judicial co-operation, and customs and police co-operation in the fight against terrorism and drug trafficking: Article K.1 of the TEU. Provision is also made for these matters to be transferred to the Community pillar without the need to amend the Treaty: Article K.9 of the TEU.

The Union's Main Objective

The first-stated *objective* of the Union in Article B TEU is indicative of what has already been achieved and what remains to be achieved:

to promote economic and social progress which is balanced and sustainable, in particular through the creation of an area without internal frontiers, through the strengthening of economic and social cohesion and through the establishment of economic and monetary union, ultimately including a single currency ...

Underlying Principles

Fundamental principles underlying the Union include, in particular, respect for the *national identities* of its Member States: Article F(1), respect for *fundamental rights* as general principles of Community law: Article F(2), and respect for the principle of *subsidiarity*: Article B, para. 2. As discussed in Chapter Three, the purpose of this latter principle is, in broad terms, to provide a practical basis on which decisions can be made as to whether it is better for Community action to be taken on a particular issue or whether the Member States are better placed to achieve the objectives in question. Some issues, by reason of scale or effects, are better suited to Community action than others: see Article 3b of the amended EEC Treaty.

It is also established under Articles C and E that the Union shall be served by a *single institutional framework*. The Parliament, the Council, the Commission and the Court of Justice will however exercise their powers on the one hand on the basis of the Treaties establishing the European Communities and on the other for the purposes of the second and third pillars of the Union where, contrary to the continued trend under the EC Treaty towards qualified majority decisions of the Council, the rule of unanimity will generally apply. (Arrangements under the two new pillars, focusing as they do on co-operation and common action between the Member States, clearly *dilute* the supranational nature of the Union, although, as seen below, scheduled developments regarding economic and monetary union more than offset this effect in these 'fledgling' areas and greatly advance (to 'Euro-sceptics' dismay) the concept of central control at the expense of national sovereignty.

Extension of Powers

As compared with the original Article 3 of the EEC Treaty (see above), the list of common policies or activities of the new European Community – EC not EEC – in Article 3 of the amended EEC Treaty (see Title II, Article G of the TEU) shows a further *strengthening or expansion of Community powers* (legal bases) in a number of economic and, particularly, social fields. Building in part on advances recognised by the Single European Act in 1986 (see above), these include the strengthening of economic and social cohesion (aid to poorer regions) and environmental policy, the promotion of research and technology, consumer protection and education and training. The new list also includes the establishment and development of trans-European transport networks, health protection, culture and (overseas) development co-operation.

Economic and Monetary Union

It will be recalled that the two means by which the Community's objectives would be achieved in Article 2 of the original EEC Treaty were the establishment of a Common Market and progressive approximation of the economic policies of the Member States. In the TEU, the first of these means remains (the '1992' Internal Market programme bringing the concept much closer to a reality) but the second, closely related, means becomes the establishment of 'an economic and monetary union' (EMU).

The origins of EMU go back to 1969 but progress was thwarted for many years by both economic and political problems. The European Council laid down the basis for a European Monetary System (EMS) in 1979, the central features of which are the *exchange rate mechanism* (ERM) for the stabilisation of exchange rates between Member States' currencies and the recognition of the *European Currency Unit* (the ECU) to replace national currencies for an increasing number of purposes. As we have seen, the Single European Act re-emphasised the need for the 'convergence' of the Member States' economic and monetary policies.

As progress proceeded towards the completion of the Internal Market in the late 1980s, the European Council came to accept a three-stage plan for the attainment of EMU as proposed by a committee chaired by Jacques Delors, the President of the Commission. The legal basis for EMU is now to be found in a new Article 3a, added to the EEC Treaty as amended by the TEU:

1. For the purposes set out in Article 2, the activities of the Member States and the Community shall include, as provided in this Treaty and in accordance with the timetable set out therein, the adoption of an economic policy which is based on the close co-ordination of Member States' economic policies, on the internal market and on the definition of common objectives, and conducted in accordance with the principle of an open market economy with free competition.

2. Concurrently with the foregoing, and as provided in this Treaty and in accordance with the timetable and the procedures set out therein, these activities shall include the irrevocable fixing of exchange rates leading to the introduction of a single currency, the ECU, and the

definition and conduct of a single monetary policy and exchange-rate policy the primary objective of both of which shall be to maintain price stability and, without prejudice to this objective, to support the general economic policies in the Community, in accordance with the principle of an open market economy with free competition.

3. These activities of the Member States and the Community shall entail compliance with the following guiding principles: stable prices, sound public finances and monetary conditions and a sustainable balance of payments.

The TEU also lays down a strict timetable for the realisation of the 'Delors Plan'. Stage one is assumed to be in existence and the second stage is scheduled to begin on 1 January 1994. A Member State's participation in the ERM is a necessary prerequisite for its participation in the second stage and the current absence of three UK, Italy and Greece from the ERM poses potential problems. Stage two is set within a prescribed framework of a high level of *economic convergence* on the part of the Member States. There are four 'convergence criteria': price stability (a low rate of inflation), a sound government financial position (no excessive budget deficit), stable exchange rates within the ERM and low interest rates: Article 109j(1) of the EC Treaty as amended. Preparation will also be made at this stage for the establishment of a European System of Central Banks (ESCB) which, in the third stage, will 'define and implement the monetary policy of the Community', and a new, similarly independent institution, the European Central Bank (ECB), which will have law-making powers within the monetary field.

The third stage, leading eventually to the adoption of a single currency (the ECU) under the control of the ECB, will begin in 1977 if a majority of Member States have met the convergence criteria. In any event, entry to the third stage of EMU cannot be delayed beyond 1 January 1999 even if only a small number of Member States fulfil the required conditions on that date. At Maastricht the UK and Denmark were unable to give a firm commitment to full participation in the third stage of EMU. The UK negotiated the right 'not to be obliged or committed to move to the third stage of economic and monetary union without a separate decision to do so by its government and Parliament'. The collision between a strict Treaty timetable and continuing economic problems in Europe raises the possibility of a 'Union' which, by the end of the century is weakened by a severe case of what is known as 'variable geometry'.

The Social Policy Protocol

At UK insistence, new social policy measures concerning 'the promotion of employment, improved living and working conditions, proper social protection', etc, were left out of the main Treaty. Eleven Member States, however, committed themselves to the harmonisation of their policies within these fields in a separate Protocol to be annexed to the Treaty, as amended.

The UK opted out on the grounds of cost and the need to combat inflation and the maintenance of a right to create jobs within its own particular market conditions free of 'interference' from Brussels. This is, of course, on the face of it, an actual not a prospective case of 'variable geometry', the effect of which may be diminished if the policy measures in the Protocol can to some extent be achieved on the basis of an *existing* Treaty base (eg Article 118 on minimum health and safety standards for workers).

Further Issues

Finally, as indicated earlier, changes to be brought about by the Maastricht Treaty to the institutional system and the law-making process of the Community will be examined in some detail in Chapter Five. However, it is important to note at this stage that, although the powers of the European Parliament will be increased as regards its right to amend or veto legislation (and in other matters also), its role in the Community's law-making process will remain inferior to that of the Council – the final decision-maker – and the Commission, the prime initiator of legislation and the body charged with the implementation of the rules laid down by the Council: see Article 155 of the Rome Treaty (unaffected by the TEU). The so-called 'democratic deficit' has not therefore been appreciably reduced. The Parliament has for some time sought a major role as co-legislator with the Council, a function which it still only exercises not, as we will see, 'across the board' but only within certain specified areas. The people's representatives therefore remain subordinate to those of the Member State governments.

This issue, together with that of subsidiarity, is of obvious significance to those in the Member States who insist that national governments retain as many powers as possible – as opposed to 'losing' them to the Community institutions. This view of the Community tends also to find favour with hose who advocate the *broadening* of the Community through the accession of new Member States, rather than a *deepening*, whereby the process of economic and political integration leads inexorably towards some form of European federal structure in which the central institutions exercise extensive powers.

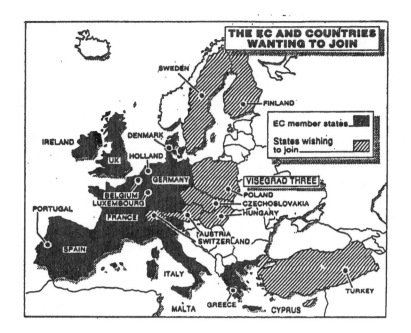

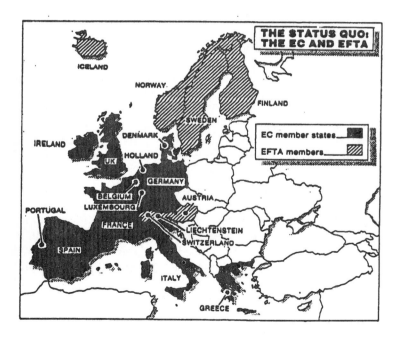

Although a 'federal' goal was omitted from the final draft of the Treaty (particularly at British insistence), ratification of the Treaty and the establishment of economic and monetary union would in fact bring the Community much closer to a federal system (see also Chapter Three).

Despite current uncertainties, the Community (Union) will continue to develop despite crucial questions of size, structure and speed of change remaining open at present. In legislative terms at least the Internal Market was virtually completed on time at the end of 1992. Earlier, in 1991, political agreement was reached on the creation of the EUROPEAN ECONOMIC AREA (EEA) made up of the EEC and the seven EFTA states (Norway, Sweden, Finland, Iceland, Austria, Switzerland and Liechtenstein: see map). Close economic relations have existed between the EEC and EFTA for many years and the purpose of the partial merger which is envisaged has been outlined as follows:

> The idea behind the EEA is to give the EFTA countries all the free-trade advantages of EC membership, without making them part of the EC political system. All the rules of Community law regarding free movement of goods (but only as regards products originating in the Contracting States), persons, services and capital apply – with only slight modifications – to the EFTA countries, as do the rules of EC law relating to competition and state aid. This has great attractions, but also serious drawbacks. In particular, it means that the EFTA countries will have to apply a system of rules in the making of which they will have virtually no say: Hartley.

In Opinion 1/91 *Re the Draft Treaty on a European Economic Area*, the Court of Justice raised certain objections to the agreement. The Court was particularly concerned to preserve the autonomy and homogeneity of the Community legal order, the position of the Court of Justice within that legal order as established by Article 164 EEC, and the binding nature of its decisions. In its Opinion 1/92, following revisions of the text, the Court was satisfied that it was compatible with Community law. (The agreement is not yet in effect as Switzerland has withdrawn following a negative response in a national referendum.)

Wishing to avoid a 'satellite status' under the EEA Agreement, several EFTA countries are seeking membership of the Community. Similarly, since freeing themselves of Communist control in 1989, Central European countries have become potential members. Following unification, East Germany has become a member through the 'back door', and what is now the 'Visegrad Four' (Poland, Hungary, the Czech and Slovak Republics) are proceeding towards special trading relations both among themselves and with the Community. A partnership and co-operation agreement between the Community and Russia (at present in the process of negotiation) could eventually lead to a free trade area relationship.

Any state which applies for membership must satisfy the three basic conditions of European identity, democratic status and respect of human rights. The applicant state must also accept the Community system and be able to implement it. The obligations of membership presuppose a functioning and competitive market economy and an adequate legal and administrative framework in the public and the private sector.

Membership entails acceptance of the Community's 'acquis', or the existing body of EC law, which includes the contents of the Treaties, including Maastricht, all legislation adopted in implementation of the Treaties, all adopted declarations and resolutions and all international agreements. This is subject to transitional measures that might be agreed in accession negotiations.

The implications of the present position (August 1993) are enormous. In Pinder's opinion:

> Enlargement may, then, carry membership beyond twenty states, and eventually even to thirty or more. The implications of this prospect for Community institutions are profound. How could unanimous agreement on difficult questions be reached among so many and such diverse governments? How, indeed, could a basically intergovernmental system function effectively or democratically among them? In any or all of the cases of possible future enlargement, the European Parliament's right to refuse accession is likely to be used to secure that widening is accompanied by deepening, in the form of strengthening and democratising the Community's institutions; and it will have some support from member states. By the time that the accession of new applicants would bring the number of members up to twenty or so, the Parliament and at least some member states are likely to withhold their consent unless the institutions are given a federal form.

It is doubtful if a Community, or Union, of twenty or more Member States is capable of achievement except over a long period. Economic integration is feasible only when the economies of the participants are at a similar stage of development and those of the former Communist countries remain perilously weak. The Community's hesitant steps towards Union, together with the political earthquake in Central and Eastern Europe, means that the continent will need to be virtually redesigned over the next decade or so. Although the economic and political problems are immense, Europe does possess the opportunity to regain a central position within the world economic and political order.

Bulletin of the European Communities, Chronology of the European Community 1957–87, Bulletin Supplement 2/1987.

Donovan, R. J., *The Second Victory: The Marshall Plan and the Revival of Europe*, 1988.

European Documentation, *European Unification: The Origins and Growth of the European Community*, Periodical 3/1986, (Office for the Official Publications of the E.C.).

Hartley, Trevor, 'The European Court and the EEA' (1992) 41 ICLQ 841.

Henig, S., *Power and Decision in Europe*, 1980.

Kapteyn, P.J.G. and VerLoren van Themaat, P., *Introduction to the Law of the European Communities* (ed. Lawrence Gormley), 1989, Chapter 1.

Kitzinger, U., *The European Common Market and Community*, 1967.

Kitzinger, U., *Diplomacy and Persuasion*, (UK entry), 1973.

Lasok, D., and Bridge, J.W., *Law and Institutions of the European Communities*, Chapter 1.

Mayne, R., 'The Contribution of Jean Monnet' (1967) *Government and Opposition* 349.

Meier, Gerald M., *Problems of Trade Policy*, 1973, Part 3 'Regional Integration: EEC' (including UK entry).

Milward, Alan S., *The Reconstruction of Western Europe* 1945–51, 1984, Chapters XII and XIII.

Monnet, Jean, *Memoirs* (trans. R. Mayne), 1978.

Nicholl, C., 'The Luxembourg Compromise' (1984) 23 JCMS 35.

Nugent, Neill, *The Government and Politics of the European Community*, 1991, Part One 'The Historical Evolution'.

Pinder, John, *European Community: The Building of a Union*, 1991.

Shonfield, Andrew, *Europe – Journey to an Unknown Destination*, 1972.

Tugendhat, C., *Making Sense of Europe*, 1986.

Urwin, Derek, *The Community of Europe* (A History of European Integration since 1945), 1991.

CHAPTER TWO

THE EVOLVING PROCESS OF EUROPEAN INTEGRATION

The European Community is a unique structure which cannot be related to any known model of government nor to any single theory of inter-state relations. In consequence, the process of economic and political integration by which the Community has proceeded and continues to develop represents a journey to an unknown, or at least disputed, destination. The 1990s may reveal more clearly what is meant by 'European Union' and the degree of consensus among the Member States as to how far they wish to go together in that direction. What seems certain is that further progress will only be achieved in a gradual way (as has been the case in the past) by a series of practical measures. At present the central issue is: How many more steps are to be taken? Is the ultimate aim some form of United States of Europe or a somewhat looser pattern of economic and political integration or co-operation involving the Member States and the Community institutions.

The history of European integration over the last forty years or so is littered with concepts and theories such as interdependence, convergence, approximation, harmonisation, common market, union, federal finality, subsidiarity, and sovereignty. In order to understand the nature of the integration process over this period, it is necessary to familiarise ourselves with these concepts and theories, their political, economic and legal dimensions, and by doing so we will be able to establish clearer guidelines to the future.

In her September 1988 speech in Bruges, Mrs Thatcher declared that the Community was 'not an institutional device to be constantly modified according to the dictates of some abstract theory'. The then Prime Minister's adherence to free market policies and the Internal Market aspects of European integration surely owed something to economic theory, and in what follows differences between the theories and models may well show up in the differences of approach displayed by the politicians and practitioners of integration. In so far as the Community is still only part of the way down the integrative road, the theories have a predictive value reflecting, for example, the 'ever closer union' of the Preamble to both the Treaty of Rome and the Maastricht Treaty or the 'willing and active co-operation between independent sovereign states' of the Bruges speech.

REGIONAL ECONOMIC CONCEPTS, INTEGRATION AND THE TREATY OF ROME

> Integration is the combination of parts into a whole, and union is a whole resulting from the combination of parts ... Negative and positive integration together comprise economic integration, whose end is economic union: John Pinder, 1968.

As we have already seen, the Preamble to the Treaty of Rome expressed this process in similar terms: 'ever closer union ... common action to eliminate barriers ... by pooling their resources ...'

Integration is therefore a process: parts/nations proceeding in political, economic and legal terms from positions of (relative) independence to some form of union. In economic terms, the process can be divided into two constituent processes: negative integration involving the removal of restrictive and discriminatory barriers between the parts/nations, and positive integration which calls for further necessary common action in order that union can be attained.

In the 1950s a number of international economists (Tinbergen, Pinder, etc) paid particular analytical attention to a number of regional economic concepts, each representing a recognisable stage in an integrative process.

The first stage is the FREE TRADE AREA in which a group of sovereign nations abolishes all tariffs and quantitative restrictions on mutual trade, but each member retains its own customs duties and quota system as regards trade with other countries. A regional arrangement of this type, whether covering all products or (as with EFTA) only industrial goods, represents only a modest form of negative economic integration and it does not necessarily advance political integration.

A basic problem with the free trade area can be illustrated as follows:

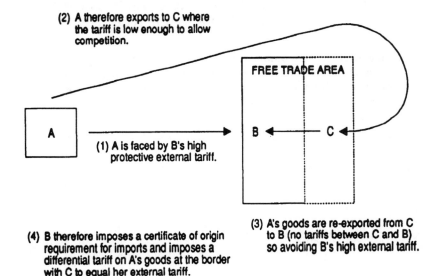

(2) A therefore exports to C where the tariff is low enough to allow competition.

FREE TRADE AREA

(1) A is faced by B's high protective external tariff.

(4) B therefore imposes a certificate of origin requirement for imports and imposes a differential tariff on A's goods at the border with C to equal her external tariff.

(3) A's goods are re-exported from C to B (no tariffs between C and B) so avoiding B's high external tariff.

The solution to this problem is for the member countries to form a CUSTOMS UNION with a *common* external tariff wall: see Article 3(a) and (b) and Article 9 EEC (and the equivalent in the amended Treaty). Agreement on a uniform level of external tariffs, on its enforcement, and on the destination and use of the revenue which accrues as goods cross the wall, all involve some loss of the member countries' sovereignty (in terms of their competence or control over international trade) which passes to a central authority composed of all member countries.

A customs union becomes a COMMON MARKET when, apart from the removal of restrictions on the free movement of goods (including agricultural products) - and services such as banking and insurance - they are also removed on the movement between the member states of the factors of production: labour, capital and enterprise, and, in particular, a system is established to ensure that competition within the Common Market is not distorted: Article 3(c) and (f) (which become 3(c) as amended and 3(g) under the TEU).

Over twenty years ago, the ultimate steps in the process of economic integration to an ECONOMIC UNION were described in the following way:

The completion of the final stage of economic union involves a full integration of the member economies with supranational authorities responsible for economic policy making. In particular, an economic union requires a single monetary system and central bank, a unified fiscal system, and a common foreign economic policy. The task of creating an economic union differs significantly from the steps necessary to establish the less ambitious forms of economic integration. A free trade area, a customs union, or a common market mainly result from the abolition of restrictions, whereas an economic union demands a positive agreement to transfer economic sovereignty to new supranational institutions: F.R. Root, 1973.

It is perfectly acceptable for economic theory to present the integration process in this way, with a series of models each in turn embodying a greater degree of integration. However, *it would be a mistake* to conclude that in practice the Community has followed this precise sequence. In 1957, the Community's legal base, the Treaty of Rome, established the framework for both a customs unions *and* a common market, together with, arguably an indication of ultimate union. This Treaty can, as we will see, therefore be seen as laying down the ground rules for both the abolition of restrictions (*negative* integration) and for *'positive* agreement' on other common and coordinated policies.

From 1958 actual progress in the 'negative' sphere was much faster than in the 'positive' for reasons that will be discussed, but it was not a case of negative integration of necessity preceding positive integration as the theory, as presented above, might suggest. Additionally, and most importantly, the Treaty (and the ECSC Treaty before it) also established supranational institutions (the Commission, Council, Parliament and Court) at the time the integrative enterprise was first launched. Indeed, some theories of integration have concentrated less on economic analysis and more on institutional and policy-making considerations. For example, Ernest Haas, the founder of one of the most influential theories (neofunctionalism), described integration as the 'process whereby political actors in several distinct national settings are persuaded to shift their loyalties, expectations and political activities towards a new and larger setting'.

However, it is essential, in order to gain real insight into the nature and structure of the EEC Treaty, that we pursue further an analysis based on the concepts of negative and positive integration. A *Common Market Law Review* editorial of 1989 on the Commission's November 1988 report on the half-way point in the 'Completion of the Internal Market' programme stated that:

The bonds between negative and positive integration are manifold, but the framework for action created by the Single Act and the 'new momentum' is basically confined to securing the free flow of goods, persons, services and capital in an area without frontiers.

NEGATIVE INTEGRATION, COMMON MARKET AND THE TREATY

It will be recalled that the two basic *means* in Article 2 of the Treaty of Rome for achieving the Community's economic, social (and political?) objectives were *the establishment of a common market* and *the progressive approximation of the economic policies of the Member States*. These two means are different in nature but they are complementary - and both are essential for the attainment of 'unity'.

Elaborating on the distinction made earlier between negative and positive integration, Pinder explains that:

Negative and positive integration together comprise economic integration, whose end is economic union ... negative integration unaccompanied by positive integration may be called a common market.

Negative integration is again used here to signify 'the removal of discrimination' and by this Pinder primarily means the removal by the Member States, as part of their Treaty obligations, of discriminatory and restrictive legal measures applied by them to a wide variety of inter-Member State business transactions (involving goods, services, labour and capital) and arising in large part from anti-competitive and protectionist national policies. (Companies themselves must comply with Community rules against restrictive and monopolistic practices).

A direct relationship therefore clearly exists between negative integration and the establishment of a Common Market. What remains to be shown is, firstly, the relationship between Pinder's 'removal of discrimination' and more specific indications in the Treaty as to how the Common Market is established and, secondly, the connection between the basic means in Article 2 described as 'the progressive approximation of the economic policies of Member States' and the other side of the integrative coin, positive integration. This he defined as:

The formation and application of co-ordinated and common policies in order to fulfil economic and welfare objectives other than the removal of discrimination.

Thirdly, it is necessary to indicate the nature of the 'bonds between negative and positive integration' - two means to form an indissoluble unity.

Article 3 EEC[2] states that, for the purposes set out in Article 2, the Community shall engage in a number of 'activities', including the following which relate to Pinder's definition of negative integration - *and* to the regional economic concepts analysis above:

Article 3

(a) the elimination, as between Member States, of customs duties and quantitative restrictions on the import and export of goods, and of all other measures having equivalent effect;

(b) the establishment of a common custom tariff and a common commercial policy towards third countries;

(c) the abolition, as between Member States, of obstacles to freedom of movement of persons*, services and capital;

(d) the adoption of a common policy in the sphere of agriculture;

(e) the adoption of a common policy in the sphere of transport;

(f) the institution of a system ensuring that competition in the common market is not distorted;

...

(h) the approximation of the laws of the Member States to the extent required for the proper functioning of the common market;

...

(*The freedom of establishment in other Member States of, for example, companies should be considered here: see Article 52 EEC.)

Writing in 1991, van Themaat confirms this Common Market listing when discussing the developing case law of the Court of Justice:

In this consistent case law, it used the notion of a Common Market also as a link between the 'five freedoms' provided for concerning goods, persons, services, capital and payments, the rules of competition (Articles 85-94), the common policies for agriculture, transport and

---

[2] As this chapter focuses on the original treaty, the Treaty of Rome, TEU amendments are not incorporated. Very few of the basic provisions have been changed, although some have been added.

external trade, Articles 95-98 on fiscal discrimination and the provisions on harmonisation of legislation.

The fundamental legal principles underpinning the Common (and the Internal) Market are those of *freedom* and *equality*. This can be seen in particular as regards the 'four fundamental freedoms' (the free movement of goods, persons, services and capital - omitting payments) and the maintenance of free and equal competitive conditions (the 'level playing-field').

The economic and legal concept of the Internal Market (Article 8A EEC introduced by the Single European Act 1986) is the particular creation of the Community. As noted in Chapter One, the Internal Market Programme 1986-92 involved an accelerated continuation and completion of those Common Market activities that had fallen badly behind schedule. (The Common Market should have been completed by the end of 1969: Article 8(1) of the Treaty.) Internal Market measures, as will be discussed in Chapter Eleven, relate largely to certain aspects of Article 3(a), (c), (e) and (h). In essence, therefore the Common (in the sense of 'single') and the Internal Market are one and the same; the later Internal Market programme was required to be more intensive but not as comprehensive as that originally laid down for the Common Market.

Some commentators on the Treaty have omitted agriculture and transport – Article 3(d) and (e) - from the concept of the Common Market. However the Spaak Report of 1956 (see Chapter One) stated that: 'One cannot conceive the establishment of a Common Market in Europe without the inclusion of agriculture'. The Common Agricultural Policy (and the same generally applies to the other sectoral policies: transport, coal and steel and atomic energy) is, nevertheless, as much concerned with interventionist market management and control as with the removal of discrimination. The prices of agricultural products are fixed on a common Community basis within a complex system of Community import levies and subsidies to producers. (The CAP has been described as 'merely a complicated kind of customs union'). One of the prime aims of the common policy is to stabilise agricultural product markets, as referred to in Article 39(1)(c), and the rules relating to the free movement of goods and competition apply to the production and distribution of agricultural products only to a limited extent. On balance, and in line with Pinder's analysis, and that of other economists, agriculture and transport are to be seen as elements of the Common Market and hence of negative integration.

The approximation (better known now as *harmonisation*) of the national laws of Member States referred to in Article 3(h) is a key element of the *legal integration* which must accompany economic integration. Differences between Member States' laws embodying discriminatory obstacles to free movement (eg differing national rules or standards relating to the contents or packaging of products which hinder free movement and make imports more expensive, or differing national rules concerning professional qualifications which hinder the free movement of persons) are removed by means of a Community-based legal process which will be examined in Chapter Five and elsewhere. However, harmonisation measures do not relate solely to the removal of discrimination as between Member States. Equal pay measures, which remove discrimination by gender *within* Member States, do have an impact on the costs and therefore the competitive position of a Member State's industries *vis-à-vis* those of the other Member States, but equal pay policy is primarily an element of Community social policy, which comes within the scope of *other* 'economic and welfare objectives', ie positive integration. (Consider also the harmonisation of national environmental and VAT laws.) Approximation (harmonisation) of national laws will therefore be included within *both* negative and positive integration.

POSITIVE INTEGRATION, ECONOMIC AND SOCIAL POLICIES AND THE TREATY

We must first of all add to Pinder's definition of positive integration his *bases* of positive integration in the Community, remembering that positive integration advances the integration process beyond the Common Market on towards full economic union. We find, therefore, - as well as and beyond the removal of discrimination' - the necessity for 'co-ordinated and common policies in order to fulfil [other] economic and welfare objectives', in particular:

(i) major common policies at Community level ... including regional, social, monetary and fiscal policies ... and

(ii) the co-ordination of monetary, budgetary and incomes policies of the member states.

This is a formulation similar to Professor Root's description above of the essential elements of the final stage of economic union. It will readily be noted that some of these policies (monetary, fiscal and social) are the subject-matter of current controversy and it will be recalled that Root explained that 'economic union demands a positive agreement to transfer economic sovereignty to new supranational institutions'.

What indications of such 'positive' policies do we find in the original 1957 version of the Treaty of Rome?

Article 3

(g) the application of procedures by which the economic policies of Member States can be co-ordinated and disequilibria in their balances of payments remedied;

(h) the approximation of the laws of Member States ...;

(i) the creation of a European Social Fund in order to improve employment opportunities for workers and to contribute to the raising of their standards of living;

(j) the establishment of a European Investment Bank to facilitate the economic expansion of the Community by opening up fresh resources;

(k) the association of the overseas and territories in order to increase trade and to promote jointly economic and social development.

The most significant difference between Article 3 activities which relate to negative integration and those associated with positive integration was, at least until 1986, that whereas the former were developed in detail in the body of the Treaty (and in secondary legislation), so giving rise to ease of legal implementation (eg in the fields of the free movement of goods and competition policy), this was generally not the case for positive agreement on common policies dealing predominantly with economic and social issues other than the removal of restrictions and discrimination. In the period prior to the new impetus established by the Single European Act in 1986, the programme of policies and procedures for positive integration was variously described as 'vague', 'feeble' and 'permissive instead of definite and mandatory' (eg no time limits were laid down). What were the reasons for this difference?

One view on the reasons for slow progress was expressed by Stuart Holland in 1980:

It is conceivable that governments with a predominantly liberal capitalist ideology should try to establish economic union on negative integration lines through a process of harmonisation of national policies which downgrades their differences to a lowest common denominator [but equally that such an ideological base] accounts for some of the major handicaps experienced in achieving planned policies for positive integration.

During the economically difficult 1975-85 period, faced with a choice between concerted action or a search for solutions along national lines, Member States exhibited little European will. The concept of supranationality flattered to deceive; Community progress was attributable less to the capacity of its institutions to function 'above' governments than to their small success in managing to stimulate their co-operation.

However, as seen in Chapter One, the Single European Act was concerned not merely with the completion of the Internal Market but also with a determination to 'improve the social and economic situation by extending common policies and pursuing new objectives'. Subsequent to the Act, Treaty of Rome provisions to be identified with the process of positive integration were to be found between Articles 102 A and 136 EEC. These articles still rest in the main on Article 3(g) – (k) of the Treaty (or parts thereof) and they were themselves amended (in part) and supplemented by the Act. For the most part they were only 'new' policies in as much as they now specifically featured in the (amended) Treaty. The groundwork for them had in fact proceeded previously, albeit slowly, over a number of years and in some cases indirectly, in a legal sense, on the basis of other Treaty articles. By far the most important of these articles applied to:

> *Co-operation in Economic and Monetary Policy*: Article 102A which provided that 'convergence' of the Member States' policies in these fields 'shall take account ... of the European Monetary System and ... the ECU'.

> Here lies the basis (subject to further amendment of the Treaty) of the Delors Plan for a Community Central Bank and a single currency.

> New *Social Policy* provisions under Articles 118A and B, to which should be linked the Commission's 'Social Charter' of 1989 which aimed to protect workers' wage levels, bargaining rights and conditions of employment in the more competitive market of post-1992 Europe (and see now the Social Policy Protocol in Chapter One).

> Provisions concerning *Economic and Social Cohesion* aimed at 'reducing the disparities between various regions and the backwardness of the least favoured regions'. Article 130B speaks of the implementation of common policies and the completion of the internal market.

> *Research and Technological Development* serving to strengthen the scientific and technological base of European industry in order to make it more competitive at the international level: Articles 130F–Q.

> *Environmental Policy* under new Articles 130 R–T directed the Community towards improvement of the quality of the environment, the protection of human health, and prudent and rational utilisation of natural resources. Policy in this field dates back to 1973 even though

protection of the environment did not appear as an express objective in the Treaty. Measures were taken as elements of free trade policy, competition policy or agricultural policy, and in 1985 the Court of Justice held that environmental protection was indeed an essential objective of the Community (and see Article 2 EEC).

Foreign Policy Co-operation under Article 30 of the Single European Act (not incorporated into the EEC Treaty) was, as seen, yet again not a totally new development but the continuation of political moves dating back to 1970: see Article 1 of the Act. Whether this and further steps taken in 1992 will help to bring forth a more definite and influential European 'voice' in international relations remains to be seen.

THE BONDS BETWEEN NEGATIVE AND POSITIVE INTEGRATION

It will have been noticed that the dividing line between negative and positive integration is not as neat in practice as in theory (eg as regards sectoral policies). Pinder recognised this when, for example, he stated that 'the Rome Treaty employs the term common market ambiguously, sometimes including, and sometimes excluding, some of the fruits of positive integration'. And in 1989 he stressed that:

> While the distinction between positive and negative integration should not be pressed too far, it is useful in helping to show why the SEM [Single European Market] brings the need for other common objectives and policies in its train.

These two points – that blurring can occur between negative and positive integration and that negative integration acts as a motor for further, positive, integration – can be illustrated in the following ways.

For example, the Common Commercial Policy of Article 3(b) which covers Community trade relations with the rest of the world is a necessary corollary to the establishment of the Common Customs Tariff and therefore an essential feature of the customs union and hence the Common Market: see Article 110 EEC. However, Common Commercial Policy has increasingly been used solely as an instrument of the Community's external trade relations and not as a guarantee for the proper operation of the Common Market. However, in the context of the current Uruguay Round of GATT (General Agreement on Tariffs and Trade) talks on the liberalisation of *world* trade, the Community is under extreme pressure from the USA to bring about drastic reductions in measures operating *within* the CAP to protect Community farmers from the rigours of world trade in agricultural products.

As regards the second point, as Pinder himself has explained:

> When the EC determines a standard for car exhausts, it is both removing the distortion whereby the differing standards previously fragmented the market; and is taking a view as to the sort of environment it wants to have ... When the EC establishes a monetary union, it is both removing the distortions of variable exchange rates and providing itself with the instruments for a common macroeconomic policy which also implies objectives beyond that of removing distortions: Pinder, 'The Single Market: a Step Towards European Union' in Lodge (ed.)

The process of linking the economic concepts of negative and positive integration to the EEC Treaty has enabled us to sketch the outlines of the *economic and social law* of the Community. Nor have these references to the substance of policies (in economic and legal terms) ignored –they have at times been inevitably linked to – questions of economic management and the respective roles of the Community's political institutions and the Member States. These are the issues which, from a legal viewpoint, comprise the remainder of this book.

In the meantime, however, having identified the integral Treaty elements of, and the relationship between, negative and positive integration – and recalling that the ultimate aim of the integration process is 'union' – an attempt must be made to say what is currently understood by that term in practice.

EUROPEAN UNION

As seen in Chapter One, Article A of Title I (Common Provisions) of the Maastricht Treaty provides that the twelve Member States of the European Community 'establish among themselves a European Union'. No definition of this Union is provided, references to a 'federal structure' were deleted, and Article A merely continues by stating that the Treaty marks 'a new [not a final] stage in the process of creating an ever closer union among the peoples of Europe'.

Commenting on the expression 'ever closer union', which of course first appeared in the Preamble to the Treaty of Rome, Wellenstein argues that:

The sense of the term is still the same, that of a political objective of a general nature. In order to give it a specific substantive meaning, one has to opt for specific common approaches to specific practical problems and to devise institutions and procedures to cope with them, like in 'custom union' (Article 9 EEC: '1. The Community shall be based on a customs union . . . etc'.)

From this, it is clear that 'union' remains an undefined objective; it remains to be achieved. That part of it which has been achieved can be identified only by singling out those 'specific practical problems' (eg customs union, equal pay, competition, the environment, monetary union, etc) which have from time to time been agreed as constituting proper Community/Union concerns, and which have been established (coped with) on a common basis through the agency of the European institutions and their procedures.

The original list of common policies and activities in Article 3 EEC has successively expanded – in 1986 and at Maastricht – to encompass new, mainly positive, objectives of an economic and social nature. Economic and monetary union now finds its place in an amended Article 2 and a new Article 3a (see Chapter One) and recognises, *as it must*, its constituent negative and positive elements, in particular the internal market, free competition and the conduct of a single monetary policy.

What of the future? For Pinder, writing in 1991:

If it is true that negative integration brings with it the need for positive integration, a completed single market after 1992 is not likely to rest in stable equilibrium. Either, if the needs for positive integration are not met, it will tend to become less integrated again, as the Community market did in the 1970s. Or the Community will, with more positive integration, move farther towards Union on federal lines. The Maastricht Treaty included a number of steps in that direction. If the new technologies, and the specialisation that goes with them, continue to press the European economies towards integration, the cost of resisting movement towards such a Union could be high.

The Community, then, can either go forwards or backwards – and where are we now? Wellenstein concludes:

So there we are. We have (that is to say, after ratification we will have) a Union without real unity, a building half-built with an institutional 'géométrie variable' and a 'rendez-vous' in 1996 to try to improve on what was achieved in Maastricht. Between today and 1996 the world, especially the European world, will remain in constant turmoil.

41

61

Curzon Price, Victoria, 'Three Models of Integration' in *Whose Europe? Competing Visions for 1992*, 1989.

George, S., *Politics and Policy in the European Community*, 1991, particularly Chapter 2, 'European Integration in Theory and Practice'.

Haas, Ernest, *The Uniting of Europe: Political, Social and Economic Forces*, 1958.

Holland, S., *Uncommon Market*, 1980.

Lodge, J., (ed.), *The European Community and the Challenge of the Future*, 1989 (particularly Chapter One).

Mandel, E. 'International Capitalism and Supranationality' in Radice (ed.) *International Firms and Modern Imperialism*, 1969.

Pinder, John, 'Positive Integration and Negative Integration: Some Problems of Economic Union in the EEC', *The World Today*, March 1968; also in Denton, G.R. (ed.) *Economic Integration in Europe*, 1969.

Pinder, John, 'Economic Integration versus National Sovereignty: Differences between Eastern and Western Europe' (1989) *Government and Opposition* 309.

Root, F.R. *International Trade and Investment - Theory, Policy Enterprise*, 1973.

The Financial Times, 21 September 1988: Mrs Thatcher's speech at Bruges (extracts).

The Financial Times, 2 November 1988: 'A Power Struggle at the Heart of the EC'.

The Times Guide to 1992, 'Conclusion – Britain, 1992 and European Union', 1991.

Webb, Carol, 'Theoretical Perspectives and Problems' in Wallace, Wallace and Webb (eds) *Policy Making in the European Community*, 1983.

Wellenstein, E.P., 'Unity, Community, Union – What's in a Name?' (1992) 29 CML Rev. 205.

Williams, R., 'The EC's Technology Policy as an Engine for Integration' (1989) *Government and Opposition* 158.

CHAPTER THREE

FEDERALISM, SOVEREIGNTY AND SUBSIDIARITY

A FEDERAL PATTERN

Taking the United States as a model, in the constitution of this federal State, sovereignty (political power or competence) is divided between the central, federal government and the governments of the associated states:

> The Constitution of the United States establishes an association of states so organised that powers are divided between a general government which in certain matters - for example, the making of treaties and the coining of money - is independent of the governments of the associated states, and, on the other hand, state governments which in certain matters are, in their turn, independent of the general government. This involves, as a necessary consequence, that general and regional governments both operate directly upon the people; each citizen is subject to two governments. It is not always easy to say what matters are within the spheres of the general and the regional governments respectively: Wheare, *Federal Government*, 1964.

The European Community cannot properly be described as a federation. It is not a state and the EC institutions do not comprise a European government. The Community's basic document is formally not a constitution but an international treaty, although it is increasingly being recognised (particularly by the Court of Justice) as a constitution, providing for institutions and European law-making machinery. The Community is perhaps best described as a hybrid or half-way house, being based, since the creation of the Coal and Steel Community, on a *federal pattern*:

> It is important to remember that with the ratification of the European treaties, concessions of sovereignty to autonomous European institutions have already occurred. An embryonic federal structure is in place, even if its powers are confined to certain areas ...: Peter Sutherland (former EC Commissioner), 1988.

It will be recalled that the prime motive behind the Community concept in the first place was to *reduce the power of the nation state* and thus the central cause of war. Therefore, over the last forty years or so, the integrative process has led to an increasing shift in the balance of power from the Member States to the Community institutions. In 1957, 1986 and (possibly) 1993, under successive Treaties or Treaty amendments, the Member States themselves agreed to enlargements of Community competence and, therefore, to corresponding reductions of their own sovereignty. However, as we have said, this does not mean that we already have a federal Europe. In 1986 Hartley outlined the position in the following way:

> The European Community is not a federation, though it may one day become one. It nevertheless possesses a number of distinctly federal elements, a fact which has led writers to coin the neologism 'supranational' to describe it ...
>
> ... it is precisely those parts of the Community constitution which are concerned with the legal and judicial system that are most federal; the parts concerned with the political system, on the other hand, are still firmly rooted in the pre-federal milieu of inter-governmental diplomatic co-operation. Thus, the main Community legislature (the Council) is not elected by the people of the Community: its members are mere delegates of the Member States and they vote on the instructions of their governments. (The European Parliament is directly elected by the people of the Community but it has no legislative power, though it does have significant powers over the Community budget.) Moreover, though the Treaties envisage qualified majority voting for the exercise of many of the Council's powers, a rule of unanimity prevails in most situations in practice. Secondly, the legislative powers of the Council are insufficient by federal standards. For instance, defense, foreign policy (except as regards international trade), monetary policy, citizenship and immigration into the Community (though not intra-Community immigration) are wholly or mainly outside the competence of the Community legislature. Thirdly, the tax powers of the Community are insufficient for its purposes. Fourthly, the Community Executive (the Commission) is not fully responsible to the elected representatives of the people (the European Parliament). These factors ... are in themselves sufficient to prevent the Community from being a federation.

Of course, since 1986, as we have seen in the preceding chapters, various developments have moved the Community/Union further in a federal direction: increased powers for the European Parliament in the legislative process, the restoration and extension of majority voting in the Council, and the bringing of the policy areas mentioned by Hartley within the three pillars of the TEU.

In 1989 Pinder explained this question of successive accretions to Community powers not only in terms of the 'bonds' between negative and positive integration (economic 'spill-over') but also in terms of the links between economic and political integration (political 'spill-over'):

... the closer the interdependence, the less effective the member states' policies become ... member states' policies are replaced or supplemented by common policies for the Community as a whole. But positive integration is harder to achieve than the removal of distortions. The making and execution of laws and policies are, after all, the task of governance, so we are expecting the Community's institutions to be capable of governance ...

... If the single market implies, in turn, the need for further stages of policy integration such as an economic and monetary union, it is hard to escape the conclusion that federal structures of government for the Community will be required. Intergovernmental cooperation would be unable to produce effective policies or democratically legitimate laws.

On this basis a European federal structure is emerging gradually, step by step, but not without opposition from those who wish to see national governments retain their sovereignty in key areas of economic policy. As Pinder explains:

This sequence of events has given rise to a neo-federalist analysis of Community development, which sees the second half of the twentieth century as a period in which federal structures and competencies, instead of being established by a single constituent act, are being created by a series of steps ... envisaging institutions of government beyond the nation state. It differs from the neo-functionalists ... by considering what institutions and competencies are adequate for the democratic governance of a single economy; and unlike the neo-functionalists, it treats each step as a political struggle between forces favouring integration and the reactions of national sovereignty, in which it is not certain which of the two will prevail.

For the 'Euro-sceptics' of the various Member States, federation means centralism, hence their stiff opposition to the Maastricht Treaty. As Anatole Kaletsky writing in 'The Times' prior to the Maastricht summit stated:

Whether or not the dreaded word 'federal' appears in the treaties, the virtual certainty of a deal on EMU [Economic and Monetary Union] makes some form of federalism inevitable. For once monetary sovereignty is removed from the nations of the European Union, the other attributes of the state are bound to follow, regardless of what provisions on political union may or may not be agreed next week.

What is clear is that these developments bring about a changing relationship between the Community and the Member States which is underpinned by the Treaties (the legal acts of the Member States) and thus by the rule of Community law. In his 1986 article, Hartley stressed that 'it is precisely those parts of the Community constitution [the Treaties] which are concerned with the legal and judicial system [as opposed to the political system] that are most federal.' In reply to the question: 'What are the essential features of a federation, as far as the courts and legal system are concerned?', he states that:

> First, obviously, there must be a federal constitution which delimits the respective spheres of the federation and the units (states, provinces, etc.)
> ...
> The Community Treaties fulfil most of the requirements of a constitution in that they establish the legislative, executive and judicial organs of the Community and grant them their powers. They do not, however, grant any powers to the Member States: it is assumed (quite correctly) that the Member States already have their powers from another source. The consequence of this is that all powers not granted to the Community remain with the Member States.

This attribution of powers by the Treaties was examined by the European Court of Justice in 1963 in the *Van Gend en Loos* case. Here the Court spoke of the establishment by the Treaty of Rome of 'institutions endowed with sovereign rights, the exercise of which affects Member States and their citizens'. It also stated that 'the States have limited their sovereign rights, albeit within limited fields'. (This case will be examined in more detail in the next chapter.)

Similarly, in litigation before the Court of Appeal in 1989, Kerr LJ stated that:

> ... there is equally no doubt that the EEC exercises powers and functions which are analogous to those of sovereign states ... the EEC enjoys certain sovereign powers to the extent to which these have been ceded to it by its members under the various EEC treaties and from this cession it has derived its own legislative, executive and judicial organs whose acts and decisions take effect within the member states. On the other hand, the EEC differs from sovereign states in that it has no sovereignty over territory as such and no nationals or citizens: *J.H. Rayner (Mincing Lane) Ltd* v *Department of Trade and Industry* (1989).
> (It will be recalled that provision for Union citizenship is to be found in the TEU: Article 8 of the EC Treaty, as amended.)

If we draw together the main points from the foregoing discussion the following picture emerges. *Transfers* of sovereignty from the Member States to the Community have taken place within certain economic and social fields. Although only partial, these transfers have assumed greater proportions as wider powers have been granted to the Community institutions by the Member States under successive agreements. The purpose of this *pooling of sovereignty* is to enable the Community to achieve those economic and social objectives laid down in the Treaties for the benefit of the Member States and their citizens. These are policies which are considered better achievable at Community rather than Member State level but they require the involvement and co-operation of all the Member States.

The *federal or supranational* nature of the Community legal (as opposed to its political) system rests on the extent to which Community law, comprising the Treaties and the law enacted by the Community institutions, is *directly binding in the Member States and has primacy over national law*. Even so, Community law is not administered solely by Community courts but by national courts also. Lasok and Bridge have summed up the position in the following terms:

> In the terms of the EEC Treaty the states endeavour to build Community institutions and to create a body of law to regulate the economic activities of the members. Although surrender of a certain portion of sovereignty is necessary in order to achieve these objectives the pooling of sovereignty is not explicit enough to create a federal state or a federal government of the Community. Therefore, at this stage of its development, the Community is merely an association of sovereign states with a federal potential.

NATIONAL SOVEREIGNTY, COMMUNITY POWERS AND SUBSIDIARITY

The current political tug-of-war between those who advocate further integration and the upholders of national sovereignty is a phenomenon which Jean Monnet himself foresaw in 1978, when he warned that the Community process 'would stop where the frontiers of political power began. Then something new would have to be invented'. A response to those who seek to stop the process of integration, before the stage of economic and monetary union is reached, is to ask to what extent nowadays do national governments independently exercise control over their economies in any case:

> The massive growth of international trade and its accompanying huge capital flows, and the emergence of multinational corporations, with

annual turnovers often in excess of the gross national products of independent countries, have made the whole world economically interdependent. As a result countries that try to isolate themselves by erecting barriers against the outside pay a heavy price in economic stagnation and backwardness, while the rest of the world moves ahead. These dramatic changes in the nature of global society have thrown up new problems that can no longer be tackled by individual countries merely looking after their own interests. Unfettered national sovereignty is obsolete, and economic and political independence is giving way to growing interdependence between nation states. The major task for the world today is to devise policies to deal with global problems and create appropriate political structures to ensure that the policies are put into effect. The same applies to individual continents or major regions within them that are affected by common problems. Amongst these, for instance, pollution, disease, crime and terrorism know no frontiers and can no longer by tackled by individual countries in isolation, but require international solutions: Wistrich.

And, from 'The Times', in June 1990:

'SOVEREIGNTY FOR 15 MINUTES'
by Nicholas Wood
Political Correspondent

British sovereignty over interest rates will boil down to a 15–minute wait before following the lead of a European central bank if the government continues to resist the Delors proposals for economic and monetary union, Sir Leon Brittan says today in a pamphlet.

In a direct assault on Margaret Thatcher's contention that monetary union would involve Britain's surrendering control over domestic monetary policy, the vice-president of the European Commission argues that the scope for independent action by the British government is already severely limited and will become more so once European Community countries have decided to embrace the single currency and a central bank.

Sir Leon points out in a paper published by the Thatcherite Centre for Policy Studies that when the Bundesbank raised interest rates last autumn, the Chancellor of the exchequer followed suit within 30 minutes, even though theoretically the government had retained full sovereignty over monetary policy by holding out against full membership of the European monetary system. 'Does anyone in this country believe that when there is a common currency for much of Europe, British interest rate decisions will not be even more tightly constrained than at present?

Let us be generous. Let us assume that if there is a European currency unit (ecu) and sterling is not part of this monetary union, that we would still have 15 minutes to decide whether to follow interest rate decisions of the 'EuroFed', before the markets took the decision for us by selling sterling and precipitating a crisis of confidence.

'Is that extra quarter of an hour of crisis really so precious an addition to sovereignty that it is worth putting British industry at a permanent competitive disadvantage ... by excluding it from the benefits of a common currency for a single market?'

It is also appropriate to ask to what extent it is true to say that sovereignty is 'lost' or 'surrendered' to Brussels. When competence is 'lost', where does it come to rest? What precisely happens when an exclusive right to legislate is ceded to a superior law-making body? The answers to these questions depend upon the view one takes of the legislative process in the Community. Monsieur Delors has said that 'it is the Council not the Commission which takes the real decisions' - the Commission merely proposes. As such it is therefore the representatives of the Member States themselves constituting the Council, often now with the co-operation of the European Parliament, who are the Community's legislators.

On this view there is no real 'surrender' of sovereignty (a word with, it is said, emotional connotations suggesting coercion on the Community's part) rather a pooling of sovereignty, jointly exercised by the Member States in order to achieve objectives which they could not attain on an individual basis:

The Council stands at the crossroads of two kinds of sovereignty, national and supranational. While it must safeguard the national interests of member states, it must not regard this as its paramount task. Its paramount task is to promote the interests of the Community; and, unless it does so, the Community will not develop: Konrad Adenauer, West German Chancellor, 1951.

The Community is based not on a loss of sovereignty but on a pooling of sovereignty, on its exercise jointly in the common good rather than its exercise separately - often selfishly and to the detriment of other people : Lord Cockfield, address to the Swiss Institute of International Affairs in Zurich, October 1988.

Nevertheless 'lukewarm' Europeans still perceive two particular threats to national interests, arising from a different view of the Community's legislative process. First, they point out that the Commission, the guardian of the Community interest, puts forward detailed proposals to a Council that has a limited right of amendment. Secondly to a reply that the Commission always works within the (widening) scope of Community competence as established by the Treaties – a contention that is itself sometimes disputed – critics observe that the post-1986 return to majority voting in the Council on a wide range of issues may well result in the demise of the national interest: the power of veto has been lost.

For example: Is vocational training for young people a matter of national education policy or one which falls within the Community competence as a question of social policy? The Court of Justice has rejected a UK claim that a Council Decision on this question lacked a sufficient legal base – Article 128 EEC which allows for a simple majority vote:

> The Council shall, acting on a proposal from the Commission and after consulting the Economic and Social Committee, lay down general principles for implementing a common vocational training policy capable of contributing to the harmonious development both of the national economies and of the common market.
> (See now Article 127 E.C., as introduced by the TEU.)

The Court would not accept the argument that Article 235 EEC, a general residual clause which requires unanimity, must be added. Article 235 states that:

> If action by the Community should prove necessary to attain, in the course of operation of the common market, one of the objectives of the Community and this Treaty has not provided the necessary powers, the Council shall, acting unanimously on a proposal from the Commission and after consulting the Assembly [Parliament], take the appropriate measures.

As integration proceeds towards union and power and control passes increasingly to the Community, a further question arises: When transfers of sovereignty occur, do the Member States lose *all* their powers within the areas concerned? As early as Case 30/59 *Limburg* v *High Authority of the ECSC* the Court of Justice stated that:

> The Community is founded on a common market, common objectives, and common institutions ... Within the specific domain of the

Community, ie for everything which relates to the pursuit of the common objectives within the common market the institutions [of the Community] are provided with exclusive authority ... Outside the domain of the Community, the governments of the Member States retain their responsibilities in all sectors of economic policy ... They remain masters of their social policy; the same undoubtedly holds true for large segments of their fiscal policy ...

This division of powers (which has clearly altered since this case was decided in 1961) should however be seen not in terms of a separation but more as a sharing of responsibilities based on the concepts of solidarity and co-operation (see, for example, Articles 5 and 177 of the Treaty of Rome). Nevertheless it remains the case that in terms of the 'moving boundary' between the Community and the Member States, the transfer of powers from the latter to the former is a continuing process with the Community increasingly in the 'driving seat'.

The Community may gain *exclusive* powers directly from the Treaties although this is so only in a limited number of areas. However, where this is the case (eg as regards Community external trade under Articles 110-116 EEC), Member States may not adopt any national measures within the area, whether or not the Community has in fact exercised its available powers. The Community may expressly delegate powers *back* to the Member States within such areas. Thus national law may still operate within the area but only if it has been authorised by the Community.

Much more significantly, the Community usually acquires exclusive competence not directly from the Treaties but from *specific enactments* based on the appropriate policy article(s) of the Treaties (see the section on 'Legal Base' in Chapter Six). It is here that the basic principle of the *supremacy* (or *primacy*) of Community law assumes great importance.

The principle of the supremacy of Community law (in relation to the national law of the Member States) means that in a case of conflict the Community measure prevails over national law. The development of common policies throughout the Community (as they supersede differing national policies or parts of them, and the law upon which they are based) requires the uniform application of Community law in all the Member States. This is a clear expression of the federal or supranational nature of Community law, although it is not laid down as such in the Treaties. The Community measures which implement such developments, and which can only be amended at Community level, thus create, in terms of competence rather than conflict, new areas of exclusive Community power.

Although Community law generally prevails over the law of the Member States in their national courts (which means that national authorities are deprived of the effective power to legislate in a manner which conflicts with Community law), this does not mean that such exclusive Community power may not itself be used to sanction derogations from, and exceptions to, Community-based rules. In such areas (eg Articles 36 and 48(3) relating to the free movement of goods and of persons), national rules will prevail within the limits laid down.

It is also important to understand that, on the basis of Community law, powers may be returned to appropriate national authorities (say, within the scope of the CAP) who are authorised and required to adopt implementing or supplementary *national* measures in order to make the underlying Community measures fully effective in an operational sense in the Member States. In this way, integrative aims can be secured through continuing co-operation between Community institutions and Member State authorities.

Similar co-operation is required (see Article 5 of the Treaty) in the case of rules of Community law which, while introducing or developing common policies (eg as regards equal pay and treatment for men and women at work), by definition require that *national powers are left intact* in order that each Member State may implement the policy according to its own choice of *form and methods* (see Article 189(3) on Directives). This was in large part the method used, under Article 100A EEC, to complete the Internal Market.

The principle of *subsidiarity*, which finds its first formal expression in the TEU, is designed to go to the heart of the question of transfers of sovereignty and the division of powers within the Community. It is essentially a response to the argument that the Community, in particular the Commission as initiator of Community policy, has acquired too much power, particularly in areas where Community-wide policies are considered to be unnecessary. It is to be seen as a countervailing force to the natural tendency of the centre to accumulate power.

On the basis of TEU, Article B, para. 2, Article 3b of the amended EC Treaty states that:

> The Community shall act within the limits of the powers conferred upon it by this Treaty and of the objectives assigned to it therein. In areas which do not fall within its exclusive competence the Community shall take action in accordance with the principle of subsidiarity only if and in so far as the objectives of the proposed action cannot be sufficiently achieved by the Member States and can therefore by reason of the scale or effects of the proposed action be better achieved by the Community.

Any action by the Community shall not go beyond what is necessary to achieve the objectives of the Treaty.

At a political level, this principle can clearly be seen as a means whereby the Member States can reassert national sovereignty and seek to move the institutional balance back from the centre. (In this respect it may be linked to the call for 'transparency' or greater 'openness' in the Community's legislative process.)

However, when the TEU comes into force, subsidiarity will become a binding legal principle which the Community must respect before taking any action under the new EC Treaty. It will be seen that the principle will only operate in areas which do not fall within the Community's exclusive competence (under TEU, Article B, para. 1, fifth indent, the 'acquis communautaire' must be fully maintained); ie it will operate in areas of *shared* competence. In policy areas of exclusive competence, the Community must act within the limits of the powers conferred upon it by the Treaty and the objectives assigned to it. In addition, such exclusive Community powers are subject to the principle of *proportionality*: no action by the Community shall go beyond what is necessary to achieve the relevant objectives. The proportionality principle also applies ('Any action by the Community ...' in the final sentence, above) where the Community does take action subsequent to an application of the principle of subsidiarity in its favour. It would therefore appear that, once Article 3b takes effect, in areas of shared competence, the Community will have the onus of showing that it (and not the Member States) should have the authority to act and also that its action is proportionate.

Establishing which policy areas are shared and so subject to subsidiarity (the environment? Social policy?) will not be easy and could lead to litigation in itself. Within areas of shared competence, it will be for the Commission to take account of the principle when putting forward policy proposals in the form of draft Community legislation and for the Council (embodying the interests of the Member States) to decide whether or not the objectives could be as well achieved at Member State level.

A final question: 'Is the principle of subsidiarity justiciable?' Is it capable, in itself, of application by a court of law? The prevailing view is that it is not. It is too imprecise for it to establish, on its own, grounds for the review of the validity of an act of the Council or Commission – under, for example, Article 173 (see Chapter Nineteen). The Court of Justice and national courts will however be in a position to apply the principle when engaged in the interpretation of Community law.

Sir Leon Brittan, a lawyer and a Vice-President of the Commission, stated in his Granada Lecture in November 1989 that subsidiarity should be seen 'as something intensely practical ... to be developed and applied with much more vigour in practice'. Perhaps the fact that 49 per cent said 'No' in the French referendum on the Maastricht Treaty in September 1992, together with the growing view that the Community has become divorced from the citizen, will mean that in future, and in accordance with Article A, para. 2 of that Treaty, decisions *will* be taken 'as closely as possible to the citizen'. Sir Leon added:

> We should ask ourselves, particularly in the social domain, is this really a decision that needs to be taken at Community level? If it is not, the Community would be wise to set out the general objective, but leave it to the individual Member State to achieve that as they wish, according to their own traditions and their own laws.

At the Edinburgh Summit of the European Council in December 1992, a memorandum was issued anticipating the adoption of an agreement in 1993 between the EC institutions on the application of the principle of subsidiarity to any new measures adopted by the Community in the future and in some cases to measures which are already in place.

TRANSFERS OF SOVEREIGNTY AND PARLIAMENTARY SOVEREIGNTY

Sovereignty is a word of many meanings. In the UK the expression *Parliamentary* sovereignty refers to the constitutional doctrine that there are no legal limits to the legislative power of Parliament except that Parliament cannot limit its own powers for the future. Thus in national law there is nothing that a statute properly enacted cannot do and therefore no act is irreversible. Now, as Collins points out:

> It is only in the sense last mentioned that the word has any useful meaning in relation to the national law of the United Kingdom. In the international sphere and in the political sphere there may have been a limitation of sovereignty but there is no reason to believe that there has yet been any limitation on the sovereignty of the United Kingdom Parliament: Collins, *European Community Law in the United Kingdom*, 1990.

Therefore, as regards transfers of *national* sovereignty as discussed earlier, it is agreed that whereas this involves the removal of legislative powers from the UK Parliament by *limiting* its authority, such transfers do not amount to an encroachment upon the doctrine of Parliamentary sovereignty:

> The stage has now been reached where the current legal and political reality is that there has been a transfer of powers to the Community. It has already been suggested that the traditional rule that Parliament may not bind its successors is not necessarily irreconcilable with the concept of a transfer of powers to another authority. It may further be suggested that whilst the political reality remains membership of the Community, such powers are unlikely in practice to be recovered, and at least to that extent the transfer can be regarded as irreversible: Usher, 1981.

Thus the European Communities Act 1972, which provides for the incorporation of Community law into the law of the UK, whilst recognising in sections 2 and 3 the supremacy of Community law (as established by the European Court of Justice), also lays down a rule of interpretation to the effect that Parliament is to be presumed not to intend any statute to override Community law. Community law will therefore always prevail over national law unless Parliament expressly states in a future Act that it is to override Community law.

In this way, the remote possibility that Parliament might some day wish to repeal the 1972 Act is not excluded and the ultimate sovereignty of Parliament is upheld:

> We have all been brought up to believe that, in legal theory, one Parliament cannot bind another and that no Act is irreversible. But legal theory does not always march alongside political reality ... What are the realities here? If Her Majesty's Ministers sign this Treaty and Parliament enacts provisions to implement it [the 1972 Act], I do not envisage that Parliament would afterwards go back on it and try to withdraw from it. But if Parliament should do so, then I say we will consider that event when it happens: Lord Denning in *Blackburn* v *Attorney-General* (1971).

Lord Denning is here referring to the unlikely eventuality of this country withdrawing from the Community. (The Treaty contains no provisions for withdrawal.)

The *reality*, therefore, is that while the UK is a member of the Community, the constitutional doctrine of Parliamentary sovereignty cannot be relied upon in the face of directly enforceable rules of Community law. Although in 1983, Sir Robert Megarry VC stated, in *Manuel* v *Attorney-General*, that 'once an instrument is recognised as being an Act of Parliament, no English court can refuse to obey it or question its validity', this statement must certainly now be modified to read 'once an instrument is recognised as being an Act of Parliament and is compatible with enforceable Community law, no English court can refuse to obey it or question its validity'. That this is the present state of the law in this country was expressed in the clearest terms and on the highest judicial authority by Lord Bridge in the *Factortame (No. 2)* case (see Chapter Twenty):

> Some public comments on the decision of the European Court of Justice, affirming the jurisdiction of the courts of Member States to override national legislation if necessary to enable interim relief to be granted in protection of rights under Community law, have suggested that this was a novel and dangerous invasion by a Community institution of the sovereignty of the United Kingdom Parliament. But such comments are based on a misconception. If the supremacy within the European Community of Community law over the national law of Member States was not always inherent in the E.E.C. Treaty it was certainly well-established in the jurisprudence of the European Court of Justice long before the United Kingdom joined the Community. Thus, whatever limitation of its sovereignty Parliament accepted when it enacted the European Communities Act 1972 was entirely voluntary. Under the terms of the Act of 1972 it has always been clear that it was the duty of a United Kingdom court, when delivering final judgment, to override any rule of national law found to be in conflict with any directly enforceable rule of Community law ... Thus there is nothing in any way novel in according supremacy to rules of Community law in those areas to which they apply and to insist that, in the protection of rights under Community law, national courts must not be inhibited by rules of national law from granting interim relief in appropriate cases is no more than a logical recognition of that supremacy.

Beaud, Michel, 'The Nation-State Questioned' in Contemporary European Affairs: *1992 and After*, Vol. 1, 1989, No. 1/2.

Bieber, Roland, 'On the Mutual Completion of Overlapping Legal Systems: The Case of the European Communities and the National Legal Orders' (1988)13 EL Rev 147.

Bradley, A.W., 'Sovereignty of Parliament' in Jowell and Oliver (eds) *The Changing Constitution.*

Brewin, C., 'The European Community: A Union of States without Unity of Government' (1987) 26 JCMS 1.

Cass, D., 'The Word that Saves Maastricht? The Principle of Subsidiarity ...' (1992) 29 CML Rev. 1107.

Cockfield, Lord, 'National Sovereignty and the European Community' (1986) 39 *Studia Diplomatica* 649.

Emiliou, N., 'Subsidiarity: An Effective Barrier Against `the Enterprises of Ambition'?' (1992) 17 EL Rev. 383.

Hartley, Trevor, 'Federalism, Courts and Legal Systems: The Emerging Constitution of the European Community' (1986)34 *American Journal of Comparative Law* 224.

Layton, C., 'The Sharing of Sovereignty' in 'One Europe, One World' (1986) *Journal of World Trade Law*, Special Supplement No. 4.

Pinder, John, 'European Community and Nation-State: A Case for a Neo-Federalism? (1986) *International Affairs* 41.

Temple Lang, John, 'European Community Constitutional Law: The Division of Powers Between the Community and the Member States' (1988) 39 *Northern Ireland Legal Quarterly* 209.

Toth, A., 'The Principle of Subsidiarity in the Maastricht Treaty' (1992) 29 CML Rev. 1079.

Turpin, Colin, *British Government and Constitution*, (sections on 'Parliamentary Sovereignty' and 'Sovereignty and the European Community').

Usher, John, *European Community Law and National Law: The Irreversible Transfer?*

Usher, John, 'The Scope of Community Competence – Its Recognition and Enforcement' (1985) 24 JCMS 121.

Wade, W.H.R., 'What has Happened to the Sovereignty of Parliament?' (1991) 107 LQR 1.

Wilke, M. and Wallace, H., 'Subsidiarity: Approaches to Power-Sharing in the European Community', Royal Institute of International Affairs Discussion Paper No. 27, 1990.

Wistrich, Ernest, *After 1992 – The United States of Europe*, 1989.

PART TWO

THE NATURE AND EFFECT

OF

COMMUNITY LAW

CHAPTER FOUR

THE NATURE AND MAIN SOURCES OF COMMUNITY LAW

THE SOURCES OF COMMUNITY LAW

... all Community law by one route or another must find its roots and its authority in a written text, that of the Treaties themselves. The bulk of Community law, as the reported cases demonstrate, is concerned with the interpretation and validity of further written texts, Community 'acts' such as directives, regulations or decisions: Lord Mackenzie Stuart, former President of the European Court of Justice.

The three major formal (as opposed to economic or social) sources of Community law are to be found in Lord Mackenzie Stuart's statement:

1. The Constitutional Treaties of the Community (which are acts of the Member States).
2. The law-making acts of the Community's political institutions.
3. The decisions of the Court of Justice (and the general principles of law and fundamental rights recognised and developed by that court).

The Treaties form the basis of the Community legal order. They are *primary* sources from which *secondary* sources are derived. Thus Community acts (Regulations, Directives and Decisions) must establish themselves upon a legal base from within the Treaties.

1 The Constitutional Treaties

The constitutional nature of the Treaties has been discussed in the preceding chapters. They do not merely create rights and duties between the Member States but establish the autonomous legislative, executive and judicial organs of the Community – each of which is granted specific powers (see Article 4) which regulate the activities of Member States, business organisations and individuals.

As we have seen, there are three founding Treaties:

The Treaty of Paris Establishing the European Coal and Steel Community, 1951 (in force 1952).

The Treaty of Rome Establishing the European Economic Community, 1957.

The Treaty of Rome Establishing the European Atomic Energy Community (EURATOM), 1957 (both in force 1958).

Revisions of the founding Treaties have been discussed, the main ones being:

The Treaty Establishing a Single Council and a Single Commission of the European Communities (the Merger Treaty) 1965 (in force 1967).

The Treaties of Accession of new Member States: The First Accessions (Denmark, Ireland and the UK) 1972 (in force 1973); The Second Accession (Greece) 1979 (in force 1981); The Third Accessions (Spain and Portugal) 1985 (in force 1986).

The Single European Act 1986 (in force 1987).

(The Treaty on European Union, agreed at Maastricht in December 1991 and signed in February 1992) [In effect 1 November 1993.]

The predominant integrative aims of the EEC Treaty* are, from a legal standpoint, facilitated by the 'self-executing' character of the Treaty. This means that upon ratification the Treaty of Rome *automatically* becomes law within the Member States and must be directly applied as such by national courts and tribunals. (This point was touched upon in the previous chapter when discussing the supranational character of Community law.) There is no *requirement*, as in the case of a 'non-self-executing' treaty (which merely creates obligations of a contractual nature binding on the signatories in international law), for the Treaty to be incorporated into the national law of the Member States by means of implementing legislation. However, as a consequence of the UK's *dualist view* of international law as being a separate system of law from national law, it became necessary upon accession, *from a national viewpoint*, for the UK to make Community law applicable within the national legal system by means of a special Act, the European Communities Act, 1972: see Chapter Eight.

The Treaty takes its 'self-executing' character from its legislative form and its constitutional design. The implementation of the Treaty is, by its terms (see Article 4) removed from the control of the Member States and the rights and duties which it establishes exist not merely between the Member States on a reciprocal international basis but on the basis of a complex set of legal relationships between the Member States, their *nationals* and the Community institutions: see, in particular, Case 26/62 *Van Gend en Loos*,

---

* The text, cases and materials will hereafter refer mainly to the EEC and the EEC Treaty. TEU amendments to that Treaty will be referred to where appropriate. In any event, article numbers generally remain the same.

discussed below, in which the Court of Justice established that certain key provisions of the Treaty are *directly effective*, ie they create rights for individuals (both natural and legal) which they may invoke in national courts in disputes with their national authorities or with other individuals. The enormous impact of the principle of direct effect, as established and developed by the Court of Justice, in terms of the Community's quasi-federal structure, its integrative goals, and the rights of Community nationals will be discussed below and in subsequent chapters.

In broad terms, the content of the Treaty can be divided into two main parts, although Community case law shows that they are very much interwoven. It embodies the *institutional* organisation of the Community and the powers and duties of the institutions in terms of law-making and law enforcement. The Treaty also contains the legal basis for the Community's economic and social policies: the *substantive* law of the Community. On the basis of Articles 2 and 3 (aims, means and objectives), it lays down in varying degrees of detail the legal framework of the interlocking processes of negative and positive integration: for example, the customs union rules, the common agricultural policy, the rules on competition, and on economic and monetary union.

2. Community Law-Making Acts (Community Legislation)

The three political institutions, the Council, the Commission and the Parliament, are responsible for the adoption of binding Community acts (secondary or derived legislation), which amplify the articles of the Treaty and enable Community law and policy to be brought fully into effect.

Such acts derive their authority from the fact that they are brought into force by institutions invested with the necessary power, *where specific articles of the Treaty so provide*: eg Article 49 which authorises the Council to issue directives or make regulations in order to bring about freedom of movement for workers; or Article 100A which grants the Council power to adopt measures for the harmonisation of the laws of the Member States in the course of the establishment and functioning of the internal market.

In that they derive their authority from the Treaty (which is an act of the Member States) and so rank below it, Community acts can be compared to delegated legislation. Whereas neither the Court of Justice nor national courts have the power to test the validity of the Treaty (the constitution), the validity of Community acts can be challenged either directly before the Court of Justice under Article 173 or indirectly in a national court on the basis of the Court's preliminary rulings jurisdiction under Article 177(1)(b) (see Chapters Nine and Nineteen).

Article 189 of the Treaty provides legal definitions of the various Community acts. The first paragraph states that:

> In order to carry out their task the Council and the Commission shall, in accordance with the provisions of this Treaty, make regulations, issue directives, take decisions, make recommendations or deliver opinions.

Article 189(1) is to be amended by the TEU to take account of the Parliament's power of co-decision with the Council in certain defined areas: see Chapter Five.

Regulations, Directives and Decisions are obligatory acts whereas recommendations and opinions are stated in Article 189(5) to 'have no binding force'. They are therefore non–obligatory and are not legal acts.

Regulations

Under Article 189(2):

> A regulation shall have general application. It shall be binding in its entirety and directly applicable in all Member States.

The 'general application' of a Regulation is indicative of its legislative character and it is the main instrument for uniformity throughout the Community.

> It is applicable ... to objectively determined situations and involves legal consequences for categories of persons viewed in a general and abstract manner: Court of Justice in Case 6/68 *Zuckerfabrik Watenstedt* v *Council*.

For example, see *Council Regulation 1612/68 on Freedom of Movement for Workers within the Community*, Official Journal, Special Edition 1968(II), 475, the first part of which is reproduced on page 67.

In Article 189(2), the provisions of Regulations are stated to be '*directly applicable*'; ie they penetrate into the legal order of the Member States without the need for any national implementing measures (cf. Treaty articles). Also, as will be seen, Regulations normally have *direct effect*, creating rights for individuals (eg workers) that must be protected by national courts: see Chapter Eight.. However, this is not the case where a Regulation states that certain of its provisions are to be implemented by the national authorities: eg

Official Journal of the European Communities

No L 257/2   Official Journal of the European Communities   19.10.68

REGULATION (EEC) No 1612/68 OF THE COUNCIL

of 15 October 1968

on freedom of movement for workers within the Community

THE COUNCIL OF THE EUROPEAN COMMUNITIES,

Having regard to the Treaty establishing the European Economic Community, and in particular Article 49 thereof;

Having regard to the proposal from the Commission;

Having regard to the Opinion of the European Parliament;

Having regard to the Opinion of the Economic and Social Committee;

[...]

PART I

EMPLOYMENT AND WORKERS' FAMILIES

TITLE I

Eligibility for employment

Article 1

1. Any national of a Member State shall, irrespective of his place of residence, have the right to take up an activity as an employed person, and to pursue such activity, within the territory of another Member State in accordance with the provisions laid down by law, regulation or administrative action governing the employment of nationals of that State.

2. He shall, in particular, have the right to take up available employment in the territory of another Member State with the same priority as nationals of that State.

Article 2

Any national of a Member State and any employer pursuing an activity in the territory of a Member State may exchange their applications for and offers of employment, and may conclude and perform contracts of employment in accordance with the provisions in force laid down by law, regulation or administrative action, without any discrimination resulting therefrom.

Article 3

1. Under this Regulation, provisions laid down by law, regulation or administrative action or administrative practices of a Member State shall not apply:

— where they limit application for and offers of employment, or the right of foreign nationals to take up and pursue employment or subject this to conditions not applicable in respect of their own nationals; or

— where, though applicable irrespective of nationality, their exclusive or principal aim or effect is to keep nationals of other Member States away from the employment offered.

This provision shall not apply to conditions relating to linguistic knowledge required by reason of the nature of the post to be filled.

2. There shall be included in particular among the provisions or practices of a Member State referred to in the first subparagraph of paragraph 1 those which:

(a) prescribe a special recruitment procedure for foreign nationals;

(b) limit or restrict the advertising of vacancies in the press or through any other medium or subject it to conditions other than those applicable in respect of employers pursuing their activities in the territory of that Member State;

(c) subject eligibility for employment to conditions of registration with employment offices or impede recruitment of individual workers, where persons who do not reside in the territory of that State are concerned.

Article 4

1. Provisions laid down by law, regulation or administrative action of the Member States which restrict by number or percentage the employment of foreign nationals in any undertaking, branch of activity or region, or at a national level, shall not apply to nationals of the other Member States.

2. When in a Member State the granting of any benefit to undertakings is subject to a minimum percentage of national workers being employed, nationals of the other Member States shall be counted as national workers, subject to the provisions of the Council Directive of 15 October 1963.[1]

[1] OJ No 159, 2.11.1963, p. 2661/63.

as regards the creation of new criminal offences in Case 128/78 *Commission v UK (Re Tachographs)*;.

Directives

Under Article 189(3):

A directive shall be binding, as to the result to be achieved, upon each Member State to which it is addressed, but shall leave to the national authorities the choice of form and methods.

Unlike a Regulation which is binding in every respect, a Directive is only binding 'as to the result to be achieved' for each Member State to which it is addressed. A Directive may be addressed to all the Member States (eg internal market harmonisation Directives issued under Article 100A) or perhaps to only one. It is therefore not necessarily of 'general application'.

... while the principal subjects governed by Regulations are agriculture, transport, customs and social security of migrant workers, Community authorities resort to Directives when they intend to harmonise national laws on such matters as taxes, banking, equality of the sexes, protection of the environment, employment contracts and the organisation of companies. Plain cooking and haute cuisine, in other words. The hope of seeing Europe grow institutionally, in matters of social relationships and in terms of quality of life, rests to a large extent on the adoption and implementation of Directives: Mancini.

An addressee Member State is under an obligation (see Article 5) to achieve the aim or purpose of a Directive but has a discretion as to the type of measure and procedure adopted at national level to achieve that result. A Directive is not therefore directly applicable. Under the scheme envisaged by Article 189(3), individuals within the scope of the Directive will *acquire rights* on the basis of the *national* implementing measure. However, where national authorities *fail to implement* Directives properly, or within the time limit laid down, rights for individuals *may* nevertheless accrue, ie Directives may have direct effect: see Chapter Eight.

On page 69 is an example of a Directive within the field of social policy. It is based on Article 100 (relating to harmonisation of national laws) and it implements in more specific terms the principle of equal pay in Article 119.

19. 2. 75 Official Journal of the European Communities No L 45/19

II

(Acts whose publication is not obligatory)

COUNCIL

COUNCIL DIRECTIVE

of 10 February 1975

on the approximation of the laws of the Member States relating to the application of the principle of equal pay for men and women

(75/117/EEC)

THE COUNCIL OF THE EUROPEAN COMMUNITIES,

Having regard to the Treaty establishing the European Economic Community, and in particular Article 100 thereof;

Having regard to the proposal from the Commission;

Having regard to the Opinion of the European Parliament (¹);

Having regard to the Opinion of the Economic and Social Committee (²);

Whereas implementation of the principle that men and women should receive equal pay contained in Article 119 of the Treaty is an integral part of the establishment and functioning of the common market;

Whereas it is primarily the responsibility of the Member States to ensure the application of this principle by means of appropriate laws, regulations and administrative provisions;

Whereas the Council resolution of 21 January 1974 (³) concerning a social action programme, aimed at making it possible to harmonize living and working conditions while the improvement is being maintained and at achieving a balanced social and economic development of the Community, recognized that priority should be given to action taken on behalf of women as regards access to employment and vocational training and advancement and as regards working conditions, including pay;

Whereas it is desirable to reinforce the basic laws by standards aimed at facilitating the practical application of the principle of equality in such a way that all employees in the Community can be protected in these matters;

Whereas differences continue to exist in the various Member States despite the efforts made to apply the resolution of the conference of the Member States of 30 December 1961 on equal pay for men and women and whereas, therefore, the national provisions should be approximated as regards application of the principle of equal pay,

HAS ADOPTED THIS DIRECTIVE:

Article 1

The principle of equal pay for men and women outlined in Article 119 of the Treaty, hereinafter called 'principle of equal pay', means, for the same work or for work to which equal value is attributed, the elimination of all discrimination on grounds of sex with regard to all aspects and conditions of remuneration.

In particular, where a job classification system is used for determining pay, it must be based on the same criteria for both men and women and so drawn up as to exclude any discrimination on grounds of sex.

(¹) OJ No C 55, 13. 5. 1974, p. 43.
(²) OJ No C 88, 26. 7. 1974, p. 7.
(³) OJ No C 13, 12. 2. 1974, p. 1.

No L 45/20 Official Journal of the European Communities 19. 2. 75

Article 2

Member States shall introduce into their national legal systems such measures as are necessary to enable all employees who consider themselves wronged by failure to apply the principle of equal pay to pursue their claims by judicial process after possible recourse to other competent authorities.

Article 3

Member States shall abolish all discrimination between men and women arising from laws, regulations or administrative provisions which is contrary to the principle of equal pay.

Article 4

Member States shall take the necessary measures to ensure that provisions appearing in collective agreements, wage scales, wage agreements or individual contracts of employment which are contrary to the principle of equal pay shall be, or may be declared, null and void or may be amended.

Article 5

Member States shall take the necessary measures to protect employees against dismissal by the employer as a reaction to a complaint within the undertaking or to any legal proceedings aimed at enforcing compliance with the principle of equal pay.

Article 6

Member States shall, in accordance with their national circumstances and legal systems, take the measures necessary to ensure that the principle of equal pay is applied. They shall see that effective means are available to take care that this principle is observed.

Article 7

Member States shall take care that the provisions adopted pursuant to this Directive, together with the relevant provisions already in force, are brought to the attention of employees by all appropriate means, for example at their place of employment.

Article 8

1. Member States shall put into force the laws, regulations and administrative provisions necessary in order to comply with this Directive within one year of its notification and shall immediately inform the Commission thereof.

2. Member States shall communicate to the Commission the texts of the laws, regulations and administrative provisions which they adopt in the field covered by this Directive.

Article 9

Within two years of the expiry of the one-year period referred to in Article 8, Member States shall forward all necessary information to the Commission to enable it to draw up a report on the application of this Directive for submission to the Council.

Article 10

This Directive is addressed to the Member States.

Done at Brussels, 10 February 1975.

For the Council

The President

G. FITZGERALD

Decisions

Under Article 189(4):
A decision shall be binding in its entirety upon those to whom it is addressed.

Community law is applied in *specific cases* by means of Decisions. They are binding in every respect upon their addressees who may be Member States, individuals or corporations. In Case 54/65 *Compagnie des Forges de Châtillon* v *High Authority*, the Court of Justice defined a decision (so distinguishing it from a non-binding communication, opinion or recommendation) as:

A measure emanating from the competent authority, intended to produce legal effects and constituting the culmination of procedure within that authority, whereby the latter gives its final ruling in a form from which its nature can be identified.

The binding nature of a Decision means that there is no room for any discretion as to the manner in which it is to be carried out. Clearly, Decisions may be taken (as legal acts) for a wide variety of purposes. Commission Decisions in the field of competition policy are of a quasi-judicial nature. Such a Decision may, on the basis of Article 86 and implementing Council Regulation 17/62, find an *undertaking* to be abusing its dominant position on a product market and impose a large fine. To take a further example, at the time of the 'mad cow disease' scare in the UK, the Commission adopted Decision 89/469 concerning 'certain protective measures relating to bovine spongiform encephalopathy in the United Kingdom'. It was in turn based on Council Directive 64/432 on 'animal health problems affecting intra-Community trade in bovine animals and swine', which was in turn based on the appropriate Treaty article: see page 70.

The bicephalous or two-headed nature of Community law-making, the fact that both the Council and the Commission have powers to act, requires some explanation. For the most part, the Commission's powers are delegated to it by the Council: see Article 145 and, more particularly, Article 155. In these cases, the Council lays down general principles, for example in a Regulation, and delegates to the Commission the task of implementing those general principles by means of detailed rules in a further measure: see Case 25/70 *Köster*.

3. 8. 89   Official Journal of the European Communities   No L 225/51

COMMISSION DECISION
of 28 July 1989
concerning certain protection measures relating to bovine spongiform encephalopathy in the United Kingdom

(89/469/EEC)

THE COMMISSION OF THE EUROPEAN COMMUNITIES,

Having regard to the Treaty establishing the European Economic Community,

Having regard to Council Directive 64/432/EEC of 26 June 1964 on animal health problems affecting intra-Community trade in bovine animals and swine (¹), as last amended by Directive 89/360/EEC (²), and in particular Article 9 thereof.

Whereas several outbreaks of bovine spongiform encephalopathy have occurred throughout the territory of the United Kingdom ;

Whereas this disease can be considered to be a new serious contagious or infectious animal disease whose presence may constitute a danger to cattle in other Member States ;

Whereas a significant risk may be considered to exist in respect of live animals ; whereas however, this risk is considered to exist only for cattle born before 18 July 1988 or born to affected cows, in view of the epidemiology and pathogenesis of the disease ;

Whereas the United Kingdom authorities have given certain guarantees to certain Member States to prevent the spread of the disease ; whereas therefore these measures should be applied to intra-Community trade to all Member States ;

Whereas the measures provided for in this Decision are in accordance with the opinion of the Standing Veterinary Committee.

HAS ADOPTED THIS DECISION :

Article 1

The United Kingdom shall not send to other Member States live cattle born before 18 July 1988 or born to females in which bovine spongiform encephalopathy is suspected or has been officially confirmed.

Article 2

The health certificate provided for in Directive 64/432/EEC accompanying cattle sent from the United Kingdom must be completed by the following :

'animals in accordance with Commission Decision 89/469/EEC of 28 July 1989 concerning bovine spongiform encephalopathy'.

Article 3

Member States shall amend the measures which they apply to trade so as to bring into compliance with this Decision three days after its notification. They shall immediately inform the Commission thereof.

Article 4

The Commission will follow developments in the situation. This Decision may be amended in the light of such developments.

Article 5

This Decision is addressed to the Member States.

Done at Brussels, 28 July 1989.

For the Commission
Ray MAC SHARRY
Member of the Commission

(¹) OJ No 121, 29. 7. 1964, p. 1977/64.
(²) OJ No L 153, 6. 6. 1989, p. 29.

To the extent that the European Parliament will have powers of co-decision with the Council in the legislative process under the TEU, it will be more appropriate to speak of the three-headed nature of Community law-making.

Article 190 (amended by the TEU to take account of the Council and Parliament acting jointly) presently provides that:

> Regulations, directives and decisions of the Council and Commission shall state the reasons on which they are based and shall refer to any proposals or opinions which were required to be obtained pursuant to this Treaty.

In Case 18/62 *Barge*, Advocate General Lagrange submitted with reference to Regulations that they must be reasoned, indicating in general terms the aims pursued, the reasons justifying them and the outline of the system adopted. Article 190 does not therefore impose a mere formal requirement:

> In imposing upon the Commission the obligation to state the reasons for its decisions, Article 190 is not taking mere formal considerations into account but seeks to give an opportunity to the parties of defending their rights, to the Court of exercising its supervisory functions and to Member States and to all interested nationals of ascertaining the circumstances in which the Commission has applied the Treaty: Court of Justice in Case 24/62 *Germany v Commission (Brennwein)*.

An absence of sufficient reasons may lead the Court to nullify an act under Article 173 on the ground of the infringement of an essential procedural requirement. This is also the case where the Council fails to obtain the opinion of the Parliament (or the Economic and Social Committee) as and when required by the relevant Treaty provision: see Case 138/79 *Roquette Frères v Council*.

Article 191 states that:

> Regulations shall be published in the Official Journal of the Community. They shall enter into force on the date specified in them or, in the absence thereof, on the twentieth day following their publication.

Directives and decisions shall be notified to those to whom they are addressed and shall take effect upon such notification.

Regulations are published in the 'L' series of the Official Journal, as are the vast majority of Directives and Decisions – a practice which is put on a proper legal footing under the TEU amendment of Article 191.

The foregoing description of Community acts suggests, in Hartley's words, 'a fairly neat and tidy system ... Unfortunately, things are not as simple as this.' Firstly, although exceptionally, the formal designation of an act is not always an accurate guide to its contents. For example, a Directive may leave very little discretion to Member States as to the choice of form and methods for its implementation. It may therefore take on the character (although not the legal status) of a Regulation. A Regulation may, at least in part, lose its general and objective character and, in deciding a specific issue, become what the Court has termed a 'disguised decision'. (As will be seen in Chapter Nineteen, this is significant in that under Article 173(2) natural and legal persons may within certain limits challenge the validity of Decisions but not Regulations or Directives.) It is the *function* of an act rather than its label which is of primary importance.

It is also significant that in Case 22/70 *Commission v Council (ERTA)* the Court of Justice ruled that the list of acts in Article 189 was *not exhaustive*. It was decided in this case (discussed more fully in Chapter Six) that a Council 'resolution' concerning the negotiating procedure for the European Road Transport Agreement was intended to have, and in practice did have, legal effects on relations between the Community and the Member States and on the relations between the institutions. The 'resolution' was held to be an act *sui generis*.

In a further development, which is significant in the light of the European Parliament's continuing campaign for real legislative powers, the Court recognised the Parliament's capacity to adopt legally binding acts in Case 294/83 *Partie Ecologiste Les Verts v Parliament*. The Court's ruling came within the context of a Article 173 challenge to a decision of the Parliament in connection with direct elections and was justified on the basis of the Parliament's enhanced status and power to pass measures which could affect the rights of third parties (see also Chapter Six).

3. Decisions of the Court of Justice

Decisions of the Court of Justice constitute a secondary source of Community law by providing authoritative *interpretations* of the Treaty and acts of the institutions made thereunder. The Treaty is a 'traité cadre', a framework Treaty, the wording of which is much removed from the precise, tightly drafted provisions of an English statute. In the course of explaining the Treaty (and derived legislation) over several decades, the Court has complemented and filled in gaps in the Community legal system in a way which has considerably enhanced the process of economic and legal integration.

Additionally, in a number of highly important decisions, the Court has gone some way beyond interpretation in the normal sense of the term and, as a policy-maker, has established, refined and developed several *basic principles* which can be said to be implied within the Treaty. In the cases discussed in the section which follows can be found the interrelated principles of the autonomy, supremacy, direct applicability and direct effect of Community law. While clarifying the relationship between Community law and national law, the Court has, in its use of these principles, also done much to increase the scope and effectiveness of Community law, not least as regards the availability of rights for individuals within the Community legal order.

A further major contribution, closely linked to the final point made above, has come about through the Court's recognition and development of *general principles of Community law* (referred to in the Treaty as 'general principles common to the laws of the Member States' in Article 215). The jurisprudence of the Court in this field has been variously described as 'a creative act of judicial legislation' and 'naked law-making'. Some of these principles are to be found in the Treaty itself, eg solidarity in Article 5 and non-discrimination on the grounds of nationality in Article 7 (Article 6 EC as amended by the TEU), but in the main they have been taken by the Court from the national legal traditions of the Member States and adapted to the Community context. They include *equality* (or non-discrimination as a *general* principle), *fundamental human rights* (to which the Treaty makes no express reference) and *proportionality*.

The principle of proportionality, for example, means that economic burdens may be placed on individuals (or corporations) for the purposes of the general Community interest (ie in the furtherance of Community policy) only to the extent that is strictly necessary for the attainment of such purposes: a question of means and ends. This definition, and the clear purpose of the other principles mentioned, indicates that the main, but not sole, function of these general principles (they may also provide a bedrock aid to interpretation) lies in the field of Community administrative law. They may be invoked by individuals and corporations and Member States in the course of challenges to action, or inaction, on the part of the Community institutions (see Chapters Ten and Nineteen).

THE COURT OF JUSTICE AND THE PRINCIPLES OF SUPREMACY AND DIRECT EFFECT OF COMMUNITY LAW

It follows from the very concept of integration, of common and co-ordinated policies, and not least from the need for the establishment and maintenance of a Common Market by institutions charged with these duties by the Treaty itself (ie by the agreement of the Member States), that Community law must have a uniform meaning and effect in all the Member States and that primacy or *supremacy* must be accorded to Community law within the national legal orders of the Member States. The Community would not be able to function properly if Member States had the power to annul Community law by adopting, or giving precedence to, national law. If this were possible Community law would lose its essential character and the legal basis of the Community would be radically impaired. The continuing development of Community policies, in the search for the attainment of the objectives in Article 2, must of necessity also involve the provision of new or enhanced legal rights for individuals (ie for both natural and legal persons) within the widening ambit of the Community's economic and social jurisdiction. The duty of the Member States under Article 5 to fulfil the obligations imposed on them by the Treaty and Community legislation entails not only the possibility of an action brought against them, normally by the Commission under Article 169, for breach of these obligations but also a duty which rests on their national courts to recognise and protect those *directly effective* rights which Community law confers on individuals and which they seek to enforce against national authorities or other individuals. Those rights, as we have indicated and shall discuss in more detail in due course, may arise under the Treaty itself or from specific provisions of the binding Community acts defined in Article 189, ie Regulations, Directive and Decisions.

Neither the supremacy of Community law nor its capability to give rise to individual rights is to be found in the Treaty, except by way of the definition of a Regulation in Article 189. These fundamental principles, lying at the heart of the Community legal system and its relationship with the law of the Member States, were established and elucidated by the Court of Justice in some of its earlier judgments. The nature and supremacy of Community law is more fully spelt out in the following policy decision:

Case 6/64 *Costa* v *ENEL*

In 1962 the Italian Government nationalised private electricity undertakings and transferred their assets to ENEL. Costa, a lawyer and former shareholder in one of the undertakings, objected to the nationalisation measures. When presented with an electricity bill for £1 by ENEL, he refused to pay it and on being sued he pleaded, amongst other things, that the nationalisation legislation was incompatible with various Treaty articles.

The Milanese magistrate sought guidance from the Court of Justice under Article 177. The Italian authorities argued that the matter was to be settled by domestic law alone and that the magistrate's request was 'absolutely inadmissible'. The Court of Justice ruled that:

The Italian Government submits that the request of the Giudice Conciliatore is 'absolutely inadmissible', inasmuch as a national court which is obliged to apply a national law cannot avail itself of Article 177.

By contrast with ordinary international treaties, the Treaty has created its own legal system which, on the entry into force of the Treaty, became an integral part of the legal systems of the Member States and which their courts are bound to apply.

By creating a Community of unlimited duration, having its own institutions, its own personality, its own legal capacity and capacity of representation on the international plane and, more particularly, real powers stemming from a limitation of sovereignty or a transfer of powers from the States to the Community, the Member States have limited their sovereign rights, albeit within limited fields, and have thus created a body of law which binds both their nationals and themselves.

The integration into the laws of each Member State of provisions, which derive from the Community and more generally the terms and the spirit of the Treaty, make it impossible for the States, as a corollary, to accord precedence to a unilateral and subsequent measure over a legal system accepted by them on a basis of reciprocity. Such a measure cannot therefore be inconsistent with that legal system. The executive force of the Community law cannot vary from one State to another in deference to subsequent domestic laws, without jeopardising the attainment of the objectives of the Treaty set out in Article 5(2) and giving rise to the discrimination prohibited by Article 7.

The obligations undertaken under the Treaty establishing the Community would not be unconditional, but merely contingent, if they could be called in question by subsequent legislative acts of the signatories. Wherever the Treaty grants the States the right to act unilaterally, it does this by clear and precise provisions ...

The precedence of Community law is confirmed by Article 189, whereby a regulation 'shall be binding' and 'directly applicable in all Member States'. This provision, which is subject to no reservation, would be quite meaningless if a State could unilaterally nullify by means of a legislative measure which could prevail over Community law.

It follows from all these observations that the law stemming from the Treaty, an independent source of law, could not, because of its special and original nature, be overridden by domestic legal provisions, however framed, without being deprived of its character as Community law and without the legal basis of the Community itself being called into question.

The transfer by the States from their domestic legal system to the Community legal system of the rights and obligations arising under the Treaty carries with it a permanent limitation of their sovereign rights, against which a subsequent unilateral act incompatible with the concept of the Community cannot prevail. Consequently Article 177 is to be applied regardless of any domestic law, whenever questions relating to the interpretation of the Treaty arise ...

These statements are based on the Court's view or interpretation of the Treaty as the legal vehicle whereby the *objects* of the Community may be achieved. It may be cited as an example of what is known as the teleological or purposive method of interpretation. However, as Hartley has explained:

... the court prefers to interpret texts on the basis of what it thinks they should be trying to achieve; it moulds the law according to what it regards as the needs of the Community. This is sometimes called the 'teleological method of interpretation' but it really goes beyond interpretation properly so-called: it is decision-making on the basis of policy.

It will be noticed that in the course of this decision, which concerned *Treaty articles*, the Court confirms the precedence of Community law by reference to the *direct applicability of Regulations*. Not only may no unilateral national legislative measure nullify a Regulation but no such measure is required to implement or transpose a Regulation into national law. Gormley has put the position in the following terms:

> The Court of Justice, however, on the basis of the Community legal order takes a quite different position from the current conception of international law, a conception which leaves the regulation of the internal effect of rules of international law to constitutional law. As a matter of fact, it appears from the case-law of the Court that Treaty provisions ... penetrate into the internal legal order without the aid of any national measure, to the extent that their character makes this appropriate ... Such provisions, like regulations (which are by nature and function in the system of Community sources of law directly applicable) must be applied by the national courts without the intervention of a legal measure designed to transpose Community law ... into domestic law.

Similarly, in Case 34/73 *Variola*, the Court of Justice stated that:

> In the fourth and fifth questions, the Court is, in effect, asked to determine whether the disputed provisions of the Regulations can be introduced into the legal order of Member States by internal measures reproducing the contents of Community provisions in such a way that the subject-matter is brought under national law, and the jurisdiction of the Court is thereby affected.

> The direct application of a Regulation means that its entry unto force and its application in favour of or against those subject to it are independent of any measure of reception into national law.
> By virtue of the obligations arising from the Treaty and assumed on ratification, Member States are under a duty not to obstruct the direct applicability inherent in Regulations and other rules of Community law.

> Strict compliance with this obligation is an indispensable condition of simultaneous and uniform application of Community Regulations throughout the Community.

Direct applicability, which strictly speaking only applies to Regulations, relates to *how* provisions of Community law enter the legal order of the Member States. The principle of *direct effect* on the other hand concerns the effectiveness of provisions of Community law once they enter the national legal systems. Although closely related, the two principles should be considered separately.

In *Costa* v *ENEL*, the Court of Justice stated that Community law binds both Member States and individuals and also that the national courts of the Member State are bound to apply Community law. As we have seen when examining the definitions of the binding Community acts in Article 189, such acts may well create rights for individuals which may be relied upon by them in national courts. And, if this is so as regards Community legislation (a secondary source), then, although the Treaty does not state as such, it must also be the case as regards Treaty provisions also (a primary source).

In the famous *Van Gend en Loos* case in 1963, the principle of direct effect, the clearest legal indicator of supranationality, was fully explained by the Court of Justice. In the course of answering questions regarding the nature and effect of one of the Treaty's customs union rules (Article 12), put to it by a Dutch court called upon to decide a case brought by a Dutch company against the national customs authorities, the Court ruled that this provision of Community law 'produces direct effects and creates individual rights which national courts must protect'. The Court stressed the constitutional nature of the Treaty – 'this Treaty is more than an agreement which merely creates mutual obligations between the contracting states' – and thus a consequent need to provide 'direct legal protection of the individual rights of ... nationals'. These rights find their Community law corollary in *obligations* which rest upon others – in this case the Dutch state. Because the article in question was 'ideally adapted to produce direct effects in the legal relationship between Member States and their subjects', it enabled the plaintiff company, threatened by the breach of its obligations by the Dutch state, to assert its rights before the national court.

As Brown and Jacobs have explained:

> The notion of the direct effect of Community law, coupled with the jurisdiction of the Court to give preliminary rulings and so to determine the scope of the individual's rights and obligations, is a more powerful weapon [than Articles 169 and 170]. The individual has no direct remedy, before the Court, against the default of a State. The remedy lies with the national court, with the use of Article 177 where necessary. In this way the national courts enforce, if necessary against their own State, the rights conferred on the individual by the Treaty.

Case 26/62 *Van Gend en Loos*

In September 1960, VG imported into the Netherlands from West Germany a quantity of a chemical product known as unreaformaldehyde.

In December 1959 a Dutch statute had been passed which brought into force modifications of the Benelux tariff system as a result of acceptance of the Brussels Nomenclature, a measure designed to secure international unification of the classification of goods for customs purposes. Regrouping of goods under the nomenclature resulted in an increase in the amount of duty payable on ureaformaldehyde to 8% on an 'ad valorem' basis.

However, Article 12, EEC had come into force as regards intra-Community trade on 1 January 1958.

Article 12: Member States shall refrain from introducing between themselves any new customs duties on imports or exports or any charges having equivalent effect, and from increasing those which they already apply in their trade with each other.

VG contended that on 1 January 1958 the duty payable under Dutch law on the product in question was 3% and they objected to paying the additional 5%.

The Customs Inspector having rejected their claim, VG appealed to the Dutch Tariefcommissie (Customs Court) in Amsterdam. Under Article 177, the Tariefcommissie certified two questions to the Court of Justice in Luxembourg regarding the nature of Article 12:

1   Does Article 12 have the effect of national law as claimed by VG, and may individuals derive rights from it which a national court must protect?

2   If the answer is affirmative, has there been an unlawful increase in customs duties or merely a reasonable modification of the duties which, although bringing about an increase, is not prohibited by Article 12?

The Governments of Belgium, West Germany and the Netherlands, and the EC Commission filed additional memoranda with the Court. All three Governments argued that Article 12 merely created obligations for Member States and did not therefore create rights for individuals. A claim might be brought against a Member State which broke its Treaty obligations under EEC Article 169 or 170.

The Court ruled as follows:

The first question of the Tariefcommissie is whether Article 12 of the Treaty has direct application in national law in the sense that the nationals of Member States may on the basis of this Article lay claim to rights which the national court must protect.

To ascertain whether the provisions of an international treaty extend so far in their effects it is necessary to consider the spirit, the general scheme and the wording of those provisions.

The objective of the EEC Treaty, which is to establish a Common Market, the functioning of which is of direct concern to interested parties in the Community, implies that this Treaty is more than an agreement which merely creates mutual obligations between the contracting states. This view is confirmed by the preamble to the Treaty which refers not only to governments but to peoples. It is also confirmed more specifically by the establishment of institutions endowed with sovereign rights, the exercise of which affects Member States and also their citizens. Furthermore, it must be noted that the nationals of the states brought together in the Community are called upon to co-operate in the functioning of this Community through the intermediary of the European Parliament and the Economic and Social Committee.

In addition the task assigned to the Court of Justice under Article 177, the object of which is to secure uniform interpretation of the Treaty by national courts and tribunals, confirms that the states have acknowledged that Community law has an authority which can be invoked by their nationals before those courts and tribunals.

The conclusion to be drawn from this is that the Community constitutes a new legal order of international law for the benefit of which the states have limited their sovereign rights, albeit within limited fields, and the subjects of which comprise not only Member States but also their nationals. Independently of the legislation of Member States, Community law therefore not only imposes obligations on individuals but is also intended to confer upon them rights which become part of their legal heritage. These rights arise not only where they are expressly granted by the Treaty, but also by reason of obligations which the Treaty imposes in a clearly defined way upon individuals as well as upon the Member States and upon the institutions of the Community.

With regard to the general scheme of the Treaty as it relates to customs duties and charges having equivalent effect it must be emphasised that Article 9, which bases the Community upon a customs union, includes as an essential provision the prohibition of the customs duties and charges. This provision is found at the beginning of the part of the

Treaty which defines the 'Foundations of the Community'. It is applied and explained by Article 12.

The wording of Article 12 contains a clear and unconditional prohibition which is not a positive but a negative obligation. This obligation, moreover, is not qualified by any reservation on the part of states which would make its implementation conditional upon a positive legislative measure enacted under national law. The very nature of this prohibition makes it ideally adapted to produce direct effects in the legal relationship between Member States and their subjects.

The implementation of Article 12 does not require any legislative intervention on the part of the states. The fact that under this Article it is the Member States who are made the subject of the negative obligation does not imply that their nationals cannot benefit from this obligation.

In addition the argument based on Articles 169 and 170 of the Treaty put forward by the three Governments which have submitted observations to the Court in their statements of the case is misconceived. The fact that these Articles of the Treaty enable the Commission and the Member States to bring before the Court a State which has not fulfilled its obligations does not mean that individuals cannot plead these obligations, should the occasion arise, before a national court, any more than the fact that the Treaty places at the disposal of the Commission ways of ensuring that obligations imposed upon those subject to the Treaty are observed, precludes the possibility, in actions between individuals before a national court, of pleading infringements of these obligations.

A restriction of the guarantees against an infringement of Article 12 by Member States to the procedures under Article 169 and 170 would remove all direct legal protection of the individual rights of their nationals. There is the risk that recourse to the procedure under these Articles would be ineffective if it were to occur after the implementation of a national decision taken contrary to the provisions of the Treaty.

The vigilance of individuals concerned to protect their rights amounts to an effective supervision in addition to the supervision entrusted by Articles 169 and 170 to the diligence of the Commission and of the Member States.

It follows from the foregoing considerations that, according to the spirit, the general scheme and the wording of the Treaty, Article 12 must be interpreted as producing direct effects and creating individual rights which national courts must protect ...

It follows from the wording and the general scheme of Article 12 of the Treaty that, in order to ascertain whether customs duties or charges having equivalent effect have been increased contrary to the prohibition contained in the said Article, regard must be had to the customs duties and charges actually applied at the date of the entry into force of the Treaty.

Further, with regard to the prohibition in Article 12 of the Treaty, such an illegal increase may arise from a re-arrangement of the tariff resulting in the classification of the product under a more highly taxed heading and from an actual increase in the rate of customs duty.

It is of little importance how the increase in customs duties occurred when, after the Treaty entered into force, the same product in the same Member State was subjected to a higher rate of duty.

The application of Article 12, in accordance with the interpretation given above, comes within the jurisdiction of the national court which must enquire whether the dutiable product, in this case unreaformaldehyde originating in the Federal Republic of Germany, is charged under the customs measures brought into force in the Netherlands with an import duty higher than that with which it was charged on 1 January 1958.

The Court has no jurisdiction to check the validity of the conflicting views on this subject which have been submitted to it during the proceedings but must leave them to be determined by the national courts ...

The costs incurred by the Commission of the EEC and the Member States which have submitted their observations to the Court are not recoverable, and as these proceedings are, in so far as the parties to the main action are concerned, a step in the action pending before the Tariefcommissie, the decision as to costs is a matter for that court.

On those grounds,

Upon reading the pleadings,

Upon hearing the report of the Judge-Rapporteur;

Upon hearing the opinion of the Advocate-General;

Having regard to Articles 9, 12, 14, 169, 170 and 177 of the Treaty establishing the European Economic Community;

Having regard to the Rules of Procedure of the Court of Justice of the European Communities;

THE COURT in answer to the question referred to it for a preliminary ruling by the Tariefcommissie by decision of 16 August 1962, hereby rules;

1   Article 12 of the Treaty establishing the European Economic Community produces direct effects and creates individual rights which national courts must protect.

2   In order to ascertain whether customs duties or charges having equivalent effect have been increased contrary to the prohibition contained in Article 12 of the Treaty, regard must be had to the duties and charges actually applied by the Member State in question at the date of the entry into force of the Treaty.

Such an increase can arise both from a re-arrangement of the tariff resulting in the classification of the product under a more highly taxed heading and from an increase in the rate of customs duty applied.

3   The decision as to costs in these proceedings is a matter for the Tariefcommissie.

The decision in *Van Gend en Loos* dramatically increased the impact of Community law in the Member States. It is a decision which ultimately rests on two related factors: first, on the Court's perception of the federal and constitutional (as opposed to international) nature of the Treaty, key provisions of which bear directly upon the individual and, secondly, on the Court's clear appreciation that the establishment of the customs union was a key element of negative integration within the Community – and that Community law must be fully effective in that respect. It is 'undoubtedly the richest and most creative of all Community cases, and one in which virtually every later development can – at least with hindsight – be seen to have its germ': Rudden.

Thus, the case law of the Court of Justice clearly shows that a *directly effective* provision of Community law, whether of the Treaty or a legally binding secondary act, always prevails (takes precedence) over a provision of national law. In such cases, individual Community rights must be protected irrespective of whether the Community provision come before, or after, the national provision. The case which follows concerns the impact of a Community Regulation within Italian national law. A Regulation, as we have seen, is directly applicable. The Court of Justice assumes that it is therefore 'a direct source of rights and duties for all those affected thereby', ie that direct effect is the norm for Regulations. (On this point and possible confusion between direct applicability and direct effect, see Chapter Eight.)

Case 106/77 *Amministrazione delle Finanze* v. *Simmenthal*

S imported a consignment of beef from France into Italy. In accordance with an Italian statute of 1970, the company was charged fees for veterinary and public health inspections made at the frontier. S sued for the return of their money in the Italian court, pleading that the charges were contrary to EEC law. Following an Article 177 reference, the Court of Justice held that the inspections were contrary to Article 30, being measures having an equivalent effect to a quantitative restriction, and the fees were contrary to Article 12 being charges equivalent to customs duties. The Court also held that this question of animal and public health had been governed by EC Regulations since 1964 and 1968.

In consequence the national court ordered the Italian Finance Ministry to repay the fees charged. The Ministry, however, pleaded the national statute of 1970 and argued that, under the Italian Constitution, this bound them until such time as it was set aside by the Constitutional Court. Following a further reference, the Court held:

The main purpose of the first question is to ascertain what consequences flow from the direct applicability of a provision of Community law in the event of incompatibility with a subsequent legislative provision of a Member State.

Direct applicability in such circumstances means that rules of Community law must be fully and uniformly applied in all Member States from the date of their entry into force and for so long as they continue in force.

These provisions are therefore a direct source of rights and duties for all those affected thereby, whether Member States or individuals, who are parties to legal relationships under Community law.

This consequence also concerns any national court whose task it is as an organ of a Member State to protect, in a case within its jurisdiction, the rights conferred upon individuals by Community law.

Furthermore, in accordance with the principle of the precedence of Community law, the relationship between provisions of the Treaty and directly applicable measures of the institutions on the one hand and the national law of the Member States on the other is such that those provisions and measures not only by their entry into force render automatically inapplicable any conflicting provision of current national law but – in so far as they are an integral part of, and take precedence in, the legal order applicable in the territory of each of the Member States – also preclude the valid adoption of new national legislative measures to the extent to which they would be incompatible with Community provisions.

Indeed any recognition that national legislative measures which encroach upon the field within which the Community exercises its legislative power or which are otherwise incompatible with the provisions of Community law had any legal effect would amount to a corresponding denial of the effectiveness of obligations undertaken unconditionally and irrevocably by Member States pursuant to the Treaty and would thus imperil the very foundations of the Community.

The same conclusion emerges from the structure of Article 177 of the Treaty which provides that any court or tribunal of a Member State is entitled to make a reference to the Court whenever it considers that a preliminary ruling on a question of interpretation or validity relating to Community law is necessary to enable it to give judgement.

The effectiveness of that provision would be impaired if the national court were prevented from forthwith applying Community law in accordance with the decision or the case-law of the Court.

It follows from the foregoing that every national court must, in a case within its jurisdiction, apply Community law in its entirety and protect rights which the latter confers on individuals and must accordingly set aside any provision of national law which may conflict with it, whether prior or subsequent to the Community rule.

Accordingly any provision of a national legal system and any legislative, administrative, or judicial practice which might impair the effectiveness of Community law by withholding from the national court having jurisdiction to apply such law the power to do everything necessary at the moment of its application to set aside national legislative provisions which might prevent Community rules from having full force and effect are incompatible with those requirements which are the very essence of Community law.

This would be the case in the event of a conflict between a provision of Community law and a subsequent national law if the solution of the conflict were to be reserved for an authority with a discretion of its own, other than the court called upon to apply Community law, even if such an impediment to the full effectiveness of Community law were only temporary.

The first question should therefore be answered to the effect that a national court which is called upon, within the limits of its jurisdiction, to apply provisions of Community law is under a duty to give full effect to those provisions, if necessary refusing of its own motion to apply any conflicting provision of national legislation, even if adopted subsequently, and it is not necessary for the court to request or await the prior setting aside of such provision by legislation or other constitutional means.

The essential point of the second question is whether – assuming it to be accepted that the protection of rights conferred by provisions of Community law can be suspended until any national provisions which might conflict with them have been in fact set aside by the competent national authorities – such setting aside must in every case have unrestricted retroactive effect so as to prevent the rights in question from being in any way adversely affected.

It follows from the answer to the first question that national courts must protect rights conferred by provisions of the Community legal order and that it is not necessary for such courts to request or await the actual setting aside by the national authorities empowered so to act or any national measures which might impede the direct and immediate application of Community rules.

The second question therefore appears to have no purpose.

On those grounds the court hereby rules:

A national court which is called upon, within the limits of its jurisdiction, to apply provisions of Community law is under a duty to give full effect to those provisions, if necessary refusing of its own motion to apply any conflicting provisions of national legislation, even if adopted subsequently, and it is not necessary for the court to request or await the prior setting aside of such provisions by legislative or other constitutional means.

The need for national courts to set aside the law of their own country when it is found to conflict with directly effective Community law is a point which will be seen to arise in many of the cases which follow, eg *Factortame (No. 2)*, see Chapter Three and Chapter Twenty. Such national law must be repealed by the national legislature and the failure to do so amounts to a breach of Article 5 of the Treaty.

Reaction in the Member States

As these cases illustrate, some Member States, at least initially, encountered difficulties in accepting the supremacy of directly effective Community law in their courts. That the Court of Justice would brook no interference with the requirement that Community rules be uniformly applied by national courts throughout the Member States is thrown into sharp relief in the following German case. It concerns the question of a possible conflict between a provision of a Regulation (secondary Community law) and fundamental human rights provisions of the West German Constitution. The case also illustrates the point that the validity of Community law may not be tested against the provisions of national law.

Case 11/70 *Internationale Handelsgesellschaft*
In order to export certain agricultural products an export licence was required. If the products were not exported during the period of the licence's validity, the exporter forfeited a deposit. The company, having lost a deposit of DM 17,000, claimed that this Community system, based on two Community Regulations and operated through the West German National Cereals Intervention Agency, was contrary to the fundamental human rights provisions of the German Constitution. In particular it was in breach of the principle of *proportionality*: it imposed obligations (relating to deposits) on individuals that were not *necessary* for the attainment of the intended objective (the regulation of the cereals market).

The question of the validity of one of the Regulations was referred to the Court of Justice under Article 177(1)(b) by the Frankfurt

Administrative Court. The Court stated that the validity of Community measures could not be judged according to the principles of national law; Community criteria only might be applied.

The Court continued:

Recourse to the legal rules or concepts of national law in order to judge the validity of measures adopted by the institutions of the Community would have an adverse effect on the uniformity and efficiency of Community law. The validity of such measures can only be judged in the light of Community law. In fact, the law stemming from the Treaty, an independent source of law, cannot because of its very nature be overridden by rules of national law, however framed, without being deprived of its character as Community law and without the legal basis of the Community itself being called in question. Therefore the validity of a Community measure or its effect within a Member State cannot be affected by allegations that it runs counter to either fundamental rights as formulated by the constitution of that State or the principles of a national constitutional structure.

However, an examination should be made as to whether or not any analogous guarantee inherent in Community law has been disregarded. In fact, respect for fundamental rights forms an integral part of the general principles of law protected by the Court of Justice.

The protection of such rights, whilst inspired by the constitutional traditions common to the Member States, must be ensured within the framework of the structure and objectives of the Community. It must therefore be ascertained, in the light of the doubts expressed by the Verwaltungsgericht, whether the system of deposits has infringed rights of a fundamental nature, respect for which must be ensured in the Community legal system ...

It follows from all these considerations that the system of licences involving an undertaking, by those who apply for them, to import or export, guaranteed by a deposit, does not violate any right of a fundamental nature. The machinery of deposits constitutes an appropriate method, for the purposes of Article 40(3) of the Treaty, for carrying out the common organisation of the agricultural markets and also conforms to the requirements of Article 43.

However, the referring Frankfurt court *did not apply* the Court's ruling that the Regulation did not contravene the Community concept of human rights. Instead it made a reference to the West German Federal Constitutional Court which, drawing attention to the absence of a 'codified catalogue of human rights' at Community level, allowed the reference and held that Community measures *were subject to the fundamental rights provisions of the German Constitution*. Nevertheless it ruled that the Community Regulation in issue was not contrary to the Constitution. Thus, although the Federal Constitutional Court refused to acknowledge the absolute supremacy of Community law, an open rift with the Court of Justice was averted.

By 1986 however the Federal Constitutional Court felt sufficiently confident regarding the protection of human rights at Community level that in *Wünsche Handelsgesellschaft* it reversed its previous decision in the following terms:

> Since 1974 the Community has advanced convincingly in the protection of human rights both in the adoption in a legally significant manner of texts whereby the institutions agree to be guided as a legal duty by respect for fundamental rights and by the development of case law by the European Court. The consequent connection of human rights guarantees in the national constitutions and European Convention on Human Rights on the one hand and the general principles of Community law on the other obviates the continuing need for a catalogue of fundamental rights. In view of these developments, it is now the position that, so long as the European Communities and particularly the case law of the European Court generally ensure an effective protection of fundamental rights as against the sovereign powers of the Community which is to be regarded as substantially similar to the protection required unconditionally by the German Constitution, and in so far as they generally safeguard the essential content of fundamental rights, the German Federal Constitutional Court will no longer exercise its jurisdiction to decide on the applicability of secondary Community law cited as the legal basis for any acts of German courts or authorities within the sovereign jurisdiction of the Federal Republic of Germany; and it will no longer review such legislation by the standard of the fundamental rights contained in the German Constitution. References to the Constitutional Court under Article 100(1) of the Constitution for that purpose are therefore inadmissible.

On the strength of this development, together with similar ones in other Member States, it is possible to say that the courts (if not some politicians) of the Member States have now accepted the doctrine of the supremacy of directly effective Community law. Following the *Factortame* decision the Master of the Rolls, Sir Thomas Bingham, has stated that: 'The supremacy of Community law has been accepted by the English courts with a readiness, and applied with a loyalty, which, if equalled in one or two other Member States, has probably been exceeded in none.'

In the light of these (at one time) controversial cases on direct effect, it is important to consider the attention they direct towards the role of the Member States in the development of the Community and the duty of solidarity which rests on them by virtue of Article 5 of the Treaty.

The Community, principally through the exercise of its Treaty powers by the Commission, is concerned to achieve full and effective implementation of the policies within its competence. However, in many cases the Commission must, in order to achieve its aims, work with and through one of a variety of national authorities (government departments, customs authorities, agricultural intervention agencies, etc.). Within this working relationship, Member States and their agencies are required to adopt certain courses of action or to refrain from doing so. This can involve an obligation to adopt new legislation (or secondary legislation), to revise existing legislation, or to repeal existing legislation.

Similarly, national courts, often in co-operation with the Court of Justice through the medium of the preliminary rulings procedure of Article 177, have a duty, based again on Article 5, to ensure the full effectiveness of Community law within the scope of their jurisdictions. Where there is a Community dimension to a case, national courts and tribunals are obliged to interpret Community law (or request an interpretation from the Court of Justice), to apply Community law and to enforce it.

As will be seen, in most cases the Court of Justice is a court of first instance *and* last resort. Its interpretations of Community law are definitive in the courts and tribunals of the Member States. It may be called upon to assess the validity of the acts of the Community institutions. It may not exceed its powers as laid down in the Treaty but it does not look to a Parliament as supreme law-maker. It is not bound by its own decisions but frequently cites such decisions to indicate a consistent line of reasoning. Its crucial role in the development of the Community will become increasingly apparent in succeeding chapters.

Collins, L., European Community Law in the United Kingdom, 1990, Chapter 1 'Introduction'.

Gormley, L.W. (ed.), Kapteyn and VerLoren van Themaat's *Introduction to the Law of the European Communities*, 1989, chapters 2, 3 and 5.

Hartley, T.C., *The Foundations of European Community Law*, 1988, Chapters 3 and 4.

Lord Mackenzie Stuart, *The European Communities and the Rule of Law*, 1977, Chapter 1.

Mancini, F., 'The Making of a Constitution for Europe' (1989) 26 CML Rev. 595.

Rudden, B., *Basic Community Cases*, 1987, Part 1.

Sorensen, Max, 'Autonomous Legal Orders' (1983) 32 ICLQ 559.

Usher, J., *European Community Law and National Law: The Irreversible Transfer*, 1981, comments on Van Gend en Loos, etc.

Weiler, J., 'The Community System: The Dual Character of Supranationalism' (1981) 1 YEL 267.

Weiler, J., 'Community, Member States and European Integration: Is the Law Relevant?' (1982) 21 JCMS 39.

Wyatt, D., 'New Legal Order, or Old?' (1982) 7 EL Rev. 147.

CHAPTER FIVE

LAW-MAKING AND THE COMMUNITY'S POLITICAL INSTITUTIONS

INTRODUCTION

Although the ECSC, the EEC and Euratom were originally endowed with separate institutions, following changes in the structure in the intervening years (as seen in Chapter One), by the time the Single European Act came into effect in 1987, it was correct in both a practical *and* formal sense to say that there was a *single* institutional framework comprising the European Parliament, the Council, the Commission and the Court of Justice: Article 4 EEC. The Maastricht Treaty preserves this unitary framework (Article 4 EC Treaty as amended by the TEU) and will add the Court of Auditors, first established in 1975, as a fifth Community institution.

Article 4 also provides that: 'Each institution shall act within the limits of the powers conferred upon it by this Treaty.' Their powers are therefore only those which have been expressly or impliedly conferred upon, or *attributed* to, them by the Member States under the Treaties. Thus, any illegal act of any of the three main *political* institutions (the Council, Commission and Parliament), for example an act of the Council beyond its Treaty-based competence, will become the basis for an action for annulment under Article 173 (see Chapter Nineteen).

Since 1958, the Council and the Commission have been assisted in an advisory capacity by the *Economic and Social Committee*, and, in a further move towards the decentralisation of policy-making, the TEU will create a similar *Committee of the Regions*: Article 4(2) EC Treaty, as amended (and see below). The *European Central Bank*, with law-making powers within the field of monetary policy, will be established by a new Article 4a and the Luxembourg-based *European Investment Bank*, which has acted since 1958 as a prime source of investment finance for Community projects, is accorded further legal recognition in a new Article 4b.

The Community's four main institutions (the three political institutions and the Court of Justice), acting within their powers, are responsible for the performance of the legislative, executive and judicial functions of the Community. However, as should already be appreciated, and contrary to basic notions of the 'separation of powers', the legislative function still rests primarily with the Council of Ministers (and to some extent the Commission) - and not on the European Parliament, although the powers of this institution within this field have, as we will see, steadily increased since

1958. The Commission, which represents the Community interest (in contrast to the Council's identification with the interests of the Member States), is not only 'the guardian of the Treaties', overseeing and if necessary enforcing (particularly *vis-à-vis* the Member States) the execution of existing Community policies, but it is also both the proposer of new Community policy initiatives (in the form of draft legislation) for consideration by the Council and Parliament and the body entrusted by the Council with the implementation of such policies as have been adopted.

Commenting on the institutional structure in 1989, Gormley has said:

> The institutional structure is of decisive importance for the balance of power within the Community. The two most important actors are undoubtedly the Council of Ministers and ... the Commission. It is on the co-operation of these two Institutions that the implementation of the Treaties is largely dependent ...

> At the outset the European Parliament – the Institution which involves the peoples of the Member States in the activities of the Community – played only a modest role. Since 1979 the Parliament has been directly elected and this role has grown in importance. The Court of Justice also plays an important part in the institutional structure as it has to ensure the observance of the law in the implementation of the Treaty by the Institutions and the Member States. Its jurisdiction enables the Court to contribute to the maintenance of the balance of rights and duties both amongst the Institutions themselves and between them and the Member States. The Court is also in the position of being able to ensure the legal protection of private parties, which is of great importance because of the limited nature of parliamentary supervision of the behaviour of the Institutions.

Over and above this view of the Community's institutional structure as based on Article 4(1), it is also essential to take due account (as in the historical survey of the Community's development in Chapter One) of a further, all important political body, the European Council.

THE EUROPEAN COUNCIL

The summit conferences of Community leaders which began in 1969 were put on a formal basis in 1974 and brought within the framework of Community law by virtue of Article 2 of the Single European Act. Article D of the TEU states that:

The European Council shall provide the Union with the necessary impetus for its development and shall define the general political guidelines thereof. The European Council shall bring together the Heads of State or of Government of the Member States and the President of the Commission ...

The European Council, which meets at least twice a year, is not engaged in the formal decision-making process, and the adoption of its policy guidelines (within the institutional, economic, social and foreign policy or security fields) rests largely with the Council of Ministers in Brussels unless Treaty amendments are involved. In terms of 'impetus', the European Council was heavily involved, amongst other things, in the establishment of the European Monetary System in 1979, the introduction of direct elections to the European Parliament in the same year, and successive enlargements of the Community. At the Maastricht Summit of December 1991, crucial questions concerning further economic and political integration – EMU, common foreign and security policy, the admission of new Member States and the reform of the institutions – all lay on the Council's table. As the following extract from an article by Adrian Hamilton, published in *The Observer* in October 1991 indicates, a complex mixture of national interests and priorities will often make for difficult decisions in the Council and, perhaps inevitably, for trade-offs and compromises:

EC's EMBRACE OF NEW ORDER LACKS POLITICAL PASSION
One immediate victim of the collapse of Communism may be the drive towards a tighter Europe. That at any rate is what John Major seems to believe and President François Mitterrand to fear, judging by their meeting last week.

They have their own reasons for voicing their separate views, of course. With little to offer at home, Mitterrand is anxious to show himself still the master of a new Europe, just as Major, with a party conference in view, would be happy to see the contentious issue of European federalism disappear into the sands of a fragmenting Soviet Union.

What is more curious is that Major seems to have been so surprised that his French host should have reaffirmed so publicly both his federalism and his suspicions that the British would try to undermine them.

The French and the British see these things differently. To the French – as to others – the European Community is very much a political association and events in Eastern Europe and the Soviet Union make it all the more imperative to accelerate the integration of its existing members.

There are good hard commercial reasons why the French should be reluctant to open up the Common Market to Polish fruit or to share too much of the wealth of the Twelve with the poorer neighbours to the east. But there are also good political reasons why the French should see in an integrated Europe a means of tying down the Germans to a common policy.

To John Major and to his Foreign Secretary, Douglas Hurd, on the other hand, the EC is primarily an economic, not a political ideal.

Despite the obvious differences with his predecessor on the style of discussion with our European colleagues (and the real differences on ERM entry), on this Mr. Major and Mrs Thatcher are as one. The Common Market should be just that. On defence, the British remain Atlanticists; on foreign policy, both Hurd and Major are essentially pragmatic nationalists who see the Community as a balance of bilateral arrangements shifting from issue to issue.

In that vision a wider Europe makes more sense than a narrower one. Not for them Delors' vision of a tighter grouping of the existing Twelve in which majority voting is the 'tiger in the tank' ...

Although it may be argued that the existence of the inter-governmental European Council has diluted the supranational character of the Community (Union), it will be recalled that Jean Monnet himself conceded that the way forward lay with the Council, as that was where 'authority' resided as the questions and answers moved into the realms of 'higher politics'. In any event, the Commission fought hard in the late 1970s for a full voice within the Council (see Jenkins in References and Further Reading at the end of the chapter) and, as the Internal Market programme illustrates, the Commission and the European Council have often forged successful partnerships.

THE COUNCIL
(Articles 145-154 EC as amended by the TEU)

Composition

The Council of Ministers of the European Communities consists of representatives of the Member States. The new Article 146 states that:

> The Council shall consist of a representative of each Member Sate at ministerial level, authorised to commit the Government of that Member State ...

Its main function is 'to take decisions' (Article 145, second indent), ie to decide whether or not to adopt Community legislation.

It is not a fixed body but whoever the representatives in attendance in Brussels are and whatever their responsibilities, the powers of the Council remain the same. When foreign and security policy, general institutional and other broad policy matters are on the agenda, the Foreign Ministers of the Member States make up what is called the General Affairs Council. For other more specialist matters, for example economic and financial affairs (the Ecofin Council), agriculture, transport or social security, the appropriate ministers will attend for the legislative and other business in hand.

The Presidency of the Council rotates among the Member States at six-monthly intervals, and although the President has the role of honest broker in the search for agreement between the Member States, he or she will usually be keen to achieve the maximum progress during his or her term of office. The latter ambition may defeat the former function as the Dutch discovered in the period leading up to the crucial decisions on further 'positive' integration scheduled for December 1991. As reported in *The Times* on 2 October of that year:

LUBBERS LICKS EC TREATY WOUNDS
from George Brock in Brussels

Ruud Lubbers, the Dutch prime minister, conferred yesterday with Hans van den Broek, his foreign minister, on how to pick up the pieces after EC foreign ministers rejected their draft for federal union by 10-2 on Monday. His government was mauled by yesterday morning's Dutch papers. 'One of the worst political blunders ever,' thundered the conservative *De Telegraaf.*

But with the return to the Luxembourg treaty draft, the pressure on Britain also returns. Jacques Delors, the federalist president of the European Commission, has treated the whole fuss over the Dutch text in a lofty 'much ado about nothing' manner and pointed out that agreement on several key points is in sight.

The outlines of a monetary union treaty are nearly all agreed. Norman Lamont, the chancellor, plainly believes his officials have helped write a treaty which both keeps Britain in and allows it to stay out. No such flexibility exists in the talks on political union. There has so far been no real meeting of minds - let alone the unanimity which would allow treaty drafting - on several questions of principle.

The EC has not agreed how to handle foreign policy. Thanks to the disappearance of the Dutch text, foreign policy is unlikely to be integrated into the central system. But most EC countries want, or say they want, majority voting in foreign policy. Britain wants co-operation decided by unanimity. Should the EC have a defence policy and armed forces independent of the United States? Britain, Germany and France have come nowhere near agreeing on this question, which will also confront them at the Nato summit next month.

Britain will probably concede that the EC should start to make policy in areas where Brussels has no law-making power at the moment. Some extension of the EC's power to set community-wide standards for education, health, welfare and transport is likely.

But the extension of majority voting is a far more sensitive issue. On that and on new powers for the European parliament, Britain does not look set to yield very much.

Although the Maastricht summit does not open until December 9, the effective deadline for settling contentious points is the middle of November, so that the treaty text can be completely ready for Maastricht. The Dutch government has scheduled a three-day meeting of EC foreign ministers in the North Sea resort of Noordwijk on November 13. That meeting will decide the treaty's fate.

Council Working Parties and COREPER

Article 4 of the Merger Treaty of 1965 (to be replaced under the TEU by a new Article 151 EC) states that:

(1) A committee consisting of the Permanent Representatives of the Member States shall be responsible for preparing the work of the Council and for carrying out the tasks assigned to it by the Council.

Before a Commission proposal reaches the Council it will be examined first by a Council working party of *national* technical experts. When agreement is reached, the proposal goes forward to the Committee of Permanent Representatives in Brussels (COREPER), as it does in the absence of agreement in the hope that it will be forthcoming at the higher level. COREPER itself is divided into two bodies, deputy Permanent Representatives (COREPER I) for technical, economic issues and Permanent Representatives (COREPER II) for more political questions.

Proposals agreed by a working party receive formal approval and proceed to Part A of a Council agenda. They will normally be adopted by the Council without further discussion. Proposals not yet agreed may be agreed by a COREPER committee and proceed as outlined above. If COREPER fails (even with Commission involvement) to agree, the matter is placed on Part B of the Council agenda. Agreement may then be reached in the Council, possibly on the basis of a 'package deal' in which several decisions are put together so that concessions made by a Member State on one issue are balanced against gains on another. Proposals on which there is failure to agree are passed back to the working party.

Decision-making and Voting

Article 145 provides that:

To ensure that the objectives set out in this Treaty are attained, the Council shall, in accordance with the provisions of this Treaty:

– ensure coordination of the general economic policies of the Member States;

– have power to take decisions;

– confer on the Commission, in the acts which the Council adopts, powers for the implementation of the rules which the Council lays down.

The Council may impose certain requirements in respect of the exercise of these powers ...

Indent one will assume increasing importance as (or if) the Community moves successful through the three stages necessary for the achievement of EMU. Indent three establishes that power to implement acts of the Council be conferred on the Commission (see below). It is the deceptively simply worded *indent two* which confers on the Council its key role regarding the adoption of secondary legislation, based upon and developing the framework established by the Treaty itself. This legislative process and the relationship of the Council to the other political institutions and other bodies within that process will be examined later in this chapter.

THE COMMISSION
(Articles 155–163 EC as amended)

Composition

Article 9 of the Merger Treaty of 1965 stated that:

A Commission of the European Communities ... is hereby established. This Commission shall take the place of the High Authority of the European Coal and Steel Community, the Commission of the European Economic Community and the Commission of the European Atomic Energy Community.

The Commission, whose headquarters are in Brussels, presently consists of 17 members (Commissioners) 'whose independence is beyond doubt' and who, although appointed by the governments of the Member States, shall in the performance of their duties 'neither seek nor take instructions from any government or from any other body'. In practice the five largest Member States each have two members and the remainder one each. Their term of office is four years (five under the TEU) and it is renewable.

The President of the Commission, whose main functions are to provide the Commission with a sense of direction (eg new initiatives or the re-launching of old ones that have lapsed) and to secure co-ordination between the various Community policies, is appointed by 'common accord' of the Governments of the Member States. The European Council makes the appointment after consulting the Parliament. An important change is introduced by the TEU (Article 158EC) in that: 'The President and the other members of the Commission thus nominated shall be subject as a body to a vote of approval by the European Parliament' – which is thereby given a right to veto the appointment of a Commission including members of which it disapproves.

The following list gives the names and responsibilities of the Commission which took office in January 1989:

The New Commission

A new European Commission took office on 6 January 1989. Its 17 members will serve until 5 January 1993. The new Commission includes eight Commissioners who served in the last Commission, including Commission President Jacques Delors. The 17 Commissioners, and their list of responsibilities, are as follows:

FRANS H.J.J. ANDRIESSEN	External Relations and trade policy, co-operation with other European countries.
DR. MARTIN BANGEMANN	Internal Market and industrial affairs, relations with the European Parliament.
SIR LEON BRITTAN	Competition policy, financial institutions.
ANTONIO CARDOSA E CUNHA	Personnel, administration and translation, energy and EURATOM supply agency, SMEs, crafts, trade, tourism, social economy.
HENNING CHRISTOPHERSEN	Economic and financial affairs, co-ordination of structural funds and statistical office.
JACQUES DELORS	President of the Commission. General secretariat and legal affairs service, monetary affairs, spokesman service, forecasting unit, interpretation-conference services, security bureau.
JEAN DONDELINGER	Audiovisual and cultural affairs, information and communications, people's Europe, publications office.
RAY MacSHARRY	Agriculture, rural development.

MANUEL MARIN GONZALEZ	Co-operation and development, fisheries policy.
ABEL MATUTES JUAN	Mediterranean policy, relations with Latin America and Asia, North-South relations.
BRUCE MILLAN	Regional policy.
PILIPPO M. PANDOLFI	Science, research & development, telecommunications information and innovation industries, Joint Research Centre.
VASSO PAPANDREOU	Employment, industrial and social affairs, human resources, education and training.
CARLO RIPA DI MEANA	Environment, nuclear safety, civil defence.
PETER M. SCMIDHUBER	Budget, financial control.
CHRISTIANE SCRIVENER	Taxes and customs union, obligatory levy questions (fiscal and social levies).
KAREL VAN MIERT	Transport, credit and investment, protection and promotion of consumers' interests.

The Commission is divided into twenty departments known as Directorates General (eg DG I External Relations; DG IV Competition Policy), each of which is headed by a Director General who is responsible to the relevant Commissioner. DGs are divided into Directorates which in turn are divided into Divisions. In addition there are a number of specialised services including the Legal Service. The Commission now has a total staff of over 16,000, almost 3,000 of whom are involved with translation and interpretation duties.

Each Commissioner is assisted by his Cabinet, a group of officials appointed by the Commissioner and responsible to him. The Chefs de

Cabinet meet at regular intervals to co-ordinate activities and prepare for Commission meetings.

Commission decisions are made on a collegiate basis either by decisions taken at its weekly meetings or by a written procedure whereby proposals are circulated to all Commissioners. If no objections are notified within a stated period, the proposal is deemed to have received assent. Objections are referred to a full Commission meeting where decisions are taken by a simple majority vote.

Functions and Powers

The Commission's functions are set out in Article 155:

In order to ensure the proper functioning and development of the Common Market, the Commission shall:
- ensure that the provisions of this Treaty and the measures taken by the institutions pursuant thereto are applied;
- formulate recommendations or deliver opinions on matters dealt with in this Treaty, if it expressly so provides or if the Commission considers it necessary;
- have its own power of decision and participate in the shaping of measures taken by the Council and by the European Parliament in the manner provided for in this Treaty;
- exercise the powers conferred on it by the Council for the implementation of the rules laid down by the latter.

1.   The first of these functions places the Commission in the role of guardian of the Treaty. In order to secure observance of the Treaty and legislative measures taken in pursuance of it, the Commission has the power to initiate proceedings not only against Member States but also against other Community institutions (but not the Court), and against individuals and legal persons, particularly business undertakings.

As regards an action against a *Member State* alleged to be in breach of its Treaty obligations (see Article 5), eg it has failed to implement a Directive or has placed a ban on intra-Community trade, the Commission may proceed on the basis of Article 169:

If the Commission considers that a Member State has failed to fulfil an obligation under this Treaty, it shall deliver a reasoned opinion on the matter after giving the State concerned the opportunity to submit its observations.

If the State concerned does not comply with the opinion within the period laid down by the Commission the latter may bring the matter before the Court of Justice.

It will be seen that the Commission gives Member States ample opportunity to remedy infringements and at present less than a third of the reasoned opinions issued lead to Article 169 rulings. As will be discussed later, the Commission also has a role to play under Article 170 (actions between Member States), and further special enforcement proceedings are available to it in relation to, for example, hindrances to the establishment of the internal market: Article 100A(4).

Proceedings against *other Community institutions* may at present be taken by the Commission against the Council or the Parliament under Article 173. (The range of this article is extended by the TEU to include, in this context, acts *jointly* adopted by the Parliament and the Council and acts of the ECB.) Such proceedings are for the purpose of enabling the Court of Justice *to review the legality of binding acts* of these bodies. (Commission acts may similarly be challenged.) An important Commission direct action for the annulment of a Council act, Case 22/70 *Commission v Council (European Road Transport Agreement)*, will be examined in Chapter Six. Under the present Article 175, the Commission may also challenge a *failure to act* by the Council or Parliament and, again, the Commission's own omissions may, in certain circumstances, be similarly challenged.

These inter-institutional conflicts indicate quite clearly the operation of the Rule of Law within the Community: the law-makers are also bound by it themselves and, in Hartley's words, 'the legality of government action should be subject to determination by an independent, impartial adjudicatory body ... the European Court.' Articles 173 and 175 will be discussed more fully in later chapters.

Proceedings brought by the Commission against individuals or, more probably, business undertakings (eg corporations) for violations of the Treaty arise within the sphere of Community *competition policy* under Article 85 (restrictive trading agreements),

Article 86 (abuse of the dominant position on a product market) and under the 1989 Merger Regulation. As will be seen in Chapter Seventeen, the Commission may impose large fines on business undertakings engaging in anti-competitive behaviour. All such Decisions made by the Commission are, however, subject to review by the Court under Article 173.

2   The second of the Commission's functions under Article 155 concerns its right to '*formulate recommendations or deliver opinions* on matters dealt with in the Treaty.' The initial policy impetus may have come from the European Council. Although under Article 189 such recommendations and opinions are not binding, this power to initiate and formulate Community policy is of great importance. Each year numerous policy proposals are put to the Council. In 1984 a proposal introducing discipline in agricultural spending was accepted by the Council, in 1985 the Commission produced its White Paper on *Completing the Internal Market* and in 1989 the Commission's 'Social Charter' was adopted by the European Council and later formed the basis of the 'social chapter' in the original draft of the TEU (finally being added as a Protocol, following the UK's failure to approve it, and thus binding only on the remaining eleven signatory States).

In 1991 the Commission proposed, in a recommendation to the Council, what was reported as 'a swingeing energy tax that would cut emissions of global warming gases, but raise some fuel costs by up to 60 per cent'. This recommendation was seen as an unprecedented attempt by the Commission to determine the tax policies of Member States and to add flames to sovereignty arguments within the Community before and since the Maastricht summit meeting. Although welcomed by environmentalists, the proposal has yet to find draft legislative form. The energy tax proposal is, however, revealing on the subject of the relationship between the Commission and the Member States. It has been said that:

... though the Commission is an independent force in its own right, it cannot fulfil its functions without the co-operation of national governments. Consequently, it is very much concerned with national interests and one of its most important tasks is the reconciliation of national policies with Community objectives: Hartley

Linked to the Commission's role as an initiator of policy is the crucial part it plays as the initial drafter of Community legislation.

3. This further role for the Commission is to be found in the third indent of Article 155, which speaks not only of that body's 'own power of decision' but also of the Commission's participation '*in the shaping of measures taken by the Council and by the European Parliament*'. Although, as we have seen, the Council of Ministers takes the final decision on most Community legislation, the normal procedure is for the Council to act on a proposal — draft legislation — formulated by the 'European' institution.

The Commission's right of initiative in this respect is drawn from the many provisions of the Treaty which empower the Council to act on a proposal from the Commission. For example:

Article 49
(as amended by the SEA)
As soon as this Treaty enters into force, the Council shall, acting by a qualified majority on a proposal from the Commission, in cooperation with the European Parliament and after consulting the Economic and Social Committee, issue directives or make regulations setting out the measures required to bring about, by progressive stages, freedom of movement for workers ...(This article is subject to amendment by the TEU as regards the procedure to be followed.)

4. With regard to the provision in Article 155 that *the Commission shall 'have its own power of decision'*, we are concerned here with the Commission's power to *bring legislation into effect in its own right*. As will be seen in (5) below, the vast majority of Commission acts (Regulations, Directives and Decisions) stem from *derived* powers and are of a *delegated* nature. They are issued on the basis of Council legislation and deal with its detailed implementation by means of specific rules.

However, the role of the Commission, as an independent legislator (as opposed to the Council, the representative of the Member States) causes some concern to some Member States, despite the fact that the extent of the *express* Treaty base for its autonomous legislative competence is not extensive:

Cases 188–190/80 *France, Italy and UK* v. *Commission;*
Article 90 of the Treaty is concerned with the application of the competition policy rules to public undertakings. In 1980 the Commission adopted Directive 80/723 on the transparency of financial relations between Member States and public undertakings. (The aim was to establish the extent to which public funds were being made available to public undertakings and the uses to which they were being put). The legal base for this measure was Article 90(3) which states that: 'The Commission shall ensure the application of the provisions of this Article and shall, where necessary, address appropriate directives or decisions to Member States.' The Directive was part of a more vigorous policy adopted by the Commission in applying the Treaty rules to state involvement in economic activity, and it was challenged under Article 173 by the three Member States with the largest public sectors.

The UK argued on a separation of powers basis that all original law-making power was vested in the Council; the Commission's powers being confined to 'surveillance and implementation' (ie executive powers). France and Italy argued that even if Article 90(3) did confer a general law-making power on the Commission, its exercise was precluded where the rules in question could have been adopted by the Council.

The Court drew attention to the Commission's 'own power of decision' under Article 155. In rejecting the applicants' arguments it stated that:
'The limits of the powers conferred on the Commission by a specific provision of the Treaty are to be inferred not from a general principle, but from an interpretation of the particular wording of the provision in question ...analysed in the light of its purpose and place in the Treaty.' The power conferred on the Commission by Article 90(3) 'thus operates in a specific field of application and under conditions defined by reference to the particular objective of that article. It follows that the Commission's power to issue the contested directive depends on the needs inherent in its duty of surveillance provided for in Article 90 and that the possibility that rules might be laid down by the Council, by virtue of its general power under Article 94, containing provisions impinging upon the specific sphere of aids granted to public undertakings does not preclude the exercise of that power by the Commission.'

In a more recent decision, the Court has held that whenever the Treaty of Rome confers a *specific task* on the Commission, it impliedly confers on the Commission the powers, including legislative powers, necessary to carry out that task:

Cases 281, 283-285 and 287/85 *Germany, France,*
the Netherlands, Denmark and the UK v *Commission;*
By Decision 85/381 the Commission required Member States to enter
into a prior communication and consultation procedure with the
Commission with regard to their policies on immigration from non-
Member States. It was to cover such matters as entry, residence and equal
treatment.

The decision was based on Article 118 EEC:
'Without prejudice to the other provisions of this Treaty and in
conformity with its general objectives, the Commission shall have the
task of promoting close co-operation between Member States in the
social field, particularly in matters relating to:
- employment;
- labour law and working conditions ...'

It is clear that, on the face of it, this article is not concerned with
immigration, nor does it confer any legislative power on the
Commission.

The Court held:
1   Immigration from non-Member States (eg 'guest workers') can affect
    employment and working conditions in the Community.
2   On the basis of the doctrine of implied powers:
    'Where an article of the EEC Treaty – in this case Article 118 –
    confers a specific task on the Commission it must be accepted, if
    that provision is not to be rendered wholly ineffective, that it
    confers on the Commission necessarily and per se the powers which
    are indispensable in order to carry out that task.'

In 1988, Hartley made the following observations on this outcome:

The consequences of this ruling could be far-reaching. There are many
provisions in the EEC Treaty conferring tasks on the Commission, one
of the most important being that in Article 155 EEC of ensuring that
Community law is applied. This task of acting as Community
policeman could in theory entitle the Commission to adopt the most
extensive measures. Are we now on the threshold of an expansion of
Commission competence comparable to the expansion of Community
treaty-making power that occurred in the 1970s? Has the European
Court adopted the policy of enhancing Commission legislative power
as its answer to the continuing difficulty of getting measures through the

Council? The answers to these questions are not yet clear but they open up intriguing possibilities.

5.   The final indent of Article 155 states that the Commission shall *'exercise the powers conferred on it by the Council for the implementation of the rules laid down by the latter'.* Additionally, and crucially, Article 145, as we have seen, states that:

> ...the Council shall ... confer on the Commission, in the acts which the Council adopts, powers for the implementation of the rules which the Council lays down. The Council may impose certain requirements in respect of the exercise of these powers. The Council may also reserve the right to specific cases, to exercise directly implementing powers itself ...

On the basis of this provision, the Council delegates to its 'European civil service' powers of an executive nature which are necessary for the carrying out of 'decisions' taken by the Council on the basis of Article 145. The amount of legislation emanating from the Commission under these delegated or secondary powers is enormous, but it is largely made up of detailed rules of policy implementation, not least in the field of agriculture. This is apparent from a typical list of the contents of an issue of the Official Journal: see page 112.

Although the Council's power to delegate in the legislative field extends only to the implementation of rules, it is clear from the case law of the Court that considerable discretionary powers may be delegated to the Commission provided the empowering Council provision establishes the basic principles in issue.

It will be seen that Article 145 lays down that the Council 'may impose certain requirements' of a procedural nature in respect of the Commission's subordinate powers. Thus the Council may provide for the establishment of committees of representatives of the national governments to which the Commission must submit drafts of measures it intends to adopt under its derived authority. The degree of control which the Council exercises over the Commission via these *advisory, management* and *regulatory* committee procedures varies considerably. However, it would appear that the system generally operates to the Commission's satisfaction but see Case 302/87 *Parliament* v *Council (Comitology)* in the next chapter.

Official Journal

of the European Communities

ISSN 0378-6978

L 172

Volume 36

15 July 1993

English edition

Legislation

Contents

1

(Continued overleaf)

Acts whose titles are printed in light type are those relating to day-to-day management of agricultural matters, and are generally valid for a limited period.
The titles of all other Acts are printed in bold type and preceded by an asterisk.

96a

The Commission's role as an *initiator* of Community legislation is examined in more detail later in this chapter, but it is clear that this function enables the Commission to act as a prime mover in the continuing process of economic (and social) integration. Nowhere was this more apparent than in the 1986-1992 programme to establish the Internal Market:

Latest status of Internal Market proposals
In November 1989 the latest status of the Internal Market legislative programme was as follows:
- 279 proposals currently comprise the programme
- 134 proposals have been finally adopted by the Council
- 7 proposals have been partially adopted by the Council
- 6 proposals have reached the stage of a Council Common Position
- 116 proposals of the Commission are with the Council
- 29 proposals are still to be presented by the Commission

THE EUROPEAN PARLIAMENT
(Articles 137-144 EC as amended)

The European Parliament was known until 1962 as the Assembly and the change of name was not officially recognised until the coming into effect of the Single European Act in 1987. The history of the European Parliament is a history of gradual and hard-won accretions of power within the institutional structure.

Article 137 EEC states that the Parliament 'shall consist of representatives of the peoples of the States brought together in the Community' but its members were appointed by and from national parliaments until 1979, the year of the first direct elections, now held every five years. Direct elections by universal suffrage constituted an important step towards reducing the so-called 'democratic deficit' within the Community. Additionally, Article 137 EEC states that the Parliament 'shall exercise the advisory and supervisory powers which are conferred upon it by this Treaty'. As amended by the TEU, the words 'advisory and supervisory' disappear from this article. The deletion of these words is indicative of the considerable and to a certain extent successful efforts the Parliament has made in the intervening years to expand its sphere of influence and power. In 1988, Davidson and Freestone explained the Parliament's position as follows:

... the EP is not a Parliament in the sense that Westminster is a parliament. It does not pass legislation, nor is the executive drawn from its members. As we have seen, the legislative and executive functions are performed by the Council and the Commission ...Built into the Treaties are specific powers which indicate that the drafters intended the EP to provide an important element of democratic accountability within the legislative and executive system ...Members of the European Parliament (MEPs) are increasingly assertive in their demands for increased influence over, and indeed share in, the legislative and executive processes of the Community.

The most important additions to the Parliament's powers over the years relate to the Community budget (under the Treaties of 1970 and 1975) and to its more influential role in the legislative process (under the Single European Act). These increased legislative powers (and further such powers, including 'co-decision' with the Council in certain areas under the TEU) will be discussed later in this chapter.

Seat and Political Parties

The Parliament's main seat, where plenary sessions are held, is the Palais de l'Europe in Strasbourg. However, its nineteen Standing Committees, covering the whole range of policy areas, usually meet in Brussels.

The make-up of the Parliament in 1992 in terms of its transnational political groups, and group membership by nationality, is shown in the following charts (and see the new Article 138a, introduced by the TEU , which states that political parties at the European level are important as a factor for integration within the Union):

	Total	B	DK	D	GR	E	F	IRL	I	L	NL	P	UK
Socialist Group	180	8	4	31	9	27	22	1	14	2	8	8	46
Group of the European People's Party	162	7	4	32	10	18	11	4	27	3	10	3	33
Liberal, Democratic and Reformist Group	45	4	3	5	–	5	9	2	3	1	4	9	–
Group for the European Unitarian Left	29	–	1	–	1	4	–	1	22	–	–	–	–
Green Group	27	3	–	6	–	1	8	–	7	–	2	–	–
Group of the European Democratic Alliance	21	–	–	–	1	2	12	6	–	–	–	–	–
Rainbow Group	15	1	4	1	–	2	1	1	3	–	–	1	1
Technical Group of the European Right	14	1	–	3	–	–	10	–	–	–	–	–	–
Left Unity	13	–	–	–	3	–	7	–	–	–	–	3	–
Non–attached	12	–	–	3	–	1	1	–	5	–	1	–	1
Total	518	24	16	81	24	60	81	15	81	6	25	24	81

From March 1991, 18 representatives from the former East Germany attended parliamentary debates as observers, and in 1992 at its Edinburgh summit meeting the European Council increased the total number of MEPs for the 1994 elections to 567: Belgium 25, Denmark 16, Germany 99, Greece 25, Spain 64, France 87, Ireland 15, Italy 87, Luxembourg 6, Netherlands 31, Portugal 25 and the UK 87.

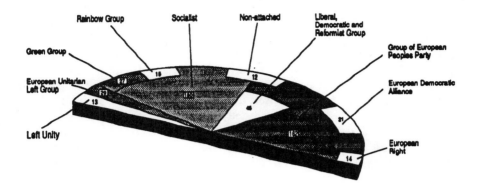

Most of the Parliament's work is done in its Standing Committees (Agriculture, Budgets, Economic and Monetary Affairs, Legal Affairs, Social Affairs, etc.) where issues are considered and reported before being debated. Resolutions of the Parliament do not have any legal effect, although it may well seek in this way to bring pressure to bear on the Commission and the Council to take appropriate action with regard to not only Community but also to international matters of concern: see also Article 138b EC, as introduced by the TEU.

Functions and Powers

Apart from its growing participation in the law-making process – as established in the Treaty base of the act in question (consultation, co-operation, co-decision or assent) – the Parliament's other main powers relate to the Community *budget* and its *supervision of the Commission*.

A significant increase in the Parliament's powers came about in 1975 under the second Budgetary Treaty, as a result of which the Parliament now exercises joint control of the Community budget with the Council. Although the Commission draws up the draft budget and the Council ultimately determines 'compulsory' expenditure (mainly on the CAP), the Parliament has, within certain constraints, the final decision on 'non-compulsory' expenditure, relating in the main to social and regional policy, research and, significantly in recent years, aid to non-Community countries such as the Central and Eastern European countries and Russia.

When, in 1985, the Parliament refused to abide by limits placed on 'non-compulsory' expenditure, the Council obtained a ruling that the decision of the President of the Parliament, declaring the 1986 budget adopted, was invalid: see Case 34/86 *Council* v *Parliament* in Chapter Six. It is however agreed, at least in a political sense, that the Council and the Parliament will co-operate on budgetary matters (Joint Declarations of the Parliament, the Council and Commission, 1975 and 1982) and, since 1988, that they will do so within a framework of 'budgetary discipline'. Since 1977 the Parliament has possessed the power under Article 203(8) to reject the budget in its entirety. It has exercised this power twice, in 1979 and 1984. (In such circumstances, until the matter is settled, the Community proceeds on the basis of the preceding year's budget allocations.)

As regards the Parliament's *supervisory powers*, under Article 140 the Commission (and, in practice, the Council) is required to answer written and oral questions from MEPs: see the official Journal, 'C' series. Roy Jenkins was President of the Commission from 1977 to 1980. In his 'European Diary' for 10th May 1978 whilst in Strasbourg he noted:

> Then into the Chamber, luckily as little Fellermaier without any notice got up on a complicated point of order which turned out to be a justified complaint about the very poor attendance and performance of the Commission at question period the previous day. Only Burke and Vredeling had been there. We had discussed this at the Commission meeting that morning, deciding that we must strengthen the team for Thursday and in the future. I therefore had an answer, but felt I had to change my plans, stay in Strasbourg and do Thursday questions myself.

The Commission is also required by Article 143 to submit to the Parliament for public debate an annual general report.

Article 144 provides that the Parliament can obtain the *en bloc* resignation of the Commission by a vote of censure passed by a two–thirds majority of votes cast, representing a majority of all members. This power has in fact never been used by the Parliament against its most pro-European ally.

New supervisory powers introduced by the TEU include the right to set up Committees of Inquiry to investigate 'alleged contraventions or maladministration in the implementation of Community law' (except where the matter is *sub judice*): Article 138c, and the Parliament will also have the power to appoint an Ombudsman empowered to receive complaints concerning instances of maladministration in the activities of the Community's political institutions. Established cases of maladministration will be reported to the Parliament and the institution concerned, the complainant being informed of the outcome: Article 138e.

OTHER COMMUNITY BODIES

The composition and powers of the Luxembourg-based *Court of Auditors* (which is not a court in the legal sense) are to be found in the EC Treaty, as amended by the TEU, Articles 188a - 188c (replacing Articles 206 and 206 A EEC). Established in 1975, the Court has been added to the list of institutions in Article 4(1) EC by the TEU, although it has no power to adopt Community acts under Article 189 and so, it would seem, cannot be subject to proceedings before the Court of Justice under Article 173 (but see Cases 193 and 194/87 *Maurissen and Others* v *Court of Auditors* in which, exceptionally, the Court of Justice allowed such an action.)

Its main functions are to examine the annual accounts of all Community revenue and expenditure (as drawn up by the Commission), to provide a statement as to the reliability of the accounts and the legality of the underlying transactions, and to examine the soundness of the financial management involved. It must provide an annual financial report, which, together with the replies to its observations from the institutions under audit, is published in the Official Journal. The Court of Auditors may also submit special reports on specific questions (eg agricultural fraud, budgetary discipline).

The Court of Auditors is the Community's financial watchdog, exercising control and supervision over the implementation of the budget and providing the Parliament with the documentation necessary for it to give discharge to the Commission in respect of the budget.

The *Economic and Social Committee*, established under the Treaty of Rome (and, similarly, see Article 4(2) EC as amended by the TEU) acts, as numerous Treaty articles testify, in an advisory capacity to both the Council and the Commission in the law-making process: see, for example, Article 100A relating to Internal Market harmonisation measures and Article 43 on the establishment of common organisations of the markets for agricultural products.

Where the Treaty provides for such consultation, a failure to take the Committee's advice amounts to a breach of an essential procedural requirement invalidating the resultant Community measure.

Under Article 193:

> ... The Committee shall consist of representatives of the various categories of economic and social activity, in particular, representatives of producers, farmers, carriers, workers, dealers, craftsmen, professional occupations and representatives of the general public.

Members are appointed by the Council on the basis of national allocations from lists provided by the Member States. Although appointed in their personal capacity, they are generally representative of employers, trade unions, consumers, farmers and professional bodies.

The new Article 194 EC provides that the members of the Committee shall be 'completely independent in the performance of their duties, in the general interest of the Community'. In addition to Treaty-based mandatory consultation, the Council and the Commission may also consult the Committee on other matters as they see fit. The Committee also produces advisory opinions on its own initiative.

The new Article 4(2)EC also establishes a *Committee of the Regions* to act in a similar advisory capacity. Article 198c provides that:

> The Committee of the Regions shall be consulted by the Council or by the Commission where this Treaty so provides and in all other cases in which one of these two institutions considers it appropriate.

The Committee will be made up of representatives of 'regional and local bodies', so providing, in furtherance of a general policy that decisions be taken 'as closely as possible to the people', a direct link between the Community institutions and representatives of, for example, the German Länder and, presumably, such Spanish regions as Catalonia and the Basque country.

Attention has already been drawn to other important Community bodies: the *European Investment Bank* (Articles 198d and 198e inserted by the TEU) and the *European Central Bank* (Article 4a, Article 106 and Protocol No. 3).

THE COMMUNITY LAW-MAKING PROCESS

It will already be apparent that there is no single Community law-making process; no single procedure whereby Community acts (Regulations, Directives and Decisions) come into effect. At the simplest level, it is said that 'the Commission proposes and the Council disposes'. Although correct in a general sense (at least prior to the TEU coming into force), the Commission's legislative powers being as we have seen mainly of a derived nature, this remark fails to take any account of the varying roles of the European Parliament in Community decision-making. Not only therefore is there no single procedure but no one institution which can be called the Community legislature.

The only safe way of determining the procedure necessary for putting into effect a particular Community policy, or element of it, is to refer to the Treaty article, or articles, which form its base. For example, in Chapter Four in the section on Community acts, attention was drawn to Council Regulation 1612/68 on freedom of movement for workers. The Preamble to that act indicates that it is based on Article 49 EEC which at that time (1968) required that the Council had regard 'to the Opinion of the European Parliament'. Earlier in this chapter, Article 49 as amended by the Single European Act 1986 was cited in full, and it will be seen that the Council is now required to act 'in co-operation with the European Parliament'. Following the coming into force of the TEU, a further amendment will come into effect and measures based on Article 49 EC must be adopted by the Council 'acting in accordance with the procedure referred to in Article 189b', the so-called 'co-decision' procedure. This single article is therefore indicative not only of three of Parliament's possible roles in the legislative process but also of that institution's growing legal status.

On the assumption that the TEU will come into force, all three of these procedures (plus the *assent* procedure, see below) will be found within the Treaty.

The *consultation procedure* was, until the amendment of the EEC Treaty by the Single European Act, the *only* legislative procedure and it only required the Council to obtain the Opinion of the Parliament, then merely an 'advisory and supervisory' body. It has *not* been eliminated by the introduction of the later procedures and can still be found in various parts of the EC Treaty, eg Article 43(2) relating to the CAP, Article 130 s (2) dealing with certain aspects of environmental policy and several articles concerning EMU.

The following steps can be identified with this 'traditional' procedure:

1. *Draft legislation is prepared by the Commission* following consultations with interested parties (eg politicians, business leaders and trade unionists) and on the advice of national experts from the civil service of the Member States.

2. *The proposal is submitted to the Council* (ie its working parties and COREPER) for consideration.

3. *The proposal is submitted by the Council to the Parliament* (and the Economic and Social Committee if required) *on a consultative basis*. The draft will be passed to the appropriate specialist Parliamentary committee before the full Parliament gives its *Opinion*: that the proposal be accepted, rejected or amended.

4.   The Commission (or the Council) may modify the proposal and *if the amendment is one of substance*, the Parliament must be consulted again: Case C-65/90 *Parliament* v *Council (Road Haulage Services)*. (In the case of more important proposals, where the Council intends not to follow the Parliament's Opinion, common ground may be sought through a joint Conciliation Committee.)

5.   *The final Council decision on the proposal is taken* (in conjunction with COREPER and its working groups). The applicable *voting procedure* must be followed (see below).

As seen in Chapter Four, this procedure must respect the Parliament's right to be consulted, otherwise the act will be annulled: Case 138/79 *Roquette Frères* v *Council*, but it gives the Parliament no legal power to affect the content of the legislation – merely the right to an Opinion which may or may not be taken into account.

The *co-operation procedure*, introduced by the Single European Act as Article 149(2)EEC, will become the subject of Article 189c EC as amended by the TEU and, strictly speaking, will become 'the procedure referred to in Article 189c'.

If the consultation procedure can be seen as involving a *single* reading (by the Parliament and the Council), the more complicated co-operation procedure gives rise to *two* readings by those institutions.

At the point where, under the consultation procedure, the Council would be in a position to adopt the act (point 5 above), under the co-operation procedure the Council is required to adopt what is termed a *'common position'*. This common position ('first reading') is reached on the basis of a qualified majority (see below) unless the Council amends the Commission's proposal in which case unanimity is required.

The Council then communicates its common position to the Parliament, with the reasons which led to its adoption and a statement of the Commission's position. The Parliament therefore has a second opportunity to consider the draft measure and react to it. The process advances as indicated in the diagram. It will be seen that the Parliament may approve the Council's position (in which case the Council will move to adopt the act) or – by an absolute majority of its Members – amend or reject it.

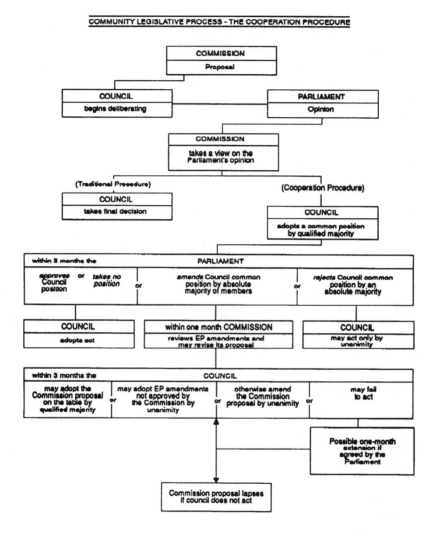

COMMUNITY LEGISLATIVE PROCESS - THE COOPERATION PROCEDURE

If its draft has been rejected, the Council can maintain it at a second reading only by a unanimous vote. It is unlikely that unanimity will be achieved where the common position was originally adopted by a qualified majority. The minority will in all probability maintain their dissenting position and the Parliament's rejection will in effect become a veto: see, eg the demise of the Commission's proposed Directive on sweeteners for use in foodstuffs of September 1990: see Earnshaw and Judge in References and Further Reading at the end of the chapter.

In many cases, the Parliament proposes amendments to the common position. Here, as seen, the Commission examines the amendments and forwards a new proposal to the Council (together with any of the Parliament's amendments that it has not adopted). On considering the new proposal, the Council may act in one of three ways:

(i)   adopt the Commission's proposal as it stands by a qualified majority, or

(ii)   amend that proposal by a unanimous vote, or (iii) adopt any of the Parliament's amendments (not adopted by the Commission) by a unanimous vote.

A great many of the measures relating to the completion of the Internal Market were adopted on the basis of the co-operation procedure: see, in particular, Article 100A, the Treaty base for most of the necessary measures for the approximation of national laws. Under the TEU the co-operation procedure will apply to action taken in various policy areas where previously only consultation was required, eg the environment, common transport policy and vocational training. Similarly, the Parliament's influence will be enhanced to the extent that 'co-decision' will replace co-operation for many of the future Internal Market measures: see the new Article 100a(1), etc.

The 'co-decision' procedure (strictly speaking, 'the procedure referred to in Article 189b') does not give the Parliament equal rights of approval in the legislative procedure, although that body's powers are further increased in those areas where the procedure will operate.

This procedure is recognised in the amended Article 189, which includes a reference to acts of 'the European Parliament acting jointly with the Council'. Similarly, the amended Article 191 refers to a requirement that acts 'adopted in accordance with the procedure referred to in Article 189b' are 'signed by the President of the European Parliament and by the President of the Council'.

This procedure follows the pattern of the co-operation procedure (except that the Commission's original proposal is submitted to both the Council and the Parliament) up to the point where the Parliament (at its second reading) either approves, rejects or amends the Council's common position:

(i)   If the Parliament approves, the position is as before – the Council adopts the act.

(ii)   If the Parliament *rejects* the common position, the Council may convene the new Conciliation Committee (made up of equal members of the Council and the Parliament, the Commission acting as honest broker). If the Parliament still rejects the common position, the proposal will lapse.

(iii)   If the Parliament *amends* the common position, then, following reconsideration by the Council and Commission, the Council (if it approves *all* the amendments) can proceed to adopt the act as amended. If it does not, the Conciliation Committee will attempt to get the two institutions to agree a joint text for adoption. If no such agreement is reached, the measure either lapses *or* it is still possible for the Council to adopt it (amended or otherwise) on a *unilateral* basis – *except* if an absolute majority of the Parliament moves to reject that text: see Article 189b for the complete procedure and note the strict time-limits set at the various stages.

The new Article 189b procedure will apply, as indicated, to most of the Internal Market legislation and to, for example, consumer protection measures, some environmental measures and trans-European networks.

Finally, the *assent procedure*, introduced by the Single European Act, does operate on a true co-decision basis: the Council may only adopt a Commission proposal having obtained the formal approval of the Parliament. It applies, amongst other matters, to decisions under Article 237 regarding applications for membership of the Community and to decisions concerning the conclusion of agreements under Article 238 which, as amended by the TEU, reads as follows:

> The Community may conclude with one or more States or international organisations agreements establishing an association involving reciprocal rights and obligations, common action and special procedures.

Such agreements have been concluded with both European and non-European countries, the most important, the Lomé Convention IV (1989) governing the relationship between the Community and 66 African, Caribbean and Pacific Ocean (ACP) countries.

Voting Procedures in the Council

Article 148(1) provides that:

Save as otherwise provided in this Treaty, the Council shall act by a majority of its members.

However, as will already be apparent, the vast majority of those Treaty articles which lay down a voting procedure do provide otherwise; in the majority of cases for a qualified majority, otherwise for unanimity.

Article 148(2) explains that where the Council is required to act by a qualified majority, the votes of its members are *weighted* as follows:

Germany, France, Italy and the UK:	10 votes each
Spain:	8 votes
Belgium, Greece, the Netherlands and Portugal:	5 votes each
Denmark and Ireland:	3 votes each
Luxembourg:	2 votes

Where the Council (as is normally the case) is acting on a proposal from the Commission, the required minimum positive vote for a qualified majority is 54, amounting to a little over two-thirds of the total of 76. Thus, for example, two of the larger (10 vote) Member States may be outvoted – giving rise, where qualified majority voting applies, to UK concern regarding national sovereignty. In other cases, 54 votes must be cast by at least eight Member States. In either situation, the interests of the smaller Member States are protected from block voting by the larger ones.

Following extensions of qualified majority voting by the Single European Act (and the TEU) – a procedure which clearly allows for quicker and more effective decision-making than one requiring consensus (see Chapter One, regarding the 'Luxembourg Compromise'), unanimity is called for only for matters of particular significance, eg decisions on 'own resources' (Article 201), harmonisation of Member States' indirect taxation legislation (Article 99) and, as seen, Council amendments of Commission proposals (Article 149(1) EEC; EC Treaty, as amended by the TEU, Article 189a (1)). Abstentions by Member States do not prevent the adoption by the Council of acts which require unanimity.

COMMENTS: THE WIDER PICTURE

Students of politics, or even Constitutional law, will not need to be told that this Treaty-based examination of the Community's law-making process tells only part of the real story. Thus, for example, 'identifying the policy context' in 1983, Carole Webb observed that:

... the Community institutions themselves represent but the tip of an iceberg. When all the facts of the wider consultative and implementive processes are exposed, and the inputs from the national systems and, on occasions, the international system, are taken into account, a much more dense network emerges.

Illustrations of the 'wider consultative' process abound in Roy Jenkins' 'European Diary'. During his four-year period as President of the Commission (1977-80), and in his search for progress towards economic and monetary union (the EMS was created in 1978), he discussed, debated and decided issues at informal and formal levels with a wide variety of individuals and institutions. For example: the Italian Minister of the Treasury, the Ecofin Council, German Chancellor Schmidt, within the Commission itself, Swiss Central Bank governors, the US Secretary of the Treasury, British bankers and businessmen, International Monetary Fund officials, the European Parliament (plenary sessions and the Economic and Monetary Affairs Committee), COREPER and the European Council, etc, etc.

From a different angle, Nugent draws attention to a wide range of 'interests' to be found within the wider context of the Community's decision-making process. Their main target is naturally the Commission as the main initiator of economic and social legislation. They include regional and local authorities, individual companies and corporations and their representative bodies such as the Confederation of British Industries (CBI), national interest groups such as environmentalists, and Euro-groups such as the European Trade Union Confederation (ETUC).

Helen Wallace, speaking of 'Negotiation, Conflict and Compromise' in 1983, concluded that:

The Community process is both diverse and intricate ... the character of Community negotiations puts pressure on the member governments to aggregate their policy priorities and so defend them in Brussels. The public visibility of Council sessions emphasises the apparent importance of overall national interests and presents an illusory image of monolithic governments, bargaining with each other, especially the governments of the larger members.

However, despite the attempt by governments to set up gatekeeping mechanisms, transnational networks of policy-making elites have emerged and become increasingly significant ...

During the 1970s a crucial change took place in the EC policy process. A less benign economic context, enlargement, and the international environment were met by disputes over the policy agenda of the EC.

There is no longer a ready consensus on what should constitute the core of collaboration within the enlarged Community comparable to the initial list of priorities to which the Treaties committed the founder members. Instead there is controversy over both the content and order of the policy agenda combined with demands for policies that are difficult to satisfy, given the limitation of resources and authority at the Community level. Inevitably therefore the bargaining on which agreement depends has become more tortuous and competitive, while the challenge of accommodating diverse interests subjects the output of policies to more public scrutiny than hitherto. The Community has thus begun to tread the tortuous path from a policy process largely concerned with issues of regulation and adjudication towards the harsher world of distributional policies, but without a policy-making system with authority and legitimacy commensurate to the task.

Bieber, R., 'Achievements of the European Parliament 1979–1984' (1984) 21 CML Rev. 283.

Bieber, R., 'Legislative Procedures for the Establishment of the Single Market' (1988) 25 CML Rev. 711.

Bieber, R., and Bradley K. St. C., 'Legal Developments in the European Parliament' (1988) 7 YEL 285.

Campbell, A., 'The Single European Act and the Implications' (1986) 35 ICLQ 932.

Earnshaw, D. and Judge D. 'The European Parliament and the Sweeteners Directive' (1993) 31 JCMS 103.

Edward, D., 'The Impact of the Single European Act on the Institutions' (1987) 24 CML Rev. 19.

Freestone and Davidson, *The Institutional Framework of the European Communities*, 1988, Chapters 3 and 4.

Gormley, L., (ed.) of Kapteyn and VerLoren van Themaat's *Introduction to the Law of the European Communities*, 1990, Chapters IV and V(3).

Hartley, T.C., *The Foundations of European Community Law*, 1988, Chapter 1.

Henig, S., 'The European Community's Bicephalous Political Authority: Council of Ministers–Commission Relations' in Lodge, J., (ed.) *Institutions and Policies of the European Community*, 1983.

Jenkins, Roy, *European Diary 1977-81*, 1989.

Lauwaars, R. H., 'The European Council' (1977) 14 CML Rev. 25.

Lenaerts, K., 'Some Reflections on the Separation of Powers in the European Community' (1991) 28 CML Rev. 11.

Lodge, J., 'EC Policy making: Institutional Considerations' and 'The European Parliament – from Assembly to Co-Legislature: Changing the Institutional Dynamics' in Lodge, J. (ed.) *The European Community and the Challenge of the Future*, 1989.

Lodge, J., 'The Single European Act: Towards a New European Dynamism?' (1986) 24 JCMS 203.

Noel, E., 'The Single European Act' (1989) *Government and Opposition* 3.

Philip, Alan Butt, 'Pressure Groups and Policy-Making in the European Community' in Lodge, J. (ed.), as above.

Noël, E. and Nuttall, R., 'The Functioning of the Commission of the European Communities' in *In Memoriam J.D.B. Mitchell* (ed. Usher, J. et al), 1983.

Nugent, Neill, *The Government and Politics of the European Community*, 1991, Part Two.

Scharpf, F. W., 'The Joint Decision Trap: Lessons from German Federalism and European Integration' (1988) 3 *Public Administration* 239.

Wallace, Wallace and Webb, *Policy Making in the European Community*, 1983, Chapters 1 and 2.

Usher, J., 'The "Good Administration" of European Community Law', *Current Legal Problems*, 1985, page 269.

Usher, J., 'The Institutions of the European Communities after the Single European Act' (1987) *Bracton Law Journal* 64.

Weiler, J., 'The Community System: The Dual Character of Supranationalism' (1981) 1 YEL 267.

Weiler, J. and Mondrall, E., 'Institutional Reform: Consensus or Majority?' (1985) 10 EL Rev 316.

CHAPTER SIX

COMMUNITY ACTS: TREATY BASIS AND CONSTITUTIONAL CHECKS AND BALANCES

TREATY BASIS

Article 189 provides that the Community's political institutions, acting in their law–making capacity, shall make Regulations, issue Directives and take Decisions *'in accordance with the provisions of this Treaty'*. Article 190 states that Community acts 'shall state the reasons on which they are based'. The Council's rules of procedure provide that every Community act which it adopts (and in future those it adopts jointly with the Parliament) shall contain a reference to the provisions on which the measure is based.

This reference is usually to a particular Treaty article (or articles), which authorises the adoption of the act and specifies both the procedure to be followed and the type of act permitted. It is usually found in the first recital to the act in question. For example (as seen in Chapter Four), Council Regulation 1612/68 on the free movement of workers was based on Article 49; Council Directive 75/117 on the approximation of Member State laws relating to the application of the equal pay principle was based on Article 100. Commission Decision 89/469 concerning BSE ('mad cow disease') in the UK was based on a Council Directive of 1964 on animal health problems, itself based on Articles 43 and 100.

However, the scope of Community powers is in practice more extensive than this analysis indicates. First, express law–making powers of a more general nature are to be found in Articles 100, 100A and 235.

Aside from Article 99 (dealing with national indirect taxation), Article 100 was the original Treaty provision empowering the Council to issue harmonisation Directives in connection with the establishment and functioning of the Common Market. It was in large part overtaken by Article 100A as introduced by the Single European Act:

Article 100A

1. By way of derogation from Article 100 and save where otherwise provided in this Treaty, the following provisions shall apply for the achievement of the objectives set out in Article 8A. The Council shall, acting by a qualified majority on a proposal from the Commission in co-operation with the European Parliament and after consulting the Economic and Social Committee, adopt the measures for the approximation of the provisions laid down by law, regulation or

administrative action in Member States which have as their object the establishment and functioning of the internal market ...

(When TEU amendments come into effect, the co-operation procedure will, as we have seen, be replaced in this article by the Article 189b 'co-decision' procedure. Article 8A, defining the Internal Market, will become Article 7a.)

As the basis for Internal Market harmonisation measures, Article 100A has been applied to a vast range of subjects. For example, as regards the removal of differing national rules relating to goods, it has been used to introduce new European standards to pressure vessels, children's toys and building materials, and in total Article 100A has formed the basis of some 280 measures within the full range of the single market programme.

Article 235 is similarly of a general nature but it serves a different purpose:

Article 235

If action by the Community should prove necessary to attain, in the course of the operation of the Common Market, one of the objectives of the Community and this Treaty has not provided the necessary powers, the Council shall, acting unanimously on a proposal from the Commission and after consulting the European Parliament, take the appropriate measures.

This article, containing a *residual* legislative power, enables the Council to act on policy matters which, whilst falling within the broad objectives of the Community, are not however specifically spelt out in the Treaty.

To illustrate the requirement that this power must be used to attain one of the Community's *objectives*, prior to the introduction of Articles 130R-T into the Treaty by the Single European Act, environmental protection was brought within Article 2 of the Treaty by regarding a 'continuous and balanced expansion' in a qualitative sense. Environmental action Directives were then based on Article 235 (or Article 100 in connection with the removal of technical barriers to trade).

In addition, action must also be 'necessary', which in practice means that a measure of discretion is left to the Council and Commission. Thirdly, although Article 235 states that the objective must be attained in the 'course of the operation of the common market', this in effect means that the action must fall within the context of the Treaty as a whole, so that the Common Market may function more effectively.

Nevertheless, it is also the case that, in the words of the Court of Justice in Case 45/86 *Commission v Council* (*Generalised Tariff Preferences*), 'it follows from the very wording of Article 235 that its use as the legal basis for a measure is justified only where no other provision of the Treaty gives the Community institutions the necessary power to adopt the measure in question'. Thus it may be that powers *are* to be found elsewhere in the Treaty but they are not considered sufficiently effective. In Case 8/73 *Hauptzollamt Bremerhaven v Massey-Ferguson*, a Regulation enacted under Article 235 on uniform rules for the valuation of goods was held to be valid since Article 27 on the same subject only provided for the issue of non-binding recommendations.

Article 235 was used extensively, prior to the 1986 amendments of the Treaty, in connection with the establishment of a basis for Economic and Monetary Union and also for the development of common regional, social, environmental, energy, and science and technology policies. Whilst, therefore, the Single European Act (and, as anticipated, the TEU) have reduced the significance of Article 235, it does still allow the Council to act, where necessary and under the conditions laid down, to the exclusion of Article 236 which, in *dealing with Treaty amendments*, calls for a conference of the Member States and the ratification of agreed amendments by each of those States.

Apart from the general powers conferred under Articles 100, 100A and 235, when examining the full range of the Community's legislative powers it is also necessary to consider the question of *implied powers*. In a narrow sense implied powers may be derived from the Council's or Commission's express powers and typically extend to such power as is necessary to permit of a *reasonable application* of such express powers; see Case 8/55 *Fédération Charbonnière de Belgique*. However, in Cases 281, 283-85, 287/85 *Germany et al v Commission*, which was discussed in relation to the Commission's powers in the previous chapter, it was seen that the Court of Justice took a wider view of the theory of implied powers. It will be recalled that the Court held in that case that where a provision of the Treaty conferred a specific *task* on the Commission, such provision was also to be regarded as impliedly conferring on the Commission 'the powers which are indispensable in order to carry out that task.'

Alleged Defects in the Treaty Basis of Adopted Measures

The legal foundation on which measures of Community legislation are based had, until recently, rarely been a contentious issue in the relations between the Community institutions, nor had alleged defects in the legal basis frequently been pleaded as a ground of invalidity of such measures. Previous literature on the subject of the legal basis of Community legislation has thus largely been confined to the question of the extent of the Community's powers under certain Treaty articles, in particular Articles 100 and 235 EEC. The spotlight has been thrown on this issue by the institutional modifications introduced by the Single European Act: the extension of the scope of majority voting within the Council, the setting up of a new legislative procedure for the adoption of measures in certain areas of Community activity and the granting of a right to veto to the European Parliament on proposed accession and association agreements: *Bradley* (1988).

Legal basis disputes can arise in a variety of ways and the challenge to an act can be set in several contexts. The *Massey-Ferguson* case (above) was an Article 177 validity reference which questioned the scope of the *Community's* powers. An allegation of a lack of competence of the adopting *institution*, the Commission, was the fundamental issue in the Article 173 annulment action brought by three Member States in Cases 188-190/80 *France, Italy and the UK v Commission* (see Chapter Five). However, of increasing significance, for the reasons set out by Bradley, are disputes where it is alleged that the correct institution (the Council) has based its measure on the wrong Treaty article.

Typically, such a challenge arises either as an *intra-Council matter*, the action being brought by a Member State out-voted in the Council at the time the measure was adopted by a qualified majority, or in the course of an *inter-institutional dispute* involving the Commission (the 'European' body) and the Council (representing the interests of the Member States). In the latter situation an added factor may be an assertion by the Parliament of its enhanced status within the institutional structure. In short, the cases are about the *division of powers*.

This first case arose shortly before Article 100A (and its qualified majority procedure) came into effect:

Case 68/86 *UK* v. *Council (Agricultural Hormones)*

The UK brought proceedings under Article 173(1) for the annulment of Council Directive 85/649 prohibiting the use of natural hormones for fattening purposes in meat production. The UK was opposed to a total prohibition and had voted (with Denmark) against the adoption of the Directive in the Council. It was submitted, *inter alia,* that the Directive had an insufficient legal basis. It had been issued on the basis of Article 43 which requires only a qualified majority; the UK arguing that it should have been based on both Article 43 and Article 100, the latter requiring unanimity. (It was claimed that Article 100 was necessary in order to cover the consumer protection aspects of the Directive.) Clearly, if Article 100 had been required the Council would not be able to impose the hormone ban at all. The Court of Justice ruled as follows on the issue of legal basis:

... Article 43 of the Treaty is the appropriate legal basis for any legislation concerning the production and marketing of agricultural products listed in Annex II to the Treaty which contributes to the achievement of one or more of the objectives of the Common Agricultural Policy set out in Article 39 of the Treaty. There is no need to have recourse to Article 100 of the Treaty where such legislation involves the harmonisation of provisions of national law in that field.

... even where the legislation in question is directed both to objectives of agricultural policy and to other objectives which, in the absence of specific provisions, are pursued on the basis of Article 100 of the Treaty, that article, a general one under which directives may be adopted for the approximation of the laws of the Member States, cannot be relied on as a ground for restricting the field of application of Article 43 of the Treaty.

The Court did, however, go on to annul the Directive because the Council had infringed its own rules of procedure. However the Council quickly readopted the Directive – only to be met by two more annulment actions.

In the following case, the Court clearly ruled that it is not possible for legal bases to be combined (as in *Hormones*) if their prescribed procedures are incompatible:

Case C-300/89 *Commission* v. *Council (Titanium Dioxide Waste)*
The Commission (supported by the Parliament) brought proceedings under Article 173(1) for the annulment of Directive 89/428 on procedures for harmonising the programmes for the reduction and elimination of pollution caused by waste from the titanium dioxide industry.

The Commission had proposed that the Directive be based on Article 100A, which involved the Council acting by a qualified majority in co-operation with the Parliament. However, despite the Parliament's objections, the Council adopted the Directive on the basis of the environmental policy Article 130S. This article provides (at present) for unanimity and merely for consultation with the Parliament.

The Court decided that Article 100A was the correct legal basis. Although the Directive had the dual objectives of environmental protection and the removal of distortions of competition (by establishing harmonised production conditions), it was not possible to have recourse to *both* Article 100A and 130A as the unanimity rule in the latter was incompatible with the co-operation procedure in the former.

In what was primarily a policy decision (which will not exclude the future use of Article 130S for waste management purposes), the Court stated that it did not wish to see the co-operation procedure 'compromised'. If that were so, 'the very objective of the co-operation procedure, which was to reinforce the participation of the European Parliament in the legislative process of the Community, would thereby be called into question.'

As a contribution towards a reduction in the Community's 'democratic deficit', the Court concluded that the participation of the Parliament was 'the reflection at the Community level of a fundamental democratic principle, according to which people were to take part in the exercise of power through the intermediary of a representative assembly.'

CONSTITUTIONAL CHECKS AND BALANCES

In the preceding chapter we examined the collaborative law-making powers of the Community institutions. However, as the foregoing legal basis case shows, this collaborative process can break down, not least on account of differing views held by the Commission (the 'European' body) and the Council (of national ministers) concerning the precise nature and scope of each other's powers within this process. Similarly, as seen, the increased status of the European Parliament within the law-making process has added a further dimension to any discussion of the institutional power structure. It is in this context that Rudden observes that 'it seems as if institutional problems which prove intractable to negotiated political solution are being passed to the Court'.

The jurisdiction of the Court of Justice as regards judicial review and annulment of acts of the Community's law-makers falls generally within the concept of Community administrative law and, as Article 173(1) EEC (subject to amendment by the TEU) demonstrates, extends beyond inter-institutional disputes:

Article 173

The Court of Justice shall review the legality of acts of the Council and Commission other than recommendations or opinions. It shall for this purpose have jurisdiction in actions brought by a Member State, the Council or Commission on grounds of lack of competence, infringement of an essential procedural requirement, infringement of this Treaty or of any rule of law relating to its application, or misuse of powers ...

However, from within this wide field of challenge and review, it is appropriate at this point that we confine our attention to those cases (concerning not only challenges to the legal basis of an act but other matters also) which involve the institutions alone. This will enable us to concentrate upon the development by the Court of the 'interdependent legal accountability' of the institutions: 'The Council, Commission and Parliament collaborate to make *laws*, but are becoming more and more answerable to the guardian of the law': Rudden. The cases which follow tend to operate on two levels: large political-constitutional issues are decided in narrow, technical terms. All the cases, with one exception, are of an inter-institutional direct challenge nature, but one case contains special features. The applicant, the French Ecology Party, was not a 'privileged plaintiff' under Article 173(1), and the act challenged was not an act of the Council or the Commission as would appear necessary under that paragraph.

In the first case, the central issue was the distribution of powers between the Community (the Commission) and the Member States (the Council) as regards the negotiation of an international treaty. In Winter's view:

> The position of the two institutions opposing each other in this legal dispute clearly reflected the interests which each has a duty to safeguard: the Commission represented the interests of the Community and its institutions; claiming that the principle of attributed (or enumerated) powers should not be applied with the utmost strictness in the field of the Community's external relations in an area with so many international aspects as transport. The Council, on the other hand, clung to a narrow definition of the Community's external powers and sought to protect the sovereignty of the Member States in the foreign field from an allegedly illegal limitation by the Community.

Case 22/70 *Commission v Council (ERTA)*

In 1962 five Member States and other European countries signed the European Road Transport Agreement, which harmonised certain social provisions (composition of crews, rest periods, etc) relating to international road transport. Before it came into force, re-negotiations were started in 1967 for its revision.

In October 1969, on the basis of a Commission proposal, Council Regulation 543/69 came into effect. It was based on Article 75 of the Treaty concerning the implementation of the EEC Common Transport Policy and covered much the same ground as ERTA.

In March 1970 the Council decided that the geographically wider-based ERTA II negotiations should continue and that the six Member States would co-ordinate their positions. It was on this basis that the six Member States re-negotiated and agreed ERTA II.

The Commission claimed that the Council proceedings and resolution of 20 March 1970 were an encroachment by the Council on the Commission's responsibilities and functions in this regard. It therefore brought legal action against the Council under Article 173(1) to annul the resolution.

The Court held:

1 The Commission's application for annulment was admissible. Although not within the terms of Article 189, the Council resolution was a reviewable act under Article 173 (see also Chapter Four). It 'had definite legal effects both on relations between the Community and the Member States and on the relationship between institutions.' Not being an act listed in Article 189, it could not be annulled for lack of reasons under Article 190. The Council's arguments on these points were therefore rejected.

2 The adoption by the Community of Regulation 543/69 in October 1969 as an element of the Common Transport Policy gave rise to a transfer of treaty-making power from the Member States to the Community: 'As and when such common rules come into being, the Community alone is in a position to assume and carry out contractual obligations towards third countries affecting the whole sphere of application of the Community legal system. With regard to the implementation of the provisions of the Treaty the system of internal Community measures may not therefore be separated from that of external relations.'

3 Most of the work on ERTA I and II having been completed, on a Member State basis, in October 1969, 'it was for the two institutions whose powers were directly concerned, namely, the Council and Commission, to reach agreement ... on the appropriate methods of co-

operation with a view to ensuring most effectively the defence of the
interests of the Community.'

4 The Commission having failed to exercise its rights as regards the
initiation of such co-operation (see Articles 75, 116 and 228), the Court
ruled that the Council had *not* acted improperly in continuing the
ERTA negotiations on a Member State basis.

By means of a skilful use of Article 173 in relation to Article 189 so as
to create an act *sui generis* (the Council resolution), and by its application of
the doctrine of 'parallelism' (whereby the exercise of *internal* powers gave rise
to *external* powers also), the Court was able to increase, at the expense of the
Member States, the competence of the Community in the field of external
relations. In this important sense the Commission won the war although it
lost this particular battle, because the Court did not wish to throw the long-
running negotiations with non-Member States into confusion by allowing
the Commission to replace the Member States at such a late date.

The Court's powers of review under Article 173(1) enable it to maintain
the institutional balance of power, while ensuring that Community activities
remain within the boundaries established by the Treaty. It is also clear from
the *ERTA* decision that, if policy requires it, the Court is prepared to extend
those boundaries. Nowhere is this more apparent than in a series of Article
173 cases involving the European Parliament. That article provides that: 'The
Court of Justice shall review the legality of acts of the Commission and the
Council ...'. There is no mention of acts of the Parliament. Nevertheless, in
the case which follows, the Court, having reviewed the growth of the
Parliament's powers since the Treaty came into force, ruled that to hold it
unaccountable as regards measures intended to have legal effects would
amount to a failure by the Court to fulfil its duty under Article 164 to ensure
that the law is observed. Commenting upon this extension by the Court of
its own jurisdiction, Hartley states that:

All courts are of course influenced by policy, but in the European Court
policy plays a particularly important role: occasionally the Court will
ignore the clear words of the Treaty in order to obtain a policy
objective.

Under certain conditions, Article 173(2) EEC allows 'any natural and
legal person' to challenge a Decision (but not a Regulation or a Directive):

Case 294/83 *Parti Ecologiste 'Les Verts'* v. *European Parliament*

The Parliament adopted a decision involving the expenditure of budgetary funds which had the effect of subsidising the expenses of parties fighting the forthcoming 1984 direct elections. The method of allocation resulted in the bulk of the money going to parties *already* represented in the Parliament. The Greens were not such a party and therefore challenged the decision under Article 173(2) EEC as being discriminatory.

Having ruled that the challenge by 'Les Verts' was admissible, the Court stated that acts of the Parliament were not expressly included in the Treaty because at that time (1958) the Parliament merely possessed powers of consultation and political control rather than the power to adopt measures which had legal effects.

In *ERTA* the Court had expressed the view that the 'general scheme' of the Treaty was to make a direct action available against 'all measures adopted by the institutions ... which are intended to have legal effects'. To exclude acts of the Parliament from the ambit of this statement would, in the Court's view, be contrary to the functions of the Court itself under Article 164 and the Treaty as a whole:

'... the European Economic Community is a Community based on the rule of law, inasmuch as neither its Member States nor its institutions can avoid a review of the question whether the measures adopted by them are in conformity with the basic constitutional charter, the Treaty ... Measures adopted by the European Parliament in the context of the EEC Treaty could encroach on the powers of the Member States or of the other institutions, or exceed the limits which have been set to the Parliament's powers, without its being possible to refer them for review by the Court. It must therefore be concluded that an action for annulment may lie against measures adopted by the European Parliament intended to have legal effects *vis-à-vis* third parties.'

The Parliament's act was annulled on the ground that 'in the present state of Community law, the establishment of a scheme for the reimbursement of election campaign expenses ... remains within the competence of the Member States.'

It is noteworthy that the Parliament itself did not claim that the action was inadmissible because it was not a named defendant in Article 173. The logic of this was that if its acts, as this case demonstrates, could be *challenged*, then at the earliest opportunity the Parliament would seek to become a *challenger*, although again not so named in Article 173.

At the time of '*Les Verts*', another case was in progress in which it was alleged that the Parliament had exceeded the limit set to its powers:

Case 34/86 *Council* v. *Parliament (Budget)*

In December 1985 the President of the Parliament acting under Article 203(7) declared the budget for 1986 to be finally adopted. This was despite increases in non-compulsory expenditure in excess of the maximum rate fixed by the Commission and in the absence of an agreement between the Parliament and the Council on a new rate: Article 203(9). The Parliament had expressed the view that the Council had failed to take into account commitments already entered into and the cost of accession of two new Member States -Spain and Portugal. Nevertheless, in A. G. Macini's opinion:

'The Parliament's strategy is inspired by the history of Western institutions ... and a basic forecast: the greater its influence in determining the budget becomes the less resistible will be its requests for new powers and, by the same token, for greater democracy in the Community system.' In this Article 173 action brought by the Council, the question of whether the President's declaration was a reviewable act was dealt with by the Court as follows:

'It is the President of the Parliament who formally declares that the budgetary procedure has been brought to a close by the final adoption of the budget and thus endows the budget with binding force *vis-à-vis* the institutions and the Member States. In exercising that function the President of the Parliament intervenes by means of a separate legal act of an objective nature at the conclusion of a procedure characterised by the joint action of various institutions.'

The Court concluded that the President's declaration had been made before the Parliament and Council had agreed the new rate of increase for non-compulsory expenditure. It was tainted with illegality and therefore annulled. The Court went on to rule that those two institutions as a matter of urgency should, in accordance with their obligation under Article 176, take steps to agree the budget.

In 1987, the European Parliament, in an attempt to establish a position as a fully privileged applicant under Article 173(1), challenged a Council Decision relating to the operation of Council regulatory committees acting in conjunction with the Commission, where the Commission is exercising powers conferred on it by the Council for the implementation of rules laid down by the latter: see Chapter Five.

As Weiler argues:

> ... it was possible (but by no means necessary) to construe the earlier case law on the position of the Parliament before the European Court (most importantly, Case 138/79 *Roquette Frères* ... Case 294/83 *Les Verts*; Case 34/86 *Budget* ...) as being informed by a judicial policy of 'equalising' the jurisdictional status of Parliament to that of the other principal Community institutions. *Comitology* might simply have become the 'logical' continuation of this case law, especially of *Les Verts*. It must have come as a disappointment to Parliament that in its judgment the European Court underscored its interest, already revealed in *Les Verts*, in having all legal acts in the Community order susceptible to judicial review and was less concerned with institutional jurisdictional 'equity'. It might nonetheless be that in negating *any* standing to Parliament under Article 173 the European Court left an unacceptable jurisdictional lacuna and compromised the very system of protection it was at pains to complete in *Les Verts*.

Case C-302/87 *Parliament v Council (Comitology)*

The Parliament contended that Article 173 should be interpreted in its favour as it had been, *against* the Parliament, in *Les Verts* and the *Budget* case. Rejecting this argument based on 'balance' and 'equity', the Court refused the Parliament's right to sue under Article 173.

Amongst other things, the Court stated that the Commission was charged with the guardianship of the Treaty under Article 155 and so could introduce an action for annulment of acts which endangered the Parliament's prerogatives.

The Court did not follow the compromise put forward by Attorney General Darmon who argued for limited rights for the Parliament under Article 173. In view of the case which follows, it is important to see that he argued that the Parliament should be entitled to challenge Council or Commission acts where its own interests or rights were directly affected, otherwise it would stand in an unfavourable position as compared with the other institutions and Member States under Article 173(1) and with private parties under Article 173(2). The case which follows had been commenced when this argument was put before the Court:

Case 70/88 *Parliament v. Council (Chernobyl)*

Parliament sought the annulment under Article 173 (and Article 146 Euratom) of Council Regulation 3954/87 which laid down permitted maximum levels of radioactive contamination of food and feeding-stuffs. It claimed that the Regulation should have been based on Article 100A, which required the opening of the co-operation procedure with the Parliament, and not on Article 31 Euratom which merely required Parliament to be consulted. The Council's action, it was claimed, amounted to a failure to observe the Parliament's post-Single European Act powers regarding its more influential role in the drawing up of legislation. The Council objected to the admissibility of the action, denying Parliament's standing under Article 173.

The Court of Justice ruled that the action *was* admissible despite its decision in *Comitology*.

In *Comitology*, the Court had stated that the prerogatives of the Parliament were sufficiently safeguarded by its own rights as a plaintiff under Article 175 (regarding an institution's *failure* to act) and indirectly by way of Article 177 references concerning an act's validity and Article 173 annulment actions brought by privileged (para. 1) and non-privileged (para. 2) applicants. Nevertheless, in *Chernobyl* a differently constituted Court felt that the existence of these other remedies was not sufficient to guarantee in all circumstances the annulment of an act of the Council or Commission which had infringed the rights of the Parliament.

However, in following Attorney General Darmon's compromise in *Comitology*, the Parliament's interest in such proceedings has been restricted to situations where an infringement of its rights is in question. Such interest is not the *general* interest of the Council, the Commission or the Member States, and the Court emphasised that proceedings brought by the Parliament in defence of its rights (relating, for example, to its proper participation in the legislative process) were not covered by Article 173 but under a right of action created by the Court to ensure respect for the institutional balance: see, however, the new Article 173 below. If it is argued that the Parliament's interest is that of its constituents, the citizens of the Community, then it may be added that at some future date that view of the Parliament's interest must be recognised. *Chernobyl* does extend the scope of judicial review of Community acts and institutional 'balance' has been somewhat restored.

These developments, and others, are reflected in Article 173 EC as amended by the TEU which now reads, in part:

> The Court of Justice shall review the legality of acts adopted jointly by the European Parliament and the Council, of acts of the Council, of the Commission and of the ECB, other than recommendations and opinions, and of acts of the European Parliament intended to produce legal effects *vis-à-vis* third parties ...

> The Court shall have jurisdiction ... in actions brought by the European Parliament and by the ECB for the purpose of protecting their prerogatives ...

Bradley, K. St. C., 'Maintaining the Balance' (1987) 24 CML Rev. 41.

Bradley K. St. C., 'The European Court and the Legal Basis of Community Legislation' (1988) 13 EL Rev. 379.

Bradley, K. St. C., 'Sense and Sensibility: *Parliament* v *Council* Continued' (Chernobyl), (1991) 16 EL Rev. 245.

McGee, A. and Weatherill, S., 'The Evolution of the Single Market – Harmonisation or Liberalisation?' Part 5 'Choice of Legal Base: the Court's Role Reasserted' (1990) 53 MLR 578.

Page, A., 'Transparency Directive Upheld' (1981) 6 EL Rev. 496.

Rudden, B., *Basic Community Cases*, 1987, Part II B 'Constitutional Checks and Balances'.

Weiler, J., 'Pride and Prejudice – *Parliament* v *Council*' (Comitology), (1989) 14 EL Rev. 334.

Winter, J., 'Annotation on Case 22/70, Re ERTA' (1971) 8 CML Rev. 550.

CHAPTER SEVEN

THE EUROPEAN COURT OF JUSTICE

INTRODUCTION

The Convention on Certain Institutions Common to the European Communities, signed in Rome in 1957, provides that the three Communities are to be served by a single Court, the Court of Justice of the European Communities. The Court of Justice, which sits in Luxembourg, is the supreme authority on all aspects of Community law. It should not be confused with the European Court of Human Rights which sits in Strasbourg and which is not a European Community institution. The Court of First Instance of the European Communities was established in 1988.

Article 164 of the EEC Treaty (unaffected by the TEU) establishes that:

The Court of Justice shall ensure that in the interpretation and application of this Treaty the law is observed.

The purpose of this chapter is to present a broad survey of the Court's various powers under the EEC Treaty (which are examined in more detail from different angles in other chapters); to outline the Court's composition and organisation, including aspects of its procedure; and to consider its role in the development of the Community and Community law.

THE COMPOSITION AND ORGANISATION OF THE COURT

The Court consists of thirteen Judges appointed by the common accord of the Governments of the Member States. In practice each Judge has been a national of a different Member State, with the office of the thirteenth judge rotating between the larger Member States. When the Court sits in *plenary session* (ie as a full court), either nine or all thirteen Judges sit (with the President presiding) depending on the difficulty or importance of the case.

The Judges do not deliver separate judgments; the practice being to frame a decision as a single collegiate judgment following secret deliberations. If necessary, decisions are taken by a majority and, although this will not be apparent on the record, the presence of dissenting voices may well affect the tenor of a judgment.

The Court is also divided into *Chambers* or divisions of three or five judges. To avoid unnecessary complications, the method of assigning cases to the full Court or to a Chamber will be examined on the basis of Article 165 EC (as amended by the TEU):

> The Court of Justice shall consist of thirteen Judges.

> The Court of Justice shall sit in plenary session. It may, however, form chambers, each consisting of three or five Judges, either to undertake certain preparatory inquiries or to adjudicate on particular categories of cases in accordance with rules laid down for these purposes.

> The Court of Justice shall sit in plenary session when a Member State or a Community institution that is a party to the proceedings so requests
> ...

The overall effect of the amendment to the original Treaty text (introducing the new third paragraph above) is to allow the Court more freedom to assign cases to Chambers, so alleviating the weight of its case load. (A Member State or Community institution counts as a 'party' for this purpose where it intervenes in a direct action or submits written observations in a reference for a preliminary ruling.)

Although the judges come from the Member States they are *Community* (not national) judges in a *European* Court which, while operating in nine different languages, has adopted French as its working language.

The appointment and status of the Judges (and Advocates General, see below) are covered by Article 167:

> The Judges and Advocates General shall be chosen from persons whose independence is beyond doubt and who possess the qualifications for appointment to the highest judicial offices in their respective countries or who are jurisconsults of recognised competence; they shall be appointed by common accord of the Governments of the Member States for a term of six years.

> Every three years there shall be a partial replacement of the Judges. Seven and six Judges shall be replaced alternately.

> Every three years there shall be a partial replacement of the Advocates General. Three Advocates General shall be replaced on each occasion.

Retiring Judges and Advocates General shall be eligible for reappointment.

The Judges shall elect the President of the Court of Justice from among their number for a term of three years. He may be re-elected.

The Judges have come from various backgrounds including membership of their national judiciary, legal practice, political or administrative office, law faculties or some combination of these.

In 1992 the constitution of the Court was as follows:

President	– Ole Due
First Advocate General	– Francis Jacobs
Judges	– Manuel Diez de Velasco
	– Constantin Kakouris
	– Paul Joan George Kapteyn
	– Fernand Gervisse
	– René Joilet
	– Francis O'Higgins
	– Giuseppe Federico Mancini
	– Jose Carlos Moitunho de Almeida
	– Gil Carlos Rodriguez Iglesias
	– Fernand Schockweiler
	– Sir Gordon Slynn
	– Manfred Zuleeg
Advocates General	– Marco Darmon
	– Walter van Gerven
	– Carl Otto Lenz
	– Jean Mischo
	– Giuseppe Tesauro

ADVOCATES GENERAL

Under Article 166:
The Court of Justice shall be assisted by six Advocates General.

It shall be the duty of the Advocate General, acting with complete impartiality and independence, to make, in open court, reasoned submissions on cases brought before the Court of Justice, in order to assist the Court in the performance of the task assigned to it in Article 164 ...

There is no equivalent to the Advocate General in the English legal system. As Brown and Jacobs explain:

> ... although a member of the Court, he acts as its independent adviser. Unlike however his counterpart in the French *Conseil d'Etat*, he *commissaire du gouvernement*, he does not attend the judges' deliberations ... even in a consultative capacity.

The prime function of an Advocate General is, in each case before the Court, to deliver an impartial and reasoned *Opinion*. This Opinion is given after the conclusion of the arguments of the parties and before the judgment of the Court. It will review the facts, the submissions of the parties and others who have taken part, examine the law (including previous decisions of the Court) and finally express a view as to how the case should be decided.

The Advocate General's Opinion is not binding on the Court, which may or may not follow his or her submissions:

> The advocate general may also see himself as in effect delivering a reserved first instance judgement in a case taken on appeal, but his opinion, while it may have authority in future cases, does not of course decide the instant case, even provisionally: *Brown and Jacobs*.

In essence, therefore, an Opinion forms an extremely valuable basis on which the Court, which is still frequently a court of both first and last instance, can arrive at its judgment. (The role of the Advocate General should be distinguished from that of the assigned *Judge Rapporteur*, whose function is to make a preliminary study of the case and prepare a report for the Court on such matters as facts to be proved and evidence to be adduced for that purpose: see Outline of Procedure before the Court of Justice, below.)

THE JURISDICTION OF THE COURT

The jurisdiction of the Court of Justice is that which is conferred upon it by the Treaty. On the basis of Article 164 it is concerned to ensure the correct interpretation and application of the Treaty and the acts of the Community institutions.

The Court's *dispute-solving* powers operate within the complex set of relationships that exist between the subjects of Community law: the political institutions, the Member States and private parties (natural and legal persons). Here the Court may be called upon to exercise a jurisdiction of a *constitutional* nature, relating either to the balance of powers between the institutions themselves (eg the *ERTA* and *Titanium Dioxide Waste* cases) or between the Community and the Member States (eg an action brought *by* a Member State against a Community institution for annulment of an act, as in the *Agricultural Hormones* case brought by the UK against the Council) or, alternatively, an action brought by the Commission *against* a Member State for failure to fulfil its Treaty obligations (eg the *Tachographs* action brought against the UK).

In other disputes concerning the interpretation and application of Community law, the Court will exercise a jurisdiction of an *administrative* character. Here its duty is the protection of Member States and private parties against the illegal acts or omissions of the institutions. As regards Member States, there is clearly an overlap with such cases as *Agricultural Hormones*. However, not only may Member States have recourse to direct action under Article 173 but private parties also, eg *Roquette Frères* v *Council* and *Les Verts* v *Parliament*. It should also be recalled that, for natural and legal persons, an alternative, *indirect* route from a national court, regarding rulings on the *validity* of acts of the institutions, exists under the Court's preliminary rulings jurisdiction: Article 177(1)(b).

The powers of the Court in relation to the *interpretation* of Community law are of particular significance within the framework of the preliminary rulings jurisdiction of Article 177. Here the keynote is one of *co-operation* between Member States (that is, their national courts and tribunals) and the Community (the Court of Justice). The Court is concerned to ensure the *uniformity* of interpretation of Community law in its *application* by these national courts. These are the courts which first refer questions of interpretation to the Court of Justice and they are the courts which, armed with that Court's interpretative ruling, must ultimately settle the disputes in the actions which have arisen before them. Many of the most important Community law cases are of this kind: *Van Gend en Loos*, *Costa* v *ENEL* and many more. They are also the cases which focus on both the legal relations between private parties and the State and between one private party and another.

Since 1989, the Court's *appellate* jurisdiction is mainly concerned with appeals from the Court of First Instance on points of law brought by undertakings under Article 173(2) against Commission Decisions under which they have been fined for breach of the Community's competition rules.

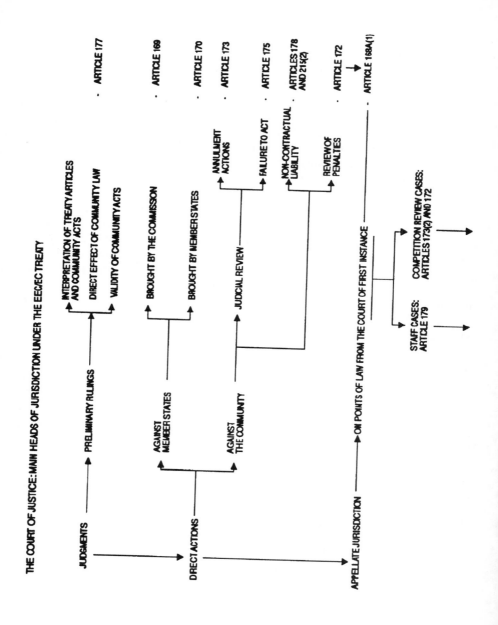

THE COURT OF JUSTICE: MAIN HEADS OF JURISDICTION UNDER THE EEC/EC TREATY

These and other of the main heads of the Court's jurisdiction are referred to in the diagram on page 150 and have been, and will be, discussed in more detail elsewhere.

PROCEDURE IN THE COURT

A lawyer from the British Isles is likely to find the procedure very strange. The oral and adversary character of English civil procedure (and its Scottish and Irish counterparts) is in marked contrast with the written and inquisitional features of the Luxembourg procedure ...: Brown and Jacobs.

The procedure of the Court is laid down in the Statutes of the Court and the Court's own Rules of Procedure: Article 188. For direct actions it is normally made up of the following stages:

(i)   Written proceedings;

(ii)   Although questions of fact are not often in dispute, the Court may decide to hold a preliminary inquiry to establish what issues of fact need to be proved and what evidence is required;

(iii)   Oral proceedings;

(iv)   Judgment.

These stages, in which the written documents play a more important part than the oral proceedings, are to be found in Title III Procedure of the Court Statute (EEC) and the diagram on page 152. (They also cover the procedure for preliminary rulings.)

Title III. PROCEDURE

Article 17

The States and the institutions of the Community shall be represented before the Court by an agent appointed for each case; the agent may be assisted by an adviser or by a lawyer entitled to practise before a court of a Member State.

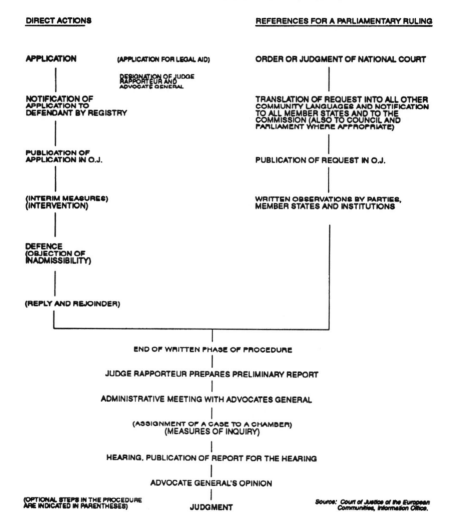

OUTLINE OF PROCEDURE BEFORE THE COURT OF JUSTICE

DIRECT ACTIONS

REFERENCES FOR A PARLIAMENTARY RULING

APPLICATION

(APPLICATION FOR LEGAL AID)

DESIGNATION OF JUDGE RAPPORTEUR AND ADVOCATE GENERAL

ORDER OR JUDGMENT OF NATIONAL COURT

NOTIFICATION OF APPLICATION TO DEFENDANT BY REGISTRY

TRANSLATION OF REQUEST INTO ALL OTHER COMMUNITY LANGUAGES AND NOTIFICATION TO ALL MEMBER STATES AND TO THE COMMISSION (ALSO TO COUNCIL AND PARLIAMENT WHERE APPROPRIATE)

PUBLICATION OF APPLICATION IN O.J.

PUBLICATION OF REQUEST IN O.J.

(INTERIM MEASURES)
(INTERVENTION)

WRITTEN OBSERVATIONS BY PARTIES, MEMBER STATES AND INSTITUTIONS

DEFENCE
(OBJECTION OF INADMISSIBILITY)

(REPLY AND REJOINDER)

END OF WRITTEN PHASE OF PROCEDURE

JUDGE RAPPORTEUR PREPARES PRELIMINARY REPORT

ADMINISTRATIVE MEETING WITH ADVOCATES GENERAL

(ASSIGNMENT OF A CASE TO A CHAMBER)
(MEASURES OF INQUIRY)

HEARING. PUBLICATION OF REPORT FOR THE HEARING

ADVOCATE GENERAL'S OPINION

(OPTIONAL STEPS IN THE PROCEDURE
ARE INDICATED IN PARENTHESES)

JUDGMENT

Source: Court of Justice of the European Communities, Information Office.

Other parties must be represented by a lawyer entitled to practise before a court of a Member State.

Such agents, advisers and lawyers shall, when they appear before the Court, enjoy the rights and immunities necessary to the independent exercise of their duties, under conditions laid down in the rules of procedure ...

Article 18

The procedure before the Court shall consist of two parts: written and oral.

The written procedure shall consist of the communication to the parties and to the institutions of the Community whose decisions are in dispute of applications, statements of case, defences and observations, and of replies, if any, as well as of all papers and documents in support or of certified copies of them.

Communications shall be made by the Registrar in the order and within the time laid down in the rules of procedure.

The oral procedure shall consist of the reading of the report presented by a Judge acting as Rapporteur, the hearing by the Court of agents, advisers and lawyers entitled to practise before a court of a Member State and of the submissions of the Advocate-General, as well as the hearing, if any, of witnesses and experts.

Article 19

A case shall be brought before the Court by a written application addressed to the Registrar. The application shall contain the applicant's name and permanent address and the description of the signatory, the name of the party against whom the application is made, the subject matter of the dispute, the submissions and a brief statement of the grounds on which the application is based.

The application shall be accompanied, where appropriate, by the measure the annulment of which is sought or, in the circumstances referred to in Art. 175 of this Treaty, by documentary evidence of the date on which an institution was, in accordance with that Article, requested to act. If the documents are not submitted with the application, the Registrar shall ask the party concerned to produce them within a reasonable period, but in that event the rights of the party shall not lapse even if such documents are produced after the time limit for bringing proceedings.

Article 20

In the cases governed by Art. 177 of this Treaty, the decision of the court or tribunal of a Member State which suspends its proceedings and refers a case to the Court shall be notified to the Court by the court or tribunal concerned. The decision shall then be notified by the Registrar of the Court to the parties, to the Member States and to the Commission, and also to the Council if the act the validity or interpretation of which is in dispute originates from the Council.

Within two months of this notification, the parties, the Member States, the Commission and, where appropriate, the Council, shall be entitled to submit statements of case or written observations to the Court.

Article 21

The Court may require the parties to produce all documents and to supply all information which the Court considers desirable. Formal note shall be taken of any refusal.

The Court may also require the Member States and institutions not being parties to the case to supply all information which the Court considers necessary for the proceedings.

...

Article 28

The hearing in court shall be public, unless the Court, of its own motion or on application by the parties, decides otherwise for serious reasons.

Article 29

During the hearings the Court may examine the experts, the witnesses and the parties themselves. The latter, however, may address the Court only through their representatives.

Article 30

Minutes shall be made of each hearing and signed by the President and the Registrar.

...

Article 32

The deliberations of the Court shall be and shall remain secret.

Article 33

Judgments shall state the reasons on which they are based. They shall contain the names of the Judges who took part in the deliberations.

Article 34

Judgments shall be signed by the President and the Registrar. They shall be read in open court.

Article 35

The Court shall adjudicate upon costs.

Article 36

The President of the Court may, by way of summary procedure, which may, in so far as necessary, differ from some of the rules contained in this Statute and which shall be laid down in the rules of procedure, adjudicate upon applications to suspend execution, as provided for in Art. 185, or to suspend enforcement in accordance with the last paragraph of Art. 192 ...

Article 37

Member States and institutions of the Community may intervene in cases before the Court.

The same right shall be open to any other person establishing an interest in the result of any case submitted to the Court, save in cases between Member States, between institutions of the Community or between Member States and institutions of the Community.

Submissions made in an application to intervene shall be limited to supporting the submissions of one of the parties.

The defendant in most of the cases before the Court is either the Community, or one of its institutions, or a Member State, or a ministry or department thereof. It is not possible in either case to obtain *execution* of the Court's judgment although it is binding on the defendant. Thus, as regards enforcement actions against Member States under Articles 169 and 170, Article 171 provides that:

If the Court of Justice finds that a Member State has failed to fulfil an obligation under this Treaty, the State shall be required to take the necessary measures to comply with the judgment of the Court of Justice.

Similarly, in relation to cases brought against an institution regarding reviewable acts or failures to act under Articles 173 and 175, Article 176 goes on to state that:

The institution whose act has been declared void or whose failure to act has been declared contrary to this Treaty shall be required to take the necessary measures to comply with the judgment of the Court of Justice.

The evidence is that Member States do comply with judgments but it may take them a year or more to do so. When France refused to comply with a judgment of the Court regarding a ban on lamb imports (mainly from Britain) until it received Community concessions which Britain was blocking in the Council, the Commission brought new proceedings and applied for an interim order under Article 186 requiring France to admit British exports of lamb. The 'lamb war' was however eventually settled on the political plane by means of trade-off concessions negotiated in the Council.

Although there are no provisions for sanctions against Member States in the EEC Treaty, the TEU will add a second paragraph to Article 171 which will give the Court power to impose financial penalties upon Member States which do not comply with the first paragraph, above. This development is discussed more fully in Chapter Twenty.

THE COURT OF JUSTICE: POLICY AND THE PROCESS OF INTEGRATION

The importance of the judicial dimension to the process of integration – to the functioning of the Community – is generally recognised. The Court of Justice has, as a basic policy objective, consistently advanced the process of integration. In its landmark decisions establishing the principles of direct effect and the supremacy of Community law (*Van Gend en Loos*, *Costa* v *ENEL*, and *Simmenthal*) and see now *Francovich* in the next chapter, it has dramatically increased the scope and effectiveness of Community law. In *ERTA* and subsequent competence cases, it has extended the powers of the Community institutions. Its continuing emphasis on the Treaty as the Community's 'constitution' rather than an international agreement follows the same path.

Remarks regarding the role of the Court of Justice attributed to the British Prime Minister, John Major, in September 1991 drew an interesting response in a letter to the editor of 'The Times' from a former President of the Court – a response which was not allowed to go unchallenged:

EC AND THE LAW
from Lord Mackenzie Stuart

Sir, According to your political editor the prime minister regards the Court of Justice of the European Communities 'as a politically motivated body that should have no role in shaping member governments' policies' (report, September 26, earlier editions). If this accurately represents the prime minister's belief, which would surprise me, then he should be rapidly disabused of this slur on the court's integrity.

The European treaties, which are agreements reached by the governments of the member states, are the result of political choice. So, too, is every act of Parliament. The court plays no part in that choice. Its function, a purely judicial one, as the Treaty of Rome provides, is to see that the law is observed.

This, of course, includes applying the old common law rule that, where possible, a legal document should be given an intelligible meaning rather than that it should be declared a nullity.

To suggest, as does your report, that the court ignores proper judicial standards, is a calumny.

Yours faithfully,

MACKENZIE STUART

(President, Court of Justice of the European Communities, 1984-8), Le Garidel, Gravières, 07140 Les Vans, France. September 27.

JUDICIAL FUNCTION OF EUROPEAN COURT
From Mr. Gavin Smith

Sir, One hesitates to take issue with a jurist of the distinction of Lord Mackenzie Stuart. However, his assertion (October 3) that the function of the European Court of Justice is a purely judicial one cannot go unchallenged.

In the opinion of many objective commentators, the court has since its inception been inspired more by a political urge to achieve European integration than by a desire to 'ensure that in the interpretation and application of the treaties the law is observed', as it is enjoined to do by article 164 of the Treaty of Rome.

Indeed, of the two most fundamental principles of EC law one (its supremacy over national law) is exclusively and the other (its direct applicability in national proceedings) largely the product of judicial inventiveness, designed to increase the impact of EC law at the expense of national law.

Perhaps Lord Mackenzie Stuart would like to comment on the recent statement made (extra-judicially) by one of his former brethren, Judge Mancini, that 'the main endeavour of the court has been to reduce the differences between the treaties and a constitution; that it 'has sought to 'constitutionalise' the treaty ... to fashion a constitutional framework for a federal-type structure in Europe' (*Common Market Law Review*, 1989). I am not aware that any present or former judges of the court have dissociated themselves from these views.

Probably the most striking recent instance of judicial policy-making by the European Court was its decision last year in the Chernobyl case (Case 70/88), where it held that the European Parliament could in certain circumstances challenge EC legislation before the court.

The relevant treaty provision (article 173) can only be construed as denying the parliament this right. However, this 'procedural lacuna' did not prevent the court from ruling, in effect, that since – in its view – the parliament *needed* such a power, it should be *granted* it.

What is particularly disturbing about that judgment is that the court must have been aware that a European Commission proposal to give the parliament this very power had been rejected by the member states only five years before, at the last revision of the treaties.

It is no doubt going too far to accuse the European Court, as did a former prime minister of France, Michel Debré, of suffering from a *mégalomanie maladive*. Nevertheless, concern at the unorthodoxy of the court's approach cannot be dismissed merely as a slur on its integrity.

Perhaps, with the issue of European federalism high on the political agenda, those commentators who display such enthusiasm for criticism of our own judges should apply themselves with equal vigour to analysis of how the European Court performs its judicial function.

Yours faithfully,

GAVIN SMITH

1 Metre Court Buildings, Temple, EC4. October 9.

As regards negative integration and the establishment and functioning of the Common/Internal market, the Court, on the basis of its jurisdiction under Article 177, has acted as a prime mover in determining and refining the obligations of the Member States. It has done this with respect not only to the free movement of goods (*Van Gend en Loos*, Case 8/74 *Dassonville* and Case 120/78 *Cassis de Dijon*; see Chapter Twelve) but also to persons (Case 2/74 *Reyners*) and capital (Cases 286/82 and 26/83 *Luisi* and *Carbone*). As Gormley has explained:

> ... the Court has sometimes been obliged with the aid of the systematic teleological method of interpretation to deduce solutions from Community law for concrete problems which should have been dealt with by the Community legislator. This has led to the Court being accused of indulging in judicial policy-making. Geelhoed has rightly observed, though, that the systematic teleological method of interpretation binds the judges to the system and aims of Community law and thus limits their freedom of policy choice.

> However, the systematic teleological approach seems to bind the judges less in some areas than in others with the result that the Court's case-law acquires a stronger aspect of judicial creativity than lawyers are used to seeing from national judges.

In the 1990s and beyond, following the establishment of the Internal Market, it may be that the Court's influence will diminish as the focus switches to *positive* economic and political integration. Alternatively, it may be that, the essential nature of the process of integration remaining the same, the same basic questions both of competence and the effectiveness of Community law will remain as questions for the Court to face.

THE COURT OF FIRST INSTANCE

As a result of the ever-increasing workload of the Court of Justice and consequently the similarly increasing length of time for a case to come to judgment, it was agreed by the Member States in the Single European Act to make provision for a new Court of First Instance.

WORKLOAD OF THE COURT OF JUSTICE

	NEW CASES	JUDGMENTS	CASES PENDING
1980	279	132	328
1988	373	238	605
1989	—	Direct actions: approximately 2 years to obtain judgment.	
	—	Article 177: approximately 18 months to obtain a preliminary ruling.	

It had also become clear that the Court of Justice was not the appropriate forum for some cases, particularly staff cases (disputes between Community institutions and their employees: 58 in 1988) and competition policy cases requiring extensive research and assessment of the economic and legal context in which the original Commission Decisions under Article 85 or 86 had been taken.

Following the Single European Act, the EEC Treaty was amended as follows:

Article 168A

1. At the request of the Court of Justice and after consulting the Commission and the European Parliament, the Council may, acting unanimously, attach to the Court of Justice a court with jurisdiction to hear and determine at first instance, subject to a right of appeal to the Court of Justice on points of law only ... certain classes of action or proceeding brought by natural or legal persons. That court shall not be competent to hear and determine actions brought by Member States or by Community institutions or questions referred for a preliminary ruling under Article 177 ...

The Court of First Instance was established in October 1988 by Council Decision 88/591 and it heard its first cases a year later. It will be seen that the new Court is 'attached' to the Court of Justice; it is not a separate institution. Under Article 3 of the Decision, the Court's jurisdiction (the 'classes of action or proceeding brought by natural or legal persons') was laid down:

(a) disputes between the Communities and their servants: Article 179 EEC;

(b) certain types of action brought by undertakings against the Commission under the ECSC Treaty;

(c) actions brought by natural or legal persons against a Community institution under Article 173(2) or Article 175(3) EEC relating to the implementation of the competition rules applicable to undertakings.

It had been thought that the CFI would also take over jurisdiction in *anti-dumping* and *subsidy* cases, as they often raise difficult factual problems similar to those in competition cases: see, for example, Article 92 on aids granted by States.

However, Article 3(3) of the Council Decision merely stated that the question of CFI jurisdiction regarding the review of anti-dumping Decisions would be re-examined after two years 'in the light of experience, including the development of jurisprudence'. (Community rules regarding non-EEC goods allegedly dumped on to the Common Market, and the protective measures that may be taken against them, are at present considered in some quarters to be unfair and not in conformity with GATT dumping rules.)

Under a TEU amendment to Article 168a, the 'classes of action or proceeding' coming within the CFI's jurisdiction (with the exception of Article 177 references) are left open, to be decided by the Council at the request of the Court of Justice. This development should lead to a significant extension of the CFI's jurisdiction by allowing it to hear actions brought by Community institutions or Member States.

The CFI is located in the same complex as the Court of Justice in Luxembourg, and comprises 12 members (one from each Member State in practice). The first British judge was Mr. D. A. O. Edwards QC who was formerly a professor of law at the University of Edinburgh, and the first President of the CFI was a Portuguese judge, Mr. J. L. da Cruz Vilaca, previously an Advocate General at the Court of Justice.

The CFI sits in chambers of three or five judges or occasionally in plenary session. There are no specially appointed Advocates General although a member may be called upon to perform that function in a particular case. By January 1990 there were 171 cases pending before the CFI most of which were staff or competition review cases. Judgments of the CFI bear the prefix 'T', for the French word *tribunal*; judgments of the Court of Justice since 1989 are distinguished by the prefix 'C'.

Appeals to the Court of Justice, on points of law only, may be brought – by an unsuccessful party, an intervening Member State or Community institution, or a directly affected natural or legal person: cf. Article 173(2) – on three grounds:

(i)   lack of competence of the CFI;

(ii) breach of procedure before the CFI which adversely affects the interests of the appellant;

(iii) infringement of Community law by the CFI.

The distinction between questions of law and questions of fact and the circumstances in which the CFI can be said to have infringed Community law will doubtless prove controversial: see, for example, Case C-132/90P *Schwedler* v *Parliament* ('P' stands for *pourvoi*, decision on appeal from the CFI).

Where the Court of Justice decides that an appeal is well-founded, it is required to quash the CFI decision. It can then give final judgment itself or refer the case back to the CFI for judgment.

If a high proportion of CFI decisions become the subject of appeals, the present reduction in the workload of the Court of Justice will be accordingly offset. Competition decisions affecting valuable commercial interests are the most likely subject of appeal, but at least the complex facts will have been determined by the CFI, leaving the Court of Justice to apply the law.

THE FUTURE

In 1993 it is clear that the heavy caseload of the Court of Justice remains a worrying matter and that in this respect the establishment of the CFI has been only partially successful. Advocate General Jacobs has concluded that:

As for the Court of Justice itself, its own caseload is likely to continue to grow, particularly as references from courts in the newer Member States become more frequent and the validity and interpretation of measures adopted to implement the Single Market programme are contested. It is therefore likely that in due course further steps will need to be taken to ensure that cases are dealt with promptly. What might these consist of?

First, the requirement laid down in the second paragraph of Article 165 of the EEC Treaty, that cases brought by a Member State or by one of the Community institutions must be heard by the Court of Justice in plenary session, could be abolished. The Court of Justice itself should be the sole judge of when it is necessary for a case to be dealt with in plenary session [see now the amendment introduced by the TEU, discussed above]. There is no need, for example, for undefended actions brought by the Commission against Member States for failure to implement directives, or financial disputes between the Commission and Member States over payments from the Community's Agricultural Fund, to be heard by the full court. An increase in the number of judges from thirteen to fifteen would then allow the Court of Justice to sit permanently in three chambers of five judges each in wider categories of cases.

Secondly, the role of the Advocates General and the way the Court of Justice deals with their Opinions might be reconsidered. It is arguable that an Advocate General's Opinion is not necessary in every case. It will be observed that many of the cases which now come within the jurisdiction of the CFI will be dealt with, at least at first instance, without the benefit of an Advocate General's Opinion. Had those cases been dealt with by the Court of Justice, an Advocate General would have been assigned to them. Where an Advocate General's Opinion is delivered and the Court of Justice broadly agrees with it, it might be asked whether it is necessary for an extensive judgment to be given. The Court of Justice could simply express its general agreement with the views of the Advocate General, it being understood that it was not necessarily to be taken as endorsing every aspect of the Opinion.

In the longer term, a further reorganisation of the Court of Justice may prove necessary, with the establishment of other specialised tribunals.

Bengoetxea, J., The Legal Reasoning of the European Court of Justice, 1993.

Brown, L. Neville, Brown and Jacobs': The Court of Justice of the European Communities, 1989.

Cappelletti, M., 'Is the European Court of Justice Running Wild?' (1987) 12 EL Rev. 3.

Dashwood, A., 'The Advocate General in the Court of Justice of the European Communities' (1982) 2 Legal Studies 202.

Due, O., 'The Court of First Instance' (1988) 8 YEL 1.

Editorial Comment, 'The Future Development of the Community's Judicial System' (1991) 28 CML Rev. 5.

Gormley, L., (ed.), Kaptyn and VerLoren Van Themaat's Introduction to the Law of European Communities, 1990, Chapter IV, Part 3.

Hartley, T., The Foundations of European Community Law, 1988, Chap 2.

Jacobs, F.G., 'The European Court of First Instance' (1990) Wig and Gavel 28.

Lenz, C. O. 'The Court of Justice of the European Communities: Its Modus Operandi and its Significance for the Sovereignty of the Member States of the European Community' (1988) 2 LIEI 1.

Millett, T., 'The New European Court of First Instance' (1989) 38 ICLQ 811.

Office for Official Publications of the E.C. (Luxembourg), Synopsis of the Work of the Court of Justice and the Court of First Instance of the E.C. in 1988 and 1989, 1991.

Rasmussen, H., On Law and Policy in the European Court of Justice, 1986.

Rasmussen, H., 'Between Self-Restraint and Activism: A Judicial Policy for the European Court' (1988) 13 EL Rev. 28.

Slynn, G., 'The Court of Justice of the European Communities' (1984) 33 ICLQ 409.

Weiler, J. H. H., 'The Court of Justice on Trial' (Review essay on Rasmussen's book listed above) (1987) 24 CML Rev. 555.

CHAPTER EIGHT

THE DIRECT EFFECT OF COMMUNITY LAW

THE DIRECT EFFECT OF TREATY ARTICLES

In 1963 in Case 26/62 *Van Gend en Loss* (see Chapter Four), it will be recalled that the Court of Justice stated that the Community constituted a 'new legal order'. The Dutch government's arguments that the 'standstill' on customs duties in Article 12 was a Treaty obligation any violation of which could be invoked only at international level (ie by an action brought either by the Commission or another Member State – a *dualist* position in international law terms) was rejected by the Court on policy grounds and in *monist* terms:

> The objective of the EEC Treaty, which is to establish a Common Market, the functioning of which is of direct concern to interested parties in the Community, implies that this Treaty is more than an agreement which merely creates mutual obligations between the Contracting States.

Such a view rests on the theory, recognised by many Member States but not the UK, that international law (including in this respect the Treaty of Rome) and municipal law (the internal law of the Member States) are a *single* (monist) system in which the former has primacy, rather than their being separate systems, the former binding states only and having effect in municipal law only when expressly incorporated by, for example, an Act of Parliament.

The Court of Justice therefore concluded that the 'subjects' of the new legal order were 'not only Member States but also their nationals':

> Independently of the legislation of Member States, Community law therefore not only imposes obligations on individuals, but is also intended to confer upon them rights ... These rights arise not only where they are expressly granted by the Treaty, but also by reason of obligations which the Treaty imposes in a clearly defined way upon individuals as well as upon Member States and upon the institutions of the Community.

Thus, not only are provisions of Community law capable by their very nature (the Treaty is of a self-executing character) of direct application in the national courts of the Member States but such application by national judges is intended to be effective in the sense of the creation of Community rights for individuals.

As we have seen, there is nothing in the Treaty itself to indicate that its provisions may have such *direct effect, ie the capacity to create directly enforceable rights which may be relied upon by an individual in an action before the national courts.* In Chapter Four it was argued that the Court wished to assert not only the federal and constitutional nature of the Treaty (individuals being subjects of both Community law and national law, subject to the principle of supremacy) but also the full effectiveness of a provision of substantive Community economic law in a case involving the customs union and an action brought by an undertaking engaged in inter-Member State trade against a national authority. It is clear that the Court was (as it remains) anxious to play its part in the promotion of European economic integration through a policy of increasing the scope and effectiveness of Community law. The Court's rulings on direct effect, whether based on its interpretive functions under Article 177 or otherwise, are crucial as regards the compliance of Member States (and, in some cases, individuals) both with the Treaty and, as will be seen, with Community legislation. They are therefore fundamental to the overall coherence and consistency of the law which underpins common and co-ordinated policies.

In *Van Gend en Loos*, the Court considered itself empowered to establish the principle of direct effect on the basis of the 'purpose, spirit and wording' of the Treaty. Except where the Treaty so provides, there must be no transformation of Community law into national law. It must be of *direct* use to Community citizens who, within their national legal orders, are enabled to exercise the 'vigilance of individuals to protect their rights' so securing 'an effective form of supervision of Member States acting in breach of the provisions of the Treaty.'

However, it should not be assumed that all Treaty articles create rights for individuals. In *Van Gend en Loos* the Court stated that Article 12 was 'ideally adapted to produce direct effects in the legal relationship between Member States and their subjects'. This was so because the provision contained a 'clear and unconditional' prohibition (an obligation *not* to increase customs duties), which was independent of the need for any further action being taken by national (or Community) authorities. Article 12 was therefore appropriate to confer rights on individuals, being in itself 'complete and legally perfect'. While observing these overlapping tests or requirements in a rather informal way, the view of the Court of Justice has increasingly been that direct effect is the *norm*, and Professor Van Gerven (presently an Advocate General) has suggested that:

... the direct effect of a provision depends mainly on whether the courts and finally the Court of Justice, feel able and sufficiently equipped to apply the provision without any further act by the authorities of the Communities or of its Member States.

The case law of the Court shows that a number of articles (or paragraphs of an article) do not create direct effects because they are insufficiently precise (eg Articles 11 and 18) or by their nature they are not capable of conferring individual rights (eg Article 100A). However a fundamentally important article such as Article 7 (Article 6 when the TEU comes into effect), which provides that discrimination on the grounds of nationality is prohibited, although of a very general character, can be either directly effective in itself or in conjunction with other Community provisions: see Case 186/87 *Cowan v Tresor Public*.

Article 119, which concerns another kind of discrimination and imposes an obligation on Member States to implement and maintain the principle of 'equal pay for equal work' for men and women, is also directly effective: see eg Case 43/75 *Defrenne v Sabena (No. 2)*. A significant feature of *Defrenne* is that, although it is addressed to Member States, Article 119 does not merely apply to public sector (state) employees. The equal pay principle must apply throughout the Community and in so doing it places *obligations* on *all* employers. Thus, as *Defrenne* and other cases show, an employee can rely on Article 119 against a private sector employer: the legal status of the defendant employer and its relation to the State is irrelevant. Article 119 is therefore an illustration of the availability of a Community provision for use by one individual against another individual or undertaking; so-called *horizontal* direct effect. The use of Article 12 in *Van Gend en Loos* against a branch of the Dutch government was a case of *vertical* direct effect. (This is a distinction which is all-important when considering the direct effect of EEC Directives.)

Since *Van Gend en Loos*, the case law of the Court on the direct enforceability of Treaty articles in national courts has extended the list of such articles not only within the field of the free movement of goods but to other policy areas such as the free movement of workers, the right of establishment, the freedom to provide services, competition policy and equal pay. (For such a list, see *Collins* in 'References and Further Reading' at the end of the chapter.)

THE DIRECT EFFECT OF COMMUNITY ACTS: REGULATIONS

Regulations, as defined in Article 189(2), are of general application; they are binding in their entirety and are directly applicable in all Member States.

Much confusion has existed in relation to the terms direct effect and direct applicability. Regulations are directly applicable in the sense that national legislation is *not* required to implement and so incorporate them into the national legal system: see Case 34/73 *Variola* in Chapter Four. The entry into force of a Regulation occurs automatically upon adoption or upon a date laid down by the Council or Commission. As Freestone and Davidson state:

> This system of Community legislation is a vital part of the Community system for regulating such matters as customs tariffs and the control of agricultural products where market structures and prices change rapidly. In order for such a system to work effectively, the legislation must take effect in all Member Sates at the same time.

Although Regulations are directly applicable, they are *not necessarily* directly effective in the sense described above, ie that they confer directly enforceable rights upon individuals. In Case 131/79 *Santillo*, AG Warner stated in his Opinion that:

> Unquestionably every provision of every regulation is directly applicable, but not every provision of every regulation has direct effect in the sense of conferring on private persons rights enforceable by them in national courts. One can point to numerous examples of provisions of regulations that confer no direct rights on individuals.

A prime source of the confusion between the two terms (in the UK at least) has been the Court of Justice itself where on many occasions the expressions have been used interchangeably in the sense of the creation of Community rights for individuals.

Although generally Member States are precluded from taking steps, for the purpose of applying a Regulation, which are intended to alter its scope or supplement its provisions, the measure may itself expressly provide otherwise:

Case 128/78 *Commission* v. *UK (Re Tachographs)*

The Commission's action under Article 169 concerned the failure of the UK to implement Article 21 of Regulation 1463/70 relating to the introduction, for health and safety reasons, of tachometers in commercial vehicles. Although Article 4 of the Regulation laid down the date from which use of the equipment became compulsory, Article 21(1) provided that: 'Member States shall, in good time and after consulting the Commission, adopt such laws, regulations or administrative provisions as may be necessary for the implementation of this Regulation. Such measures shall cover, *inter alia*, the reorganisation of, procedure for, and means of carrying out, checks on compliance and the penalties to be imposed in case of breach.'

This vague and conditional provision could not become effective and, for example, create any new criminal offence except through specific implementation at national level spelling out the nature of the offence, responsibility for it, penalties and defences.

The Court of Justice ordered the UK to implement the provision as required.

The normal position as regards Regulations is however illustrated by the following case:

Case 93/71 *Leonosio* v. *Italian Ministry of Agriculture*

L brought a claim in the Italian courts for payments due from the national Ministry under Community Regulations relating to a scheme to reduce dairy herds and over-production of dairy products. Although the Community rules established that payments to farmers should be made within two months of their slaughter of dairy cows, the Italian government delayed final implementation of the scheme until the necessary budgetary provision was made to meet that part of the cost falling on the national authorities.

In a preliminary ruling, the Court of Justice held that the Regulations were of direct effect, creating a right in the applicant L to a payment which could not be conditional or altered by national authorities, and which was immediately enforceable in the national courts. The Court referred to Article 5, para (1) of the Treaty: 'Member States shall take all appropriate measures, whether general or particular, to ensure fulfilment of the obligations arising out of this Treaty or resulting from action taken by the institutions of the Community'.

If the objections of the Italian State had been recognised, Italian farmers would have been placed in a less favourable position than those in the other States. This would have involved a disregard of the fundamental principle that Regulations must be uniformly applied throughout the whole Community.

In view of the fact that a Regulation is of 'general application', it follows, providing its relevant provisions are sufficiently 'clear and unconditional', that they may be invoked in national courts both against other individuals (ie horizontally) and against the State (ie vertically). Additionally, it will be recalled that, as with Treaty articles, such directly effective provisions of a Regulations take priority over conflicting national law: see Case 106/77 *Simmenthal (No. 2)* and Case 11/70 *Internationale Handelsgesellschaft* in Chapter Four.

DECISIONS

As we have seen in Chapter Four, a Decision of the Council or Commission is binding in its entirety upon those to whom it is addressed: Article 189(4). Unlike a Regulation, which is of 'general application', it may be addressed to a Member State(s), an individual(s) or an undertaking(s). By definition, Decisions are formal acts imposing rights or obligations on their addressees.

In Case 9/70 *Grad v Finanzamt Traunstein*, the plaintiff haulage contractor challenged a West German tax alleged to be in breach of a Council Decision addressed to the Member States providing for the application of the common VAT system to road haulage (and other methods of transporting goods) and a harmonisation Directive which laid down the deadline for the implementation of the Decision. On the question of the Decision having direct effect, and thus creating rights in favour of G, the Court of Justice ruled that Article 189 does not prevent individuals from founding their actions in national courts upon Decisions (and Directives) addressed to Member States:

> ... the provision according to which decisions are binding in their entirety on those to whom they are addressed enables the question to be put whether the obligation created by the decisions can only be invoked by the Community institutions against the addressee or whether such a right may possibly be exercised by all those who have an interest in the fulfilment of this obligation. It would be incompatible with the binding effect attributed to decisions by Article 189 to exclude in principle the possibility that persons affected might invoke the obligation imposed by a decision.

In each particular case, stated the Court –

> ... it must be ascertained whether the nature, background and wording of the provision in question are capable of producing direct effects in the legal relationships between the addressee of the act [here, the West German tax authorities] and third parties [such as Grad].'

In Case 249/85 *ALBAKO*, a Berlin margarine producer sought an order in the national courts to restrain the German agricultural intervention agency from distributing in West Berlin 900 tonnes of free butter from the EEC 'butter mountain' in accordance with a Commission Decision addressed to the Federal Republic. The applicant claimed that the agency's proposed action was in breach of German competition law. Following an Article 177 reference, the Court of Justice observed that the circumstances of the case were different from those in *Grad*. In that case the Decision in question had required national law to be modified and it had been invoked in order to prevent the application to G of provisions of national law which G claimed had not been amended in accordance with the Decision's requirements.

In *ALBAKO*, the Commission's Decision did not require any rules of general application to be adopted by the Federal Republic which, through its intervention agency, had duly complied with it. Unlike *Grad* there was consequently no question of protecting a litigant from the adverse consequences of a Member State failing to comply with its obligations under Community law. The Commission's valid Decision obliged the Federal Republic to act and left it no margin of discretion. Its binding character had to be respected by all the organs of the addressee State including its courts. By virtue of the primacy of Community law, national courts had to refrain from giving effect to all provisions of national law the application of which would interfere with the implementation of a Community Decision.

DIRECTIVES: CAN THEY CREATE RIGHTS FOR INDIVIDUALS?

The question of the direct effect of Directives has aroused a great deal of controversy and considerable case law. It would appear from Article 189 that no question of direct effect should arise. Article 189(3) provides that:

> A directive shall be binding, as to the result to be achieved, upon each Member State to which it is addressed, but shall leave to the national authorities the choice of form and methods.

From this several points emerge:

1. Directives are *not* of general application: they may be addressed to one or more Member States.

2. As they are required to be implemented by national authorities, it is clear that they are *not directly applicable* as defined above. *When issued* by the Council or the Commission, Directives are not designed to be law in that form in the Member States.

3. This being so, they only take effect − *or should take effect* − on the basis of appropriate and properly implemented *national* measures, which will secure for individuals whatever rights the Community measure seeks to confer upon them. Member States to whom a Directive is addressed must implement its obligations within the *time-limit* laid down in the Directive.

4. Directives are of a somewhat different character from Regulations; they are in several ways a more flexible instrument. They can be addressed merely to one or more Member States where particular problems are found or, of necessity, to all the Member States, eg Internal Market harmonisation Directives. Also they leave a discretion to the Member States, not as regards 'the result to be achieved', but as to the 'form and methods' by which that result is brought about.

For example, Article 6 of Council Directive 76/207 on the implementation of the principle of equal treatment for men and women as regards access to employment, promotion, etc. requires all Member States to 'introduce into their national legal systems *such measures as are necessary* to enable all persons who consider themselves wronged' by discrimination 'to pursue their claims by judicial process'. (Emphasis added.) In answer to an Article 177 question from a German court as to whether the Directive required certain *specific* sanctions (compulsory engagement or substantial damages), the Court of Justice replied that

> ... Member States are required to adopt measures which are sufficiently effective to achieve the objective of the directive ... However, the directive does not prescribe a specific sanction, it leaves Member States free to choose between the different solutions suitable for achieving its objectives.

Despite the fact that the authors of the Treaty did not intend Directives to have direct effect, individual rights being provided by the implementing national law, significant failures by Member States to fulfil their obligations under Article 189(3) eventually led the Court of Justice to apply the principle of direct effect, at least to a limited extent, to Directives.

An early major development in a long line of decisions arose in a case involving the question of (a) the direct effect of a Treaty article which did not appear to contain an absolute, unqualified rule but rather one incorporating a discretionary element, and (b) the direct effect of a Council Directive which fleshed out that Treaty article:

Case 41/74 *Van Duyn* v. *Home Office*

Ms D, a Dutch national and scientologist, arrived at Gatwick Airport on 9 May 1973. Her purpose in coming to the UK was to take up a post as secretary at the British headquarters of the Church of Scientology of California. She was refused leave to enter by the immigration authorities on grounds of public policy. In particular, the Home Secretary considered it 'undesirable' to allow anyone to enter the UK on the business or employment of the Church of Scientology. This decision was based on Government policy to the effect that the Church's activities, although not illegal, were harmful to the mental health of those involved.

Ms. D claimed in the High Court that she was entitled under EEC law to enter and remain in the UK for the purpose of employment. She relied first on Article 48 of the Treaty which grants workers the right of free movement between Member States, subject in para. (3) to 'limitations justified on grounds of public policy, public security or public health.' She further relied on Article 3(1) of Directive 64/221 which particularises and limits the powers of Member States as laid down in Article 48(3). Thus measures taken by them on public policy grounds must be 'based exclusively on the personal conduct of the individual concerned'. Ms D claimed that this provision was directly effective and gave her the right to enter – her argument being that her exclusion was based on the UK Government's declared policy towards the Church of Scientology generally and not on account of any 'personal conduct' on her part. (The UK had not implemented Directive 64/221, relying instead on pre-existing immigration rules which did not however state that entry could be refused only on the basis of personal conduct.)

In the first ever Article 177 reference from the UK, the High Court put to the Court of Justice questions regarding the direct effect of both the Treaty article and the Directive.

The Court ruled that Article 48 imposed on Member States a precise and immediate obligation regarding the free movement of workers. A Member State's right to invoke the limitations on that freedom in para. (3) of the article was, as stated in the Directive, 'subject to judicial control' in national courts and it did not prevent the article from conferring on individuals rights which were enforceable by them.

On the question of the creation of individual rights on the basis of the Directive, the Court's main ground for declaring that Article 3(1) of the Directive was directly effective was not the UK Government's failure to implement the Directive (there was, as stated earlier, no provision in national law that entry could be refused *only* on basis of the 'personal conduct' of a would-be immigrant such as Ms D) but the Court's policy decision that, given the nature, general scheme and wording of the provision, its *effectiveness* would be greater if individuals were entitled to invoke it in national courts. Therefore Article 3(1) of the Directive was also directly effective.

At the end of the day, however, Ms D lost her case: the Court of Justice ruled that *present association* with an organisation considered socially harmful by a Member State does amount to 'personal conduct'. (Later decisions in this area suggest that 'the Court may have been very indulgent towards the UK'; see Rudden, *Basic Community Cases.*)

In a broader context, the Court of Justice had established a principle: Directives were capable of creating rights for individuals who might enforce them in national courts. Member States were put on warning regarding their duty under Article 5 to fulfil their Treaty obligations; here, to transpose Directives into national law so that individuals might secure their Community rights in the manner envisaged by those who had drafted Article 189. In addition, proper transposition of Directives by Member States would mean that pressure might be taken off the Commission regarding the bringing of enforcement proceedings under Article 169 against defaulting Member States.

In the case with follows, the Italian State had clearly failed to implement a harmonisation Directive within the time-limit laid down in the measure itself:

Case 148/78 *Pubblico Ministero* v. *Ratti*

R, who was in business selling solvents and varnishes, fixed labels to certain dangerous substances in a manner which was in conformity with Directive 73/173, but which contravened the relevant Italian legislation of 1963. Italy had failed to implement the Directive within the time limit laid down (8 December 1974). This would have necessitated amending the national legislation.

R was prosecuted for breach of the Italian labelling law and he pleaded the provisions of the Directive in his defence. The Milan Court, being unsure 'which of the two sets of rules should take precedence', referred the following question to the Court of Justice: 'Does Council Directive 73/173/EEC of 4 June 1973, in particular Article 8 thereof, constitute directly applicable legislation conferring upon individuals personal rights which the national courts must protect?' (Note the use here of the word 'applicable'.)

The Court held that:

This question raises the general problem of the legal nature of the provisions of a directive adopted under Article 189 of the Treaty.

In this regard the settled case-law of the Court ... lays down that, whilst under Article 189 regulations are directly applicable and, consequently, by their nature capable of producing direct effects, that does not mean that other categories of acts covered by that article can never produce similar effects.

It would be incompatible with the binding effect which Article 189 ascribes to directives to exclude on principle the possibility of the obligations imposed by them being relied on by persons concerned.

Particularly in cases in which the Community authorities have, by means of directive, placed Member States under a duty to adopt a certain course of action, the effectiveness of such an act would be weakened if persons were prevented from relying on it in legal proceedings and national courts prevented from taking it into consideration as an element of Community law.

Consequently a Member State which has not adopted the implementing measures required by the directive in the prescribed periods may not rely, as against individuals, on its own failure to perform the obligations which the directive entails.

It follows that a national court requested by a person who has complied with the provisions of a directive not to apply a national provision incompatible with the directive not incorporated into the internal legal order of a defaulting Member State, must uphold that request if the obligation in question is unconditional and sufficiently precise.

Therefore the answer to the first question must be that after the expiration of the period fixed for the implementation of a directive a Member State may not apply its internal law – even if it is provided with penal sanctions – which has not yet been adapted in compliance with the directive, to a person who has complied with the requirements of the directive.

In relation to a second prosecution for the selling of varnishes, improperly labelled under the national law of 1963, the Court of Justice held that R could not rely on Directive 77/128 relating to varnishes because the time-limit for implementation into national law (9 November 1977) had not been reached at the relevant time. The obligation was not then directly effective.

Article 189 states that a Directive is binding, as to the result to be achieved, upon a Member State. Thus where a Member State fails to implement a Directive within the time-limit laid down (or implements it in a defective manner, eg beyond the limits of the State's discretion: see Case 51/76 *VNO*) and as a result deprives individuals of their Community rights, such individuals may nevertheless, in the face of conflicting national provisions, rely upon the Directive (providing its relevant provisions are 'unconditional and sufficiently precise'). In these circumstances Directives create enforceable rights for individuals as plaintiffs or defendants – *against the State* – by means of what has been described as a 'reflex or ricochet effect rather in the nature of estoppel':

> ... the European Court of Justice has developed a doctrine which is akin to estoppel. It works this way. If a citizen sues a Member State in the national courts claiming that the State has caused him damage by acting in a way which is contrary to the directive, and has done so at a time when, if the State had fulfilled its duty under Community law, national law would have been amended to make such action unlawful, the State is not permitted to defend itself on the basis that its actions were lawful in terms of national law. It is otherwise if the defendant is a private person: *Foster* v *British Gas* per Sir John Donaldson M.R.

It must be stressed that all the cases considered so far have involved a dispute between a private individual (or undertaking) and the State (ie State authorities). They establish that Directives may have *vertical* direct effect, ie they may be used as a sword, to sue a Member State which has failed to implement (properly) a Directive: see *Van Duyn* and *VNO*, or as a shield against a Member State which seeks to enforce conflicting national legislation against the individual: *Ratti*.

The next question regarding the attribution of direct effect to Directives was, and remains, a controversial one. It may be put several ways: Is it open to an individual to rely on a Directive in litigation *not* against a Member State but against another individual? Can Directives impose *obligations*, and not merely confer rights, on individuals? Are Directives capable of creating *horizontal* direct effect?

Both provisions of the Treaty (see Case 43/75 *Defrenne* regarding Article 119) and Regulations (which are of 'general application': Article 189) may confer rights and impose obligations on private individuals, ie they may be both vertically and horizontally directly effective. The main argument *against* Directives imposing obligations on individuals is that they are not binding on individuals but on the Member State to whom they are addressed and a defaulting Member State should not take advantage of its own wrong. This is not an argument that can be employed against individuals.

There seems little doubt that the Court of Justice was anxious to maximise the 'effet utile' of Directives in the sense of securing rights for individuals that *should be* available through proper implementation in national law. However, in the face of a serious revolt by some superior national courts to the concept even of the *vertical* direct effect of Directives (see eg the French Conseil d'Etat in the *Cohn-Bendit* case in 1978, when it refused to follow *Van Duyn*, see Chapter Nine, although the attitude of this national court has since changed), the Court of Justice not only did not extend the concept but eventually clearly decided in the *Marshall* case against horizontal direct effect.

Nevertheless, not least because the *Marshall* decision, whilst affirming the vertical direct effect of Directives but denying any horizontal effect, created a serious anomaly, the Court moved later, in the *Von Colson* case, to rectify the position and, by an alternative route, seek to maximise the effect of Directives via national law:

Case 152/84 *Marshall* v. *Southampton and S.W. Hampshire*
Area Health Authority;

Miss M was employed by the AHA which had a policy of compulsory retirement for women at 60 and men at 65. M was dismissed at 62 on the sole ground that she was over the retirement age for women. The Sex Discrimination Act 1975 excluded from the ambit of its prohibition on discrimination by an employer on the ground of sex 'provision in relation to death or retirement'. M, who wished to remain in employment, alleged sex discrimination by the AHA contrary to Council Directive 76/207 (the Equal Treatment Directive).

The UK had adopted the Directive in 1976 but had not amended the 1975 Act as it considered that the Directive permitted discrimination in retirement ages.

The Court of Appeal referred to the Court of Justice questions as to whether the dismissal was an act of unlawful discrimination and whether the Directive could be relied upon by an individual in the national courts.

The Court of Justice answered both these questions in the affirmative:

1. The different compulsory retirement ages amounted to discrimination on the grounds of sex contrary to Article 5(1) of the Equal Treatment Directive.

2. Article 5(1) could be relied upon as against a State authority acting in its capacity as employer in order to avoid the application of any national provision (section 6(4) of the Sex Discrimination Act) which did not conform to Article 5(1).

The Court stressed that the defendant Health Authority was a *public* body and that a person in Miss Marshall's position was able to rely on the Directive as against the State regardless of the capacity in which the latter was acting – whether public authority or employer. Thus, while not accepting the UK Government's contention that as an employer the State was no different from a private employer (ie an individual), the Court did accept that:

> With regard to the argument that a directive may not be relied upon against an individual, it must be emphasised that according to Article 189 of the EEC Treaty the binding nature of a directive, which constitutes the basis for the possibility of relying on the directive before a national court, exists only in relation to 'each Member State to which it is addressed'. It follows that a directive may not of itself impose obligations on an individual and that a provision of a directive may not be relied upon as such against such a person.
>
> ...
>
> The argument submitted by the United Kingdom that the possibility of relying on provisions of the directive against the respondent qua organ of the State would give rise to an arbitrary and unfair distinction between the rights of State employees and those of private employees does not justify any other conclusion. Such a distinction may easily be avoided if the Member State concerned has correctly implemented the directive in national law.

Following Miss Marshall's success, it being conceded when the ruling was remitted that the AHA was a 'public authority', it nevertheless remained the case that where a Directive has not been implemented or has been implemented incorrectly, its effectiveness against the State but not against a private individual (eg employer) could clearly lead to anomalies. As has been said:

> Making the right to rely on a directive by an employee dependent on the status of his employer seems a remarkably arbitrary criterion for setting the parameters of an important component of Community social law: Morris.

The problems surrounding the 'public/private' dichotomy can be mitigated or removed in several ways. Firstly, while it may be said that for the Court to argue that the blame lies with Member States who fail to act correctly and in time is idealistic, the duty so to act does exist under Article 5 of the Treaty. A failure properly to implement a Directive can bring about an Article 169 action by the Commission, which, as we have seen, will under the TEU be backed by the possibility of sanctions against a defaulting Member State in the form of financial penalties (not that this is of direct assistance to the individual). Secondly, it is clear that the Court of Justice is intent on giving 'the State' the widest possible interpretation:

Case C-188/89 *Foster and Others* v. *British Gas plc*

In the Court of Appeal the appellants, who were former employees of the (then nationalised) British Gas Corporation, claimed discrimination by their employer contrary to Article 5(1) of Council Directive 76/207 on Equal Treatment, in that they had been compulsorily retired at 60 whereas their male colleagues were not required to retire until 65. Their dismissals were not unlawful under the national legislation in force at the time (the Sex Discrimination Act 1975). As in *Marshall*, the domestic rules had not yet been amended to bring them in line with the Directive's insistence on equal treatment in regard to, inter alia, the conditions of dismissal. (They were amended in 1986).

The Court of Appeal held that the Directive was only vertically directly effective, ie so as to provide rights for an individual employee against the non-compliant State (as employer) or any organ or emanation thereof: see *Marshall*, which makes it clear that the task of determining whether a defendant is part of the State rests on national courts. Relying on domestic case law, 'most of it concerning post-war nationalisation measures light years removed from the social policy objectives embodied in the Equal Treatment Directive' (see Morris), the Court held that British Gas was not an organ or emanation of the State. It was therefore not bound by the Directive and the appeal failed.

On further appeal, the House of Lords sought a preliminary ruling under Article 177 on the basic question: What is the State in the context of the direct effect of Directives?

The Court of Justice held:

1. (On a preliminary issue), that it was the function of the Court of Justice to determine the categories of person against whom a Directive might be relied. It was for national courts to decide if a party fell within one of those categories.

2. Article 5(1) of the Equal Treatment Directive might be relied upon in a claim for damages against a body, whatever its legal form, which had been made responsible, pursuant to a measure adopted by a public authority, for providing a public service under the control of that authority and had for that purpose special powers beyond those which resulted from the normal rules applicable in relations between individuals.

Earlier, in Case 222/84 *Johnston* v *Chief Constable of the Royal Ulster Constabulary*, the Court had observed that the Chief Constable was:

... an official responsible for the direction of the police service. Whatever its relations may be with other organs of the State, such a public authority, charged by the State with the maintenance of public order and safety, does not act as a private individual. It may not take advantage of the failure of the State, of which it is an emanation, to comply with Community law.

There was, therefore, following the ruling in *Foster*, little doubt that the appellants in that case would be able to rely on the Equal Treatment Directive when the case returned to the House of Lords. Thus, as Lord Templeman stated in applying the ruling:

Applying those words, it seems to me that the 1972 Act created a body, the BGC, which provided a public service, the supply of gas to citizens of the State generally under the control of the State, which could dictate its policies and retain its surplus revenue; the BGC was equipped with a special monopoly power which was created and could only have been created by the legislature. The BGC is therefore a body against which the relevant provisions of the equal treatment directive may be enforced.

For the purpose of the enforcement of social policy Directives, the Court of Justice therefore established appropriate guidelines for national courts regarding the scope of 'the State' within all the Member States. However, this decision merely redrew the line between 'public' and 'private'; it did not remove the distinction.

Thus, in another compulsory retirement case, *Doughty* v *Rolls Royce* (1992), the Court of Appeal, applying the *Foster* guidelines, held (1) that the 100 per cent. control exercised over RR by the State as its sole shareholder was irrelevant, albeit (2) the service provided by RR was under control of the State; (3) that RR traded *with* the State at arm's length and in no way could be said to have been made responsible, pursuant to a measure adopted by the State, for providing a public service, and (4) that RR had not been granted any special powers. RR was not therefore an appropriate body against which to invoke the Directive and the appeal was dismissed.

A solution, *at least in some cases*, to the problems surrounding the vertical/horizontal, public/private dichotomy was in fact available as a result of earlier decisions of the Court of Justice in two West German references which again involved the Equal Treatment Directive: Case 14/83 *Von Colson* (in which the defendants were the provincial authorities of North-Rhine Westphalia) and Case 79/83 *Harz* (in which the defendant was a private company). Contrary to the position in *Marshall* and *Foster*, the Equal Treatment Directive *had* been implemented in West Germany but the national law did not appear to provide an adequate remedy for the discrimination that had taken place. Could therefore the two plaintiffs have recourse to the Directive?

Case 14/83 *Von Colson v. Land Nordrhein-Westfalen*

This case and *Harz* were referred to the Court of Justice from the West German Labour Court. C had been discriminated against on grounds of sex when applying for the post of prison social worker, and H when applying to join a training programme with a commercial company.

The national court considered that it only had power to award nominal damages to the plaintiffs under the provisions of the German implementing law. C and H claimed that such implementation of Article 6 of the Equal Treatment Directive failed to achieve that article's intended aim. Article 6 states that:

'Member States shall introduce into their national legal systems such measures as are necessary to enable all persons who consider themselves wronged by failure to apply to them the principle of equal treatment ... to pursue their claims by judicial process after possible recourse to other competent authorities.'

C and H contended that they either had the right to be offered the posts they had applied for or substantial damages. The national court referred questions to the Court of Justice to establish:

(a) whether Directive 76/207 required Member States to provide for particular sanctions or other legal consequences to attach to cases of discrimination on grounds of sex against a person seeking employment;

(b) whether the provisions of Directive 76/207 were directly effective.

The Court replied that the Directive did not impose an obligation on the employer to conclude a contract of employment with a job applicant who had been discriminated against.

Next, in view of the obvious inconsistency that would arise from the public/private dichotomy for two plaintiffs in otherwise identical circumstances, the Court pursued a solution which ignored the question of the vertical, but not horizontal, direct effect of Directives.

The Court did not say that a Directive could be invoked against a private party (the defendant in *Harz*) but it did state that domestic law, *particularly* that introduced to implement a Directive, must be interpreted by national courts *to achieve the results required* by the Directive whether the defendant was the State *or a private party*.

In any event, the Court found that Article 6 of the Directive did not include 'any unconditional and sufficiently precise obligation as regards sanctions for discrimination' which could be relied upon by individuals to obtain particular sanctions – these were a matter for national law. Thus, continued the Court:

It should, however, be pointed out to the national court that although Directive No. 76/207/EEC, for the purpose of imposing a sanction for the breach of the prohibition of discrimination, leaves the Member States free to choose between the different solutions suitable for achieving its objective, it nevertheless requires that if a Member State chooses to penalize breaches of that prohibition by the award of compensation, then in order to ensure that it is effective and that it has a deterrent effect, that compensation must in any event be adequate in relation to the damage sustained and must therefore amount to more than purely nominal compensation such as, for example, the reimbursement only of the expenses incurred in connection with the application. It is for the national court to interpret and apply the legislation adopted for the implementation of the directive in conformity with the requirements of Community law, in so far as it is given discretion to do so under national law.

The duty of the national court to secure an *effective* sanction arises quite apart from direct effects. It rests on Article 189(3) and the duty of Member States (including their courts) under Article 5 of the Treaty to fulfil their obligations regarding the result envisaged by the Directive.

When the case returned to the German Labour Court, it reinterpreted the relevant implementing rules and discovered that it did possess the power to award damages (to *both* parties) not exceeding six months gross salary. In this way, *Von Colson* achieves what has been called the *indirect effect* of Directives. The principle enables the equivalent of the horizontal direct effect of a Directive to be achieved; domestic law is to be interpreted in such a way that the Directive is applied indirectly.

The Court stated that the *Von Colson* principle applied to 'national law and *in particular* the provisions of a national law specifically introduced in order to implement' the Directive. Thus, not being limited to implementing legislation, the principle could, it appeared, also be applied to national law adopted *before* the Directive. However, placing national courts under a duty to review domestic law enacted prior to a Directive, so as to comply with it, raises difficult questions regarding legal certainty and non-retroactivity. The rights of individuals who have arranged their affairs on the basis of such legislation, with a legitimate expectation that it would not suddenly be changed (reinterpreted) in this way, must be safeguarded. Thus in Case 80/86 *Kolpinghaus Nijmegen* the Court of Justice stated that the duty to interpret national law on the basis of the *Von Colson* principle was limited by the general principles of legal certainty and non-retroactivity (see further Chapter Ten). It follows that where Community law is not directly effective, national courts are not required to interpret domestic law to comply with it in violation of these principles.

In a subsequent case the Court of Justice reviewed the operation of the *Von Colson* principle:

Case C-106/89 *Marleasing SA* v. *La Comercial Internacional de Alimentación SA;*
M brought a claim in the Spanish courts for a declaration of nullity regarding the founders' contract establishing the defendant company. The claim was based on certain articles of the Spanish civil code and alleged

that the contract was void on the grounds of 'lack of cause', being a bogus and fraudulent transaction. In reply, the defendants argued that Article 11 of the first Company Directive (Directive 68/151), which exhaustively lists the grounds on which the nullity of a company may be declared, did *not* include the grounds on which M. relied.

Directive 68/151 *not* having been implemented by Spain as required, as from the date of its accession to the European Communities, the Spanish court asked the Court of Justice whether Article 11 of the Directive had direct effect such as to bar a declaration of nullity for reasons other than those listed in Article 11.

The Court drew attention to its consistent line of case law (*Marshall.* etc) denying to Directives any *horizontal* direct effect: a Directive may not of itself impose obligations on any individual and therefore its provisions may not be relied upon as such against an individual – such as a Spanish public limited company.

Nevertheless the Court chose to re-word the question referred in terms of an obligation to interpret national law in conformity with the provisions of a Directive on the basis of its judgment in *Von Colson*.

The purpose of Directive 68/151 was to co-ordinate safeguards for the protection of members of companies and others – to make such safeguards equivalent throughout the Community – and the Court of Justice informed the Spanish court that it was obliged so far as was possible, to interpret its national law, *whether it pre-dated or post-dated the Directive*, in the light of its terms.

As a result, the Spanish court was placed under a duty to endeavour to interpret the (pre-dated) Spanish Civil Code in such a way as to exclude from it a declaration of nullity based on any ground other than those listed in Article 11 of the (unimplemented) Directive.

While in one part of its ruling, the Court appears to lay down that national courts are prohibited from interpreting national law (even pre-dated legislation, which was not introduced to comply with a Directive) inconsistently with a Directive, this can hardly be the case where to do so would be in breach of individuals' legitimate expectations: see Case 80/86 *Kolpinghaus Nijmegen*, above. As we will see shortly, in *Duke* v *GEC Reliance Ltd* (1988), the House of Lords refused to engage in 'purposive' or 'sympathetic' interpretation of pre-dated national law so as to impose obligations contained in a non-implemented Directive upon an individual (company), as this would have been 'unfair' and in breach of the company's legitimate expectations.

In any event, the *Von Colson* principle, as elaborated in *Marleasing*, can surely not apply where national law is clearly incompatible with the terms of the Directive. To apply the principle in such a case would be to stretch the concept of 'purposive' interpretation beyond all bounds. Thus, even the *Von Colson* principle may fail to provide individuals with their Community law rights. Thus, in 1992, on the heels of vertical direct effect and indirect effect, the Court of Justice provided individuals with the basis for a quite different solution which depends neither on direct effect nor the *Von Colson* principle: an action for *damages* brought by the individual against the Member State that has deprived him of his Community rights.

However, before examining this decision, in *Francovich* v *Italian State*, it is appropriate at this point to look more closely at the impact of the principle of direct effect in the UK.

DIRECT EFFECT AND THE IMPLEMENTATION OF COMMUNITY LAW IN THE UK

The European Communities Act 1972

In Chapter Four it was pointed out that the UK approach to international law is of a dualist character. Treaties entered into by the UK do not in themselves affect the law applied in the UK courts. Although binding in international law, a treaty only has effect in the domestic legal system if an Act of Parliament incorporates it. It was on this footing that the European Communities Act 1972 was passed to make provision for British membership of the Community and to supply the *national* legal basis for enforceable Community rights for individuals, ie. the direct effect of Community law in the UK.

Under section 2(1) what the Act terms 'directly enforceable rights' are given effect in the UK, and the combined effect of section 2(1) and (4) and section 3 is to make the principle of the supremacy of directly effective Community law part of UK law. Thus, on the basis of section 2(4), domestic legislation 'shall be construed and have effect' subject to the principle of supremacy. Section 3 directs national courts to follow the principles laid down by the Court of Justice:

> 3.-(1) For the purposes of all legal proceedings any question as to the meaning or effect of any of the Treaties, or as to the validity, meaning or effect of any Community instrument, shall be treated as a question of law (and, if not referred to the European Court, be for determination as such in accordance with the principles laid down by and any relevant decision of the European Court).

Thus, in the House of Lords in 1983, in a case involving Article 86 of the Treaty, a competition policy article first established as being of direct effect by the Court of Justice in 1974, Lord Diplock said:

> The rights which the article confers on citizens in the United Kingdom fall within Section 2(1) of the 1972 Act. They are without further enactment to be given legal effect in the United Kingdom and enforced accordingly.

Later, in 1990, in the highly controversial and much publicised *Factortame* litigation, Lord Bridge stated that:

> Under the terms of the Act of 1972 it has always been clear that it was the duty of a United Kingdom court, when delivering final judgment, to override any rule of national law found to be in conflict with any directly enforceable rule of Community law ... there is nothing in any way novel in according supremacy to rules of Community law ...

In this series of cases, in which it was eventually decided that provisions of the Merchant Shipping Act 1988 conflicted with the plaintiff's directly enforceable Treaty rights, Lord Bridge concluded that section 2(1) of the 1972 Act had the same effect as if a section had been incorporated into the 1988 Act which in terms laid down that the 1988 Act was to be *without prejudice to* the plaintiffs' (or any other EEC national's) directly effective rights (see also Chapters Three and Twenty).

It has often been observed that the 1972 Act does not expressly accord supremacy to Community law and that Parliament remains free to repeal the Act itself. Supremacy is recognised by denying effectiveness to UK legislation while we are a member of the Community to the extent that it conflicts with directly effective Community law. Section 2(4) provides that UK legislation shall be construed and have effect subject to the principle of supremacy, leaving open the perhaps theoretical possibility of Parliament *expressly* withdrawing from the Community (see Chapter Three regarding Parliamentary sovereignty).

No question of the construction or interpretation of the Merchant Shipping Act arose in *Factortame*. The Court of Justice declared that the Act was in breach of the plaintiffs' directly effective rights. Community law took priority and in accordance with the *Simmenthal* decision on supremacy (see Chapter Four), the Act was amended to comply with Community law. Similarly, following the *Marshall* decision on equal treatment regarding retirement ages for men and women, national law was amended in 1986 to make discriminatory retirement ages illegal (but not in time for Mrs. Duke, see below).

A survey of the English case law in which the question of the supremacy of directly effective Community law has been the issue shows that our courts have generally been ready and willing to comply with the principle. This has been done in some cases, as in *Factortame*, by a direct application of Community law in the face of the conflicting domestic law. In other cases, 'conflicting' national law has been subjected to 'purposive' interpretation in accordance with section 2(4) of the 1972 Act in order to secure compliance.

A purposive or teleological interpretation of national law will seek to achieve the purpose or aims of the relevant directly effective Community law. In 1982, in *Garland* v. *British Rail Engineering*, an equal pay case, Lord Diplock stated (*obiter*) that:

> The instant appeal does not present an appropriate occasion to consider whether, having regard to the express direction as to the construction of enactments 'to be passed' which is contained in section 2(4), anything short of an express positive statement in an Act of Parliament passed after January 1, 1973, that a particular provision is intended to be made in breach of an obligation assumed by the United Kingdom under a Community treaty, would justify an English court in construing that provision in a manner inconsistent with a Community treaty obligation of the United Kingdom, however wide a departure from the prima facie meaning of the language of the provision might be needed in order to achieve consistency.

The House of Lords proceeded to construe the Equal Pay Act to comply with Article 119 of the Treaty 'without any undue straining of the words' of the Act. Their Lordships did not directly apply Article 119, which is capable of both vertical and horizontal direct effect, but instead sought a ruling from the Court of Justice as to whether that Article conferred directly enforceable rights on the facts of this particular case. (The Court of Justice ruled that it did: see Chapter Fourteen.)

The case of *Pickstone* v *Freemans plc* (1989) concerned a claim for equal pay for work of *equal value*. The Equal Pay Act 1970 (operative 1975) did not allow for 'equal value' claims, but it was amended by statutory instrument in 1983, on the basis of section 2(2) of the European Communities Act 1972, in order to comply with the 1975 Equal Pay Directive. The Court of Appeal found it impossible to construe the 1983 amendment (which was in terms of 'outstanding obscurity') in the plaintiff's favour but instead directly applied Article 119 (read in conjunction with the Directive) against the private sector employer. In the House of Lords, however, the 'purposive' *Garland* approach was approved and their Lordships chose to 'interpret' the national regulations amending the Equal Pay Act (to the extent of reading certain words into them) in order to achieve a result compatible with the Directive as interpreted by the Court of Justice.

These cases show the English courts willing to give full effect to Community law: on the basis of the priority of directly effective Treaty provisions (*Factortame*) or by a purposive interpretation of national law on the basis of section 2(4) of the 1972 Act to comply with directly effective Community provisions (*Garland* and *Pickstone*).

Alternatively, in *Litster* v *Forth Dry Dock and Engineering Co. Ltd.* (1990), in an action brought against a private sector employer, the House of Lords, proceeding in line with *Von Colson*, were prepared to interpret national law introduced for the purpose of complying with a Directive in a way which was contrary to its prima facie meaning. Their Lordships adopted a purposive construction of UK regulations made in 1981 under section 2(2) of the Act in order to implement a 1977 Council Directive on the protection of employees' rights on the transfer of a business from one employer to another. Additional words were implied into the regulations to ensure that they complied with the obligation in the Directive that it should apply not only to employees who were employed in the business immediately before its transfer, but also to employees who would have been so employed if they had not been unfairly dismissed in contemplation of the transfer. Lord Oliver stated that:

> The critical question, it seems to me, is whether, even allowing for the greater latitude in construction permissible in the case of legislation introduced to give effect to this country's Community obligations, it is possible to attribute to regulation 8(1) when read in conjunction with regulation 5, the same result as that attributed to article 4 [of the Directive] in the *Bork* case [1989] IRLR 41. Purely as a matter of language, it clearly is not. Regulation 8(1) does not follow literally the

wording of article 4(1) ... If this provision fell to be construed by reference to the ordinary rules of construction applicable to a purely domestic statute and without reference to Treaty obligations, it would, I think be quite impermissible to regard it as having the same prohibitory effect as that attributed by the European Court to article 4 of the Directive. But it has always to be borne in mind that the purpose of the Directive and of the Regulations was and is to 'safeguard' the rights of employees on a transfer and that there is a mandatory obligation to provide remedies which are effective and not merely symbolic to which the Regulations were intended to give effect. The remedies provided by the Act of 1978 in the case of an insolvent transferor are largely illusory unless they can be exerted against the transferee as the Directive contemplates and I do not find it conceivable that, in framing Regulations intending to give effect to the Directive, the Secretary of State could have envisaged that its purpose should be capable of being avoided by the transparent device to which resort was had in the instant case. *Pickstone* v *Freemans Plc* [1989] AC 66, has established that the greater flexibility available to the court in applying a purposive construction to legislation designed to give effect to the United Kingdom's Treaty obligations to the Community enables the court, where necessary, to supply by implication words appropriate to comply with those obligations: see particularly the speech of Lord Templeman, at pp. 120-121 ...

However, in an earlier decision in 1988 involving a claim by a former employee against her private sector employer, a purposive interpretation of national law on behalf of the plaintiff was not embarked upon by their Lordships. It is a decision which should be viewed in the light of both *Von Colson* (1983) and *Marleasing* (1989):

Duke v. GEC Reliance Ltd (1988)

Mrs. Duke's equal treatment claim regarding compulsory retirement at 60 was essentially the same as that in the earlier case of *Marshall*. Their Lordships were urged to construe the Sex Discrimination Act 1975 as amended in 1986 to comply with the 1976 Equal Treatment Directive as interpreted by the Court of Justice in *Marshall* to make discriminatory retirement ages unlawful. However, the 1986 amendment had not been made retrospective and D's claim for damages related to a period, as in *Marshall*, prior to the amendment. In addition, her company employers were not, as in *Marshall*, to be regarded as an arm of the State; ie there was no question of the vertical direct effect of the Directive itself.

It was argued on D's behalf that the effect of section 2(4) of the European Communities Act ('... any enactment passed or to be passed ... shall be construed ...') was to make the Sex Discrimination Act 1975 subject to the ban on discriminatory retirement ages in the 1976 Directive.

It was held that a purposive construction could not be given to legislation *pre-dating* a Directive and which was not enacted to give effect to its provisions. Nor did their Lordships feel obliged to distort the meaning of a domestic statute to comply with a Community provision which was not directly effective. Lord Templeman stated that section 2(4) 'does no more than reinforce the binding nature of legally enforceable rights and obligations imposed by appropriate Community law.' Therefore section 2(4), relating to section 2(1) and to directly effective rights only, had, in their Lordships' view, no application in this case.

The House of Lords felt it would be 'most unfair' to allow this claim against a private sector employer by interpreting the Sex Discrimination Act, which prior to its amendment allowed for differing retirement ages, against its literal meaning so as to comply with the *later* Directive – and certainly not when the 1986 amendment operated prospectively not retrospectively.

Of the various factors at play in this case:

1. The *raison d'être* of the *Von Colson* principle is that it applies in respect of Community law which is *not* directly effective ('horizontal' situations such as *Litster*).

2. Section 2(1) of the 1972 Act is not confined to directly effective Community law; the better view being that it encompasses directly applicable law also (eg Article 177 regarding references to the Court of Justice, which, in the main, is not directly effective.)

3. The way was therefore open for their Lordships to attempt a purposive interpretation of the pre-dated national law on the basis of *Von Colson* (as explained in *Marleasing*).

4. Nevertheless, even if their Lordships had felt able to construe section 6(4) of the Sex Discrimination Act 1975 (which excluded retirement ages from the prohibition on discrimination) contrary to its literal meaning so as to comply with the Directive, the powerful point remains that this would have been an infringement of the private employer's legitimate expectation (that the English statute meant what it said and that meaning would not suddenly be changed in a retrospective manner): see Case 80/86 *Kolpinghuis Nijmegen*, above.

A FURTHER DEVELOPMENT: THE *FRANCOVICH* PRINCIPLE OF STATE LIABILITY

Marshall, Foster, Von Colson and *Marleasing* have all played their part in enabling individuals to secure rights to be found in Community Directives – in some instances adopted by the Member State in a defective manner (*Marshall* and *Foster*, existing national law, as claimed, not meeting the terms of the Directive), or implemented in an apparently insufficient manner (*Von Colson*, where national law appeared not to provide an effective remedy), or not implemented at all (*Marleasing*).

At the same time, and particularly since 1986, as the Community has sought to complete the Internal Market, mainly by the use of Directives, Member States have been falling behind in their obligation to implement those Directives (and others) in time. The TEU will introduce penalties, in the amended Article 171 EC, to be imposed on Member States which fail to fulfil their Treaty obligations (not merely as regards Directives), but this will not secure compensation for individuals who have thereby suffered loss. That Member States might be liable in damages on a non-contractual (tortious) basis to individuals who have suffered loss as a result of their breach of Community law has been discussed in the literature, and suggested by the Court of Justice, over a number of years. In *Francovich* v *Italian State*, decided in 1992, that possibility becomes rather more than a probability:

> Joined Cases C-6/90 and C-9/90 *Francovich* v *Italian State*
> and *Bonifaci* v *Italian State;*
>
> Council Directive 80/987 on the protection of employees in the event of the insolvency of their employers requires Member States to ensure that payment of employees' outstanding claims arising from the employment relationship and relating to pay is guaranteed by 'guarantee institutions'.

In the UK the Employment Protection (Consolidation) Act 1978 (as amended) meets the Directive's requirements and payments are made out of the Redundancy Fund. However, in Case 22/87 *Commission* v *Italy*, the Court of Justice held in Article 169 proceedings that Italian legislation was insufficient for the proper implementation of the Directive. This was still the position in 1991 when these cases come before the Court.

Mr. Francovich was owed 6,000,000 lire by his insolvent employers, CDN Elettronica, and, being unable to enforce judgment against them, he brought an action against the Italian Government for sums due in accordance with the terms of Directive 80/987 or for compensation in lieu. (The position of Mrs Bonifaci and others, employees of another insolvent employer, was the same.)

The Italian courts referred questions to the Court of Justice for a preliminary ruling which the Court examined on the following basis: (1) whether the provisions of the Directive in relation to payment of the guaranteed debts were directly effective, and (2) whether there was State liability in damages arising from its failure to implement the Directive.

The Court reached the following conclusions:

1. Interested parties may not assert their rights to obtain guarantees of payment against the State because the relevant provisions of the Directive did not make it clear that it was the State itself which should guarantee the sums owed by the employer. (Although the beneficiaries of the guarantee and its content could be identified, the discretion allowed by the Directive did not enable the Court to identify the *debtor* with sufficient clarity).

2. It is a general principle 'inherent in the scheme of the Treaty' that 'a Member State is liable to make good damage to individuals caused by a breach of Community law for which it is responsible'.

Liability for failure to take the steps necessary in order to achieve the result required by a Directive depends on the following conditions: (i) the result required by the Directive includes the conferring of rights for the benefit of individuals, (ii) the content of those rights is identifiable by reference to the Directive, and (iii) there exists a causal link between the breach of the State's obligations and the damage suffered by persons affected.

Where these conditions are fulfilled (as they were in these cases) the individual is entitled to damages as a matter of Community law.

Building on its own case law on supremacy and direct effect, the Court stressed that it was necessary to provide full protection of the rights of individuals, *in particular* where those rights were conditional on the Member States taking certain action and where, as a result of a Member State's breach of Community law, such individuals were unable to rely on their Community rights.

It is apparent from this statement of principle regarding State liability and from the Court's reliance on Article 5 of the Treaty – which requires

Member States to take all appropriate measures to ensure the fulfilment of their Treaty obligations including those under Article 189(3) – that *Francovich* will have an impact beyond the failure to implement Directives. Advocate General Mischo was of the opinion that this principle was 'capable of being extended to cover any failure of Member States to observe Community law ... whether the failure is in breach of the Treaty, Regulations or Directives, whether they have direct effect or not.' Thus Member States which act in a manner contrary to the Treaty (which are in breach of their fundamental Community obligations, as, for example, was the case with the UK in *Factortame*) will now come within the scope of the *Francovich* decision and may be liable for loss caused until such time as the infringement is terminated or relief granted: see also Chapter Twenty.

The claim for compensation is based on the State's breach of Community law, *such as* its clear failure to implement a Directive. It is not based on direct effect and so may remove public sector *employers*, for example, out of that particular firing line. In any event, one result of this decision would appear to be that where a Directive has not been implemented and either (i) it is not enforceable against the State owing to its lack of precision (it has no vertical direct effect) as in *Francovich*, or (ii) it is not enforceable against another individual (it has no horizontal effect as decided in *Marshall*), an individual who nevertheless suffers harm may sue the State as tortfeasor as a result of the State's default so long as the three conditions laid down are met. As regards the protection of rights for individuals, gaps have been closed and *Marleasing* may be overshadowed by this development.

However, as Steiner (1993) points out: 'The problem with *Francovich* lies not in the decision itself but in its implications.' In *Francovich* there was a serious failure by the Italian State to fulfil a fundamental Treaty obligation (as decided in Case 22/87). However, given the potential scope of the decision, Steiner asks: 'If Member States are to be liable for breach of any binding Community obligation, under what circumstances will they be liable? This question concerns the nature and gravity of the breach.'

> ... *Francovich* will be invoked to support a claim in respect of other, lesser failures. A failure to fulfil a Community obligation can take many forms, embracing a broad spectrum of culpability. At its most blatant it can be a deliberate or knowing breach of Community law, for example a clear failure to implement an obligation, as in *Francovich* itself. It may be a partial failure, where implementation measures have been adopted, but they are faulty or inadequate. Such failures may be deliberate, knowing, negligent or innocent. Implementation measures may not have been adopted because existing national law was deemed to be adequate. Here the failure may be negligent or innocent.

The failures may be legislative or executive. They will normally comprise a wrongful act or omission; the enactment of measures, or failure to amend, repeal or introduce legislation, in breach of Community law ...

It is submitted that even where the other conditions for liability under *Francovich* are met not all the above failures should give rise to non-contractual liability on the part of the State. They would not do so under the majority of laws of Member States, nor under the principles of Community liability.

For what kind of failures, then, should a state be liable? On what principles is this to be decided? And are these matters of national or Community law?

Member State courts will be obliged to settle these questions within the context of national law on State liability and provide real and effective protection for individuals' Community law rights. Steiner concludes that although 'States should not escape liability for damage caused by any wrongful acts, legislative or otherwise, both the nature of Community law and the principles of certainty and equity demand that States should not, in this context, be liable in the absence of fault.' However:

... whilst all States provide for the non-contractual liability of public authorities, their law, in the vast majority of (perhaps all) cases, will be inadequate to provide effective protection for individual rights under *Francovich*. Moreover, national laws governing the non-contractual liability of public authorities differ considerably from State to State. Thus, if *Francovich* is to be fully and fairly applied in all Member States it will be necessary to develop a framework of common Community rules.

Francovich is also discussed in Chapter Twenty 'Member States and their Community Obligations'.

Bebr, G., Case note on Francovich (1992) 29 CML Rev. 557.

Craig, P. P., 'Once Upon a Time In the West; Direct Effect and the Federalization of EEC Law' (1992) 12 OJLS 453.

Curtin, D., 'Effective Sanctions and the Equal Treatment Directive: *The Von Colson* and *Harz* Cases' (1985) 22 CML Rev. 505.

Curtin, D., 'The Province of Government: Delimiting the Direct Effect of Directives in the Common Law Context' (1990) 15 EL Rev. 195.

Dashwood, A., 'The Principles of Direct Effect in European Community Law' (1978) JCMS 220.

De Búrca, G., 'Giving Effect to European Community Directives' (1992) 55 MLR 215.

Fitzpatrick, B., 'The Significance of EEC Directives in UK Sex Discrimination Law' (1989) 9 OJLS 336.

Freestone and Davidson, *The Institutional Framework of the European Communities*, 1988, Chapter 2.

Morris, P.E., 'The Direct Effect of Directives — Some Recent Developments in the European Court — I and II' (1989) JBL 233 and 309.

Pescatore, P., 'The Doctrine of `Direct Effect': An Infant Disease of Community Law' (1983) 8 EL Rev. 155.

Shaw, J., 'European Community Judicial Method: Its Application to Sex Discrimination' (1990) 19 ILJ 228.

Steiner, J., 'Coming to Terms with EEC Directives' (1990) 106 LQR 144.

Steiner, J. 'From Direct Effects to *Francovich*: Shifting Means of Enforcement of Community Law' (1993) 18 EL Rev. 3.

Winter, T. A., 'Direct Applicability and Direct Effects' (1972) 9 CML Rev. 425.

Wyatt, D., 'Direct Effects of Community Law, not forgetting Directives' (1983) 8 EL Rev. 241.

Wyatt D., 'Enforcing EEC Social Rights in the United Kingdom' (1989) 18 ILJ 197.

*   See also case notes on the cases discussed to be found in the *European Law Review*, the *Common Market Law Review*, the *Modern Law Review*, etc.

CHAPTER NINE

REFERENCES FOR PRELIMINARY RULINGS: ARTICLE 177

As we have seen, particularly in the last chapter on direct effect, many of the difficult questions regarding the correct interpretation and therefore application of Community law (Treaty articles, Regulations, Directives and Decisions) are raised in the national courts and tribunals of the Member States. This situation gives rise to an obvious danger: that different interpretations and applications of Community law will emerge from Member State to Member State. Because it follows from the principle of the supremacy of Community law that it must have the same meaning and effect in all the Member States, this is a situation that would be inimical to the proper, effective functioning of the Community. The mechanism provided by the Treaty to avert this danger is the preliminary rulings procedure in Article 177. This procedure supplies the vital, *co-operative* link between national courts and tribunals and the Court of Justice, whereby questions of Community law may – or must – be referred by them to Luxembourg for an authoritative ruling.

Article 177

The Court of Justice shall have jurisdiction to give preliminary rulings concerning:

(a) the interpretation of this Treaty;

(b) the validity and interpretation of acts of the institutions of the Community;

(c) the interpretation of the statutes of bodies established by an act of the Council, where those statutes so provide.

Where such a question is raised before any court or tribunal of a Member State that court or tribunal may, if it considers that a decision on the question is necessary to enable it to give judgment, request the Court of Justice to give a ruling thereon.

Where any such question is raised in a case pending before a court or tribunal of a Member State, against whose decisions there is no judicial remedy under national law, that court or tribunal shall bring the matter before the Court of Justice.

(The TEU will add the words 'and of the ECB' to para. 1(b).)

It must be stressed that Article 177 does not provide an appeals procedure. The jurisdiction of the Court of Justice is limited to *preliminary* rulings on specific issues referred to it by a national court (not by a party), and the answers given are remitted to the national court which must itself *apply* them when finally deciding the case before it. In the *CILFIT* case (see below), the Court stated, in response to a question raised by an Italian court relating to the correct interpretation of Article 177 itself:

> In order to answer that question it is necessary to take account of the system established by Article 177, which confers jurisdiction on the Court of Justice to give preliminary rulings on, *inter alia*, the interpretation of the Treaty and the measures adopted by the institutions of the Community.

> The second paragraph of that article provides that any court or tribunal of a Member State may, if it considers that a decision on a question of interpretation is necessary to enable it to give judgment, request the Court of Justice to give a ruling thereon. The third paragraph of that article provides that, where a question of interpretation is raised in a case pending before a court or tribunal of a Member State against whose decisions there is no judicial remedy under national law, that court or tribunal shall bring the matter before the Court of Justice.

> That obligation to refer a matter to the Court of Justice is based on cooperation, established with a view to ensuring the proper application and uniform interpretation of Community law in all Member States, between national courts, in their capacity as courts responsible for the application of Community law, and the Court of Justice. More particularly, the third paragraph of Article 177 seeks to prevent the occurrence within the Community of divergences in judicial decisions on questions of Community law.

THE MAIN PROVISIONS UPON WHICH REFERENCES MAY BE BASED

Article 177(1)(a) covers the interpretation of the EEC Treaty and all Treaties amending or supplementing it. Article 177(1)(b) extends to both the interpretation and *validity* of acts of the Community institutions. The vast majority of these will be acts of the Council and Commission, and the case of law of the Court shows that they include not only the binding acts of Article 189 (whether directly effective or not) but also those which are not binding. In Case C-322/88 *Grimaldi*, in which a Belgian tribunal referred a question relating to the possible direct effect of a *recommendation*, the Court stated that Article 177 conferred upon it the jurisdiction to give preliminary rulings on the interpretation and validity of *all* acts adopted by the institutions. As explained earlier by AG Warner in Case 113/75 *Frecassetti*:

> I do not think it correct to say that the interpretation of a recommendation can never be relevant to an issue before a national court. Where, for example, a national statute has been passed for the express purpose of giving effect to a recommendation the correct interpretation of that statute may well depend on that of the recommendation. Whether it does so depend or not is a matter for the national court concerned.

The Court of Justice may also be asked whether a provision of Community law produces direct effects.

THE COURTS OR TRIBUNALS WHICH MAY OR MUST REFER

Article 177(2) states that 'any court or tribunal of a Member State' may request a ruling from the Court of Justice. What is a 'court or tribunal' for this purpose is a matter of Community law, based by the court on general criteria against which, however, the rules of national law governing the composition, status and functions of the body in question must be measured. For example, in Case 14/86 *Pretore di Salo v X*, the Court observed that:

> ... the Pretori are judges who, in proceedings such as those in which the questions referred to the Court in this case were raised, combine the functions of a public prosecutor and an examining magistrate. The Court has jurisdiction to reply to a request for a preliminary ruling if that request emanates from a court or tribunal which has acted in the general framework of its task of judging, independently and in accordance with law, cases coming within the jurisdiction conferred on it by law, even though certain functions of that court or tribunal in the proceedings which give rise to the reference for a preliminary ruling are not, strictly speaking, of a judicial nature.

In essence the Court will accept a reference from any body which exercises judicial, as opposed to investigatory or advisory, functions: ie a body which, through its relationship to the State, possesses the power to make binding decisions affecting the legal rights and obligations of individuals.

Under Article 177(3), if a question of Community law is raised before 'a court or tribunal of a Member State, against whose decisions there is no judicial remedy under national law', that court or tribunal *must* refer it to the

Court of Justice. For such a body, therefore, referral is not, as in Article 177(2), discretionary or 'permissive' but (within the terms of the article) mandatory: see, however, *CILFIT*, below.

Case 6/64 *Costa* v *ENEL* concerned a reference made by an Italian magistrate in a case involving less than £2. Under Italian law there was no right of appeal from the magistrate's decision because the amount in question was so small. Although not expressly called upon to rule on the matter, the Court of Justice was of the opinion that:

> By the terms of the Article ... national courts against whose decisions, as in the present case, there is no judicial remedy, must refer the matter to the Court of Justice so that a preliminary ruling may be given upon the 'interpretation of the Treaty' whenever a question of interpretation is raised before them.

On the basis of this statement it can be said that the *obligation* to refer applies to *any* court or tribunal whose decision in the particular case is not subject to appeal (the 'concrete' theory), rather than merely to those courts and tribunals whose decisions are never subject to appeal (the narrower, 'abstract' theory). This view of the matter clearly provides litigants with wider opportunities for references to be made on the *interpretation* of Community law. (However, as will be seen, the position is different as regards questions of validity.)

In *Hagen* v *Fratelli D. & G. Moretti* (1980), it was stated in the Court of Appeal that if leave to appeal to the House of Lords is refused, the Court of Appeal is the ultimate court for the purposes of Article 177(3).

NATIONAL COURTS AND THE DISCRETION UNDER ARTICLE 177(2)

Under Article 177(2), national courts or tribunals whose decisions *are* subject to a judicial remedy (basically, an appeal) under national law have a discretion as to whether or not to ask for a preliminary ruling on a point of Community law that they are called upon to decide. Obviously, if the question is one of interpretation and the court decides not to refer, the court must interpret the Community provision itself. On possible dangers in taking this course of action, and for questions of *validity*, see below.

The national court may refer when an appropriate question of Community law has been raised in the proceedings and the court considers that a decision on that question is *necessary* to enable it to give judgment.

Thus in Case 166/73 *Rheinmuhlen*, the Court of Justice stated that the power to make a reference arises:

> ... as soon as the judge perceives either of his own motion or at the request of the parties that the litigation depends on a point referred to in the first paragraph of Article 177.

In this case, the Court ruled that the discretion to refer in Article 177(2) could not be fettered by national rules of precedent:

> ... the existence of a rule of domestic law whereby a court is bound on points of law by the rulings of the court superior to it cannot of itself take away the power provided for by Article 177 of referring cases to the Court of Justice.

If the national court exercises its discretion in favour of a referral, this does not in itself mean that everything must be thought to hinge on the Community point; rather that it is potentially a determining factor of significance in the final outcome.

Although it is for the national court itself to decide at what stage in the proceedings it is appropriate to refer, in Joined Cases 36 and 71/80 *Irish Creamery Milk Suppliers Association* v. *Ireland* the Court of Justice stated that:

> The need to provide an interpretation of Community law which will be of use to the national court makes it essential ... to define the legal context in which the interpretation requested should be placed. From that aspect it might be convenient, in certain circumstances, for the facts in the case to be established and for questions of purely national law to be settled at the time the reference is made to the Court of Justice so as to enable the latter to take cognizance of all the features of fact and of law which may be relevant to the interpretation of Community law which it is called upon to give.

> However, those considerations do not in any way restrict the discretion of the national court, which alone has a direct knowledge of the facts of the case and of the arguments of the parties, which will have to take responsibility for giving judgment in the case and which is therefore in the best position to appreciate at what stage in the proceedings it requires a preliminary ruling from the Court of Justice.

> Hence it is clear that the national court's decision when to make a reference under Article 177 must be dictated by considerations of procedural organisation and efficiency to be weighed by that court.

In the UK the courts have on various occasions been drawn into a discussion of 'considerations of procedural organisation and efficiency' and attempts have been made to establish guidelines as to how the discretion to ask for a preliminary ruling should be exercised. (This will be discussed shortly.)

As stated earlier, the national court may of course decide the interpretive point of Community law itself without seeking any guidance from the Court of Justice. It may well consider exercising its discretion in this way where the correct application of the Community rule appears so clear as to leave no room for doubt. (See, however, the discussion of *CILFIT*, below: What is obvious to one judge, in one Member State, may not be obvious to another.)

> In *R v Henn and Darby* (1978), the Court of Appeal decided that national legislation banning certain imports was not contrary to Article 30 of the Treaty on the ground that the term 'quantitative restrictions' in that article connotated restrictions 'concerned with quantity' and not total prohibitions. The defendants appealed to the House of Lords, which referred this and other matters to the Court of Justice. There it was found, not surprisingly, that the prohibition *was* a quantitative restriction.

> In the House of Lords, Lord Diplock warned that English judges should not be 'too ready to hold that because the meaning of the English text (which is one of six of equal authority) seems plain to them no question of interpretation can be involved'.

Where a doubt exists the national court should refer. In *Garland v British Rail Engineering* (1983), the House of Lords, operating under Article 177(3) but examining whether there was in reality a 'question' to be referred, did refer on certain equal pay matters despite there not being 'any serious doubt'. This was because there was not, in their Lordships' opinion, in existence at the time

> ... so considerable and consistent a line of case law of the Court of Justice on the interpretation and direct applicability of Article 119, as would make the answer too obvious and inevitable to be capable of giving rise to what could properly be regarded as a 'question' within the meaning of Article 177: Lord Diplock.

From another angle, it should also be borne in mind that the Court of Justice is free to depart from its previous decisions – interpretive or otherwise. Even if the identical point of interpretation has already been ruled upon, the national court may refer:

In Cases 28-30/62 *Da Costa en Schaake*, the Dutch court referred questions on Article 12 which were identical to those in *Van Gend en Loos*, judgment in which was given a fortnight before the oral hearing in these cases. The Commission argued that no 'question' remained and the request for a ruling should be dismissed for lack of substance.

The Court stated that the fact that an interpretive ruling had already been given might absolve a national court even from a *duty* to refer if the meaning of the disputed provision was not clear. (The Dutch court was covered by Article 177(3).) However, *no* national court could be deprived of the opportunity to refer a question on a provision which had already been interpreted.

This is because (i) Article 177 always allows a national court whether operating under paragraph (2) or paragraph (3), if it considers it necessary, to refer questions of interpretation to the Court again; (ii) the national court may not fully understand, and therefore encounter difficulty in applying, an interpretation already given (eg the House of Lords reference in the *B & Q* Sunday trading case following the Court's earlier interpretive ruling on Article 30 in *Conforama*: see Chapter Twelve; and (iii) the national court may consider the previous ruling to be wrong, and therefore seek a reversal, as in Case C-10/89 *Sucal* v *Hag*: see Chapter Seventeen. (In *Da Costa* the Court of Justice ruled that there was no ground for giving a new interpretation of Article 12).

A national court acting within the area of discretionary jurisdiction, faced with a question of interpretation of Community law must therefore first ask: Is an interpretive ruling a *necessary* step in reaching a decision? Only if the answer to this question is in the affirmative does a second question arise: How should the discretion be exercised? In other words: should a referral be made or should the national court provide its own interpretation?

On the first question, authoritative guidelines were provided by the Court of Justice in Case 283/81 *CILFIT* v *Ministry of Health*. This was a reference from the Italian Supreme Court but the three main criteria apply equally to national courts whose decisions are subject to appeal or review:

> ... it follows from the relationship between the second and third paragraphs of Article 177 that the courts or tribunals referred to in the third paragraph have the same discretion as any other national court or tribunal to ascertain whether a decision on a question of Community law is necessary to enable them to give judgment. Accordingly, those courts or tribunals are not obliged to refer to the Court of Justice a question concerning interpretation of Community law raised before them if that question is not relevant, that is to say, if the answer to that

question, regardless of what it may be, can in no way affect the outcome of the case.

If, however, those courts or tribunals consider that recourse to Community law is necessary to enable them to decide a case, Article 177 imposes an obligation on them to refer to the Court of Justice any question of interpretation which may arise.

The question submitted by the Corte di Cassazione seeks to ascertain whether, in certain circumstances, the obligation laid down by the third paragraph of Article 177 might nonetheless be subject to certain restrictions.

It must be remembered in this connection that in its judgment of 27 March 1963 in Joined Cases 28 to 30/62 (*Da Costa* v. *Nederlandse Belastingadministratie* [1963] ECR 31) the Court ruled that: 'Although the third paragraph of Article 177 unreservedly requires courts or tribunals of a Member State against whose decisions there is no judicial remedy under national law ... to refer to the Court every question of interpretation raised before them, the authority of an interpretation under Article 177 already given by the Court may deprive the obligation of its purpose and thus empty it of its substance. Such is the case especially when the question raised it materially identical with a question which has already been the subject of a preliminary ruling in a similar case.'

The same effect, as regards the limits set to the obligation laid down by the third paragraph of Article 177, may be produced where previous decisions of the Court have already dealt with the point of law in question, irrespective of the nature of the proceedings which led to those decisions, even though the questions at issue are not strictly identical.

However, it must not be forgotten that in all such circumstances national courts and tribunals, including those referred to in the third paragraph of Article 177, remain entirely at liberty to bring a matter before the Court of Justice if they consider it appropriate to do so.

Finally, the correct application of Community law may be so obvious as to leave no scope for any reasonable doubt as to the manner in which the question raised is to be resolved. Before it comes to the conclusion that such is the case, the national court or tribunal must be convinced that the matter is equally obvious to the courts of the other Member States and to the Court of Justice.

However, having set down the three situations where a reference would *not* be 'necessary' (irrelevance, previous interpretation and obvious application – the last two instances being of an *acte clair* (clear provision) nature, see further below), the Court hedged round its statement with a series of qualifications which have led Rasmussen to conclude that:

> The real strategy of *CILFIT* is not to incorporate an *acte clair* concept into Community law. It is to call the national judiciaries to circumspection when they are faced with problems of interpretation and application of Community law.

What the Court proceeded to say in *CILFIT* was as follows:

> However, the existence of such a possibility [of not referring] must be assessed on the basis of the characteristic features of Community law and the particular difficulties to which its interpretation gives rise.

> To begin with, it must be borne in mind that Community legislation is drafted in several languages and that the different language versions are all equally authentic. An interpretation of a provision of Community law thus involves a comparison of the different language versions.

> It must also be borne in mind, even where the different language versions are entirely in accord with one another, that Community law uses terminology which is peculiar to it. Furthermore, it must be emphasised that legal concepts do not necessarily have the same meaning in Community law and in the law of the various Member States.

> Finally, every provision of Community law must be placed in its context and interpreted in the light of the provisions of Community law as a whole, regard being had to the objectives thereof and to its state of evolution at the date on which the provision in question is to be applied.

These are considerations which the national court should keep in mind when directing its attention to the second question above. A decision on the point being necessary, should it refer or not? An indication of how national courts have viewed their responsibilities within this process can be seen from the following statements by two High Court judges.

In *R* v. *H. M. Treasury, ex parte Daily Mail and General Trust* (1987), McPherson J. based his decision to refer on the following grounds:

I do not refer the case simply because a serious point of Community law arises, but I do so for the following reasons:

1. The relevant facts are not in dispute. The case before mein its written form and the documents before me set out the facts which are substantially, if not wholly, agreed.
2. The point raised will in my judgment be substantially determinative of the case.
3. There is no Community authority precisely or indeed in my judgment closely in point.
4. The point raised and indeed the case itself are both put forward in good faith and without any adverse motive. Of course the applicants wish to improve their financial and fiscal position. Of course the Revenue wish to maintain this source of tax. Neither of these wishes is improper in any way.
5. I am convinced that at some stage in its life the case will be or will have to be referred to Europe.
6. I do not find the point free from doubt. And I feel justified in asserting that I am not (in Lord Denning's words) shirking my responsibilities by referring this case. It seems to me to be tailor-made for reference here and now.

In the course of his decision to refer in *Customs and Excise Commissioners* v *Samex ApS* (1983), Bingham J. clearly acknowledges the advantages possessed by the Court of Justice when dealing with Community law matters:

> In endeavouring to follow and respect these guidelines I find myself in some difficulty, because it was submitted by counsel on behalf of the defendant that the issues raised by his client should be resolved by the Court of Justice as the court best fitted to do so, and I find this a consideration which does give me some pause for thought. Sitting as a judge in a national court, asked to decide questions of Community law, I am very conscious of the advantages enjoyed by the Court of Justice. It has a panoramic view of the Community and its institutions, a detailed knowledge of the Treaties and of much subordinate legislation made under them, and an intimate familiarity with the functioning of the Community market which no national judge denied the collective experience of the Court of Justice could hope to achieve. Where questions of administrative intention and practice arise the Court of

Justice can receive submissions from the Community institutions, as also where relations between the Community and non-Member States are in issue. Where the interests of Member States are affected they can intervene to make their views known. That is a material consideration in this case since there is some slight evidence that the practice of different Member States is divergent. Where comparison falls to be made between Community texts in different languages, all texts being equally authentic, the multinational Court of Justice is equipped to carry out the task in a way which no national judge, whatever his linguistic skills, could rival. The interpretation of Community instruments involves very often not the process familiar to common lawyers of laboriously extracting the meaning from words used but the more creative process of supplying flesh to a spare and loosely constructed skeleton. The choice between alternative submissions may turn not on purely legal considerations, but on the broader view of what the orderly development of the Community requires. These are matters which the Court of Justice is very much better placed to assess and determine than a national court.

Later in his judgment, Bingham J. drew attention to questions of time and cost:

The reference to the Court of Justice would be unlikely to take longer than appeals have normally taken to reach the Court of Appeal, at least until recently, and unlikely to cost much more. If, at the Court of Appeal stage, a reference were held to be necessary, the delay and expense would be roughly doubled.

Generally speaking, however, should a reference not be made at first instance or from the Court of Appeal, Article 177(3) comes into play in the House of Lords. Subject to the *CILFIT* guidelines, 'that court ... shall bring the matter before the Court of Justice'.

MANDATORY REFERENCES: ARTICLE 177(3)

Although the *CILFIT* guidelines may be taken to extinguish the *obligation* to refer placed by Article 177(3) on a court or tribunal of last resort in the instant case, such court or tribunal, as we have seen, *may* in such circumstances nevertheless refer if it considers it desirable, ie the *power* to refer remains. On the other hand, if the question of interpretation, in, for example, a recently adopted Regulation, is important, is novel and is not free from doubt, it would seem clear that the obligation in the third paragraph would apply: a ruling from the Court of Justice on the question would be 'necessary'. (We will deal with questions of validity below.)

The *CILFIT* decision aroused considerable controversy in so far as the Court of Justice was seen as giving its qualified approval to the principle that where the Community provision is regarded as *clear* and free from doubt, even though the Court has not ruled on it, the obligation to refer is removed. This is a particular application of the French *acte clair* principle whereby a clear provision does not require interpretation – and, therefore, in the Community context, falls outside the scope of Article 177; there is no 'question' on which a decision is necessary.

Attention has already been drawn to the fact that what is clear to one national court may well be a source of doubt, or be clear in quite a different sense, to another court in the Community, including the Court of Justice. In the case of lower courts which under Article 177(2) are not obliged to make a reference and which mistakenly decide that a Community provision is 'clear', the matter can be cleared up on the basis of an appeal (as in *R v. Henn and Darby*). However, with regard to final courts and Article 177(3), such a problem, in the light of the requirements of co-operation and the uniform interpretation and proper application of Community law in all the Member States, can obviously result in an irretrievable misapplication of Community law to the detriment of one of the parties. It is for this reason that the Court of Justice subjected the 'acte clair' principle to so many qualifications in *CILFIT*; qualifications described as being so 'intimidating to an English judge' as to make it seem likely that UK courts will hesitate long before deciding, at least without the aid of a previous line of authority from the Court of Justice, that a Community provision is clear.

This is not to say that there are no instances of courts of last resort failing to meet their responsibilities under Article 177(3). Particularly noticeable are cases where the national court has been faced with the question of the direct effect of a Directive. In *Minister of the Interior v. Cohn-Bendit* (1980), C-B ('Red Danny', a leader of student unrest in Paris in 1968) was refused entry when he tried to return to France. He sought to rely on Directive 64/221 on the freedom of movement of persons, which had been held to be directly effective in Case 41/74 *Van Duyn v. Home Office*, see Chapter Eight. The French Conseil d'Etat, the supreme administrative court, was advised that it must either follow *Van Duyn* or refer to the Court of Justice under Article 177(3). Instead the Court held that Directives could not be invoked by individuals against administrative acts of the government; the Directive was not directly effective.

Similar problems with Directives have led the German Federal Constitutional Court to declare that a court operating within Article 177(3), which knowingly deviates from the case law of the Court of Justice and fails to make a reference is in breach of Article 101 of the German Constitution. In 1989 in *Re Patented Feedingstuffs*, the Constitutional Court stated that it would review an 'arbitrary' refusal to co-operate with the Court of Justice by such a court:

> The main types of case of an arbitrary misconception of the obligation to refer which come into consideration for these purposes are first of all cases in which a court of final instance judging the main issue gives no consideration at all to a reference under Article 177(3) in spite of the relevance (in the court's view) of the question of Community law to its judgment although the court itself entertains doubts as to the correct answer to the question; secondly there are the cases in which the court of final instance deciding the main issue consciously departs in its judgment from the judgments of the European Court on relevant questions in issue and nevertheless does not make a reference or does not make a fresh reference.

> The first kind of case constitutes a fundamental misconception of the obligation to make a reference; a case of the second sort must be categorised as being in itself an arbitrary act. Finally, a further kind of arbitrary misconception of the obligation to make a reference under Article 177(3) ... may occur typically where either there is not as yet any decisive judgment of the European Court on a question of Community law relevant to the issue or where, although such judgment or judgments have been given, they may possibly not have provided an exhaustive answer to the relevant question or there may appear to be a more than remote possibility of a further development of the case law of the European Court on the issue.

> In such cases there is only an arbitrary misconception of the obligation to seek a ruling under Article 177(3) and therefore a breach of Article 101(1), second sentence, of the Constitution if the court of final instance trying the main issue has exceeded to an indefensible extent the scope for its exercise of the discretion which it must necessarily have in such cases; that will occur where there may be contrary views on the relevant question of Community law which should obviously be given preference over the view put forward by the court.

MISUSE OF THE PRELIMINARY RULINGS PROCEDURE

Exceptionally the Court of Justice has rejected a reference from a national court. This occurred in Case 104/79 *Foglia* v *Novello (No. 1)* in which the Court held that there was no genuine dispute between the parties.

The collusive litigation between the Italian parties in their national court was, in the Court's view, an artificial device designed to obtain a ruling that the law of another Member State was contrary to Community law. (See the arguments for and against this decision in Wyatt and in Barav in the References and Further Reading at the end of the chapter.)

In Case C-83/91 *Meilicke* v *ADV/ORGA F.A. Meyer*, some ten pages of questions regarding the compatibility of the West German legal theory of disguised non-cash subscriptions of capital with the Second Company Law Directive were referred by the Hanover Regional Court to the Court of Justice. The Court stated that from the file submitted by the national court it was apparent that it had not been established that the conditions for the application of the theory were present in the dispute between M and the defendant company. The questions raised were therefore hypothetical, as the Court did not have before it those elements of fact and national law necessary for it to provide a useful answer to the questions. M. was the author of a German law book on the theory in question.

A series of cases in the UK (and elsewhere in the Community), concerning the compatibility of domestic legislation which restricts trading on Sundays with Treaty provisions on the free movement of goods within the Community, has thrown up a situation whereby financially powerful business interests, trading illegally on Sundays, have set up this 'Euro-defence' which national courts have felt compelled to refer to the Court of Justice. The defence, which has eventually been shown to have no legal merit and has therefore been struck down by the Court of Justice, was designed to protract, and succeeded in protracting, the litigation for several years (through references, appeals and fresh references) and enabled the firms involved to continue in the meantime with their illegal trading: see in particular Case C-169/91 *Stoke City Council and Norwich City Council* v *B. & Q. plc* in Chapter Twelve.

PRELIMINARY RULINGS ON VALIDITY

It will be recalled that Article 177(1)(b) covers the jurisdiction of the Court of Justice to give preliminary rulings concerning 'the validity ... of acts of the institutions of the Community' but the article does not expressly give the Court exclusive jurisdiction on this matter. Thus a 'permissive' reading of Article 177(2) would seemingly give a national court (other than one of last resort) the power to exercise its discretion in such a way as to declare a Community act, say a Regulation, invalid. Such a result would clearly be contrary to the aim of preventing a body of case law coming into existence in any Member State which is not in accordance with Community law.

This matter was put to rest by the Court of Justice in Case 314/85 *Foto-Frost*, where it was held that no national court can declare a Community act invalid; the power to declare such an act invalid is reserved to the Court of Justice. A national court can declare a Community act valid but should a real doubt be raised, providing a decision on the question is necessary, then the matter should be referred. CILFIT and the *acte clair* principle are only relevant to questions of interpretation.

In *Foto-Frost*, the Court stated that:

In enabling national courts against whose decisions there is a judicial remedy under national law to refer to the Court for a preliminary ruling questions on interpretation or validity, Article 177 did not settle the question whether those courts themselves may declare that acts of Community institutions are invalid.

Those courts may consider the validity of a Community act and, if they consider that the grounds put forward before them by the parties in support of invalidity are unfounded, they may reject them, concluding that the measure is completely valid. By taking that action they are not calling the existence of the Community measures into question.

On the other hand, those courts do not have the power to declare acts of Community institutions invalid ... the main purpose of the powers accorded to the Court by Article 177 is to ensure that Community law is applied uniformly by national courts. That requirement of uniformity is particularly imperative when the validity of a Community act is in question. Divergences between courts in the Member States as to the validity of Community acts would be liable to place in jeopardy the very unity of the Community legal order and detract from the fundamental requirement of legal certainty.

The same conclusion is dictated by consideration of the necessary coherence of the system of judicial protection established by the Treaty. In that regard it must be observed that requests for preliminary rulings, like actions for annulment, constitute means for reviewing the legality of acts of the Community institutions. As the Court pointed out in its judgment of 23 April 1986 (Case 294/83 *Parti écologiste 'Les Verts'* v. *Parliament* [1986] ECR 1339), 'in Articles 173 and 184, on the one hand, and in Article 177, on the other, the Treaty established a complete system of legal remedies and procedures designed to permit the Court of Justice to review the legality of measures adopted by the institutions'.

Since Article 173 gives the Court exclusive jurisdiction to declare void an act of a Community institution, the coherence of the system requires that where the validity of a Community act is challenged before a national court the power to declare the act invalid must also be reserved to the Court of Justice ...

It should be added that the rule that national courts may not themselves declare Community acts invalid may have to be qualified in certain circumstances in the case of proceedings relating to an application for interim measures; however, that case is not referred to in the national court's question.

The answer to the first question must therefore be that national courts have no jurisdiction themselves to declare that acts of Community institutions are invalid.

The relationship between Article 177 (as regards such indirect challenges to Community acts) and, particularly, Article 173 (direct challenges to Community acts in the Court of Justice) has been noted already and will be examined more closely in Chapter Nineteen.

The suggestion, in the penultimate paragraph of the extract from the Court's judgment, that national courts might have jurisdiction to declare Community acts invalid in interlocutory proceedings where, for reasons of urgency, it was not practical to refer and wait for the Court's ruling, was taken a step further in Joined Cases C-143/88 and C-92/89 *Zuckerfabrik Süderdithmarschen*. In this case, following a reference to the Court of Justice by the German court regarding (a) the validity of a Regulation and (b) the power of a national court to suspend a *national* administrative act based on the disputed Regulation, the Court stated that, for the protection of a party in the context of an Article 177 reference, a national court should possess such a right of suspension but within strictly defined limits. This case will also be discussed in more detail in Chapter Nineteen.

THE EFFECTS OF PRELIMINARY RULINGS

The ruling given by the Court of Justice under Article 177 is sent back to the national court which originally made the reference. That court must apply the ruling, which is binding upon it, in its resumed proceedings. This may, for example, require the court to refuse to apply conflicting provisions of national law – the point which was at the heart of Case 106/77 *Simmenthal (No. 2)*, a leading case on supremacy: see Chapter Four.

The ruling (on interpretation or validity) may operate as a precedent for *all* national courts in subsequent cases involving the same Community provision:

for the UK see section 3(1) of the European Communities Act, although, as seen, a national court is not precluded from making a further reference.

A ruling that a Community act is invalid will mean that the measure will be treated as void for all purposes unless, in the interests of legal certainty, the Court of Justice limits the effect of its ruling on past transactions: see, eg, Case 66/80 *International Chemical Association*. Similar considerations can, exceptionally, apply to the temporal effect of rulings on interpretation. On a number of occasions the Court has stated that a preliminary ruling on interpretation:

> ... clarifies and defines where necessary the meaning and scope of that rule as it must or ought to have been understood and applied from the time of its coming into force. It follows that the rule as thus interpreted may, and must, be applied by the courts even to legal relationships arising and established before the judgment ruling on the request for interpretation.

> ... It is only exceptionally that the Court may, in the application of the general principle of legal certainty inherent in the Community legal order and in taking into account the serious effects which its judgments might leave, as regards the past, on legal relationships established in good faith, be moved to restrict for any person concerned the opportunity of relying on the provision as thus interpreted with a view to calling in question those legal relationships.

> Such a restriction may, however, be allowed only in the actual judgment ruling upon the interpretation sought ... it is for the Court of Justice alone to decide upon the temporal restrictions to be placed on the interpretation which it lays down: Case 61/79 *Denkavit Italiana*.

Thus, in Case 43/75 *Defrenne (No. 2)*, the Court decided that its ruling on the direct effect of equal pay Article 119 should, 'for important considerations of legal certainty', only apply to future cases and those lodged prior to judgment. Member States had, in the main, not implemented the equal pay principle, perhaps considering that the broad principle in Article 119 required further implementation. However, in spite of warnings from the Commission, no proceedings had been taken against them under Article 169. This situation had, in the Court's view, consolidated 'the incorrect impression as to the effects of Article 119' prior to the Court's decision.

It has been argued that to shield *employers* (including the State) in this way from 'an avalanche of similar claims' was at the expense of legal principle: 'if Article 119 was directly effective for Miss Defrenne, it must have been directly effective for all other workers; claims for back pay might be affected by national statutes of limitation, but there was no legal ground for making the date of the judgment in the *Defrenne* case decisive': see Hartley, *The Foundations of Community Law.*

Alexander, W., 'The Temporal Effects of Preliminary Rulings' (1988) 8 YEL 11.

Arnull, A., 'The Use and Abuse of Article 177 EEC' (1989) 52 MLR 622.

Arnull, A., 'References to the European Court' (1990) 15 EL Rev. 375.

Barav, A., 'Preliminary Censorship? The Judgment of the European Court in .c5.Foglia v Novello' (1980) 5 EL Rev. 443.

Bebr, G., 'Preliminary Rulings of the Court of Justice – their Authority and Temporal Effect' (1981) 18 CML Rev. 475.

Bebr, G., 'The Reinforcement of the Constitutional Review of Community Acts under Article 177 EEC' (*Foto-Frost and 'Berlin Butter'*) (1988) 25 CML Rev. 684.

Collins, L., *European Community Law in the United Kingdom*, section on 'Preliminary Rulings by the European Court'.

Harding, C., 'The Impact of Article 177 on the Review of Community Action' (1981) 1 YEL 93.

O'Keefe, D., 'Appeals against an Order to Refer under Article 177 of the EEC Treaty' (1984) 9 EL Rev. 87.

Rasmussen, H., 'The European Court's *Acte Clair* Strategy in CILFIT' (1984) 9 CML Rev. 242.

Toth, A., 'The Authority of Judgments of the European Court of Justice; Binding Force and Legal Effects' (1984) 4 YEL 1.

Waelbroeck, M., 'May the Court of Justice Limit the Retrospective Operation of its Judgments?' (1981) 1 YEL 115.

Wyatt, D., 'Following up *Foglia*: Why the Court is Right to Stick to its Guns' (1981) 6 EL Rev. 447.

PART THREE

ASPECTS OF COMMUNITY ECONOMIC

AND

SOCIAL LAW

COMMUNITY ECONOMIC AND SOCIAL LAW: ITS NATURE AND THE IMPACT OF GENERAL PRINCIPLES OF COMMUNITY LAW

COMMUNITY ECONOMIC AND SOCIAL LAW

The legal basis for the economic and social policies of the Community is to be found in the EEC Treaty, as amended by the Single European Act and the Treaty on European Union. (Coal and steel and atomic energy come under their respective Treaties.) In the TEU, apart from the new Articles 7 and 7a–c of the European Community Treaty relating to the Common Market and the Internal Market, these policies are to be found in Part Three (Community Policies: Articles 9–130y) and Part Four (Association of the Overseas Countries and Territories: Articles 131–136a).

The EC Treaty, like its forerunner, lays down the basis for the implementation of these policies and for their enforcement. As we have seen in Chapter One, the scope of these policies, widened by the 1986 Act, is extended even further by the Maastricht Treaty. The full list of these policies can be found in Article 3(a) - (t) EC:

For the purposes set out in Article 2, the activities of the Community shall include, as provided in this Treaty and in accordance with the timetable set out therein:

(a) the elimination, as between Member States, of customs duties and quantitative restrictions on the import and export of goods, and of all other measures having equivalent effect;

(b) a common commercial policy;

(c) an internal market characterized by the abolition, as between Member States, of obstacles to the free movement of goods, persons, services and capital;

(d) measures concerning the entry and movement of persons in the internal market as provided for in Article 100c;

(e) a common policy in the sphere of agriculture and fisheries;

(f) a common policy in the sphere of transport;

(g) a system ensuring that competition in the internal market is not distorted;

(h) the approximation of the laws of Member States to the extent required for the functioning of the common market;

(i) a policy in the social sphere comprising a European Social Fund;

(j) the strengthening of the economic and social cohesion;

(k) a policy in the sphere of the environment;

(l) the strengthening of the competitiveness of Community industry;

(m) the promotion of research and technological development;

(n) encouragement for the establishment and development of trans-European networks;

(o) a contribution to the attainment of a high level of health protection;

(p) a contribution to education and training of quality and to the flowering of the cultures of the Member States;

(q) a policy in the sphere of development cooperation;

(r) the association of the overseas countries and territories in order to increase trade and promote jointly economic and social development;

(s) a contribution to the strengthening of consumer protection;

(t) measures in the spheres of energy, civil protection and tourism.

At the heart of Community economic law, by reference to the first of the two means in Article 2 and hence to the concept of negative integration (the removal of restrictions and discrimination), lie the rules relating to the establishment and maintenance of the Common Market. As seen in the early

chapters, these include the rules governing the free movement of goods
(including the customs union rules), the free movement of persons
(particularly workers, and including the right of establishment of companies
and self-employed persons), the free movement of services (including banking
and insurance) and the free movement of capital flows.

Closely linked to the rules on the free movement of goods and services
are the common rules on competition within the Common Market. Of
particular significance are the rules which apply to undertakings which, either
jointly or individually, seek to control markets for goods and services and so
restrict competition to the detriment of inter-Member State trade.

Sectoral policies embrace agriculture (and the establishment and
maintenance of common organisations of the markets for agricultural
products such as cereals, wine and sheepmeat), fisheries, the transport
infrastructure, coal and steel (under the Treaty of Paris) and atomic energy
(under the Euratom Treaty). Harmonisation of the laws of the Member States
proceeds to the extent required for the proper functioning of the Common
Market.

'Positive' policies (those co-ordinated and common policies the main
aim of which is to achieve economic and welfare objectives other than the
removal of discrimination) are to be seen in the context of the second of the
two means in Article 2 – 'the approximation of the economic policies of the
Member States' in the Treaty of Rome, which becomes 'economic and
monetary union' under the Maastricht Treaty. Under the later Treaty are to be
found economic and monetary policy, common commercial (external trade)
policy, economic and social cohesion (aimed at 'reducing disparities between
the various regions'), protection of the environment, promotion of research
and technological development and consumer protection, etc.

Social measures (Articles 117-129 EC) relate in particular to such issues
as equal pay and treatment for men and women within the field of
employment, to eligibility for social security benefits for those persons (and
their families) who exercise their right of free movement, health and safety at
work, education and vocational training, culture and public health.

As regards the implementation and enforcement of Community
economic and social law, it is important to remember that Community law
creates a complex of legal relationships involving the Community's policy-
makers, a wide range of national authorities engaged in the implementation
of Community policies, and business undertakings and individuals who are
affected in one way or another by such policies. Consider, for example, the
customs union rules and *Van Gend en Loos*, the competition rules directed at
undertakings, and equal pay and treatment measures which impact not only on
individual employees and employers but also, because of the costs involved,

on the economies of the Member States. Hence, when discussing the concept of the Community law of the economy, Lasok and Bridge state that:

> The dual role of the law as a force of integration is that of organising the Community and its economy. Therefore the Community law of the economy is the body of rules addressed to the Member States, individuals and private and public corporations which in their entirety purport to govern the economic and social life both at a state and individual level.

In slightly different terms, the economic and social law of the Community can be seen as encompassing:

(a) policies adopted by the Community institutions for the attainment of economic, social (and political) *objectives*;

(b) *economic management* functions assumed by the Community institutions, particularly the Commission, within the 'market and plan' pattern underlying European economic integration;

(c) active participation by competent *authorities within the Member States* (including their courts) in the development of the Community and their involvement in the decision-making processes of the Community.

Community law, while assuming a market economy operating on the basis of effective competition, also provides for varying degrees of 'economic dirigisme' (economic direction or control) on the part of the Community institutions and the Member States.

As Mertens de Wilmars has pointed out:

> This was already the case in economic systems of the 'Soziale Marktwirtschaft' [Social Market Economy] type where the essential aims of such intervention were, on the one hand, to create the conditions for 'workable competition' and to oblige to abide by the rules regarded as appropriate to ensure self-regulation of the market economy and, on the other hand, to redress, by means of systems involving direct or indirect transfers of income, the socially or culturally unfavourable consequences of market mechanisms.

The basic legal instruments for the implementation (and enforcement)
of Community economic and social law are those which were introduced in
Chapter Four: Treaty provisions themselves and the secondary legislation
derived from them – Regulations, Directives and Decisions of the political
institutions. Legal integration goes hand in hand with economic and social
integration and rests on the twin principles of supremacy and direct effect as
established by the Court of Justice.

GENERAL PRINCIPLES OF COMMUNITY LAW

The written sources of Community law (the Treaties and the acts of the
institutions) cannot possibly in themselves provide a solution for every
question that comes before the Court of Justice (or the Court of First
Instance). Thus, in the exercise of its jurisdiction under Article 164 regarding
the interpretation and application of Community law, the Court has
developed (as noted in Chapter Four) a form of 'unwritten' law, a body of
general principles, in order to assist it in its duties and to fill gaps in the
written sources.

These general principles may be used in the following main ways:

1.   As a basis for the *interpretation* of written Community law, which
      must be interpreted in accordance with them.

2.   As a basis for the *review by the Court of the legality of acts of the
      Community institutions* and of the Member States when they take
      measures to implement Community law, on this second point see
      Case 230/78 *Eridania*.

3.   In the context of *claims for damages against Community institutions*
      brought by undertakings or individuals who have suffered loss as a
      result of an illegal or allegedly illegal act (see Chapter Nineteen).

The clear relevance of these general principles to the body of rules
which 'purport to govern the economic and social life both at a state and
individual level', and, therefore, their relevance to the vital question of the
protection of the individual was explained in 1982 by Professor Mertens de
Wilmars, a former President of the Court of Justice. He drew attention to the
increasingly wide range of interventionary powers of public authorities
(including the Community's institutions) in mixed economies and the new

economic management methods available to such bodies. Accordingly, 'the problem of controlling the exercise of discretionary powers has acquired greater significance and new dimensions'. Such control, particularly through the medium of judicial review, which traces 'the boundary between the lawful and unlawful exercise of a discretionary power', must rest on the basis of 'general criteria which may be transposed from one case to another'. Such criteria are to be 'found in a number of general legal principles whose aim and effect are both to guarantee the freedom of action given to the authority and to place such restrictions on it as are necessary in order to avoid arbitrariness.'

Legal Basis and Sources

The Treaty basis for the development of these general principles by the Court, and their incorporation into the general body of Community law, can be justified by reference to the following articles (emphasis added):

> The Court of Justice shall ensure that in the interpretation and application of this Treaty *the law is observed*: Article 164. ('the law' being a body of law beyond the text of the Treaty.)

> The Court of Justice shall review the legality of acts of the Council and Commission ... on grounds of lack of competence, infringement of an essential procedural requirement, infringement of this Treaty *or of any rule of law* relating to its application ... : Article 173(1).

> In the case of non-contractual liability, the Community shall, in accordance with *the general principles common to the laws of the Member States*, make good any damage caused by its institutions ... : Article 215(2).

The main source of the general principles of Community law (such as equality, proportionality and legal certainty) is the national laws of the Member States, in particular national administrative and economic law. Recognition by the Court of Justice of *fundamental human rights*, as found both in the national legal systems of the Member States and in the European Convention on Human Rights of 1950, a Council of Europe treaty to which all the Member States (but not the Community) are signatories, led to a declaration by the Court that such rights *also* form an integral part of the general principles of law which it is bound to uphold. (Article F, paragraph (2) of the Maastricht Treaty provides that: 'The Union shall respect fundamental rights, as guaranteed by the European Convention for the

Protection of Human Rights and Fundamental Freedoms signed in Rome on 4th November 1950 and as they result from the constitutional traditions common to the Member States, as general principles of Community law.')

With respect to the Court's 'discovery' of general principles, it has been said that it is

> ... largely an exercise in comparative law. This use of the comparative technique is not governed by an *a priori* intent to find the highest common denominator; rather it is governed by an intent to trace elements from which Community legal principles and rules can be built up which will offer an appropriate, fair and viable solution for the questions with which the Court is confronted: *Gormley*.

Before examining these 'unwritten' general principles individually, it should be noted that *the Treaty itself* contains the 'written' general principle of *solidarity* in Article 5, which governs the relationship between the Member States and the Community and in particular, as seen, the duty of the Member States to fulfil their Community obligations. Article 7 (which will become Article 6 when the TEU comes into effect) contains the general principle of *non-discrimination on grounds of nationality* within the scope of application of the Treaty, and Article 119 embodies the general principle of *non-discrimination on the grounds of sex* within the field of employment.

General principles should not, however, be confused with the basic principles of autonomy, supremacy and direct effect, nor with the four *fundamental freedoms of movement* – goods, services, persons and capital, which make up the concept of the unity of the market.

In his discussion of general principles, Mertens de Wilmars draws a distinction between:

1. Principles borrowed from the foundations of the democratic system: *respect for fundamental rights and freedoms* and the principle of *equality or non-discrimination*.

2. Principles of sound and proper administration, including the *balancing of interests, proportionality* and the *protection of legitimate expectations*.

3. General principles relating to the concept of *legal certainty*: laws must not be *retroactive* and *vested rights* must be protected.

Respect for Fundamental Rights and Freedoms

The Treaty of Rome contained no reference to fundamental rights and freedoms (but note the Maastricht Treaty, above). For many years this was a matter of great concern to some Member States, particularly West Germany where, despite or as a consequence of the *Internationale Handelsgesellschaft* case (see Chapter Four), this omission for some time posed a threat to the supremacy of Community law. Nevertheless since that time the Court of Justice has developed a considerable body of case law on human rights — *within the context of the structure and aims of Community law.*

It is unlikely that this case law will be concerned with fundamental human rights such as freedom of expression or the right of peaceful assembly. This is not surprising in a Community which is essentially of an *economic* nature. Nevertheless, it is clear that the rights which have been recognised by the Court can serve to protect the individual or an undertaking from the administration by curtailing the legislative powers of the Community and the Member States.

As seen in Chapter Four, Case 11/70 *Internationale Handelsgesellschaft* concerned the validity of a Community measure as implemented by a national agency. The issue was whether the system of forfeitable deposits introduced under Regulation 120/67 was, as the company claimed, contrary to various fundamental rights provisions (including the right of economic freedom and the principle of proportionality) of the German Basic Law. The Court of Justice refused to test the validity of the Community measure against principles of national constitutional law. Instead it held that respect for such rights formed part of the general principles of law recognised in the *Community* legal order. The Court nevertheless held that the system of forfeitable deposits was justifiable in order to support the effective functioning of the common organisation of the market in cereals: see also *Wünsche* (1987) in Chapter Four. In this case the German Constitutional Court expressed satisfaction with Community progress in the field of human rights.

In another German case, *Nold*, a case of judicial review under Article 173(2), the rights at issue related to the protection of commercial interests, discrimination and denial of economic opportunities. While drawing attention to both national constitutional traditions and international treaties as inspiration for respect for fundamental rights at the Community level, the Court held that the pleas made on behalf of the German undertaking failed when assessed against the market rationalization scheme pursued under the Coal and Steel Treaty. The Court declared that such rights are not 'unfettered prerogatives' but are subject to limitations 'justified by the overall objectives pursued by the Community':

Case 4/73 *Nold K G* v. *Commission*

Nold, a West German wholesale coal undertaking, sought the annulment of a Commission Decision which provided that coal wholesalers could not buy Ruhr coal direct from the selling agency unless they agreed to purchase a minimum quantity. Nold was not in a position to meet this requirement and dealing through an intermediary proved more costly.

The Court of Justice ruled:

As to the objection based on an alleged violation of fundamental rights:

The applicant asserts finally that certain of its fundamental rights have been violated, in that the restrictions introduced by the new trading rules authorized by the Commission have the effect, by depriving it of direct supplies, of jeopardizing both the profitability of the undertaking and the free development of its business activity, to the point of endangering its very existence.

In this way, the Decision is said to violate, in respect of the applicant, a right akin to a proprietary right, as well as its right to the free pursuit of business activity, as protected by the Grundgesetz of the Federal Republic of Germany and by the Constitutions of other Member States and various international treaties, including in particular the Convention for the Protection of Human Rights and Fundamental Freedoms of 4 November 1950 and the Protocol to that Convention of 20 March 1952.

As the Court has already stated, fundamental rights form an integral part of the general principles of law, the observance of which it ensures.

In safeguarding these rights, the Court is bound to draw inspiration from constitutional traditions common to the Member States, and it cannot therefore uphold measures which are incompatible with fundamental rights recognized and protected by the Constitutions of those States.

Similarly, international treaties for the protection of human rights on which the Member States have collaborated or of which they are signatories, can supply guidelines which should be followed within the framework of Community law.

The submissions of the applicant must be examined in the light of these principles.

If rights of ownership are protected by the constitutional laws of all the Member States and if similar guarantees are given in respect of their right freely to choose and practice their trade or profession, the rights thereby guaranteed, far from constituting unfettered prerogatives, must be viewed in the light of the social function of the property and activities protected thereunder.

For this reason, rights of this nature are protected by law subject always to limitations laid down in accordance with the public interest.

Within the Community legal order it likewise seems legitimate that these rights should, if necessary, be subject to certain limits justified by the overall objectives pursued by the Community, on condition that the substance of these rights is left untouched.

As regards the guarantees accorded to a particular undertaking, they can in no respect be extended to protect mere commercial interests or opportunities, the uncertainties of which are part of the very essence of economic activity.

The disadvantages claimed by the applicant are in fact the result of economic change and not of the contested Decision.

It was for the applicant, confronted by the economic changes brought about by the recession in coal production, to acknowledge the situation and itself carry out the necessary adaptations.

This submission must be dismissed for all the reasons outlined above.

The European Convention on Human Rights has also been invoked by the Court of Justice in a number of cases concerning the actions of *national* authorities and the administration of justice at Member State level (see also balancing of interests and procedural rights, below):

Case 63/83 *Kent Kirk*

Captain Kirk, a Danish fisherman, was prosecuted for fishing on 6 January 1983 within 12 miles of the UK coast contrary to the Sea Fish Order 1982, which was ostensibly a conservation measure. Following a reference to the Court under Article 177, it was held that at the relevant time the Order had expired and the penal provisions of Council Regulation 170/83, which allowed for similar discriminatory exclusion but which had not come into effect until 25 January 1983, did not have

retroactive effect so as to justify enforcement of the criminal penalties to
be found in the Order.

The Court declared that:

'The principle that penal provisions may not have retroactive effect is
one which is common to all the legal orders of the Member States and
is enshrined in Article 7 of the European Convention ... as a
fundamental right; it takes its place among the general principles of law
whose observance is ensured by the Court of Justice.'

In Case 222/84 *Johnston* v *Chief Constable of the Royal Ulster
Constabulary* (an equal treatment case discussed in detail in Chapter Fourteen),
it was argued that a certificate relating to national security and public safety,
signed by the Secretary of State for Northern Ireland under the Sex
Discrimination (Northern Ireland) Order 1976, prevented the national court
from hearing the applicant's discriminatory treatment claim. Mrs. Johnston
had formerly been a policewoman in Northern Ireland. The Court of Justice
referred to Article 6 of Council Directive 76/207 on Equal Treatment which
requires Member States 'to enable all persons who consider themselves
wronged by discrimination to pursue their claims by judicial process'. The
Court stressed that the requirement of effective judicial control stipulated by
the Directive reflected a *general principle of law* which underlies the
constitutional traditions of the Member States and which is laid down in
Article 6 of the European Convention on Human Rights.

Equality or Non-Discrimination

Referring to the operation of the principle of equality (as a basis for
judicial review of Community acts), Mertens de Wilmars states that:

The principle of non-discrimination is merely the transposition into
economic law of the constitutional principle of the equality of citizens
before the law and with regard to taxes.

The principle of equality or non-discrimination permeates the whole
fabric of Community law. As stated previously, it is to be found (within
limited contexts) in several provisions of the Treaty itself and in many
provisions of Community legislation. Article 7 of the Treaty of Rome
established the principle of non-discrimination on grounds of *nationality*
across the whole range of the Treaty, and the principle operates in the case law
in conjunction with other articles to provide rights for individuals: see, for
example, Case 186/87 *Cowan* v *Tresor Public* (Article 59 relating to Cowan's

freedom, as a tourist, to *receive* services; the action being against an arm of the French State) and Case C-221/89 *R* v *Secretary of State for Transport, ex parte Factortame Ltd* (Article 52 concerning the right of establishment; see Chapter Twenty). Article 119 of the Treaty provides for equal pay for equal work irrespective of sex and Directive 76/207 implements the principle of equal treatment for men and women in the field of employment.

The principle of equality also constitutes a basic element of the Common Market, being an integral part of the concept of free movement. For example, it operates, as has been seen, to strike down national measures which discriminate against, and obstruct the free movement of, goods imported from other Member States. (Nevertheless, within this context, similar situations may be treated differently on the basis of overriding, objectively justifiable grounds of public concern. Article 36 allows for derogation from the principle of free movement of goods for a number of reasons including the protection of the health and life of humans, animals or plants. See also Article 48(3) as regards the free movement of persons.)

The Court of Justice has deduced an 'unwritten' general principle of equality from these various Treaty provisions. In Case 1/72 *Frilli*, a Belgian state pensions case, it was declared that:

> The absence of any agreement of reciprocity may not ... be validly raised against such a worker, such a condition being incompatible with the rule of equality of treatment, which is one of the fundamental principles of Community law, embodied in this matter in Article 8 of Regulation 3.

The principle in its various applications means that *similar* situations (a question which can call for careful consideration and judgment) must be treated in the same way; different treatment must not be arbitrary, ie based on uninformed or random decision, as this will amount to discrimination.

Economic policy decisions of the Community institutions and national agencies regarding the reduction of agricultural surpluses have not infrequently been the subject of challenges by producers on the grounds of discrimination: see, eg, Case 114/76 *Bela-Mühle* v *Grows-Farm* (discussed below in the section on proportionality, a second ground for complaint) and Cases 103 and 145/77 *Royal Scholten-Honig* v *Intervention Board for Agricultural Produce*. In the latter case, a Regulation imposed an onerous levy on the production of isoglucose, a product which in certain respects competes with sugar, which was in surplus to the extent of creating a 'sugar mountain'. Isoglucose manufacturers indirectly challenged the Regulation in national court proceedings, claiming that it threatened to put them out of business. Following a reference under Article 177(1)(b), the Court of Justice held that the provisions of the Regulation 'offend against the general principle of equality of which the prohibition on discrimination set out in Article 40(3) of the Treaty is a specific expression'. In *Bela-Mühle*, the Advocate General defined non-discrimination as being 'concerned with the relationship between various groups of persons [eg isoglucose and sugar manufacturers] and takes the form of equality of treatment by bodies vested with public authority'.

The Balancing of Interests and Procedural Rights

It will be recalled that Mertens de Wilmars' second category of general principles concerns *sound and proper administration*. The case law of the Court indicates that the first of these, the balancing of interests, is, in his own words, 'one transposed into the administrative field from the area of legal proceedings: *audi alterem partem*'. Thus:

> Public authorities, when adopting an administrative decision [are obliged] to take into account all the interests involved and in particular not to take decisions which are likely to damage the interests of private individuals without giving them an opportunity to make their views known in advance.

In Case 17/74 *Transocean Marine Paint Association* v *Commission*, an administrative (quasi-judicial) Decision by the Commission, pursuant to Article 85(3) of the competition law rules, renewed, subject to new conditions (one of which TMPA claimed was unduly onerous), an exemption for the association from the prohibitions in Article 85(1) relating to anti-competitive trading agreements. In its review of this Decision under Article 173(2), the Court of Justice stated that:

> The applicants claim that at no time could they infer from this statement that the Commission intended to impose on them a condition such as that contained in the provision in issue, and one to which they would not be able, by reasons of its breadth, to adhere and which, without good reason, would harm their interests. If they had been in a position to realize the Commission's intentions they would not have failed to make known their objections on this matter so as to draw the Commission's attention to the inconvenience which would result from the obligation in issue and to the illegality by which it is vitiated. Since they were not given this opportunity, they allege that the Decision, insofar as the obligation in issue is concerned, must be annulled since it is vitiated by a procedural defect.

Where individual rights and interests are likely to be affected, Community law generally provides express procedural safeguards but in this case natural justice and the right to a fair hearing were invoked. The Commission had not afforded the applicant the opportunity to make its views known and was therefore in breach of 'an essential procedural requirement' necessary as a safeguard for the protection of substantive rights.

The decision in the *Johnston* case above can be seen in the same light. The Secretary of State's certificate purported to deny Mrs. Johnston access to the legal process and thus to effective judicial control as regards her employer's compliance with Community law in the form of the Equal Treatment Directive.

Also at national level, the House of Lords in the *Factortame (No. 2)* case was called upon, following a ruling by the Court of Justice to that effect, to grant an interim injunction against the Crown in order to protect the interests of a party, at least until a decision had been reached regarding directly effective rights to which that party laid claim. Their Lordships stated that as regards the balance of convenience (or interests), matters of considerable weight had to be put in the balance to outweigh the desirability of enforcing, in the *public* interest, what was on the face of it the law of the land (in this case, provisions of the Merchant Shipping Act 1988). It was enough however to swing the balance if the applicant could 'show that there was a serious case to be tried'. (This case is discussed in more detail in Chapter Twenty where it will be seen that the Act's provisions were disapplied.)

Proportionality

Derived from German law concerning fundamental rights and freedoms (and possessing a clear relationship with the English law concept of reasonableness), this principle has been explained by Hartley in the following terms:

> According to the principle of proportionality, a public authority may not impose obligations on a citizen except to the extent to which they are strictly necessary in the public interest to attain the purpose of the measure. If the burdens imposed are clearly out of proportion to the object in view, the measure will be annulled. This requires that there exists a reasonable relationship between the end and the means ... the means must be reasonably likely to bring about the objective, and ... the detriment to those adversely affected must not be disproportionate to the benefit to the public ...

> Proportionality is particularly important in the sphere of economic law, since this frequently involves imposing taxes, levies, charges or duties on businessmen in the hope of achieving economic objectives.

In Case 11/70 *Internationale Handelsgesellschaft* (discussed above and in Chapter Four), the Court of Justice gave an Article 177(1)(b) ruling on the validity of certain Community Regulations to the effect that a CAP system, whereby a West German exporter lost a deposit of DM 17,000 on failing to export cereals during the period of validity of an export licence granted to him by the National Cereals Intervention Agency, was 'appropriate' and did not violate the principle of proportionality. However, in Case 181/84 *R v Intervention Board for Agricultural Produce, ex parte Man (Sugar) Ltd.*, the exporter lost a deposit of £1,670,000 when its application for a licence reached the Commission four hours past the deadline. In this action against the Board which, on the basis of the relevant Community legislation, had declared the deposit forfeit, the Court of Justice ruled (following a validity reference from the English Court) that:

> ... the automatic forfeiture of the entire security, in the event of an infringement significantly less serious than the failure to fulfil the primary obligation [to export the sugar] which the security itself is intended to guarantee, must be considered too drastic a penalty in relation to the export licence's function of ensuring the sound management of the market in question.

The forfeiture was a disproportionate act and the company recovered the entire sum with interest and costs.

In the *Bela-Mühle* case referred to above, and others which arose out of the Community's attempt to reduce the skimmed-milk powder 'mountain', Regulation 563/76 had obliged animal feed producers to purchase expensive skimmed-milk powder in place of soya as the protein ingredient of their product. The Court held that the Regulation was invalid. It was contrary to the principle of equality in that it obliged feed producers to purchase skimmed-milk powder at such a disproportionate price that it was equivalent to a discriminatory distribution of the burden of costs between the various agricultural sectors.

Apart from its application in the context of challenges to Community secondary legislation, the principle also operates in the context of substantive Treaty articles. It has been seen that Member States may seek to justify derogations from the principle of free movement of goods on specified grounds under Article 36 and as regards free movement of persons under Article 48(3). The case law of the Court of Justice clearly demonstrates that such restrictive national measures must hinder trade no more than is necessary to achieve the desired objective. For instance, in Case 178/84 *Commission v Germany (Re Purity Requirements for Beer)*, sixteenth-century German legislation required beer to be produced from a limited number of natural ingredients. This absolute ban on additives had the effect of preventing beers from other Member States which contained additives from being sold in Germany. All the additives at issue were allowed under German law to be used in other foodstuffs. The ban was found to be contrary to Article 30 (as regards measures having an effect equivalent to a quantitative restriction) and could not be justified on public health grounds under Article 36. That objective could be achieved by less restrictive means (eg labelling). Not being 'necessary', the ban was disproportionate. (For various other examples see Chapter Twelve.)

Legal Certainty

It is customary to link the next general principle referred to by Mertens de Wilmars, the protection of legitimate expectations, to those relating to the retroactivity of laws and the protection of vested rights under the general heading of *legal certainty*. This is how they will be treated here. As Brown and Jacobs put it: 'these principles shade into one another, and the same case may raise one or more of them'.

The significance of the general principle of legal certainty (together with its related or component principles) is at its most apparent within the relationship between Community undertakings and Community or national administrative bodies in a highly regulated sector such as agriculture. Of course, economic agents must act within the law but they may also legitimately operate on the basis of reasonable expectations or predictions as to the way they *will be* treated by an administrative body in the future application of Community law. Thus Wyatt and Dashwood explain that:

> The principle of legal certainty requires that those subject to the law should not be placed in a situation of uncertainty as to their rights and obligations. The related concept of legitimate expectation constitutes an important corollary to this principle: those who act in good faith on the basis of the law as it is or seems to be should not be frustrated in their expectations.

Thus, Community measures should not take effect without adequate notice to those concerned: see Case 98/78 *Racke*, and, even more so, should not take effect retroactively from their date of publication. For example, a new Community measure should not apply to an act or transaction which has been *completed* before the measure came into effect. If it does so, in principle it offends against respect for *vested or acquired rights*, ie those rights which have been acquired by an individual (or undertaking) within the legal

framework and according to due process. In Case 100/78 *Rossi*, the Court
explained that:

> The Community rules could not, *in the absence of an express exception
> consistent with the aims of the Treaty*, be applied in such a way as to
> deprive [individuals] of the benefit of a part of the legislation of a
> Member State. (Emphasis added)

Neither should a new Community measure apply to an act or
transaction which has begun and is *in the process of completion*. Here the offence
is against the principle of the *protection of the legitimate expectations* of the
individual concerned rather than against the principle of non–retroactivity.

For expectations to be legitimate, they must be held by a prudent
person acting in accordance with the law. Such a person's reliance on the
certainty of the law should be rewarded by the protection of his *confidence* in
the system. It should not be disrupted by a sudden, unforeseeable change in the
law to his detriment in the absence of an overriding matter of public, rather
than individual, interest. As regards this final point, to put the situation in
perspective and looking at it from the point of view of the legislator,
Sharpston has explained that:

> The background to all economic activity is that economic operators live
> in an uncertain world. Changes in the regulatory framework within
> which they operate are one further hazard. Indeed, one might say that, in
> the general economic interest (as distinct from the interest of any
> particular individual economic agent), there should probably be a
> presumption of legislative freedom: legislators should normally be left
> with their hands untied, free to modify the regulatory framework in
> order to implement desired policy in the face of changing economic
> circumstances. At the simplest level of argument, therefore, expectations
> should never be permitted to invalidate legislative change.

Case 108/81 *Amylum* v *Council*

At a time of concern regarding the size of the Community 'sugar
mountain', a system of quotas and levies was imposed on sugar
producers and also, under Regulation 1293/79, on producers of
isoglucose, which competes with sugar. This Regulation was annulled
by the Court, not on substantive grounds but because the Council had
failed to consult the Parliament on the matter (a breach of an essential
procedural requirement).

The Council therefore issued another Regulation, having this time
consulted the Parliament, reimposing the scheme with retrospective

effect. This new Regulation was challenged (like its predecessor it was a 'disguised decision', see Chapters Four and Nineteen) by Amylum and other isoglucose producers under Article 173(2) as being in breach of the principle that Community measures may not have retroactive effect. The Court of Justice ruled:

I – First submission: Breach of the principle that Community measures may not have retroactive effect

As the Court has already held ... although in general the principle of legal certainty, as the applicant states, precludes a Community measure from taking effect from a point in time before its publication, it may exceptionally be otherwise where the purpose to be achieved so demands and where the legitimate expectations of those concerned are fully respected.

As regards the first of those two conditions it is well to call to mind certain matters of fact or law which are moreover well known to the parties. During the period of application of the contested regulation sugar producers were, in particular, subject to quotas and production levies. Isoglucose is a product which may be substituted for sugar and is in direct competition with it. Any Community decision concerning one of those products necessarily has repercussions on the other. Having regard to that situation, although by judgments of 29 October 1980 the Court declared Regulation No 1293/79 void for infringement of an essential procedural requirement, namely the absence of the Parliament's opinion, the Court nevertheless considered that it was a matter for the Council, in view of the fact that isoglucose production was contributing to an increase in sugar surpluses and that it was open to it to impose restrictive measures on that production, to take such measures in the context of the agricultural policy as it judged to be useful, regard being had to the similarity and interdependence of the two markets and the specific nature of the isoglucose market.

If, following the declaration of the nullity of Regulation No 1293/79, the Council had adopted no measure restrictive of isoglucose production – in the present case the reinstatement with effect from 1 July 1979 of the quotas allocated and the levies imposed on the producers – the objective, which it was pursuing, namely the stabilization, in the general interest, of the sugar market, could not have been achieved or could only have been achieved to the detriment of sugar producers, who alone would have had to finance the costs of Community surpluses, or even to the detriment of the Community as a whole, whilst isoglucose producers whose production competed with that of sugar undertakings would have escaped all restraints ...

Thus the Council was lawfully entitled to consider that the objective to be achieved in the general interest, namely the stabilization of the Community market in sweeteners without arbitrary discrimination between traders, required the contested provisions to be retroactive in nature and thus the first of the conditions which the Court lays down for the applicability *ratione temporis* of a Community measure to a date prior to the date of its publication may be regarded as satisfied.

To ascertain whether the second of the conditions set out above is satisfied it is necessary to inquire whether the action of the Council in publishing on 17 February 1981 Regulation No 387/81 has frustrated a legitimate expectation on the part of the applicants to the effect that the production of isoglucose would not be regulated during the period from 1 July 1979 to 30 June 1980, the period to which that regulation makes applicable Article 9 relating to quotas and production levies on isoglucose which it inserted in Regulation No 1111/77.

It should first be pointed out that the contested provisions of Regulation No 387/81 do not include any new measures and merely reproduce the provisions of Council Regulation No 1293/79 declared void by the Court on 29 October 1980.

In view of the fact that Council Regulation No 1293/79 of 25 June 1979 retained its full effect within the Community legal order until it was declared void, so that the national authorities responsible for its implementation were required to subject the production of isoglucose to the restrictive system which it laid down, such a legitimate expectation could only be founded on the unforeseeability of the reinstatement with retroactive effect of the measures contained in Regulation No 1293/79 declared void by the Court.

In the present case the applicant cannot claim any legitimate expectation worthy of protection.

In the first place the traders concerned by the rules in question are limited in number and are reasonably well aware of the interdependence of the markets in liquid sugar and isoglucose, of the situation of the Community market in sweeteners and therefore of the consequences which, following the declaration that Regulation No 1293/79 was void, the imposition on the production of sugar in respect of the period from 1 July 1979 to 30 June 1980 of stabilization measures from which the production of isoglucose would have been entirely exempt might have had.

As this case shows, legitimate expectations must be reasonable expectations. Would a reasonably experienced and prudent isoglucose manufacturer have relied on the expectation? If not, the expectation does not merit protection. The plaintiffs in the next case, a damages claim – not a direct challenge under Article 173(2) – were more successful:

Case 74/74 *CNTA* v *Commission*

CNTA, producers of colza oils, alleged, in support of a claim for damages against the Community under Article 215(2), the illegality of Regulation 189/72. This measure had, without warning, discontinued agricultural compensatory amounts (introduced earlier following a devaluation of the French franc) in dealings in colza seeds. The company claimed that this sudden curtailment frustrated the legitimate expectations of the persons concerned that the compensatory amounts would be maintained for deliveries in progress, which had been severely disrupted by the curtailment; traders thereby suffering extensive losses.

It was argued that even a prudent trader might in such circumstances fail to cover himself by insurance, as he could legitimately expect that no unforeseeable change would be made such as unexpectedly to expose him to exchange risks and unavoidable loss.

The Court of Justice stated that the monetary compensatory amounts could not be seen as providing a guarantee to exporters that they would not suffer loss as a result of fluctuations in the exchange rate. Nevertheless, continued the Court:

In these circumstances, a trader may legitimately expect that for transactions irrevocably undertaken by him because he has obtained, subject to a deposit, export licences fixing the amount of the export subsidy in advance, no unforeseeable alteration will occur which could have the effect of causing him inevitable loss, by re-exposing him to the exchange risk.

The Community is therefore liable if, in the absence of an overriding matter of public interest, the Commission abolished with immediate effect and without warning the application of compensatory amounts in a specific sector without adopting transitional measures which would at least permit traders either to avoid the loss which would have been suffered in the performance of export contracts, the existence and irrevocability of which are established by the advance fixing of the export subsidies, or to be compensated for such loss.

In the absence of an overriding matter of public interest, the
Commission has violated a superior rule of law, thus rendering the
Community liable, by failing to include in Regulation 189/72
transitional measures for the protection of the confidence which a trader
might legitimately have had in the Community rules.

Whereas Community acts may only have retroactive effect in these
exceptional circumstances where individual rights must give way to Treaty-
based economic and social policy considerations, conversely Court of Justice
rulings, as we have seen in the previous chapter with regard to preliminary
rulings, are in normal circumstances retroactive. Its judgments are *declaratory*,
stating the law as it always has been. Thus an interpretative ruling clarifies and
defines the meaning of a rule of Community law, which should have been
understood and applied since the time of its coming into force: see, eg the
meaning and effect of Article 12 in *Van Gend en Loos*. The national court is
required to apply the rule as so interpreted even to legal relationships
established *before* the preliminary ruling was made, except again where, in
exceptional circumstances, 'important considerations of legal certainty' have
been called in aid by the Court to validate a finding that its ruling should
only apply prospectively – as in *Defrenne (No. 2)* and a handful of other cases.

Akehurst, M., 'The Application of General Principles of Law by the Court of Justice of the European Communities' (1981) BYIL 29.

Arnull, A., *The General Principles of EEC Law and the Individual*, 1989.

Dallen, R. M., 'An Overview of EEC Protection of Human Rights' (1990) 27 CML Rev. 761.

Dauses, M., 'The Protection of Fundamental Rights in the Community Legal Order' (1985) 10 EL Rev. 398.

Hartley, T., *European Community Law*, Chapter 5.

Koopmans, T., 'European Public Law: Reality and Prospects' (1991) PL 53.

Lamoureux, F., 'The Retroactivity of Community Acts in the Case Law of the Court of Justice' (1983) 20 CML Rev. 269.

Mancini, G. F., 'The Making of a Constitution for Europe' (1989) 26 CML Rev. 544.

Martens de Wilmars, J., 'The Case Law of the Court of Justice in Relation to the Review of the Legality of Economic Policy in Mixed-Economy Systems' (1982) 1 LIEI 1.

Schermers, H., 'The European Community Bound by Fundamental Human Rights' (1990) 27 CML Rev. 249.

Schwartz, J., 'The Tendency towards a Common Administrative Law in Europe' (1991) 16 EL Rev. 3.

Sharpston, E., 'Legitimate Expectations and Economic Reality' (1990) 15 EL Rev. 103.

Shonfield, A., 'The Politics of the Mixed Economy in the International System of the 1970s' (1980) *International Affairs* 1.

Snyder, F., 'New Directions in European Community Law' (1987) 14 JLS 167.

Tillotson, J., 'The Scope and Teaching of Economic Law – A Note' (1978) 13 JALT 104.

Usher, J., 'The Influence of National Concepts on Decisions of the European Court' (1976) 1 EL Rev. 359.

Weiler, J., 'Eurocracy and Distrust ...' (the Court of Justice and Human Rights) (1986) 61 *Washington Law Review* 1103.

Wyatt and Dashwood's *European Community Law*, section on 'The General Principles of Community Law' in Chapter 4.

CHAPTER ELEVEN

COMMON MARKET AND INTERNAL MARKET: THE FOUR FREEDOMS

COMMON MARKET

A clear relationship was established in Chapter Two between the economic concept of *negative integration* (the removal of restrictions and discrimination) and the Community law concept of Common Market as found in Article 2 of the Treaty. Of those Community 'activities' or objectives listed in Article 3 which are necessary for the establishment and functioning of the Common Market – objectives 3(a) to (f) and 3(h) – it is apparent that they are to a considerable extent concerned with the question of *free movement*. (References, where we are discussing developments since 1957, are to the EEC Treaty. Maastricht TEU amendments are noted where appropriate.)

Article 3

For the purposes set out in Article 2, the activities of the Community shall include ...

(a) the elimination, as between Member Sates, of customs duties and of quantitative restrictions on the import and export of goods, and of all measures having equivalent effect;

(b) the establishment of a common customs tariff and a common commercial policy towards third countries ...

The fundamental principle of *free movement of goods* within intra-Community trade is embodied in Article 3(a). Article 3(a) and (b) constitute the basis for the Community's *customs union* and Article 3(a) requires not only the abolition of tariffs and quota restrictions on inter-Member State trade but also the removal of other 'measures' (*non-tariff barriers*) such as significantly differing national standards and technical requirements relating to goods.

The Common Customs (or External) Tariff was established for the original six Member States primarily on the basis of an unweighted average of the import duties of the four customs territories (France, Germany, Italy and the Benelux Customs Union). It was completed by mid-1968 and progressively adopted by the new Member States. (There is no reference to it in Article 3(b) of the Maastricht Treaty.) As a result of Community participation in *international* tariff negotiations within the GATT (the General Agreement on Tariffs and Trade), the level of external tariffs has been reduced in subsequent years. Community agricultural products are, however, subject to a different legal regime from industrial products. Protection from fluctuations in world market prices, through a system of Community import levies and export refunds, lies at the heart of difficulties experienced in 1992–93 between the Community and the USA within the GATT Uruguay Round, which seeks to extend trade liberalization to agricultural products.

Article 3

...

(c) The abolition, as between Member States, of obstacles to freedom of movement for persons, services and capital ...

The Maastricht Treaty rephrases Article 3(c) in terms of the Internal Market to include goods. In any event, the Treaty therefore encompasses not only those *factors of production* which make up the mobile resources or input of economic enterprise: *labour* and *management* (in as much as the Treaty provisions on persons apply to workers, self-employed persons, and business undertakings on the basis of the right of establishment) and *capital*, but it also applies to the output or end-products of such enterprise (*goods* and *services*).

The Court of Justice has on many occasions stated that the free movement of goods is a fundamental principle of Community law – and so too the other freedoms in Article 3. In Case 203/80 *Casati*, the Court explained that:

The first question concerns the effects of Article 67 and, more particularly, Article 67(1), after the expiry of the transitional period. That article heads the chapter on capital which belongs to Title II, 'Free movement of persons, services and capital', incorporated in Part Two of the EEC Treaty, entitled 'Foundations of the Community'. The general scheme of those provisions is in keeping with the list, set out in Article 3 of the EEC Treaty, of the methods provided for the attainment of the Community's objectives. Those methods include, according to Article 3(c) 'the abolition, as between Member States, of obstacles to freedom of movement for persons, services and capital'. Thus the free movement of capital constitutes, alongside that of persons and services, one of the fundamental freedoms of the Community. Furthermore, freedom to move certain types of capital is, in practice, a pre-condition for the effective exercise of other freedoms guaranteed by the Treaty, in particular the right of establishment.

However, capital movements are also closely connected with the economic and monetary policy of the Member States ...

What is of particular importance in this extract from the Court's judgment is its insistence on the *inter-relationship* between the freedoms, particularly here between capital movements and the right of undertakings to *establish* themselves in other Member States. Also the Court makes a clear link between free movement of capital (an element of *negative* integration) and the convergence of the economic and monetary policies of the Member States (a key aspect of *positive* integration) in the movement towards economic and monetary union: see 'The Bonds between Negative and Positive Integration' in Chapter Two.

Effective functioning of the Common Market therefore entails effective functioning of the four freedoms. As regards free movement of goods, the 'cornerstone' of the Common Market, whereas the customs duties and quota restrictions of Article 3(a) have been almost entirely eliminated for 'the Twelve', other national barriers and discriminatory practices remain and are in practice still only in the process of being removed. Therefore, in order to obtain a more comprehensive picture of what the establishment of a 'true' Common Market entails, it is necessary to draw attention to a wider range of protectionist and anti-competitive non-tariff barriers than merely the 'measures' – particularly, differing national rules and standards applied to goods – in Article 3(a):

1. *The anti-competitive practices* both of individual large firms which dominate markets for goods (and services) and of firms which act together to, for example, fix prices and share markets. Such activities (of undertakings not Member States) are contrary to the Common Market and they are subject to the Community's *competition policy* rules which seek to establish and maintain fair and effective competition: Article 3(f) as developed in Articles 85-90 (see Chapters Fifteen to Seventeen).

2. Discriminatory and anti-competitive *State aids* to national industries, which are incompatible with the Common Market, subject to certain exceptions, under Articles 92-94.

3. Differences in national *indirect taxation*, particularly Value Added Tax (VAT) and excise duties, as regards scope and rates, and subject to *harmonisation* measures under Article 99 (see Chapter Twelve).

4. *Nationalistic public purchasing policies of Member State governments*, which exclude foreign undertakings from procurement contracts, and which are subject now to Community legislation designed to

introduce effective competition on a Community-wide basis, eg Directive 89/440 on Public Works Tendering.

5.   Frontier checks and formalities which cause delays to the transport of goods and increase costs to an estimated value of 80p of every £10 spent by consumers, and which are subject to abolition or simplification under the Internal Market programme (see below and Chapter Twelve).

It should also be noted that a fifth freedom, *free movement of payments*, is currently to be found in Articles 106 and 67(2). Such payments include payments for goods imported and dividends on capital invested in another Member State. The 'basic' freedoms (to the extent to which they are themselves liberalized) would clearly be ineffective if the financial benefits arising from the transactions involved could not be 'repatriated'. Remaining *exchange controls* in relation to capital and as affecting financial services are being removed either through Commission action or the Member States' own volition.

COMMON MARKET AND INTERNAL MARKET

Article 8(1) of the 1957 Treaty laid down that:

The Common Market shall be progressively established during a transitional period of twelve years.

Although considerable progress was made in the fields of trade liberalization and the free movement of persons by the time of the expiry of the transitional period at the end of 1969, the objective expressed in Article 8(7) was not achieved:

Save for the exceptions and derogations provided for in this Treaty, the expiry of the transitional period shall constitute the latest date by which all the rules laid down must enter into force and all the measures required for establishing the common market must be implemented.

It was not until the mid-1980s, and the initiative provided by the Commission White Paper on Completing the Internal Market (Com (85) 310), that renewed political will on the part of the Member States, as evidenced by the Single European Act of 1986, introduced not only a new programme but also a new Community law concept, the Internal or Single European Market.

Article 8A of the EEC Treaty (Article 7a EC), incorporated from the Single European Act, states that:

> The internal market shall comprise an area without frontiers in which the free movement of goods, persons, services and capital is ensured in accordance with the provisions of this Treaty.

The concept of the Internal Market, focusing as it does on the four freedoms, is therefore narrower in scope than that of the Common Market as found in the original Treaty and the case law of the Court of Justice. However the words 'without frontiers' have raised new questions in relation to border controls and the movement of, for example, drugs and terrorists. In essence the completion of the Internal Market by the end of 1992

> ... represents a plan for a large-scale onslaught on the 'omissions' in the 'acquis' with respect to Treaty obligations crucial to market integration, and a simultaneous endeavour to make progress on issues where the Treaty provides a permissive legal basis but no obligations: *Pelkmans and Winters*. (The second part of this sentence relates to 'positive' measures.)

Following its acceptance of the White Paper, the European Council instructed the Council to introduce an action programme, priority to be given to:

(i)   the removal of *physical* barriers to the free movement of goods within the Community. (The aim being not merely to simplify frontier controls, which cause expensive delays, but to remove frontiers in relation to the movement of goods – and persons);

(ii)   the removal of *technical* barriers to the free movement of goods within the Community (particularly differing national rules and standards which fragment the market);

(iii)   the creation of a free market in *financial services* (eg banking and insurance) and in *transport* (still subject to national transport quotas);

(iv)   the creation of full freedom of establishment for the *professions*;

(v)   the liberalisation of *capital* movements.

The '1992' Internal Market programme involved almost 300 legislative measures (virtually all Directives) to be adopted by the Community and implemented by the Member States in the time-scale provided, and the Single European Act provided for decisions in most of the areas involved to be taken by a qualified majority vote in the Council (acting in co-operation with the Parliament): Article 100A(1). Thus the primary legal mechanism for the completion of the Internal Market is 'the approximation of the provisions laid down by law, regulation or administrative action in Member States' and unanimity is only required as regards fiscal provisions and those relating to the free movement of persons and the rights and interests of employed persons: Article 100A(2).

As will be seen in the following chapter, of particular importance are those measures concerning the harmonisation of the many differing national rules and standards which have continued to impede the free movement of goods. Similarly significant are the measures relating to professional qualifications, the free movement of services and public procurement.

As Pelkmans and Winters indicate, the Internal Market programme does not focus on all Common Market activities, only on 'omissions'; those aspects of the original programme where progress was limited. However developments in related fields continue: for example, the regulation of corporate mergers (see Chapter Seventeen), the extension of competition policy further into the fields of air and sea transport, reform of the Common Agricultural Policy, and participation by the Community in the liberalization of world trade in the GATT Uruguay Round.

In 1989 Owen and Dynes listed ten actual or potential benefits of the Single (Internal) Market:

- EASIER TRAVEL. Frontier controls will be all but abolished at the EC's internal frontiers, although not at its external points of entry (if anything, external controls will be increased to ensure that non-EC citizens do not find 'soft' entry points and then go on to exploit the benefits of the single market.) Computer-read, single-format EC passports will cut down delays, and police and immigration forces will tackle crime more through behind-the-scenes co-ordination than through frontier controls. Duty-free sales will disappear, and by way of compensation ferry companies – which stand to lose over £160 million from the abolition of duty-frees – are planning floating offshore superstores, using converted roll-on-roll-off ferries.

- A BUSINESS BOOM. 320 million customers await the efforts of EC business, from Britain to Denmark to Greece and Portugal, with all firms competing on equal terms in a huge open market. One of the key provisions obliges public authorities to give enterprises from any EC nation an equal opportunity to win high-value contracts.

- BORDER SAVINGS. Frontier delays for goods vehicles (many trucks and lorries now wait at borders for eight hours or more) cost an estimated £17 billion, according to European Parliament. Restrictions on tendering for public contracts cost a further £60 billion. The simplified customs procedures of the Single Administrative Document – which Britain was one of the first EC countries to introduce – will save costs. However, the Kangaroo Group (an EC 1992 pressure group founded by the late Basil de Ferranti, Conservative MEP and a determined campaigner for border abolition) says that hold-ups at borders still cost British and European consumers 80p for every £10 they spend.

- JOB RECOGNITION. A teacher from Glasgow will be able to teach in Lyons or Copenhagen, and an accountant from Brighton could go and work in Naples or Frankfurt, all on the basis of mutually recognized qualifications and diplomas. Linguistic barriers will still cause problems – and will work against the British, since as a nation, our grasp of Continental languages is still poor.

- FINANCIAL SERVICES. Restrictions on capital movements are to be lifted in 1990. EC citizens will be able to open bank accounts in due course or take out mortgages anywhere in the Community, with some exceptions in Southern Europe. There is a long-term plan (still under discussion) for a European Central Bank.

- CONSUMER PROTECTION. EC states will no longer be able to block imports of foodstuffs or toys because they do not meet national labelling, health or safety standards. Broad criteria and common standards are being devised.

- FREE COMPETITION. Protectionist practices preventing free competition – including competition in transport by road, sea and air – will become illegal. The first stages of liberalization in aviation and road haulage are already in effect, preventing cartels and quotas and allowing smaller operators increased market access.

- **VAT AND INDIRECT TAXES HARMONISED.** This is a controversial area because of the Government's electoral commitment not to allow the abolition of VAT zero rating on basic goods such as food and children's clothes. However, the basic principle of the 1992 programme is that, once border controls have gone, trade in the integrated market will be distorted if there are large differentials between VAT rates.

- **TELEVISION AND BROADCASTING.** Technical standards for television and satellite technology are to be harmonized in conjunction with the 1992 programme to ensure that the twelve EC nations do not have incompatible systems, obstructing sales and communication. To prevent European television being dominated by American or Australian soap operas, a 'majority' of programmes 'where practicable' will have to be of EC origin once the Commission's plans are approved.

- **THE TELECOMMUNICATIONS MARKET.** This is being opened up, under a plan (tabled by the Commission in June 1987) for ending the monopoly supply of customer terminal equipment and telecommunications services, including databases and electronic mailboxes. Eventually, electrical plugs and sockets may also be standardized so that travellers do not have to carry adaptors or change plugs – but at the moment this seems unlikely.

It must be remembered, however, as many commentators have stressed and as the Single European Act and the Maastricht Treaty demonstrate, that:

> ... it is hard to see how a transnational unified common marketplace could be created and remain viable without adequate monetary and fiscal powers ... the achievement of the single market will necessitate far greater attention to the formation of common economic policies and major changes in the decisional processes of the Community. The need for such policies was, indeed, foreshadowed in the opening articles of the [Rome] Treaty: the programme set out in articles 2 and 3 EEC remains today, as it was in 1958 when the Treaty came into force, a truly inspired and radical blueprint for European integration: Bieber et al (1988).

In particular, integrationists strongly argue that the lack of a common currency and a European Central Bank to manage it are major weaknesses of the Internal Market.

In June 1992 the status of the Internal Market legislative programme was as follows:

- 282 proposals comprised the programme
- 228 proposals had been finally adopted by the Council
- 5 proposals had been partially adopted by the Council
- 4 proposals had reached the stage of a Council Common Position
- 2 proposals had reached the stage of a Council Political Agreement

(Figures supplied by the DTI in June 1992.)

Transposition of these measures into national law is proceeding but in some cases not as speedily as was required to meet the non-binding deadline of 31 December 1992. (As regards these obligations of the Member States, see also Chapter Eight concerning the *Francovich* decision and the agreed, but not yet ratified, Article 171(2) EC.)

FREE MOVEMENT OF PERSONS, SERVICES AND CAPITAL

The basis of free movement is best explained in terms of the economic concept of the *optimum division of labour.*

... the object of optimum division of labour within the Community can be inferred from the objectives of Article 2. This optimum division of labour not only implies ensuring a free outlet for the economically most favourable supply of certain goods or services throughout the common market. It also implies the requirement of optimum allocation of production factors within the Community. Besides the necessity of mobility of the principal production factors – capital, labour, technical and managerial know-how – this latter requirement also entails the requirement of equal possibilities of establishment and exercise of a trade or profession in the most favourable place of establishment which may be attractive either on account of its shorter distance from buyers ... or because the general socio-economic, fiscal and financial climate is more favourable: *Gormley.*

Freedom of movement of persons and services and the right of establishment are dealt with in separate chapters of the Rome Treaty although from an economic standpoint they are closely related. Article 48 provides for the free movement of *workers* and, via the expression 'nationals of a Member State', Articles 52 and 59 provide for employers (including *companies and firms*: see Article 58) and the *self-employed, eg professional persons.* Such 'nationals' may or may not be in business to provide *services.* (The substantive aspects of these articles are not affected by the TEU.)

The obligations placed upon Member States to secure free movement of workers and services and the right of establishment are underpinned by the prohibition of discrimination on grounds of nationality to be found in Article 7 (Article 6 EC), and, as in the case of goods (but not capital), the main Treaty provisions are directly effective.

Article 48 of the Treaty provides that freedom of movement for *workers*:

> 2. ... shall entail the abolition of any discrimination based on nationality between workers of the Member States as regards employment, remuneration and other conditions of work and employment ...

The term 'worker' extends not only to a person in permanent employment in a Member State other than that of which he or she is a national but also, according to the case law of the Court of Justice, to others (whose Community rights are usually more limited) such as work-seekers and involuntarily unemployed workers. In addition members of an immigrant worker's *family* are covered, even if they are not workers, as regards rights of entry and residence.

Provision is made in Article 51 and Community Regulations for the transferability and aggregation of the social security rights of immigrant workers and their dependants. This *social*, rather than economic, aspect of free movement is also apparent with respect to Directives issued in 1990 granting rights of free movement to persons who are not economically active: students, retired persons and persons of independent means: see also the new Articles 8-8e EC on citizenship of the Union.

Articles 52-58 governing the *right of establishment* cover both self-employed persons and companies and firms. The rights which are granted cover both the right of an individual to become established as a self-employed person on a *permanent basis* in another Member State and the right of a company incorporated in one Member State to set up a subsidiary or branch in another Member State. Such a person or company may be established in order to provide services in that other Member State, but if such provision of services is merely on a *temporary* basis, the rules relating to the provision of cross-border services, and not those on the right of establishment, will apply. Thus Article 52(2) provides that:

> Freedom of establishment shall include the right to take up and pursue activities as self-employed persons and set up and manage undertakings, in particular companies and firms ... under the conditions laid down for

its own nationals by the law of the country where such establishment is effected ...

Thus, the basic principle of non-discrimination applies: X or X Ltd. shall be treated in the same way as nationals of the host Member State. The main problems which have arisen in this respect, and which have to some extent been solved on the basis of harmonisation measures, concern mutual recognition of professional qualifications (eg doctors, architects and lawyers) and obstacles arising from differences in the laws of Member States relating to companies, not least those providing banking and insurance services.

Articles 59-66 deal with the *provision of services* of an industrial, commercial or professional character. Under the Treaty regime the provision of services is seen as an act, or series of acts, carried out from an establishment in one Member State, the services being provided for a person situated *in another Member State*. Under Article 59 'restrictions on freedom to provide services within the Community shall be progressively abolished' and Article 60 provides that such services are those which are 'normally provided for remuneration'. Persons to whom these provisions would apply include consulting engineers, architects and advertising agents engaged on a *temporary or spasmodic basis* by a client in another Member State. Article 60(3) states that:

> ... the person providing a service may, in order to do so, temporarily pursue his activity in the State where the service is provided, under the same conditions as are imposed by that State on its own nationals.

Thus a host state's binding professional rules 'justified by the general good' (and see above as regards harmonisation) may be applied to the cross-border provider of a service. It has rightly been said that:

> The difference between the right of establishment and the right to provide services is one of degree rather than kind. Both apply to business or professional activity pursued for profit or remuneration: Steiner, *Textbook on EEC Law.*

The Court of Justice has held that tourists, as *recipients* of services, are entitled to immigration rights and, more significantly, to equal treatment in the country visited: see Case 186/87 *Cowan*. Similarly, on the basis of, amongst other things, Article 7 (Article 6 EC) and the concept of vocational training, the Court has extended the principle of non-discrimination to most university students who are nationals of a Member State.

The basic provisions relating to the abolition of restrictions on the *free movement of capital* throughout the Community are at present to be found in

Article 67 EEC. We are concerned here primarily with the movement of funds for investment in industry and commerce from one Member State to another. Examples would include *direct* investment by a company establishing a subsidiary in another Member State (attainable under the right of establishment rules), the provision of long-term loans for industry by a bank or building society, and the cross-border acquisition of bonds or shares.

Liberalisation involves the removal of restrictions on the underlying transaction, eg exchange control restrictions on the transfer of investment funds *into* (and profits such as dividends *out* of) the host Member State. Other obstacles, amenable to harmonisation measures, include differing national tax laws and stock exchange rules.

Capital movements have an immediate bearing on government short-term economic and budgetary policy and therefore Community action in this area is, as seen, closely linked to the further progress of the process of positive integration towards economic and monetary union, including the introduction of a single currency. The links between capital movements and the provision of financial services by banks and insurance companies are also close: see Article 61(2). Development in all these fields leads to the concept of a European Financial Area.

Reference was made earlier to a fifth freedom, *the free movement of payments*, to be found in Articles 67(2) and 106 EEC. For example:

Article 106

1. Each Member State undertakes to authorise, in the currency of the Member State in which the creditor or the beneficiary resides, any payments connected with the movement of goods, services or capital, and any transfers of capital or earnings, to the extent that the movement of goods, services, capital and persons between Member States has been liberalised pursuant to this Treaty.

In the past *exchange controls* operated by national governments have proved a more effective instrument for maintaining protectionist policies than any other restrictive measure. Freedom of payments allows goods to be paid for (prior to the establishment of a single currency) in the seller's currency and similarly allows the migrant worker to transfer earnings home: see also Articles 70 and 71.

On the basis of the TEU, Articles 67-73 EEC on Capital are due to be replaced as from 1 January 1994 by the more extensive provisions of Articles 73b-g on Capital and Payments. Article 73b EC states that:

1. Within the framework of the provisions set out in this Chapter, all restrictions on the movement of capital between Member States and between Member States and third countries shall be prohibited.

2. ... all restrictions on payments between Member States and between Member States and third countries shall be prohibited.

Finally, it is important to understand that Member States' obligations regarding free movement are *not* absolute. Derogations or escape clauses are to be found in the Treaty itself with respect to all aspects of free movement. Some of these will be examined in detail at the appropriate point. Examples include:

Article 36

The provisions of Arts. 30 to 34 shall not preclude prohibitions or restrictions on imports, exports or goods in transit justified on grounds of public morality, public policy or public security; the protection of health and life of humans, animals or plants; the protection of national treasures possessing artistic, historic or archaeological value; or the protection of industrial and commercial property ...

Article 48

Freedom of movement for workers ... shall entail the right, subject to limitations justified on grounds of public policy, public security or public health:

(a) to accept offers of employment actually made;

(b) to move freely within the territory of Member States for this purpose ...

Bieber, R. et al (eds), *1992: One European Market*, 1988.

Brearley, M. and Quigley, C., '*Completing the Internal Market of the European Community*, 1989.

Ceccini, P., *The European Challenge*: – 1992, *The Benefits of a Single Market*, 1989.

Curzon Price, Victoria, 1992 – *Europe's Last Chance? From Common Market to Single Market*, IEA Occasional Paper, 1988.

Deloitte's *1992 Guide*, 1989.

Dudley, R. 1992: *Strategies for the Common Market*, 1990.

EC Commission White Paper on Completing the Internal Market, COM (85) 310 Final.

EC Commission, 'Fifth Report of the Commission ... Concerning the Implementation of the White Paper on the Completion of the Internal Market', COM (90) final, March 1990: Part II.

EC Commission, 'Implementation of the Legal Acts Required to Build the Single Market', COM (90) 473 final, October 1990.

Forwood, N. and Clough, M., 'The Single European Act and Free Movement' (1986) EL Rev. 383.

Gormley, L. W. (ed.), Kapteyn and VerLoren van Themaat's *Introduction to the Law of the European Communities*, 1989, Chapter 7(1) etc.

Legal Issues of European Integration, Special Issue on the Internal Market (Goods, Persons, Institutional Aspects, etc) 1989/1.

Owen, Richard and Dynes, Michael, *The Times Guide to 1992*, 1989.

Pelkmans, J. and Robson, P., 'The Aspirations of the White Paper' (1987) 25 JCMS 181.

Pelkmans J., and Winters, A., *Europe's Domestic Market*, 1988.

Pinder, J., 'The Single Market: A Step Towards European Union' in Lodge, J. (ed.) *The EC and the Challenge of the Future* (1989).

Pinder, J., *European Community: The Building of a Union*, 1991, Chapter 4.

Shave, A., 'Policy Europe Without Frontiers', *European Access*, 1989: 1, February.

Swann, D., *The Economics of the Common Market*, 1990.

Taylor, P., 'The New Dynamics of EC Integration in the 1980s' in Lodge, J. (ed.) *The EC and the Challenge of the Future*, 1989.

Thompson, I., 'Internal Market Developments', *European Access*, 1990 onwards (published 6 times a year).

Weatherill, S., *Cases and Materials on EEC Law*, Chapter 5.

CHAPTER TWELVE

FREE MOVEMENT OF GOODS

A NOTE ON THE ECONOMICS OF INTERNATIONAL TRADE

It has been generally accepted by economists that an international free trade policy is desirable to optimise world output and income levels in the long run. Free trade is the condition in which the flow of goods (and services) in international exchange is neither restricted nor encouraged by direct government intervention.

In an ideal world, on the basis of the economic law of comparative advantage, it is economically beneficial for countries to specialise in producing and exporting goods in the production of which their resource endowments make them relatively more efficient, and to import from other countries the goods which they are relatively less efficient in producing. However, where governments are involved in regulating overseas trade this picture is distorted. The most visible means of affecting the distribution and levels of international trade are import tariffs, import quotas, export subsidies and currency exchange controls.

The purpose of import restrictions is to divert expenditure away from foreign-produced goods in favour of domestic products. Such controls can correct a balance of international payments problem. They may also be imposed in order to protect the market of a domestic industry, which may be less efficient and therefore less competitive. Where, as with tariffs (customs duties) and taxes, the controls increase the price of imported goods, such restrictions also have a revenue-raising purpose.

In the nineteenth century the prevailing concept of economic liberalism and the doctrine of laissez-faire promoted the strongest support for a free trade policy. However, the first major breaks in this policy came early in the twentieth century:

> There is much truth in the claim that war is the ultimate experience of, and justification for, protection; and the First World War left a heavy legacy of increased protection. Not only did protection of industrial products increase – even Britain made a major breach in its traditional policy of free trade, largely on the grounds of defence considerations – but the European countries took steps to protect their farmers against the competition of cheap grains from North and South America,

Australia, and South Africa: Johnson, *The World Economy at the Crossroads* (1965).

In the inter-war period economic nationalism reached a peak and free trade was abandoned for protectionism. In line with its new 'isolationalist' policy, the US Congress enacted the Hawley-Smoot Tariff Act in 1930. Originally designed to help farmers suffering from declining agricultural prices, the scope of the Act was later widened to include industrial products. The Act led to massive resentment and retaliation throughout the world at a time following the Wall Street stock market crash of 1929: 'Italy objected to duties on hats and bonnets of straw, wool-felt hats, and olive oil; Spain reacted sharply to increases on cork and onions': Kindelberger.

Following the Great Crash — and the Great Depression — came a period of severe monetary disorganisation from which countries sought to rescue themselves at each other's expense by resorting to greatly increased protection, combined with preferential trading arrangements (for example, the British Imperial Preference and Sterling Bloc systems) and bilateral agreements. The result was an enormous contraction of the volume and a choking-up of the channels of international trade.

After the Second World War, the major economic powers, and the USA in particular, sought to establish a new world economic order. The International Monetary Fund was devised to deal with monetary matters. The General Agreement on Tariffs and Trade (GATT) was established in 1957 and, through the medium of GATT negotiating 'Rounds', has remained the focal point of international trade bargaining ever since.

As Swann explains:

> GATT gave rise to rules concerning international trade matters. Those required that tariff bargaining should be based on reciprocity and should not give rise to discrimination. The latter was particularly important in the context of EEC trade policy. It implied that if a country offered to cut its import duties on goods coming from country A, then it should also apply that treatment to all other countries — this is called most-favoured-nation treatment. The reader may wonder how the Community was able to form a customs union and still stay within GATT rules. Obviously, a customs union is discriminatory — import duties on partner goods are eliminated but are maintained on goods coming from third countries. The answer to that question is quite simple, GATT provided an exception in the case of customs unions (and free trade areas). Various rules were devised, including the requirement that in the case of a customs union the CET (Common External Tariff) should on the whole be no higher than the general incidence of duties which the parties had imposed prior to the union. The EEC drew

attention to the fact that the CET was based on the arithmetic average of the previous national duties and that therefore it had not breached GATT rules.

It is important, therefore, that initially it is appreciated that the liberalisation of trade *within* the Common Market (ie the establishment and maintenance of the free movement of goods on a *regional* basis) must be seen in the wider context of GATT efforts since the end of the Second World War to liberalise trade on a *global* basis. Article 18 of the Treaty of Rome (in the section on the setting up of the custom's union's Common Customs or External Tariff wall *vis-à-vis* third countries' products) acknowledges this point and indicates that customs duties on goods entering the Community will be reduced as a result of the Community's participation in GATT negotiating Rounds:

Article 18

The Member States declare their readiness to contribute to the development of international trade and the lowering of barriers to trade by entering into agreements designed, on a basis of reciprocity and mutual advantage, to reduce customs duties below the general level of which they could avail themselves as a result of the establishment of a customs union between them.

Similarly,

Article 110

By establishing a customs union between themselves, Member States aim to contribute, in the common interest, to the harmonious development of world trade, the progressive abolition of restrictions on international trade and the lowering of customs barriers.

FREE MOVEMENT OF GOODS IN THE COMMON MARKET: INTRODUCTION

Economic integration through competitive interpenetration of national markets depends in large part on the fundamental Community law principle of the free movement of goods. Trade liberalisation within the Community involves the removal of a variety of obstacles or barriers to inter-Member State trade. Although obstacles may be created by business undertakings (see, in particular, Chapters Fourteen and Fifteen on

Competition Law), they are, as has already been seen, generally put in place by States themselves through the medium of national law.

The EEC Treaty recognised the following main obstacles to intra-Community trade:

1. Customs duties (tariffs) on imports (and exports): Article 3(a) and Articles 9 and 12, etc.

2. Charges having an equivalent effect to customs duties: Article 3(a) and Articles 9 and 12, etc.

3. Discriminatory internal taxation of imports: Article 95.

4. Quantitative restrictions (quotas) on imports (and exports): Article 3(a) and Articles 30 and 34, etc.

5. Measures having an equivalent effect to quantitative restrictions: Article 3(a) and Articles 30, 34 and 100A, etc.

6. State monopolies of a commercial character: Article 37.

7. State aids to national industries or undertakings: Articles 92–94.

(Note also Member States' public procurement policies which favour national suppliers: see Council Directives 88/295 and 89/440 on Public Supply Contracts and Public Works Contracts.)

For reasons of space, we will concentrate on the first four of these obstacles to free movement.

In the period 1958 to 1986, considerable progress was made, particularly by the Commission and the Court of Justice, in removing, in whole or in part, customs duties (and charges), quantitative restrictions (QRs) and equivalent measures (MEEQRs, such as different national rules and standards relating to goods) that had hindered inter-Member State trade. This was so despite successive enlargements of the Community.

However, as a result of fears of renewed protectionism and the need for a new impetus, the Internal Market programme was launched by the Single European Act 1986. A little earlier the Commission's White Paper of 1985 on the Completion of the Internal Market (see Chapter Eleven) identified three sets of barriers which still significantly hindered the free movement of goods (and, in certain respects, persons, services and capital also):

1. Physical barriers

2. Fiscal barriers

3. Technical barriers

Although this categorisation of barriers might not immediately relate to that found in the Treaty (see above), the following extract explains the position:

... the categorisation by the EC of these three types of barrier is somewhat arbitrary. Physical barriers are concerned with frontier controls on the movement of goods and persons. Fiscal barriers consist of all impediments and substantial distortions among member states that emanate from differences in the commodity base as well as in the rates of VAT and the duties on excises ... All remaining impediments fall into the category of technical barriers. Therefore, this category comprises not only barriers arising from absence of technical harmonisation and public procurement procedures, but also institutional impediments on the free movement of people, capital and financial services, including transport and data transmission. It also comprises a miscellaneous collection of obstacles to the business environment which take the form of an inadequately harmonised company law, the lack of an EC patent and an EC trade mark, together with issues of corporate taxation and several diverse problems concerned with the national application of EC law: El-Agraa (ed.), *Economics of the European Community*.

As regards the free movement of *goods* therefore, the Commission's Internal Market programme focused on the continuing need to remove frontier controls (physical barriers), to harmonise VAT and other forms of indirect taxes on goods (fiscal barriers), and to harmonise those differing national rules and standards relating to goods (MEEQRs) that still proliferated in inter-Member State trade (technical barriers). Discriminatory public procurement procedures and problems relating to patents and trade marks were also targeted.

However, before examining those aspects of the post-1986 programme of Community legislation which were designed to complete the Internal Market in relation to the free movement of goods, it is clearly necessary to look at problems posed and progress made in the earlier period. It will be seen that the attack on trade barriers is essentially two-pronged: *elimination* as a result of litigation in the Court of Justice or national courts and *harmonisation* of national rules by the Commission. An important link between the two attacks is to be found in the *Cassis de Dijon* decision, which will be examined in due course.

A number of further introductory points must be made. First, subject to certain exceptions, the rules laid down for the establishment of the Common Market, and hence the rules relating to the free movement of goods, apply to agricultural products as well as industrial goods: Article 38.

Secondly, the free movement rules apply both to goods which originate in a Member State and to those which come from a third country and are in free circulation in a Member State. Such goods are in free circulation when they have crossed the Common External Tariff wall with all import formalities complied with and duties or charges paid: Article 10(1).

Thirdly, although the free movement provisions of the Treaty are addressed to the Member States, the more important articles are *directly effective* and may be invoked by individuals (and undertakings) in their national courts, eg Article 12 in *Van Gend en Loos* (see also the list in Collins, *European Community Law in the United Kingdom*, Chapter 2).

Finally, the case law of the Court of Justice clearly demonstrates that the Court's primary aim is to establish the *effect* (not the purpose) of a national rule on the fundamental concept of the unity of the market. If it is in breach of the free movement rules, the national measure will be struck down, unless it comes within one of the restrictively interpreted derogations or exceptions provided for in the Treaty. For example, Article 36 allows Member States to prohibit imports on grounds of the protection of the life and health of humans. However, even where derogation has been allowed on this or other meritorious grounds, the creation of a single market demands that to the extent that they differ such national rules be *harmonised* at Community level to ensure that, whilst the objective of the national rules is maintained, so is the principle of free movement.

The creation of a single market encompassing the twelve Member States and, under the Agreement on the European Economic Area, a further six EFTA countries, will result in the formation of a regional trading bloc capable of competing on the world market with the USA and Japan.

INTERNAL FISCAL BARRIERS: CUSTOMS DUTIES AND CHARGES (ARTICLES 9-17)

Article 9(1) of the Treaty establishes the Community's *customs union* (an integral part of the Common Market):

> The Community shall be based on a customs union which shall cover all trade in goods and which shall involve the prohibition between Member States of customs duties on imports and exports and of all charges having equivalent effect, and the adoption of a common customs tariff in their relations with third countries.

For 'the Six', Article 12 operated as a 'standstill' provision regarding all customs duties and charges (see *Van Gend en Loos*) and Articles 13-17 provided either specific timetables for their progressive elimination or powers whereby the Commission could establish such a timetable. As regards tariffs, Member States were allowed to 'accelerate' their abolition and it was announced in mid-1968 that all tariffs had been abolished – eighteen months ahead of schedule (the end of the twelve-year transitional period):

> The customs union continued to fulfil high expectations through the 1960s. Trade among the Community's member states grew twice as fast as trade in the wider international economy, quadrupling in the first decade after the Community was established in 1958 ... There was no way of knowing how much of this growth was due to the creation of the customs union ... but the Community had evidently provided a framework in which it had been possible: Pinder, *European Community: The Building of a Union*.

When the UK, Ireland and Denmark joined the Community in 1973, they were allowed a five-year period in which to dismantle their various forms of protection. Greece, joining in 1981, was given a similar period to adapt and Spain and Portugal, which became full members in 1986 were allowed seven years. On this basis, therefore, inter-Member State trade can now be said to be free, at least of customs duties, although it is more than possible that some of the less visible charges (see below) remain. (A Member State facing severe economic difficulties may seek authorisation from the Commission to take 'necessary protective measures' in derogation from the free movement provisions of the Treaty: Article 115 (amended by the TEU).)

The nature and purpose of the Treaty provisions on the elimination of customs duties and charges were explained by the Court of Justice in Cases 2 and 3/69 *Social Fund for Diamond Workers*:

> It was submitted that a small levy imposed under Belgian law on imported diamonds could not be in breach of Articles 9 and 12 because (i) it had no protectionist purpose as Belgium did not produce diamonds, and (ii) the levy's purpose was to provide social security benefits for Belgian diamond workers. The Court explained that:

> In prohibiting the imposition of customs duties, the Treaty does not distinguish between goods according to whether or not they enter into competition with the products of the importing country. Thus, the purpose of the abolition of customs barriers is not merely to eliminate their protective nature, as the Treaty sought on the contrary to give general scope and effect to the rule on elimination of customs duties and charges having equivalent effect in order to ensure the free movement of goods. It follows from the system as a whole and from the general and absolute nature of the prohibition of any customs duty applicable to goods moving between Member States that customs duties are prohibited independently of any consideration of the purpose for which they were introduced and the destination of the revenue obtained

therefrom. The justification for this prohibition is based on the fact that any pecuniary charge – however small – imposed on goods by reason of the fact that they cross a frontier constitutes an obstacle to the movement of such goods.

This definition of a charge having equivalent effect to a customs duty was elaborated by the Court in Case 24/68 *Commission v Italy* (*Re Statistical Levy*), a case in which a levy was imposed on goods exported to other Member States in order to fund the compilation of statistical data relating to trade patterns:

> ... any pecuniary charge, however small and whatever its designation and mode of application, which is imposed unilaterally on domestic or foreign goods by reason of the fact that they cross a frontier and which is not a customs duty in the strict sense ... even if it is not imposed for the benefit of the State, is not discriminatory or protective in effect and if the product on which the charge is imposed is not in competition with any domestic product.

The charge in this case was found to be in breach of Article 16 (relating to *exports*).

Similarly, in Cases 2 and 3/62 *Commission v Luxembourg and Belgium* (*Gingerbread*), charges were defined by the Court of Justice as

> ... duties whatever their description or technique, imposed unilaterally, which apply specifically to a product imported by a Member State but not to a similar national product and which by altering the price, have the same effect upon the free movement of goods as a customs duty.

In this case, the Court disallowed a 'tax' levied by the two Member States on imported gingerbread, the object of which was to offset the competitive disadvantage of domestic gingerbread, the price of which was higher due to the incidence of a national tax on rye, an ingredient of gingerbread.

In the *Statistical Levy* case above, the Italian Government argued that the disputed charge constituted the 'consideration for a service rendered' for the benefit of traders. It was, it was claimed, part of a commercial transaction and could not be designated as a charge having equivalent effect to a customs duty. The Court accepted that a fee might be levied as consideration for a *specific benefit* actually conferred on the importer. However, whatever advantages traders gained from the statistics, they were so general and so difficult to assess (applying to the economy as a whole) that, in the Court's view, the argument failed.

It is an argument which has similarly failed in respect of charges or fees imposed for compulsory veterinary and public health inspections carried out on imported products at frontiers: Case 87/75 *Bresciani* (raw cowhides) and Case 39/73 *Rewe-Zentralfinanz* (plant health inspection on imported apples). In these cases the Court held that the inspections were not for the specific benefit of the traders themselves but were rendered for the benefit of the public as a whole. It should also be appreciated that such inspections may themselves be contrary to the free movement rules. If, by means of a harmonisation Directive, a common system of health controls and standards to be applied *away from* frontiers (in the exporting State) has been established, then further unilateral requirements imposed by the importing State may amount to a discriminatory *technical* barrier to trade in the form of a measure having an equivalent effect to a quantitative restriction (MEEQR): see Case 4/75 *Rewe-Zentralfinanz (San José Scale)*, a companion to the charges case above. In this case, no comprehensive Community system of inspections existed and the national inspections were *justified* on public health grounds under Article 36. A charge cannot be justified in this way.

In the context of the 'fee for services' argument, the Court has held that 'a charge may escape prohibition as a charge having equivalent effect if the charge in question is the consideration for a service actually rendered to the importer and is of an amount commensurate with that service', eg temporary storage facilities requested by a trader: Case 132/82 *Commission* v *Belgium*. Member States are also permitted to recoup from traders the cost of compliance with *Community* measures, as above, designed to facilitate the flow of inter-Member State trade: Case 18/87 *Commission* v *Germany (Re Animals Inspection Fees)*.

DISCRIMINATORY INTERNAL TAXATION (ARTICLE 95)

Article 95

No Member State shall impose, directly or indirectly, on the products of other Member States any internal taxation of any kind in excess of that imposed directly or indirectly on similar domestic products.

Furthermore, no Member State shall impose on the products of other Member States any internal taxation of such a nature as to afford indirect protection to other products.

A Member State's 'internal taxation' comprises financial charges levied within a *general system* applying systematically to both domestic and imported products. Such taxation must not discriminate against imported products where those products are the same or similar to domestic products, ie the level of tax on imports must not exceed that on the domestic products: Article 95(1). Neither must internal taxation be applied to imported products in order to protect the market position of a domestic product which, while not the same or similar, nevertheless competes in the same market: Article 95(2). In Case 170/78 *Commission* v *UK (Re Excise Duties on Wine)*, a competitive relationship was established between beer and more highly taxed imported wines of the cheaper variety, and as a result the relative tax burden on wine reduced.

The purpose of Article 95 was explained by the Court of Justice in Case 171/78 *Commission* v *Denmark*:

> The above-mentioned provisions supplement, within the system of the Treaty, the provisions on the abolition of customs duties and charges having equivalent effect. Their aim is to ensure free movement of goods between the Member States in normal conditions of competition by the elimination of all forms of protection which result from the application of internal taxation which discriminates against products from other Member States. As the Commission has correctly stated, Article 95 must guarantee the complete neutrality of internal taxation as regards competition between domestic products and imported products.

It follows that a charge on imported goods falls *either* under Articles 12 and 13 *or* Article 95. The two regimes are mutually exclusive and cannot be applied at the same time to the same situation. Articles 12 and 13 abolish charges having equivalent effect to a customs duty which are imposed specifically on imported products by reason of their crossing a frontier (domestic products bearing no such charge), whereas Article 95 *permits* the taxation of imported products provided similar, or otherwise competing, domestic products bear the same taxes. The tax system must have what is called 'origin neutrality'.

Much of the case law focuses on the question of whether the domestic and imported products are sufficiently similar or compete with each other so as to bring Article 95(1) or (2) into play. All Member States tax the various types of alcoholic drinks (frequently in a complicated way) for both social and revenue-raising purposes. There is an obvious tendency to favour domestic products. A higher tax on the imported products is usually defended on the basis that they are not similar to the domestically produced drinks. Case 168/78 *Commission* v *France (Re Taxation of Spirits)* involved French legislation which imposed a higher tax on grain-based spirits (imported whisky and gin, etc.) than on fruit-based spirits (home produced brandy and armagnac). The Court held that 'similar' must be interpreted widely from the point of view of the consumer. The home–produced and imported products were broadly in competition and the French legislation was discriminatory and so contrary to Article 95. In the *UK Excise Duty on Wine* case above the issue, as seen, centred not on similarity but on competitiveness and Article 95(2).

The issue was somewhat different in Case 112/84 *Humblot*, in which the French government, using 'objective' criteria, taxed cars over a certain power rating more heavily than those below it. Below a 16 CV power rating, annual car tax increased in a graduated way in proportion to the car's power up to a maximum of 1,100 francs. For cars rated above 16 CV, a flat rate of 5,000 francs was imposed. H was charged this amount on his imported 36 CV car but, on discovering that no French produced car was rated above 16 CV, he claimed the tax was in breach of Article 95. Following an Article 177 reference, the Court stated that:

> Article 95 of the EEC Treaty prohibits the charging on cars exceeding a given power rating for tax purposes of a special fixed tax the amount of which is several times the highest amount of the progressive tax payable on cars of less than the said power rating for tax purposes, where the only cars subject to the special tax are imported, in particular from other Member States.

The basis of this ruling was that:

> ... the special tax reduces the amount of competition to which cars of domestic manufacture are subject and hence is contrary to the principle of neutrality with which domestic taxation must comply.

Of particular significance among the internal taxation systems of the Member States, at least as regards *indirect* taxation applied to goods and services, is Value–Added Tax (VAT). The essential feature of this tax is that a supplier of goods or services is liable for tax assessed on the value of the product when he disposes of it, and may set off against this liability the tax paid on the value of the product when he acquired it, in other words the net liability is to pay tax on the added value.

On the basis of Article 99 of the Treaty much work has been done over the years to harmonise various aspects of indirect taxation and, in particular, to develop a Community system of VAT. This involves harmonisation of the *base* or scope of the tax (some countries allow zero rating for some goods), harmonisation of the *number* of rates and harmonisation of the *actual rates*. It would now appear to be agreed that identical rates throughout the Member States are not necessary, and that if they are brought sufficiently close together this will prevent any significant distortion of trade and competition. It is envisaged that an agreed Community-wide VAT system will be in operation before 1997, which will not discriminate between goods and services according to where they are produced with the EC. This is a result which will achieve the elimination through the harmonisation process of a *fiscal* barrier to the free movement of goods between Member States and which will eliminate elaborate bureaucratic procedures at frontiers regarding the collection of VAT (*physical* barriers). Similar work is proceeding in relation to *excise duties* and in 1991 the Member States accepted the principle of binding minimum excise rates on petrol, tobacco and alcohol.

INTERNAL TECHNICAL BARRIERS: QUANTITATIVE RESTRICTIONS AND MEASURES HAVING EQUIVALENT EFFECT

As with customs duties and charges, the Treaty basis for the Community's attack on these *non-tariff* barriers is Article 3(a). The more detailed rules are to be found in Articles 30–36:

Article 30

Quantitative restrictions on imports and all measures having equivalent effect shall, without prejudice to the following provisions, be prohibited between Member States.

Article 34 makes similar provision as regards exports. The scheme laid down by the Treaty broadly corresponds to that applied to customs duties and charges: 'standstill' provisions and gradual elimination by the end of the twelve-year transitional period at the latest (ie by the end of 1969). However, as seen in Chapter Eleven, Article 36 allows Member States to *derogate* from the free movement in Articles 30–34 within strictly defined limits for the purpose of protecting certain listed interests of general public importance, eg public health. Such national rules as are justified under Article 36 are nevertheless not allowed to remain as obstacles to the free movement of goods between Member States. By a process of harmonisation, the interests they protect are secured – but on the basis of *common* Community standards which the goods of all Member States must meet.

There is no definition of a QR (or quota) in the Treaty but it was defined by Ehlermann in 1972 as follows:

Any governmental measure adopted in a general form and directed to individuals which provides that a certain amount of goods, defined either by quantity or value, may be imported or exported during a specific period of time.

It includes any prohibition which amounts to a partial or total (zero quota) restraint on imports or exports: see Case 34/79 *R v Henn and Darby*.

Quantitative restrictions on imports (total or partial) can clearly prove more effective as protectionist measures than customs duties. Partial restraints reduce the supply of imported goods, raise their price, and so reduce or eliminate any competitive advantage they may have over domestic products. However, in terms of free movement within the Community, national quota systems dating from the years before or during the Second World War had ceased to be a major problem by the time the Community was established in 1958, due to measures of liberalization achieved in the more immediate post-war years within the framework of GATT and the Organization for European Economic Co-operation (OEEC).

Nevertheless cases do still arise involving specific import restraints which Member States seek to justify under Article 36. For example:

In Case 40/82 *Commission v UK (Re Imports of Poultry Meat)*, an import licence requirement for poultry was introduced in the UK which had the effect of a total ban on imports from six Member States. The requirement was allegedly designed to prevent the spread of 'Newcastle disease' (a contagious disease affecting poultry) and was defended on the basis of Article 36.

In Article 169 proceedings, the Court of Justice found that the UK measure did not form part of a seriously considered health policy; it operated as a disguised restriction on trade and was contrary to Article 30.

At the height of concern in the UK in late 1989 about 'mad cow disease' (BSE), West Germany banned UK beef products on the grounds that they were a danger to human health and life: see Article 36. The ban was eventually lifted and no legal action was taken. Arguments against such a ban included the existence at Community level of a comprehensive, harmonised health safety system operating within exporting States.

National measures which are contrary to Article 30, in that they amount to measures having an equivalent effect to quantitative restrictions (MEEQRs), are many and various. They frequently operate in a subtle and disguised way with the purpose of protecting home-produced products from imports. They operate to isolate national markets, contrary to the concept of a common market, and such fragmentation has the effect of increasing the costs (and prices) of producers, who are required to meet the differing requirements of different Member States.

Normally such measures discriminate, either directly or indirectly, against imported goods but, for the Court of Justice, the prime mark of an MEEQR is its *restrictive effect* on inter-Member State trade.

Article 2 of Commission Directive 70/50 on the abolition of MEEQRs on imports states that:

1. This Directive covers measures, other than those applicable equally to domestic or imported products, which hinder imports which could otherwise take place, including measures which make importation more difficult or costly than the disposal of domestic products.

2. In particular, it covers measures which make imports or the disposal, at any marketing stage, of imported products subject to a condition – other than a formality – which is required in respect of imported products only, or a condition differing from that required for domestic products and more difficult to satisfy. Equally, it covers, in particular, measures which favour domestic products or grant them a preference, other than an aid ...

Article 2(3)(a)–(s) contains a long, non-exhaustive list of such measures which it is not necessary to refer to here.

The Directive provides clear indications of the Commission's view of Article 30 as applied to MEEQRs. Article 2 covers national measures which apply *only* to imports, which directly discriminate against them and which are overtly protective. They have been referred to as *'distinctly applicable'* measures. In respect of such a measure (as with a QR), a *derogation* from Articles 30–34 under Article 36 will only be allowed if it can be justified under one of the six heads in Article 36 and does not constitute a means of arbitrary discrimination or a disguised restriction on trade between Member States.

Expressly omitted from Article 2(1) of the Directive are national measures which are 'applicable equally to domestic or imported products' ('*indistinctly applicable*' or '*equally applicable*' measures). These are to be found in Article 3:

This Directive also covers measures governing the marketing of products which deal, in particular, with shape, size, weight, composition, presentation, identification or putting up and which are equally applicable to domestic and imported products, where the restrictive effect of such measures on the free movement of goods exceeds the effects intrinsic to trade rules.

This is the case, in particular, where:
- the restrictive effects on the free movement of goods are out of proportion to their purpose;
- the same objective can be attained by other means which are less of a hindrance to trade.

National technical rules and standards of the type listed may have a justifiable purpose regarding, for example, the protection of public health or environmental protection. If such is the case, measures of this kind will generally only breach Article 30 where their 'restrictive effects on the free movement of goods are out of proportion to their purpose' (ie they are subject to the principle of proportionality). As we have already seen in the case of allowable Article 36 *derogations* from the free movement rules in Article 30 for distinctly applicable national measures, where, as here, equally applicable national rules reflecting the public interest (in what are termed 'mandatory requirements') override Article 30, obstacles to free movement will again remain. In both cases, the national rules embodying such obstacles must be harmonised so that common 'European' standards can be set as the criterion for goods from all the Member States.

'Equally applicable' measures are frequently indirectly discriminatory in their effect. In practice, whereas *domestic* products will meet the technical rules and minimum standards laid down, goods from other Member States, which meet their own national requirements, may well not do so and hence may be excluded from the market of the importing state – subject, as above, to the measure being justifiable and complying with the principle of proportionality. Alternatively, where an equally applicable national measure serves *no* purpose of public interest but merely acts as a ban on imports, it will be struck down as being in its effect a disguised restriction on inter-Member State trade which partitions the market: see, in particular, the decision of the Court of Justice in Case 120/78 *Cassis de Dijon*, below.

Although, on occasion, the Court has referred to Directive 70/50 (the main purpose of which was to provide guidance on MEEQRs to the Member States), it has laid down its own definition of MEEQRs on imports. In Case 8/74 *Dassonville*, it defined them as:

FREE MOVEMENT OF GOODS WITH SPECIAL REFERENCE TO ARTICLES 30-36

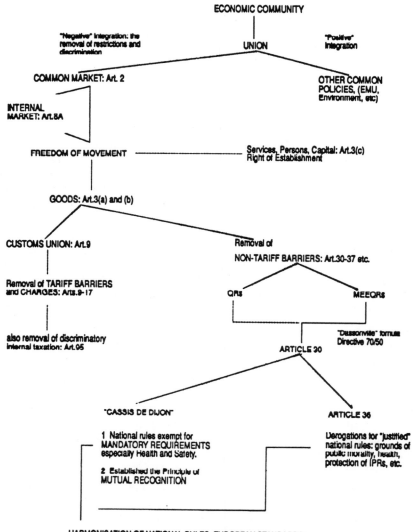

All trading rules enacted by Member States which are capable of hindering, directly or indirectly, actually or potentially, intra-Community trade.

The phrase 'rules enacted by Member States' apparently excludes the activities of undertakings and private individuals acting independently without backing from the State: see Case 249/81 *Commission* v *Ireland* below. It should also be recalled that, although Article 30 is addressed to Member States, it is directly effective. Thus the cases which follow cover both Article 169 enforcement actions brought by the Commission against Member States and Article 177 references arising out of actions brought by traders against a variety of public authorities in national courts. They are merely a sample of the several hundred that have already been decided.

DISTINCTLY APPLICABLE MEASURES (AS IN ARTICLE 2(1) AND (2) OF DIRECTIVE 70/50)

1. Conditions imposed on imports but not on similar domestic products and differing conditions which hinder imports.

Case 4/75 *Rewe-Zentralfinanz (San José Scale)*

Plant health inspections (obstacles of a physical and technical nature) applied by regional West German authorities only to imported apples were caught by Article 30. However, being designed to control a pest called San José Scale, which was not to be found in domestic apples, the inspections were found to be justified on health grounds under Article 36. There was a genuine risk of the harmful organism spreading if no inspection was held on importation. The discrimination against imports was therefore not arbitrary.

The Court stressed the fact that frontier inspections make imports more difficult or costly (although any charges made, as we have seen, are contrary to Articles 12 and 13). Common rules for the control of the pest in exporting states under Directive 69/446 did not disallow protective measures taken by importing States.

As regards 'a condition differing from that required for domestic products and more difficult to satisfy' (Article 2(2) of the Directive), an illustration is provided by Case 42/82 *Commission* v *France (Re Italian Table Wines)*:

277

Italian wine imported into France was first tested by the Italian authorities. At French customs it was delayed for an excessive period of time pending analysis to ensure it complied with French quality standards. Although the Court conceded that random checks might be made, it found that the French measures, involving systematic testing greatly in excess of that required for domestically produced wine, were discriminatory. A defence plea for derogation on public health grounds under Article 36 failed as the French tests did not comply with the principle of proportionality.

2   *Measures which make imports more difficult by, for example, discriminating between channels of trade.*

The following case, like *San José Scale*, similarly concerned a measure affecting imports only – Belgian rules concerning certificates of origin for imported Scotch whisky:

Case 8/74 *Procureur du Roi v. Dassonville*

D, a Belgian importer of Scotch whisky, was unable to obtain, as required by Belgian law, a British certificate of origin made out in his name from his French suppliers. He therefore produced one of his own making and was charged with forgery. He pleaded that the national rule was contrary to Article 30.

The Court of Justice held that the Belgian legislation favoured direct importers as distinct from traders importing the authentic product from other Member States where it was already in free circulation.

3.   *Measures which favour domestic products or grant them a preference.*

Case 152/78 *Commission v. France (Re Advertising of Alcoholic Beverages)*

The French government adopted measures which placed restrictions on the advertising of grain spirits (whisky, gin, vodka, etc.) which were almost entirely imported. Restrictions were not placed on the advertising of fruit-based spirits such as brandy.

The Court held that national rules on advertising may amount to MEEQRs if there is a possibility that they may affect the marketing prospects of goods imported from other Member States.

Case 249/81 *Commission v. Ireland (Re 'Buy Irish' Campaign)*

In 1978 the Irish government introduced a three-year 'Buy-Irish' campaign to help promote Irish products (at the expense of imports). The campaign was conducted by a company known as the Irish Goods

Council. The aims of the campaign were decided by the Ministry of Industry, which also provided financial support particularly for a massive advertising campaign.

The Court held that the activities in question were in breach of Article 30. In the Court's view:

Such a practice cannot escape the prohibition laid down by Article 30 of the Treaty solely because it is not based on decisions which are binding upon undertakings. Even measures adopted by the government of a Member State which do not have binding effect may be capable of influencing the conduct of traders and consumers in that State and thus of frustrating the aims of the Community as set out in Article 2 and enlarged upon in Article 3 of the Treaty.

A distinction was made by the Court in a case with similar facts. In Case 222/82 *Apple and Pear Development Council* v *Lewis*, the Court stated that:

... a body such as the Development Council, which is set up by the government of a Member State and is financed by a charge imposed on growers, cannot under Community law enjoy the same freedom as regards the methods of advertising used as that enjoyed by producers themselves or producers' associations of a voluntary character.

In particular, such a body is under a duty not to engage in any advertising intended to discourage the purchase of products of other Member States or to disparage those products in the eyes of consumers. Nor must it advise consumers to purchase domestic products solely by reason of their national origin.

On the other hand, Article 30 does not prevent such a body from drawing attention, in its publicity, to the specific qualities of fruit growing in the Member State in question or from organizing campaigns to promote the sale of certain varieties, mentioning their particular properties, even if those varieties are typical of national production.

See also Case 72/83 *Campus Oil* v *Minister for Industry and Energy* which is discussed later.

DEROGATION FROM ARTICLES 30–34 UNDER ARTICLE 36

Article 36

The provisions of Articles 30 to 34 shall not preclude prohibitions or restrictions on imports, exports or goods in transit justified on grounds of public morality, public policy or public security; the protection of health and life of humans, animals or plants; the protection of national treasures possessing artistic, historic or archaeological value; or the protection of industrial and commercial property. Such prohibitions or restrictions shall not, however, constitute a means of arbitrary discrimination or a disguised restriction on trade between Member States.

Although in terms Article 36 applies to 'prohibitions or restrictions on imports...' generally (both QRs an MEEQRs), since the Court of Justice in Case 120/78 *Cassis de Dijon* established, as regards *indistinctly* applicable measures (MEEQRs), that where they are necessary for the protection of mandatory requirements (as noted above), they will not breach Article 30 at all, *derogation from* Article 30 under Article 36 normally only applies to *distinctly* applicable national measures (and QRs).

Article 36 can be broken down into three overlapping parts:

1. *An exhaustive list of possible grounds for derogation*: a Member State seeking to defend its restrictive rules must show that they fall within one of those grounds. Thus, in Case 95/81 *Commission* v *Italy* (*Re Advance Payments for Imports*) and other cases, the Court held that Article 36 does not justify derogation from Article 30 on the grounds of the protection of consumers (but see *Cassis de Dijon*, below).

2. *A stipulation that any prohibition or restriction must be justified*. A national trading rule is justified if it can be proved to be *necessary*, and no more than necessary, to achieve its particular objective, eg the protection of health and life of humans. Derogation therefore involves compliance with the principle of *proportionality*.

3. *The proviso in the second sentence* that national prohibitions or restrictions must not constitute a means of arbitrary discrimination or a disguised restriction on trade. These requirements must be considered in conjunction with the questions of justification and proportionality above. Arbitrary discrimination cannot be justified on objective grounds: in the *San José Scale* case discussed earlier, the

discrimination against the imported apples was justifiable in terms of the necessity of inspecting the applies in the face of the risk of the insect disease spreading. Similarly, a failure to stay within the bounds of the proportionality principle can result in a measure being struck down as a disguised restriction on trade, eg the excessive testing of Italian wine at the French frontier in Case 42/82 *Commission* v *France*, also discussed earlier.

What all this amounts to is that Article 36, although allowing derogation from the fundamental principle of the free movement of goods, must, for that reason, be interpreted strictly. Obstacles to free movement will delay the establishment of a genuine Common Market at least until the national rules which remain to create such obstacles are harmonised.

Turning to the six grounds in Article 36 upon which prohibitions or restrictions may be justified, the case law on the protection of industrial and commercial property (eg patent and trade mark rights established under national law) is closely related to certain aspects of competition policy and is therefore dealt with separately in Chapter Eighteen. It will be seen that the grounds for derogation are essentially of a non-economic nature:

It follows that such objects as the promotion of employment or investment, curbing inflation and controlling the balance of payments fall outside Article 36: Oliver.

Protection of the Health and Life of Humans, Animals and Plants

Much of the case law on Article 36 (some of which has already been referred to, eg the inspections of imported apples in the *San José Scale* case and Italian wine in Case 42/82 *Commission* v *France* concerns the protection of health. To be capable of justification, a measure must form part of a 'seriously considered health policy'. This, as seen, was not the case in Case 40/82 *Commission* v *UK (Re Imports of Poultry Meat)* in which, shortly before Christmas 1981, the Ministry of Agriculture, Fisheries and Food suddenly imposed what amounted to a ban (QR) on imports of French turkeys. It sought to justify this measure on the basis that it was necessary to control Newcastle disease (which affects poultry) and that the measures taken to do this in France were insufficient. There had been no outbreak of Newcastle disease in France for five years. The Court held that the ban was excessive and constituted a disguised restriction on trade. (See as a sequel to this case *Bourgoin* v *MAFF* (1986) in Chapter Twenty).

Similarly, the French authorities' attempt to justify their restrictions on the advertising of (largely imported) grain spirits on the ground of the protection of health, when no such restrictions were imposed on home-produced brandy and armagnac, was not accepted by the Court of Justice: Case 152/78 *Commission* v *France* (see also above).

In Case 104/75 *De Peijper*, the Court stated that:

> Health and the life of humans rank first among the property or interests protected by Article 36 and it is for the Member States, within the limits imposed by the Treaty, to decide what degree of protection they intend to assure and in particular how strict the checks to be carried out are to be.

> Nevertheless it emerges from Article 36 that national rules or practices which do restrict imports of pharmaceutical products or are capable of doing so are only compatible with the Treaty to the extent to which they are necessary for the effective protection of health and life of humans.

> National rules or practices do not fall within the exception in Article 36 if the health and life of humans can be as effectively protected by measures which do not restrict intra-Community trade so much.

Difficult scientific and dietary questions can arise in relation to national rules regarding the composition of foodstuffs, in particular the presence of additives. An added *legal* complication is that although such rules are general, ie they amount to indistinctly applicable MEEQR's applying to *both* imported and domestic products, where the issue is that of the protection of health the Court of Justice may choose to deal with it on the basis of Article 36 rather than under the *Cassis de Dijon* 'mandatory requirements' of which the protection of health is one. Clearly, Article 36 would be pleaded in cases prior to the *Cassis de Dijon* decision in 1979.

Case 174/82 *Sandoz BV*

Muesli bars to which vitamins had been added were subjected to no marketing restrictions in West Germany and Belgium. In the Netherlands, where it was considered that the vitamins could be a danger to public health, prior authorisation was required from the Dutch health authorities. S. imported such bars into the Netherlands but was refused permission to market them.

Following a reference to the Court of Justice under Article 177, the Court held that the Dutch rules were in breach of Article 30. On the question of derogation under Article 36, the Court stated that:

It appears from the file that vitamins are not in themselves harmful substances but on the contrary are recognized by modern science as necessary for the human organism. Nevertheless excessive consumption of them over a prolonged period may have harmful effects, the extent of which varies according to the type of vitamin: there is generally a greater risk with vitamins soluble in fat than with those soluble in water. According to the observations submitted to the Court, however, scientific research does not appear to be sufficiently advanced to be able to determine with certainty the critical quantities and the precise effects.

... in so far as there are uncertainties at the present state of scientific research it is for the Member States, in the absence of harmonization, to decide what degree of protection of the health and life of humans they intend to assure, having regard however for the requirements of the free movement of goods within the Community.

Those principles also apply to substances such as vitamins which are not as a general rule harmful in themselves but may have special harmful effects solely if taken to excess as part of the general nutrition, the composition of which is unforeseeable and cannot be monitored. In view of the uncertainties inherent in the scientific assessment, national rules prohibiting, without prior authorization, the marketing of foodstuffs to which vitamins have been added are justified on principle within the meaning of Article 36 of the Treaty on grounds of the protection of human health.

Nevertheless the principle of proportionality which underlies the last sentence of Article 36 of the Treaty requires that the power of the Member States to prohibit imports of the products in question from other Member States should be restricted to what is necessary to attain the legitimate aim of protecting health. Accordingly, national rules providing for such a prohibition are justified only if authorizations to market are granted when they are compatible with the need to protect health.

Such an assessment is, however, difficult to make in relation to additives such as vitamins the above-mentioned characteristics of which exclude the possibility of foreseeing or monitoring the quantities consumed as part of the general nutrition and the degree of harmfulness of which cannot be determined with sufficient certainty. Nevertheless, although in view of the present stage of harmonization of national laws at the Community level a wide discretion must be left to the Member States, they must, in order to observe the principle of proportionality, authorize marketing when the addition of vitamins to foodstuffs meets a real need, especially a technical or nutritional one.

The first question must therefore be answered to the effect that Community law permits national rules prohibiting without prior authorization the marketing of foodstuffs lawfully marketed in another Member State to which vitamins have been added, provided that the marketing is authorized when the addition of vitamins meets a real need, especially a technical or nutritional one.

Similar questions arose regarding (equally applicable) German rules, which in practice constituted an absolute ban on the marketing of beers containing additives, in Case 178/84 *Commission v Germany (Re Beer Purity Laws)*. The German legislation dated back to the sixteenth century. The ban being in breach of Article 30, on the question of derogation on the ground of the protection of health under Article 36 – the German government pointed out the high consumption of beer by German drinkers – the Court ruled that:

> It must be observed that the German rules on additives applicable to beer result in the exclusion of all the additives authorised in the other Member States and not the exclusion of just some of them for which there is concrete justification by reason of the risks which they involve in view of the eating habits of the German population; moreover those rules do not lay down any procedure whereby traders can obtain authorisation for the use of a specific additive in the manufacture of beer by means of a measure of general application.

> ... Consequently, in so far as the German rules on additives in beer entail a general ban on additives, their application to beers imported from other Member States is contrary to the requirements of Community law as laid down in the case-law of the Court, since that prohibition is contrary to the principle of proportionality and is therefore not covered by the exception provided for in Article 36 of the EEC Treaty.

Public Morality

Case 34/79 *R v Henn and Darby* involved a criminal prosecution following a seizure (a QR) of pornographic literature imported by the defendants from Denmark into the UK. Their 'Euro-defence' was that the legislation on the basis of which the customs authorities had impounded the goods was contrary to the free movement rules in Article 30. This was met by the argument that the seizure was justified on the grounds of public morality under Article 36. Following a somewhat surprising finding that there was no lawful domestic trade in such literature in the UK, the Court, pursuing an equally applicable or equal treatment line, held that the prohibition did not amount to arbitrary discrimination.

Similar questions arose later in Case 121/85 *Conegate v Customs and Excise Commissioners* but led to a different outcome:

C imported a consignment of inflatable rubber 'love dolls' from West Germany. The customs authorities seized the goods on the ground that they were 'indecent or obscene' and therefore subject to a prohibition on importation under the Customs Consolidation Act 1876. When C claimed that the seizure was in breach of Article 30, the customs authorities relied on the 'public morality' justification in Article 36.

There was no ban on the manufacture of such goods in the UK although their marketing was subject to certain restrictions. Following a reference to the Court of Justice under Article 177, the Court stated that:

[This] question raises, in the first place, the general problem of whether a prohibition on the importation of certain goods may be justified on grounds of public morality where the legislation of the Member State concerned contains no prohibition on the manufacture or marketing of the same products within the national territory.

So far as that problem is concerned, it must be borne in mind that according to Article 36 of the EEC Treaty the provisions relating to the free movement of goods within the Community do not preclude prohibitions on imports justified 'on grounds of public morality'. As the Court held in its judgment [in *Henn and Darby*], in principle it is for each Member State to determine in accordance with its own scale of values and in the form selected by it the requirements of public morality in its territory.

However, although Community law leaves the Member States free to make their own assessments of the indecent or obscene character of certain articles it must be pointed out that the fact that goods cause offence cannot be regarded as sufficiently serious to justify restrictions on the free movement of goods where the Member State concerned does not adopt, with respect to the same goods manufactured or marketed within its territory, penal measures or other serious and effective measures intended to prevent the distribution of such goods in its territory.

Public Policy and Public Security

Very few cases have raised these issues of general interest. However, public policy and public security were both argued by the Irish government in Case 72/83 *Campus Oil* v *Minister for Industry and Energy*:

> Irish legislation required importers of petroleum products to purchase up to 35 per cent of their requirements from Ireland's only (State-owned) refinery at prices fixed by the Minister. The measure was clearly discriminatory and protective and contrary to Article 30. It was argued, however, that the measure was necessary on the ground that the importance of oil for the maintenance of the life of the country made it indispensable to maintain refining capacity on the national territory and the system under question was the only means of ensuring that the refinery's output could be marketed.

> The Court accepted that an interruption of supplies of petroleum products could be regarded as a matter of public security (even though the measure also achieved purely economic objectives). The Court held that:

> 1. The purchasing obligation could only be continued if no less restrictive measure was capable of achieving the same objective.

> 2. The quantities covered by the scheme must not exceed the minimum supply requirements without which the public security of the State would be affected or the level of production necessary to keep the refinery's production capacity available.

INDISTINCTLY (OR EQUALLY) APPLICABLE MEASURES (AS IN ARTICLE 3 OF DIRECTIVE 70/50)

It will be recalled that Article 3 of the Directive covers measures governing the marketing of products which deal with such matters as their shape, size, composition or identification. Unlike the measures covered in Article 2, they apply to both domestic and imported goods. On the basis of Article 3 such measures will be in breach of Article 30, in particular, where:

- the restrictive effects on the free movement of goods are out of proportion to the purpose; [or]

- the same objective can be attained by other means which are less a hindrance to trade.

Thus, for example, in Case 261/81 *Walter Rau*, Belgian rules required margarine to be packed in cube-shaped boxes. The alleged purpose of the rules was to enable consumers to distinguish margarine from butter. The Court held that the rules were in breach of Article 30; the same objective could be achieved by labelling, which was less a hindrance to trade.

The Belgian rules were not overtly discriminatory; they did not expressly treat similar products (domestic and imported margarine) in different ways. However in so far as they were *different from* similar rules (if any) in other Member States, they had the effect of treating different situations in the same way. In practice, an apparently neutral criterion (cube-shaped), which would presumably be met by domestic producers, would probably not be met by producers in other Member States, unless they went to the expense of putting another production line into operation in order to meet the Belgian requirement. The real intention behind the rules *may* have been of a discriminatory and protectionist nature.

In the most important case on indistinctly or equally applicable measures of this kind, the Court concentrated on the exclusionary *effects* of such rules in the face of the need to establish and maintain the free movement of goods within the Common Market:

Case 120/78 *Rewe (Cassis de Dijon)*

German legislation laid down that certain fruit liqueurs (such as Cassis) could only be marketed if they contained a minimum alcohol content of 25 per cent. German products met this requirement but it made it impossible for Rewe lawfully to import and sell French 'Cassis de Dijon', which had an alcohol content of between 15 and 20 per cent.

Rewe brought an action against the German alcohol monopoly, and the national court asked the Court of Justice if the German rules were consistent with Article 30.

The Court concentrated first on the exclusionary nature of the German rule and examined whether there might exist grounds for its justification:

The plaintiff takes the view that the fixing by the German rules of a minimum alcohol content leads to the result that well-known spirits products from other Member States of the Community cannot be sold in the Federal Republic of Germany and that the said provision therefore constitutes a restriction on the free movement of goods between Member States which exceeds the bounds of the trade rules reserved to the latter.

In its view it is a measure having an effect equivalent to a quantitative restriction on imports contrary to Article 30 of the EEC Treaty.

In the absence of common rules relating to the production and marketing of alcohol – a proposal for a regulation submitted to the Council by the Commission on 7 December 1976 (Official Journal, C309, p.2) not yet having received the Council's approval – it is for the Member States to regulate all matters relating to the production and marketing of alcohol and alcoholic beverages on their own territory.

Obstacles to movement within the Community resulting from disparities between the national laws relating to the marketing of the products in question must be accepted in so far as those provisions may be recognised as being necessary in order to satisfy mandatory requirements relating in particular to the effectiveness of fiscal supervision, the protection of public health, the fairness of commercial transactions and the defence of the consumer.

Having introduced the concept of *mandatory requirements* in relation to obstacles to free movement arising from disparities between national marketing rules, the Court rejected claims by the German authorities that the minimum alcohol rule was necessary for the protection of public health (based on a dubious 'tolerance' argument) and for the protection of the consumer against unfair commercial practices (based on the argument that Cassis, with a lower alcohol content, gained an unfair competitive advantage; tax on alcohol being the most expensive cost item). As a result:

It is clear from the foregoing that the requirements relating to the minimum alcohol content of alcoholic beverages do not serve a purpose which is in the general interest and such as to take precedence over the requirements of the free movement of goods, which constitutes one of the fundamental rules of the Community.

The actual effect of such a rule was explained by the Court of Justice in the following terms:

In practice, the principle effect of requirements of this nature is to promote alcoholic beverages having a high alcohol content by excluding from the national market products of other Member States which do not answer that description.

It therefore appears that the unilateral requirement imposed by the rules of a Member State of a minimum alcohol content for the purposes of the sale of alcoholic beverages constitutes an obstacle to trade which is incompatible with the provisions of Article 30 of the Treaty.

> *There is therefore no valid reason why, provided that they have been lawfully produced and marketed in one of the Member States, alcoholic beverages should not be introduced into any other Member State*; the sale of such products may not be subject to a legal prohibition on the marketing of beverages with an alcohol content lower than the limit set by the national rules. (Emphasis added.)

In the first part of the final paragraph, the Court introduced the principle of *mutual recognition*, which has *general* effect as a *presumption*. It applies, in the pursuit of free movement, unless national rules can be justified on the basis of mandatory requirements. The relationship between (1) mutual recognition, (2) what is termed the *mandatory requirements* 'rule of reason', which takes a national rule *outside* Article 30, and (3) the Commission's drive to harmonise national rules has been explained by Swann:

> In the process of delivering its judgment the Court of Justice also made the point that any product legally made and sold in one member state must in principle be admitted to the markets of the others. National rules and standards can only create barriers where they are necessary to satisfy 'mandatory' requirements such as public health, consumer protection, etc. Moreover, and this is the key point, any rule must be the 'essential guarantee' of the interest, the protection of which is regarded as being justified. It will be remembered that in the *Cassis* case the German Government defended its minimum alcoholic content rule on grounds of consumer protection. But the Court noted that that objective could have been achieved by merely requiring the label to show the actual alcoholic content. The rule was not essential to guarantee the protection of the consumer. It does not follow that in the light of *Cassis* the need to harmonize no longer exists. There will be some situations where the need to have rules is essential and goods not conforming to them will be excluded. In such cases the only way forward is to harmonize. But there will be many cases where the differences of standards as between states are really relatively trivial and are not essential to protect the public. In such cases harmonization will no longer be required.

Where differences between standards are 'relatively trivial', mutual recognition will apply; where mandatory requirements must be preserved, the rules which embody them (like the rules embodying justifiable Article 36 derogations) must be *harmonised* to ensure the free movement of goods *as well*.

In *Cassis de Dijon*, the Court of Justice *in effect* provided new grounds for derogation from Article 30 where obstacles to free movement arise from disparities in national marketing rules (*equally* applicable MEEQRs), although strictly speaking in the cases involving the mandatory requirement argument, national rules are examined in the context of Article 30 to establish if they are in breach of that article at all.

Article 36, with its *closed* list of justifiable derogations, remains to be applied in cases involving *distinctly* applicable measures, although, as we have seen, the protection of public health features in both lists, leading the Court on occasion to apply Article 36 to equally applicable, albeit clearly discriminatory rules: see, for example, Case 124/81 *Commission* v *UK (Re UHT Milk)*, in which the Court held that there was no genuine health risk because exporting States maintained standards and controls equivalent to those in the UK.

Since *Cassis de Dijon*, the Court of Justice has added to the list of mandatory requirements. Apart from the protection of public health, the original list included, 'in particular', three further issues of public interest: 'the effectiveness of fiscal supervision' (eg national rules applied to goods and designed to prevent and detect tax evasion), 'the fairness of commercial transactions' (eg passing off rules) and 'the defense of the consumer' (eg bans on false or misleading labelling of products: see Case 788/79 *Gilli and Andres*).

In Case 240/83 *Brûleurs d'Huiles Usagées*, environmental protection was added (and argued unsuccessfully in Case 302/86 *Commission* v *Denmark* (*Re Disposable Beer Cans*). In Case 155/80 *Oebel*, the Court recognised that legitimate interests of economic and social policy, such as the improvement of working conditions, might, so long as they were consistent with the Treaty, constitute mandatory requirements. In a similar vein, the Court has held that restrictions arising from national rules governing the opening hours of retail premises on Sundays (or governing the working hours of employees in such premises) might be justified by reference to 'national or regional socio-cultural characteristics': see Case C-169/91 *Stoke-on-Trent City Council and Norwich City Council* v *B. & Q. plc*. In Cases 60 and 61/84 *Cinéthèque*, the Court upheld a non-discriminatory French rule prohibiting the sale or hire of video-cassettes of films within a year of their first showing at a cinema. Although the rule restricted the import of videos from other Member States, the Court held the restriction to be justified and not in breach of Article 30. No specific category of mandatory requirement was stated by the Court but Advocate General Slynn had argued in terms of the protection of the film industry – a cultural basis?

Of the many cases where national marketing rules have failed the mandatory requirements test, the following are taken as illustrations, in addition to those discussed above:

> A British regulation *requiring* retail goods such as clothing and textiles to be marked with their country of origin. Manufacturers remained free to indicate their own national origin if they wished but it was not necessary to compel them to do so: Case 207/83 *Commission* v *UK (Re Origin Marking of Retail Goods)*.

> National rules restricting the name 'Edam' to cheese having a minimum fat content of 40 per cent: Case 286/86 *Deserbais*. Similarly, in Case C-196/89 *Italy* v *Nespoli*, in a similar situation, consumer protection and public health arguments failed to impress the Court.

> German rules designed to protect the 'Bocksbeutel' (a distinctive bulbous-shaped bottle) and its contents, a quality wine from a particular region, from unfair competition. The Court did not allow the rules to restrict the importation of Italian wine traditionally produced in similar bottles. The principle of mutual recognition overrode the rules' discriminatory and protective effects: Case 16/83 *Prantl*.

> National rules prohibiting the use of common wheat flour in the production of pasta products: Case 407/85 *Drei Glocken GmbH*.

In Case 113/80 *Commission* v *Ireland (Re Restrictions on Importation of Souvenirs)*, the Court held that Irish Orders requiring that imported souvenirs either be marked 'Foreign' or with their country of origin were

> not measures which are applicable to domestic products and to imported products without distinction but rather a set of rules which apply only to imported products and are therefore discriminatory in nature, with the result that the measures in issue are not covered by the decisions cited above which relate exclusively to provisions that regulate in a uniform manner the marketing of domestic products and imported products.

'The decisions cited above' included *Cassis de Dijon* and *Gilli and Andres*. Therefore the Irish government's attempt to justify the Orders on the grounds of consumer protection failed — and also failed under Article 36 as consumer protection does not feature in that article as a ground for derogation.

Nevertheless, there is an important link between Article 36 and mandatory requirements. Just as a distinctly applicable measure must comply with the principle of proportionality in order to qualify for derogation from Article 30 under Article 36, the same principle also applies to claims that equally applicable national marketing rules are 'necessary' in order to meet mandatory requirements. In *Walter Rau*, the Court stated that:

> It is also necessary for such rules to be proportionate to the aim in view. If a Member State has a choice between various measures to attain the same objective it should choose the means which least restrict the free movement of goods.

Thus, in *Cassis de Dijon* itself, even if the protection of public health and fairness of commercial transactions claims were genuine, the minimum alcohol content rule was not necessary to achieve those aims. Clear labelling and pricing were all that was necessary and the consumer could exercise his right to choose. (Remember the last two sentences of Article 3 of Directive 70/50.)

In the Sunday trading cases (see, particularly, Case C-312/89 *Conforama*, Case C-332/89 *Marchandise*, Case C-169/91 *Stoke-on-Trent City Council and Norwich City Council v B & Q plc*), the Court of Justice eventually clearly held that the restrictions in issue (eg the Shops Act 1950) escaped Article 30 under the rule of reason. The restrictions on opening hours were no more than necessary to achieve their socio-cultural aims, although just what those aims are in precise terms is open to various interpretations. The rules in question are equally applicable, they are not discriminatory and they do not offend the principle of proportionality. In fact, there is a strong body of academic opinion (see both White and Steiner in 'References and Further Reading') that such rules pose no threat to the single market and should not fall to be *considered* under Article 30 at all. They merely restrict, in equal measure, the volume of sales of both imported and domestic goods by certain undertakings (chain stores, DIY and garden centres, etc.).

HARMONISATION MEASURES, THE FREE MOVEMENT OF GOODS AND THE INTERNAL MARKET

It will be recalled that under Article 8A EEC (Article 7a EC when the TEU comes into effect) the Internal Market 'shall comprise [amongst other things] an area without internal frontiers in which the free movement of goods ... is ensured'. We have seen how, to this end, the Commission's White Paper of 1985 on the completion of the Internal Market by the end of 1992 initiated a massive legislative programme to eliminate remaining physical, fiscal and technical barriers to the free movement of goods (see the Introduction to this chapter). The main legal instrument for putting this programme into effect was the harmonisation Directive, which, while maintaining common 'European' standards, eliminates obstacles to free movement: see Article 100A.

In the course of discussing the Court's case law on free movement from the early 1960s, we have already seen how, for example, expensive delays (physical barriers) could arise from frontier controls applied to goods as a result of the need to subject them to import VAT at every internal Community frontier (a fiscal barrier), or from the perceived need to examine, test and certify imported food products at frontiers in accordance with national criteria in the interests of public health (technical barriers). We have also seen how differing national rules and standards fragment the market, increase production costs and hinder free movement irrespective of frontiers.

In many of the free movement cases already considered, the Court's decision has been given in the light of 'the present stage of Community law' in which there were 'no common rules'. That is, in the absence of Community legislation which has established a common (or complete) regime of control. Where Directives have been in place, we have seen the onus for, say inspections and certification, move from the frontier and the authorities of the importing State to the production centres of the exporting State.

Although the categorisation of barriers into physical, fiscal and technical is somewhat arbitrary and overlapping, the problems concerning frontier controls have been graphically illustrated by Pelkmans and Winter (1988):

Box 2.1 The cost of selling in Europe – transport

One man in a laden lorry travelling from London to Glasgow and back can cover 750 miles in 36 hours without violating government regulations. If, instead, he transported the same goods in the same lorry from London to Milan, which is a similar distance, he would take at least 58 hours (excluding the time necessary to cross the Channel). Much of the difference is accounted for by compulsory rest periods, but the need for these arises from the 6 to 10 extra 'working hours' entailed in inter-member trade. These extra hours are lost to Customs and commercial port formalities, which include:

- passport and health controls;
- transport quota checks – indeed, if permits for direct shipments of some goods between two EC countries have been used up, then the shipments must be rerouted via other EC countries whose quotas have not been used up;

- checks on cargoes carried by the lorry, since within the EC it was (until 1 January 1988) necessary to have one Community transit document for each country passed through en route to the destination, while for exporting outside the EC all that has been necessary is one TIR document;

- safety checks confirming that vehicles meet all weight and dimension regulations and that drivers' hours are not excessive;

- the requirement that lorry drivers purchase fuel from particular service stations at ports; and

- the non-coordination of border-post closing times on the two sides of certain frontiers. Some major (ie busy) border posts are not even open 24 hours a day.

All these formalities require significant amounts of queuing and waiting. Of course, the 58 hours could be drastically reduced by having three drivers to a lorry, but this hardly constitutes a solution. – Source: Information from SITPRO.

It has been estimated that barriers such as these cost the Community around £5.5 billion a year, and the White Paper stated that the Commission's aim was 'not merely to simplify the existing system but to do away with the internal frontier controls in their entirety.'

In 1993, in the Commission's opinion the Internal Market programme had come to fruition – albeit as yet more in a legislative than a practical sense. In terms of the free movement of goods, the following developments are of particular significance. First, with regard to *physical* barriers:

1. The Commission has stated that all checks on goods (and on lorries) at border crossings between Member States have been eliminated.

2. It was reported in May 1993 that work is progressing towards the elimination of national transport quotas.

3. An estimated 60 million customs clearance documents a year (at a cost to industry of an average ECU 70/£50 per consignment) have been replaced by a Single Administrative Document, a single customs and entry and transit document, itself replaced by CADDIA (Co-operation in the Automation of Data and Documentation for Imports, Exports and Agriculture).

In the field of *fiscal* barriers:

1. Until 1993 all goods traded between Member States were subject to import VAT at frontiers and exempt from VAT in the exporting Member State. Frontier formalities in connection with the

collection of VAT have now disappeared and VAT will be levied in the country of destination via normal VAT returns. A computerised information system, VIES (VAT Information Exchange System) has been set up at Community level to check that VAT payments and exemptions are in order and to prevent tax evasion.

2   The Member States have agreed on the approximation of VAT rates. The lower limit for the standard rate of VAT is now 15 percent (UK 17.5 per cent, France 18.6 per cent, Germany 15 per cent, etc.) Agreement on reduced rates or exemptions for goods and services of particular social or cultural significance (food, medicines and water supply, etc) has yet to be reached.

With regard to *technical* barriers (taking us back to the MEEQRs of Article 30, including not only Member States' differing health, safety and packaging standards, etc. but also their various inspection and certification procedures), it is here that the harmonisation process of Article 100A has played a major role. It has been an enormous undertaking. The Cecchini Report on the Internal Market found, for example, 200 such cost-increasing non-tariff barriers in ten food and drink products alone in the five largest Member States.

It is now the case that a Member State may no longer unilaterally seek either to derogate from Article 30 on the grounds listed in Article 36, or plead that Article 30 does not apply to its trade restrictions on the grounds of protection of mandatory requirements as established in *Cassis de Dijon* and later cases, where Community legislation (normally a harmonisation Directive) provides for the protection of the interests in question. (This will *not* be the case in, for example, cases involving public morality.) These developments have been referred to several times in the earlier parts of this chapter and were explained by the Court of Justice in Case 25/88 *Wurmser*.

Since *Cassis de Dijon*, and as outlined in the White Paper of 1985, the Commission has been in the position of being able to concentrate its efforts regarding the adoption of harmonisation measures designed to secure the free movement of goods whilst at the same time protecting these interests of general public concern because it can rely on the *Cassis de Dijon* principle of mutual recognition to operate towards the elimination of the restrictive effect of what Swann called 'trivial' differences between national marketing rules. In such cases, it will be recalled that the presumption is that goods lawfully produced and marketed in one Member State (ie in accordance with the Member State's rules) are to be freely admitted into other Member States.

The Commission's new freedom to concentrate on the provision of essential guarantees in the fields of health and safety and environmental and consumer protection was enhanced by the further change brought about by the

Single European Act whereby, in the context of the completion of the Internal Market, the unanimity voting requirement of Article 100 was replaced by majority voting in the Council under Article 100A(1): see also Chapter Six on Treaty Basis.

Article 100A

1. By way of derogation from Article 100 and save where otherwise provided in this Treaty, the following provisions shall apply for the achievement of the objectives set out in Article 8A. The Council shall, acting by a qualified majority on a proposal from the Commission in cooperation with the European Parliament and after consulting the Economic and Social Committee, adopt the measures for the approximation of the provisions laid down by law, regulation or administrative action in Member States which have as their object the establishment and functioning of the internal market.

2. Paragraph 1 shall not apply to fiscal provisions, to those relating to the free movement of persons nor to those relating to the rights and interests of employed persons.

3. The Commission, in its proposals envisaged in paragraph 1 concerning health, safety, environmental protection and consumer protection, will take as a base a high level of protection.

(Note: under the TEU, Article 8A becomes Article 7A EC and the co-operation procedure becomes 'the procedure referred to in Article 189b'.)

Harmonisation was frequently a slow, laborious process prior to Article 100A but nevertheless Community legislation was adopted which by its *comprehensive* regulation of the issue in question therefore *excluded* the application of national rules. For example:

Case 28/84 *Commission* v. *Germany (Re Compound Feedingstuffs)*
The Commission contended that Council Directives adopted in 1970, 1974 and 1979 constituted a complete and exhaustive set of rules covering the whole field of production and marketing of compound animal feedingstuffs, including questions of public health raised by the use of certain ingredients.

The Court held that the Directives did establish a comprehensive system as regards the composition and preparation of animal foodstuffs with the effect that German rules on the minimum and maximum levels of certain ingredients could not apply.

(In Case 73/84 *Denkavit Futtermittel*, it was held that the same Directives did *not*, however, regulate health inspections of animal foodstuffs and so did not preclude (at that time) national health inspections justifiable under Article 36.)

Putting the main point here another way: once a Directive which lays down a comprehensive system for the marketing of goods, including such matters as health controls, is law within the Member States, goods which comply with its provisions are in a position to be marketed anywhere within the Community: see, for example, Case 148/78 *Ratti* (dealing with the packaging and labelling of solvents and varnishes). in Chapter Eight and Case 60/86 *Commission* v *UK (Re Dim-Dip Headlights)* in which the Court said:

> It follows that the Member States cannot unilaterally require manufacturers who have complied with the harmonized technical requirements set out in Directive 76/756/EEC to comply with a requirement which is not imposed by that directive, since motor vehicles complying with the technical requirements laid down therein must be able to move freely within the common market.

> It must therefore be declared that, by prohibiting, in breach of Council Directive 76/756/EEC of 27 July 1976, the use of motor vehicles manufactured after 1 October 1986 and put into service after 1 April 1987 which are not equipped with a dim-dip device, the United Kingdom has failed to fulfil its obligations under Community law.

However, it should be noted that *Community* law itself may permit or require Member States to carry out inspections of imports on a sample basis away from frontiers.

The 'New Approach' to Harmonisation

In 1987 Pelkmans drew attention to the disadvantages and shortcomings of the 'traditional' approach to technical harmonisation and standardization. They included time-consuming and cumbersome procedures, excessive uniformity, the need for unanimity in the Council under Article 100, and neglect of the problems of testing and certification. By the time a Directive was adopted, it might be technically obsolete.

Already, in 1980, the Commission had announced that, following *Cassis de Dijon*, it would concentrate on steps for the harmonisation of national laws which could still hinder inter-Member State trade (ie Article 36 derogations and mandatory requirements). The Council Resolution of 7 May

1985 set out a 'new approach to technical harmonisation and standards' which was essential for the improvement of the competitiveness of Community industry.

In an annex, the Council laid down the four fundamental principles on which the new approach was to be based:

(i)   legislative harmonization is limited to the adoption, by means of Directives based on Article 100 of the EEC Treaty, of the essential safety requirements (or other requirements in the general interest) with which products put on the market must conform, and which would therefore enjoy free movement throughout the Community.

(ii) the task of drawing up the technical specifications needed for the production and placing on the market of products conforming to the essential requirements established by the Directives, while taking into account the current stage of technology, is entrusted to organizations competent in the standardization area,

(iii) these technical specifications are not mandatory and maintain their status of voluntary standards,

(iv) but at the same time national authorities are obliged to recognize that products manufactured in conformity with harmonized standards (or, provisionally, with national standards) are presumed to conform to the 'essential requirements' established by the Directive. (This signifies that the producer has the choice of not manufacturing in conformity with the standards but that in this event he has an obligation to prove that his products conform to the essential requirements of the Directive.)

In order that this system may operate it is necessary:

(i)   on the one hand that the standards offer a guarantee of quality with regard to the 'essential requirements' established by the Directives.

(ii) on the other hand that the public authorities keep intact their responsibility for the protection of safety (or other requirements envisaged) on their territory.

The Council further explained that: 'In following this system of legislative harmonisation in each area in which it is feasible, the Commission intends to be able to halt the proliferation of excessively technical separate Directives for each product. The scope of Directives according to the 'general reference to standards' formula should encompass wide product categories and types of risk'. On this basis the Commission proceeded to establish codes of essential requirements incorporating 'European' standards.

Codes of Essential Requirements

By this method, any product lawfully manufactured and marketed in one Member State will enjoy free circulation throughout the Community *provided* certain minimum standards are met. To this end, the Council need now only agree, on a majority basis under Article 100A, 'codes of essential requirements' for broad, sufficiently homogeneous product areas or types of risk, thus leaving manufacturers greater flexibility in deciding how to meet such requirements.

Under the terms of Article 100A(3), these framework harmonisation codes (measures other than Directives may be used: Article 100A(1)) are restricted to essential health and safety requirements and environment and consumer protection. Measures have been adopted relating to health (eg food additives), to safety (eg toys and construction products), to the environment (eg air pollution by gaseous emissions from motor vehicles) and consumer protection (eg indications of prices).

These Directives have a common format covering such matters as definitions, rules about placing the product on the market, essential safety requirements, the obligation on Member States to respect the principle of free movement of goods, proof of and means of attestation to conformity, etc: see, for example, Council Directive 88/378 on the Safety of Toys.

Goods complying with a framework Directive must be given free circulation, so ensuring that mutual recognition is made of Member States' individual product composition rules and quality standards provided they conform to the essential requirements. As the Council Resolution of 1985 indicated, this will involve close co-operation between the Commission, European standardization organisations (see below) and national bodies such as the British Standards Institute (BSI):

> The quality of harmonized standards must be ensured by standardization mandates, conferred by the Commission, the execution of which must conform to the general guidelines which have been the subject of agreement between the Commission and the European standardization organizations. In so far as national standards are concerned their quality must be verified by a procedure at Community level managed by the Commission, assisted by a standing committee composed of officials from national administrations.

In addition, and again in line with the Council Resolution, the Commission is charged with developing common criteria for the evaluation of testing laboratories and certification agencies in order to achieve mutual recognition of testing throughout the Community:

At the same time safeguard procedures must be provided for, under the management of the Commission assisted by the same committee, in order to allow the competent public authorities the possibility of contesting the conformity of a product, the validity of a certificate or the quality of a standard.

European Standards

The second principle in the Council Resolution above states that 'the task of drawing up the technical specification' [regarding design and composition, etc] for products which will be deemed to conform to the 'essential requirements' established by the Directives, 'while taking into account the current state of technology, is entrusted to organizations competent in the standardization area'. Such bodies are the Comité Européen de la Normalisation (CEN), the Comité Européen de la Normalisation Electronique (CENELEC) and the European Telecommunications Standards Institute: see, for example, the Preamble to the Toy Safety Directive. The British Standards Institute (BSI) serves British interests on these bodies. Over 800 European standards were adopted between 1984 and 1990, three times as many as in the previous twenty years.

As an illustrative indication of how the 'new approach' works, the Preamble to Council Directive 88/378 on the safety of toys states, in part:

> ... the laws, regulations and administrative provisions in force in the various Member States relating to the safety characteristics of toys differ in scope and content ... such disparities are liable to create barriers to trade and unequal conditions of competition within the internal market without necessarily affording consumers in the common market, especially children, effective protection against the hazards arising from the products in question;

> ... these obstacles to the attainment of an internal market in which only sufficiently safe products would be sold should be removed ... for this purpose, the marketing and free movement of toys should be made subject to uniform rules based on the objectives regarding protection of consumer health and safety as set out in the Council resolution of 23 June 1986 concerning the future orientation of the policy of the European Economic Community for the protection and promotion of consumer interests;

> ... to facilitate proof of conformity with the essential requirements, it is necessary to have harmonized standards at European level which concern, in particular, the design and composition of toys so that products complying with them may be assumed to conform to the essential

requirements ... these standards harmonized at European level are drawn up by private bodies and must remain non–mandatory texts ... for that purpose the European Committee for Standardization (CEN) and the European Committee for Electrotechnical Standardization (CENELEC) are recognized as the competent bodies for the adoption of harmonized standards ...

... in accordance with the Council resolution of 7 May 1985 on a new approach to technical harmonization and standards, the harmonization to be achieved should consist in establishing the essential safety requirements to be satisfied by all toys if they are to be placed on the market.

... toys placed on the market should not jeopardize the safety and/or health either of users or of third parties ...

... compliance with the essential requirements is likely to guarantee consumer health and safety ... all toys placed on the market must comply with these requirements and, if they do, no obstacle must be put in the way of their free movement;

... toys may be presumed to comply with these essential requirements where they are in conformity with the harmonized standards, reference numbers of which have been published in the *Official Journal of the European Communities* ...

... cases might arise where a toy does not satisfy the essential safety requirements ... in such cases, the Member State which ascertains this fact must take all appropriate measures to withdraw the products from the market or to prohibit their being placed on the market ... a reason must be given for this decision and, where the reason is a shortcoming in the harmonized standards, these, or a part thereof, must be withdrawn from the list published by the Commission;

... the Commission is to ensure that the harmonized European standards in all the areas covered by the essential requirements listed in Annex II are drawn up in sufficient time to enable Member States to adopt and publish the necessary provisions by 1 July 1989 ... the national provisions adopted on the basis of this Directive should consequently become effective on 1 January 1990 ...

In Annex II 'Essential Safety Requirements for Toys', particular risks are listed under the headings physical and mechanical properties, flammability, chemical properties, electrical properties, hygiene and radioactivity.

The 'new approach' is nevertheless not without its critics (see, for example, materials in Weatherill, Chapter 16 under the heading 'Harmonisation Policy') and problems have arisen and will continue to arise:

> For example, a cellular phone may enjoy free circulation, but for technical reasons (ie it is only compatible with its own domestic network), it cannot be used in another Member State. Therefore, where necessary, the Commission aims to develop specific European standards, so that not only can the product in question enjoy free circulation to other Member States, but can actually be used there. This will also entail some harmonisation of testing procedures, so that each country accepts certificates awarded in other Member States: *Deloitte's 1992 Guide.*

Similarly, an article by James Erlichman (Consumer Affairs Correspondent) in *The Guardian* in February 1991 under the heading 'EC Reopens Door to Foam Fire Hazard' reported that:

> Highly flammable furniture foam, banned in Britain two years ago, will go back on sale unless fire chiefs and consumer groups can force changes to new European Community law.

> The old style foam was removed from new bedding and furniture after fire chiefs blamed its noxious smoke for the death of 24 people in house fires during the Christmas period in 1988. Their campaign won public sympathy and forced the Government to require manufacturers to use only safer 'combustion modified foam' after February 1989.

> Deaths from house fires have fallen since the introduction of the new foam, which is harder to ignite and gives off much less toxic smoke.

> But an EC draft directive requires furniture foam to pass only a simple ignition test. It does not limit the amount and speed of toxic smoke from ignited foam. 'This omission will allow the old-style conventional foam back on the market', said Bob Graham, assistant chief fire officer for Greater Manchester, who led the fight to have the lethal foam banned. 'The standard is being determined by businessmen, not by scientists and consumers.'

> Critics say the draft directive is weak because it is being written by DG3, the European Commission department concerned only with creating a single market. The regulations would also lower British standards for foam furniture in cinemas, discos and other public buildings ...

Article 100A(4): 'Major Needs'

4. If, after the adoption of a harmonisation measure by the Council acting by a qualified majority, a Member State deems it necessary to apply national provisions on grounds of major needs referred to in Article 36, or relating to protection of the environment or the working environment, it shall notify the Commission of these provisions.

The Commission shall confirm the provisions involved after having verified that they are not a means of arbitrary discrimination or a disguised restriction on trade between Member States.

By way of derogation from the procedure laid down in Articles 169 and 170, the Commission or any Member State may bring the matter directly before the Court of Justice if it considers that another Member State is making improper use of the powers provided for in this Article.

Under paragraph (4), any Member State may seek to retain or introduce national provisions on grounds of 'major needs' as listed, where it considers that harmonised rules (European standards), adopted under Article 100A by a qualified majority, do not constitute a sufficient guarantee of the particular public interest objective in question. Such provisions, which seek to safeguard higher national requirements, must be confirmed by the Commission according to the procedure laid in the second sentence of paragraph (4), which incorporates the same conditions as those laid down by the proviso to Article 36.

At the time of its introduction, there were fears that Member States would regularly turn to Article 100A(4) — the so-called 'price paid for majority voting' — and so undermine the 'new approach' to harmonisation. This has not proved to be the case: in only one instance, concerning Council Directive 91/173 on the marketing and use of dangerous substances, has the Commission had cause formally to confirm the national provisions in question. These provisions related to a substance known as pentachlorophenol (PCP) which is dangerous to both health and the environment.

International Trade

Buckley, P. J. and Brooke, M. Z., *International Business Studies*, 1992, Part 2.5 'Barriers to World Trade'.

Hine, R. C., *The Political Economy of European Trade*, 1986.

Kindelberger, C. P., 'Commercial Policy Between the Wars' in *The Cambridge Economic History of Europe*, Vol. XIII.

Swann, D., *The Economics of the Common Market*, Chapters 4 and 5.

Charges and Taxation

Danusso, M. and Denton, R., 'Does the European Court of Justice look for a Protectionist Motive under Article 95?' (1990) 1 LIEI 67.

Easson, A. J., 'Fiscal Discrimination: New Perspectives on Article 95' (1981) 18 CML Rev. 521.

Van der Zanden, J. B. and Terra, B. J. M., 'The Removal of Tax Barriers' (1989) 1 LIEI 137. (Harmonisation).

Non-Tariff Barriers: Articles 30–36

Arnull, A., 'What Shall We Do on Sunday?' (1991) 16 EL Rev. 112.

Dashwood, A., 'The *Cassis de Dijon* Line of Authority' in *In Memoriam J. D. B. Mitchell*, 1983.

Diamond, P., 'Dishonourable Defences: The Use of Injunctions and the EEC Treaty – Case Study of the Shops Act 1950' (1991) 54 MLR 72.

Evans, A. C., 'Economic Policy and the Free Movement of Goods in EEC Law' (1983) ICLQ 577.

Oliver, P., *Free Movement of Goods in the EEC* (Articles 30–36), 1990.

Oliver, P. 'Measures of Equivalent Effect: A Reappraisal' (1982) 19 CML Rev. 217.

Steiner, J., 'Drawing the Line: Uses and Abuses of Article 30 EEC' (1992) 29 CML Rev. 749 (Sunday trading).

White, E., 'In Search of Limits to Article 30 of the EEC Treaty' (1989) 26 CML Rev. 235 (Sunday trading).

See also case notes, particularly in the Common Market Law Review and the European Law Review and surveys of cases on the free movement of goods in those journals, eg Gormley (1990) 27 CML Rev. 825.

Internal Market and Harmonisation

Bieber, R. et al (eds), 1992: One European Market?, 1988.

Brearley, M. and Quigley, C., Completing the Internal Market of the European Community, 1989, sections on 'Control of Goods' and 'Free Movement of Goods'.

E C Commission, 'Completing the Internal Market', White Paper from the Commission to the European Council, 14 June 1985, COM (85) 310.

E C Commission, 'Fifth Report of the Commission ... Concerning the Implementation of the White Paper on the Completion of the Internal Market', COM (90)90, March 1990: Part II.

E C Commission, 'Implementation of the Legal Acts Required to Build the Single Market', COM (90) 473, October 1990.

Gormley, L. W., 'Some Reflections on the Internal Market and Free Movement of Goods' (1989) 1 LIEI 9.

Langton, M., 'Standards and the Single European Market', *European Access*, 1990. 1, February.

Pelkmans, J., 'The New Approach To Technical Harmonisation and Standardisation' (1987) 25 JCMS 249.

Pelkmans, J. and Winter, A., *Europe's Domestic Market*, 1988.

Shave, A., 'Policing Europe Without Frontiers', *European Access*, 1989:1, February.

Thompson, I., 'Internal Market Developments: September – November 1990', *European Access*, 1990:6, December (regularly updated).

Vignes, D., 'The Harmonisation of National Legislation and the EEC' (1990) 15 EL Rev. 358.

Weatherill, S., *Cases and Materials on EEC Law*, Chapter 16(B) Harmonisation Policy, (C) Methods of Harmonisation.

CHAPTER THIRTEEN

SOCIAL POLICY: SEX DISCRIMINATION

Community law relating to sex discrimination operates within the context of employment and the working population as broadly defined. It comprises two basic principles: the principle of *equal pay for equal work* for men and women (Article 119 and Directive 75/117) and the principle of *equal treatment* for men and women as regards access to employment, promotion and dismissal, etc (Directive 76/207). In *Defrenne* (discussed in Chapter Eight and see below), the Court of Justice described the equal pay principle as one of the 'foundations of the Community' and laid emphasis on the *social* aims of Article 119.

In addition to these 'employment equality' provisions, the Community has adopted additional 'welfare equality' measures which govern equal treatment in *social security* matters, eg State retirement pensions: Directive 79/7, and equal treatment in *occupational*, eg company, *pension schemes*: Directive 86/378.

A very significant trend in the development of the law in this field at Community level has been the increasing willingness of the Court of Justice to recognise claims, relating for example to redundancy payments and some pensions, as coming within the ambit of 'pay'. The equality principle is thereby enhanced in two ways. First, such claims come within the scope of the (horizontally and vertically) directly effective Article 119. Secondly, claims are removed from the scope of the 'welfare equality' provisions, which are subject to several exceptions from the equal treatment principle, not least as regards the continuing ability of Member States to determine different pensionable ages under State social security schemes (eg 65 for men, 60 for women) for the purposes of retirement pensions *and the possible consequences thereof for other benefits.*

A considerable number of the cases discussed in this chapter concern the relationship between English law in this area and the Community measures. There have been considerable problems, as Collins has pointed out:

> There can be no doubt that the United Kingdom Government has caused much unnecessary litigation and the expenditure of much unnecessary cost by taking the position that implementation of the Equal Pay and Equal Treatment Directives required only the continuation of, or minor amendments to, the Equal Pay Act 1970 and the Sex Discrimination Act 1975, rather than new law based specifically on the Directives: *European Law in the United Kingdom.*

EQUAL PAY FOR EQUAL WORK

Article 119

Each Member State shall during the first stage ensure and subsequently maintain the application of the principle that men and women should receive equal pay for equal work.

For the purpose of this Article, 'pay' means the ordinary basic or minimum wage or salary and any other consideration, whether in cash or in kind, which the worker receives, directly or indirectly, in respect of his employment from his employer ....

Although Article 119 speaks only of 'equal pay for equal work' and not of 'remuneration for work of equal value', the wider concept adopted by the International Labour Organisation Convention No. 100 of 1951, the subsequent adoption by the Community of the Equal Pay Directive in 1975 meant that Community law was brought into line with ILO concepts and principles: see Case 149/77 *Defrenne (No. 3)*.

In the late 1950s, it was generally thought that it was necessary for 'the Six' to implement Article 119 by means of national measures in order to make the equal pay principle effective. This they failed to do but the Commission took no enforcement actions against them. (Article 119 states that the principle shall be brought into effect 'during the first stage', ie during the period 1958-62). It was not until the *Defrenne* litigation of the 1970s that a breakthrough was made – by Belgian activists and the Court of Justice:

Case 43/75 *Defrenne* v. *Sabena (No. 2)*

Miss Defrenne was employed by the Belgian airline, Sabena, as an air hostess. In the Belgian courts she claimed compensation for discrimination in terms of the pay she received as compared with cabin stewards doing the same work. Her action was based on Article 119 and the Court de Travail asked the Court of Justice if Article 119 could be relied upon before national courts, independently of national legislation. The Court ruled:

1. Article 119 pursued a double aim: (a) economic, by the removal of the competitive disadvantage suffered by undertakings which had implemented the equal pay principle as compared to those which had not, and (b) social, by the improvement by common action of living and working conditions for workers throughout the Community. As such, the principle of equal pay formed one of the foundations of the Community.

2. In interpreting Article 119 it was not possible to base any argument on the dilatoriness and resistance which had delayed the implementation of the basic principle.

With reference to the actual provisions of Article 119 the Court held that:

3. Article 119 was directly effective and gave rise to individual rights which national courts must protect in cases of discrimination which could be identified by the court solely with the aid of the criteria based on equal work and equal pay in Article 119 itself.

4. Such cases included those which had their origins in legislative provisions or in collective labour agreements and which might be detected on the basis of a purely legal analysis of the situation. There was certainly no difficulty in applying Article 119 where the facts clearly showed that a woman worker was receiving lower pay than a male worker performing the same task in the same establishment or service – whether *public or private*; ie Article 119 is both vertically and horizontally directly effective.

5. For cases of discrimination which could only be identified by reference to more explicit implementing provisions of a Community or national character, the Court stated that:

'It is impossible not to recognise that the complete implementation of the aim pursued by Article 119, by means of the elimination of all discrimination between men and women workers, not only as regards individual undertakings but also entire branches of industry and even of the economic system as a whole, may in certain cases involve the elaboration of criteria whose implementation necessitates the taking of appropriate measures at Community and national level.'

Therefore, in such latter cases Article 119 is not sufficient, at least on its own, to secure the equal pay objective – further Community or national measures will be required, as we will see below.

The Court's ruling that in essence its decision should only have prospective (not retrospective) effect was discussed at the end of Chapter Ten. This is what the Court said:

The Governments of Ireland and the United Kingdom have drawn the Court's attention to the possible economic consequences of attributing direct effect to the provisions of Article 119, on the ground that such a decision might, in many branches of economic life, result in the introduction of claims dating back to the time at which such effect came into existence.

In view of the large number of people concerned such claims, which undertakings could not have foreseen, might seriously affect the financial situation of such undertakings and even drive some of them to bankruptcy.

Although the practical consequences of any judicial decision must be carefully taken into account, it would be impossible to go so far as to diminish the objectivity of the law and compromise its future application on the ground of the possible repercussions which might result, as regards the past, from such a judicial decision.

However, in the light of the conduct of several of the Member States and the views adopted by the Commission and repeatedly brought to the notice of the circles concerned, it is appropriate to take exceptionally into account the fact that, over a prolonged period, the parties concerned have been led to continue with practices which were contrary to Article 119, although not yet prohibited under their national law.

The fact that, in spite of the warnings given, the Commission did not initiate proceedings under Article 169 against the Member States concerned, on grounds of failure to fulfil an obligation was likely to consolidate the incorrect impression as to the effects of Article 119.

Therefore, the direct effect of Article 119 cannot be relied on in order to support claims concerning pay periods prior to the date of this judgment, except as regards those workers who have already brought legal proceedings or made an equivalent claim.

In these circumstances, it is appropriate to determine that, as the general level at which pay would have been fixed cannot be known, important considerations of legal certainty affecting all the interests involved, both public and private, make it impossible in principle to reopen the question as regards the past.

The first UK equal pay case to be referred to the Court of Justice raised a slightly different question from that in *Defrenne (No. 2)*:

Case 129/79 *Macarthys Ltd v. Smith*

S brought an equal pay claim on the basis that she was paid £10 per week less than the man who had held the same position four months previously. In the Court of Appeal, a majority found that the wording of section 1(2)(a) and (b) of the Equal Pay Act ('where the woman *is* employed') limited the right to equal pay to situations of contemporaneous (and not sequential) employment. Following a reference to the Court of Justice on the interpretation of Article 119, the Court ruled that:

As the Court indicated in the *Defrenne* judgment of 8 April 1976, that provision applies directly, and without the need for more detailed implementing measures on the part of the Community or the Member States, to all forms of direct and overt discrimination which may be identified solely with the aid of the criteria of equal work and equal pay referred to by the article in question. Among the forms of discrimination which may be thus judicially identified, the Court mentioned in particular cases where men and women receive unequal pay for equal work carried out in the same establishment or service.

In such a situation the decisive test lies in establishing whether there is a difference in treatment between a man and a woman performing 'equal work' within the meaning of Article 119. The scope of that concept, which is entirely qualitative in character in that it is exclusively concerned with the nature of the services in question, may not be restricted by the introduction of a requirement of contemporaneity.

It must be acknowledged, however, that, as the Employment Appeal Tribunal properly recognised, it cannot be ruled out that a difference in pay between two workers occupying the same post but at different periods in time may be explained by the operation of factors which are unconnected with any discrimination on grounds of sex. That is a question of fact which it is for the court or tribunal to decide.

Thus the answer to the ... question should be that the principle that men and women should receive equal pay for equal work, enshrined in Article 119 of the EEC Treaty, is not confined to situations in which men and women are contemporaneously doing equal work for the same employer.

On the question of pay differences (arising in this case following a lapse of time), which can be shown to have a basis in factors *unconnected* with sex, see the *Bilka Kaufhaus* case and others, below.

It would seem that the Court of Justice has left open the question whether the comparison between pay and work based on Article 119 is to be confined to the same employer or whether it can be extended to the situation prevailing at other undertakings operating in the same field: Case 143/83 *Commission* v *Denmark* (*Re Equal Pay Concepts*).

DISCRIMINATION: THE SCOPE OF ARTICLE 119

The following case shows that Article 119 extends to what is termed 'indirect discrimination', such as a 'gender-neutral' distinction made between full-time and part-time workers:

> Case 96/80 *Jenkins* v. *Kingsgate (Clothing Productions) Ltd*
> Mrs J worked part-time for K Ltd. She received an hourly rate of pay lower than that of her male (and female) colleagues employed full-time on the same work. All the part-time workers except one were women. The Employment Appeal Tribunal referred several questions to the Court of Justice under Article 177. The Court ruled as follows:

It appears from the first three questions and the reasons stated in the order making the reference that the national court is principally concerned to know whether a difference in the level of pay for work carried out part-time and the same work carried out full-time may amount to discrimination of a kind prohibited by Article 119 of the Treaty when the category of part-time workers is exclusively or predominantly comprised of women.

The answer to the questions thus understood is that the purpose of Article 119 is to ensure the application of the principle of equal pay for men and women for the same work. The differences in pay prohibited by that provision are therefore exclusively those based on the difference of the sex of the workers. Consequently the fact that part-time work is paid at an hourly rate lower than pay for full-time work does not amount per se to discrimination prohibited by Article 119 provided that the hourly rates are applied to workers belonging to either category without distinction based on sex.

If there is no such distinction, therefore, the fact that work paid at time rates is remunerated at an hourly rate which varies according to the number of hours worked per week does not offend against the principle of equal pay laid down in Article 119 of the Treaty in so far as the difference in pay between part-time work and full-time work is attributable to factors which are objectively justified and are in no way related to any discrimination based on sex.

Such may be the case, in particular, when by giving hourly rates of pay which are lower for part-time work than those for full-time work the employer is endeavouring, on economic grounds which may be objectively justified, to encourage full-time work irrespective of the sex of the worker.

By contrast, if it is established that a considerably smaller percentage of women than of men perform the minimum number of weekly working hours required in order to be able to claim the full-time hourly rate of pay, the inequality in pay will be contrary to Article 119 of the Treaty where, regard being had to the difficulties encountered by women in arranging to work that minimum number of hours per week, the pay policy of the undertaking in question cannot be explained by factors other than discrimination based on sex.

Where the hourly rate of pay differs according to whether the work is part-time or full-time it is for the national courts to decide in each individual case whether, regard being had to the facts of the case, its history and the employer's intention, a pay policy such as that which is at issue in the main proceedings although represented as a difference based on weekly working hours is or is not in reality discrimination based on the sex of the worker.

The reply to the first three questions must therefore be that a difference in pay between full-time workers and part-time workers does not amount to discrimination prohibited by Article 119 of the Treaty unless it is in reality merely an indirect way of reducing the level of pay of part-time workers on the ground that that group of workers is composed exclusively or predominantly of women.

Approximately 90% of part-time workers in the Community are women, mostly married women with other responsibilities.

In Case 170/84 *Bilka-Kaufhaus*, which again involved a claim by a part-time worker, the Court made it clear that it was for *the employer*, in his defence, to prove to the satisfaction of the national court an *objective justification* for the wage differential in question. The plaintiff's complaint was that, as a part-time worker, she was excluded from the benefits of the employer's *occupational pension scheme*, at least until she had worked for the firm for at least 15 out of a total of 20 years. The scheme, which supplemented the state pension scheme, originated in a collective agreement; it was incorporated into contracts of employment and was financed solely by employer contributions. (It will be recalled that Article 119 in defining pay speaks of 'indirect' consideration received by a worker from his employer in respect of his employment):

Case 170/84 *Bilka-Kaufhaus*

Ms Weber, a female part-time worker, challenged BK's pension scheme as being indirectly discriminatory on the basis that the long service requirement applied only to part-time workers (not full-timers) and the majority of part-timers were women. Men comprised 28% of the total work force, but male part-time workers comprised only 2.8% of the total work force. The long service requirement therefore disproportionately disadvantaged women.

In Article 177 proceedings, the Court of Justice was asked if the exclusion of part-time workers from the scheme could be in breach of Article 119. The Court referred to its decision in *Jenkins* (above) and held that if it was found that a considerably smaller percentage of men than of women worked part-time, and if the difference in treatment could not be explained by any other factor than sex, the exclusion of part-time workers from the occupational pension scheme would be contrary to Article 119.

The difference in treatment would however be permissible if the employer could explain it by *objectively justified factors* unrelated to discrimination based on sex. To do this the employer must prove that the measures giving rise to the difference in treatment:

(a) 'correspond to a real need on the part of an undertaking',

(b) 'are appropriate with a view to achieving the objectives pursued', and

(c) 'are necessary to that end'.

This 'economic objectives' test (which is similar to that applied to 'mandatory requirements' in *Cassis de Dijon*, see Chapter Twelve) was met by the employer in *Bilka-Kaufhaus* with the argument that part-timers were less economic and less willing to work evening and Saturday shifts, and there was a need to provide incentives to full-time employment. As a defence, these claims would have to be proved to the satisfaction of the national court and shown to satisfy the principle of proportionality, ie that they were necessary, but no more than necessary. Where the employer has a choice as to how he may achieve a legitimate economic objective, he must choose the least discriminatory method.

The *Bilka-Kaufhaus* test has been applied in the UK when dealing with a 'genuine material difference' under section 1(3) of the Equal Pay Act 1970. In *Rainey v Greater Glasgow Health Board* (1987) Lord Keith, speaking of the need to consider the circumstances of the case, stated that:

These may well go beyond what is not very happily described as 'the personal equation' ... In particular, where there is no question of intentional sex discrimination whether direct or indirect, a difference which is connected with economic factors affecting the efficient carrying on of the employer's business or other activity may be relevant.

Thus, in *Benveniste v University of Southampton* (1989), B had been appointed in 1981 at a time of great financial stringency in British universities. She had been appointed six points below the point on the salary scale at which a person of her age would normally have been appointed. It was argued that this need for financial stringency was a genuine material factor within the terms of section 1(3), but Neil L.J. held that 'the material difference between the appellant's case and the case of the comparators evaporated when the financial constraints were removed' in 1982. For a doubtful argument (added economic burdens on employers) upholding a justifiable 'real need' to discriminate between full-time and part-time employees (in a UK statute), see the Divisional Court decision in *R v Secretary of State for Employment, ex parte Equal Opportunities Commission* (1992).

THE CONCEPT OF PAY

As some of the cases already discussed show, Article 119 is not confined to wages and salaries alone. It also covers:

> ... any other consideration, whether in cash or in kind, which the worker receives, directly or indirectly, in respect of his employment from his employer.

As regards *benefits in kind*:

> Case 12/81 *Garland v. British Rail Engineering Ltd*
> BRE employees and their families were entitled to special rail travel concessions. On retirement, however, families of female ex-employees lost these concessions while those of male ex-employees continued to enjoy them.

> The Court ruled that such benefits constituted 'pay' within the meaning of Article 119, even though employment had ceased, providing they were granted *as a result of* the employment relationship. It was immaterial that (a) the entitlement was not part of any contractual obligation and (b) the discrimination related to the worker's family and not to the benefits accruing to the ex-employee herself.

The case of *Kowalska* shows that, in respect of *benefits arising from a collective wage agreement*, the terms of such an agreement may be contrary to Article 119 if they indirectly discriminate against women and cannot be objectively justified by factors unrelated to sex:

Case C-33/89 *Kowalska*

Under a German 'white collar', public services collective agreement, employees normally working less than 38 hours per week were excluded from its severance payments provisions. The purpose of severance money was to help employees who involuntarily left employment (eg on retirement or through disability) to adjust to their new situation.

The Court of Justice ruled that severance pay constituted pay within the terms of Article 119, and, since a higher proportion of part-time workers were women, the agreement was contrary to Article 119 unless it could be shown that the exclusion was justified by objective factors unrelated to sex. If not, both full and part-timers were to receive a severance payment on a proportionate basis.

In a similar case, Case C-184/89 *Nimz*, the Court of Justice stated that:

Where there is indirect discrimination in a provision in a collective agreement, the national court is required to disapply that provision, without requesting or awaiting its prior removal by collective negotiation or any other procedure, and to apply to members of the group which is disadvantaged by that discrimination the same arrangements which are applied to other employees, arrangements which, failing the correct application of Article 119 of the EEC Treaty in national law, remain the only valid system of reference.

It would appear therefore that those indirectly discriminated against in such circumstances can look to the application of an equality clause where the discriminatory term has been incorporated into their contracts of employment or at least to a declaration that they are to enjoy comparable rights.

From the standpoint of *part-time workers*, such cases as *Kowalski* and *Nimz* and Case 171/88 *Rinner-Kühn*, in which a part-time office cleaner had been excluded from sick pay entitlement (prima facie a statutory social security benefit), indicate that national legislation which *allows* certain categories of workers (eg part-timers) to be treated differently *by employers*, ie discriminated against, is in breach of Article 119. As Steiner has pointed out, these cases 'will have profound implications for employers of part-time workers in the UK, since the majority of statutory employment rights allow for derogation in the case of part-time workers'. (National 'welfare' legislation which currently *requires* certain groups to be treated differently, eg state social security schemes providing, say, for different 'pensionable' ages for men and women for the purposes of granting old age and retirement pensions, still remains outside Article 119.)

It is in relation to the Court's extension of the concept of 'pay' under Article 119 to cover *employers' contributions to employees' pension schemes* that considerable complications have arisen. Only the main issues will be considered here.

In Case 12/81 *Garland* (see above), the Court stated that pay covered any consideration

> whether immediate or future, provided that the worker receives it, albeit indirectly, in respect of his employment from his employer.

However, in Case 80/70 *Defrenne (No.1)*, in which D challenged Belgian Royal Decrees laying down rules governing retirement and pensions in the civil aviation industry, the Court had said that:

> A retirement pension established within the framework of a social security scheme laid down by legislation does not constitute consideration which the worker receives indirectly in respect of his employment from his employer within the meaning of the second paragraph of Article 119 of the EEC Treaty.

This ruling appeared to *exclude* from Article 119 all social security benefits directly governed by legislation and available to workers generally or to certain categories of workers. In *Defrenne (No.1)* the employer made different contributions to the scheme in respect of male and female employees but the Court stated that the benefits arising from such a statutory social security scheme were 'no more emoluments paid directly by the employer than are roads, canals or water drains'. What were not considered in this case were *employers' occupational pension schemes*.

The nature of one such scheme was outlined by the Court in Case 69/80 *Worringham and Humphreys* v *Lloyds Bank Ltd*:

> Lloyds applies to its staff two retirement schemes, one for men and one for women. Under these retirement benefits schemes, which are the result of collective bargaining between the trade unions and Lloyds and which have been approved by the national authorities under the Finance Act 1970 and certified under the Social Security Pensions Act 1975, the member contracts out of the earnings-related part of the State pension scheme and this is replaced by a contractual scheme.

In 1986 the Court of Justice held that occupational pension benefits fall within the scope of 'pay' in Article 119 notwithstanding that they are fitted into a statutory framework:

Case 170/84 *Bilka-Kaufhaus*

A pension scheme, adopted in accordance with German legislation, originated however in a collective agreement and was incorporated into contracts of employment. This occupational pension *supplemented* the state pension scheme and was financed solely by employer contributions.

The Court ruled that the scheme fell within Article 119 and that (as seen above) a long service requirement for part-time workers could amount to indirect discrimination. The Court stressed that:

'The contractual, and not the statutory, origin of the disputed scheme is confirmed by the fact that the scheme and its rules are considered ... to form an integral part of the contracts of employment between Bilka and its employees'. The supplementary nature of the pension and its relationship to the employment involved were factors which overrode the social security and social policy aspects of the scheme. The benefit constituted consideration paid by the employer *indirectly* (via the pension fund) to the employee in respect of his employment.

In this next case, the Court held that Article 119 applied to UK employers' contracted-out occupational pension schemes (see the *Worringham* reference above) in a situation where benefit was subject to an *age requirement* which was discriminatory, the difference in age resulting in a difference in 'pay'. In addition, Article 119 was applied to all redundancy payments. Thus only statutory social security schemes still remain outside the ambit of Article 119.

Case C-262/88 *Barber v. Guardian Royal Exchange Assurance Group*

B was a member of GRE's contracted-out occupational pension scheme, ie it was contracted out of the *state* earnings related pension scheme (SERPS) and was a *substitute* for it. The scheme had been established by his employer and was wholly financed by GRE. The pensionable age for employees in his category was 62 for men and 57 for women. However, contracts of employment further provided that, under severance terms, employees made redundant were entitled to an immediate pension if they were aged 55 for men and 50 for women.

B was made redundant at 52 and he claimed an immediate pension – which he would have received if he had been a woman. (The 5-year age difference reflected the different *state* pensionable ages for men and women.) He also claimed entitlement to redundancy benefit.

The Court of Appeal referred various questions to the Court of Justice under Article 177, particularly as regards whether contracted-out pensions and statutory redundancy payments came within Article 119.

The Court held:

1. Benefits paid to an employee by his employer in connection with his *redundancy* fall in principle within the concept of pay for the purposes of Article 119. This is so whether such benefits are paid under a contract of employment, under statute (*prima facie* a social security payment), or on a voluntary basis: see also *Garland* (1982) 1 CMLR 696, para. 5. The 'employment relationship' is paramount.

2. Unlike the benefits (eg pensions) awarded by national statutory social security schemes, a pension paid under a contracted-out scheme constitutes consideration paid by the employer to the worker in respect of his employment and so falls under Article 119: see *Bilka-Kaufhaus*. (Note also that the payment is made *indirectly*, via the pension fund.)

3. It is contrary to Article 119 to impose an *age condition* which differs according to sex in respect of pensions paid under a contracted-out scheme. It is therefore discriminatory for a man made compulsorily redundant to be entitled to claim only a deferred pension, when a woman in the same position is entitled to an immediate pension as the result of the application of an age condition that varies according to sex in the same way as is provided for by the national statutory pension scheme: cf. *Marshall* as regards equality in *retirement*, as opposed to pension ages.

4. Each *element* of the consideration must comply with Article 119 to ensure transparency of the pay system.

5. The direct effect of Article 119 to the situation in issue was confirmed: if a woman was entitled to an immediate retirement pension when she was made compulsorily redundant and a man of the same age was only entitled to a deferred pension, then the result was unequal pay within Article 119, identifiable by a national court.

6. The judgment was limited to entitlement to pensions with effect from the date of the judgment (17 May 1990), except for cases already pending before the national courts: cf. the Court's ruling in

the *Defrenne* (No. 2) equal pay case. The justification for this was that in the light of the *exemption* from the equal treatment principle in Article 9 of the Occupational Social Security Directive 86/378 of the 'determination of pensionable age for the purposes of granting old-age or retirement pensions, and the possible implications for other benefits', Member States and the parties concerned were reasonably entitled to consider that Article 119 did not apply to pensions paid under contracted-out schemes and that, accordingly, it was permissible to discriminate (Article 9 has apparently been construed out of existence by the Court's decision in *Barber*.)

Concern regarding the precise meaning of the Court's temporal limitation on its judgment and its effect on pensions and pension funds was so great as to lead to the addition of a Protocol to Article 119 at the Maastricht Summit conference. The protocol makes it clear that, subject to the Court's proviso in (6) above, *benefits* under occupational social security schemes are not to be considered as pay -and so do not attract the equality principle in the directly effective Article 119 – insofar as they are attributable to periods of employment prior to 17 May 1990. In other words companies will not be required to provide equal pension benefits for men and women for any period of service prior to that date – so saving British industry an estimated £50 billion.

On the urgent practical problem facing pension fund managers with respect to achieving equality in pension ages, Curtin (1990) speculated along the following lines:

The full extent to which pension funds are obliged to change current practices is arguably not entirely clear which is why *legislative* guidance, taking full account of the terms of Article 119, is urgently required. Occupational pension schemes are faced with some very difficult problems in dealing with the current morass in which many of them find themselves swamped. For example, where occupational schemes wish to reduce the male pension age to that applicable to female members, they are nevertheless confronted, in some Member States, with the consequences of the disparity arising from the present system of State provision. The highly unclear situation thus lends urgency to those Member States with unequal statutory pension ages to give a clear commitment about their equalisation.

Advocates of changes of the pension age in occupational schemes are met with the argument that to the extent that the resultant costs would be funded by employers, competitiveness of the industry would be reduced thereby damaging prospects for jobs. For these reasons it is not unlikely that many occupational schemes faced with the necessity of taking immediate and unplanned action will simply opt to raise the female pension age to the male one, the cheapest of all options open. Indeed it would allow significant savings to be made in the cost of pension payments. The only viable alternative is perceived by the pensions industry as setting the pension age at 63 or 64 based on an arithmetical calculation where the costs balance out. The probable unpopularity of such moves stems from the perception of women's position having been relatively worsened; this would be exacerbated by the fact that any transitional periods in the implementation of the principle of equal treatment are probably not permissible and yet special terms are imperative if contractual problems *vis-à-vis* existing employees are to be avoided.

ARTICLE 119 AND THE EQUAL PAY DIRECTIVE: WORK OF EQUAL VALUE

Under Article 1 of Council Directive 75/117 on the approximation of the laws of the Member States relating to the application of the principle of equal pay for men and women (adopted under Article 100):

> The principle of equal pay for men and women outlined in Article 119 of the Treaty, hereinafter called 'principle of equal pay', means, for the same work or for work to which equal value is attributed, the elimination of all discrimination on grounds of sex with regard to all aspects and conditions of remuneration.

> In particular, where a job classification system is used for determining pay, it must be based on the same criteria for both men and women and so drawn up as to exclude any discrimination on grounds of sex.

Although this article appears to introduce the concept of 'work of equal value' into Community law, the Court of Justice has held that the Directive merely restates the equal pay principle in Article 119, ie it applies not only to the same work but to work of equal value as well. Thus where, in an *equal value* case, the national court is able to identify discrimination purely by reference to Article 119, that article will be directly effective, eg where a collective agreement assigns equal value to various types of work but men and women working within such a grouping do not receive equal pay.

If, on the other hand, discrimination can only be identified by the national court with the *additional* aid of further criteria, such as a job classification scheme laid down by national law (see Article 1, para. 2), then, whilst Article 119 is not directly effective, the combined effect of that article and the national implementing rules will be sufficient to secure equality if discrimination exists.

The Directive (see Article 1, para. 2 and Article 6) does not make job evaluation schemes compulsory, but Member States must establish some effective machinery whereby it can be decided whether work is of equal value:

Article 6

Member States shall, in accordance with their national circumstances and legal systems, take the measures necessary to ensure that the principle of equal pay is applied. They shall see that effective means are available to take care that this principle is observed. ['Equal pay' including, of course, equal pay for work of equal value.]

Where this is not the case, an employee will be deprived of her/his enforceable rights under Article 2:

Article 2

Member States shall introduce into their national legal systems such measures as are necessary to enable all employees who consider themselves wronged by failure to apply the principle of equal pay to pursue their claims by judicial process after possible recourse to other competent authorities.

In Case 61/81 *Commission v UK (Re Equal Pay for Equal Work)*, under UK legislation (the Equal Pay Act 1970, as amended by the Sex Discrimination Act 1975) equal pay was required in cases where a man and a woman were employed in work 'rated as equivalent' on the basis of a job evaluation scheme. Such schemes could, however, only be implemented with the consent of the employer. The Court held that the UK was in breach of its Community obligations. UK law as brought into line in 1983 by the Equal Pay (Amendment) Regulations under which machinery was provided whereby independent experts were required to report to an industrial tribunal on 'equal value' claims in the absence of a job evaluation scheme.

As early as the mid-1970s, in *Defrenne (No.2)*, the Court of Justice had, as seen, been prepared to speculate on the full implications of the equal pay principle:

It is impossible not to recognise that the complete implementation of the aim pursued by Article 119 EEC, by means of the elimination of all discrimination, direct or indirect, between men and women workers, not only as regards individual undertakings but also entire branches of industry and even the economic system as a whole, may in certain cases involve the elaboration of criteria whose implementation necessitates the taking of appropriate measures at Community or national level.

The scope of the comparisons which may be necessary in order fully to implement Directive 75/117 was indicated by A G VerLoren van Themaat in Case 143/83 *Commission* v *Denmark (Re Equal Pay Concepts)*:

> As appears from the second sentence of Article 1 of the Directive however a comparison of duties within the same fixed establishment of an undertaking or even within a single undertaking will not always be sufficient. In certain circumstances comparison with work of equal value in other undertakings covered by the collective agreement in question will be necessary ... in sectors with a traditionally female workforce comparison with other sectors may even be necessary. In certain circumstances the additional criterion of 'the same place of work' for work of equal value may therefore place a restriction on the principle of equal pay laid down in Article 119 of the E.E.C. Treaty and amplified in the Directive in question. The mere fact that such a supplementary condition for equal pay which has no foundation in Article 119 or the Directive has been added must in any event be regarded as an infringement of the Treaty. That supplementary condition limits the scope, governed by the Treaty, of the extension of the principle of equal pay for men and women to equal value ... which is recognised in Denmark.

The establishment of agreed methods for making the wider equal value comparisons indicated here on a uniform basis throughout the Member State clearly presents enormous difficulties, not the least of which is the resistance of employers (and national governments) in the face of the cost burdens involved. Uniformity can only be achieved on the basis of further clarification and harmonisation at Community level. Some guidance has been forthcoming from the Court of Justice. It will prove helpful to view these cases in the light of the following provisions of Directive 75/117:

Article 3

Member States shall abolish all discrimination between men and women arising from laws, regulations or administrative provisions which is contrary to the principle of equal pay.

Article 4

Member States shall take the necessary measures to ensure that provisions appearing in collective agreements, wage scales, wage agreements or individual contracts of employment which are contrary to the principle of equal pay shall be, or may be declared, null and void or may be amended.

...

Article 7

Member States shall take care that the provisions adopted pursuant to this directive, together with the relevant provisions already in force, are brought to the attention of employees by all appropriate means, for example at their place of employment.

Case 143/83 *Commission v Denmark (Re Equal Pay Concepts)*

In this case the Court of Justice ruled that where collective bargaining was the dominant basis for wage structures, a Member State was nevertheless under a duty to provide effective protection for *all* workers, particularly non-union members and those in sectors where collective bargaining did not cover or fully guarantee the equal pay principle. Relying on general principles of law (the principle of legal certainty and the protection of the individual), the Court ruled that all workers required an unequivocal statement of the rights flowing from Directive 75/117 so that national courts were in a position to ensure that its obligations were being observed.

Case 237/85 *Rummler v. Dato-Druck*

R challenged the classifications used in the framework wage-rate agreement for the German printing industry. She claimed that her work should have been placed in a higher category since her job as a packer involved lifting parcels weighing more than 20 killogrammes, which, for a woman, represented heavy physical work.

On a reference for a preliminary ruling, the Court of Justice held that a job classification scheme based on such factors as the strength and physical effort required to perform the work was not contrary to the provisions of Directive 75/117 as long as:

(a) the system as a whole precluded discrimination on grounds of sex, and

(b) the criteria employed were objectively justified, ie they must:
  (i) be appropriate to the tasks to be carried out, and
  (ii) correspond to a genuine need of the undertaking.

The scheme must also take into account the criteria for which *each sex* has a particular aptitude. Criteria based exclusively on the attributes of one sex contained 'a risk of discrimination'.

Case 109/88 *Danfoss*

A trade union backed claim was brought on behalf of a group of women workers who earned on average 7% less than male workers covered by the relevant collective agreement. Although the same *basic* wage was applied to all workers, the employer was able to supplement this on the basis of various neutral criteria including 'flexibility', professional training and 'seniority'. There was no clarification of how and when the criteria were being used and the applicants alleged that the criteria must be discriminatory. The Court ruled that where a pay system showed a 'total lack of transparency' (ie where the criteria for determining pay increments were not clear to those affected) and where the system operated to the patent disadvantage of women, there must be a partial reversal of the burden of proof such that the employer must prove that the criteria employed were justified. By reference to Article 6 of Directive 75/117, without knowledge of how the criteria applied, the complainants would be denied access to an effective remedy.

It has been stated as recently as 1991 that 'few Member States have in fact intervened in order to establish if sex discrimination is checked within their existing job classification and payment systems': Nielson and Szyszczak.

DIRECTIVE 76/207: THE PRINCIPLE OF EQUAL TREATMENT

Council Directive 76/207 governs the implementation of the principle of equal treatment for men and women as regards access to employment, vocational training and promotion, and working conditions (including those governing dismissal). As no Treaty article specifically provides for the application of this principle, except in relation to pay, the Directive was based on the residual legislative powers embodied in Article 235. However, the Directive should be seen in the light of Article 117 EEC which states that the 'Member States agree upon the need to promote improved working conditions and an improved standard of living for workers, so as to make possible their harmonisation while the improvement is being maintained.'

Equal treatment in matters of *social security*, referred to in Article 1 of the Directive, and covering *national statutory schemes* providing protection against sickness, invalidity, old age, accidents at work or occupational diseases, and unemployment, was implemented by means of Directive 79/7 (effective 1984). The principle of equal treatment in *occupational* (as opposed to statutory) *pension schemes* was implemented by Directive 86/378 which was not fully effective until 1 January 1993.

However, as *Barber*, which was decided in 1990, demonstrates, discrimination claims in respect of occupational pension benefits may be decided on the basis of 'pay' under the directly effective terms of Article 119 (as may also sick pay claims: see *Rinner-Kühn*, above).

Litigation in the UK regarding Directive 76/207 has mainly focused on Article 5 and challenges to different retirement ages:

Article 5

1. Application of the principle of equal treatment with regard to working conditions, including the conditions governing dismissal, means that men and women shall be guaranteed the same conditions without discrimination on grounds of sex.

2. To this end, Member States shall take the measures necessary to ensure that:

   (a) any laws, regulations and administrative provisions contrary to the principle of equal treatment shall be abolished;

   (b) any provisions contrary to the principle of equal treatment which are included in collective agreements, individual contracts of employment, internal rules of undertakings or in rules governing the independent occupations and professions shall be, or may be declared, null and void or may be amended ...

As previously indicated, in this country the ages at which men and women retire from employment have been linked to the differing ages at which they qualify for state pensions: 65 for men and 60 for women. Thus, as seen in Case 152/84 *Marshall* in Chapter Eight, section 6(4) of the Sex Discrimination Act 1975 excluded from the prohibition of discrimination by an employer on the ground of sex 'provision in relation to ... retirement'. Article 5 of the Directive applies the equal treatment principle to 'the conditions governing dismissal'. However, Article 7(1)(a) of Directive 79/7 on equal treatment in matters of social security does allow 'Member States to exclude from its scope ... the determination of pensionable age for the purposes of granting old-age and retirement pensions and the possible consequences thereof for other benefits.' (In Case C-9/91 *R v. Secretary of State for Social Security, ex parte Equal Opportunities Commission*, the Court of Justice stated that the exceptions to the principle of equal treatment for men and women provided for in Directive 79/7 were intended to allow Member States to maintain temporarily the advantages accorded to women with respect to retirement in order to permit them progressively to modify their pension schemes in this respect without disrupting the complex financial equilibrium of those systems.)

Although the decision of the Court of Justice in the first case to be discussed has been undermined (impliedly overruled) in subsequent decisions, it represents an important step in understanding the development of law in this area:

Case 19/81 *Burton* v. *British Railways Board*

Under the BRB scheme, women were entitled to apply for voluntary early retirement, and the receipt of appropriate redundancy payments and pension benefits, at 55 and men at 60. Mr B. aged 58, alleged that the scheme was discriminatory. A claim in national law being blocked by section 6(4) of the Sex Discrimination Act 1975, B sought to rely on Directive 76/207.

Following a reference under Article 177, relating to Article 119, Directive 75/117 and Directive 76/207, the Court of Justice held that:

1. The claim, relating as it did to *conditions of access* to BRB's early retirement scheme, could only be covered, if at all, by Directive 76/207 on equal treatment.

2. The word 'dismissal' in Article 5 was to be widely construed to cover termination of employment even under a voluntary redundancy scheme.

3. However, it was not contrary to Directive 76/207 to provide unequal access to such payments and benefits since the ages of retirement under the BRB scheme were calculated by reference to, and tied to, the *minimum statutory retirement* ages, and since Directive 79/7 explicitly allowed Member States to exclude from the scope of the equal treatment principle the determination of minimum pensionable age 'and the possible consequences thereof for other benefits'.

It should also be noted, with reference to the question of the *direct effect of Directives* as examined in Chapter Eight, that the Court in *Burton*, having held that the claimant's action lay *outside* the scope of Directive 76/207, was able to avoid the then (early 1980s) controversial issue of the possible horizontal direct effect of a Directive. This, as we have seen, was a question which was answered in the negative by the Court of Justice in 1986 in the next case. Although *Marshall* again involved a claim under Directive 76/207, her action concerned an allegation of discriminatory *compulsory* retirement. As with *Burton* she was faced by section 6(4) of the 1975 Act plus the view of the

UK Government that the Equal Treatment Directive permitted discrimination in compulsory retirement ages:

Case 152/84 *Marshall* v. *Southampton and SW Hampshire AHA*

The area health authority's normal retirement policy was linked to the state pension age: 60 for women, 65 for men. Miss M, who had been allowed to stay on after the normal age, was compulsorily retired at 62. As she wished to continue working, she challenged the defendant's policy as being discriminatory. Following a reference from the Employment Appeal Tribunal, the Court of Justice held that:

1. The retirement scheme was a 'condition governing dismissal' within Article 5 of Directive 76/207.

2. It was possible to distinguish Burton, which concerned benefits tied to a national scheme for which different pensionable ages were allowed. Article 7 of Directive 79/7 only allowed differing pensionable ages in the context of 'granting old-age and retirement pensions and the possible consequences thereof for other benefits'. Where differing pensionable ages were being used for other purposes, as here, for the purpose of retirement, discrimination was not allowed. (The question of dismissal was therefore separated from the issue of the exclusion of state pension ages from the equal treatment principle.)

3. Directive 76/207 could be invoked against the Area Health Authority ('an emanation of the State') in its capacity as employer (see Chapter Eight).

The upshot of this decision was that an employee could not be dismissed *merely* because she qualified for a state pension.

In the next case, a female employee made redundant at the age of 53 attempted to justify her claim of discrimination as regards access to early retirement benefits by tying her dismissal, as in *Burton*, to the differing qualifying ages for pensions under the state pension scheme:

Case 151/84 *Roberts* v. *Tate and Lyle Industries Ltd*

TLI agreed with the unions that *all* employees made redundant aged 55 and over would be entitled to immediate accelerated pension rights under the company's occupational pension scheme. (This replaced a previous agreement, linked to State pension ages, whereby immediate pensions were payable to women at 55 and men at 60; ie up to 5 years before their entitlement under the scheme would normally arise).

R claimed that the revised scheme was discriminatory since women were not entitled to a pension until five years before their normal retirement age, whereas men received an immediate pension up to ten years before their normal retirement age. A ten-year rule for both men and women, tied to State pension ages, would have brought R within the scope of entitlement. The Court ruled that the case was concerned exclusively with dismissal and was therefore covered by Article 5 of Directive 76/207, and not by Article 7 of Directive 79/7 which related to the consequences which *pensionable* age may have for social security benefits. As the *retirement* age was fixed at 55 for both men and women the scheme was not discriminatory.

Examining these last three cases, Greenwood summed up the position at that time in the following way:

> Nevertheless, the problems inherent in the distinction between pensionable age and retirement age may be seen in a comparison between *Marshall* and *Burton* v *British Railways Board* [1980] Q.B. 1080 (Case 19/81), in which the Court rejected an argument that a male employee had been the object of discrimination under an early retirement scheme offered to employees less than five years below the statutory pensionable age, so that a woman aged fifty-five was eligible under the scheme but a man of the same age was not. The two decisions can be reconciled. *Burton* was about access to a pension and post-retirement benefits, *Marshall* concerned continued access to employment. Yet to allow discrimination in the former case but not the latter is absurd, for both concern the problems of retirement. *Roberts* v *Tate and Lyle Industries Ltd* [1986] 2 All E.R. 602 (Case 151/84) may create further difficulties since it suggests that, even in relation to the pensionable age, Article 7 of Directive 79/7 may apply only to State, not private, pension schemes. However, such arbitrary distinctions are the price of the Member States' refusal to eliminate discrimination from State pension schemes.

Similarly, Steiner in 1990 stated that:

> Thus Member States' power under Article 7 of Directive 79/7 to exclude from the equal treatment principle 'the determination of pensionable age' has, in view of the fundamental importance of the principle of equal treatment (*Marshall*), been given the narrowest scope. It seems it will only apply where the difference in age is *for the purpose* of the granting of old age and retirement *pensions* and the possible consequences thereof for the other benefits 'falling within the statutory [or occupational] social security schemes' (*Marshall*, para. 35). *Burton* v *British Railways Board* (Case 19/81) appears to have been distinguished out of existence.

Having added the words 'or occupational' to para. 35 of the Court's judgment in *Marshall*, Steiner recognised that *Barber* (at the time only the AG's opinion was available) might, *as it eventually did*, call for their deletion: 'it may be possible to bring a claim in respect of *pension benefits paid by the employer*, even under a statutory scheme, which are discriminatory as a *result* of a difference in retirement ages for men and women, under the umbrella of 'pay'.' (Emphasis added and see Steiner, 3rd edition, 1992.)

However, before fitting *Barber* more fully into these developments, it is important to note that, following the decision in *Marshall*, the Sex Discrimination Act 1986 was passed and discriminatory *retirement* (not pensionable) ages were made unlawful, thereby amending section 6(4) of the 1975 Act. (The amendment did not have retrospective effect: see *Duke* v *GEC Reliance* in Chapter Eight – and it should be remembered that Directive 76/207 does not have horizontal direct effect – which leads us on to *Von Colson* (an equal treatment case) and the case law as it has developed in that area; currently as far as *Francovich*.)

Further, again at the national level, under the Employment Act 1989 men and women enjoy an equal right to receive redundancy benefits up to the age of 65, or the normal retirement age for their occupation, if that is less than 65. However, neither this Act nor that of 1986 was in force *at the time Mr Barber's claim arose*.

At Community level, the key to Barber's success as regards occupational pension benefits, resting on the decision by the Court of Justice that they fall within the concept of pay under the directly effective Article 119 and not the non-horizontally effective Equal Treatment Directive, was the Court's earlier decision in Case 170/84 *Bilka-Kaufhaus* (see above). There the German employer's *contractual* occupation pension scheme, albeit negotiated within a statutory framework laying down minimum requirements, was differentiated from the statutory State scheme which it supplemented. In *Barber* the British employer's occupational pension scheme was similar, being at least in part a *substitute* for the statutory scheme (the State earnings related pension scheme, SERPS). As regards the finding in *Barber* that, again, redundancy payments fall within the equal pay principle in Article 119, the Court, it will be recalled, stressed that where the benefit is received by the worker from his employer as a result of the employment relationship, the employment nexus is decisive (see *Defrenne No. 2*) and overrides the social policy aspect of statutory redundancy payments –and this was so even though the discrimination arose directly from legislative provisions. The payment was the employer's responsibility – but only as a result of a statutory obligation.

As Fitzpatrick explains:

Until recently, it had been presumed that payments made under statutory obligation were outside the scope of employment equality measures. However, the ECJ in *Rinner-Kühn* [see above] concluded that sick pay paid directly to the employer was still 'pay' within Article 119/EEC, even if dictated by legislation. The more reasoned re-affirmation of this position in *Barber*, in relation to both statutory redundancy pay and also the minimum statutory obligations applicable to contracted-out OP schemes, is not, in itself, surprising.

Derogations from the Equal Treatment Principle: Article 2(2)-(4) of Directive 76/207

Article 2(2) allows for exemption from the equal treatment principle 'those occupational activities and, where appropriate, the training leading thereto, for which, by reason of their nature or the context in which they are carried out, the sex of the worker contributes a determining factor'. Thus, in Case 165/82 *Commission* v *UK* (*Re Equal Treatment for Men and Women*), the UK's refusal to allow men full access to training for midwifery, on the basis of section 41 of the Sex Discrimination Act, was held to fall under Article 2(2) as the profession was one 'in which respect for the patient's sensitivities is of particular importance.'

In Case 248/83 *Commission* v *Germany* (*Re Sex Discrimination Laws*), in relation to the scope of the derogations in Article 2(2), the Court stated that it was for the Member States:

> ... to complete a verifiable list, in whatever form, of the occupations and activities excluded from the application of the principle of equal treatment and to notify the results to the Commission.

Otherwise, in the Court's opinion, the Commission would be prevented from exercising effective supervision, and individuals would have difficulty in defending their rights.

Article 2(3) allows for special protection to be afforded to women in relation to pregnancy and maternity. In particular it is concerned to protect two types of female need:

(i)   the biological condition of women during and after pregnancy, and
(ii)   the relationship between mother and child during the period following pregnancy and birth: see Case 184/83 *Hofmann* v *Barmer Ersatzkasse*.

Articles 2(2) and 2(3) came under consideration by the Court of Justice in the following case which has, however, much wider significance:

333

Case 224/84 *Johnston v. Chief Constable of the RUC*

In view of the deteriorating situation in Northern Ireland, the Chief Constable decided that: (i) men in the RUC and RUC Reserve would in future carry firearms in the normal course of duties, (ii) women would not be equipped with firearms nor be trained in their use, (iii) policewomen should no longer be asked to perform general duties (which might involve the use of firearms), and (iv) women in the RUC Reserve would only be required to perform duties which were assigned to women officers only.

Mrs Johnston had been an unarmed member of the RUC Reserve performing general duties for several years. In 1980 her three-year contract came up for renewal but the Chief Constable refused to renew it on the basis of the new policy towards female officers.

Mrs. J challenged this refusal and her exclusion from firearms training arguing that these amounted to unlawful sex discrimination.

In the face of a certificate issued by the Secretary of State which, under Article 53 of the Sex Discrimination (Northern Ireland) Order 1976, amounted to 'conclusive evidence' that the Chief Constable's refusal was 'for the purpose of safeguarding national security or of protecting public safety or public order', Mrs J sought to rely on the Equal Treatment Directive 76/207. Following an Article 177 reference regarding the interpretation of various provisions of the Directive, in particular the scope for derogation from the equal treatment principle, the Court of Justice ruled:

1. *Article 53 of the Order and Article 6 of the Directive*: the obligation imposed upon Member States under Article 6 was for them to introduce into their national legal systems the measures necessary to enable alleged victims of sex discrimination 'to pursue their claims by judicial process'. Article 53 of the Order was 'contrary to the principle of effective judicial control laid down in Article 6' because it enabled the individual to be deprived of the 'possibility of asserting by judicial process' the right that the Directive conferred.

   The principle of effective judicial control was, said the Court, 'a general principle of law which underlies the constitutional traditions common to the Member States. That principle was also laid down in Articles 6 and 13 of the European Convention for the Protection of Human Rights and Fundamental Freedoms (see Chapter Ten). Member States must ensure that the rights conferred by the Directive 'may be effectively relied upon before the national courts by the persons concerned.'

2. *The protection of public safety*: derogations on the grounds of national security, public safety or public order such as those found in Articles 36, 48, 56, 66, 223 and 224 of the Treaty were concerned with 'exceptional and clearly defined cases': the question of derogations from the equal treatment principle was to be dealt with in the light of the specific provisions of the Directive.

3. *The derogation in the Directive*: in terms of the permitted derogation in Article 2(2) relating to 'occupational activities' and 'training' for them, the crucial question was whether, in view of the *'context'* in which police work in Northern Ireland was carried out, the sex of police officers could amount to being 'a determining factor'.

The Court reviewed the reasons underlying the Chief Constable's change of policy: (i) if women were armed, they might more frequently become targets for assassination attempts and their firearms could fall into the hands of their attackers; (ii) the carrying of firearms by women conflicted too much with the ideal of an unarmed police force; (iii) policewomen would be hindered in carrying out of their valuable social work if they were armed.

In considering whether these reasons were covered by Article 2(2), the Court stressed that that provision, as a derogation from the fundamental principle of equal treatment (see Chapter Ten), must be interpreted strictly. However the Court did accept that:

'the possibility cannot be excluded that in a situation characterised by serious internal disturbances the carrying of firearms by policewomen might create additional risks of their being assassinated and might therefore be contrary to the requirements of public safety.

In such circumstances, the context of certain policing activities may be such that the sex of police officers constitutes a determining factor for carrying them out. If that is so, Member States may therefore restrict such tasks, and the training leading thereto, to men.'

It was for *the national court* (i) to assess whether the Chief Constable's reasons were well founded and thus justified his refusal to renew Mrs J's contract, and (ii) to ensure that the principle of proportionality was respected and so determine 'whether the refusal ... could not be avoided by allocating to women duties which, without jeopardising the aims pursued, can be performed without firearms'. (ie if there was a less discriminatory way of ensuring that the demands of public safety were met, the principle of proportionality was not satisfied.)

The Court dismissed Article 2(3) of the Directive as irrelevant and (as seen above) it would appear that the provision only permits derogations from equal treatment where they relate to 'a woman's biological condition and the special relationship which exists between a woman and her child'. The Court stated that: '... the Directive does not therefore allow women to be excluded from a certain type of employment on the ground that public opinion demands that women be given greater protection than men against risks which affect men and women in the same way and which are distinct from women's specific needs for protection, such as those expressly mentioned.'

1. *The question of the Directive's direct effect*: here the question was not the direct effect of the general principle of equal treatment. This had been properly implemented in Northern Ireland. The crucial issue was whether an individual could rely on the Directive as against a derogation laid down by the national authorities (in the Northern Ireland Order) which was found to have exceeded what was permitted by the Directive. The answer, in so far as it was held that a public authority responsible for the direction of the police was an 'emanation of the State', was in affirmative:

   'Whatever its relations may be with other organs of the State, such a public authority, charged by the State with the maintenance of public order and safety, does not act as a private individual. It may not take advantage of the failure of the State, of which it is an emanation, to comply with Community law.' (See also *Marshall* and the guidelines as to what constitutes 'the State' in the later case of *Foster* in Chapter Eight.)

   The Court held that *Article 6 of the Directive had direct effect* as regards *access to the judicial process* and the obligation to provide an effective judicial remedy in the national court. (This finding is to be contrasted with that in *Van Colson* where the Court stated that Article 6 was *not* directly effective as regards the provision of *specific sanctions*, not being unconditional or sufficiently precise in that respect).

In a perceptive comment on this case, Arnull states that:

The *Johnston* decision represents an attempt by the European Court to reconcile the need to promote the *effet utile* of the Directive with a reluctance to interfere with the discretion of the Chief Constable in a situation of serious internal disorder. That attempt seems to have been largely successful, although the Court perhaps gives the impression of accepting a little too readily the justifications advanced by the Chief

Constable for refusing to allow women to be trained in the use of firearms. The idea that armed policewomen would more frequently be subject to assassination attempts than male officers and that their guns might fall into the hands of their attackers seems somewhat fanciful. In addition, while it is probably true that the public would not relish the sight of armed policewomen, it must be doubtful whether the carrying of guns by male officers is particularly welcome. Arming women does not conflict with the ideal of an unarmed police force any more than arming men: to treat it as if it does is simply discriminatory. Moreover, even if women police officers were to be armed on some occasions, there would be no necessity for them to carry guns while performing duties of a social nature. It is therefore to be hoped that the Industrial Tribunal takes seriously the duty imposed on it by the European Court to examine whether these reasons were in fact well founded and justified the specific measure taken in Mrs. Johnston's case.

Finally, with regard to the question of restrictive interpretation of a derogation from a fundamental principle and the operation of the principle of proportionality, Docksey concludes that:

> As a result, it is difficult to imagine how to argue that public safety in Northern Ireland could only be effectively protected by restricting general policing to men equipped with firearms.

This case was eventually settled; the Chief Constable agreeing to pay thirty former policewomen £250,000. He also agreed to provide equal access for men and women to all forms of employment opportunities and to consider possible re-instatements. It has since been reported that RUC policewomen are carrying firearms.

Current Developments

In the light of evidence that discrimination against women in the workplace, both as regards pay and treatment, was a continuing problem in the Community, the Commission has, since 1982, initiated a series of Social Action programmes designed to eliminate remaining inequalities. One of its priorities under its 'Equal Opportunities for Men and Women: Third Action Programme (1991-95) is the improved application and development of existing legislation. In late 1990, the Commission introduced several draft Directives designed to abolish existing inequalities between part-time and temporary workers and full-time workers, which would, as we have seen, clearly benefit female employees. UK opposition to these measures has been largely instrumental in blocking Council approval, but it may well be that they will become law in the eleven Member States which (unlike the UK) signed the Agreement on Social Policy at Maastricht in December 1991.

Arnull, A., 'Article 119 and the Principle of Equal Pay for Work of Equal Value' (1986) 11 EL Rev. 200.

Arnull, A., 'The Beat Goes On': case note on Case 222/84 *Johnston* v *C.C. of the RUC* (1987) EL Rev. 56.

Arnull, A., *The General Principles of EEC Law and the Individual*, 1990.

Bourne, C., and Whitmore, J., *The Law of Discrimination and Equal Pay* (UK and EEC), 1989.

Curtin, D., 'Effective Sanctions and the Equal Treatment Directive: the *Von Colson* and *Harz* Cases' (1985) 22 CML Rev. 505.

Curtin, D., 'Scalping the Community Legislator: Occupational Pensions and 'Barber'.' (1990) 27 CML Rev. 475.

Docksey, C., 'The Principle of Equality Between Women and Men as a Fundamental Right under Community Law' (1991) ILJ 258.

Fitzpatrick, B., 'Equality in Occupational Pensions – The New Frontiers after *Barber*' (1991) 54 MLR 271.

Foster, N., 'Equal Treatment and Retirement Ages': case note on Case 152/84 *Marshall* (1986) 11 EL Rev. 222.

Greenwood, C., 'Directives – Time to Retire': case note on Case 152/84 *Marshall* (1987) 46 CLJ 9.

Honeyball, S. and Shaw, J., 'Sex, Law and the Retiring Man': case note on Case 262/88 *Barber* (1991) 16 EL Rev. 47.

Neilson, R., and Szyszczak, E., *The Social Dimension of the European Community*, Copenhagen, 1991.

Shaw, J., 'European Community Judicial Method: Its Application to Sex Discrimination Law' (1990) ILJ 228.

Steiner, J., 'Sex Discrimination under UK and EEC Law: Two plus Four Equals One' (1983) 32 ICLQ 399.

Szyszczak, E., 'Pay Inequalities and Equal Value Claims' (1985) 48 MLR 139.

Wyatt, D., 'Enforcing EEC Social Rights in the UK' (1989) ILJ 197.

CHAPTER FOURTEEN

COMPETITION LAW : RULES APPLYING TO UNDERTAKINGS – ARTICLE 85

At one moment they would be battling fiercely for markets, cutting prices, trying to undersell one another; at the next, they would be courting one another, trying to make an arrangement to apportion the world's markets among themselves; at still the next, they would be exploring mergers and acquisitions. On many occasions they would be doing all three at the same time in an atmosphere of great suspicion and mistrust, no matter how great the cordiality at any given moment: Yergin, *The Prize: the Epic Quest for Oil, Money and Power*.

INTRODUCTION TO COMMUNITY COMPETITION POLICY

As we have seen, Article 3 of the Treaty sets out the activities to be carried on by the Community in order to achieve fulfilment of the two related aims of Article 2: the establishment of a Common Market and an Economic and Monetary Union. Within the context of the first aim, Article 3(f) (Article 3(g) following ratification of the TEU) requires:

the institution of a system ensuring that competition in the common market is not distorted. [Article 3(g) EC substitutes 'internal market' for 'common market'.]

Article 3(f) is implemented by the 'Rules of Competition' comprising Articles 85-94 of both the EEC Treaty and EC Treaty as amended by the TEU. Articles 85-90 contain the rules applying to undertakings (private and public). Only these rules will be discussed here – to the exclusion of the obsolete, transitional period Article 91 on *dumping* (the penetration of one Member State's market by goods exported from another Member State at loss-making prices), and Articles 92-94 on *State aids* which distort competition by favouring national undertakings.

In its Fifth General Report on the Activities of the EEC (1971), the Commission drew attention to the close relationship between the free movement of goods principle and Community competition policy, whilst highlighting the two main targets of the latter:

The creation and development of this unified market would be difficult if not impossible if while conventional trade barriers among the Six were being speedily reduced, other obstacles, less visible but equally restrictive, were allowed to persist. These may arise from Member States applying different economic and fiscal regulations, or systems of State aid, *or from the abuse of dominant positions on the part of private firms or from agreements to restrict competition among them* (emphasis added).

Community competition policy (as distinct from the national competition policies of Member States) is therefore mainly directed towards the following anti-competitive activity:

1. Restrictive trading agreements between otherwise independent firms (undertakings) which may affect trade between Member States and which distort competition within the Common Market: Article 85. Restrictive agreements may be designed, for example, to fix prices or otherwise control markets for goods or services.

2. Abusive (anti-competitive and exploitative) practices of large undertakings (which dominate markets for goods or services) which, again, may affect trade between Member States: Article 86. Dominant firms may, for example, have the power to charge excessive and unfair prices to their customers; also

3. In that they can lead to or strengthen conditions of market dominance, major mergers (concentrations) between undertakings are subject to control under Council Regulation 4064/89.

Although the Community has thus established a regulatory framework – a system of law within which competition between undertakings is encouraged – the Treaty does not define competition. The following extract from a late 1980s American antitrust (competition policy) case provides valuable insights:

Competition is the driving force behind our free enterprise system. Unlike centrally planned economies, where decisions about production and allocation are made by government bureaucrats who ostensibly see the big picture and know to do the right thing, capitalism relies on decentralised planning – millions of producers and consumers making hundreds of millions of individual decisions each year – to determine what and how much will be produced. Competition plays the key role in this process: it imposes an essential discipline on producers and sellers of goods to provide the consumer with a better product at a lower cost; it drives out inefficient and marginal producers, releasing resources to higher-valued uses; it promotes diversity, giving consumers choices to fit a wide array of personal preferences; it avoids permanent concentrations of economic power, as even the largest firm can lose market share to a feistier and hungrier rival. If, as the metaphor goes, a market economy is governed by an invisible hand, competition is surely the brass knuckles by which it enforces its decisions.

When competition is impaired, producers may be able to reap monopoly profits, denying consumers many of the benefits of a free market. It is a simple but important truth, therefore, that our antitrust laws are designed to protect the integrity of the market system by assuring that competition reigns freely. While much has been said and written about the antitrust laws during the last century of their existence, ultimately the court must resolve a practical question in every monopolisation case: is this the type of situation where market forces are likely to cure the perceived problem within a reasonable period of time? Or, have barriers been erected to constrain the normal operation of the market, so that the problem is not likely to be self-correcting? In the latter situation, it might well be necessary for a court to correct the market imbalance; in the former, a court ought to exercise extreme caution because judicial intervention in a competitive situation can itself upset the balance of market forces, bringing about the very ills the antitrust laws were meant to prevent.

The opinions – of economists, politicians and lawyers – vary over time, from one country or political system to another, regarding the degree of regulation or intervention through law to which markets should be subjected by public authorities. The shift by the former Soviet Union and the countries of Central and Eastern Europe from centrally planned economies to free market economies, in which the forces of demand and supply will largely determine prices, is a clear illustration of this point.

Competition policy (and law) must therefore be dynamic, changing in terms of direction and objectives as political and economic situations change and develop. In its First Report on Competition Policy in 1972 the Commission stated that:

Competition is the best stimulant of economic activity since it guarantees the widest possible freedom of action to all. An active competition policy pursued in accordance with the provisions of the Treaties establishing the Communities makes it easier for the supply and demand structures continually to adjust to technological development. Through the interplay of decentralised decision-making machinery, competition enables enterprises continuously to improve their efficiency, which is the *sine qua non* for a steady improvement in living standards and employment prospects within the countries of the Community.

From this point of view, competition policy is an essential means for satisfying to a great extent the individual and collective needs of our society.

This statement focuses upon freedom of action for undertakings (and hence wide choice for their customers), upon the pressure on firms to invest in research and to innovate in line with changes in technology and consumer preferences, and thus upon the improved efficiency of firms in free market conditions. Human and material resources will be allocated effectively to meet demand for goods and services when and where it exists. Above all, competition keeps suppliers under pressure to keep costs and prices as low as possible in order not to lose sales to more efficient undertakings.

This somewhat idealised picture of the attractions of competition becomes obscured in the real world, not least in times of continued inflation. Although competition and free markets reflect the basic tenets of capitalism and western democracy, all the Member States operate what are called 'mixed' economies. On the basis of nationalisation measures, governments have moved undertakings or whole sectors of their economies out of private into public ownership. In this way legal monopolies have been created. This has applied particularly to public services such as gas, electricity, health services and rail transport. In such cases competition and the profit motive have not necessarily been eliminated (gas can compete with electricity) but have been subordinated to social welfare principles – or, rather, *were* until Thatcherite privatisation policies moved such sectors, in varying degrees, back to positions where, with more undertakings free to operate, market forces have become stronger.

Within the private sector itself, there is a natural tendency for concentrations of economic power to develop in markets for goods and services. The forces of competition themselves tend to throw up large and dominant, often multinational, corporations. Alternatively firms may agree to act in concert in order to obtain a greater degree of market power. Market structures within the Community may therefore be viewed according to the degree of *concentration* they exhibit, that is, according to the extent to which market power is concentrated in the hands of one or a few suppliers (or buyers).

It is against this background that it has been said that Community competition law and policy must aim to achieve '*workable competition*', ie competition which is effective and secures the most efficient allocation of available resources, against a background in which a variety of economic and social factors (eg the environment, regional imbalances, equal pay policy, consumer protection) must be weighed and kept in balance:

What is needed is to ensure access to the markets in question, for changes in supply and demand to be reflected in prices, for production and sales not to be artificially restricted and for the freedom of action and choice of suppliers, buyers and consumers not to be compromised': Commissioner von der Groeben in 1969.

Later, the Court of Justice in Case 26/76 *Metro (No.1)* spoke of workable competition in terms of market structures and Treaty objectives, particularly the creation of a single market:

The requirement contained in Articles 3 and 85 of the EEC Treaty that competition shall not be distorted implies the existence on the market of workable competition, that is to say the degree of competition necessary to ensure the observance of the basic requirements and the attainment of the objectives of the Treaty, in particular the creation of a single market achieving conditions similar to those of a domestic market.

In accordance with this requirement the nature and intensiveness of competition may vary to an extent dictated by the products or services in question and the economic structure of the relevant market sectors.

Workable competition will ensure that a market participant, be he one of many or of a few, or even the only one, is exposed to the competitive action of existing, or potential, competitors. Markets of this type fall somewhere between the two polar market models of economic theory:

(i)   the *perfectly competitive market* in which many small firms compete in the supply of a single product, and no single firm (seller or buyer) has sufficient power to have an impact on market price, and

(ii)   the *monopolistic market* in which a single firm, responsible for the supply of the total output of the product, is able, in the absence of substitutes, to control its price. Such a monopolist will maximise his profits at some point where his output is less than it would be under perfect competition, ie where demand exceeds supply, so ensuring him a high monopoly price.

A monopolistic market can be broken down if new firms are able to enter the market. This will probably involve overcoming considerable entry barriers. These may be exceptionally high investment costs, control by the monopolist of production methods covered by patents granted under national law, or even, as we have seen, the granting of monopoly power to an undertaking by the State, eg British Telecom before privatisation.

BASIC OBJECTIVES OF COMMUNITY COMPETITION POLICY

In its Ninth Report on Competition Policy (1980), the Commission stated that undistorted competition was 'a prerequisite for the proper functioning of the common market, which is the rock on which economic integration is to be founded'.

The introduction to the Ninth Report outlined four basic objectives of the Community's policy:

1.   An open and unified market - not partitioned by restrictive, anti-competitive agreements between undertakings.

2.   The right amount of effective competition in markets not subject to over-concentration or the abuses of dominant firms.

3.   Fairness in the market place - hence support for small and medium sized businesses, consumer protection measures and the attack on illegal state aids.

4.   Maintenance of the Community's competitive position vis-à-vis its main rivals (the USA and Japan) within the world economy.

The conclusion reached (at a time of severe economic difficulties arising in large part from large increases in oil prices) was that:

> The sheer scale of the common market and its inextricable enmeshment in world trade dictate that the need for a universal regulator of economic activity throughout the Community can only be answered by a Community competition policy. To yield to the persuasions of those who would respond to the crisis by a retreat into self-sufficient isolation would simply aggravate the situation beyond redemption by deepening the trauma of the structural changes thrust upon Europe by the shifting patterns of world trade. If we delude ourselves that we can dispense with the forces of competition and a decentralised economy and can steer through the necessary restructuring by purely legislative means, we run the

irremediable risk of cutting our Community off from the economic reality of its surroundings.

In several respects Community competition policy involves the Commission in a delicate balancing act. The market integration function of competition policy will not cease with the establishment of the Internal Market - not with a number of EFTA and Central European countries waiting to join the Community. The encouragement of small and medium-sized firms must not be at the expense of the need for some firms to achieve optimum size in order to operate effectively not only throughout the Common Market but in competition with large scale undertakings in the USA and Japan. The attack on agreements which restrict competition must not stifle efficiency:

> Competition policy fosters market integration in a positive way as well. Subject to the maintenance of an adequate level of competition, it allows scope for cooperation between firms likely to further technical and economic progress, especially in research and development and the transfer of technology. Hence the Commission can take favourable decisions on inter-company cooperation or government intervention that is in the wider Community interest and not just the interest of the firms or countries concerned. This is especially evident in the case of measures which stimulate R & D and innovation, as well as boosting dynamic growth, or which help realise the growth potential of underdeveloped areas.

> These two sides of the Commission's competition policy, control of the action of governments and of firms, thus pursue the same aim of ensuring open, efficient markets in which firms determine their prices and output independently according to market conditions. It is this type of environment in which firms can best develop and can take on world competition: Sixteenth Commission Competition Report.

THE ENFORCEMENT OF COMMUNITY COMPETITION LAW

On the basis of Article 87, Council Regulation 17/62 provides for the 'balanced application of Arts. 85 and 86 in a uniform manner in the Member States'. The administration and enforcement of the competition rules applying to undertakings is entrusted to the Commission (in particular Directorate General IV and the Legal Service), 'acting in close and constant liaison with the competent authorities of the Member States'. Such competent authorities include the Office of Fair Trading in the UK and the German Bundeskartellamt.

Under Regulation 17/62 the Commission is empowered, amongst other things, for the purpose of bringing to an end infringements of Articles 85 and 86, to address non-judicial *Decisions* to undertakings, enforceable by means of fines and periodic penalty payments. In addition, the Commission has sole power under Article 9(1) of the Regulation to grant exemption under Article 85(3) of a notified agreement caught by Article 85(1) which nevertheless produces economic or other benefits which outweigh its anti-competitive effects. Block exemptions may also be granted under Article 85(3) to 'categories of agreements' by way of Commission Regulations.

Decisions made by the Commission under Articles 85 and 86 are, since 1989, subject to review by the Court of First Instance (previously by the Court of Justice) under Article 173(2) in challenges brought (usually) by undertakings on the various grounds stipulated in that article. Article 172 also applies to the CFI, giving it unlimited jurisdiction as regards penalties imposed on undertakings by the Commission. Fines or penalty payments may be cancelled, reduced or increased. As seen in Chapter Seven, decisions of the CFI are subject to a right of appeal to the Court of Justice on points of law.

In that Article 85(1) imposes a clear, direct and unconditional obligation upon undertakings as regards anti-competitive concerted behaviour, it produces *direct effects* and creates rights which national courts must protect: see Case 127/73 *BRT* v *SABAM*. If, for example, an agreement between undertakings falls within Article 85(1), not only will it be 'automatically void' under Article 85(2) in respect of its offending provisions, but also other parties injured by such infringement may be in a position to pursue a civil claim in the national courts for damages and/or an injunction. The courts of the Member States may therefore be called upon to apply Community competition law - within certain limits. The same principles apply in general to Article 86 relating to an undertaking's abuse of a dominant position. Many of the points raised in this introduction to enforcement will be elaborated and seen in action in the cases which follow and, more particularly, in Chapter Seventeen.

ARTICLE 85 : RESTRICTIVE AGREEMENTS, DECISIONS AND CONCERTED PRACTICES

Article 85

1. The following shall be prohibited as incompatible with the Common Market: all agreements between undertakings, decisions

by associations of undertakings and concerted practices which may affect trade between Member States and which have as their object or effect the prevention, restriction or distortion of competition within the Common Market, and in particular those which:

(a)   directly or indirectly fix purchase or selling prices or any other trading conditions;

(b)   limit or control production, markets, technical development, or investment;

(c)   share markets or sources of supply;

(d)   apply dissimilar conditions to equivalent transactions with other trading parties, thereby placing them at a competitive disadvantage;

(e)   make the conclusion of contracts subject to acceptance by the other parties of supplementary obligations which, by their nature or according to commercial use, have no connection with the subject of such contracts.

2. Any agreements or decisions prohibited pursuant to this article shall be automatically void.

3. The provisions of paragraph 1 may, however, be declared inapplicable in the case of:

–   any agreement or category of agreements between undertakings;

–   any decision or category of decisions by associations of undertakings:

–   any concerted practice or category of concerted practices;

which contributes to improving the production or distribution of goods or to promoting technical or economic progress, while allowing consumers a fair share of the resulting benefit, and which does not:

(a)   impose on the undertakings concerned restrictions which are not indispensable to the attainment of these objectives;

(b)   afford such undertakings the possibility of eliminating competition in respect of a substantial part of the products in question.

In broad terms, Article 85 is directed against forms of co-operation between firms which are anti-competitive. The article formulates (1) a prohibition (followed by a non-exhaustive list of anti-competitive practices), (2) (some of) the consequences attached to that prohibition, and (3) a qualification concerning the Commission's power to grant an exemption from the prohibition to agreements, etc which achieve beneficial ends which outweigh the harm to competition. There are two positive conditions and two negative conditions.

Commenting on Article 85 Sharpston explains that:

We are dealing with heavily economic law: what is being assessed and approved or condemned is the effect of certain types of behaviour on markets, prices and product availability.

Article 85(3) is essentially an economic balancing act: will the benefits from a particular arrangement (in terms of enhanced product choice or better quality service, or similar) be deemed to outweigh the costs (in terms of the associated reduction in competition)? If so, the agreement may be exempted; if not, it will continue to be caught by the general prohibition contained in Art 85(1).

'Assessment' implies an assessor – in this case, Directorate General IV of the Commission of the European Communities: the Commission's view of the likely effects of a proposed or implemented arrangement does not necessarily coincide with the client company's.

The power to exempt under Art 85(3) is a discretionary power: the Commission is not obliged to grant an exemption in a particular case.

The very first decision of the Court of Justice on Article 85 illustrates, amongst other things, (1) the close relationship between competition policy and the free movement of goods and (2) the need to establish a Common Market based on the competitive interpenetration of existing national markets for goods and services:

Cases 56 and 58/64 *Consten and Grundig* v. *Commission*
In 1957, as part of its international distribution network, the German company Grundig appointed Consten as its exclusive distributor in France. G agreed to supply only C in France and to ensure that its distributors outside France did not deliver G's radio, television and recording equipment into France. In return C undertook not to sell competing products and not to sell G's products to other countries.

By means of the *export bans* included in these exclusive distributorship agreements, C, and G's other dealers, were granted a position of '*absolute territorial protection*' within their contract areas. In addition, C was granted exclusive rights in France to G's GINT (Grundig International) trade mark.

UNEF, a French firm, bought G's products in Germany and, as a result of price differentials in the German and French markets, was able to sell them in France below the prices charged by C.

C sued the parallel importer UNEF in the French courts for breach of the GINT trade mark. On an application by UNEF to the Commission that the Grundig-Consten agreement was in breach of Article 85(1), the Commission issued a Decision to that effect. G and C sought to annul that Decision under Article 173(2). The Court of Justice struck down those clauses of the agreement, relating to the export ban and the supplementary use of the trade mark, which sought to partition the market and so prevent the creation of a Common Market. This was so despite strong economic arguments which sought to justify the arrangements in question.

The Court ruled, in part, as follows:

The complaints relating to the concept of 'agreements ... which may affect trade between Member States'

The applicants and the German Government maintain that the Commission has relied on a mistaken interpretation of the concept of an agreement which may affect trade between Member States and has not shown that such trade would have been greater without the agreement in dispute.

The defendant replies that this requirement in Article 85(1) is fulfilled once trade between Member States develops, as a result of the agreement, differently from the way in which it would have done without the restriction resulting from the agreement, and once the influence of the agreement on market conditions reaches a certain degree. Such is the case here, according to the defendant, particularly in view of the impediments resulting within the Common Market from the disputed agreement as regards the exporting and importing of Grundig products to and from France.

The concept of an agreement 'which may affect trade between Member States' is intended to define, in the law governing cartels, the boundary between the areas respectively covered by Community law and national law. It is only to the extent to which the agreement may affect trade between Member States that the deterioration in competition caused by the agreement falls under the prohibition of Community law contained in Article 85; otherwise it escapes the prohibition.

In this connection, what is particularly important is whether the agreement is capable of constituting a threat, either direct or indirect, actual or potential, to freedom of trade between Member States in a manner which might harm the attainment of the objectives of a single market between States. Thus the fact that an agreement encourages an increase, even a large one, in the volume of trade between States is not sufficient to exclude the possibility that the agreement may 'affect' such trade in the above mentioned manner. In the present case, the contract between Grundig and Consten, on the one hand by preventing undertakings other than Consten from importing Grundig products into France, and on the other hand by prohibiting Consten from re-exporting those products to other countries of the Common Market, indisputably affects trade between Member States. These limitations on the freedom of trade, as well as those which might ensue for third parties from the registration in France by Consten of the GINT trade mark, which Grundig places on all its products, are enough to satisfy the requirement in question.

Consequently, the complaints raised in this respect must be dismissed.

The complaints concerning the criterion of restriction on competition
The applicants and the German Government maintain that since the Commission restricted its examination solely to Grundig products the decision was based upon a false concept of competition and of the rules on prohibition contained in Article 85(1), since this concept applies particularly to competition between similar products of different makes; the Commission, before declaring Article 85(1) to be applicable, should, by basing itself upon the 'rule of reason', have considered the economic effects of the disputed contract upon competition between the different makes. There is a presumption that vertical sole distributorship agreements are not harmful to competition and in the present case there is nothing to invalidate that presumption. On the contrary, the contract in question has increased the competition between similar products of different makes.

The principle of freedom of competition concerns the various stages and manifestations of competition. Although competition between producers is generally more noticeable than that between distributors of products of the same make, it does not thereby follow that an agreement tending to restrict the latter kind of competition should escape the prohibition of Article 85(1) merely because it might increase the former.

Besides, for the purpose of applying Article 85(1), there is no need to take account of the concrete effects of an agreement once it appears that it has as its object the prevention, restriction or distortion of competition.

Therefore the absence in the contested decision of any analysis of the effects of the agreement on competition between similar products of different makes does not, of itself, constitute a defect in the decision.

It thus remains to consider whether the contested decision was right in founding the prohibition of the disputed agreement under Article 85(1) on the restriction on competition created by the agreement in the sphere of the distribution of Grundig products alone. The infringement which was found to exist by the contested decision results from the absolute territorial protection created by the said contract in favour of Consten on the basis of French law. The applicants thus wished to eliminate any possibility of competition at the wholesale level in Grundig products in the territory specified in the contract essentially by two methods.

First, Grundig undertook not to deliver even indirectly to third parties products intended for the area covered by the contract. The restrictive nature of that undertaking is obvious if it is considered in the light of the prohibition on exporting which was imposed not only on Consten but also on all the other sole concessionaires of Grundig, as well as the German wholesalers. Secondly, the registration in France by Consten of the GINT trade mark, which Grundig affixes to all its products, is intended to increase the protection inherent in the disputed agreement, against the risk of parallel imports into France of Grundig products, by adding the protection deriving from the law on industrial property rights. Thus no third party could import Grundig products from other Member States of the Community for resale in France without running serious risks.

The defendant properly took into account the whole distribution system thus set up by Grundig. In order to arrive at a true representation of the contractual position the contract must be placed in the economic and legal context in the light of which it was concluded by the parties. Such a procedure is not to be regarded as an unwarrantable interference in legal transactions or circumstances which were not the subject of the proceedings before the Commission.

The situation as ascertained above results in the isolation of the French market and makes it possible to charge for the products in question prices which are sheltered from all effective competition. In addition, the more producers succeed in their efforts to render their own makes of product individually distinct in the eyes of the consumer, the more the effectiveness of competition between producers tends to diminish. Because of the considerable impact of distribution costs on the aggregate cost price, it seems important that competition between dealers should also be stimulated. The efforts of the dealer are stimulated by competition between distributors of products of the same make. Since the agreement thus aims at isolating the French market for Grundig products and maintaining artificially, for products of a very well-known brand, separate national markets within the Community, it is therefore such as to distort competition in the Common Market.

It was therefore proper for the contested decision to hold that the agreement constitutes an infringement of Article 85(1). No further considerations, whether of economic data (price differences between France and Germany, representative character of the type of appliance considered, level of overheads borne by Consten) or of the corrections of the criteria upon which the Commission relied in its comparisons between the situations of the French and German markets, and no possible favourable effects of the agreement in other respects, can in any way lead, in the face of above mentioned restrictions, to a different solution under Article 85(1).

As seen, the Court confined its decision to the export bans imposed on the distributors and the related agreement regarding the use of the 'GINT' trade mark. It also annulled for lack of reasoning (see Article 190) that part of the Commission's Decision condemning the obligation on Grundig not to make direct deliveries in France except to Consten (and see also Case 56/65 *Société-Technique Minière*, below).

As a result of this decision, it is clear that:

1. Article 85 applies not only to *horizontal* agreements between competing firms but also to *vertical* agreements between non-competing firms which seek to exclude others from the market.

2. An agreement may be caught by Article 85(1), even though it encourages trade between Member States, if, as a result of (a) the export bans and (b) the use of national industrial property rights (the GINT trade mark), the agreement nevertheless has an adverse effect on competition and the free movement of goods.

3. Article 85 covers not only agreements which restrict competition between competing manufacturers, ie *inter-brand competition*, but also agreements which restrict competition between distributors of a single manufacturer's products; *intra-brand* competition.

4. The consumer interest in choice and fair prices is a constituent element in the concept of workable or effective competition.

Critics of this decision point out that market power (inter-brand competition) and not regulation would ensure that Grundig's products could not be sold at unreasonably high prices. In the USA, the Supreme Court, in *Continental TV Inc* v *GTE Sylvania Inc* (1977) stated that:

> Interbrand competition ... is the primary purpose of antitrust law ... When interbrand competition exists ... it provides a significant check on the exploitation of intrabrand market power because of the ability of consumers to substitute a different brand of the same product.

It may be argued that, unlike the Court of Justice in 1964 (and later), the Supreme Court in 1977 was not concerned with the establishment of a single market. Further developments, regarding both the case law and subsequent legislative measures in relation to exclusive distribution agreements, are considered later in this chapter.

INTERPRETATION OF ARTICLE 85: ITS CONSTITUENT ELEMENTS

'AGREEMENTS ... DECISIONS ... AND CONCERTED PRACTICES'

For Article 85(1) to apply there must be an *agreement* between undertakings, *or a decision by an association of undertakings* or a *concerted practice*. The case law shows that these concepts may overlap and, for example, an informal agreement may also be a concerted practice.

'*Agreements*' covers not only binding contracts but also so-called 'gentlemen's agreements': Case 41/69 etc *ACF Chemiefarma* (the *Quinine* cases). An agreement may be inferred from the circumstances of the case but, although it may be caught by Article 86, action taken by an undertaking without any form of agreement by another does not infringe Article 85(1).

It may be the case that an apparently 'unilateral' action in fact amounts to a tacit understanding between the parties. Thus a supplier's restrictive sales policy may be regarded as implicitly accepted by that supplier's distributors so as to give rise to an agreement within the meaning of Article 85(1):

Cases 25 and 26/84 *Ford Werke AG* v. *Commission*

The Court upheld the Commission's refusal to grant exemption under Article 85(3) for Ford Werke's apparently acceptable standard distribution agreement. Ford Werke was refusing to supply its distributors in Germany with right–hand–drive cars likely to be exported to the UK where prices were high. This action was taken following complaints from Ford's UK dealers who were being undercut by these parallel imports. This was seen by the Court as a tactic designed to partition the market and to maintain different price levels in different Member States.

Although there was no evidence of an express agreement or of concerted action, the Court ruled that the refusal to supply had been impliedly accepted by the distributors, so forming a sufficient basis for a contract between Ford Werke and its distributors. (See also Case C-279/87 *Tipp-Ex*.)

Both horizontal agreements (eg between two or more competing suppliers) and, as seen in *Consten and Grundig*, vertical agreements (eg between a supplier and a distributor) may fall with Article 85(1).

'*Decisions by associations of undertakings*' typically covers the rules, decisions *and* recommendations of trade associations which apply to their members and produce the results prohibited under Article 85(1): see, for example, Cases 96/82 etc *NV IAZ International Belgium*.

'*Concerted practices*' amount to a form of co-ordination between undertakings which, without amounting to an agreement, knowingly substitutes practical co-operation for the risks of competition. Leading cases on concerted practices include Case 48/69 *ICI* v *Commission (Dyestuffs)*; Cases 40/73 etc *Suiker Unie* v *Commission (Sugar)* and Cases T-1/89 etc *Rhone Poulenc and Others* v *Commission (Polypropylene)*.

Case 48/69 *ICI* v. *Commission (Dyestuffs)*

Three uniform price increases were introduced by the leading producers of aniline dyes in Benelux and Italy in 1964, 1965 and 1967. The Commission held that the parties were guilty of concerted practices and it imposed heavy fines. The Commission's decision was based, among other things, upon (i) the uniform identity of the rates of increase, (ii) the similarity of the dates upon which the increases were announced or applied, (iii) the simultaneous despatch of instructions to subsidiaries, and (iv) the fact and nature of informal contact between the undertakings in question.

Following a challenge under Article 173(2), the Court upheld the Commission's decision.

Cases T-1/89 etc *Rhone Poulenc and Others* v. *Commission*
(Polypropylene)

At meetings of competing polypropylene (thermoplastic materials used for films, fibres, etc.) suppliers, RP disclosed company price and production figures. The Commission's finding that the meetings had the purpose of influencing market conduct within the industry was confirmed by the Court. In the Court's view, mere attendance at the meetings (passive contact) would amount to participation in a concerted practice.

In the *Dyestuffs* case (in 1969 ICI was a non-EEC undertaking, controlling an EEC subsidiary), it was argued that the price increases were parallel increases made *without* collusion and were a natural feature of what is known as an *oligopolistic* market. This is a market dominated by a small number of suppliers of a (relatively) homogeneous product, eg petrol. Price is thus a crucial determinant of demand and if one company reduces prices, the others will follow *independently* in order to retain their market share. If costs increase, all are affected and prices rise - not as a result of collusion but on the basis of what is known as mutual interdependence or conscious parallelism of action.

In *Dyestuffs*, the Court held that the defendants must prove that parallel prices were not collusive and thus that the absence of effective competition arose from the oligopolistic nature of the market:

> Although parallel behaviour may not by itself be identified with a concerted practice, it may however amount to strong evidence of such a practice if it leads to conditions of competition which do not correspond to the normal conditions of the market, having regard to the nature of the products, the size and number of the undertakings, and the volume of the said market..

The Court went on to say that:

> Although every producer is free to change his prices, taking into account in so doing the present or foreseeable conduct of his competitors, nevertheless it is contrary to the rules on competition contained in the Treaty for a producer to co-operate with his competitors, in any way whatsoever, in order to determine a coordinated course of action relating to a price increase and to ensure its success by prior elimination of all uncertainty as to each other's conduct regarding the essential

elements of that action, such as the amount, subject-matter, date and place of the increases.

The oligopoly argument was rejected by the Court, which was of the view that the more powerful of the producers might indeed have been in a position to refrain from following an increase by a price-leader, and have attempted to increase their market share by maintaining existing price levels. On the facts, however, the price collusion found by the Court had, in practice, the effect of dividing the Common Market into five national markets with different price levels and structures.

Bearing in mind that effective competition may be curtailed both by collusion, caught by Article 85(1), or oligopolistic conscious parallelism falling short of collusion, it is perhaps surprising that it was not until the mid 1980's that the Commission moved against oligopolies, primarily on the basis of the words of Article 86 - 'one or more undertakings' - and the concept of joint dominance of the relevant market. In 1989, in *Italian Flat Glass*, the Commission decided that three Italian glass manufacturers:

> ... as participants in a tight oligopoly, enjoy a degree of independence from competitive pressures that enables them to impede the maintenance of effective competition, notably by not having to take account of the behaviour of other market participants.

This case will be discussed later in the context of Article 86: see Chapter Fifteen.

'BETWEEN UNDERTAKINGS'

The concept of 'undertaking' covers all legal and natural persons engaged in economic or commercial activity, eg limited companies, sole traders and State corporations. Such undertakings may be concerned with the supply of goods or the provision of services: see, eg Case 155/73 *Sacchi* (television broadcasts), *UNITEL* (1978) (opera singers).

In a number of cases, the Court has focused attention on the corporate group rather than the separate legal units which comprise it. A parent company and its subsidiaries are not considered as separate undertakings for the purpose of Article 85 where the subsidiary is not economically independent of the parent.

In practice it is unlikely that an agreement between parent and subsidiary will be found to fall within Article 85(1); financial and/or directorial control by the former being readily assumed. For example, in Case 15/74 *Centrafarm*, the Court stated that:

Article 85, however, is not concerned with agreements or concerted practices between undertakings belonging to the same concern and having the status of parent company and subsidiary, if the undertakings form an economic unit within which the subsidiary has no real freedom to determine its course of action on the market, and if the agreements or practices are concerned merely with the internal allocation of tasks as between the undertakings.

A parent company may however be liable for the acts of its subsidiary in relation to third parties when the subsidiary is acting on the instructions of the parent. In Case 22/71 *Béguelin:*

B was appointed exclusive distributor for Belgium and France for WIN gas pocket lighters by Oshawa, the Japanese manufacturers.

B later transferred the exclusive concession for France to its wholly dependent subsidiary in that country. The French company concluded an agreement to that effect with Oshawa.

B and its subsidiary brought actions against a parallel importer of the lighters in the French courts in circumstances similar to those in the *Consten and Grundig* case.

The Court of Justice held, *inter alia*, that:
1. The agreement between B and its French subsidiary could not affect competition between the parties but it could do so between one of the parties and third parties such as the defendants.

2. The fact that one of the undertakings which are parties to an agreement is situated outside the Community does not prevent the application of Article 85 when the agreement is operative *within* the Common Market.

Further implications of (i) the 'integrated undertaking' or 'enterprise entity' principle, and (ii) the extra-territorial reach of Community competition law will be examined in due course.

'WHICH MAY AFFECT TRADE BETWEEN MEMBER STATES'

These words determine the jurisdiction of the Community in that if an agreement has no such effect, EEC rules will not apply - although national competition rules may do so.

Nevertheless, an agreement between two undertakings situated within the *same* Member State may be examined under Article 85 in order to establish whether, within the context of similar national agreements, they are capable *in aggregate* of affecting inter-Member State trade. Case 23/67 *Brasserie de Haecht* concerned a typical 'tied-house' or beer supply agreement between a Belgian cafe proprietor and Belgian brewery. In this Article 177 reference, the Court's concern was whether such national agreements might (in aggregate) significantly foreclose outlets in Belgium to breweries situated in other Member States and so partition the Common Market. Clearly, in terms of our next section, it was not the 'object' of this particular agreement to restrict competition such as to effect trade between Member States, but the Court was anxious to establish the practical 'effect' of Belgian 'tied-house' agreements in general: see also Case 234/89 *Delimitis* v *Henniger Brau* in which the tenant/purchaser was, however, allowed to obtain supplies from other Member States. There is no decision to date that a brewery tie does infringe Article 85(1) and the position is now covered by block exemption Regulation 1984/83.

Similar questions arise in relation to horizontal agreements which extend throughout a Member State. In Case 8/72 *Cementhandelaren*, a price-fixing cement cartel sought to argue that their agreement could not affect trade between Member States because it was limited to the Netherlands and did not apply to imports or exports. The Court of Justice held that the agreement by its very nature had the effect of reinforcing the compartmentalisation of markets on a national basis and of impeding the establishment of a Common Market.

In order for an agreement, etc to affect trade between Member States, the basic test was laid down by the Court in Case 56/65 *Société Technique Minière* v *Maschinenbau Ulm*:

> ... it must be possible to foresee with a sufficient degree of probability on the basis of a set of objective factors of law or fact that it may have an influence, direct or indirect, actual or potential, on the pattern of trade between Member States, such as might prejudice the aim of a single market in all the Member States.

The case law shows that this requirement is easily met and it is sufficient that the goods or services are traded, or likely to be traded, between Member

States. As the *Consten and Grundig* case shows, it is irrelevant that the agreement produces an increase in trade since the prime aim of the Treaty is to create a system of undistorted competition. The Grundig agreement infringed Article 85 mainly because it partitioned the market, its export bans being designed to prevent parallel imports and the competitive interpenetration of markets which the Treaty is designed to bring about. This question also arose in the *Société Technique Minière* case which is discussed below.

Horizontal market-sharing agreements between otherwise competing producers: see Article 85(1)(c), can readily be seen as serious infringements of Article 85(1). In Cases 40/73 etc *Suiker Unie (Sugar)*, the parties agreed to keep out of each other's territory. In Case 41/69 etc *ACF Chemiefarma (Quinine)*, the parties also jointly fixed the prices at which they would sell their products in the various national markets of 'the Six'. Such perpetuation of national markets was held to deny consumers the benefits of competition: see also Article 85(1)(a).

'OBJECT OR EFFECT THE PREVENTION, RESTRICTION OR DISTORTION OF COMPETITION'

In Case 172/80 *Zückner (Bank Charges)*, which concerned uniform service charges imposed by banks with respect to transfers of money by cheque from one Member State to another, the Court of Justice made the following statement of principle:

> A basic principle of the EEC competition rules is that each trader must determine independently the policy which he intends to adopt on the common market and the conditions which he intends to offer to his customers. This does not prevent the traders adapting themselves intelligently to the existing or anticipated conduct of their competitors; it does, however, strictly preclude any direct or indirect contact between such traders the object or effect of which is to create conditions of competition which do not correspond to the normal conditions of the relevant market, in the light of the nature of the products or services offered, the size and number of the undertakings and the size of the market.

Horizontal price-fixing and market-sharing agreements of the cartel type clearly have the *object* of preventing, restricting or distorting competition. However in many other situations, where the agreement is not *designed* to restrict competition within the Common Market, eg *Brasserie de Haecht* above, an examination of its *effect* will often require a detailed analysis of the surrounding economic and legal circumstances:

Case 56/65 *Société Technique Minière* v. *Maschinenbau Ulm*

A German manufacturer of heavy earth-moving equipment MBU, granted exclusive distribution rights in France to STM. MBU agreed not to compete with STM in France and STM agreed not to sell competing machines. However, as no exports bans were imposed on STM (nor it would appear on other distributors of MBU's products), distributors were not given 'absolute territorial protection' and there were no impediments to parallel imports.

The Commission claimed that the restriction accepted by MBU not to compete with STM necessarily brought the agreement within Article 85(1). The Court disagreed and held that exclusive distribution agreements did not in themselves ('of their very nature') restrict competition within the meaning of Article 85(1).

The conclusions reached by the Court distinguished this case from *Consten and Grundig* and (following the analysis by Bellamy and Child) yield the following propositions:

1. In deciding whether Article 85(1) applies, it is first necessary to consider 'the object' of the agreement. The export bans in *Consten and Grundig* were 'of their nature' restrictive of competition irrespective of their actual effects. Thus the *object* of the agreement in that case was to restrict competition and it was not necessary to examine the effects. The agreement in *Consten and Grundig* was therefore of a type (like horizontal price-fixing agreements) which restrict competition *per se*. They may only be exempt, if at all, under Article 85(3). There were no export bans in the agreement between STM and MBU, which was not part of a large network and concerned companies of only modest importance. The agreement was therefore *not necessarily* restrictive of competition. Whether or not this was the case depended on the '*effects*' of the agreement, taking into account the economic context in which it operated.

2. In judging the effect of an agreement, regard must be had to the competition which would occur in the absence of the agreement in question. The effect on competition must be appreciable: the introduction of a '*de minimis*' rule, see below.

    Taking into account in particular (a) the market shares of the parties in the relevant market; (b) whether the agreement stood alone or as part of a network; and (c) whether the agreement precluded the possibility of parallel imports, the Court stated that 'it may be doubted whether there is an interference with competition if the said agreement [between MBU and STM] seems really necessary for the penetration of a new area by an undertaking.'

The conclusions reached by the Court (for the benefit of the referring national court) are said to be based on a '*rule of reason*', which carries disputed agreements *outside* the scope of Article 85(1) altogether. Such agreements may contain restrictions on competition (eg *MBU's* acceptance that it would not compete with STM within its contract territory) but so long as they do not have the 'object' of restricting competition, their anti-competitive 'effect' will be weighed against any pro-competitive advantages (in *STM/MBU* the need to penetrate a new territory through the medium of a national distributor in touch with the market in question). Where the latter outweigh the former, the restrictions will be seen as 'necessary' in the circumstances and the 'rule of reason' adopted by the Court will mean that no breach of Article 85(1) has taken place. The agreement poses no real threat to competition or the functioning of a single market. (Compare the operation of a 'rule of reason' here to that in *Cassis de Dijon* in Chapter Twelve.)

This 'rule of reason' approach (not expressly acknowledged as such by the Court) can also be seen applied to 'necessary' or 'essential' restrictions in agreements in the following examples:

Case 26/76 *Metro (No. 1)*: *selective* distribution systems do not infringe Article 85(1) where dealers are chosen on the basis of *objective* criteria of a qualitative nature (relating to such matters as specialist expertise, adequacy of premises, qualified staff and after-sales service) and the conditions for the application of such criteria are laid down uniformly for all potential resellers. Such 'restrictions' as those above (which generally exclude discount stores and the like) may be objectively justified on the basis of a business policy consideration such as the need to ensure the proper distribution of quality products, for example, top range motor cars, electronic goods and luxury perfumes.

Case 258/78 *Nungesser*: restrictive but 'necessary' clauses in licences of plant breeders' rights in order to encourage the licensee to take the business risk of adopting a new and untried technology: see also Chapter Eighteen.

Case 42/84 *Remia*: a non-competition clause imposed on the seller of a business, 'necessary' for the protection of the goodwill taken over by the buyer. (The ten year restriction was however excessive; compare with the English common law restraint of trade approach.)

Case 161/84 *Pronuptia*: a case involving the application of Article 85(1) to a franchise agreement. Such agreements have as their object the establishment of a special distribution system whereby the franchisor provides for the franchisee, in addition to goods (in this case wedding dresses and accessories), certain trade names, trade marks, merchandising material and services. The Court of Justice, in response to an Article 177 reference stated that:

> The compatibility of franchise agreements for the distribution of goods with Article 85(1) depends on the provisions contained therein and on their economic context.

> Provisions which are strictly necessary in order to ensure that the know-how and assistance provided by the franchisor do not benefit competitors do not constitute restrictions of competition for the purposes of Article 85(1).

> Provisions which establish the control strictly necessary for maintaining the identity and reputation of the network identified by the common name or symbol do not constitute restrictions of competition for the purposes of Article 85(1).

> Provisions which share markets between the franchisor and the franchisee or between franchisees constitute restrictions of competition for the purposes of Article 85(1).

> The fact that the franchisor makes price recommendations to the franchisee does not constitute a restriction of competition, so long as there is no concerted practice between the franchisor and the franchisees or between the franchisees themselves for the actual application of such prices.

> Franchise agreements for the distribution of goods which contain provisions sharing markets between the franchisor and the franchisees or between franchisees are capable of affecting trade between Member States.

Thus, the Court's 'rule of reason' approach, which clearly narrows the scope of Article 85(1) itself, only operates to take provisions of an agreement outside Article 85(1) where they are economically justifiable ('necessary') in terms of the agreement's purpose and where their restrictive effect poses no danger to the Common Market.

Provisions which do not meet these requirements may however still escape Article 85(1) by means of exemption under Article 85(3), together with less likely candidates whose *object* is to distort competition within the meaning of Article 85(1). There are, therefore, in effect two filters at work: one at Article 85(1), adopted where appropriate by the Court of Justice, another at Article 85(3) in the *sole* hands of the Commission. This is not helpful in terms of coherence in the application of Article 85.

The Commission's favoured approach is to give Article 85(1) a wide interpretation, which, as seen in *Société-Technique Minière*, can catch provisions which the Court has nevertheless later excluded under the 'rule of reason'. On this 'wide' view, restrictions on competition are only allowed if the Commission (the Court of Justice, the Court of First Instance and national courts possess no such power) grants an individual or block exemption under Article 85(3). A national court which finds that an agreement falls *within* Article 85(1) only has the option of declaring the agreement void or adjourning its proceedings until the Commission reaches a decision taking Article 85(3) into account.

The structure of Article 85 clearly indicates an intention on the draftsman's part that the Commission alone should weight the pro and anti-competitive effects of an agreement – and weigh them under Article 85(3). Coherence and uniformity of interpretation would in this way be forthcoming. What the draftsman apparently did not envisage was the massive pressure on the Commission brought about in the 1960s by the receipt of many thousands of notified agreements containing applications for individual exemption. The delay and uncertainty which resulted, and which continues, cannot be relieved by national courts. Advocates of the 'rule of reason' therefore point to the effect it has on reducing the Commission's burden and propose that national courts should have it at their disposal.

In practice, the most important development, which has gone some way to solving these problems, has been for the Commission increasingly to use its powers to issue *block* exemption Regulations: exemption of *categories* of agreements, see Article 85(3). Business parties whose agreements fall within such a category (eg exclusive distribution agreements, franchising agreements or research and development agreements) merely have to ensure that the terms of their agreement comply with the exemption rules to be found in the appropriate Regulation: see below.

A final point on the 'rule of reason' takes us back to the *de minimis* rule mentioned in the *Société-Technique Minière* case analysis.

In Case 5/69 *Völk*, the Court established that an agreement falls outside Article 85(1) if it is unlikely to have an appreciable effect on competition and inter-Member State trade even if its object is plainly restrictive of competition. The exclusive distribution agreement in this case sought to establish absolute territorial protection for the Dutch distributor of a small-scale German washing machine manufacturer. On the basis that the manufacturer's share of the relevant market was less than 1 per cent, it was decided that the 'de minimis' principle applied and no breach of Article 85(1) had occurred. (In Case 19/77 *Miller International*, the Court held that a 5 per cent share in the product market did not come within the 'de minimis' principle, and see also the Commission's Notice on Minor Agreements 1986).

'WITHIN THE COMMON MARKET'

As seen, *Béguelin* and the *ICI (Dyestuffs)* cases (and others) show that a non-EEC undertaking may be liable under Article 85(1) where the effects of its agreements or participation in concerted practices are felt *within* the Common Market. Three of the companies fined for price-fixing in *Dyestuffs*, including at that time ICI, were situated outside the EEC. The Court ruled on the basis of the 'enterprise entity' principle that the fact that a parent (eg ICI) had the ability to control the activities of its subsidiary within the Common Market was sufficient to justify the application of Article 85(1) against the parent: see also the Article 86 *Commercial Solvents* case and others in the next chapter.

In a more recent case, the 'enterprise entity' principle did not apply and the Court had to consider the *effects doctrine* of jurisdiction under international law, ie that jurisdiction under the Community's competition rules could be founded on proof of an appreciable effect on competition within the EEC of activities outside the Community by non-EEC undertakings:

> Case 89/85 etc *Ahlstrom and Others* v. *Commission (Wood Pulp)*
> Forty-three forestry undertakings in Finland, Sweden and Canada were held by the Commission to have infringed Article 85(1) as regards concerted price-fixing in respect of supplies of wood pulp to the paper industry in the Community. Considerable fines were imposed.

Although the Commission had based its decision on the 'effects doctrine', ie jurisdiction existed because the producers' agreement exerted effects within the Community, the Court, by stating that the determining factor was the place where the agreement was *implemented*, avoided explicit adoption of the 'effects doctrine' in favour of a territorial nexus. The Court explained that:

The applicants have submitted that the decision is incompatible with public international law on the grounds that the application of the competition rules in this case was founded exclusively on the economic repercussions within the Common Market of conduct restricting competition which was adopted outside the Community.

It should be observed that an infringement of Article 85, such as the conclusion of an agreement which has had the effect of restricting competition within the Common Market, consists of conduct made up of two elements: the formation of the agreement, decision or concerted practice and the implementation thereof. If the applicability of prohibitions laid down under competition law were made to depend on the place where the agreement, decision or concerted practice was formed, the result would obviously be to give undertakings an easy means of evading these prohibitions. The decisive factor is therefore the place where it is implemented.

The producers in this case implemented their pricing agreement within the Common Market. It is immaterial in that respect whether or not they had recourse to subsidiaries, agents, sub-agents, or branches within the Community in order to make their contacts with purchasers within the Community.

Thus, although the Commission had held that the effects doctrine applied, the Court preferred to develop what may be called the implementation doctrine.

ARTICLE 85(2)

Agreements or decisions prohibited by Article 85(1) are 'automatically void' under Article 85(2). However, as established by the Court of Justice in Cases 56 and 58/64 *Consten and Grundig*, only the offending clauses in an agreement are void. The effect of the nullity of the prohibited parts on the rest of the agreement is a matter for national courts to determine. Thus, under English law, the contract rules of severance will apply. By application of the 'blue pencil' test, it may be possible to cut out offending clauses (eg export bans) and uphold the remainder of the agre ment, bearing in mind, however, the words of Buckley L.J. in the leading case of *Chemidus Wavin* v *TERI* (1978):

It seems to me that, in applying Article 85 to an English contract, one may well have to consider whether, after the excisions required by the

Article of the Treaty have been made from the contract, the contract could be said to fail for lack of consideration or on any other ground, or whether the contract would be so changed in its character as not to be the sort of contract that the parties intended to enter into at all.

Being directly effective, Article 85 may be invoked either by a plaintiff or a defendant in a national action (ie as a sword or a shield). In both the *Brasserie de Haecht* and *Société-Technique Minière* cases, the defendant pleaded Article 85 as a reason for claiming he was not bound by the agreement. Similarly, following the House of Lords decision in *Garden Cottage Foods Ltd* v *Milk Marketing Board* (1984), it has been generally accepted that an action both for an injunction and for damages for breach of statutory duty can be brought by anyone harmed by an infringement of Articles 85 or 86. (Such person's directly effective rights must be protected on the basis of section 2(1) of the European Communities Act 1972).

There are dangers to enforcement of Community law by national courts in this way. In the absence of a Directive harmonising national laws in this area, there exists a serious difficulty regarding differing, and unequal, treatment of undertakings.

Apart from these civil consequences of Article 85(2), the Commission may, on the basis of a formal Decision under Article 15 of Regulation 17/62 inflict heavy (non-criminal) fines upon undertakings guilty of an infringement of Article 85(1) or Article 86. Such fines range from 1000 to 1,000,000 ECU, or a sum in excess of this limit but not exceeding 10 per cent of turnover. In Case 100/80, etc *Pioneer*, involving price-fixing and market-sharing, fines totalling almost 7 million ECU were imposed. The Commission may also impose penalties ranging from 50 to 1000 ECU per day in order to put an end to an infringement. (1 ECU presently equals approximately 75p.) Enforcement of the competition rules is dealt with in more detail in Chapter Seventeen.

ARTICLE 85(3)

Even when the prohibition in Article 85(1) does apply (in contrast to when the 'rule of reason' applies), it is, as we have seen, nevertheless possible that an exemption from Article 85(1) may be obtained under Article 85(3).

Article 85(3) provides that the provisions of Article 85(1) may be declared inapplicable in the case of:

- any agreement or category of agreements between undertakings, any decision or category of decisions of associations of undertakings and any concerted practice or category of concerted practices' which fulfils all of the following four conditions:

(a)   contributes to improving the production or distribution of goods or to promoting technical or economic progress; and

(b)   allows consumers a fair share of the resulting benefit; and

(c)   imposes on the parties only restrictions which are indispensable to the attainment of these objectives; and

(d)   does not afford such undertakings the possibility of eliminating competition in respect of a substantial part of the products in question.

In essence therefore exemption may be granted in cases where the anti-competitive effects of an agreement, etc are outweighed by its economic benefits. Exemption may be either on the basis of an individual decision by the Commission or by 'category', ie on the basis of a Commission block or group exemption Regulation.

Block Exemption

As already referred to, as a result of the administrative burdens placed on the Commission's limited resources in following the procedure laid down in Regulation 17/62 for granting individual exemptions, and the delay and resulting uncertainty for undertakings, the Commission (using the experience gained from the Court's case law and its own granting of individual exemptions in the early years) has, since the mid-1960s, increasingly relied on its power to grant block exemption by means of Regulations.

Undertakings should therefore first consider whether their agreement has been drafted in compliance with the terms of an applicable block exemption. An agreement which benefits from block exemption does not have to be notified (see below). It is automatically valid and enforceable despite containing restrictive but 'necessary' clauses.

The main block exemptions which have been issued to date cover:

1.   Exclusive distribution agreements: Regulation 1983/83.

2.   Exclusive purchasing agreements (with special provisions relating to the supply of beer and petrol): Regulation 1984/83.

3.   Patent licensing agreements: Regulation 2349/84.

4.   Selective distribution in the motor vehicle sector: Regulation 123/85.

5.   Specialisation agreements: Regulation 417/85.

6.   Research and development agreements: Regulation 418/85.

7.   Franchise agreements: Regulation 4078/88.

8.   Know-how licensing agreements: Regulation 556/89.

In broad terms, a similar pattern is followed throughout these Regulations. They lay down the permitted restrictions deemed essential to the achievement of economic advantages of general public interest (the 'white' list), followed by a list of restrictions which are incompatible with the Common Market and therefore forbidden (the 'black' list). Some Regulations (eg patent licensing) also contain a 'grey' list of restrictions subject to an 'opposition' procedure. If such a restriction is adopted it must be notified to the Commission. If not opposed within six months it may be considered exempt from Article 85(1).

For a detailed discussion of these Regulations, reference should be made to one of the specialised texts on competition law listed at the end of the chapter. A closer examination of the Regulations covering (vertical) exclusive distribution agreements and (horizontal) specialisation agreements will follow in due course.

Individual Exemption

Where, for example, undertakings find that their agreement cannot be tailored to meet the requirements of the appropriate block exemption Regulation, an individual exemption under Article 85(3) may be applied for by first *notifying* the agreement to the Commission, the only body with the power to grant or refuse such an application. Exemptions may now only be granted for a specified period, conditions may be attached, and the exemption may be renewed or revoked.

As regards *notification*, the procedure for obtaining an exemption is laid down in Regulation 17/62 (Articles 4, 19 and 21, etc). It is advisable to make the formal application on Form A/B for either *negative clearance* or exemption. Negative clearance involves a formal Commission Decision that Article 85(1) does not apply *at all*: see Article 2 of Regulation 17/62. This may be because, for example, no anti-competitive object or effects can be discerned or because the 'de minimis' principle applies to the agreement. (The main provisions of Regulation 17/62 can be found in Chapter Seventeen.)

When submitting Form A/B for exemption purposes, it is necessary to set out the reasons why, in the opinion of the parties, the economic or other advantages of the agreement outweigh its 'necessary' anti-competitive effects.

Because of the delays (two to three years) involved in fulfilling the requirements of Regulation 17/62 (each decision must be fully reasoned and translated), it is only in a small minority of cases that the Commission now undertakes a full investigation of an agreement and invokes the procedure governing the hearing of the parties before it issues a Decision: see Case 17/74 *Transocean Marine Paint*. Formal Decisions are reserved for priority cases and otherwise, perhaps after informal meetings, an administrative communication, known as a '*comfort letter*', may be sent to the parties. The letter will state that, in the Commission's opinion, the agreement notified either does not infringe Article 85(1) at all or is of a type that qualifies for exemption. The file is then closed, although it may be re-opened if the material legal or factual circumstances change. Unless this happens the parties have a legitimate expectation that the Commission will take no further action.

Whilst cutting down delays, 'comfort letters' are of only persuasive authority in national courts and, as non-binding measures, they cannot (as can a Commission Decision) be challenged before the Court of Justice under Article 173(2) either by the parties themselves or by a third party who is directly and individually concerned: see, eg Case 99/79 *Lancome v ETOS BV*.

Many of the individual exemptions granted by the Commission in the early days have now been superseded by block exemptions. Of the Commission's general policy under Article 85(3), Bellamy and Child state that:

> Although not always clearly stated, the Commission's policy is to encourage those agreements which it considers to be, on balance, pro-competitive. Broadly speaking, in respect of production, and the introduction of new technology, the Commission's policy is to permit agreements to co-operate in manufacture, or in joint research and development, that seem genuinely likely to lead to better use of resources, such as rationalisation of production, the achievement of economies of scale, or the faster, or more effective, development of new products, particularly where the firms concerned are likely to be better able to compete with third parties. Article 85(3) may also be used to assist the process of change in older industries, particularly through restructuring agreements to remove excess capacity. At the distribution level, in broad terms the Commission's policy is to permit certain restrictions in exclusive dealing, exclusive purchase or selective distribution agreements if they enable new markets to be developed, or if they ensure better regularity of supply, or a genuinely better service to the consumer, but only on condition that there is no absolute impediment to the free flow of the goods throughout the common market.

Horizontal agreements which almost certainly will not be exempted under Article 85(3) include price-fixing agreements, agreements limiting production or controlling markets, and those seeking to protect a particular national market. Such agreements are unlikely to be notified in the first place. Also, as already discussed, export bans in vertical agreements, and other measures to inhibit parallel imports, are highly unlikely to be granted individual exemptions (and see the 'black' list in Regulation 1983/83, below).

The Conditions for Individual Exemption

Positive Conditions

1. *The agreement (or decision) must contribute to improving the production or distribution of goods (or, by analogy, services) or to promoting technical or economic progress;* and

2. *The agreement must allow consumers (buyers) a fair share of the resulting benefit.*

Negative Conditions

1. *The agreement (or decision) must not impose on the undertakings concerned restrictions which are not indispensable to the attainment of these objectives;* and

2. *The agreement must not afford the undertakings the possibility of eliminating competition in respect of a substantial part of the products in question.*

To obtain exemption, both the positive and negative conditions must be satisfied. An agreement which met all these requirements was the subject of an individual exemption in the following Commission Decision:

Vacuum Interrupters (No. 1) (1977)

Two UK undertakings, AEI and Reyrolle Parsons, who were important competing manufacturers of heavy electrical equipment, including switchgears, entered into a joint venture. Previously they had independently tried to develop vacuum interrupters as a commercially viable alternative form of circuit breaker in switchgears. (In the event of a fault, a circuit breaker cuts off the flow of electric current in a fraction of a second). The research being difficult and expensive, AEI and RP agreed to pool resources to develop, manufacture and sell vacuum interrupters through Vacuum Interrupters Ltd, a jointly owned subsidiary.

The ten-year agreement stipulated that VIL would only manufacture vacuum interrupters and not the switchgear into which they would be installed; that AEI and RP would not compete with VIL, and would obtain all their requirements of vacuum interrupters from VIL except if a customer stipulated otherwise.

At the time of the Commission's Decision in 1977, VIL's products were first coming on to the market and VIL, the only EEC manufacturer of vacuum interrupters, faced strong competition from non-EEC manufacturers.

The Commission decided that Article 85(1) applied as, at the time of the joint venture agreement, AEI and RP were *potential* competitors in the vacuum interrupter field within the Common Market and the agreement brought the possibility of such competition to an end.

However, the Commission granted an exemption under Article 85(3). The sharing of risks and technical skills facilitated the development, manufacture and sale of an efficient product at a reasonable cost, quicker than otherwise possible, and to the benefit of consumers. VIL were able to sell their interrupters independently to switchgear manufacturers other than AEI and RP, and continued research would promote technical progress to allow VIL to compete with American and Japanese manufacturers.

The Commission was also satisfied that the agreement contained only 'indispensable' restrictions. It therefore accepted the provisions whereby the parties agreed not to compete with VIL and to buy their requirements from VIL unless the customer specified otherwise. (A change in circumstances led the Commission to issue a new decision in *Vacuum Interrupters (No.2)*(1981).

Other Commission Decisions illustrative of the conditions applicable to individual exemption under Article 85(3) include:

Improvements in Production: a specialisation agreement likely to lead to a wider range of products produced at lower cost: *Sopelem/Langen* (1972), and see now Regulation 417/85, below.

Improvements in Distribution: a collaborative joint sales arrangement between small and medium-sized manufacturers which, although amounting to a horizontal market-sharing agreement, allowed them to compete with large-scale firms in the field: *Transocean Marine Paint Association* (1967).

Technical Progress: horizontal agreements on technical standards may infringe Article 85(1) by limiting production or preventing the parties from selling differentiated products. However, in *X/Open Group* (1987), an industry standard was granted exemption as it would enable computer users to switch the hardware and software from different sources, so facilitating the development of new programmes.

Economic Progress: in *International Energy Agency* (1984), it was held that concerted practices contributed to the distribution of oil throughout Western Europe and thereby promoted economic progress and reduced the economic difficulties that would be caused if supplies to any one participating country were substantially interfered with.

A Fair Share of Resulting Benefits to Consumers: where vigorous interbrand-competition exists, the Commission assumes that benefits are passed on to anyone who acquires the goods or services. ('Consumers' is interpreted in this broad sense). In *United Reprocessors* (1976), a joint venture involving the allocation of markets in the reprocessing of nuclear fuels enabled the cost of electricity to be reduced because of the improved stability of the reprocessing service.

Indispensable Restrictions Only: each clause in the agreement will be examined by the Commission to determine whether it is indispensable to the attainment of proven objective benefits. A clause seeking to achieve absolute territorial protection will rarely be acceptable: *Consten and Grundig*, but note the special circumstances of *Transocean Marine Paint*. In Case 161/84 *Pronuptia*, the Court of Justice indicated that limited territorial protection for a franchisee might be acceptable. In *Carlsberg Beers* (1985) an eleven year co-operation agreement under which Grand Metropolitan agreed to buy 50 per cent of its lager from Carlsberg was exempted on the ground that the requirement was necessary to enable Carlsberg to gain access to the UK market and develop its distribution network.

No Substantial Elimination of Competition: there must be no possibility of the elimination of competition in respect of a substantial part of the products in question. The greater the combined market share of the parties, the greater the threat to competition but, alternatively, the greater the pressure of inter-brand competition (from within the Common Market or from outside: see *Vacuum Interrupters*) the more likely exemption will be granted.

BLOCK EXEMPTION OF EXCLUSIVE DISTRIBUTION AGREEMENTS

The Court's *Consten and Grundig*, *Société-Technique Minière* and *Béguelin* decisions in the mid-60s (see above) clearly showed that the export ban was the principle sign of an exclusive distribution agreement that would *not* be accepted:

> The Commission had become fully aware that it is the removal of export bans which enables the parallel movement of goods through unofficial channels of distribution, whose availability keeps downward pressure on price levels that otherwise ... might tend to rise: *Goyder.*

Exclusive distribution agreements made up the largest proportion of the large number of agreements notified to the Commission and which required detailed examination. In so far as these agreements contained many pro-competitive features, and restrictions which fell within the letter and spirit of Article 85(3), it was felt that the way forward was to proceed by way of block exemption ('exemption by category').

The Commission first proceeded (on the basis of Council Regulation 19/65) by means of Regulation 67/67 for specified forms of exclusive distribution and exclusive purchasing. (In the latter case, the distributor is not allocated a contract territory and there is no obligation on the supplier not to sell to other distributors in the area; eg brewery ties as in *Brasserie de Haecht* and see now Regulation 1984/83).

Many of the advantages of exclusive dealing were outlined in the Preamble to Regulation 67/67:

> ...
>
> (5) Whereas exclusive distribution agreements lead in general to an improvement in distribution because the undertaking is able to concentrate its sales activities, does not need to maintain numerous business relations with a larger number of dealers and is able, by dealing with only one dealer, to overcome more easily distribution difficulties in international trade resulting from linguistic, legal and other differences;
>
> (6) Whereas exclusive distribution agreements facilitate the promotion of sales of a product and lead to intensive marketing and to continuity of supplies while at the same time rationalising distribution; whereas they stimulate competition between the products of different manufacturers; whereas the appointment of an exclusive distributor who will take over sales promotion, customer services and carrying of stocks is often the most effective way, and sometimes indeed the only way, for the manufacturer to enter a market and compete with other manufacturers already present; whereas this is particularly so in the case of small and medium-sized undertakings; whereas it must be left to the contracting parties to

decide whether and to what extent they consider it desirable to incorporate in the agreements terms providing for the promotion of sales;

(7) Whereas, as a rule, such exclusive distribution agreements also allow consumers a fair share of the resulting benefit as they gain directly from the improvement in distribution, and their economic and supply position is improved as they can obtain products manufactured in particular in other countries more quickly and more easily; ...

Although Regulation 67/67 has been replaced by Regulation 1983/83 as regards exclusive distribution, the basic pattern has been retained: (References are to the 1983 Regulation).

1. *The exemption applies to agreements to which only two undertakings — the supplier (S) and the distributor (D) - are party*: Article 1. Distribution networks do not offend this requirement but it does strike at horizontal arrangements or collusion either between suppliers or dealers.

2. *The goods must be for resale and not for use*: Article 1.

3. *It is acceptable for S to agree to supply only D within the whole or a specified part of the Common Market*: Article 1. (Regulation 67/67 did not allow an agreement which covered the entire Community; see *Duro-Dyne/Europair International* (1975): individual exemption.) In addition, S may also agree that he himself will not sell the contract goods in D's territory: Article 2(1).

The Regulation does not permit S to accept any other restrictions which may affect competition, such as an obligation to impose *export bans* in respect of D's territory upon other distributors including those in S's own Member State. D's exclusivity is therefore qualified and may be subject to parallel imports.

The *only* acceptable restrictions on competition which may be imposed on D are as follows:

4. *Where D agrees to purchase the goods for resale only from S and further agrees not to manufacture or distribute goods which compete with the contract goods during the period of the contract*: Article 2(2)(a)

and (b). It should be noted that this restriction strikes at both intra-brand and inter-brand competition. (A post-termination restriction of a further year was allowed under Regulation 67/67.)

5. *Where D agrees not seek customers for the contract goods outside the contract territory* eg by advertising; nor must he set up a branch or warehouse outside his territory. D is thus free to sell the contract goods outside his territory only as a *passive recipient* of orders.

D remains free to determine his prices and terms of resale and S must not impose restrictions upon D as to the persons to whom he may resell if, in the circumstances, such provisions are restrictive of competition. D may be required by S to purchase complete ranges of goods or minimum quantities, to sell goods under S's trade marks, and to provide an adequate sales network, stock, staff and sales services: Article 2(3).

Article 3(d) provides that Regulation 1983/83 shall not apply where:

One or both of the parties makes it difficult for intermediaries or users to obtain the contract goods from other dealers inside the common market or, in so far as no alternative source of supply is available there, from outside the common market, in particular where one or both of them:

1. exercises industrial property rights so as to prevent dealers or users from obtaining outside, or from selling in, the contract territory properly marked or otherwise properly marketed contract goods;

2. exercises other rights or takes other measures so as to prevent dealers or users from obtaining outside, or from selling in, the contract territory contract goods.

Clearly these provisions are aimed at measures which the parties might adopt to protect D against parallel imports, such as the improper use of trade mark rights (*Consten and Grundig*) and differential pricing according to the territory into which the goods are to be delivered: *Distillers* (1978); low prices for 'home trade' which did not apply if the goods were to be exported).

Regulation 1983/83 does not apply to certain drinks and petroleum agreements: see Regulation 1984/83. It expires at the end of 1997 but (as previously) it may be renewed in the same or a modified form.

BLOCK EXEMPTION OF SPECIALISATION AGREEMENTS

Specialisation agreements are a form of horizontal co-operation between undertakings involving an allocation of the products to be produced by competing or potentially competing parties. For example under their agreement:

(i)   X agrees to specialise in the production of products A and B to the exclusion of products C and D, which are to be produced by Y;

(ii) X agrees to obtain products C and D exclusively from Y, who similarly agrees to obtain products A and B from X.

Although such arrangements restrict the competitive freedom of the parties (subject to the *de minimis* rule), as the Preamble to block exemption Regulation 417/85 states:

> Agreements on specialisation in production generally contribute to improving the production or distribution of goods, because undertakings concerned can concentrate on the manufacture of certain products and thus operate more efficiently and supply the products more cheaply. It is likely that, given effective competition, consumers will receive a fair share of the resulting benefit.

> Such advantages can arise equally from agreements whereby each participant gives up the manufacture of certain products in favour of another participant and from agreements whereby the participants undertake to manufacture certain products or have them manufactured only jointly.

The following case, decided by the Commission three years after the first block exemption Regulation was published in 1972, is illustrative of a specialisation agreement made between two undertakings from a high technology sector of the economy, in which investment costs are high and where there is considerable research and development involved:

Bayer/Gist-Brocades (1976)

B, a Germany company, and G-B a Dutch company, were large drug manufacturers. Each produced raw penicillin and an intermediate penicillin product called 6-APA. In order to increase overall production, a specialisation agreement was entered into under which G-B would specialise in the production of raw penicillin, whilst B would concentrate on 6-ABA. Most of G-B's raw penicillin was to be delivered to B at favourable prices for processing into intermediate products and B agreed to meet orders for 6-ABA from G-B again at favourable prices. Each party was free to carry on their own research and development but research results were to be exchanged. Improved new manufacturing processes developed by one were to be licensed to the other. The agreement also involved a joint investment scheme.

The Commission found that Article 85(1) applied. Neither party could gain a competitive advantage over the other in research; competition was restricted in relation to the products produced and the degree of mutual dependence created meant that the parties would tend not to deal with third parties. However, on balance, as (i) the agreement resulted in increased production of raw penicillin and 6-ABA, (ii) the restrictions were indispensable for achieving this, and (iii) there was no substantial reduction in competition in the *world* market, an individual exemption was granted under Article 85(3) subject to stringent reporting conditions.

Under the current Regulation, three requirements must be met if the agreement is to obtain the automatic benefit of the block exemption:

1.   The agreement must be of the kind described in Article 1:

Pursuant to Article 85(3) of the Treaty and subject to the provisions of this Regulation, it is hereby declared that Article 85(1) of the Treaty shall not apply to agreements on specialisation whereby, for the duration of the agreement, undertakings accept reciprocal obligations:

(a) not to manufacture certain products or to have them manufactured, but to leave it to other parties to manufacture the products or have them manufactured; or

(b) to manufacture certain products or have them manufactured jointly.

In *Prym/Beka* (1973), it was decided that a *non*-reciprocal obligation whereby P agreed to cease the production of needles and to purchase its requirements from B was not within the Regulation. In *Italian Cast Glass* (1982) agreements in the form of specialisation agreements were found to be in reality designed to fix quotas and divide the market.

2   The agreement must contain only those further restrictions set out in Article 2 which are indispensable to the purpose of the agreement:

(a) an obligation not to conclude with third parties specialisation agreements relating to identical products or to products considered by users to be equivalent in view of their characteristics, price and intended use;

(b) an obligation to procure products which are the subject of the specialisation exclusively from another party, a joint undertaking or an undertaking jointly charged with their manufacture, except where they are obtainable on more favourable terms elsewhere and the other party, the joint undertaking or the undertaking charged with manufacture is not prepared to offer the same terms;

(c) an obligation to grant other parties the exclusive right to distribute products which are the subject of the specialisation provided that intermediaries and users can also obtain the products from other suppliers and the parties do not render it difficult for intermediaries or users thus to obtain the products.

This is the Regulation's permissible 'white list'.

3. The products covered by the agreement, and the parties thereto, must fulfil the requirements as to market share and aggregate turnover set out in Article 3 (and see Articles 6 and 7). Where the aggregate turnover of the parties exceeds the permitted limits, but otherwise the agreement satisfies Regulation 417/85, individual exemption under the 'opposition procedure' may be available pursuant to Article 4. This requirement relates to the question of the possibility of the elimination of competition in respect of a substantial part of the products in question.

The current Regulation came into force in 1985 and was very recently amended.

Bellamy and Child, *Common Market Law of Competition*, 1987 (and Supplement 1, 1991) particularly Chapters 1-6.

EC Commission Reports on Competition Policy.

Forrester, I. and Norall, C., 'The Laicisation of Community Law: Self-Help and the Rule of Reason' (1984) 21 CML Rev. 11.

Frazer, T., 'Competition Policy after 1992 – the Next Step' (1990) 53 MLR 609.

Goebel, R., 'Metro II's Confirmation of the Selective Distribution Rules' (1987) 24 CML Rev. 605.

Goyder, D. G., *EEC Competition Law*, 1993.

Green, N., 'Article 85 in Perspective' (1988) 9 ECLR 190.

Green, Hartley and Usher, *The Legal Foundations of the Single European Market*, 1991, Part III.

Hornsby, S., 'Competition Policy for the 80s: More Policy, Less Competition' (1987) 12 EL Rev. 79.

Kalmansohn, M. E., 'The Application of EEC Articles 85 and 86 to Foreign Multinationals' (1984) 1 LIEI 1.

Korah, V., *Exclusive Dealing Agreements in the EEC: Regulation 67/67 Replaced*, 1984.

Korah, V., 'EEC Competition Policy: Legal Form or Economic Efficiency' (1986) 39 CLP 85.

Lange, J. B., and Sandage, D., case note on *Wood Pulp* (1989) 26 CML Rev. 137.

Sharpston, E., 'When is an Agreement Anti-Competitive? (1991) *Solicitors Journal* 1186.

Shaw, J., 'Group Exemptions for Exclusive Distribution and Purchasing Agreements in the EEC' (1985) 34 ICLQ 190.

Slot, P., 'The Application of Articles 3(f), 5 and 85 to 94' (1987) 12 EL Rev. 179.

Snyder, F. G., 'Ideologies of Competition in European Community Law' (1989) 52 MLR 149.

Steindorff, E., 'Article 85 and the Rule of Reason' (1984) 21 CML Rev. 639.

Toepke, U., 'EEC Law of Competition: Distribution Agreements and their Notification' (1985) 19 *International Law* 117.

Turner, J., 'Competition and the Common Market after *Maize Seeds*' (1983) 8 EL Rev. 103.

Vandenhove, P., 'The New Commission Regulations 1983/83 and 1984/83 ...' (1984) 2 LIEI 41.

Van Gerven, W., 'Twelve Years of EEC Competition Law (1962-1973) Revisited' (1974) 11 CML Rev. 38.

Walker-Smith, A., 'Collusion: Its Detection and Investigation' (1991) 12 EL Rev. 71.

Whish, R., *Competition Law*, 1989.

Whish, R. and Sufrin, B., 'Article 85 and the Rule of Reason (1987) 7 YEL 1.

CHAPTER FIFTEEN

COMPETITION LAW: ABUSE OF A DOMINANT POSITION – ARTICLE 86

While Article 85 primarily concerns anti-competitive horizontal and vertical agreements between undertakings, Article 86, which is similarly based on Article 3(f), (Article 3(g) EC), is primarily aimed at an abusive use of market power by a single undertaking which dominates a market for goods or services. A market which is dominated by such an economically powerful undertaking is characterised by a high degree of *concentration* (see the Introduction to Chapter Fourteen).

Such concentration of power clearly weakens the structure of competition in the market in question. The case law shows that the degree of concentration may, albeit rarely, amount to a pure monopolist's 100 per cent control: see, eg Case 226/84 *British Leyland* (a state-created monopoly indulging in excessive pricing of a service), but more usually it amounts to a lesser degree of dominance in the hands of a single undertaking, a corporate group (an integrated undertaking) or, possibly, in the light of recent developments, an oligopolistic group of undertakings.

Dominance or 'bigness' is not in itself contrary to Article 86. The optimum size needed to be able to compete effectively in large, perhaps global, markets frequently means that undertakings must acquire massive financial and other resources. What is incompatible with the Common Market is an *abuse* of that dominant position. According to the Court of Justice in Case 85/76 *Hoffman-La Roche*, this involves conduct on the part of an undertaking which

> ... has the effect of hindering the maintenance of the degree of competition still existing on the market or the growth of that competition.

The opening paragraph of Article 86 is therefore directed to ensuring that market conduct on the part of a dominant undertaking (no matter how that dominance was achieved) does not impair the maintenance of effective competition in the Common Market. It should also be borne in mind that where an abuse is proved, heavy fines may be imposed by the Commission.

Article 86

Any abuse by one or more undertakings of a dominant position within the Common Market or in a substantial part of it shall be prohibited as incompatible with the Common Market in so far as it may affect trade between Member States. Such abuse may, in particular, consist in:

(a) directly or indirectly imposing unfair purchase or selling prices or unfair trading conditions;

(b) limiting production, markets or technical development to the prejudice of consumers;

(c) applying dissimilar conditions to equivalent transactions with other trading parties, thereby placing them at a competitive disadvantage;

(d) making the conclusion of contracts subject to acceptance by the other parties of supplementary obligations which, by their nature or according to commercial usage, have no connection with the subject of such contracts.

Article 86(a) – (d) gives an indication of such conduct which covers unfair behaviour: Article 86(a), prejudicial behaviour: Article 86(b), and discriminatory behaviour: Article 86(c). Taking just two examples from the list, an abuse of a dominant position can come about through the charging of discriminatory prices or through a refusal to supply an existing customer. The dominant firm is able to act in this way, to the detriment of customers, who may be driven out of the market (to the detriment of consumers), because there is insufficient competitive pressure on the firm to prevent it from using such tactics.

Article 86 therefore has the same broad aim as Article 85: the maintenance of effective competition within the Common Market. In deciding whether any particular action falls within Article 86, the three most important questions are:

1. Whether there exists a *dominant position* held by one or more *undertakings* in the Common Market or a substantial part of it;

2. Whether there has been an *abuse* of that dominant position;

3. Whether *trade between Member States* may thereby be affected.

DOMINANT POSITION AND RELEVANT MARKET

The Court of Justice defined a dominant position under Article 86 in Case 27/76 *United Brands* as:

a position of economic strength enjoyed by an undertaking which enables it to hinder the maintenance of effective competition on the relevant market by allowing it to behave to an appreciable extent independently of its competitors and customers and ultimately of consumers.

In *AKZO Chemie* (1986), the Commission added a further dimension:

The power to exclude effective competition is not ... in all cases coterminous with independence from competitive factors but may also involve the ability to eliminate or seriously weaken existing competitors or prevent potential competitors from entering the market.

In order for the Commission to establish dominance, it is clearly first necessary to determine what it is that is allegedly being dominated. The extract from the decision in *United Brands* shows that this is the *'relevant market'*. Secondly, it is necessary, by means of various criteria, to assess whether the *market strength* of the undertaking amounts to the dominant position required by Article 86.

Swann has explained that:

... it may be that a firm is deemed to be in a position of absolute dominance because it controls the whole supply of a particular product. But it may be that there are close substitutes to which consumers can turn if the price of the product in question is raised. In other words to be absolutely dominant at any moment in time a firm must have total control over all the products which are substantially interchangeable.

From this it is apparent that at the heart of a definition of the relevant market lie questions relating to the *product* involved –and possible substitutes for it. Questions must also be answered as regards the *territorial scope* of the relevant market; Article 86 speaks of a 'dominant position within the Common Market or in a substantial part of it.' Swann also indicates a *temporal* dimension concerning the durability of a dominant position. We will see that dominance must have a considerable degree of permanence. Dominance is thus a dynamic, not a static concept. An enquiry into the relevant market may show a real likelihood of actual or potential rivals eroding the dominant firm's position.

Dominance: The Relevant Product Market

In economic theory the relevant product market is one in which products are substantially interchangeable as regards their end uses: see Swann, above. On the basis of this test of *demand* substitutability, it is necessary to determine which products are sufficiently similar in terms of function, price and attributes to be regarded by *users* as reasonable substitutes for each other. Such products will determine the nature and size of the relevant product market, and it is implied that there can be effective competition between them. To take some examples: bananas and other fresh fruit? One brand of soap powder as opposed to another? Tyres for heavy goods vehicles and tyres for motor cars?

The case law of the Court of Justice shows that in practice identification of the relevant product market is often very difficult indeed. Tests of interchangeability may only provide the basis for the necessary analysis. Whish has explained that identification of the relevant product market, using tests of substitutability

> ... should be simply the beginning of the enquiry: having identified it, it is then necessary to consider the extent of the competitive pressures upon the firms in that market. At *this* stage it is perfectly possible that a firm faces competition both from within *and from outside* the relevant market.

And later:

> The mistake is to suppose that in the commercial world there is a whole series of independent, discrete relevant product markets which exert no influence on one another. In fact in business there exists a complex web of interlocking markets and sub-markets which may have an influence on one another in a more or less tangential way. Once that has been recognised, the danger of identifying the market too narrowly ceases to be a problem, because the identification of the market is seen to be only a staging post on the way to the really important question which is whether a firm is in a position to behave independently of its competitors [*within* the defined product market and from those other markets *outside* it].

Fortunately, in some cases the problem of identifying the relevant market presents no difficulty. For example, there may be no interchangeable goods or services. In Case 226/84 *British Leyland*, BL held a state-created monopoly to issue national type approval certificates to dealers and individuals who wished to import left-hand drive BL cars. The Court stated that an abuse had occurred 'where [a company] has an administrative monopoly and charges for its services fees which are disproportionate to the economic value of the service provided.'

In *United Brands*, a case in which the US undertaking was found guilty of various breaches of Article 86 (see below), full-blown investigations of demand substitutability were carried out. The preliminary question was whether bananas made up the relevant product market (as claimed by the Commission), or whether it consisted of fresh fruit as a whole (as claimed by United Brands). Clearly the narrower the relevant product market is defined on the basis of substitutability, the easier it is for the Commission to establish dominance. The Court of Justice agreed with the Commission that bananas formed a separate market, and a market on which United Brands were dominant. The analysis involved the use of the economic concept of *cross-elasticity* (of demand). Thus, for example, where a fall in the price of product A has little or no effect on the demand for product B, cross-elasticity is not significant and the products are not to be regarded as substitutes: limited interchangeability is not enough. The Court ruled as follows on this point:

> The applicant submits in support of its argument that bananas compete with other fresh fruit in the same shops, on the same shelves, at prices which can be compared, satisfying the same needs: consumption as a dessert or between meals...

> The applicant concludes ... that bananas and other fresh fruit form only one market and that UBC's operations should have been examined in this context for the purpose of any application of Article 86 of the Treaty.

> The Commission maintains that there is a demand for bananas which is distinct from the demand for other fresh fruit especially as the banana is a very important part of the diet of certain sections of the community.

> The specific qualities of the banana influence customer preference and induce him not to readily accept other fruits as a substitute.

> The Commission draws the conclusion from the studies quoted by the applicant that the influence of the prices and availabilities of other types of fruit on the prices and availabilities of bananas on the relevant market is very ineffective and that these effects are too brief and too spasmodic for such other fruit to be regarded as forming part of the same market as bananas or as a substitute therefor.

For the banana to be regarded as forming a market which is sufficiently differentiated from other fruit markets it must be possible for it to be singled out by such special features distinguishing it from other fruits that it is only to a limited extent interchangeable with them and is only exposed to their competition in a way that is hardly perceptible ...

Since the banana is a fruit which is always available in sufficient quantities the question whether it can be replaced by other fruits must be determined over the whole of the year for the purpose of ascertaining the degree of competition between it and other fresh fruit.

The studies of the banana market on the Court's file show that on the latter market there is no significant long term cross-elasticity any more than — as has been mentioned — there is any seasonal substitutability in general between the banana and all the seasonal fruits, as this only exists between the banana and two fruits (peaches and table grapes) in one of the countries (West Germany) of the relevant geographic market.

As far as concerns the two fruits available throughout the year (oranges and apples) the first are not interchangeable and in the case of the second there is only a relative degree of substitutability.

This small degree of substitutability is accounted for by the specific features of the banana and all the factors which influence consumer choice.

The banana has certain characteristics, appearance, taste, softness, seedlessness, easy handling, a constant level of production which enable it to satisfy the constant needs of an important section of the population consisting of the very young, the old and the sick.

As far as prices are concerned two FAO studies show that the banana is only affected by the prices — falling prices — of other fruits (and only of peaches and table grapes) during the summer months and mainly in July and then by an amount not exceeding 20% ...

It follows from all these considerations that a very large number of consumers having a constant need for bananas are not noticeably or even appreciably enticed away from the consumption of this product by the arrival of other fresh fruit on the market and that even the personal peak periods only affect it for a limited period of time and to a very limited extent from the point of view of substitutability.

Consequently the banana market is a market which is sufficiently distinct from the other fresh fruit markets.

In Case 6/72 *Europemballage Corp. and Continental Can*, the Commission's finding that the American company CC, through its subsidiary SLW, held a dominant position in the German market for light metal containers for meat products, light metal containers for fish products, and metal closures for glass containers was rejected by the Court of Justice. As regards demand substitutability, the Court was of the view that the Commission, when defining the market, should have considered whether purchasers of the cans for these purposes could readily have switched their production lines so as to be able to use different cans. The Court also considered the question of *production substitution* on the supply side:

> ... a dominant position on the market for light metal containers for meat and fish cannot be decisive, as long as it has not been proved that competitors from other sectors of the market for light metal containers are not in a position to enter this market, by a simple adaptation, with sufficient strength to create a serious counterweight.

The argument here is as follows: if the allegedly dominant firm raises its prices quite considerably, are other suppliers, not currently in the market as identified, in a position to move *into* that market with substitutes for the product in question? If so, such potential competition must be taken into account. A sufficiently high cross-elasticity of supply will draw these competitors into the market and weaken the position of the allegedly dominant firm.

In the following case, demand-side substitutability was relevant in order to answer the question whether a *purchaser* could (as in *Continental Can*) readily switch from the product in question to another to satisfy his particular purpose. If not, that product made up the relevant product market.

Cases 6 and 7/73 *Istituto Chemicoterapico Italiano SpA and Commercial Solvents Corporation* v. *Commission*

CSC (an American company) and its Italian subsidiary ICI cut off supplies to another Italian company, Zoja, of a chemical, aminobutanol, an effective and cheap raw material used in the production of ethambutol, a drug for treating tuberculosis. CSC, which had (allegedly) almost a world-wide monopoly in aminobutanol, was considering manufacturing ethambutol itself in Italy through ICI. Substitutable end products existed in the form of other drugs based on different but less effective raw materials.

The Commission having decided that CSC and ICI had abused a dominant position on the raw material (aminobutanol) market, the applicants (an integrated undertaking) argued that, amongst other things, the relevant product market was the end product, anti-tuberculosis drugs, a market in which there was effective competition and on which they were not dominant.

The Court rejected this argument as irrelevant where the complaint was the refusal to supply aminobutanol, the raw material.

The desired effect of CSC's refusal to supply Zoja was to eliminate one of the main manufacturers of ethambutol in the Common Market and a potential competitor of ICI. The Court was not prepared to accept that Zoja could readily adapt its production facilities to other raw materials for the manufacture of ethambutol. Only if other raw materials could be substituted without difficulty could they be regarded as acceptable substitutes.

This was not the case and the Court upheld the Commission's Decision that the relevant product market was aminobutanol and that CSC and ICI has abused their dominant position on that market. (The case is therefore illustrative of the need to protect competition at the manufacturing level, ie on the supply side). Apart from the fine imposed, CSC was ordered to resume supplies to Zoja.

The Geographic Market: Dominance 'within the Common Market or a substantial part of it.'

Sir Leon Brittan, a former head of DG IV has explained that:

... market power makes no sense whatsoever as a concept unless a market is first defined, both in product or service terms and in geographical terms. Geography here is not political, it is economic. For some products or services, there is a Community market; for others there are still markets covering one or more Member States. There are even world markets for some products or services ...

Where necessary, therefore, the 'substantial part' requirement of Article 86 (which gives rise to a *de minimis* rule) is to be assessed on a simple geographic basis but in terms of the *economic importance* of the area as defined.

Defining the geographic market may be an easy matter, as in the case of a national state monopoly, eg *British Leyland* (above) or *British Telecom*, a Commission decision of 1983. Similarly, in *ICI (Soda Ash)* (1991), the Commission established that the UK was the relevant geographic market as follows:

For the purpose of assessing ICI's market power, the EEC can be divided into two broad zones or 'spheres of influence', one dominated by SOLVAY, the other by ICI.

Conditions in the United Kingdom are, for reasons set out earlier, both relatively homogeneous and separate from those prevailing in other EEC Member States. ICI is the sole national producer and neither SOLVAY nor the other West European producers market their product in its 'home' territory. ICI's important customers in the EEC are all located in the United Kingdom.

The second paragraph indicates that the geographic market of which the dominant firm is a part forms an area in which the conditions of competition applying to the product are the same or sufficiently similar for all participants. In Article 9 of Merger Regulation 4064/89 where the question of a 'distinct' market is addressed, it is stated that:

7. The geographical reference market shall consist of the areas in which the undertakings concerned are involved in the supply and demand of products or services, in which the conditions of competition are sufficiently homogeneous and which can be distinguished from neighbouring areas because, in particular, conditions of competition are appreciably different in those areas. This assessment should take into account in particular of the nature and characteristics of the products or services concerned, of the existence of entry barriers or of consumer preferences, of appreciable differences of the undertaking's market shares between the area concerned and neighbouring areas or of substantial price differences.

The main sales area of the dominant firm may be coterminous with the relevant geographic market as defined above and as in *ICI (Soda Ash)*, but within the total sales area there may be factors at play which distinguish certain sectors and mark them off as displaying different patterns of demand and supply.

In *United Brands*, the Court stated that the opportunities for competition under Article 86 must be considered

... with reference to a clearly defined geographic area in which [the product] is marketed and where the conditions are sufficiently homogeneous for the effect of the economic power of the undertaking concerned to be able to be evaluated.

United Brand's bananas were sold throughout the Community but the Commission excluded the UK, France and Italy from the geographic market because each of these countries applied a different preferential system for banana imports. The UK, for example, gave preferential treatment to bananas from the Commonwealth.

The Court agreed that in the remaining six Member States, taking into account differing transport costs and other charges, the conditions of competition were sufficiently similar for all traders. There were no factors of sufficient weight to disturb the unity of that geographic market.

A total of six Member States, in terms of the economic importance of the market situated there, would certainly amount to a 'substantial part' of the Common Market. The same would apply to any one of the larger Member States. In Cases 40/73 etc *Suiker Unie (Sugar)*, which involved market-sharing, it was established that there was a significant volume of business in sugar in Belgium and Luxembourg, the area in which wrongful economic pressure had been brought to bear (by the undertaking RT) on Belgian dealers. On this point the Court ruled:

> The Commission takes the view that RT brought economic pressure to bear on the Belgian dealers Export and Hottlet, hereinafter called 'the dealers', with the object of compelling them only to resell the sugar supplied to them to specific customers or destinations and to impose these restrictions on their own customers...

II. *Examination of the Submission*

RT's main submission is that the Belgo-Luxembourg market is not a substantial part of the Common Market, that it does not occupy a dominant position on this market and has not abused its position, so that the Commission infringed Article 86 of the Treaty when it applied this provision to its conduct.

1. *The question whether the Belgo-Luxembourg market is a substantial part of the Common Market*

RT considers that in view of the relatively small volume of Belgian production and the number of consumers in Belgium and Luxembourg this question must be answered in the negative.

For the purpose of determining whether a specific territory is large enough to amount to a 'substantial part of the Common Market' within the meaning of Article 86 of the Treaty the pattern and volume of the production and consumption of the said product as well as the habits and economic opportunities of vendors and purchasers must be considered.

So far as sugar in particular is concerned it is advisable to take into consideration in addition to the high freight rates in relation to the price of the product and the habits of the processing industries and consumers the fact that Community rules have consolidated most of the special features of the former national markets.

From 1968/69 to 1971/72 Belgian production and total Community production increased respectively from 530,000 to 770,000 metric tons and from 6,800,000 to 8,100,000 metric tons (cf. contested decision, p. 18, paragraphs 3 and 5).

During these marketing years Belgium consumption was approximately 350,000 metric tons whereas Community consumption increased from 5,900,000 to 6,500,000 metric tons (cf. loc.cit.).

If the other criteria mentioned above are taken into account these market shares are sufficiently large for the area covered by Belgium and Luxembourg to be considered, so far as sugar is concerned, as a substantial part of the Common Market in this product.

Dominance: The Temporal Dimension

Markets change over time particularly in terms of technological innovation and refinement (for example, the markets for fountain pens, coal or computers), and market power must be sustained in the face of such possible changes over a considerable period of time for a position of dominance to be established under Article 86. It has been suggested that a period of less than three years would be too short a period for a high market share to be an indicator of dominance. See also the extract from the Court's decision in *Hoffman-La Roche*, below.

In general terms, a dominant firm in a stable market, which possesses massive technical and financial resources and a high market share can feel reasonably secure in as much as its position cannot be undermined by those already in the market or, owing to entry barriers, those who might wish to do so.

Market Power and Dominance

In *United Brands* (1976), the Commission stated that:

> Undertakings are in a dominant position when they have the power to behave independently without taking into account, to any substantial extent, their competitors, purchasers and suppliers. Such is the case where an undertaking's market share, either in itself or when combined with its know-how, access to raw materials, capital or other major advantage such as trade-mark ownership, enables it to determine the prices or to control the production or distribution of a significant part of the relevant goods. It is not necessary for the undertaking to have total dominance such as would deprive all other market participants of their commercial freedom, as long as it is strong enough in general terms to devise its own strategy as it wishes, even if there are differences in the extent to which it dominates individual submarkets.

Of the various factors which may account for a position of dominance, a highly important one is the existence of a large market share. As the Court explained in Case 85/76 *Hoffman-La Roche*:

> An undertaking which has a very large market share and holds it for some time by means of the volume of production and the scale of the supply which it stands for − without those having much smaller market shares being able to meet rapidly the demand from those who would like to break away from the undertaking which has the largest market share − is by virtue of that share in a position of strength which makes it an unavoidable trading partner and which, already because of this secures for it, at the very least during relatively long periods, that freedom of action which is the special feature of a dominant position.

Market Share: absolute and relative values

In *Hoffman-La Roche* market shares over a three-year period of 75 per cent to 87 per cent in various vitamins markets were held to be 'so large that they are in themselves evidence of a dominant position.' However, in *United Brands*, a market share of between 40 per cent and 45 per cent did not 'permit the conclusion that UBC automatically controls the market. It must be determined having regard to the strength and number of the competitors.' UBC's best placed competitor, Castle and Cooke, had a 16 per cent share of the market, the other competitors coming far behind. Together with other factors, this was 'evidence of UBC's preponderant strength.'

Overall the cases indicate that once market share reaches 30–35 per cent, dominance becomes an issue.

Financial and Technical Resources

Ownership of, or ready access to, massive financial resources will clearly greatly assist an undertaking in the pursuit or maintenance of market power. A firm's ability to establish and maintain a lead in product development or technical services may well be a contributory factor to a dominant position. This will be more likely in newer, high technology markets and will only be possible if the firm also possesses very considerable financial resources.

Financial power (relative to its competitors) can assist an undertaking in maintaining dominance through large-scale advertising of its product, eg United Brand's 'Chiquita' banana. Financial strength ('deep pockets') can allow an undertaking to remove a competitor, and also increase its dominance, by means of persistent price-*cutting*, which the smaller firm cannot match: see Case C-62/86 *AKZO Chemie*, below. Perhaps most important of all, such resources enable an undertaking to own or control its sources of supply and its distributive outlets. This strategy of backward and forward vertical integration is discussed next.

Scale of Activities: Vertical Integration

A significant feature of the *United Brands* case was that the US corporation controlled virtually all the various stages of its banana production and distribution. Its activities reached back to ownership of banana plantations and to specially designed refrigerated transport facilities used to move the perishable product both from the plantations and to the consumer via its distribution system. The scale of its capital investment at each stage of the production and distribution process enabled it to react more easily than its competitors to changes in demand, so giving it a strategic advantage and appreciable independence from its competitors, customers and consumers. United Brands possessed what are termed 'economies of scale' that were not available to other suppliers:

> The Commission bases its view that UBC has a dominant position on the relevant market on a series of factors which, when taken together, give UBC unchallengeable ascendancy over all its competitors: its market share compared with that of its competitors, the diversity of its sources of supply, the homogeneous nature of its products, the organisation of its production and transport, its marketing system and publicity campaigns, the diversified nature of its operations and finally its vertical integration.
>
> ...
>
> In general a dominant position derives from a combination of several factors which, taken separately, are not necessarily determinative.

In order to find out whether UBC is an undertaking in a dominant position on the relevant market it is necessary first of all to examine its structure and then the situation on the said market as far as competition is concerned.

...

UBC is an undertaking vertically integrated to a high degree. This integration is evident at each of the stages from the plantation to the loading on wagons or lorries in the ports of delivery [in Europe] and after those stages, as far as ripening and sale prices are concerned, UBC even extends its control to ripener/distributors and wholesalers by setting up a complete network of agents.

At the production stage UBC owns large plantations in Central and South America.

...

The effects of natural disasters which could jeopardise supplies are greatly reduced by the fact that the plantations are spread over a wide geographic area and by the selection of varieties not very susceptible to diseases.

...

At the production stage UBC therefore knows that it can comply with all the requests which it receives.

At the stage of packaging and presentation on the premises UBC has at its disposal factories, manpower, plant and material which enable it to handle the goods independently.

The bananas are carried from the place of production to the port of shipment by its own means of transport including railways.

At the carriage by sea stage it has been acknowledged that UBC is the only undertaking of its kind which is capable of carrying two thirds of its exports by means of its own banana fleet.

...

In the field of technical knowledge and as a result of continual research UBC keeps on improving the productivity and yield of its plantations by improving the draining system, making good soil deficiencies and combating effectively plant disease.

It has perfected new ripening methods in which its technicians instruct the distributor/ripeners of the Chiquita banana.

...

This general quality control of a homogeneous product makes the advertising of the brand name effective.

Since 1967 UBC has based its general policy in the relevant market on the quality of its Chiquita brand banana.

...

UBC has made this product distinctive by large-scale repeated advertising and promotion campaigns which have induced the consumer to show a preference for it in spite of the difference between the price of labelled and unlabelled bananas (in the region of 30 to 40%) and also of Chiquita bananas and those which have labelled with another brand name (in the region of 7 to 10%).

...

It has thus attained a privileged position by making Chiquita the premier banana brand name on the relevant market with the result that the distributor cannot afford not to offer it to the consumer.

Industrial Property Rights

The ownership of industrial property rights may contribute to establishing dominance. For example, the granting to an inventor of patent rights over an innovatory and highly efficient industrial process confers a *legal* 'monopoly' (under national law) upon the owner for a number of years. This may help the owner/undertaking to dominate the market through its ability to impede effective competition unless (or until) alternative patented processes and products can be developed by other participants in the market.

Establishment of the brand name 'Chiquita' in the eyes of consumers was a factor in United Brand's position of dominance. (On industrial property rights, see Chapter Eighteen.)

Barriers to Entry

The very fact that an undertaking with a dominant position is able to earn high monopoly profits is likely to attract *new* competition. However, the presence of barriers to entry into the market may prevent such competition and threat to the dominant firm from arising: see, for example, the legal barrier in Case 226/84 *British Leyland*, above.

Bellamy and Child have explained this factor as follows:

Many of the foregoing factors, whether technical resources, overall strength, economies of scale, intellectual property rights or other attributes possessed by the dominant firm may give rise to 'barriers to entry', a compendious phrase used to describe difficulties new undertakings face in entering the market. Barriers to entry may also arise for legal or financial reasons, or because of the structure of the market. The presence or absence of barriers to entry will be highly relevant to an assessment of dominance. Sometimes the risks faced by new undertakings in attempting to enter the market to compete with established undertakings may of themselves indicate dominance.

The impact of barriers to entry in *United Brands* was similarly explained by the Court of Justice:

UBC's economic strength has thus enabled it to adopt a flexible overall strategy directed against new competitors establishing themselves on the whole of the relevant market.

The particular barriers to competitors entering the market are the exceptionally large capital investments required for the creation and running of banana plantations, the need to increase sources of supply in order to avoid the effects of fruit diseases and bad weather (hurricanes, floods), the introduction of an essential system of logistics which the distribution of a very perishable product makes necessary, economies of scale from which newcomers to the market cannot derive any immediate benefit and the actual cost of entry made up *inter alia* of all the general expenses incurred in penetrating the market such as the setting up of an adequate commercial network, the mounting of very large-scale advertising campaigns, all those financial risks, the costs of which are irrecoverable if the attempt fails.

Thus, although, as UBC has pointed out, it is true that competitors are able to use the same methods of production and distribution as the applicant, they come up against almost insuperable practical and financial obstacles.

That is another factor peculiar to a dominant position.

ABUSE OF A DOMINANT POSITION

The illustrative list of abuses in Article 86(a)-(d) focuses attention on behaviour in its business relations by the dominant firm which *exploits* (takes advantage of for its own ends) other trading parties (buyers and sellers) and consumers. Such conduct may be unfair, prejudicial or discriminatory. Thus a monopolist's market power may allow him to charge unfair high prices; conduct which for a firm operating under normal competitive conditions would spell disaster. Production may be limited so that, with demand exceeding supply, monopoly prices again prevail in the market to the prejudice of consumers. The practice of charging different prices in different parts of the Common Market for the same product means that the dominant firm is in a position to charge what the different national markets will bear, contrary to the integrative aims of the Treaty.

However, the case law of the Court of Justice shows that the scope of Article 86 is wider than exploitative abuse of market power. In *Continental Can*, the Court, drawing upon Article 3(f) of the Treaty, which provides for a system that competition in the Common Market is not distorted, stated that Article 86

> ...is not only aimed at practices which may cause damage to consumers directly, but also at those which are detrimental to them through their impact on an effective competition structure.

Thus, for example, where a dominant firm's predatory pricing policy (see *AKZO Chemie*) succeeds in driving the target firm out of the market, a competitor is eliminated and the market becomes more concentrated, most probably to the detriment of the consumer (certainly as regards choice). It is true that such conduct could be called unfair or prejudicial but the dominant firm's primary objective is the elimination of a competitor. (Many abuses fall into both the exploitative and anti-competitive categories).

The Court's classic, often-quoted statement regarding abuse was made in Case 85/76 *Hoffmann-La Roche*:

> The concept of abuse is an objective concept relating to the behaviour of an undertaking in a dominant position where, as a result of the very presence of the undertaking in question, the degree of competition is weakened and which, through recourse to methods different from those which condition normal competition in products and services on the basis of the transactions of commercial operators, has the effect of hindering the maintenance of the degree of competition still existing in the market or the growth of that competition.

Bellamy and Child sum up the position by saying that:

> In general the governing principle of Article 86 is that conduct by a dominant firm which seriously and unjustifiably distorts competition within a properly defined relevant market will be prohibited, in so far as it effects trade between Member States.

Illustrations

(1) Excessively High Selling Prices

There is not a great deal of case law in this area. In theory at least monopoly profits will attract new entrants into the market, unless barriers to entry are insuperable. This would be the case with a statutory monopoly (eg in electricity or gas supply), and even a private sector dominant firm in a high technology sector can justify, or purport to justify, the need to secure very high profits in order to finance research and development.

The following case concerns a statutory monopoly:

Case 26/75 *General Motors*

Under Belgian law, GM had an exclusive inspection service for imported second-hand Opel cars. The Commission decided that it had charged excessive prices for the legally required certificates of conformity.

The Court adopted a test of unfairness based on the relationship between the price and the 'economic value' of goods or services provided and held that GM's prices were excessive. (As GM had amended its charges and reimbursed excessive charges, the finding of an abuse was not sustained.) 'Economic value' is inferred by ascertaining the costs of the relevant goods or services or by examining the prices of comparable goods or services.

Cost/price analysis may present formidable problems and instead, in *United Brands*, the Commission operated mainly from the fact that United Brands' prices differed widely from one Member State to another. On the assumption that the prices charged in Ireland were sufficiently high to yield a profit (which UB denied), and considering that prices in other Member States were perhaps double the Irish price, the Commission reached the conclusion that such prices and profits were excessive. As the Commission had not examined UB's costs, a task which the Court thought did not present any insuperable problems, the Court decided that the unfair pricing charge had not been proved.

(2) Predatory Pricing

Heavy and persistent price cutting (even below cost) by a dominant firm aimed at a financially weaker, but not necessarily less efficient, rival with the aim of eliminating it from (or preventing it from entering) the market may well be contrary to Article 86. Short term gains by consumers will probably become longer term losses when the dominant firm, having improved or consolidated its position, raises its prices again.

Case C-62/86 *AKZO Chemie* v. *Commission*

AKZO held a dominant position within the Community in the market for benzole peroxide, used in the manufacture of plastics and for the blanching of flour. In order to prevent a British firm, Engineering and Chemical Supplies, a small-scale competitor of AKZO's in the flour additives market, from entering the market in organic peroxides for plastics, AKZO initiated a series of massive and prolonged price cuts aimed at ECS customers in the flour additives market. Following complaints to the Commission by ECS, AKZO was fined 10 million ECU. AKZO appealed under Article 173(2) against the Commission's Decision.

The Court of Justice reaffirmed its statement of principle made in *Hoffman-La Roche* regarding the concept of abuse, see above. In the Court's view it therefore followed that Article 86 prohibited a dominant undertaking from eliminating a competitor and thereby reinforcing its position by having recourse to means other than those based upon competition on merit. In that context, not all competition based on price could be regarded as legitimate.

The only interest for a dominant undertaking in applying such prices was to eliminate competitors in order, subsequently, to raise its prices and thus profit by its monopoly situation, since every sale would result in its suffering a loss.

Such prices might remove from the market undertakings which might be just as efficient as the dominant undertaking but which, because of their lesser financial capacity, were unable to resist such competition against them.

The Court upheld the Commission's decision in large part, but reduced the fine to 7,5000,00 ECU.

(3) Discriminatory Prices

In *United Brands,* the Court held that UB, selling one product, unloaded at one place (Rotterdam or Bremerhaven), should charge one quayside price for all customers, the ripener-distributors, whatever the ultimate destination of the bananas. Selling the bananas at the European port of unloading to customers from the various Member States at widely different prices fell within Article 86(c): the application of dissimilar prices to equivalent transactions with other trading parties, thereby placing those charged higher prices at a competitive disadvantage.

It was certainly true, as UB pointed out, that retail prices for ripened bananas did vary considerably from one Member State to another for a variety of reasons (eg transportation charges and wage rates). However the Court held that UB were not entitled to take account of market pressures at the retail level as they did not operate directly at that level. UB's aim was to obtain maximum profits by fixing its prices at the highest level each of the national markets would bear. The national markets were isolated, preventing ripener-distributors from any Member State who did have a price advantage via-à-vis their counterparts in other Member States from exerting competitive interpenetration of the latters' markets, by means of, amongst other things, a *restriction on distribution* imposed by UB under what was known as the 'green banana' clause in UB's conditions of sale. Under this clause, ripener-distributors, who all required suitable storage facilities, were not allowed to resell bananas while they were still green. Cross-border trade was therefore generally unpracticable:

> ... by reason of its dominant position UBC, fed with information by its local representatives, was in fact able to impose its selling price on the intermediate purchase. ... These discriminatory prices, which varied according to the circumstances of the Member States, were just so many obstacles to the free movement of goods and their effect was intensified by the clause forbidding the resale of bananas while still green and by reducing the deliveries of the quantities ordered. A rigid partitioning of national markets was thus created at price levels which were artificially different, placing certain distributor/ripeners at a competitive disadvantage, since compared with what it should have been competition had thereby been distorted.

(4) Exclusive Rights of Supply : Abusive Discounts

Discounts granted by a dominant supplier to a dealer in its products must be objectively justifiable, for example where bulk buying by the dealer enables the supplier to reduce costs. On the other hand, Article 86 catches 'loyalty' or 'fidelity' discounts granted by a dominant supplier on condition that the dealer enters into an obligation to purchaser *all or a very high percentage* of his requirements from the dominant firm. Such discounts are regarded as both anti-competitive (they create a barrier to entry to potential suppliers) and discriminatory as between different customers.

In Case 85/76 *Hoffman-La Roche*, the Commission based its finding of abuse against HLR, the largest pharmaceutical company in the world, with a dominant position in seven separate vitamins markets, on the following grounds:

(a) The fact that customers are bound by an exclusive or preferential purchasing commitment in favour of Roche for all or for a very large proportion of their requirements either as a result of an express obligation of exclusivity, or fidelity rebates, or other means.

(b) The fact that the price advantages granted are based not on the differences in costs borne by Roche in relation to the quantities supplied, but on the supply of all or a very large proportion of a customer's requirements.

(c) The fact that in certain cases the rebate is based on all purchases, so that purchases of vitamins of one group are aggregated with purchases of vitamins of other groups ('across-the-board' rebates).

(d) The fact that the agreements generally contain a provision known as the 'English clause', the significance of which is as follows; purchasers are obliged to inform Roche of offers from other manufacturers more favourable than those of Roche; should Roche not match such offers, purchasers are free to purchase from such manufacturers without losing the rebate in respect of purchases made from Roche. In some agreements Roche stipulate that the offers should emanate from 'reputable' manufacturers (thereby excluding dealers and brokers).

(5) Refusal to Supply

A dominant firm's refusal to supply goods or services in the ordinary course of business, or a refusal to supply except on very unreasonable terms, may constitute a breach of Article 86: see particularly Article 86(b) and (c). A refusal must be capable of objective justification (eg *force majeure*, see Case 77/77 *BP* v *Commission*), otherwise it will be regarded as unfair, anti-competitive and exclusionary in so far as a trading partner is denied his source of supply or at least his best source of supply.

In Cases 6 and 7/73 *Commercial Solvents* (discussed above with reference to the relevant product market), the refusal to supply the raw material was motivated by the wish to replace the customer, Zoja, in the market for the end product. The Court of Justice stated that:

When Zoja sought to obtain further supplies of aminobutanol, it received a negative reply. CSC had decided to limit, if not completely to cease, the supply of nitropropane and aminobutanol to certain parties in order to facilitate its own access to the market for the derivatives.

However, an undertaking being in a dominant position as regards the production of raw material and therefore able to control the supply to manufacturers of derivatives, cannot, just because it decides to start manufacturing these derivatives (in competition with its former customers) act in such a way as to eliminate their competition which, in the case in question, would amount to eliminating one of the principal manufacturers of ethambutol in the Common Market. Since such conduct is contrary to the objectives expressed in Article 3(f) of the Treaty and set out in greater detail in Articles 85 and 86, it follows that an undertaking which has a dominant position in the market in raw materials and which, with the object of reserving such raw material for manufacturing its own derivatives, refuses to supply a customer, which is itself a manufacturer of those derivatives, and therefore risks eliminating all competition on the part of this customer, is abusing its dominant position within the meaning of Article 86. In this context it does not matter that the undertaking ceased to supply in the spring of 1970 because of the cancellation of the purchases by Zoja, because it appears from the applicants' own statement that, when the supplies provided for in the contract had been completed, the sale of aminobutanol would have stopped in any case [ie there was no objective justification for the refusal].

In Case 27/76 *United Brands*, the dominant supplier of bananas to most of the Member States was, as we have seen, guilty of several abuses, one of which was its decision to discontinue supplies of green bananas to Olesen, a Danish ripener – distributor. The Court stated that:

It is advisable to assert positively from the outset that an undertaking in a dominant position for the purpose of marketing a product – which cashes in on the reputation of a brand name known to and valued by the consumers – cannot stop supplying a long standing customer who abides by regular commercial practice, if the orders placed by that customer are in no way out of the ordinary.

Such conduct is inconsistent with the objectives laid down in Article 3(f) of the Treaty, which are set out in detail in Article 86, especially in paragraphs (b) and (c), since the refusal to sell would limit markets to the prejudice of consumers and would amount to discrimination which might in the end eliminate a trading party from the relevant market.

It is therefore necessary to ascertain whether the discontinuance of supplies by UBC in October 1973 was justified.

The reason given is in the applicant's letter of 11 October 1973 in which it upbraided Olesen in no uncertain manner for having participated in an advertising campaign for one of its competitors.

Later on UBC added to this reason a number of complaints, for example, that Olesen was the exclusive representative of its main competitor on the Danish market.

This was not a new situation since it goes back to 1969 and was not in any case inconsistent with fair trade practices.

Finally UBC has not put forward any relevant argument to justify the refusal of supplies.

Although it is true, as the applicant points out, that the fact that an undertaking is in a dominant position cannot disentitle it from protecting its own commercial interests if they are attacked, and that such an undertaking must be conceded the right to take such reasonable steps as it deems appropriate to protect its said interests, such behaviour cannot be countenanced if its actual purpose is to strengthen this dominant position and abuse it.

Even if the possibility of a counter-attack is acceptable that attack must still be proportionate to the threat taking into account the economic strength of the undertakings confronting each other.

The sanction consisting of a refusal to supply by an undertaking in a dominant position was in excess of what might, if such a situation were to arise, reasonably be contemplated as a sanction for conduct similar to that for which UBC blamed Olesen.

In fact UBC could not be unaware of the fact that by acting in this way it would discourage its other ripener/distributors from supporting the advertising of other brand names and that the deterrent effect of the sanction imposed upon one of them would make its position of strength on the relevant market that much more effective.

Such a course of conduct amounts therefore to a serious interference with the independence of small and medium sized firms in their commercial relations with the undertaking in a dominant position and this independence implies the right to give preference to competitors' goods.

In this case the adoption of such a course of conduct is designed to have a serious adverse effect on competition on the relevant banana market by only allowing firms dependent upon the dominant undertaking to stay in business.

Important features of this extract from the Court's decision include UB's aim to *strengthen* its dominant position and the Court's use of the principle of proportionality.

A further, interesting refusal to supply case is *British Brass Band Instruments* v *Boosey & Hawkes* (1988), a Commission Decision regarding a discontinuance by B & H of supplies to BBBI to prevent its emergence as a competitor in the relevant product market (instruments for British style Brass Bands) in which B & H possessed a 90 per cent market share. BBBI obtained an interim order requiring B & H to resume supplies.

Cases involving refusals to supply *information* have raised problems in connection with a dominant firm's copyright or other rights over such information. In essence, can the withholding of such information from another be classed as abusive exploitation or anti-competitive conduct?

Case 238/87 *Volvo* v. *Erik Veng Ltd*

Volvo did not have a dominant position in the motor vehicle market but did hold such a position as regards Volvo spare parts. One issue was whether Volvo could refuse to license its UK *design rights* for certain Volvo parts to Veng, an independent parts manufacturer who wished to produce them.

The Court of Justice ruled that the specific subject matter ('core', see Chapter Eighteen) of Volvo's rights included the right to decide whether or not to license third parties. There was therefore no abuse of Article 86 in this case, although in the circumstances it would be an abuse for Volvo (i) to over-price the parts in question, (ii) to refuse to supply the finished product, or (iii) to under-produce the parts such that demand was not satisfied.

The Court of First Instance has adopted a different position in Cases T-69, 70 and 76/89 *RTE, BBC and ITP* v *Commission (Magill TV Guide)*, two of which are subject to appeal to the Court of Justice:

The Irish magazine publisher, Magill, attempted to put on the market a new weekly advance TV listings magazine covering RTE, BBC and Independent Television programmes. The three authorities each owned the copyright in the advance listings of their programmes and each published its own weekly advance guide. Interim injunctions were obtained preventing further publication of the Magill guide in breach of the authorities' copyrights.

The CFI upheld the Commission's finding that the exercise of copyright in this manner *exceeded* the scope of the specific subject matter of that right (the ensuring of a reward for creative effort). The companies had used their copyright in listings to secure a monopoly in the derivative market of weekly TV guides and they had abused their dominant position. Daily publications of listings were allowed in newspapers and in weekly publications in Member States other than Ireland and the UK. The Court was therefore of the view that the authorities were using their respective copyrights to exclude competition from the market in their own Member States. The authorities were required to supply the information under licence.

It should also be noted that in these refusal to supply information cases, there was no existing relationship between the parties. An order for a compulsory licence (as in the *Magill* case) is made in order to create effective competition.

(6) Acquisition of Exclusive Access to Critical Technology

In Case T-51/89 *Tetra Pak*, the company held a dominant position on the market for aseptic cartons and the equipment used for their manufacture. TP acquired a small undertaking in the same market which was the exclusive licensee of a patent for new and important technology in the field of sterilisation of milk cartons. As a result, TP effectively became the only company within the Community with access to this technology. It was held that TP had reinforced its dominant position on the market for liquid food packaging. The acquisition of the technology had the effect of preventing, or at least considerably delaying, the entry of any new competitor into a market where little if any competition remained. (As seen in the previous chapter, the exclusive licence itself fell within block exemption Regulation 2349/84 for the purposes of Article 85(3), but this did not prevent the application of Article 86 in the circumstances of this case.)

EFFECT ON TRADE BETWEEN MEMBER STATES

Only very rarely has the expression 'which may affect trade between Member States' as found in Article 86 precluded its application, in that the effects of abusive conduct have been held to be confined to one Member State. The required effect may come about through the diversion of the flow of goods or services from its normal channels or through a modification of the structure of competition within the Common Market. Thus, in *Commercial Solvents*, although Zoja exported the vast majority of its anti-TB drug to the Third World, the Court held that its elimination from the market, having an effect on the competitive structure of the Common Market, would have the required effect on inter-Member State trade. Evidence that abusive conduct *might* affect trade between Member States is also sufficient : Case 226/84 *British Leyland*.

However, in Case 22/78 *Hugin*, the Court of Justice held that H's refusal to supply had no perceptible repercussions beyond the UK. The Swedish manufacturer of cash registers (dominant in the market for its spare parts) had, following a disagreement, refused to supply Liptons, an independent London-based company, with spare parts used by L to service and repair Hugin machines almost entirely within a 50-mile radius of London. The Court of Justice held that (i) the supply of spare parts from Sweden did not involve trade between Member States, and (ii) H's new policy of only supplying spares to its European subsidiaries did not entail the diversion of trade in them from channels they would otherwise have followed within the Community. A purchaser such as L, if unable to obtain spares from his local distributor, was very unlikely to approach a distributor in another Member State but instead, in normal circumstances, would purchase them directly from Hugin in Sweden.

JOINT DOMINANCE : 'ONE OR MORE UNDERTAKINGS'

In the context of Article 86, where the 'enterprise entity' or 'integrated undertaking' principle applies (a subsidiary having no *economic* independence from its legally distinct parent company: see Chapter Fourteen), the policies and conduct on the market of the subsidiary will be attributed to the parent. If a corporate group is regarded on this basis as an 'undertaking', this cannot amount to a case of joint dominance.

However, this is not to say that the 'enterprise entity' principle has not played an important part in Article 86 cases, not least when tying the activities of a subsidiary established *within* the Common Market to its parent established outside: in the USA (*Continental Can*, *Commercial Solvents*, *United*

Brands) or elsewhere (eg *Hoffman-La Roche* in Switzerland). In *United Brands*, for example, the US parent and its Dutch subsidiary were fined 1 million units of account (later reduced by the Court).

The reference in Article 86 to 'one or more undertakings' would therefore appear to apply to dominance held by two or more *independent* undertakings (or corporate groups). We have seen in the previous chapter that an *oligopistic* market is one which is dominated by a small number of suppliers. However, not only does the conscious parallelism of action between such suppliers (as regards 'follow my leader' pricing, etc) in itself fall short of collusion under Article 85 (see *Dyestuffs*) but, in *Hoffman-La Roche*, the Court held that Article 86 did not apply either:

> A dominant position must also be distinguished from parallel courses of conduct which are peculiar to oligopolies in that in an oligopoly the courses of conduct interact, while in the case of an undertaking occupying a dominant position the conduct of the undertaking which derives profits from that position is to a great extent determined unilaterally. (Advocate General Lenz stated that there was a problem in knowing 'where a collective monopoly ends and an oligopoly begins.')

In the mid-1980's the Commission investigated the concept of 'shared dominance' (see Sixteenth Commission Competition Report, 1986) and developed an approach to oligopolies based on 'tacit collusion' between closely interdependent undertakings, each of which was *aware* of 'the probably unfavourable consequences of adopting a competitive attitude'.

If it proved difficult or impossible to provide evidence of such tacit collusion sufficient to show that a concerted practice existed under Article 85, the 'awareness' of the undertakings concerned (none of which is dominant alone) might manifest itself in abusive conduct on the market sufficient to satisfy Article 86:

Italian Flat Glass (1990)

The Commission decided that three major Italian glass firms, FP, SIV, and VP, ('a tight oligopoly') were not only in breach of Article 85 as regards price-fixing and market-sharing, but that they also shared a position of collective dominance which they had abused by means of identical pricing and discounts. They enjoyed a degree of independence from competitive pressures that enabled them to impede the maintenance of effective competition, notably by not having to take into account the behaviour of other market participant (the test in *United Brands,* etc.).

The Commission noted (i) a joint market share of between 79 and 95 per cent for various types of glass, (ii) significant insularity from competition; (iii) high barriers to entry into the market (large-scale investment was required at a time when demand for the products was unlikely to rise significantly over the next ten years).

The Commission's analysis of collective dominance was, in part, as follows:

'The undertakings present themselves on the market as a single entity and not as individuals.

...

The main producers jointly maintain special links with a group of wholesalers who are the main glass distributors in Italy; they instigate the meetings, and they do everything possible to get them to accept price list changes and to ensure that the changes are passed on downstream in a consistent manner, so as to prevent any individual decisions by the wholesalers from creating commercial pressures on each producer leading to changes in market equilibria.
The business decisions taken by the three producers display a marked degree of interdependence with regard to prices and terms of sale, relations with customers and business strategies.

The three undertakings have in addition established among themselves structural links relating to production through the systematic exchange of products ... The exchanges are, firstly, the result of some undertakings' structural lack of primary products or of certain processed products and, secondly, the expression and instrument of their desire to prevent this situation from resulting in changes in their relative positions on the market and in existing relations between them.'

The glass producers appealed against the Commission's Decision and in Cases T–68/89 etc. *SIV and Others v Commission*, the Court of First Instance held that the Commission had only provided sufficient proof that two of the producers had infringed Article 85(1) by engaging in concerted practices. Whether, and on what facts, Article 86 will be applied to a collective dominant position remains in the future.

Bellamy and Child, *Common Market Law of Competition*, 1987 (and Supplement 1, 1991), particularly Chapter 8.

Bishop, W., 'Price Discrimination under Article 86: Political Economy in the European Court' (1981) MLR 282.

Dashwood, A., 'New Light on Article 86 in the Banana Case' (1978) 3 EL Rev. 314.

EC Commission Reports on Competition Policy.

Fox, E., 'Monopolization and Dominance in the US and the EC: Efficiency, Opportunity and Fairness' (*United Brands, Hugin,* etc). (1986) 61 *Notre Dame Law Review* 981.

Fuller, C. Baden, 'Economic Analysis of the Existence of a Dominant Position: Article 86 of the Treaty' (1979) 4 EL Rev. 423.

Goyder, D.G., *EEC Competition Law*, 1993, particularly Chapter 17.

Green, Hartley and Usher, *The Legal Foundations of the Single European Market*, 1991, Part III.

Gyselen, L., and Kyriazis, N., 'Article 86 EEC: The Monopoly Power Measurement Issue Revisited' (1986) 11 EL Rev. 134.

Korah, V., 'The Concept of a Dominant Position within the meaning of Article 86' (1980) 17 CML Rev. 395.

Litvak, I., and Maule, C., 'Transnational Corporations and Vertical Integration: The Banana Case' (1977) *Journal of World Trade Law* 537.

Pathak, A., 'Vertical Restraints in EEC Competition Law' (1988) 2 LIEI 15.

Raybould and Firth, *Law of Monopolies*, 1991.

Schodermeier, M., 'Collective Dominance Revisited' (1990) 11 ECLR 28.

Sharpe, T., 'Refusal To Supply' (1983) 99 LQR 36.

Sharpe, T., 'Predation' (1987) 8 ECLR 53.

Smith, P., 'The Wolf in Sheep's Clothing; the Problem of Predatory Pricing' (1989) 14 EL Rev. 209.

Swann, D., *Competition and Industrial Policy in the European Community*, 1983.

Vajda, C., 'Article 86 and a Refusal to Supply' (1981) 2 ECLR 97.

Van Bael and Bellis, *Competition Law of the EEC*, 1987.

Walker-Smith, A., 'Collusion: Its Detection and Investigation' (1991) 12 ECLR 71.

Whish, R., *Competition Law*, 1989.

Case notes on all the important Article 86 decisions are to be found in the *European Competition Law Review*, the *Common Market Law Review* and the *European Law Review*, etc.

CHAPTER SIXTEEN

COMMUNITY MERGER CONTROL

INTRODUCTION

Mergers between undertakings (also known as acquisitions and takeovers) can take a variety of forms but generally involve the purchase by one company of another company's shares (particularly its equity or voting shares which give access to legal control) or of its assets. A purchase of shares can proceed by way of a recommended offer, where the directors of the target company recommend to their shareholders that the offer be accepted, or by a contested takeover bid, for example:

> Shark's hostile strike for control of Target, the cement maker, took the market by surprise and sent Target shares climbing above the 80p offer price to close on Friday at 91p. Clearly, the market expects a higher offer from Shark or a counter-bid.

> The battle lines are classic: Shark has highlighed Target's low margins on its branded businesses, its high level of debt which has prompted a cutback in capital expenditure and is sharply critical of Target's current management. The Target defece is that it is highly geared to recovery, is already beginning to see signs of that recovery and the Shark strike grossly undervalues Target's potential. All very standard stuff for the opening skirmishes in a bid that promises to be hard fought and bitter.

Where the offer or bid is successful and results in a complete merger (described as a *concentration* under the Community rules), the purchasing company taking control of the target company, the two undertakings become a new, single and larger, economic entity. Unless taking cash for their shares, the shareholders of the target company will now hold shares in the new, merged entity (eg Cadbury-Schweppes, Allied-Lyons).

A *horizontal* merger, whereby one company takes control of a *competitor* in the same product (or services) market and at the same level of production or distribution, can have serious consequences for competition. As well as bringing about a *lasting* change in the *structure* of the undertakings involved, such a merger has brought about a change in the structure of the market in question. The number of independent operators has been reduced and the level of concentration in the market has been increased. Such a merger may lead to what is called, in terms of Article 86, a dominance situation — and to possible abuse of that dominant position. For example, X Ltd in the UK merges with Y Ltd in France. The companies previously exported to each other's national market. After the merger these competitive trade flows cease. The market has become less competitive; competition may even have been eliminated.

Vertical mergers between an undertaking and its suppliers and distributors can lead to the scale of activity and control at various stages in the same market that characterised the *United Brands* case.

A merger may however be only of a *partial* nature. For example, two or more competing undertakings may merge part of their operations into a separate, subsidiary undertaking; the parent companies jointly owning the new undertaking's shares but otherwise remaining independent. Such a merger may have a cartel-like effect on competition, bringing it arguably within the scope of Article 85(1). Competition may be distorted depending upon the degree of co-operation between the companies brought about by their joint ownership.

The combined economic strengths of fully merged, or the co-operation between partly merged, undertakings can be viewed in terms of market control and the distortion or elimination of competition, but such mergers may also be defended on the basis of economies of scale, increased efficiency, and optimum size and strength in the struggle to compete effectively with economically powerful firms which are based outside the Community. The *legal* control of mergers must therefore strike a balance. This is particularly the case in the context of the completion of the Internal Market:

> The dismantling of internal frontiers can be expected to result in major corporate reorganisations in the Community, particularly in the form of concentrations ... Such a development must be welcomed as being in line with the requirements of dynamic competition and liable to strengthen the competitiveness of European industry, to improve the conditions of growth and raise the standard of living in the Community ... It must be ensured that the process of reorganisation does not give rise to lasting damage to competition [and] the system of undistorted competition must therefore include provisions governing those concentrations which may impede effective competition in the common market: see Recitals 3-5 of the Preamble to the 1989 Merger Control Regulation.

CONTROL PRIOR TO THE MERGER CONTROL REGULATION

At the time the Treaty of Rome came into effect in 1958, merger activity was not a prominent feature of Western European economies and in any event it was felt that merger activity (national or transnational) should be encouraged in the context of the integration of the European market. Hence there is no reference to the control of mergers or concentrations in the EEC Treaty. (Article 66 of the ECSC Treaty did however cover merger activity in the coal and steel sectors.) Later, when foreign investment and industrial consolidation in the Community was leading to greatly increased merger activity, concern was expressed at the absence of adequate legal tools for merger control.

In 1973, Article 86 was pressed into service by the Commission in Case 6/72 *Europemballage Corp. and Continental Can* v. *Commission*, certain aspects of which have been dealt with in the previous chapter. In this case, the Court agreed with the Commission that a merger contravenes Article 86 where an undertaking already in a dominant position strengthens or extends that position by acquiring *control* of another undertaking in circumstances whereby the residual competition remaining in the market in question is substantially restricted.

Continental Can, a US-based multinational manufacturing metal packaging, held a dominant position in West Germany through its subsidiary Smalbach. Its acquisition, through another subsidiary, of Thomassen & Drijver, the largest manufacturer of metal cans in the Benelux countries was held to be an abuse of that position. Its effect was virtually to eliminate competition in the market. Although the principle was upheld by the Court, as seen in the previous chapter the Commission's Decision was annulled by the Court of Justice as being based on a faulty analysis of the relevant product market, the Commission having primarily failed to examine the question of product (ie supply-side) substitution.

The main defect of Article 86 for the control of mergers (its use for this purpose not being intended by the drafters of the Treaty) is that it does not apply to the *creation* of a dominant position but only to a strengthening of it. Neither has it provision for authorising mergers beneficial to the consumer on the lines of Article 85(3). The Commission has not formally applied Article 86 to a merger since the *Continental Can* case.

In 1973, at the time of *Continental Can*, the Commission put to the Council a draft Regulation providing for rules and procedures for the control of concentrations with a significant transnational element. Despite various amendments, the draft was persistently blocked by some Member States in the Council who did not wish to see competence pass to the Community.

It was not until late 1989 that the Regulation was finally adopted. Shortly before that date, at a time when agreement on a new proposal was being urged on the Council and while the Internal Market programme was in progress, the Court of Justice, contrary to previous thinking on the question, ruled that Article 85(1) could *in principle* apply to a merger situation:

> Cases 142 and 156/84 *British American Tobacco and Reynolds* v. *Commission*
>
> The Community cigarette market, described by the Court as stagnant and oligopolistic, was dominated by six large companies. One such company, Philip Morris, entered into an agreement with a South African company which controlled Rothman International, one of PM's competitors. The agreement, for the sale of shares and other rights, gave PM power to influence RI's strategic policies.
>
> The Commission objected to the agreement, which was modified to give PM only a *minority* shareholding interest in RI with 25% of the voting rights. The Commission held that the new agreement did not infringe Article 85(1). However, this Decision was challenged by BAT and Reynolds, two further operators on the EC cigarette market, under Article 173(2).
>
> The Court of Justice upheld the Commission's Decision but laid down the principle that an agreement to buy shares in a competitor *might* infringe Article 85 if the acquisition was likely to restrict competition as a result of the acquiror obtaining legal or *de facto* control of the market activity of the other company.

The Court did stress that the case itself did not involve a *concentration* as Philip Morris was only acquiring a minority interest in Rothmans and the companies were to remain independent undertakings with no change of structure. Article 85(1) might apply to an agreement where independence in this sense remained but control of commercial conduct passed to the purchasing company. It is doubtful if Article 85(1) can apply where control passes *and* the undertakings concerned become a single economic unit – a concentration. (The Court also held that the acquisition of a minority interest in a competitor can only give rise to an abuse of a dominant position under Article 86 'where the shareholding in question results in effective control of the other company or at least some influence on its commercial policy', which was not established on the facts in the *Philip Morris* case.

This decision was a potent factor in speeding up agreement in the Council on the draft merger Regulation. Article 85 is quite unsuitable for merger control and the *Philip Morris* case provided no clear guidelines for industry:

> A system for the scrutiny and control of mergers should be designed to cause minimum interference with the efficient operation of the capital markets. It should produce quick and clear decisions before each merger is completed and should not require a reference to more than one authority: Berwin's *Company Law and Competition.*

To have to wait for an Article 85 decision from the Commission (or from the Court) that the merger is exempt (for a limited period of years) on pro-consumer or other grounds under Article 85(3) could well take years and would therefore be the death of the proposed merger.

Another fundamental weakness of merger control under the Treaty's competition rules was its failure to provide a 'one-stop' system. For example, a proposed merger in 1975 between the UK company, Guest, Keen and Nettlefolds, and the West German clutch manufacturer, Sachs A.G., fell to be scrutinized by the Commission under both Article 86 EEC and Article 66 ECSC, by the Office of Fair Trading in the UK and by the West German Cartel Office. It was cleared by the first three authorities but was eventually vetoed under West German law. It is to be hoped that the 1989 Regulation has put merger control on an easier and firmer footing.

COUNCIL REGULATION 4064/89 ON THE CONTROL OF CONCENTRATIONS BETWEEN UNDERTAKINGS

Merger activity within the context of the completion of the Internal Market is on the increase. Companies are acquiring other companies in other Member States in order to widen their geographic market and maximise economies of scale. Merger activity may however, as we have seen, have another aim – a dominance situation or a cartel situation -whereby, although national frontiers are being eliminated, market control can nevertheless be exerted and competition distorted.

The Merger Regulation (based on Articles 87 and 235, the latter requiring unanimity) applies to all concentrations *with a Community dimension*: Article 1(1). Its main provisions relate to:

Concentrations

A concentration (which brings about a durable change in the *structure* of the undertakings concerned) arises either where, for example:

(a) two or more *previously independent* undertakings merge (a complete merger to form a single economic unit), or

(b) an undertaking acquires, through the purchase of shares or assets, *control* of the whole or part of another undertaking (eg through acquisition of a majority interest): see Article 3(1)(a) and (b).

'Control' entails 'the possibility of exercising decisive influence' on an undertaking. (A 39 per cent stake was sufficient for this in *Arjomari-Prioux/Wiggins Teape* as decided by the Commission in 1990.)

Under Article 3(2) para. 2, the creation of a *joint venture* performing on a *lasting* basis all the functions of an *autonomous economic entity*, which does *not* give rise to co-ordination of the competitive behaviour of the parties among themselves or between them and the joint venture, shall constitute a concentration within the meaning of Article 3(1)(b): see, for example, *Renault/Volvo* (1990). Such a joint venture is to be distinguished from a *collaborative* joint venture dealt with under Article 85.

Community Dimension/Thresholds

Under Articles 4 and 21, the Commission must be notified and has the task of appraising concentrations exceeding the following turnover thresholds. ('Turnover' means after-tax receipts for all goods and services in the preceding financial year.):

(a) where the combined world-wide turnover of all the undertakings concerned exceeds 5 billion ECU (approx. £3.5 billion), *and*

(b) where the combined Community-wide turnover of at least two of the undertakings involved exceeds 250 million ECU (approx. £175 million): see Article 1(2).

However, even though these thresholds are met, if more than two-thirds of the Community-wide turnover of *each* of the undertakings concerned is achieved within one and the same Member State, the Regulation does not apply. In such a case, Member States are free to apply their own national merger controls. Such rules are well developed in Germany, France and the UK but Member States lacking adequate domestic legislation for the control of mergers (eg Italy, the Netherlands and Belgium) may request the Commission to apply the Regulation to a concentration that does not possess a Community dimension: Article 22(3). In June 1993, a Commission Press Release announced that the *British Airways/Dan Air* case was the first in which a Member State had referred a concentration that fell below the thresholds of the Merger Regulation to the Commission pursuant to Article 22(3). The Commission examined, therefore, whether the acquisition by British Airways of Dan Air could create or strengthen a dominant position which would significantly impede competition on the Belgian territory. Because there were three major competitors flying between Brussels and London that had a significant share of a rapidly growing market, and in the light of the fact that Dan Air only flew between Gatwick airport and Brussels (slots for new competitors between these two airports being available for new entrants), it was decided that no dominant position would be created or strengthened which would significantly impede competition in Belgium. The Commission therefore approved the merger.

Appraisal by the Commission

Concentrations with a Community dimension are appraised by the Commission's DG IV Merger Task Force as regards their compatibility with the Common Market: see Article 2(1). Compatibility is determined on the basis of *dominant position* analysis. Only if the concentration *creates or strengthens* a dominant position 'as a result of which effective competition would be significantly impeded in the Common Market or a substantial part of it' will it be declared incompatible: see Article 2(2) and also, as regards *significant* impediment, see the *de minimis* 25 per cent or less combined market share presumption in Recital 15 to the Regulation.

> In deciding whether a concentration creates or strengthens a dominant position such as to impede competition, the Commission is required to take into account on the one hand the need to preserve effective competition within the Common Market in the light of the structure of, and play of competition within the markets concerned; and on the other hand the market position of the companies concerned in relation to other market players. The Commission is also required to take into account the interests of consumers and the development of technical and economic progress: Rodford, *European Access*, 1990:3, June.

The economic analysis required is clearly wide-ranging and complex, beginning with the need to establish the relevant product and geographic markets. Internal and external (world-wide) factors are relevant but the maintenance of effective competition *within* the Common Market is of paramount importance.

Procedures and Timetables

Within one month of notification the Commission must reach one of the following decisions:

  a)   that the merger falls within the scope of the Regulation and, as serious doubts are raised as to its compatibility with the Common Market, proceedings must be initiated;

  b)   that it is covered by the Regulation but does not raise such doubts and so will not be opposed;

  c)   that it is not covered by the Regulation: see Article 6.

Where the Commission has initiated proceedings, they must be closed by one of the following Decisions:

  (a)   The concentration is compatible with the Common Market. (It may be that the undertakings concerned have been required to make modifications to the merger in order to achieve this result.) The Decision must be taken as soon as the serious doubts as to the concentration's compatibility with the Common Market have been removed, and in any event within four months of the date on which the proceedings were initiated.

  (b)   The concentration is incompatible with the Common Market. The Decision to this effect must be issued within four months.

  (c)   In the case of a merger that has already been implemented, the concentration may be 'unscrambled' in order to restore conditions of effective competition: Article 8.

The Commission's powers of investigation and enforcement, including the imposition of fines, are dealt with in the next chapter.

Commission Powers and National Competition Law

Under Article 21(1) the Commission has sole jurisdiction to take the Decisions provided for in the Regulation – subject to review by the Court of Justice. Therefore, as a general rule, no Member State may apply its national competition law to a concentration which has a Community dimension. However the Commission is required to work in close liaison with national competition authorities under the terms of Article 19, which provides for the setting up of an Advisory Committee of Representatives from the competent national bodies.

There are, however, two exceptions to the 'one-stop' provision in Article 21(1). Under Article 9 and the so-called 'German clause', where a notified concentration threatens to create a dominant position on a *national* market, which presents all the characteristics, in product or service and geographic terms, of a *distinct* market (whether a substantial part of the Common Market or not), the Commission may decide to deal with the case itself under the Regulation *or* refer it to the national competition authority to be dealt with under that Member State's national competition law: see, for example, *Steetley/Tarmac* (1992). The Council and the Commission have issued a joint statement indicating that where the distinct market represents a substantial part of the Common Market, the referral procedure should be applied only in exceptional cases where the competition interests of the Member State concerned could not be adequately protected in any other way: see [1990] 4 CMLR 314.

Also, as seen above, under Article 22(3), the 'Dutch clause' provides a reverse situation, allowing the Commission to deal with a concentration which, although falling *below* the Regulation's 'Community dimension' thresholds, occurs in a Member State which does not possess adequate merger controls. The Commission may only act at the request of the Member State and only where the 'national' concentration may nevertheless have an effect on trade between Member States.

Article 21(3) also allows Member States to take 'appropriate measures' (which comply with Community law) to safeguard legitimate *non-competition* interests as regards such matters as public security (eg in relation to defence interests), plurality of the media (eg newspaper mergers) and prudential rules (eg a merger putting a financial institution into the hands of a person who is unfit to have such control).

The Application of Articles 85 and 86 to Concentrations

As a matter of policy, in the light of the uncertainties following the *Philip Morris* decision (see above) and the aim of the Regulation to provide 'one-stop' merger control, it is very unlikely that the Commission will now attempt to apply the Treaty provisions to mergers. It *must* proceed against mergers with a Community dimension under the Regulation and it has indicated that it does not otherwise intend to apply Articles 85 and 86 to concentrations.

Regulation Case Law

Of the many concentrations notified to the Commission since it came into effect on 30 October 1990 (50 in the first twelve months), there is, at the time of writing, only one instance of a merger failing to obtain clearance. This may indicate that the 'Community dimension' thresholds are not, as the Commission has argued, set too high. The Commission is however concerned to establish a 'level playing field' and reduce multiple control by national authorities. (The thresholds have now been reviewed and in late July 1993 the Commission announced that, the business community being broadly in favour of the status quo, no change would be made at present.)

Two Commission decisions will be considered: a clearance and the one concentration so far caught by the Regulation:

ICI/Tioxide

Commission Decision of November 28, 1990

Tioxide Group plc is the world's second largest supplier of titanium dioxide. It was owned 50/50 between ICI and Cookson. Cookson agreed to sell its 50 per cent to ICI.

ICI, which previously exercised joint control (or joint decisive influence) over Tioxide, would henceforth exercise sole control. This change in the quality of control was considered to be a concentration:

'Article 3(3) refers to control by whatever means, conferring the possibility of exercising decisive influence on an undertaking. Decisive influence exercised simply is substantially different to the decisive influence exercised jointly, since the latter has to take into account the potentially different interest of the other party or parties concerned.'

Taking into account the turnovers of ICI and Tioxide, the thresholds of Article 1 were met.

The notified agreement was subject to a number of conditions before it became effective, such as the approval of Cookson's shareholders in a general meeting and the Commission's approval. The question thus arose whether a conditional agreement constituted an agreement within the meaning of Article 4(1). The question was thus resolved:

'The 'agreement' referred to in Article 4(1) of the Merger Regulation must be an agreement which is legally binding between the parties involved. This is the case with the agreement under consideration as it cannot be rescinded unilaterally and intends to create a legal relationship on which each party can rely.'

As titanium dioxide is used mainly in the manufacture of paint, and ICI is the world's largest paint supplier, the effects of the operation were examined both on the titanium dioxide and paint markets.

No definition of the relevant geographic market is given, but it is considered to be at least the Community. The possibility of imports from outside the EEC is examined. This indicates that the Commission will not feel itself bound to limiting its definition of the relevant geographic market to the territory of the EEC for products traded world-word.

The position of ICI on the paint markets and Tioxide on the titanium dioxide market is examined, but no competition problems are identified. An Article 6(1)(b) decision, clearing the operation, is therefore adopted.

Comment

This decision indicates the Commission's position on two questions of interpretation of the Regulation:

— the meaning of 'agreement' under Article 4(1). According to that Article, undertakings must notify the concentration within one week of the relevant agreement. The Commission considers that once an agreement has been concluded that is unilaterally irrevocable by both parties, it must to notified. This requirement is irrespective of the existence of certain conditions which must be fulfilled prior to completion if the meeting of those conditions is outside the control of the two undertakings;

— the passage from joint control to sole control constitutes a concentration within the meaning of the Regulation. It is difficult to imagine that this change in the quality of control will result in such an overwhelming change that a dominant position will be created or strengthened. However, it is just imaginable that it might, and this view thus appears justified.

(Personal analysis and comment by Colin Overbury, Director of the Merger Task Force of DG IV, see 'References and Further Reading'.)

Aerospatiale/Alenia/de Havilland
Commission Decision of October 2, 1991

The French company Aerospatiale and the Italian company Alenia planned jointly to acquire the assets of the Canadian de Havilland division from Boeing Company. The Decision refused authorization for the transaction, on the grounds that it would create a powerful and unassailable dominant position in the market for turbo-prop ('commuter') aircraft. The world's number one producer would have bought the world's number two; this would have had an unacceptable impact on customers' freedom of choice and the balance of competition in the European Community market.

The Commission's Decision was based on an exhaustive analysis following extensive inquiries in which it consulted the companies involved, their competitors in industry, and their customers. In the Commission's view, the proposed merger would have given Aerospatiale, Alenia and de Havilland 50% of the world market for commuter aircraft and 67% of the Community market. Their market share would have been even greater in the case of the larger planes within this market: 63% of the world market and 74% of the Community market for planes with around 50 seats, and 76% of the world market and 75% of the Community market for those with around 70 seats. These were the segments which were expected to grow more quickly.

The merger would have resulted in increased market share without leading to economies of scale in production. Moreover, exhaustive analysis showed that existing competitors, which included European producers, would probably have been forced to withdraw from the market for commuter aircraft if the merger had gone ahead, and potential entrants would have been discouraged from entering it, given that market growth was expected to level out in a few years.

There were various reactions, mainly negative, to this Decision. An editorial in the Common Market Law Review stated that:

> As the case did not involve ordinary privately-controlled enterprises, but state-owned enterprises, the reactions from government officials from some of the Member States concerned was extremely emotional, ranging from the criticism that the Commission has misused the MCR, to the accusation that the interests of Europe and the Member States involved have been betrayed ... What ... comes to the surface is the basic ideological split between those who think that competition policy should serve the development of a strong European industry, and those who believe in preserving competitive market structures without an 'industrial policy' bias.

A resolution of the European Parliament, while recognizing the need to preserve competition and avoid market dominance within the Community, stated that the Regulation should be revised to require Decisions on any proposed merger to take account of its likely impact on European industrial strength. The resolution concluded that measures should be taken to stimulate the global competitiveness of the European aerospace industry.

In defending the Decision, the then head of DG IV, Sir Leon Brittan, explained that as regards the relevant market:

> The criteria for appraisal of concentrations under the Merger Regulation are the same for concentrations involving only European companies as for those involving also companies from outside the Community. Where a global market exists into which the Community market is fully

integrated, the Commission takes this into account. In [this case], the Commission based its analysis on the world market for commuter aircraft in assessing the impact that the proposed concentration would have on the balance of competition in the Community.

Even so a minority within the Advisory Committee on Concentrations (see above) stated that not only had the Commission's flawed statistical analysis of the market given the highest possible shares to the parties but the Commission had also underestimated the strength of competitors and customers in the market, exaggerated de Havilland's strength and ignored the potential new entrants.

The above editorial also drew attention to the availability of judicial review of Commission Decisions in actions brought either by Member States under Article 173(1) or natural or legal persons under Article 173(2). Such persons (other than those involved in the concentration) must establish that the Decision is of 'direct and individual concern' to them (see Chapter Nineteen) or, arguably, on the basis of Case 169/84 *COFAZ*, that they are persons whose market position is materially affected by the concentration and who, as persons with 'sufficient interest', have also made a material contribution to the pre-contentious merger control proceedings under Article 18(4) of the Regulation.

Bellamy and Child, *Common Market Law of Competition*, Supplement 1, 1991; Chapter 9 'Mergers and Acquisitions'.

Berwin, S. J. & Co., *Company Law and Competition*, 1989, Chapter 9 'Growth by Acquisition – Takeovers and Mergers'.

Brittan, Sir Leon, 'The Law and Policy of Merger Control in the EEC' (1990) 15 EL Rev. 351.

Brittan, Sir Leon, *Competition Policy and Merger Control in the Single European Market* (Part II), 1991.

Cook, J. and Kerse, C., *EEC Merger Control (Regulation 4064/89)*, 1991.

Downes, T. A. and Ellison, J., *The Legal Control of Mergers in the European Communities*, 1991.

Editorial Comments, 'Judicial Review and Merger Control' (1992) 29 CML Rev. 1.

European Competition Law Review, various commentaries 1990 – date (see Fine, Pathak, Soames, Ridyard, Bright, Elland, etc.).

Fairburn, J. A. and Kay, J. A. (eds), *Mergers and Merger Policy*, 1990.

Hawkes, Leonard, 'The EC Merger Control Regulation: Not an Industrial Policy Instrument: the De Havilland Decision' (1992) 1 ECLR 34.

Overbury, Colin, 'First Experiences of European Merger Control' (1991) EL Rev. Competition Law Checklist 1990, page 79.

Report of the House of Lords Select Committee on the European Communities, 'Merger Control' (Session 1988-89, 6th Report, HL 31).

Siragusa, M. and Subiotto, R., 'The EEC Merger Control Regulation: the Commission's Evolving Case Law' (1991) 28 CML Rev. 877.

Venit, J., 'The Merger `Control' Regulation: Europe Comes of Age ... Caliban's Dinner' (1990) 27 CML Rev. 7.

CHAPTER SEVENTEEN

ENFORCEMENT OF THE COMPETITION RULES

COMMISSION POWERS AND PROCEDURAL SAFEGUARDS: REGULATION 17

The Commission's key role in the enforcement of Articles 85 and 86 has been seen in action in the preceding chapters. The original Treaty basis for the Commission's powers is to be found in Article 87 which empowers the Council to adopt measures to give effect to the principles set out in Articles 85 and 86. The second paragraph of Article 87 provides (in part) that such measures shall be designed in particular:

(a) to ensure compliance with the prohibitions laid down in Article 85(1) and in Article 86 by making provision for fines and periodic penalty payments;

(b) to lay down detailed rules for the application of Article 85(3), taking into account the need to ensure effective supervision on the one hand, and to simplify administration to the greatest possible extent on the other;

...

(d) to define the respective functions of the Commission and of the Court of Justice in applying the provisions laid down in this paragraph;

(e) to determine the relationship between national laws and the provisions contained in this Section ...

In 1962 the Council acted on Article 87 when it adopted Regulation 17. A review of the main features of this Regulation will enable us to draw together a variety of matters (some already referred to) regarding not only the Commission's powers, and the strict procedural requirements under which it must operate, but also the role of national courts and individuals in the enforcement of the competition rules.

REGULATION 17/62

...

Article 2 Negative clearance

Upon application by the undertakings or associations of undertakings concerned, the Commission may certify that, on the basis of the facts in its possession, there are no grounds under Article 85(1) or Article 86 of the Treaty for action on its part in respect of an agreement, decision or practice.

Article 3 Termination of infringements

1. Where the Commission, upon application or upon its own initiative, finds that there is infringement of Article 85 or Article 86 of the Treaty, it may by decision require the undertakings or associations of undertakings concerned to bring such infringement to an end.

2. Those entitled to make application are:

   (a) Member States;

   (b) natural or legal persons who claim a legitimate interest...

Article 4 Notification of new agreements, decisions and practices

1. Agreements, decisions and concerted practices of the kind described in Article 85(1) of the Treaty which come into existence after the entry into force of this Regulation and in respect of which the parties seek application of Article 85(3) must be notified to the Commission. Until they have been notified, no decision in application of Article 85(3) may be taken...

...

Article 8 Duration and revocation of decisions under Article 85(3)

1. A decision in application of Article 85(3) of the Treaty shall be issued for a specified period and conditions and obligations may be attached thereto.

2. A decision may on application be renewed if the requirements of Article 85(3) of the Treaty continue to be satisfied.

3. The Commission may revoke or amend its decision or prohibit specified acts by the parties...

Article 9 Powers

1. Subject to review of its decision by the Court of Justice, the Commission shall have sole power to declare Article 85(1) inapplicable pursuant to Article 85(3) of the Treaty.

2. The Commission shall have power to apply Article 85(1) and Article 86 of the Treaty; this power may be exercised notwithstanding that the time limits specified in Article 5(1) and in Article 7(2) relating to notification have not expired.

3. As long as the Commission has not initiated any procedure under Articles 2, 3 or 6, the authorities of the Member States shall remain competent to apply Article 85(1) and Article 86 in accordance with Article 88 of the Treaty.

Article 10 Liaison with the authorities of the Member States

1. The Commission shall forthwith transmit to the competent authorities of the Member States a copy of the applications and notifications together with copies of the most important documents lodged with the Commission for the purpose of establishing the existence of infringements of Articles 85 or 86 of the Treaty or of obtaining negative clearance or a decision in application of Article 85(3).

2. The Commission shall carry out the procedure set out in paragraph 1 in close and constant liaison with the competent authorities of the Member States; such authorities shall have the right to express their views upon the procedure.

3. An Advisory Committee on Restrictive Practices and Monopolies shall be consulted prior to the taking of any decision following upon a procedure under paragraph 1, and of any decision concerning the renewal, amendment or revocation of a decision pursuant to Article 85(3) of the Treaty...

Article 11 Requests for information

1. In carrying out the duties assigned to it by Article 89 and by provisions adopted under Article 87 of the Treaty, the Commission may obtain all necessary information from the Governments and competent authorities of the Member States and from undertakings and associations of undertakings.

2. When sending a request for information to an undertaking or association of undertakings, the Commission shall at the same time forward a copy of the request to the competent authority of the Member State in whose territory the seat of the undertaking or association of undertakings is situated.

3. In its request the Commission shall state the legal basis and the purpose of the request and also the penalties provided for in Article 15(1)(b) for supplying incorrect information...

...

Article 14 Investigating powers of the Commission

1. In carrying out the duties assigned to it by Article 89 and by provisions adopted under Article 87 of the Treaty, the Commission may undertake all necessary investigations into undertakings and associations of undertakings. To this end the officials authorised by the Commission are empowered:
    (a)   to examine the books and other business records;
    (b)   to take copies of or extracts from the books and business records;

431

(c)   to ask for oral explanations on the spot;

(d)   to enter any premises; land and means of transport of undertakings.

2. The officials of the Commission authorised for the purpose of these investigations shall exercise their powers upon production of an authorisation in writing specifying the subject matter and purpose of the investigation and the penalties provided for in Article 15(1)(c) in cases where production of the required books or other business records is incomplete. In good time before the investigation, the Commission shall inform the competent authority of the Member State in whose territory the same is to be made of the investigation and of the identity of the authorised officials.

3. Undertakings and associations of undertakings shall submit to investigations ordered by decision of the Commission. The decision shall specify the subject matter and purpose of the investigation, appoint the date on which it is to begin and indicate the penalties provided for in Article 15(1)(c) and Article 16(1)(d) and the right to have the decision reviewed by the Court of Justice.

4. The Commission shall take decisions referred to in paragraph 3 after consultation with the competent authority of the Member State in whose territory the investigation is to be made...

Article 15 Fines

1. The Commission may by decision impose on undertakings or associations of undertakings fines of from 100 to 5,000 units of account where, intentionally or negligently:

(a)   they supply incorrect or misleading information in an application pursuant to Article 2 or in a notification pursuant to Articles 4 or 5; or

(b)   they supply incorrect information in response to a request made pursuant to Article 11(3) or (5) or to Article 12, or do not supply information within the time limit fixed by a decision taken under Article 11(5); or

(c)   they produce the required books or other business records in incomplete form during investigations under Article 13 or 14, or refuse to submit to an investigation ordered by decision issued in implementation of Article 14(3).

2. The Commission may by decision impose on undertakings or associations of undertakings fines of from 1,000 to 1,000,000 units of account, or a sum in excess thereof but not exceeding 10% of the turnover in the preceding business year of each of the undertakings participating in the infringement where, either intentionally or negligently:

(a)   they infringe Article 85(1) or Article 86 of the Treaty; or

(b)   they commit a breach of any obligation imposed pursuant to Article 8(1). In fixing the amount of the fine, regard shall be had both to the gravity and to the duration of the infringement ...

...

5. The fines provided for in paragraph 2(a) shall not be imposed in respect of acts taking place:

(a)   after notification to the Commission and before its decision in application of Article 85(3) of the Treaty, provided they fall within the limits of the activity described in the notification...

6. Paragraph 5 shall not have effect where the Commission has informed the undertakings concerned that after preliminary examination it is of opinion that Article 85(1) of the Treaty applies and that application of Article 85(3) is not justified.

Article 16 Periodic penalty payments

1. The Commission may by decision impose on undertakings or associations of undertakings periodic penalty payments of from 50 to 1,000 units of account per day, calculated from the date appointed by the decision, in order to compel them:

(a)   to put an end to an infringement of Article 85 or 86 of the Treaty, in accordance with a decision taken pursuant to Article 3 of this Regulation;

(b)   to refrain from any act prohibited under Article 8(3);

(c)   to supply complete and correct information which it has requested by decision taken pursuant to Article 11(5);

(d)   to submit to an investigation which it has ordered by decision taken pursuant to Article 14(3) ...

Article 17 Review by the Court of Justice

The Court of Justice shall have unlimited jurisdiction within the meaning of Article 172 of the Treaty to review decisions whereby the Commission has fixed a fine or periodic penalty payment; it may cancel, reduce or increase the fine or periodic penalty payment imposed.

...

Article 19 Hearing of the parties and of third persons

1. Before taking decisions as provided for in Articles 2, 3, 6, 7, 8, 15 and 16, the Commission shall give the undertakings or associations of undertakings concerned the opportunity of being heard on the matters to which the Commission has taken objection.

2. If the Commission or the competent authorities of the Member State consider it necessary, they may also hear other natural or legal persons. Applications to be heard on the part of such persons shall, where they show a sufficient interest be granted.

3. Where the Commission intends to give negative clearance pursuant to Article 2 or take a decision in application of Article 85(3) of the Treaty, it shall publish a summary of the relevant application or notification and invite all interested third parties to submit their observations within a time limit which it shall fix being not less than one month. Publication shall have regard to the legitimate interest of undertakings in the protection of their business secrets.

[Note: The rights of undertakings in Article 19(1) and (2) hearings are supplemented by Regulation 99/63 on Hearings, and see also Case 17/74 *Transocean Marine Paint* v *Commission* in Chapter Ten.]

Article 20 Professional secrecy

1. Information acquired as a result of the application of Articles 11, 12, 13 and 14 shall be used only for the purpose of the relevant request or investigation.

2. Without prejudice to the provisions of Articles 19 and 21, the Commission and the competent authorities of the Member States, their officials and other servants shall not disclose information acquired by them as a result of the application of this Regulation and of the kind covered by the obligation of professional secrecy.

3. The provisions of paragraphs 1 and 2 shall not prevent publication of general information or surveys which do not contain information relating to particular undertakings or associations of undertakings.

Article 21 Publication of decisions

1. The Commission shall publish the decisions which it takes pursuant to Articles 2, 3, 6, 7 and 8.

2. The publication shall state the names of the parties and the main content of the decisions; it shall have regard to the legitimate interest of undertakings in the protection of their business secrets.

...

Important though the Commission's powers are under Regulation 17/62 (and similar powers in relation to mergers in Regulations 4064/89 and 2367/90, see below), as are the procedural safeguards it provides for undertakings, to put the Commission's guardianship of the competition rules in true perspective it is necessary to consider the Regulation in context.

First, as the list of block exemption Regulations grows, it is increasingly the case that agreements can be drafted within the terms of the appropriate Regulation and where this is so the notification requirement does not apply. Alternatively, if companies and their advisers are not sure whether a proposed course of action complies with the EC competition rules, they can take the opportunity of discussing it with DG IV officials in Brussels. Many agreements have been modified in this way to bring them within the rules — informally and at little expense. We have also noted the increasing use by the Commission of comfort letters and the operation of an 'opposition' procedure with respect to 'grey' restrictions in some block exemption Regulations (see the discussion of Article 85(3) in Chapter Fourteen).

Although such informal and administrative procedures are speedier and less costly than those under Regulation 17/62, the 'soft' clearance or exemption provided by a comfort letter does not provide the degree of certainty which negative clearance or individual exemption will (eventually) bring. A comfort letter does however ensure immunity f:)m fines since the agreement remains a notified agreement.

Where individual exemption is required, an agreement should be formally notified as soon as possible since protection from fines does not exist for any period of operation of an agreement prior to notification; see Article 15(5)(a) of the Regulation but note also Article 15(6).

Clearly, as regards both individual exemption applications and the bringing to light of non-notified agreements and practices in breach of Article 85 (and abusive conduct under Article 86), the Commission's powers under Articles 11 and 14 of the Regulation concerning information and investigation are vitally important. The case law of the Court of Justice in this area indicates the need to maintain a balance between effective enforcement of the competition rules and protection of the rights of the undertakings covered by those rules. In Case 46/87 *Hoechst* v *Commission*, the Court stated that:

> ... in all the legal systems of the Member States, any intervention by the public authorities in the sphere of private activities of any person, whether natural or legal, must have a legal basis and be justified on the grounds laid down by law, and, consequently, those systems provide, albeit in different forms, protection against arbitrary or disproportionate intervention. The need for such protection must be recognised as a general principle of Community law.

Suspecting Hoechst of being involved in anti-competitive activities, Commission officials, armed with the requisite authorisation (a Decision, as required by Articles 14(2) and (3) of the Regulation), arrived without warning at Hoechst's business premises – as they are entitled to do (see Case 136/79 *National Panasonic*) – in order to carry out search and seizure operations. Hoechst refused them admission until a search warrant had been obtained. The Commission imposed financial penalties on Hoechst for refusal to comply with the original Decision. In this challenge under Article 173(2), the Court held that the Commission had acted within its powers under Article 14 of the Regulation.

The onset of a Commission investigation not infrequently leads to the resolution of a dispute between the undertaking involved and another party operating on the market. However, where otherwise the Commission is of the opinion that there is a serious and urgent risk that irreparable harm will be caused to such a party or to the public interest, and the investigation shows that there is a *prima facie* case of infringement, the Commission has the power to take an interim Decision for the alleged infringement of the competition rules to be terminated. In Case 792/79R *Camera Care Ltd.* v. *Commission*, the Court annulled a Commission Decision refusing to make an interim order requiring a camera manufacturer to supply Camera Care with its cameras. The Commission had taken the position that it had no powers under Regulation 17/62 to issue interim orders, but on a broad interpretation of Article 3 the Court decided that such a power was implied.

Similarly, in the *AKZO Chemie* Article 86 predatory pricing litigation (see Chapter Fifteen), ECS complained to the Commission about AKZO's price-cutting policy, which they alleged was designed to exclude ECS from the market. The Commission carried out an investigation at AKZO's premises in the Netherlands and the UK and later issued an interim Decision requiring AKZO's UK subsidiary to return to the price and profit levels applied before the alleged predatory pricing policy was implemented against ECS.

A further question which may arise out of a Commission investigation is that of professional privilege and confidentiality. In Case 155/79 *AM & S Europe Ltd.* v. *Commission*, the Court of Justice held that, in general, correspondence between an *EEC-based* independent lawyer and his client undertaking was privileged (particularly as regards documents relating to the defence of the client after the initiation of proceedings by the Commission) but dealings with an in-house lawyer were not privileged. (It has been said that the limitation of privilege to EEC lawyers is discriminatory.) A Commission Decision ordering the handing over of documents which a party considers privileged is open to challenge under Article 173(2).

It will also be seen in Article 21(2) of the Regulation that the Commission 'shall have regard to the legitimate interest of undertakings in the protection of their business secrets' (see also Article 20 on professional secrecy). The decision as to whether a document contains business secrets rests with the Commission but if it intends to pass documents allegedly containing such secrets to a third party, it must issue a Decision informing the undertaking in question who may challenge the Decision under Article 173(2). On the general obligation of professional secrecy in Article 214 of the Treaty as it applied to the Commission in Case 145/83 *Adams v Commission*, see Chapter Nineteen.

The Commission's power to impose *fines* (of a non-criminal law nature) and *periodic penalty* (or default) *payments* on undertakings is to be found in Articles 15 and 16 of the Regulation. Fines may relate to substantive infringements of Article 85(1) or Article 86 or to infringements arising out of Commission investigations, eg supplying incorrect or misleading information or failing to co-operate in an investigation. Periodic penalty payments may be imposed in order to enforce a requirement to put an end to an infringement of Article 85 or 86, to ensure compliance with an order for interim measures, or as otherwise laid down in relation to investigations, etc in Article 16.

As seen in Article 15(2), as regards fines for substantive infringements of the competition rules, the Commission will first establish whether the infringement is intentional or negligent, and, in fixing the amount of the fine, it will have regard 'both to the gravity and to the duration of the infringement'. In Case 100/80 etc *Musique Diffusion Française (Pioneer)*, the Court of Justice said that

> ... regard must be had to the duration of the infringements established and to all the factors capable of affecting the gravity of the infringements, such as the conduct of each of the undertakings, the role played by each of them in establishing the concerted practices, the profit which they were able to derive from those practices, their size, the value of the goods concerned and the threat that infringements of that type pose to the objectives of the Community.

The Court has also stated that the purpose of fines is to 'suppress illegal activities and to prevent any recurrences'. In addition, fines have a general deterrent effect on other undertakings. In recent years there has been a considerable increase in the level of fines: in the *AKZO Chemie* (1985) and *Tetra Pak* (1991) Article 86 predatory pricing cases, the two undertakings were fined 10 million and 75 million ECU respectively (both have appealed, AKZO's fine being reduced by the Court, see Chapter Fifteen). Article 85 market sharing and price fixing cases have attracted fines in some instances of over 1 million ECU, reaching a total of 23 million ECU in *PVC* (1989) and 60 million ECU in *Polyethylene* (1989), both under appeal. Export ban cases persist: in *Pioneer Hi-Fi Equipment* (1980) a total fine of almost 7 million ECU was imposed by the Commission but it was later halved by the Court of Justice under Article 172 on the question of duration. In *John Deere* (1985), total fines of 2 million ECU were imposed. Appeals under Article 173(2) have only rarely resulted in total annulment of the Commission's Decision.

Commission Powers and Procedures: Merger Control

The powers of the Commission and the procedures it must follow with respect to *concentrations* which fall within the Community merger control rules are to be found in Council Regulation 4064/89 (see Chapter Sixteen) and Commission Regulation 2367/90, which provides further details regarding notifications, time limits and hearings. Although Regulation 17 is not applicable, the Commission's powers and procedures remain broadly the same.

In terms of Regulation 4064/89, this is the case with reference to:

— requests for information from undertakings: Article 11. The provision of misleading information gives rise to fines.

— the co-operation of national competition authorities in Commission investigations: Article 12.

— wide investigative powers granted to the Commission regarding entry of premises, the examination of business documents and requests for oral explanations 'on the spot': Article 13. These powers are subject to procedural requirements similar to those in Regulation 17 (see above).

— the Commission's power to impose fines and periodic penalty payments: Articles 14 and 15.

— review of Commission decisions by the Court of Justice under Article 172 (as regards fines and default payments) and Article 173(2) of the Treaty: see Articles 16 and 21(1).

— professional secrecy: Article 17.

— the hearing of the parties and third persons; the latter covering natural or legal persons showing 'a sufficient interest' and especially members of the managements of the undertakings involved and union representatives: Article 18.

ENFORCEMENT AT NATIONAL LEVEL:
ARTICLE 9(3) OF REGULATION 17

The availability of remedies for private parties in national courts on the basis of a breach of the *Community* competition rules stems from the decision of the Court of Justice in Case 127/73 *BRT* v *SABAM*, where it ruled that Articles 85 and 86 are directly effective (both vertically and horizontally). As a result a party may claim:

(i) that an agreement is void under Article 85(2),

(ii) that an injunction should be granted to enforce the competition rules,

(iii) damages for breach of Article 85 or 86.

However, it is important to remember that although national courts have jurisdiction concurrent with the Commission to apply Article 85(1) –or to refuse to apply it – the Commission has the sole power to grant individual exemption under Article 85(3): Regulation 17/62, Article 9(1). (The national court does have power to establish whether an agreement falls within a block exemption.)

As indicated in Chapter Fourteen, as between the parties to an agreement, Article 85 may be used as a shield by, for example, a party seeking to break away from a contractual tie without incurring liability. In Case 56/65 *Société Technique Minière* and Case 23/67 *Brasserie de Haecht*, defendant distributors pleaded the unenforceability of the agreements with their suppliers on the ground that the agreements were contrary to Article 85(1) and therefore void under 85(2). However, as we have seen, if Article 85(2) does apply, it only applies to those provisions of the agreement which fall within the prohibition of Article 85(1). The doctrine of severance may apply: having excised the offending provisions, an English court may be satisfied that what remains does not significantly differ from what was originally agreed and be prepared to enforce it.

In *Potato Marketing Board* v *Robertsons* (1983), in the Oxford County Court, the defendant firm, when sued for payment of the potato farming levy, unsuccessfully pleaded that the plaintiff Board occupied a dominant position on the British market and, in breach of Article 86, had abused that position. The case was characterised by sharp differences of opinion on issues of fact 'largely concerned with economic matters' (ie the concepts of dominant position and abuse) between counsel for the plaintiffs (the joint author of a leading textbook on Community competition law) and the main witness for the defence (a professor of economics).

In *Garden Cottage Foods Ltd.* v *Milk Marketing Board* (1984), interlocutory proceedings which reached the House of Lords, Article 86 was used by the plaintiff undertaking as a sword. (This case will be discussed more fully in Chapter Twenty in the general context of the obligation of national courts to provide remedies for the breach of an individual's directly effective rights.) GCF, who had previously been a regular customer of MMB, alleged that the Board had acted in breach of Article 86 by cutting off its supplies of bulk butter. As will be seen, this interlocutory decision has been taken to establish that there is clear authority that a private law action for breach of Article 86 against an undertaking sounds in damages. GCF had applied for an interim injunction to force the Board to resume supplies but the House of Lords ruled that damages would, in this case, be an adequate remedy.

However, it is also now quite firmly established that, in appropriate circumstances, an injunction will be available to prevent the continuation of an alleged breach of Article 86 (or Article 85(1)), at the suit of an individual claiming harm. (For circumstances in which the UK court is *bound* to grant interim relief, where there is no adequate remedy in damages, see the *Factortame* case in Chapter Twenty.) In the *AKZO Chemie* litigation, referred to above, not only did the Commission grant interim relief against alleged predatory pricing but also the High Court in an *ex parte* application. An interlocutory injunction was also obtained in the following case:

> *Cutsforth* v. *Mansfield Inns Ltd* (1986)
> C supplied gaming machines to pubs and clubs in the Humberside area. M took over a number of tied outlets in the area and required their new tenants only to install gaming machines from suppliers on an approved list. C was excluded from the list. As well as complaining to the Commission, C sought an interim injunction in the High Court on the basis of Article 85(1) and Regulation 1984/83 (the exclusive purchasing block exemption Regulation relating to beer supplies) to restrain M from enforcing the new tenancy agreements to the extent that they excluded him from this previous area of business.

It was held that a restriction of competition of this nature infringed Article 85(1) and could not benefit from the block exemption Regulation since the restrictive clause in question was to be found in the 'black list' in that Regulation. The injunction was granted to protect C from the consequences of M enforcing the new tenancy agreements. Sir Neil Lawson stated that there was a serious case to be considered and directions were given for a speedy trial. (The case was in fact settled.)

Referring to C's complaint to the Commission under Article 3(2) of Regulation 17/62, the Judge was critical of speed of 'the mills of Brussels', but it will be recalled that, following *Camera Care* (above), the Commission has the power to grant interim relief and did so with commendable speed (just over four months) in *British Brass Instruments v Boosey & Hawkes* (1988), see also Chapter Fifteen. The Commission explained that:

> Where a dominant firm has taken a series of measures to exclude a potential competitor from the market, including a refusal of supplies, the Commission will require to be satisfied on the following points before granting interim measures in the form of an order to supply:
>
> (a) that there is a reasonably strong *prima facie* case establishing an infringement;
> (b) that there is a likelihood of serious and irreparable harm to the applicant unless measures are ordered; and
> (c) that there is an urgent need for protective measures.

It should however be appreciated that although the Commission can fine an undertaking in breach of the competition rules, it cannot award damages. On the other hand, the Commission's powers of investigation under Regulation 17/62 put it in a far better position to obtain and assess information regarding a possible breach of the rules than a High Court judge. The costs to the applicant will also be far less than those incurred in domestic litigation.

Although *Garden Cottage Foods* represents a firm pointer to the availability of damages in the national courts for breach of Article 86, or Article 85(1), there is as yet no actual decision to that effect. Nor is there general satisfaction with the clear indication by Lord Diplock in that case that an award would rest on what has been termed the 'notoriously unpredictable' tort of breach of statutory duty. As will be seen in Chapter Twenty, it is a fundamental principle of Community law that national courts must ensure the legal protection which individuals derive from the direct effect of Community law. The remedies available at the national level must be no less favourable than those relating to similar actions of a domestic nature: see, eg, Case 45/76 *Comet*. However, where national competition policy, as in the UK, is enforced mainly by the Office of Fair Trading through administrative procedures similar to those of the Commission, it is clear that difficult questions remain to be answered concerning the availability of the damages remedy for breach of the Community's competition rules. After commenting on the *Garden Cottage Food* case, Bellamy and Child (with an eye to uniformity) conclude:

> More generally, there is the question whether any or all of these issues should be settled at Community, rather than national, level.

In early 1993, the Commission adopted 'The Notice on Co-operation between National Courts and the Commission in Applying Articles 85 and 86'. The Notice has been welcomed, but in a recent analysis it has been suggested that it 'is aiming at the wrong target. The most effective contribution that can be made to the enforcement of EC competition law, at the current stage of EC integration [ie in the absence of harmonised procedures and remedies where EC competition rights are pleaded] is to give the NCAs a greater role.' The NCAs are the national competition authorities of the Member States. In the UK the 'competent authority' jointly comprises the Office of Fair Trading and the Department of Trade and Industry. Under Article 9(3) of Regulation 17 NCAs already possess the power to apply Articles 85 and 86 so long as the Commission has not initiated any procedure. Some NCAs, particularly in France and Spain, do use Articles 9(3): see further, Riley in the 'References and Further Reading'.

Bellamy and Child, *Common Market Law of Competition*, 1987 (and Supplement 1, 1991) Chapter 10 'Civil Remedies' and Chapter 12 'Enforcement and Procedure'.

EC Commission Reports on Competition Policy.

Davidson, J., 'Actions for Damages in the English Courts for Breach of EEC Competition Law' (1985) 34 ICLQ 178.

Feinberg, R. M., 'The Enforcement and Effects of European Competition Policy – Results of a Survey of Legal Opinion' (1985) 23 JCMS 373.

Harris, B., 'Problems of Procedure in EEC Competition Law' (1989) NLJ 1452.

Hoskins, M., 'Garden Cottage Revisited: The Availability of Damages in the National Courts for Breaches of EEC Competition Rules' (1992) 6 ECLR 257.

Joshua, J. M., 'The Element of Surprise: EEC Competition Investigations under Article 14(3) of Regulation 17' (1983) 8 EL Rev. 3.

Joshua, J. M., 'Information in EEC Competition Law Procedures' (1986) 11 EL Rev. 409.

Kerse, C., EEC *Anti-Trust Procedure.*

Pagone, M., 'Legal Professional Privilege in the European Communities' (1984) 33 ICLQ 663.

Riley, A. J., 'More Radicalism, Please: The Notice on Co-operation between National Courts and the Commission in Applying Articles 85 and 86 of the EEC Treaty' (1993) 3 ECLR 91.

Usher, J., 'Exercise by the European Court of its Jurisdiction to Annul Competition Decisions' (1980) 5 EL Rev. 287.

Van Bael, I. 'The Anti-Trust Settlement Practice of the EC Commission' (1986) 23 CML Rev. 61.

Waelbroeck, D., 'New Forms of Settlement of Anti-Trust Cases and Procedural Safeguards: Is Regulation 17 Falling into Abeyance?' (1986) 11 EL Rev. 268.

CHAPTER EIGHTEEN

INDUSTRIAL PROPERTY RIGHTS, FREE MOVEMENT AND COMPETITION

THE DELICATE BALANCE BETWEEN NATIONAL RIGHTS AND THE FREE MOVEMENT OF GOODS

The 'industrial and commercial property' which may be protected under Article 36 in derogation from the free movement of goods principle comprises certain valuable rights relating to the production and distribution of goods and services and which are to be found in patents, trade marks, copyrights and other analogous rights. (The expression 'intellectual property' is also generally used to describe these rights although it does not appear in the Treaty.) Key features of such rights are their *exclusive* and *national* character. As recognised by the various national legal systems of the Member States, special rights or protection are granted to the owner of such industrial property (the term which will be used here). A form of legal monopoly is acquired which may last indefinitely, as is the case with trade marks in the UK, or for a certain period of years: in the UK 20 years for patents and the author's lifetime plus 50 years for copyrights.

The proprietary rights which are granted may serve to protect important and valuable technical information (as for a patented industrial process) or may protect the individuality and selling power of an established product (as is the case with trade marks). The justification for such protection may be expressed as a reward for innovation, industrial progress and efficiency or, more generally, in terms of the effort, perhaps creative, and the expense involved. For example, a patentee (or, similarly, a person to whom the patent has been assigned or licensed) is the person – such rights are often held by undertakings – who alone is entitled to manufacture and distribute the patented product for the first time within the State granting the patent. A breach of these rights by a third party can attract infringement proceedings in national law.

To the extent that varying national industrial property laws allowed a patentee (or, for example, a trade mark holder) absolute territorial protection of this kind, it appeared, in the early days of the Community that, for goods that were protected by such rights, the Common Market could be partitioned on a national basis in a manner obviously contrary to the pursuit of single market integration. The difficulties posed by industrial property rights in this way have been summed up as follows:

> The potential uneasiness of the case of industrial property in the Common Market results from the basic contradiction between on the one hand, a Common Market which eliminates all economic barriers between the Member States and, on the other hand, the territorial monopolies resulting from the industrial property rights in the Member States: Jehoram.

At the root of the problem, as the case law of the Court of Justice demonstrates, is the fact that identical goods may be the subject of parallel industrial property rights registered in a *number* of Member States. For example, patent or other rights may have been registered in several Member States by the inventor and manufacturer himself, or licensed by him to undertakings in other Member States. Such undertakings may well be his own subsidiary companies. (Alternatively, similar and competing goods may be the subject of rights which have been established under the national law of Member States in isolation from each other.)

To take one possibility: as we have seen, a patent holder, X (UK) Ltd., has in national law an exclusive right to put the patented product into circulation for the *first time* on the UK market. (However, after this first sale the company's rights are *exhausted* so far as the goods sold are concerned; once on the market they can be resold at will.) However, sales of the goods *elsewhere*, which are subject to parallel national rights, do not amount to the exercise of its rights by X (UK) Ltd. This can lead to a situation where X (UK) Ltd. might, as a matter of *national* law, oppose the sale in the UK of the same (lower priced) goods imported by Y from Belgium where a parallel patent exists which is held by X (UK) Ltd's subsidiary, X (Belgium) Ltd., which itself first put these goods on the Belgian market.

Such a situation, and others similar, clearly present problems for the fundamental principle of the free movement of goods. In an early ruling on patents, Case 24/67 *Parke, Davis* v *Probel*, the Court stated that:

> The national rules relating to the protection of industrial property have not yet been unified within the Community. In the absence of such unification, the national character of the protection of industrial property and the variations between the different legislative systems on this subject are capable of creating obstacles both to the free movement of the patented products and to competition within the common market.

The Court of Justice has made it clear that the 'protection' afforded by Article 36 leaves national industrial property rights intact in the sense that their *existence* cannot be incompatible with Articles 30-34. In addition, Article 222 of the Treaty lays down that:

This Treaty shall in no way prejudice the rules in Member States governing the system of property ownership. [The Community may nevertheless seek to harmonise such national legislation, see the statement by the Court, above.]

Thus, as Gormley points out:

The patentee or trade work owner may be able to restrain importation of the product involved by an undertaking in another Member State which has made an imitation of the relevant product protected in the importing Member State by a patent or which has illegally applied the mark protected in the importing Member State to its own products, without his consent.

It will also be recalled that, although Article 36 allows for derogation from Articles 30-34 in respect of 'the protection of industrial and commercial property', this is not the case where such rights 'constitute a means of arbitrary discrimination or a disguised restriction on trade between Member States'. It is therefore only restrictions on imports which are 'justified', ie necessary (but no more than necessary), for the protection of industrial property which are allowable under Article 36. What this means in practice rests on a distinction drawn by the Court of Justice between the '*existence*' of national rights and the '*exercise*' of those rights. To stay within Article 222, the Court allows the derogation from free movement to operate but only in respect of those rights making up the '*specific subject-matter*' (or essential core) of the property in question. These may be protected at the expense of free movement. The Court defined the specific subject-matter of a patent in Case 15/74 *Centrafarm* v *Sterling Drug* as

... the guarantee that the patentee, to reward the creative effort of the inventor, has the exclusive right to use an invention with a view to manufacturing industrial products and putting them into circulation for the first time, either directly or by the grant of licences to third parties as well as the right to oppose infringements.

In this way a patentee's 'first time' monopoly profit is recognised and safeguarded and he may oppose manufacturing or 'first time' marketing by third parties. However, the use of a patent (or other industrial property right) to obtain something further, or incidental, from the right will be in breach of Article 36 (or Article 85 if used in conjunction with a restrictive trading agreement: see the next section) if:

a) the exercise is not made for the *bona fide* protection of the specific subject-matter of the property, and

b) its object is to frustrate the fundamental principle of free movement of goods (or the related objectives of the Community's competition policy).

The distinction drawn by the Court of Justice between the existence and exercise of rights has been criticised as being artificial. A patent, for example, is a bundle of rights under national law and if some of those rights cannot be exercised under Community law then the property is to that extent diminished. On the other hand it has been said that: 'Metaphorically, the conception is that while the ownership of a motor car is allowed, its use may in certain circumstances be prevented, eg when the alcohol content of the driver's blood exceeds a certain level': Barounos et al, *EEC Anti-Trust Law*.

Exhaustion of Rights: Consent

The Court's approach to trade marks is essentially the same as for patents and the following cases illustrate both this point and the operation of the *exhaustion of rights* principle in the context of the free movement of goods. Case 15/74 *Centrafarm* v *Sterling Drug* was concerned with patents and Case 16/74 *Centrafarm* v *Winthrop* with trade marks:

UK and Dutch patents relating to the process of manufacturing a medicament marketed under the trade name 'Negram' were owned by an American company, Sterling Drug, which had granted a patent licence to its marketing subsidiary in each of those Member States. Sterling Drug had also assigned the trade mark 'Negram' to those subsidiaries, Sterling Winthrop in the UK and Winthrop in the Netherlands.

Centrafarm, an independent Dutch company, bought 'Negram' on the open market in the UK and imported it for resale into the Netherlands. The price in the UK was around half that on the Dutch market as a result of UK government price control policies.

Sterling Drug and its subsidiaries invoked their patent and trade mark rights before the Dutch courts to prevent the parallel imports. The Dutch court referred a series of questions to the Court of Justice under Article 177.

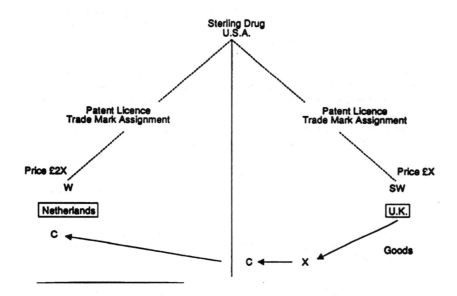

In the course of its ruling in the *Sterling Drug* patent case, the Court of Justice stated that:

> As a result of the provisions in the Treaty relating to the free movement of goods and in particular of Article 30, quantitative restrictions on imports and all measures having equivalent effect are prohibited between Member States.

> By Article 36 these provisions shall nevertheless not include provisions or restrictions justified on grounds of the protection of industrial or commercial property.

> Nevertheless, it is clear from its same article, in particular its second sentence, as well as from the context, that whilst the Treaty does not affect the existence of rights recognised by the legislation of a Member State in matters of industrial and commercial property, yet the exercise of these rights may nevertheless, depending on the circumstances, be affected by the prohibitions in the Treaty.

Inasmuch as it provides an exception to one of the fundamental principles of the Common Market, Article 36 in fact only admits of derogations from the free movement of goods where such derogations are justified for the purpose of safeguarding rights which constitute the specific matter of this property.

In relation to patents, the specific subject matter of the industrial property is the guarantee that the patentee, to reward the creative effort of the inventor, has the exclusive right to use an invention with a view to manufacturing industrial products and putting them into circulation for the first time, either directly or by the grant of licences to third parties, as well as the right to oppose infringements.

An obstacle to the free movement of goods may arise out of the existence, within a national legislation concerning industrial and commercial property, of provisions laying down that the patentee's right is not exhausted when the product protected by the patent is marketed in another Member State, with the result that the patentee can prevent importation of the product into his own Member State when it has been marketed in another State.

Whereas an obstacle to the free movement of goods of this kind may be justified on the ground of protection of industrial property where such protection is invoked against a product coming from a Member State where it is not patentable and has been manufactured by third parties without the consent of the patentee and in cases where there exist patents, the original proprietors of which are legally and economically independent, a derogation from the principle of the free movement of goods is not, however, justified where the product has been put onto the market in a legal manner, by the patentee himself or with his consent, in the Member State from which it has been imported, in particular in the case of a proprietor of parallel patents.

In fact, if a patentee could prevent the import of protected products marketed by him or with his consent in another Member State, he would be able to partition off national markets and thereby restrict trade between Member States, in a situation where no such restriction was necessary to guarantee the essence of the exclusive rights flowing from the parallel patents ...

The question referred should therefore be answered to the effect that the exercise, by a patentee, of the right which he enjoys under the legislation of a Member State to prohibit the sale, in that State, of a product protected by the patent which has been marketed in another Member State by the patentee or with his consent is incompatible with the rules of the EEC Treaty concerning the free movement of goods within the Common Market.

Similarly, in the *Winthrop* trade mark case, the Court ruled that:

In relation to trade marks, the specific subject-matter of the industrial property is the guarantee that the owner of the trade mark has the exclusive right to use that trade mark, for the purpose of putting products protected by the trade mark into circulation for the first time, and is therefore intended to protect him against competitors wishing to take advantage of the status and reputation of the trade mark by selling products illegally bearing that trade mark.

An obstacle to the free movement of goods may arise out of the existence, within a national legislation concerning industrial and commercial property, of provisions laying down that a trade mark owner's right is not exhausted when the product protected by the trade mark is marketed in another Member State, with the result that the trade mark owner can prevent importation of the product into his own Member State when it has been marketed in another Member State.

Such an obstacle is not justified when the product has been put onto the market in a legal manner in the Member State from which it has been imported, by the trade mark owner himself or with his consent, so that there can be no question of abuse or infringement of the trade mark.

In fact, if a trade mark owner could prevent the import of protected products marketed by him or with his consent in another Member State, he would be able to partition off national markets and thereby restrict trade between Member States, in a situation where no such restriction was necessary to guarantee the essence of the exclusive right flowing from the trade mark.

The question referred should therefore be answered to the effect that the exercise, by the owner of a trade mark, of the right which he enjoys under the legislation of a Member State to prohibit the sale, in that State, of a product which has been marketed under the trade mark in another Member State by the trade mark owner or with his consent is incompatible with the rules of the EEC Treaty concerning the free movement of goods within the Common Market.

The exhaustion principle has been applied by the Court of Justice within the context of Article 36 not only to patents and trade-marks but also to copyrights and analogous rights such as industrial designs. In essence, in

Community law the owner's exclusive right is exhausted by his putting the product in question into circulation *anywhere* within the Community. First time sale in such cases therefore has a Common Market not a national dimension.

In Cases 55 and 57/80 *Musik Vertrieb Membran* v *GEMA*, the Court held that the performing rights society GEMA could not rely on its German copyright in sound recordings to prevent parallel imports of records from the UK which had been put on the market there with its consent. Nor could GEMA collect the additional 2.25 per cent royalty rate reflecting the difference between the lower, statutorily-imposed rate in the UK and the rate applying in Germany. However, in Case 341/87 *EMI Electrola* v *Patricia*, records were exported to Germany from Denmark. However they had *not* been put on the Danish market with the consent of the German EMI company. These sales had arisen because the copyright protection in Denmark was for a shorter period than in Germany and had expired. The Court of Justice held that until such time as the rules were harmonised it was for national law to determine the period of copyright protection and that EMI could rely on its German copyright to prevent the parallel imports: the right to do so was indissolubly linked to the exclusive right conferred under German copyright law.

The case law of the Court therefore reveals that the *consent* (or otherwise) of the owner of the rights in question to the first marketing elsewhere in the Common Market is the key factor in these decisions. Consent can arise where the owner markets the goods himself, where he does so through a subsidiary company, or where the owner and the undertaking responsible for the first marketing are under common control: see *Centrafarm* v *Sterling Drug*, above. In these instances the owner who is seeking an injunction to prevent the lawfully marketed parallel imports cannot rely on national industrial property rights legislation, which will constitute a measure having equivalent effect to a quantitative restriction on imports under Article 30. Such an exercise of the right in question is not justified within the terms of Article 36. It amounts to a disguised restriction on trade and a means to partitioning the Common Market along national lines. The price of the parallel imports will in all probability be considerably less than that of the product on the home market, but it is immaterial whether the difference is due to government regulation in the exporting state or merely market forces.

Other patent cases similarly rest on the consent rule. In Case 187/80 *Merck* v *Stephar*, a Dutch patentee was unable to prevent the importation into the Netherlands of a pharmaceutical product previously marketed with its consent by its subsidiary in Italy. However at that time the drug was not patentable in Italy and therefore there was no possibility of earning a monopoly profit there. Although this is no longer the case, this decision was criticised as leading to products only being sold where patent protection was available; a division of the Common Market as serious as differential pricing. In Case 19/84 *Pharmon* v *Hoechst*, a Dutch patentee was able to invoke Article 36 to prevent imports of products originally marketed in the UK by a licensee holding a *compulsory* licence granted under UK law. (This can occur where the patent would not otherwise be commercially exploited.) The element of consent was absent and the patent owner could assert his basic rights.

Other trade mark cases have addressed the situation where the proprietor of a trade mark in one Member State has marketed the same goods in another Member State under a different mark. For example, in Case 3/78 *Centrafarm* v *American Home Products*, AHP sold a tranquilliser as 'Serenid' in the UK and as 'Seresta' in the Netherlands. The two products were pharmaceutically identical but chemically different and tasted different. Centrafarm imported 'Serenid' into the Netherlands from the UK having changed its name to 'Seresta'. Centrafarm were thus able to establish the identity of the goods in the Netherlands, were able to take advantage of AHP's promotion of 'Seresta', and were able to compete with, and undercut, AHP there. The Court of Justice was asked if AHP could rely on its Dutch rights to stop such imports. It ruled that in principle the trade mark proprietor was justified in opposing a sale by a third party in such circumstances even where the product had been marketed in the other Member State (under a different mark) by the same proprietor. Otherwise the essential guarantee for consumers of a product's origin would be compromised. The Court did however add, in the light of the second sentence of Article 36, that whereas there might be good reasons for using different trade marks in respect of the same products in different Member States (eg to avoid problems of similarity with existing marks causing confusion), such a strategy would amount to a disguised restriction on trade if it were used for anti-competitive and market-splitting purposes. This was a matter for the national court to decide.

In the later Case 1/81 *Pfizer* v *Eurim-Pharm*, the Court held that a trade mark owner may not oppose the parallel importation of goods (again pharmaceuticals) lawfully marketed by a subsidiary in another Member State where the importer has put properly labelled external packaging on the product without interfering with the internal packaging or obscuring the original trade mark.

Common Origin

The delicate balance between national trade mark rights (as possible MEEQRs) and the free movement of goods has also been influenced in a different way by the concept of *common origin*:

Case 192/73 *Van Zuylen Frères* v. *Hag AG*

H, a German company, owned trade marks for its decaffeinated coffee in several countries for many years. In the late 1930s and during the war its rights in Belgium and Luxembourg were held by its subsidiary Café Hag SA of Liege. Having been confiscated and sold off as enemy property in 1944, the Belgian company's trade mark eventually passed to VZF.

When H began exporting its coffee from Germany to Luxembourg, VZF brought infringement proceedings. The question of exhaustion of rights did not arise because the German company had not consented to the original transfer of its trade mark. H and VZF legitimately owned the same mark and H was exporting directly into VZF's 'territory'.

On an Article 177 reference, the Court of Justice ruled that the free movement principle must prevail over the national trade mark rights: the right claimed by VZF would have the effect of partitioning the market indefinitely (on account of the indefinite duration of trade mark rights) and consumer interests could be safeguarded by appropriate labelling regarding the origin of the products. Thus: '... one cannot allow the holder of a trade mark to rely upon the exclusiveness of a trade mark right ... with a view to prohibiting the marketing in a Member State of goods legally produced in another Member State under an identical trade mark having the same origin.'

This decision did not meet with general approval and meant that neither holder of such a 'split' mark (of common origin) could prevent goods legitimately bearing the mark from being imported and sold either by the other holder or by purchasers from him in the Member State where he owned the mark. Hag had not consented to the use of the mark by VZF but, as we have seen in the *Pharmon* case decided in 1985, a patentee *was* able to invoke Article 36 to protect his rights and prevent imports originally put on the market in another Member State by a *compulsory* licensee. In 1990 the Court of Justice considered it necessary to review its ruling in the first *Hag* decision 'in the light of the case law which had gradually developed':

Case C-10/89 *Sucal* v *Hag*

This case presented a reverse-fact situation to that in 1974. VZF had become a company, trading as Sucal (and owned by Suchard of Switzerland). VZF's trade mark rights, originally held by Hag (Belgium), having passed to Sucal, Hag was seeking an injunction in the German courts to restrain Sucal from supplying coffee under the 'Hag' mark to the German market.

Following a reference to the Court of Justice under Article 177, the Court held that Articles 30 and 36 EEC did not prevent national

legislation from allowing an undertaking, which was the proprietor of a
trade mark in one Member State, from opposing the importation from
another Member State of similar goods lawfully bearing an identical or
confusingly similar trade mark to the protected mark, even though the
mark under which the disputed product had been imported had initially
belonged to a subsidiary of the undertaking which was opposing the
importation and had been acquired by a third undertaking following the
expropriation of that subsidiary.

In the course of its decision the Court now stressed both the absence of
consent between two undertakings with no legal or economic ties and also
the possibility of confusion amongst consumers. The original *Hag* 'free
movement' decision had led some commentators to fear that it would be
applied to defeat attempts by trade mark owners in one Member State to
prevent the use in that State of another trade mark originating from another
Member State that might be confusingly similar, even where there was no
question of common origin and there were no legal or economic ties
between the parties.

However the Court had quelled those fears in Case 119/75 *Terrapin
(Overseas) Ltd.* v *Terranova Industrie*, in which the German firm, Terranova,
successfully invoked Article 36 to prevent an English firm, Terrapin, from
registering its trade mark in Germany. The marks had been acquired by
different proprietors under different national laws; there were no links between
the firms (and therefore presumably no question of the use of the different
marks as a disguised restriction on trade), and the similarity between the names
could give rise to confusion as both firms supplied building materials.

Unification of Industrial Property Law

Diverging or uncoordinated national laws lie at the root of most of
the problems faced by the Court of Justice in the above cases. Time and again
the Court has explained that its ruling is set in the context of 'the present state
of Community law' in the area and has drawn attention to 'the divergences
which remain in the absence of any unification of national rules concerning
industrial property'. Goyder has summed up the position as follows:

> If the founders of the Community were to be allowed today to redraw
> both the Treaty of Rome and Member State legislation in the way
> required to preserve the essential characteristics of the original Treaty,
> whilst providing a completely fresh basis for the framing of the rules
> relating to national rights of intellectual property, the experience of the
> last thirty years would mean that their objectives would clearly have to
> include the definition of such rights and their essential characteristics in a

way which could be accepted as valid throughout the Community, rather than allowing the perpetuation by individual Member States of such national rights varying in both classification and content, and which through their very diversity raise major problems for the free movement of goods and commercial integration. While Article 36 includes the 'protection of industrial and commercial property' as one of the exceptions to the basic principle of free movement of goods, there is no doubt that the attainment of an integrated market will remain difficult, if not impossible, so long as such varied exceptions to the basic rules are preserved. The harmonisation, therefore, of the law relating to intellectual property within the Community, in particular that relating to patents and trade marks, as well as the gradual harmonisation of the classification and definition of all the other various intellectual property rights found to exist within Member States covering rights as varied as copyright, registered design, and rights against unfair competition, remain an objective of great importance.

The tension between, on the one hand, national systems of industrial property rights and, on the other, the free movement of goods and fair and effective competition throughout the Common Market can only be satisfactorily removed through the acceptance by the Member States of Community *Regulations* which replace the national territoriality principle with grants of industrial property rights covering the territory of the whole Community.

Progress along these lines has been very slow. The possibility of introducing a Community patent was first discussed in 1959. The *European Patent Convention* 1973 (an international convention involving a number of European countries including, since 1992, *all* the Member States of the Community; it is not a Community act) merely established a system whereby the European Patent Office in Munich can grant a 'batch' of national patents, so obviating the need for a patentee to take out individual patents in the required number of different European countries. The Convention brought about no change in the substantive national patent law of the contracting states.

The *Community Patent Convention* signed in 1975 is not yet in force. Its purpose is to introduce a unitary patent for the Community as the only available form of European patent available in the Member States. The rights of the owner of such a patent will be exhausted once he puts the protected product on the market anywhere within the Community. It will not be possible to partition the Common Market by granting patent licences limited to certain territories. National patents will still be available, but not for an invention covered by a Community patent, and the exhaustion of rights principle as developed by the Court of Justice (as above) will apply. In 1988 the Council proposed an inter-governmental conference for the purpose of finalising the text of the Convention for entry into force on 1 January 1993. Further developments however are still awaited.

In 1980 the Commission put forward proposals for a Council Directive on the approximation of the laws of the Member States relating to trade marks and for a Council Regulation on a *Community Trade Mark*. The harmonisation measure was adopted in 1989 (Directive 89/104). It was initially intended that the Member States should implement it by the end of 1991 but this deadline has been extended. The Directive which aims to apply the rules established by the Court of Justice, defines the rights relating to the ownership of trade marks and the limitations on those rights within a single market. A common basis for the refusal of registration, for invalidity and for the loss or exhaustion of rights is provided but otherwise national trade mark law is unchanged.

The trade mark Regulation, which aims to establish Community marks which will supersede existing national registrations, remains to be agreed by the Council, together with a proposed Regulation on fees payable to the Community Trade Mark Office, the location of which is proving to be a problem.

So far as they go these latest developments stem from the Commission's view, expressed in its 1985 White Paper on the completion of the Internal Market that national industrial property laws still have

> a direct and negative impact on intra-Community trade and on the ability of enterprises to treat the common market as a single environment for their economic activities.

INDUSTRIAL PROPERTY RIGHTS AND THE COMPETITION RULES

In line with the decisions of the Court of Justice in connection with the free movement of goods, the mere *existence* of nationally protected industrial and commercial property rights does not infringe Articles 85 or 86. In Case 24/67 *Parke, Davis* v *Probel*, the Court stated that:

1. The existence of rights granted by a Member State to the holder of a patent is not affected by the prohibitions contained in Article 85(1) and 86 of the Treaty.

2. The exercise of such rights cannot of itself fall either under Article 85(1), in the absence of any agreement, decision or concerted practice prohibited by this provision, or under Article 86, in the absence of any abuse of a dominant position.

It follows therefore, as we have seen with regard to the free movement rules, that the competition rules may be invoked to prevent the improper *exercise* of industrial property rights. In fact the distinction between the existence of such rights and their exercise was first brought out by the Court in Cases 56 and 58/64 *Consten and Grundig v Commission* (see Chapter Fourteen). It will be recalled that, within the terms of G's exclusive distributorship agreement with C, its French dealer, the German company granted C exclusive use of its GINT trade mark in France. The Court ruled that G's purpose was not to protect the essential core or 'specific subject-matter' of the trade mark (in order, for example, to prevent other goods being passed off as Grundig products) but to enable C to prevent parallel imports of Grundig products from other Member States, so reinforcing the absolute territorial protection for C, and in a similar manner for G's other dealers in other Member States, which the network of distribution agreements was designed to achieve. It was contrary to Article 85(1) for C to bring a trade mark infringement action in the French national courts pursuant to an agreement which had the object or effect of partitioning the Common Market. As stated by the Court:

> The injunction ... to refrain from using rights under national trade mark law in order to set an obstacle in the way of parallel imports does not affect the grant of those rights but only limits their exercise to the extent necessary to give effect to the prohibition under Article 85(1).

Similarly, the mere existence of a patent, trade mark or other industrial property right does not mean that the owner has a dominant position in terms of Article 86. Nor is the exercise of such a right by an undertaking in a dominant position in itself abusive. However, an anti-competitive or exploitative exercise of industrial property rights by a dominant firm can infringe Article 86. In Case 238/87 *Volvo* v *Erik Veng Ltd* (see also Chapter Fifteen):

Volvo were the holders of registered design rights in the UK for spare parts for Volvo vehicles. The company brought an action to prevent Veng from acting in breach of their exclusive rights by copying the parts in question. Veng argued that this amounted to an abuse of Volvo's dominant position by excluding any competition in Volvo spare parts. To avoid this result, it was claimed, Volvo should be ordered to grant a licence of their rights.

Following a reference from the High Court under Article 177 regarding the applicability of Article 86, the Court ruled that, in the present state of Community law, it was solely a matter for national law to determine what protection to grant to designs -even for such functional goods as motor vehicle spare parts.

Accordingly, the Court continued: 'the right of the proprietor of a protected design to prevent third parties from manufacturing and selling or importing, without its consent, products incorporating the design constitutes the very subject-matter of his exclusive right. It follows that an obligation imposed upon the proprietor of a protected design to grant to third parties, even in return for a reasonable royalty, a licence for the supply of products incorporating the design would lead to the proprietor thereof being deprived of the substance of his exclusive right, and that a refusal to grant such a licence cannot in itself constitute an abuse of a dominant position.

It must however be noted that the exercise of an exclusive right by the proprietor of a registered design in respect of car body panels may be prohibited by Article 86 if it involves, on the part of an undertaking holding a dominant position, certain abusive conduct such as the arbitrary refusal to supply spare parts to independent repairers, the fixing of prices for spare parts at an unfair level or a decision no longer to produce spare parts for a particular model even though many cars of that model are still in circulation, provided that such conduct is liable to affect trade between Member States.'

(Note however the more restrictive view of the television companies' copyrights by the CFI in Case T-69/89 etc. *Magill TV Guide*, presently subject to appeal: see Chapter Fifteen.)

Article 86 has been applied on several occasions to the activities of what are known as collecting societies. These are formed by authors, performing artists and others who pool their copyrights within the society so as to enhance their bargaining position when negotiating with record companies and the media. In *GEMA*, a Commission decision of 1971, it was held that the German society held a dominant position in authors' copyright and had abused that position in a variety of ways, particularly as regards discrimination against authors from other Member States.

Patent Licences and Similar Agreements

It is primarily in relation to the application of Article 85 to patent licences and similar agreements that the competition rules have been invoked. Van Gerven has defined a licence agreement as

> an agreement by which the proprietor of an industrial property right – usually a patent or trade mark, but also for example a plant breeder's right – or a (non-industrial) intellectual property right, particularly copyright or know-how rights, permits another party, the licensee, under certain limitations of time, space and scope defined in the agreement, to perform various production or distribution activities which fall within the legal or factual monopoly right...

It has often been asked why the Commission is concerned to regulate patent licences at all. Such a licence may be said to 'open the door' on the patentee's monopoly, allowing the licensee to operate where he could not do so before. As in the Article 30 free movement cases, the Community authorities must attempt to strike a balance and seek to differentiate between the terms in a licence which relate to the *existence* of patent rights and those which relate to their *exercise*. The Commission has stated that Article 85(1) may only apply 'if a grant is accompanied by terms which go beyond the need to ensure the existence of an industrial property right'. As we have seen, the very opportunity to exploit a patent or other right through licences in return for royalties is recognised as an element of the 'specific subject matter' of a patent, as is a 'field of use' restriction in a patent licence which prevents the licensee from manufacturing a certain product which falls within the patent specification. However, Article 85(1) will, for example, be applied by the Commission, in its pursuit of economic integration within the Common

Market, to terms similar to those in exclusive distribution agreements which grant licensees 'absolute territorial protection' or which establish minimum prices at which protected products may be sold.

Article 85(1) applies to licence agreements on the same basis as other agreements, ie where their terms adversely affect trade between Member States and prevent, restrict or distort competition within the Common Market to an appreciable extent. Exemption may be obtained under Article 85(3) and Commission Regulation 2349/84 provides a block exemption for certain bilateral patent licence agreements and agreements which combine the licensing of patents and the transfer of related know-how. It is clearly in the interests of the parties to draft their agreement within the terms of the Regulation, but for agreements which do not fall squarely within its terms the parties may of course apply for individual exemption under Article 85(3). Article 4 of the Regulation provides for an accelerated 'opposition procedure' for obtaining such exemption: see Chapter Seventeen.

Regulation 2349/84 is complex measure operating in a field where decisions tend to be made on a case-by-case basis. Article 1 exempts from the prohibition of Article 85(1) various obligations relating to exclusivity and territorial protection. Article 2 lists those clauses which generally do not restrict competition and are considered not to fall under Article 85(1) at all: the 'white list'. Article 3 contains the 'black list' of provisions which are unacceptably anti-competitive and which will have to be removed or modified for the licence agreement to qualify for exemption. It is not possible to deal here with all the questions raised in these and other articles of the Regulation. Attention will be focused on two important areas in which the Court of Justice has reached significant conclusions.

The first of these is the question of exclusivity and the possibility that licensing agreements may isolate national markets. For example:

> A licensee may consider that the risk involved in the exploitation of the patented product or the high level of capital investment required are so great that it would not be worth taking a licence at all unless it can be offered some degree of immunity from intra-brand competition from the licensor, other licensees and their customers ...

> ... The licensor could agree to grant an exclusive right to manufacture the goods in a particular territory and to refrain from granting similar rights to anyone else there. In this situation the licensor retains the right to produce the goods in the territory itself, and such a licence is often called a 'sole' licence. It may be distinguished from an 'exclusive' manufacturing licence where the licensor also agrees not to produce the goods in the licensee's territory itself. This of course puts the licensee in a better position to exploit its licence. The licensor could go even

further and grant the licensee sole or exclusive selling rights as well. In this situation the licensee could prevent anyone who manufactured the goods outside its territory from selling them in it.

The licensee's position may be further reinforced by the licensor agreeing to impose terms on its other licensees preventing them, or requiring them to prevent their customers, from invading the licensed territory. Apart from imposing export bans, there are indirect ways of achieving the same thing: for example a term fixing the maximum quantities of goods that a licensee may produce can be so calculated that it can produce only sufficient to satisfy the demand on its domestic market. In the absence of legal constraints it would be possible for a licensor to give a licensee absolute territorial protection against any form of intra-brand competition. It would be foolish for the law to intervene and to prevent exclusivity if the result would be to deter firms from accepting licences to exploit new technology altogether. On the other hand the conferment of geographical exclusivity is precisely the type of practice most likely to alert the EEC competition authorities: Whish.

As with exclusive distribution agreements (covered by Regulation 1983/83), the Community authorities have to strike a balance. There is a conflict and, as Bellamy and Child explain, whereas on the one hand a patent licence appears to be 'restrictive', on the other hand 'the acceptance of the restrictions may well have led to the successful conclusion of the licence, with the prospect of the dissemination of new technology, increased innovation, and better exploitation of the patented invention'.

In the case which follows, concerning not a patent but the licence of plant breeder's rights, the Court of Justice followed a similar line to that in Case 56/65 *Société Technique Minière* (see Chapter Fourteen) where it held that an agreement which merely granted exclusive *distribution* rights, but conferred no absolute territorial protection and contained no export ban, did not necessarily fall within the prohibition of Article 85(1), especially if the exclusivity was necessary for the penetration of a new market. In *Nungesser* the Court was concerned that the licensee should not be deterred from accepting the commercial risks involved in dealing with a new product and should be encouraged to exploit new technology:

Case 258/78 *Nungesser* v. *Commission (Maize Seeds)*
The French research institute INRA held plant breeder's rights for certain new varieties of maize seeds. INRA granted licences in France and it also granted an exclusive right to produce and sell the varieties in West Germany to Nungesser. INRA undertook to ensure that INRA seeds would not be exported to West Germany except via Nungesser.

In 1972, dealers in France acquired the certified seed and attempted to sell it in the Federal Republic. They were restrained from doing so by Nungesser although it would appear that any industrial property rights had been exhausted by the licensed French growers' sale of the seed to the dealers. (This was prior to the decision in 1974 in *Centrafarm* v. *Sterling Drug* (see the earlier 'free movement' part of this chapter).

The Commission condemned the exclusive licence under Article 85(1) and refused to grant an exemption under Article 85(3). In Article 173(2) proceedings, the Court of Justice drew a distinction between (i) the obligations on INRA not to produce or sell the seeds in West Germany either themselves or through other German licensees and (ii) the obligation to prevent third parties from exporting the seeds to Germany.

The Court characterised a licence which merely extended to obligations of the first type as an 'open' exclusive licence; one which, in a case such as that before the Court, was *not incompatible* with Article 85(1). However a licence additionally containing obligations of the second type, which eliminated competition from third parties particularly parallel importers, would in the Court's view usually fall under Article 85(1). The Court upheld that part of the Commission's refusal to grant an Article 85(3) exemption in respect of the absolute territorial protection conferred by the licence.

The Court referred to INRA's years of research and experimentation and to the considerable financial risk attached to the commercial exploitation of the new seeds to justify the exclusivity (which normally means higher royalties), but in trying to prevent the French licensees from exporting, INRA had gone beyond permissible bounds:

> As it is a question of seeds intended to be used by a large number of farmers for the production of maize, which is an important product for human and animal foodstuffs, absolute territorial protection manifestly goes beyond what is indispensable for the improvement of production or distribution or the promotion of technical progress ...

In terms of length of research and risk involved with a new product, the Commission has limited the decision in *Nungesser* to those special circumstances (see Recital 11 in the Preamble to Regulation 2349/84), with the result that exclusive manufacturing and sale provisions in a *patent* licence may be caught by Article 85(1), subject to exemption under Article 85(3) on the basis of the block exemption Regulation.

Article 1 of Regulation 2349/84 *exempts* the following obligations relating to exclusivity and territorial protection from the prohibition of Article 85(1), providing the licence agreement contains no other provisions that infringe Article 85(1):

1. The licensor's agreeing not to license other undertakings in the licensee's territory: a 'sole' licence.

2. The licensor's agreeing not to exploit the licensed invention himself in the licensed territory: a combination of obligations (1) and (2) amount to an 'exclusive' licence.

3. The licensee's agreeing not to manufacture or use the licensed product or use the patented process in other licensees' territories within the Common Market.

4. The licensee's agreeing not to pursue an *active* sales policy within other licensees' territories within the Common Market (cf. the exclusive distribution Regulation 1983/83).

5. The licensee's agreeing not to sell even passively in other licensees' territories (ie in response to orders) for a period of five years from when the product is first marketed in the Community by the licensor or one of his licensees.

Among the 'black list' of Article 3 are provisions which *forbid* requirements in the licence to the effect that the parties shall not meet orders from undertakings in their own territories which intend to resell them within other Member States, and attempts to impede parallel imports from elsewhere in the Community of products which have been lawfully put on the market by the patentee or with his consent (cf. *Consten and Grundig*).

Finally, it is appropriate to examine a further patent licence decision of the Court of Justice concerning issues other than exclusivity and territorial protection. The case arose before Regulation 2349/84 came into effect but, as will be seen, it would still fall outside its exempting provisions.

Case 193/83 *Windsurfing International* v. *Commission*

WI obtained a German patent for the rig (mast, sail and spars) attached to a sailboard. Boards and rigs are usually sold as a complete unit. The Court agreed with the Commission that all but one of the following restrictions in WI's patent licences with its German licensees were contrary to Article 85(1):

1. An obligation on the licensee to sell only complete sailboards, ie the patented rig and a board which had been approved by WI. The

patent covered only the rig and WI's control over boards could *not* be seen as an allowable quality control, tying arrangement necessary for a technically satisfactory exploitation of the licensed products (such a clause is permissible under Article 2(1) of Regulation 2349/84). The clause in question arbitrarily restricted the licensee's freedom and it fell outside the specific subject matter of the patent.

2. An obligation on the licensee to pay royalties on the total selling price of the complete sailboard rather than on the patented rig alone. Unlike the Commission, the Court found no objection to this provision because it was shown that this method of calculating royalties produced a sum no greater than that which would have been fair and acceptable in relation to the rig alone. According to the Commission, if this had not been so, and the licensee's competitive position had been disadvantaged by having to bear costs for which he was 'not compensated through the advantages conferred by the exploitation of the patent', the obligation would have fallen under Article 85(1) – and see also Article 3(4) of the Patent Regulation's 'black list'.

3. A requirement that the licensee fix a notice on the board stating that it was 'licensed' by the licensor. This clause gave the erroneous impression that the boards were covered by WI's patent and it was not covered by the specific subject matter of the patent. It was likely to reduce consumer confidence in the licensees as being less technically competent than they in fact were and accordingly allow WI to gain a competitive advantage for itself (see also Article 2(6) of the Patent Regulation).

4. Obligations on the licensee not to challenge the validity of WI's patent and trade mark. A licensee is obviously well placed to detect any possible flaws in the patentee's title but such a clause, which seeks to prevent a licensee from being released from a burdensome, and invalid, licence is not within the specific subject matter of a patent and it is in the public interest that such an obstacle to economic activity be eliminated. The no-challenge clauses were contrary to Article 85(1) – and see also Article 3(1) of the Regulation's 'black list'.

5. A restriction on the licensee against manufacturing the sailboard except in certain factories in Germany. WI's argument that this was an essential quality control provision was rejected by the Court.

This case is important in particular for the light it throws on the distinction made between restrictions imposed by industrial property right holders which emanate from the inherent subject matter of the right and are allowable as forming part of the right itself and those other restrictions which represent an attempt to extend the holder's rights further in a manner which tilts the balance into unjustifiable anti-competitive activity.

As a postscript, it is also important to appreciate with respect to industrial property rights, their existence and their exercise, that the prohibitions in Articles 30 and in Articles 85 and 86 apply in a cumulative manner. In *Nungesser*, the Court stated that:

> ... one of the powers of the Commission is to ensure, pursuant to Article 85 of the Treaty and the regulations adopted in implementation thereof, that agreements and concerted practices between undertakings do not have the aspect or the effect of restricting or distorting competition, and that ... the power of the Commission is not affected by the fact that persons or undertakings subject to such restrictions [relating to absolute territorial protection] are in a position to rely upon the provisions of the Treaty relating to the free movement of goods in order to escape such restrictions [through the operation of the exhaustion of rights principle].

Baden Fuller, C.W.F., 'Economic Issues Relating to Property Rights in Trade Marks: Export Bans, Differential Pricing, Restrictions on Resale and Repackaging' (1981) 6 EL Rev. 162.

Bellamy and Child, *Common Market Law of Competition*, Chapter 7 and Supplement 1, 1991.

Bonet, G., Intellectual Property (1989) 9 YEL 315.

Carroll, F. 'Intellectual Property: The Current Legislative Status of Proposals Contained in the 1985 White Paper', *European Access*, 1989:4, August.

EC Commission, Reports on Competition Policy.

European Intellectual Property Review.

Evans, A. C., 'Trade Marks and Consumer Interests in EEC Law' (1983) 32 ICLQ 241.

Friden, G., 'Recent Developments in EEC Intellectual Property Law' (1989) 26 CML Rev. 193.

Goyder, D., *EEC Competition Law*, Chapter 16.

Helbach, E. A. van N., 'Industrial Property, The Centrafarm Judgments' (1976) 13 CML Rev. 37.

Jehoram, H. C., The Delicate Balance between Industrial Property and European Law: The Law as It Stands' (1976) 1 LIEI 71.

Marenco, G. and Banks, K., 'Intellectual Property and the Community Rules on Free Movement: Discrimination Unearthed' (1990) 15 EL Rev. 224.

Redies, B., 'Liberties and Risks in the Present System of Patent Protection in the EC' (1989) 11 EIPR 192.

Stone, J., 'Some Thoughts on the Windsurfing Judgment' (1986) 8 EIPR 242.

Turner, J.D.C., 'Competition and the Common Market after Maize Seeds' (1983) 8 EL Rev. 103.

Whish, R., *Competition Law*, Chapter 19.

PART FOUR

REMEDIES AND THE ENFORCEMENT

OF COMMUNITY LAW:

AT COMMUNITY AND NATIONAL LEVELS

CHAPTER NINETEEN

JUDICIAL REVIEW AND SUPERVISION OF THE COMMUNITY INSTITUTIONS

INTRODUCTION

In Chapter Six, we examined the jurisdiction of the Court of Justice under Article 173(1) regarding judicial review of acts of the Community's law-makers in the context of inter-institutional disputes (see 'Constitutional Checks and Balances'). The first of the cases discussed raised a question regarding the distribution of powers between the Commission (representing the Community interest) and the Council (representing the interests of the Member States): Case 22/70 *Commission* v *Council (European Road Transport Agreement)*.

We also saw how the Court extended the scope of its powers of review in Case 294/83 *Les Verts* v *European Parliament* to cover acts of the Parliament despite the Parliament not being a named defendant in Article 173. A further act of the Parliament was successfully challenged in Case 34/86 *Council* v *Parliament (Budget)*. In Case C-70/88 *Parliament* v *Council (Chernobyl)*, it was seen that the Parliament was entitled to *challenge* Council or Commission acts where its prerogatives (eg its right to participate in the legislative process as laid down by the Treaty) were directly affected under a special right of action devised by the Court akin to Article 173(1).

However, as pointed out when discussing these cases, questions of direct challenge to acts of the institutions, of supervision or judicial review of such acts and their possible annulment, are not merely an inter-institutional matter. Indeed, it was argued in Case 70/88 that unless Parliament was entitled to challenge Commission or Council acts, it would stand in an unfavourable position as compared not only with the other institutions but also with the Member States under Article 173(1), and with private parties (natural and legal) under Article 173(2):

Article 173

The Court of Justice shall review the legality of acts of the Council and the Commission other than recommendations or opinions. It shall for this purpose have jurisdiction in actions brought by a Member State, the Council or the Commission on grounds of lack of competence, infringement of an essential procedural requirement, infringement of this Treaty or of any rule of law relating to its application, or misuse of powers.

Any natural or legal person may, under the same conditions, institute proceedings against a decision addressed to that person or against a decision which, although in the form of a regulation or a decision addressed to another person, is of direct and individual concern to the former.

The proceedings provided for in this article shall be instituted within two months of the publication of the measure, or of its notification to the plaintiff, or, in the absence thereof, of the day on which it came to the knowledge of the latter, as the case may be.

When the TEU comes into effect, the European Parliament will be brought within the scope of Article 173 EC (in part as a result of the Court's decisions), as will the European Central Bank. The changes and additions to Article 173 EEC are as follows:

[Paragraph 1]
The Court of Justice shall review the legality of acts adopted jointly by the European Parliament and the Council, of acts of the Council, of the Commission and of the ECB, other than recommendations and opinions, and of acts of the European Parliament intended to produce legal effects *vis-à-vis* third parties.
...

[Paragraph 3]
The Court shall have jurisdiction under the same conditions in actions brought by the European Parliament and by the ECB for the purpose of protecting their prerogatives.

[Paragraph 4]
Any natural or legal person ...

The action for annulment occupies a central place among the judicial remedies provided for in the Treaty, and, although the procedure was modelled on that found in French administrative law, supervision of the legality of administrative acts is to be found, in one form or another, in the legal systems of all the Member States:

As in the Member States, so in the Communities the administrative agencies have only limited powers of rule-making and individual decision. The Treaties serve as constitutional documents to define those powers, including those of the Council when acting as a legislature. The Treaties also vest in the Court the necessary jurisdiction to control the lawful exercise of such power: Brown and Jacobs (and compare with Mertens de Wilmars in Chapter Ten).

Article 173 therefore provides the basis for the Council, the Commission, the Parliament (within limits) and the Member States as 'privileged' applicants under para. 1, to challenge the validity of Community acts, ie Regulations, Directives, Decisions and acts *sui generis* of the Council and Commission and binding measures brought into effect by the Parliament. Under para. 2, (para. 3 post-Maastricht) natural or legal persons may, within the limits laid down, only challenge Decisions. In all cases the Court's function is to determine the validity or otherwise of a governmental act on the basis of the assumption that such an act is valid.

Actions under Article 173 are referred to as *direct actions*; they are at *Community level* and brought before the *Court of Justice* or, since 1989, mainly as regards appeals against Commission Decisions against undertakings under the competition rules, the Court of First Instance (see Chapter Seventeen.)

However, it is important to appreciate that, apart from their limited rights under the present Article 173(2), natural and legal persons may be able to challenge the validity of Community acts (not merely Decisions) by means of an *indirect action* at *national level*. This will normally arise where a national authority has, by way of implementation of Community legislation, brought into effect a measure which effects the rights of such natural or legal person. A challenge to the national measure will be based on the claim that its legal base, the relevant Community act, is invalid. This will fall to be determined by the Court of Justice under Article 177(1)(b):

> The Court of Justice shall have jurisdiction to give preliminary rulings concerning:
>
> ...
>
> (b) the validity ... of acts of the institutions of the Community ...

Article 173 will now be examined more closely, together with the relationship between the present Article 173(2) and Article 177(1)(b).

Later it will be necessary to look briefly at Article 184, which allows for *indirect* challenges at *Community level*, Article 175 which (at present, see below) allows actions to be brought against the Council or the Commission for a *failure to act* (where there is a duty to act) and Articles 178 and 215 which enable '*non-contractual*' *claims* for damages to be brought against the Community institutions for loss suffered as a result of unlawful action.

ARTICLE 173: DIRECT ACTIONS FOR ANNULMENT

Five questions arise from the provisions of Article 173:

1. Which acts may be challenged, ie are susceptible to judicial review?
2. Who has the right to challenge? (This is a question of capacity or *locus standi*.)
3. What are the relevant time limits?
4. On what grounds may the challenge be made?
5. What are the effects of annulment?

1. Reviewable Acts

Acts which have legal effect are reviewable by the Court of Justice whatever their nature and form. The binding acts of Article 189 are therefore covered, and the Court itself has so far added a Council resolution (in Case 22/70 *ERTA*, see Chapter Six), a Commission Communication (withdrawing immunity from fines under the competition rules) which amounted to a Decision in Cases 8-11/66 *Re Noordwijk's Cement Accord* and a measure adopted by the Court of Auditors in Cases 193 and 194/87 *Maurissen and Others v Court of Auditors*. We have also seen in Chapter Six, as noted above, how the Court has extended its jurisdiction under Article 173 to binding acts of the Parliament.

2. *Locus Standi* (The Status or Standing of the Applicant)

As 'privileged' applicants, the Council, the Commission and the Member States have an unlimited right to challenge and review under Article 173(1). (Following the *Chernobyl* decision, the Parliament might be said to be a 'semi-privileged' applicant, and see the changes to Article 173 by the TEU, above). The basis for this 'privileged' position is that every Community act is deemed to affect these parties (cf. the position of the Crown in English administrative law) and they are considered to have a direct interest in any such act. As regards Member States, see Case 166/78 *Italy v Council*.

The position is somewhat different for 'any natural or legal person' under Article 173(2). It is clear that a Decision, which is 'binding in its entirety upon those to whom it is addressed' (Article 189) and which is applied in specific cases, may be challenged by the person(s) to whom it is addressed. However, in exceptional circumstances, Regulations (normally of 'general application') and Decisions which are addressed to *others*, may also be challenged.

The wording of Article 173(2) shows that a 'non-privileged' applicant may challenge:

a) a Decision addressed to the applicant, or

b) a Decision *in the form of* a Regulation which is however of direct and individual concern to the applicant, or

c) a Decision addressed *to another person* which is again of direct and individual concern.

A Decision Addressed to the Applicant

Little difficulty arises in the case of a Decision addressed to the applicant. The Commission's quasi-judicial Decisions against specific undertakings under Articles 85 and 86 (and the Merger Regulation) are frequently challenged and subject to review under Article 173(2): see Chapter Seventeen.

A Decision in the Form of a Regulation

In the implementation of Community policy, the Commission frequently acts on the basis of Regulations. This is particularly the case concerning matters relating to the Common Agricultural Policy. For example, production levies may be imposed, subsidies may be withdrawn or imports from third countries may be restricted. Being of a *general*, legislative nature does not however mean that a Regulation may not have serious adverse consequences for some *persons*. Nevertheless a genuine Regulation cannot be successfully challenged by such a person under Article 173(2):

> ### Case 101/76 *KSH* v. *Council and Commission*
>
> At a time of over-production of sugar within the Community, the Council and the Commission introduced Regulations which the applicant alleged discriminated against him as one of only four large manufacturers of a new product, isoglucose, which in some respects competed with sugar. The challenge was inadmissible; the measures were true Regulations and KSH therefore had no *locus standi*.

Nevertheless, as seen in Chapter Four, although a Regulation is almost invariably a Regulation both in form *and* substance, it may, at least in part, lose its general, objective character and, in deciding upon a specific issue, become in substance what the Court has called a 'disguised decision'. An individual or undertaking adversely affected by such a measure may be able to show 'direct and individual concern' as required by Article 173. A measure is of direct concern to an applicant if it is the direct cause of an effect on him (see below). We will first look in more detail at the rather difficult concept of 'individual concern' in the context of disputed 'Regulations.'

In the case which follows, a Regulation was seen by the Court as a bundle of Decisions addressed to each applicant for an import licence:

Cases 41-44/70 *International Fruit Co. v. Commission*

Under Community based rules, importers of dessert apples from non-EEC countries were required to apply in advance for import licences to the appropriate national authority. Applications were passed to the Commission on a weekly basis. The Commission then enacted a measure in the form of a Regulation laying down rules for deciding on the application in question.

In this challenge to the Commission measure, IF argued that, in that it referred back to a *named group of applicant importers,* it concerned a *closed category* of which IF was a member. The measure, it was claimed, was therefore not a true Regulation.

The Court ruled as follows:

It is indisputable that Regulation No. 983/70 was adopted [on 28 May 1970] with a view on the one hand to the state of the market and on the other to the quantities of dessert apples for which applications for import licences had been made in the week ending on 22 May 1970.

It follows that when the said regulation was adopted, the number of applications which could be affected by it was fixed. No new application could be added. To what extent, in percentage terms, the applications could be granted, depended on the total quantity in respect of which applications had been submitted.

Accordingly, by providing that the system introduced by Article 1 of Regulation No. 565/70 should be maintained for the relevant period, the Commission decided, even though it took account only of the quantities requested, on the subsequent fate of each application which had been lodged.

Consequently, Article 1 of Regulation No. 983/70 is not a provision of general application within the meaning of the second paragraph of Article 189 of the Treaty, but must be regarded as a conglomeration of individual decisions taken by the Commission under the guise of a regulation pursuant to Article 2(2) of Regulation No. 459/70, each of which decisions affects the legal position of each author of an application for a licence.

Thus, the decisions are of individual concern to the applicants.

In his perceptive analysis of Article 173(2), Hartley draws attention to two tests which are embodied in the *International Fruit* decision: (i) Is the act a Regulation or a disguised Decision? This is a question of construction. (ii) Is the applicant a member of a closed category and therefore individually concerned? A closed category is one the membership of which is fixed and determined when the measure comes into force (as opposed to a general class or open category). Hartley continues:

> If the applicant is named or otherwise individually identified in the measure, so that the first test is satisfied [ie the act is in substance a decision], it must necessarily follow that he will be individually concerned as well. On the other hand, it is quite possible for the second test to be satisfied, even if the first is not. This will occur when the measure, though framed in general terms, applies only to a closed category of persons.

Reviewing the cases concerning Regulations, in which the Commission is implementing policy and has a margin of discretion, Hartley is of the opinion that, on the basis of its use of these tests, 'it is hard to avoid feeling that the Court decides first whether it wants the application to be admissible and then applies whichever test will produce the desired result'. A good example is one of the isoglucose cases, *KSH* v *Council and Commission*, discussed above. At the time there were only four groups of companies operating in the high-investment isoglucose production field. They were virtually a closed category but, with sugar and wheat over-production in mind, the Court chose to deny the company's appeal against production levies by concentrating on the first test and finding the act to be a Regulation in both form and substance.

Although there are exceptions (*International Fruit Company*, above, decided in 1971 is one), the case law on Article 173(2), particularly since 1980, shows that where the act in question is in form a Regulation and the Commission is implementing Community policy thereby, the Court will not consider whether it is dealing with a situation where a closed category is involved, but will decide the matter on the basis of the wording of the Regulation. If it is expressed in general, abstract terms, the private applicant will not have *locus standi*. Other cases decided on this first (true Regulation) test as opposed to the second (closed category) test include Cases 103-109/78

Beauport v. *Council and Commission* (sugar refineries which had previously been allocated a sugar quota; challenge inadmissible), Cases 789 and 790/79 *Calpak* v *Commission* (complaint regarding production aid to an identifiable class of producers of preserved pears inadmissible).

(It is however worthy of note that in several of these cases, the Advocate General was in favour of the admissibility of the challenge. The Court's restrictive attitude to private applicants under Article 173(2) has not been free from criticism: see below.)

In another isoglucose case, an undertaking within a closed category *was* allowed to challenge an act in the form of a Regulation, although it could be argued that the measure was, at least in part, a Decision and so met the requirements of the first test of construction:

Case 138/79 *Roquette Frères* v. *Council*

The Council applied production quotas for isoglucose under Regulation 1293/79. This measure concerned a closed group of isoglucose producers who had previously been subjected to quota restrictions under an earlier Regulation which the Court had found to be discriminatory in an Article 177(1)(b) validity case: Cases 103 and 145/77 *RSH* v. *Agricultural Intervention Board*.

In this case, in addition to the closed group argument, RF was able to point to an annex in the Regulation which listed the isoglucose producers by name and stated their precise quotas under the new rules. The Court ruled on admissibility that:

It follows that Article 9(4) of Regulation No. 1111/77 (as amended by Article 3 of Regulation No. 1293/79) in conjunction with Annex II, itself applies the criteria laid down to each of the undertakings in question who are addressees and thus directly and individually concerned. Regulation No. 1293/79 therefore is a measure against which the undertakings concerned manufacturing isoglucose may bring proceedings for a declaration that it is void pursuant to the second paragraph of Article 173 of the Treaty.

(The Court later held that, although the Regulation infringed neither the principle of equality of treatment nor that of proportionality, it was void on the procedural ground that the Council had not, as required, consulted the Parliament.)

A Decision Addressed to Another Person: Individual Concern

The question of whether the measure is a Regulation or a Decision obviously does not arise but the applicant, not being the addressee of the Decision, may well have difficulty establishing 'direct and individual concern'. As regards individual concern (direct concern is dealt with below), the applicant will have to show that the decision affects him by reason of factors which distinguish him individually – just as in the case of the person addressed. He will be able to do this if he can show that he is a member of a *closed group*:

Case 25/62 *Plaumann* v. *Commission*

Under the Common Customs Tariff, importers of clementines from non-EEC countries had to pay a customs duty of 13 per cent. The German Government asked the Commission for permission under Article 25(3) of the Treaty partially to suspend this duty. When the Commission issued a Decision refusing the Government's request, P, one of thirty importers of clementines, challenged this refusal. The Commission claimed that P was not directly and individually concerned. On the question of admissibility, the Court ruled as follows:

Under the second paragraph of Article 173 of the EEC Treaty 'any natural or legal person may ... institute proceedings against a decision ... which, although in the form of ... a decision addressed to another person, is of direct and individual concern to the former'. The defendant contends that the words 'other person' in this paragraph do not refer to Member States in their capacity as sovereign authorities and that individuals may not therefore bring an action for annulment against the decisions of the Commission or of the Council addressed to Member States.

However, the second paragraph of Article 173 does allow an individual to bring an action against decisions addressed to 'another person' which are of direct and individual concern to the former, but this Article neither defines nor limits the scope of these words. The words and the natural meaning of this provision justify the broadest interpretation. Moreover, provisions of the Treaty regarding the right of interested parties to bring an action must not be interpreted restrictively. Therefore, the Treaty being silent on the point, a limitation in this respect may not be presumed.

It follows that the defendant's argument cannot be regarded as well founded.

The defendant further contends that the contested decision is by its very nature a regulation in the form of an individual decision and therefore action against it is no more available to individuals than in the case of legislative measures of general application.

It follows however from Articles 189 and 191 of the EEC Treaty that decisions are characterised by the limited number of persons to whom they are addressed. In order to determine whether or not a measure constitutes a decision one must enquire whether that measure concerns specific persons. The contested Decision was addressed to the government of the Federal Republic of Germany and refuses to grant it authorisation for the partial suspension of customs duties on certain products imported from third countries. Therefore the contested measure must be regarded as a decision referring to a particular person and binding that person alone.

Under the second paragraph of Article 173 of the Treaty private individuals may institute proceedings for annulment against decisions which, although addressed to another person, are of direct and individual concern to them, but in the present case the defendant denies that the contested decision is of direct and individual concern to the applicant.

It is appropriate in the first place to examine whether the second requirement of admissibility is fulfilled because, if the applicant is not individually concerned by the decision, it becomes unnecessary to enquire whether he is directly concerned.

Persons other than those to whom a decision is addressed may only claim to be individually concerned if that decision affects them by reason of certain attributes which are peculiar to them or by reason of circumstances in which they are differentiated from all other persons and by virtue of these factors distinguishes them individually just as in the case of the person addressed. In the present case the applicant is affected by the disputed Decision as an importer of clementines, that is to say, by reason of a commercial activity which may at any time be practised by any person and is not therefore such as to distinguish the applicant in relation to the contested Decision as in the case of the addressee.

For these reasons the present action for annulment must be declared inadmissible.

Plaumann, therefore, being affected by the Decision (addressed to the German Government) only as a member of a general and open class was not individually concerned and so lacked *locus standi*.

In the following case the challenge was held to be admissible.

Cases 106 and 107/63 *Toepfer* v *Commission*

The relevant German authorities mistakenly set the levy on maize imported from France at zero. When T and others applied for import licences for a substantial amount of maize free of levy (so ensuring themselves large profits), the German intervention agency realised its error and refused to grant any licences. Three days later the Commission confirmed the ban and authorised the German authorities to raise the levy on imports 'including those at present and duly pending'.

T brought an action under Article 173(2) to annul the Commission's Decision addressed to the German authorities.

The Court held that T and the other importers who had applied for licences *before* the ban was imposed were individually concerned.

It will be seen that, as in *Plaumann*, 'another person' may include a Member State, and also, as in the *International Fruit* case, which involved a 'disguised Decision' individual concern was established where the measure was of a retrospective nature, ie at the time it was made, the Commission knew, or was in a position to know, exactly to whom it applied. However, it would appear that where such retrospective effect is missing 'the possibility of determining more or less precisely the number or even the identity of the persons to whom a measure applies by no means implies that it must be regarded as being of individual concern to them': Case 123/77 *UNICME* v *Council*. In such a case the applicant is seen as being a member, at least theoretically, of an open class.

In *Toepfer*, the Decision addressed to Germany was annulled by the Court, the Commission only having the power to authorise a ban on imports if, as was not the case here, they threatened to cause 'serious disturbances' to the market.

Special Cases

A case with a number of unusual features, not least as regards Article 173(2), is Case 294/83 *Les Verts* v *European Parliament* (see also Chapter Six). The Decision in question was taken by the Parliament in 1982; it was addressed to itself and it involved the use of Community funds to subsidise the election expenses of the parties fighting the 1984 elections to the Parliament. The Greens, who did not exist at Community level at the time the Decision was made, challenged the Decision in that, by awarding the bulk of the money to parties already represented in the Parliament, it discriminated against them.

The Greens were clearly members of an open category (new parties who could contest the election), and the Decision applied generally to all political parties who decided to put up candidates. However, in what was clearly a policy decision, the Court held that Les Verts were individually concerned. They also held that the Parliament had no power to allocate funds for this purpose at all; the Decision was void. Hartley puts forward the following explanation:

> Thus if a plainly illegal act were challenged by an applicant who had no alternative means of bringing the matter before the Court, and if the only persons with *locus standi* [parties already represented in the Parliament] would have no interest in bringing proceedings, the Court might well feel obliged to stretch a point in order to declare the application admissible.

Special considerations also apply, in respect of individual concern, when the Commission takes a Decision (not addressed to the applicant) which relates not to the implementation of Community policy (a function that contains a discretionary element) but which amounts to what has been called a 'quasi-judicial' determination. Such decisions of fact and law apply in competition, anti-dumping and illegal state aids proceedings.

The Court adopts a much less rigorous approach in these cases. Thus an undertaking which made the original *complaint of injury* (see Article 3(2)(b) of Regulation 17/62 in Chapter Seventeen) as a result of another company's alleged breach of Article 85 was held to be individually concerned and so able to challenge the Commission's Decision, which was that no breach of the competition rules had taken place: Case 26/76 *Metro* v *Commission*. Anti-dumping duties are imposed against undertakings from outside the Community by means of Regulations. Nevertheless, in Case 264/82 *Timex* v *Council and Commission*, the Court decided that a complaint on behalf of the only British manufacturer of mechanical watches that the duty imposed on mechanical watches from the Soviet Union was too low was 'a decision which is of direct and individual concern to Timex'. (See also the 'special situation' identified by the Court in Case C-358/89 *Extramet* v *Council* as being sufficient to enable the main importer and user of a product subject to a Council anti-dumping Regulation to establish individual concern).

Direct Concern

Direct concern is a matter of cause and effect: under Article 173(2) a non-privileged applicant will be directly concerned where there is a direct casual link between the challenged Decision and its impact on the applicant. The question usually arises where the Commission issues a Decision to a Member State requiring or authorising it to act in a particular way. If the power granted to the Member State is merely discretionary, the fact that the power would, if exercised, affect the applicant does not mean that he has *locus standi* to challenge the Commission's original Decision. He is not directly concerned by it owing to the interposition of the autonomous will of the Member State between the Decision and its effect upon him (cf. the position regarding direct effect).

However, if the Member State's power is *not* discretionary (as in the *International Fruit* case, concerning the implementation of the Commission's weekly Decisions regarding the availability of import licences for apples) or if a Member State exercises its power first and the Commission confirms it later (as in *Toepfer*, another import licence case), these are situations where no independent will stands between the Decision and its effect on the applicant, who will be directly concerned. The national measure is equated to the Community Decision, which accordingly directly affects (concerns) the private party.

It is however difficult to perceive a consistent line of approach by the Court regarding direct concern. In Case 69/69 *Alcan* v *Commission*, the Commission rejected (by a Decision) a request by the Belgian Government which, if granted, would have authorised the Government to act to the benefit of Alcan. As, theoretically at least, the Belgian Government might have decided not so to act (but why did it make the request in the first place?), Alcan was held not to be directly concerned and could not challenge the Commission's refusal. Conversely, in Case 11/82 *Piraiki-Patraiki* v *Commission*, a Commission Decision authorised the French Government to impose a general quota system on imports of Greek yarn. Here the Court considered that the possibility that the Government would not implement the Community Decision was 'purely theoretical'. France was not legally obliged to exercise the power granted but was in fact already exercising a restrictive system of licences for such imports from the new Member State. The Greek applicants were held to be directly concerned (and individually concerned so far as they had entered into export contracts, prior to the Decision, to be performed subsequently). This, however, was a point specially taken into account by a provision of the Greek Act of Accession).

This generally restrictive approach of the Court of Justice concerning the ability of private parties to establish *locus standi* under Article 173(2) is tempered, as indicated in the introduction to this chapter, by the possible availability to such a party of an *indirect challenge to a Community act* (not merely a Decision) via an action *at national level against the national authority which implemented that act*. The Court itself has on several occasions drawn attention to this alternative route, usually, as in Case 97/85 *Union Deutsche Lebensmittelwerke*, to an unsuccessful Article 173(2) applicant:

> The applicants' argument to the effect that this application should be declared admissible so as to enable them to enjoy full legal protection must be rejected. It must be pointed out that, in support of an action challenging a national measure implementing a Community decision, the applicant may plead the illegality of that decision and thereby require the national court to adjudicate on all the allegations formulated in that respect, if necessary after making a reference to the Court of Justice for a ruling on the validity of the decision in question. The fact that the national court is empowered to determine which questions it intends to submit to the Court is an inherent feature of the system of means of redress established by the Treaty and is not therefore an argument which is capable of justifying a broad interpretation of the conditions of admissibility laid down in the second paragraph of Article 173 of the EEC Treaty.

Indirect challenges on the basis of Article 177(1)(b) will be discussed shortly.

3. Time Limits

Article 173 lays down a time limit of two months for bringing proceedings to annul. This period is calculated for Regulations (which must be published in the Official Journal) from the fifteenth day after such publication. Although Directives and Decisions are normally published, they are addressed to Member States and individuals and time runs from receipt of such notification.

The two-month limit does not apply to indirect challenges under Article 177 although national limitation rules will apply.

4. Grounds for Annulment

Four grounds for annulment are set out in Article 173(1). An applicant may plead any one or more of these grounds; they are of an overlapping nature and the Court does not necessarily state upon which ground(s) it has decided a successful challenge:

(a) Lack of Competence (or Authority)

As we have seen, an institutional act must have a legal foundation in a Treaty provision – either directly or indirectly via another institutional act. If an institution adopts an act which has no sufficient legal base, that institution has acted, in English law terms, *ultra vires*. It has acted beyond its powers and the act will be annulled for lack of competence.

The availability of residual legislative powers under Article 235 and the scope of the doctrine of implied powers (see Chapter Six) means that this ground is very rarely invoked.

(b) Infringement of an Essential Procedural Requirement

Similar to the English legal concept of procedural *ultra vires*, this ground has usually been invoked where there has been either an alleged failure to give adequate reasons for the act as required by Article 190, or where it has been claimed that the Council has failed to consult the Parliament where the Treaty so prescribes.

In Case 24/62 *Germany* v *Commission (Brennwein)*, the Court struck down a Commission Decision because of the 'inadequacy, the vagueness and the inconsistency of the statement of reasons'. In Case 138/79 *Roquette Frères* v *Council* (yet another isoglucose case; see above and also Rudden in the References and Further Reading at the end of this chapter), a Council Regulation was annulled on the ground that the Council had not properly consulted the Parliament as required under Article 43(2) of the Treaty.

(c) Infringement of the Treaty or any Rule of Law relating to its Application

This ground, while encompassing the previous two, goes further and is pleaded in almost all cases. In particular, 'any rule of law' relating to the application of the Treaty brings into play those general principles of law developed by the Court (see Chapter Ten) against which the validity of Community acts must be measured. Case law illustrations, which have been examined elsewhere (see, eg Chapter Ten) include Case 17/74 *Transocean Marine Paint* v *Commission* (breach of the principle of natural justice, in particular the rule of *audi alterem partem*), Case 112/77 *August Töpfer* v *Commission* (Decision annulled for breach of the of legal certainty) and Case 4/73 *Nold* v *Commission* (an alleged breach of fundamental human rights).

(d) Misuse of Powers

A claim under this head alleges use of a legitimate power in an illegitimate way or for an illegitimate end. It is a ground which is very rarely invoked as it means that the applicant must establish the intentions of the institution in question.

5. The Effect of Annulment

Article 174

If the action is well founded, the Court of Justice shall declare the act concerned to be void.

In the case of a regulation, however, the Court of Justice shall, if it considers this necessary, state which of the effects of the regulation which it has declared void shall be considered as definitive.

Article 176

The institution whose act has been declared void or whose failure to act has been declared contrary to this Treaty shall be required to take the necessary measures to comply with the judgment of the Court of Justice . . .

(The TEU extends Article 176 to the European Parliament and the European Central Bank.)

The effect of Article 174(2) is that, where it is necessary in the interests of legal certainty and to avoid undue damage to the Community or others, an annulled Regulation may be kept in force, at least in part, until it is replaced. It will also be recalled that in Cases 56 and 58/64 *Consten and Grundig* and Case 27/76 *United Brands* the Court held that the Commission's Decisions were only partly valid.

The series of isoglucose cases illustrates in a graphic way successive attempts by the Council and Commission to adopt Regulations to control the market in the face of a number of challenges to the Community measures by the manufacturers of that product. As will be seen below, a ruling by the Court that an act is void may lead to a further claim by the applicant for compensation in accordance with Article 178 and Article 215(2) regarding the non-contractual liability of the Community.

ARTICLE 177(1)(B): INDIRECT ACTIONS FOR ANNULMENT AT NATIONAL LEVEL

Where a Community act requires and has achieved implementation by means of a national measure (this is particularly so in the agricultural field), provided a cause of action against such *national* measure can be established by an individual or an undertaking (probably judicial review proceedings), it is possible to claim before the national court or tribunal that the relevant Community act upon which the national measure is based is invalid. By means of a reference to the Court of Justice under Article 177(1)(b) this claim can then be determined.

Where such indirect challenge is possible, the plaintiff avoids the difficult question of 'direct and individual concern' and the two-month time limit in Article 173. In addition, Article 177(1)(b) lays down no limitation as to the type of Community act which may be challenged; it does not limit the challenge to Decisions, disguised or otherwise. This article therefore provides a significant, further form of protection for individuals under the Treaty. (However, it must be remembered that national courts themselves have no jurisdiction to declare that acts of the Community institutions are invalid: Case 314/85 *Foto Frost*, see Chapter Nine.)

The isoglucose cases clearly illustrate the relationship between Articles 173(2) and 177(1)(b). In Case 101/76 *KSH* v *Commission and Council*, the applicant isoglucose producer, as seen above, failed to establish *locus standi* in its challenge under Article 173(2) to a Regulation which it alleged discriminated against isoglucose in favour of sugar. When the Dutch Intervention Agency, in pursuance of the Regulation in question, claimed payment of a substantial levy from KSH, the company brought an action in the Dutch courts against the Agency's decision and again claimed that the Regulation was invalid: Case 125/77 *KSH* v *Netherlands Intervention Agency*. This case raised the same (previously inadmissible) claims regarding the Regulation as in the Article 173(2) challenge: its stated reasons were inadequate, it was discriminatory, the speed with which it had been adopted was a breach of the principle of legal certainty and it represented a misuse of power.

Following a reference to the Court of Justice on the basis of Article 177(1)(b), the Court ruled that 'consideration of the questions raised has disclosed no factor of such a kind as to affect the validity of Council Regulation (EEC) no. 1862/76 and Commission Regulation (EEC) no. 2158/77.'

A similar situation arose in connection with the Commission's Berlin butter scheme. In Case 97/85 *Union Deutsche Lebensmittelwerke v Commission*, a German margarine producer sought annulment of a Commission Decision addressed to Germany authorising a scheme for selling cheap butter on the West Berlin market. The scheme was for only a short period of time and it had the object of researching into consumer demand for butter. UDL's challenge under Article 173(2) failed for lack of individual concern. The following case arose out of the same set of facts:

Case 133/85 *Walter Rau v BALM*

WR and other German margarine producers challenged the German measures which implemented the Commission's cheap butter scheme on the basis that the Commission Decision was invalid on several grounds including that of lack of proportionality. On the basis of a reference from the German national court under Article 177(1)(b), the Court of Justice ruled that:

It must be emphasised that there is nothing in Community law to prevent an action from being brought before a national court against a measure implementing a Decision adopted by a Community institution where the conditions laid down by national law are satisfied. When such an action is brought, if the outcome of the dispute depends on the validity of that Decision the national court may submit questions to the Court of Justice by way of a reference for a preliminary ruling, without there being any need to ascertain whether or not the plaintiff in the main proceedings has the possibility of challenging the Decision directly before the Court.

The answer to the first question must therefore be that the possibility of bringing a direct action under the second paragraph of Article 173 of the EEC Treaty against a Decision adopted by a Community institution does not preclude the possibility of bringing an action in a national court against a measure adopted by a national authority for the implementation of that Decision on the ground that the latter Decision is unlawful ...

Next, it must be emphasised that the operation constituted, as it was intended to, the basis of a scientific survey from which the Commission was able to derive useful information. Furthermore, the Commission chose the West Berlin market because of its isolated geographical location and the possibility of carrying out there, in view of its limited size, an operation at relatively low cost. In so doing, the Commission would not appear to have exceeded the discretion conferred upon it by the Council in Article 4 of Regulation No 1079/77.

Accordingly, the answer to the eighth question must be that consideration of the Decision of 25 February 1985 has not disclosed any evidence of a breach of the principle of proportionality.

On the basis of the Court's decision in Case 66/80 *International Chemical Corporation*, the effect of a successful indirect challenge (see, for example, Case 181/84 *R* v *Intervention Board, ex parte Man (Sugar) Ltd* in Chapter Ten) is that although the Court's ruling is only binding on the national court which made the reference, 'it is sufficient reason for any other national court to regard that act as void', although a further ruling may be requested by such a court. (Although the Treaty is silent on the matter, the grounds for annulment following a reference under Article 177(1)(b) are the same as those under Article 173.)

Another Article 177 validity case decided in 1991 is of considerable importance in two respects: (i) the Court's concern to develop effective remedies for individuals, here interim relief, and (ii) its insistence on there being a coherent and inter-related system of remedies in this area at both Community and national level:

Case C-143/88 *Zuckerfabrick Süderdithmarschen* v. *HZA Itzehoe*
Administrative decisions taken by German customs authorities under a duty to implement Council Regulation 1914/87 relating to the sugar sector led to sugar producer ZS being required to pay over DM 3.5 million by way of 'special elimination levy'. In the course of national proceedings, questions arose as to the validity of the Regulation and the power of a national court to suspend a national administrative act adopted on the basis of a disputed Regulation.

Questions were submitted to the Court of Justice under Article 177(1)(a) on the interpretation of the Treaty; in particular: under what conditions might a national court order stay of execution of a national measure based on a Community Regulation on the ground of doubts which it might have on the validity of that Regulation? The Court was also asked on the basis of Article 177(1)(b) to consider the validity of Regulation 1914/87. On these questions the Court ruled that:

1. Suspension of such a national measure could be granted by a national court provided (i) that court had serious doubts as to the validity of the Community act, and (ii) if the question of that act's validity had not already been referred, the national court *must* refer it; (iii) there must be urgency, the applicant being threatened by serious and irreparable harm; (iv) the national court must give due

consideration to the Community interest particularly where a stay of execution was likely to lead to a financial risk for the Community.

2. No grounds had been revealed to affect the validity of Regulation 1914/87.

The significance of this decision is as follows: In the context of an application for annulment of a Community act under Article 173, the Court may, under Article 185, 'if it considers that the circumstances so require, order that application of the contested act be suspended.' In the interests of coherence of the system of provisional protection, the Court felt that national courts should similarly possess the right to suspend a national measure based on a disputed Community Regulation (or, presumably any other Community act).

Thus, in a case such as this, in national proceedings concerning an implementing measure, and where, as an ancillary matter, the validity of the originating Community Regulation is seriously disputed, protection should be afforded a party in the context of an Article 177 reference to the Court of Justice, which alone can decide on the Regulation's validity: Case 314/85 *Foto-Frost*.

The Court found additional support for this decision in its *Factortame* ruling where, for the protection of a party, similar suspensory rights had been afforded national courts regarding the application of disputed national legislation in the context of problems relating to its compatibility with Community law. (For a discussion of Case C-213/89 *R* v *Secretary of State for Transport, ex parte Factortame*, see the next Chapter.)

The Court's Restrictive Approach under Article 173(2)

The case law shows quite clearly that most claims brought under Article 173(2) fail. As will be seen, it is similarly rare for claims brought by natural and legal persons to succeed (in fact few are brought) under Article 175 (failure to act) or under Articles 178 and 215(2) (actions for damages against the Community).

While this general lack of success of private parties who bring direct actions against the Community has been the subject of criticism from various commentators, it must be recognised that any system of administrative law must have due regard for those institutions which have a duty to implement policy, which are in possession of discretionary powers in the fulfilment of this duty, and which, it is argued, should not be unduly hindered in the exercise of their duty.

With respect to Article 173(2), Hartley is of the opinion that, following the experience with the equivalent provision in the ECSC Treaty, 'a deliberate choice in favour of a more restrictive system' was made by the drafters of the EEC Treaty:

> It is possible that the authors of the EEC Treaty (representatives of national governments) thought it unnecessary to provide for such extensive judicial control of the Commission (since its powers were less [than under the earlier Treaty]) and undesirable to have too much judicial control of the Council (since this represented the Member States).

The practice of the Court of Justice in cases involving Article 173(2) has done little to change this position. Individuals and undertakings are the subjects of wide-ranging and continuously growing public regulatory powers. Reasonableness in the exercise of these powers and the right to a hearing when there is a seemingly genuine case for challenge are matters of great importance for private parties.

Commenting on the Court's restrictive approach to Article 173(2) in 1980, Rasmussen drew attention to the fact that in several such direct actions, the Court referred to the applicant's right to the alternate, indirect claim before his national court under Article 177(1)(b). In as much as the national court can declare a Community act valid (but not void), this, so the argument runs, is a system whereby claims which lack merit can be excluded at national level. Only strong claims will reach the Court of Justice on the preliminary ruling basis. In this respect, Rasmussen concluded that 'the European Court of Justice may well be shaping a European system of appellate jurisdiction, or something very like it'.

There are however two problems. First, preliminary rulings are no longer handed down in seven months as was the case in 1980. It is now more likely eighteen months. Second, as Rasmussen acknowledges, in order for a case to proceed from national to Community level, there must be an appropriate issue of national law in which the question of the validity of the Community act may be raised, when challenging the national authority charged with implementing the disputed Community act. Nevertheless, the prospect of interim relief against the national measure as provided by the *Zuckerfabrik Süderdithmarschen* decision is a development to be welcomed by private parties.

ARTICLE 184: INDIRECT CHALLENGE AT COMMUNITY LEVEL

Although the two-month time limitation on direct challenges under Article 173 can be justified in the interest of legal certainty, and the *locus standi* restrictions for individuals under Article 173(2) prevent undue constraints being placed on the implementation of Community policy, this does mean that an illegal act, 'perfected' by lapse of time, may form the basis of further illegal acts.

The terms of Article 184 therefore provide, for example, for a situation where a Regulation, a general act, which has become immune from annulment by lapse of time, nevertheless forms the legal basis for a Decision of direct and individual concern to the applicant:

Article 184

Notwithstanding the expiry of the period laid down in the third paragraph of Article 173, any party may, in proceedings in which a regulation of the Council or of the Commission is in issue, plead the grounds specified in the first paragraph of Article 173, in order to invoke before the Court of Justice the inapplicability of that regulation.

(The TEU extends Article 184 to Regulations adopted jointly by the Parliament and the Council and to Regulations adopted by the European Central Bank.

The Decision may be challenged by the person affected and set aside if the Court is satisfied that the Regulation upon which it is based is tainted with illegality on one or more of the grounds specified in Article 173. Where the Regulation is found to be 'inapplicable', the Decision becomes invalid in that it has no legal foundation.

The operation of Article 184 was explained by the Court of Justice in Case 294/83 *Les Verts* in the following terms:

... Natural and legal persons are ... protected against the application to them of general measures which they cannot contest directly before the Court by reason of the special conditions of admissibility laid down in the second paragraph of Article 173 of the Treaty. Where the Community institutions are responsible for the administrative implementation of such measures, natural or legal persons may bring a direct action before the Court against implementing measures which are addressed to them or which are of direct and individual concern to them

and, in support of such an action, plead the illegality of the general
measure on which they are based ...

Thus, Article 184 does not give rise to a separate cause of action and in
a leading case on Article 184, Case 92/78 *Simmenthal* v *Commission*, an Italian
meat importer directly challenged a Commission Decision (under Article 173)
on the basis that, in line with Article 184, several Regulations and notices on
which the Decision was based (and which could not themselves be challenged
for reasons of standing and time limits) were invalid. Although querying
whether a notice of invitation to tender could be indirectly challenged in this
way, the Court went on to state that:

> The field of application of the said article must therefore include acts of
> the institutions which, although they are not in the form of a
> regulation, nevertheless produce similar effects and on those grounds
> may not be challenged under Article 173 by natural or legal persons
> other than Community institutions and Member States.

> This wide interpretation of Article 184 derives from the need to provide
> those persons who are precluded by the second paragraph of Article 173
> from instituting proceedings directly in respect of general acts with the
> benefit of a judicial review of them at the time when they are affected by
> implementing decisions which are of direct and individual concern to
> them.

> The notices of invitations to tender of 13 January 1978 in respect of
> which the applicant was unable to initiate proceedings are a case in
> point, seeing that only the decision taken in consequence of the tender
> which it had submitted in answer to a specific invitation to tender could
> be of direct and individual concern to it.

> There are therefore good grounds for declaring that the applicant's
> challenge during the proceedings under Article 184, which relates not
> only to the above-mentioned regulations but also to the notices of
> invitations to tender of 13 January 1978, is admissible, though the latter
> are not in the strict sense measures laid down by regulation.

Where an illegality plea is successful, the Regulation (or other act) in
question is declared inapplicable. It will be withdrawn with the effect of
removing the legal basis of any Decision adopted under it. Although
seemingly providing a useful supplement to Article 173 for non-privileged
applicants, the 'plea of illegality' under Article 184 is rarely brought before the
Court of Justice.

ARTICLE 175: DIRECT ACTIONS FOR FAILURE TO ACT

As we have seen, Article 173 governs challenges to allegedly unlawful acts of the institutions; Article 175 concerns challenges to omissions or failures to act where there is a duty to act:

Article 175

Should the Council or the Commission, in infringement of this Treaty, fail to act, the Member States and the other institutions of the Community may bring an action before the Court of Justice to have the infringement established.

The action shall be admissible only if the institution concerned has first been called upon to act. If, within two months of being so called upon, the institution concerned has not defined its position, the action may be brought within a further period of two months.

Any natural or legal person may, under the conditions laid down in the preceding paragraphs, complain to the Court of Justice that an institution of the Community has failed to address to that person any act other than a recommendation or an opinion.

Under the TEU, the Parliament is added to the named institutions in para. 1 *against whom* proceedings may be brought (a fourth paragraph adds the European Central Bank as either applicant or defendant). In the *Transport* case in the early 1980s (see below), the Court of Justice held that the Parliament, as one of the 'other institutions of the Community' in para. 1 had a right to *bring* proceedings under Article 175. It will therefore be the case, following the coming into force of the Maastricht Treaty, that the position of the European Parliament under both Articles 173 and 175 as applicant and as defendant institution, will be broadly in line with that of the other political institutions. This development, brought about initially by the Court of Justice in *Les Verts*, the *Budget* case and *Chernobyl* (Article 173) and the *Transport* case (Article 175) (as traced in this chapter and the second part of Chapter Six) in large part reflects the increasingly enhanced powers of the Parliament in relation to the Community budget and in the legislative process, now to be seen in the new Article 189b (a form of 'co-decision') and Article 189c (the 'co-operation procedure').

Returning to Article 175 and the *Transport* case:

Case 13/83 *Parliament* v. *Council*

The Parliament called for a declaration that the Council had infringed the Treaty by failing to introduce a Common Transport Policy as required by Article 74 and by failing to act on sixteen Commission proposals relating to transport.

The Court held that:

1. The Parliament had a right to bring an action under Article 175 (although it did not, at that time, have any such right under Article 173).
2. The Council had been 'called upon to act' in the correct manner under Article 175(2) and the Council had failed to define its position: 'The reply neither denied nor confirmed the alleged failure to act nor gave any indication of the Council's views as to the measures which, according to the Parliament, remained to be taken'.
3. The Council's obligation to introduce a Common Transport Policy was insufficiently precise to amount to an enforceable obligation. Although no complete nor consistent set of Regulations existed, the discretionary nature of the Council's policy role was such that its failure to act further was 'not necessarily a failure to act sufficiently specific in nature to fall within the purview of Article 175.'
4. Other specific obligations should have been implemented by the Council before the end of the transitional period and to that extent the Council had failed to act.

Although privileged applicants may challenge any failure to act (which therefore may include non-binding acts), natural and legal persons have limited *locus standi* under Article 175(3). Such an applicant may only bring an action as regards a binding act that an institution has 'failed to address' to him. It would therefore appear that the action must relate to a legally binding measure which should have been adopted and of which the applicant *would have been the addressee*. In Case 15/71 *Mackprang* v *Commission*, the Court held that a measure of a *general* nature (a Decision addressed to the Member States) could not be described as an act which could be addressed to the applicant. Case 246/81 *Lord Bethell* v *Commission* lays down that the applicant must be seeking the adoption of an act which he was 'legally entitled to claim'.

There are very few cases in which an applicant under Article 175(3) has succeeded. This has been because the institution has defined its position or because the applicant lacked *locus standi*:

Case 246/81 *Lord Bethell* v. *Commission*

Lord Bethell, an MEP and Chairman of the Freedom of the Skies Committee, attempted to force the Commission to act under Article 89 of the Treaty against alleged anti-competitive practices of various European airlines regarding passenger fares. He wrote to the Commission to this effect and not being satisfied with the reply, he brought proceedings under Article 175 (claiming that the Commission's reply was a failure to act) and alternatively under Article 173 (claiming that the Commission's reply was an act which should be annulled).

The Court ruled as follows:

In the words of the second paragraph of Article 173, any natural or legal person may, under the conditions laid down in that article, institute proceedings 'against a decision addressed to that person or against a decision which, although in the form of a regulation or a decision addressed to another person, is of direct and individual concern to the former'.

According to the third paragraph of Article 175, any natural or legal person may, under the conditions laid down in the article, complain to the Court that an institution of the Community 'has failed to address to that person any act other than a recommendation or an opinion'.

It appears from the provisions quoted that the applicant, for his application to be admissible, must be in a position to establish either that he is the addressee of a measure of the Commission having specific legal effects with regard to him, which is, as such, capable of being declared void, or that the Commission, having being duly called upon to act in pursuance of the second paragraph of Article 175, has failed to adopt in relation to him a measure which he was legally entitled to claim by virtue of the rules of Community law.

In reply to a question from the Court the applicant stated that the measure to which he believed himself to be entitled was 'a response, an adequate answer to his complaint saying either that the Commission was going to act upon it or saying that it was not and, if not, giving reasons'. Alternatively the applicant took the view that the letter addressed to him on 17 July 1981 by the Director-General for Competition was to be described as an act against which proceedings may be instituted under the second paragraph of Article 173.

The principal question to be resolved in this case is whether the Commission had, under the rules of Community law, the right and the duty to adopt in respect of the applicant a decision in the sense of the request made by the applicant to the Commission in his letter of 13 May 1981. It is apparent from the content of that letter and from the explanations given during the proceedings that the applicant is asking the Commission to undertake an investigation with regard to the airlines in the matter of the fixing of air fares with a view to a possible application to them of the provisions of the Treaty with regard to competition.

It is clear therefore that the applicant is asking the Commission not to take a decision in respect of him, but to open an enquiry with regard to third parties and to take decisions in respect of them. No doubt the applicant, in his double capacity as a user of the airlines and a leading member of an organisation of users of air passenger services, has an indirect interest, as other users may have, in such proceedings and their possible outcome, but he is nevertheless not in the precise legal position of the actual addressee of a decision which may be declared void under the second paragraph of Article 173 or in that of the potential addressee of a legal measure which the Commission has a duty to adopt with regard to him, as is the position under the third paragraph of Article 175.

It follows that the application is inadmissible from the point of view of both Article 175 and Article 173.

It is clear that once the institution has defined its position (that it will act in a certain way or will not act) within the prescribed time, a claim in relation to Article 175 can go no further. However, a party to whom this definition of position has been addressed may be in a position to attack it (if it is a Decision) under Article 173.

However, where an application for the annulment of Commission Decisions (addressed to third parties) failed on the basis of a lack of direct and individual concern under Article 173, a further claim that the Commission's failure to revoke the Decisions was actionable under Article 175 was rejected by the court. To provide an applicant 'with a method of recourse parallel to that of Article 173', which was not subject to that Article's conditions as to time limits, did not satisfy the requirements of Article 175.

Under Article 176, an institution whose failure to act has been declared contrary to the Treaty will be required by the Court to take remedial action so as to comply with the Court's judgment. This may not be the action required by the applicant. In the Transport Policy case (see above), the Court stated that 'it was for the Council to introduce the measures which it considered necessary ... and to decide in what order such measures should be adopted'.

ARTICLES 178 AND 215(2): NON-CONTRACTUAL LIABILITY OF THE COMMUNITY – ACTIONS FOR DAMAGES

Article 178

The Court of Justice shall have jurisdiction in disputes relating to the compensation for damage provided for in the second paragraph of Article 215.

Article 215

The contractual liability of the Community shall be governed by the law applicable to the contract in question.

In the case of non-contractual liability, the Community shall, in accordance with the general principles common to the laws of the Member States, make good any damage caused by its institutions or by its servants in the performance of their duties.

These Treaty articles vest in the Court of Justice exclusive jurisdiction over the 'non-contractual liability' of the Community institutions as public authorities. As yet, the case law of the Court demonstrates the need for proof of fault in actions under Article 215(2) although no such requirement is expressed in the Treaty.

This liability of the Community has therefore been classed by various commentators as tort liability and in this respect it is of interest to note the recent difficulties of the English courts regarding *Anns* v *Merton LBC* (1978) and, overruling that decision, *Murphy* v *Brentwood DC* (1990). However, the view taken by Lasok and Bridge is that:

Regarding the principles governing the non-contractual liability of the Community it has to be borne in mind that the concept cannot be construed in the sense of 'tort' or unlawful act of private law giving rise to a civil remedy of damages and/or injunction but has to be seen in the context of the activities of the Community institutions.

These activities include the exercise of administrative and legislative functions and, like any state system, may fall occasionally below the standard of sound and efficient administration ... Such malfunctioning would reveal a fault of the system (*faute de service*) for which the state should be responsible.

Elaborating on Community liability under Article 215(2), Lasok has explained that it must

> ... be seen in the context of the activities of the Community institutions which are charged with various tasks (mainly administrative and legislative) falling in the domain of sound and efficient administration. Thus the elements of damage and conduct of an institution or the persons who administer the system have to be balanced up, for it is unthinkable that every damage should be made good and every misconduct could lead to compensation. We have to think in terms of the 'fault of the system' in an objective sense rather than 'culpability' in a moral sense.

As stated in Article 215(2), the nature of such liability is to be based on 'the general principles common to the laws of the Member States'. In as much as there is no common body of legal principles regarding State non-contractual liability within the Member States, it has been said that:

> The Court is not obliged to seek the highest common denominator in the Member States' laws on administrative liability, but should focus on tracking down the elements from which Community legal principles and rules can be construed which yield an appropriate, fair and viable solution to the problem of Community liability: Gormley

In Case 4/69 *Lütticke v Commission*, the Court held that the 'general principles' in Article 215(2) required that the following conditions must be satisfied in order to establish liability against the Community:

1. Actual damage to the plaintiff;
2. A causal link between the damage claimed and the conduct alleged against the institution;
3. The illegality of this conduct (ie a wrongful act or omission on the part of the institution, or its servants).

In the *Lütticke* litigation (Cases 48/65 and 4/69):

> The German government imposed a levy on L's imports of powdered milk. L complained to the Commission that the rate of levy was in breach of Article 95 (on discriminatory internal taxation) and urged the Commission to bring Article 169 proceedings against the German government for breach of its Treaty obligations.

The Commission refused to bring such proceedings and L brought a claim against the Commission under Article 175 for *failure to act*. The Commission responded by defining its position – again refusing to act; the decision as to whether or not to bring Article 169 proceedings being a matter within the Commission's discretion. The Court held that once the Commission had defined its position, the failure to act was at an end and the claim was inadmissible. Having also failed in a claim under Article 173 to annul the Commission's Decision *not* to act, L sued the Commission for damages in a separate action under Article 215(2): Case 4/69. (Actions under Article 215 are subject to a generous limitation period of five years: Article 43 of the Statute of the Court.)

L now argued that it had suffered loss as a result of the Commission's failure to address a Directive or Decision to Germany requiring it to modify the taxes it had been obliged to pay. The Court rejected the Commission's contention (which had been successful in an earlier case) that the claim was merely an attempt to circumvent the restrictions imposed by Article 175 regarding failure to act. The Court stated that:

'It would be contrary to the independent nature of this action as well as to the efficacy of the general system of forms of action created by the Treaty to regard as a ground of inadmissibility the fact that, in certain circumstances, an action for damages might lead to a result similar to that of an action for failure to act under Article 175'.

Although admissible, the Court held that the action failed on the merits, there being no failure of duty on the Commission's part. It had conducted extensive negotiations with the German authorities (who had eventually withdrawn the levy) and no more could be expected of it.

The Court has stated that the action for damages differs from an action for annulment 'in that its end is not the abolition of a particular measure but compensation for damage caused by an institution in the performance of its duties'. Nevertheless a claim under Article 215(2) will be more likely to succeed if annulment of the act (or condemnation of the inaction) on which the claim is based has already taken place.

Attention has been drawn to the extremely limited rights of private parties regarding challenges to the validity of Community acts of a legislative or administrative nature. However, where an act has been declared invalid by the Court on one or more of the grounds specified in Article 173, this amounts to proof of *faute de service*. (A failure to act is treated in the same way).

This means of course that the Community may, albeit exceptionally, be liable in damages in respect of its *legislative* functions. In Case 5/71 *Zuckerfabrik Schöppenstedt* v *Council*, ZS brought an action for damages under Article 215(2) against the Council on the basis of an allegedly invalid Regulation adopted in the furtherance of a Treaty policy. The claim was held to be admissible on the basis of the reasoning in *Lütticke*, it being distinct from a clearly inadmissible application by an individual for the annulment of a genuine Regulation under Article 173(2). However, the Court went on to discuss in very restrictive terms the question of the Community's liability in damages in respect of 'legislative action involving measures of economic policy':

> In the present case the non-contractual liability of the Community presupposes at the very least the unlawful nature of the act alleged to be the cause of the damage. Where legislative action involving measures of economic policy is concerned, the Community does not incur non-contractual liability for damage suffered by individuals as a consequence of that action, by virtue of the provisions contained in Article 215, second paragraph, of the Treaty, unless a sufficiently flagrant violation of a superior rule of law for the protection of the individual has occurred. For that reason the Court, in the present case, must first consider whether such a violation has occurred.

Later statements of the '*Schöppenstedt* formula' by the Court make it clear that the legislative measures to which it refers involve 'choices of economic policy' and that they are therefore discretionary. Considering the nature of the Community, virtually all Community legislation is of this character. Therefore, for liability to follow three conditions must be met (in addition to the general rules stated above concerning damage and causation):

1. *There must be a breach of a superior rule of law:*
    Subsequent case law shows that the breach of such general principles as proportionality and non-discrimination: Case 83/76 etc *Bayerische HNL* v. *Council and Commission,* and legal certainty and the protection of legitimate expectations: Case 74/74 *CNTA* v. *Commission* (see Chapter Ten) are to be counted among such superior rules. In all probability, any rule of Community law which would normally be a ground for annulment of the measure in question will also amount to a superior rule for these purposes.

2. *The breach must be sufficiently serious:*

The breach must be 'manifest' and 'grave' and even if the act complained of has been annulled this does not mean that damages will automatically be awarded. It would seem to be necessary to show that the Community institution charged with discretionary powers has disregarded in a sufficiently serious or flagrant manner the limits on its exercise of such powers. In the relevant *Isoglucose* cases (Cases 116 and 124/77 *Amylum and Tunnel Refineries* and Case 143/77 *KSH* v. *Council and Commission*), the Court held that the Community would only be liable if its conduct was 'verging on the arbitrary'. Despite the producers succeeding in having Regulations imposing production levies annulled, and despite suffering enormous financial loss, no damages were recovered by them. In Case 20/88 *Roquette Frères* v. *Commission*, the Court held that the Commission's fault was merely a 'technical error'.

Nevertheless in the *Quellmehl and Gritz* cases (Case 90/78 *Granaria*, Case 238/78 *Ireks-Arkady*, etc), decided at virtually the same time as the *Isoglucose* cases, the Court was more concerned with the seriousness of the *consequences of the breach* for the undertakings in question, stating that their loss 'went beyond that inherent in business' and was recoverable. As a result it has been put forward that a complainant will only succeed in meeting this condition if *both* his scale of loss *and* the degree of the Community's breach of the rule of law are sufficiently serious: see, for example, Joined Cases C-104/89 and C-37/90 *Mulder and Others* v *Council and Commission*.

3. *The superior rule of law must be one for the protection of the individual:*

Any of the general principles established by the Court of Justice, such as equality, proportionality and the protection of fundamental human rights, constitutes a superior rule of law for the protection of the individual. In the *Ireks-Arkady* case, for example, the Court drew particular attention to the following points:

In the first place it is necessary to take into consideration that the principle of equality, embodied in particular in the second subparagraph of Article 40(3) of the EEC Treaty, which prohibits any discrimination in the common organisation of the agricultural markets, occupies a particularly important place among the rules of Community law intended to protect the interests of the individual. Secondly, the disregard of that principle in this case affected a limited and clearly defined group of commercial operators. It seems, in fact, that the number of quellmehl producers in the Community is very limited. Further, the damage alleged by the applicants goes beyond the bounds of the economic risks inherent in the activities in the sector concerned. Finally, equality of treatment with the producers of maize starch, which had been observed from the beginning of the common organisation of the market in cereals, was ended by the Council in 1974 without sufficient justification.

The '*Schöppenstedt* formula' only applies where the claim for damages relates to a legislative act involving measures of economic policy. Outside this field, the Community may be liable in respect of individual, non-discretionary acts (see Case 175/84 *Krohn*, below) and, vicariously, on other *faute de service* grounds:

Case 145/83 *Adams* v *Commission*

A supplied the Commission with information which led to his employers, the Swiss firm of Hoffman-La Roche being heavily fined for breaches of Article 86. A Commission official carelessly allowed A to be identified as their informant, in breach of the duty of confidentiality in Article 214 of the Treaty.

A was arrested by the Swiss police for economic espionage and held in solitary confinement. His wife committed suicide and he suffered financial ruin. The Court found the Commission liable for the breach of confidentiality and awarded £200,000 damages for mental anguish and economic loss plus £200,000 costs.

The *Krohn* case referred to above raises difficult questions regarding Community liability under Article 215(2) where, as is often the case, a national authority is carrying out Community instructions:

Case 175/84 *Krohn Import-Export* v. *Commission (No. 1)*

K claimed under Article 215(2) for loss suffered as a result of the refusal of the German Intervention Agency to grant an import licence for manioc from Thailand. K's application was refused on the basis of mandatory instructions (a Decision) from the Commission given within the scope of the governing Regulation.

K alleged that the Commission's Decision was illegal and he also brought an action against the Agency in national law to compel them to grant the licence. Although the national case had not reached final judgement (previous case law of the Court had, in these circumstances laid down the principle that normally the plaintiff should first pursue his rights in the national courts and exhaust his local remedies), the Court allowed the claim for damages because the national claim would not compensate K for the loss incurred.

On the merits, the Court ruled that as K had failed to comply with the necessary licensing requirements regarding preferential imports of manioc, the Commission's Decision to refuse the licence was justified.

In this case, the alleged unlawfulness on which the action was based emanated from a Community institution and, being of a mandatory nature, could not be attributed to the national body. Prima facie, the Community was therefore liable. However, as Lasok has concluded:

> ... the Community is only exceptionally vicariously liable for the acts of national authorities administering Community law or a Community policy. Such liability occurs where the relevant Community Institution has exercised effective control over the national authority in a manner which gives rise to non-contractual liability of the Community. However an action against the Community is not a soft option. Therefore, in grey areas [ie where a real issue of concurrent liability has arisen], it seems safer to proceed before the national courts on the assumption that Member States are duty bound to provide remedies for breach of Community law by their institutions and that doubts may be resolved through the machinery of a reference for a preliminary ruling.

Brown and Jacobs have suggested an alternative approach to this problem:

> The drastic alternative would be a revision of the Treaties so as to confer jurisdiction upon the Court of Justice in respect of actions against Member States for non-contractual liability arising out of the administration of Community law by national authorities. The Communities and the Member States could then be sued jointly in the one Community Court, which could allocate liability between them as it thought fit. If the Communities alone were sued (and the plaintiff might often prefer to proceed thus) then the Communities would be able to join the Member State as a party and claim a contribution or even a complete indemnity from it, as appropriate.

Adams, Stanley, *Roche versus Adams*, 1984.

Barav, A., 'Direct and Individual Concern: An Almost Insurmountable Barrier to the Admissibility of Individual Appeals to the EEC Court' (1974) 11 CML Rev. 191.

Bebr, G., 'The Reinforcement of the Constitutional Review of Community Acts under Article 177 EEC' (1988) 25 CML Rev. 684.

Bradley, K.St.C., 'The Variable Evolution of the Standing of the European Parliament in Proceedings Before the Court of Justice' (1988) 8 YEL 27.

Brown, L. Neville, Brown and Jacobs *The Court of Justice of the European Communities*.

Dinnage, J., 'Locus Standi and Article 173 EEC' (1974) 4 EL Rev. 15.

Gormley, L.W. (ed.), Kapteyn and VerLoren van Themaat's *Introduction to the Law of European Communities*, 1990.

Greaves, R.M., 'Locus Standi under Article 173 when Seeking Annulment of a Regulation' (1986) 11 EL Rev. 119.

Harding, C., 'The Impact of Article 177 of the EEC Treaty on the Review of Community Action' (1981) 1 YEL 93.

Harding, C., 'The Private Interest in Challenging Community Action' (1980) 5 EL Rev. 345.

Harding, C., 'The Choice of Court Problem in Cases of Non-Contractual Liability under EEC law' (1979) 16 CML Rev. 389.

Hartley, T.C. *The Foundations of European Community Law*, Part IV Administrative Law.

Kirchner, E. and Williams, K., 'The Legal, Political and Institutional Implications of the Isoglucose Judgments 1980' (1983) 22 JCMS 173.

Lasok, D., 'European Community Liability for Contractual and Non-Contractual Obligations I and II' (1990) *Student Law Review*, Autumn Issue 35 and (1992) *Student Law Review*, Spring Issue 37.

Lasok and Bridge, *Law and Institutions of the European Communities*.

March Hunnings, N., 'The Stanley Adams Affair or the Biter Bit' (1987) 24 CML Rev. 65.

Oliver, P., 'Interim Measures: Some Recent Developments' (1992) 29 CML Rev. 7.

Rasmussen, H., 'Why is Article 173 Interpreted Against Private Plaintiffs?' (1980) 5 EL Rev. 112.

Rasmussen, H., 'Between Self-Restraint and Activism: A Judicial Policy for the European Court' (1988) 13 EL Rev. 28.

Rudden, B., *Basic Community Cases*, Part III Community Blunders: The Isoglucose Story.

Schermers, H.G., *Judicial Protection in the European Communities*.

CHAPTER TWENTY

MEMBER STATES AND THEIR COMMUNITY OBLIGATIONS : ACTIONS AGAINST THEM AT COMMUNITY AND NATIONAL LEVEL

SUPERVISION AT COMMUNITY LEVEL

Enforcement Actions against Member States : Article 169

Proceedings may be brought in the Court of Justice either by the Commission or by a Member State against a Member State which is alleged to be in breach of its Community obligations:

> Article 169
>
> If the Commission considers that a Member State has failed to fulfil an obligation under this Treaty, it shall deliver a reasoned opinion on the matter after giving the State concerned the opportunity to submit its observations.
>
> If the State concerned does not comply with the opinion within the period laid down by the Commission the latter may bring the matter before the Court of Justice.

> Article 170
>
> A Member State which considers that another Member State has failed to fulfil an obligation under this Treaty may bring the matter before the Court of Justice.
>
> Before a Member State brings an action against another Member State for an alleged infringement of an obligation under this Treaty, it shall bring the matter before the Commission.
>
> The Commission shall deliver a reasoned opinion after each of the States concerned has been given the opportunity to submit its own case and its observations on the other party's case both orally and in writing.
>
> If the Commission has not delivered an opinion within three months of the date on which the matter was brought before it, the absence of such

opinion shall not prevent the matter from being brought before the Court of Justice.

To date only one action has proceeded to judgment under Article 170: Case 141/78 *France* v *UK* in which France claimed that UK fishery conservation measures were contrary to Community law. The Commission's reasoned opinion supported the French claim but the matter was pressed to the litigation stage at which the Court gave judgment against the UK. Disputes of this nature between Member States are better resolved by political means rather than by such direct confrontation. In any event, if the matter is left to the Commission to initiate proceedings under Article 169, the procedure laid down in that article enables a satisfactory outcome to be reached on a non-contentious basis (prior to the litigation stage) in the majority of cases.

The Commission has increasingly resorted to enforcement actions under Article 169 in recent years. Whereas there were 166 such actions brought between 1953 and 1981, a total of 163 were brought in the two years 1988 and 1989. It will be recalled that under Article 155 it is the Commission's duty to 'ensure that the provisions of this Treaty and the measures taken by the institutions pursuant thereto are applied'. In addition, as we have also seen, Member States have a duty under Article 5 to 'take all appropriate measures ... to ensure fulfilment of the obligations arising out of this Treaty or resulting from action taken by the institutions of the Community'.

Over the years the increase both in the number of Member States and the extent of their obligations has inevitably lead to an increase in the number of violations. Although the principle of direct effect may be relied upon by individuals to secure the enforcement of Treaty obligations – in 1962 in *Van Gend en Loos* the Court did not wish to restrict 'the guarantees against an infringement of Article 12 to the procedures under Article 169 and 170' – and the enforcement of Regulations, increased vigilance by the Commission as regards the full implementation of Directives has been necessitated both by problems regarding the direct effect of those measures and by the need for the Commission to secure the establishment, by means of harmonisation Directives, of the Internal Market by the end of 1992. Indeed, in its Fifth Annual Report (1988) the Commission stated that:

> Article 169 of the EEC Treaty is now an instrument for the achievement of policy, and not solely an essential legal instrument. The objective of Article 8a of the Treaty, namely to achieve by 1992 an area without internal frontiers, is now the Commission's priority objective and requires a strict application of existing Community law. It is Article 169 which makes it possible to monitor this application and ensures its observance by the Member States.

At Community level, the introduction by the Treaty on European Union of a power vested in the Court of Justice to impose financial sanctions upon a Member State which has not only failed to fulfil a Treaty obligation but has also failed to comply with a judgment of the Court to that effect (see Article 171(2) EC), and, at national level, the *Francovich* decision, which enables an individual to bring an action for damages against the State as tortfeasor for loss suffered as a consequence of the State's failure to fulfil its Treaty obligations (eg as regards the implementation of a Directive), will significantly increase the pressure on Member States to fulfil their Community obligations. (Those developments will be discussed in due course.)

The procedure laid down in Article 169 follows two distinct stages: the *administrative* and the *judicial*. The administrative stage, the purpose of which is to enable the Member State to justify its position or comply with the Treaty, itself falls into three possible parts. The Commission first warns the Member State of its alleged breach, outlines its grounds of complaint, and invites comments. In many instances, the breach is acknowledged at this point and the matter is settled. If not, the Commission will formally invite the Member State to submit its observations on the alleged breach. If the question still cannot be settled, the Commission may next issue a *reasoned opinion* setting out the nature of the infringement and requiring the Member State to take the necessary action to bring it to an end (normally within a specified time). Many cases are brought to an end at this final pre-contentious stage. If, however, it is clear that a Member State is not willing to comply with its opinion, the Commission *may* bring the matter before the Court (see, for example, the *Lütticke* litigation in the previous chapter).

A Member State may even concede its failure to fulfil its obligations *after* the case has gone to the Court but before judgment, and the Commission in such circumstances will normally ask the Court to remove the case from the register: eg Case 301/84 *Commission* v *UK* concerning 'Buy-British', preferential car purchase loan schemes applied by local authorities, see Official Journal, 1985, C 276/6. In any event, it is clear that the procedure under Article 169 (which is an improvement on the rules normally applying in public international law where a State fails to fulfil its treaty obligations) is aimed primarily at avoiding rather than achieving a condemnation of a defaulting Member State. (Probably only around 10 per cent of recorded infringements reach the stage of judgment by the Court).

Where a Member State has failed to remedy its alleged breach in compliance with the Commission's reasoned opinion within the stipulated time limit, and the Commission has exercised its power to move the matter to the judicial stage, the Court of Justice will examine the merits of the case and decide *de novo* whether a breach of Community law has occurred. The proceedings do not constitute a review of the Commission's reasoned opinion, although at this stage its legality may be questioned. In Case 293/85 *Commission* v *Belgium* (*Re University Fees*), the action by the Commission against Belgium for its failure to implement the decision in Case 293/83 *Gravier* in a satisfactory manner was dismissed as the Commission had not given the Belgian authorities sufficient time to respond to its complaints, either before or after the issue of its reasoned opinion.

In recent months, in the field of environmental policy alone, the Commission has pursued successful Article 169 actions against the UK for its failure to implement Directives on the quality of drinking water and on bathing water standards. The Commission has however dropped formal proceedings against the UK for infringing EC environment impact requirements at a BP industrial site in Scotland. The Commission had argued that BP had gained planning permission to increase its liquid gas installation without a prior environment impact assessment. Following BP's agreeing to put forward plans for public consultation, the Commission announced that the requirements of the Directive had been satisfied.

The 1985 Environment Assessment Directive was also at the heart of the dispute beginning in 1991 between the Commission and the UK concerning seven large-scale construction and transport projects in the south of England, valued at £500 million and including the controversial construction of the M3 link through Twyford Down in Hampshire. The Commission's opening of formal proceedings was accompanied by a request from the Environment Commissioner, Signor Carlo Ripa di Meana, to the Secretary of State for Transport that work on the projects should stop. This request was branded in this country as 'an unwarranted intrusion into Britain's national affairs' on the basis that the projects had no environmental effect on other Member States.

The key issues appeared to be whether the necessary permission at national level to proceed with the projects had been given before the Directive came into effect and, if it had not, the extent of the UK's discretion under the Directive in determining whether or not to subject projects (such as modifications to existing motorways or long-distance rail links) to an environmental impact assessment. In July 1992 the Commission abandoned proceedings regarding five of the seven projects, including that relating to the M3 motorway extension.

Article 169 cases that go to judgment usually go against the defendant Member State. In 1989 Dashwood and White reported how:

> In the small minority of cases that have run their full course the Member State concerned has almost always taken the steps necessary to comply with the judgment, although sometimes after a considerable delay.

Ireland, for example, took three years to amend the legislation on origin marking that gave rise to the *Irish Souvenirs* case (Case 113/80); while it was only in 1986 that France complied with judgments of 1980 and 1982 relating to discriminatory legislation on alcohol advertising (Cases 152/78, 83/82). In the *Mutton and Lamb* case (Case 232/78) an eventual solution was found through political negotiations.

These cases suggest that the EEC system might benefit from the conferment on the European Court of a power to impose financial sanctions, as an incentive to timely compliance and to discourage opportunism. However, the ultimate guarantee of the effectiveness of infringement proceedings is Member States' recognition that respect for the rule of law in the Community is a condition of its survival. A Member State that adopted a policy of ignoring adverse judgments of the European Court would not be able to remain a member of the Community for very long.

As noted earlier, a power to impose financial sanctions was introduced by the TEU by means of a new second paragraph of Article 171:

Article 171

1. If the Court of Justice finds that a Member State has failed to fulfil an obligation under this Treaty, the State shall be required to take the necessary measures to comply with the judgment of the Court of Justice.

2. If the Commission considers that the Member State concerned has not taken such measures it shall, after giving that State the opportunity to submit its comments, issue a reasoned opinion specifying the points on which the Member State concerned has not complied with the judgment of the Court of Justice.

   If the Member State concerned fails to take the necessary measures to comply with the Court's judgment within the time-limit laid down by the Commission, the latter may bring the case before the Court of Justice. In so doing, it shall specify the amount of the lump sum or penalty payment to be paid by the Member State concerned which it considers appropriate in the circumstances.

   If the Court of Justice finds that the Member State concerned has not complied with its judgment it may impose a lump sum or penalty payment on it.

This procedure shall be without prejudice to Article 170.

Before the introduction of Article 171(2), the Commission's only legal weapon was a second Article 169 action against the Member State for breach of Article 171: see, eg Cases 24 and 97/80R *Commission v France (Re Restrictions on Imports of Lamb)*.

As regards the declaratory nature of a judgment of the Court against a defaulting Member State, it is clear that it is for the Member State to 'take the necessary measures to comply' with its Treaty obligations. The Commission's reasoned opinion will have spelt out the acts which have given rise to the breach and Member States are required to draw the necessary inferences from the Court's judgment. Thus, if for example the breach consists in the enactment of legislation contrary to Community law, the Court of Justice has no power to annul the offending national measure but, following its ruling that the measure conflicts with Community law, the Member State has a duty to amend its own law: see, in particular, the *Factortame* case discussed below.

In the majority of Article 169 cases, the defendant Member State has failed to implement the obligations of a Directive, but in the case which follows (discussed also in Chapter Eight), a Regulation stated that national measures were required in order to bring it fully into effect. The Court (as it almost invariably does) brushed aside the defences raised by the UK in the face of the principle of the equality of Member States before Community law and the duty of solidarity accepted by them on the basis of Article 5:

Case 128/78 *Commission v. UK (Re Tachographs)*

Regulation 1463/70 relating to the introduction of tachographs ('the spy in the cab') in commercial vehicles laid down that its use was to be compulsory from a specified date. In this action brought by the Commission against the UK for failure to comply, the Court ruled that:

It is not denied that provision for the installation and use of the recording equipment has been made by the British legislation only on an optional and voluntary basis as regards both vehicles engaged in intra-Community transport and those engaged in national transport. On the other hand, the British legislation has maintained in force the obligations relating to the keeping of an individual control book which were abolished by the said Regulation.

The defendant claims that this arrangement is sufficient to meet the objectives of promoting road safety, of social progress for workers and of the harmonisation of conditions of competition. It maintains that the implementation of Regulation No 1463/70 on its territory is best achieved by the installation and use of the recording equipment on a voluntary basis, though this may be made compulsory at an appropriate time. It adds that implementation of the Regulation involving compulsory measures would meet with active resistance from the sectors concerned, in particular the trade unions, which would result in strikes in the transport sector and would therefore seriously damage the whole economy of the country.

It contends that since, in the case of the United Kingdom, the objectives of the Community policy in this field can be achieved just as satisfactorily by the maintenance of the system of the individual control book as by the compulsory introduction of recording equipment, the alleged failure to fulfil an obligation is of a purely technical nature and, in view of the difficulties referred to, should not be taken into account. Moreover the installation and use of recording equipment is in practice already guaranteed in respect of intra-Community transport by the fact that the other Member States have made it compulsory.

Article 189 of the Treaty provides that a Regulation shall be binding 'in its entirety' in the Member States. As the Court has already stated in its judgment of 7 February 1973 (Case 39/72 *Commission* v *Italian Republic* (1973) ECR 101) it cannot therefore be accepted that a Member State should apply in an incomplete or selective manner provisions of a Community Regulation so as to render abortive certain aspects of Community legislation which it has opposed or which it considers contrary to its national interests. In particular, as regards the putting into effect of a general rule intended to eliminate certain abuses to which workers are subject and which in addition involve a threat to road safety, a Member State which omits to take, within the requisite period and simultaneously with the other Member States, the measures which it ought to take, undermines Community solidarity by imposing, in particular as regards intra-Community transport, on the other Member States the necessity of remedying the effects of its own omissions, while at the same time taking an undue advantage to the detriment of its partners.

As the Court said in the same judgment, practical difficulties which appear at the stage when a Community measure is put into effect cannot permit a Member State unilaterally to opt out of fulfilling its obligations. The Community institutional system provides the Member State concerned with the necessary means to ensure that its difficulties be given due consideration, subject to compliance with the principles of the common market and the legitimate interests of the other Member States.

In these circumstances, the possible difficulties of implementation alleged by the defendant cannot be accepted as a justification.

Further, as the Court said in the case mentioned above, in permitting Member States to profit from the advantages of the Community, the Treaty imposes on them also the obligation to respect its rules. For a State unilaterally to break, according to its own conception of national interest, the equilibrium between the advantages and obligations flowing from its adherence to the Community brings into question the equality of Member States before Community law and creates discrimination at the expense of their nationals. This failure in the duty of solidarity accepted by Member States by the fact of their adherence to the Community strikes at the very root of the Community legal order.

It appears therefore that, in deliberately refusing to give effect on its territory to the provisions of Regulation No 1463/70, the United Kingdom has markedly failed to fulfil the obligation which it has assumed by virtue of its membership of the European Economic Community.

Special Enforcement Procedures

The Treaty also provides the Commission with special enforcement procedures against Member States, which operate in derogation from the provisions of Articles 169 and 170, in the fields of disputed state aids (Article 93(2)) and the allegedly improper use of emergency powers granted to Member States faced by various threats to their national security (see Articles 223–225). The procedure under Article 225 is of a direct, accelerated nature, as it also is under Article 100A(4), para. 3 relating to the Internal Market. As seen in Chapter Twelve, under this provision, the Commission (or another Member State) may bring a Member State directly before the Court of Justice if it considers that the State is making improper use of powers provided in Article 100A(4), para. 1 to 'apply national provisions on grounds of major needs referred to in Article 36 or relating to protection of the environment or the working environment'.

Interim Measures

Article 186

The Court of Justice may in any cases before it prescribe any necessary interim measures.

In Case 61/77R *Commission v Ireland (Re Fisheries Conservation Measures)*, the Court of Justice ruled that interim measures, ordering a Member State to act in a certain way, eg to *suspend* national rules considered by the Commission to be contrary to the Treaty, might be granted at the Commission's request within the ambit of Article 169 proceedings. The availability of such a remedy, akin to an interlocutory injunction in English law, means therefore that, somewhat anomalously, the Court possesses wider powers in interim proceedings than at the final declaratory judgment stage.

Interim relief will however only be granted in exceptional circumstances. Article 83(2) of the Rules of Procedure of the Court of Justice states that interim measures may not be ordered 'unless there are circumstances giving rise to urgency and factual and legal grounds establishing a prima facie case for the measures applied for'.

The Court will therefore take into account the following considerations:

1. As regards the main proceedings under Article 169, whether the Commission has established a prima facie case: one that 'does not appear to be without foundation'.

2. The question of urgency, which must be assessed in relation to the prevention of serious and irreparable damage.

This second consideration will normally involve the weighing of a balance of interests. The Commission will be required to show that serious and irreparable damage to the Community interest will occur if the Court does *not* grant the order. However, the defendant Member State may well argue that such damage to its interests will result if the order *is* granted.

These considerations were examined by the Court of Justice in the following case in which the Commission pursued its action against the UK under Articles 169 and 186:

Case 246/89R *Commission v. UK (Re Merchant Shipping Rules)*

The UK government had taken steps to prevent Spanish business interests from 'quota-hopping', ie fishing in vessels registered in Britain against

UK fishing quotas as laid down under the Common Fisheries Policy but landing their catch in Spain. These steps culminated in the passing of the Merchant Shipping Act 1988 which in essence required that vessels be under British ownership.

The Commission initiated an Article 169 action against the UK on the basis that the 1988 Act contravened Treaty rules prohibiting discrimination on grounds of nationality in particular Article 7 and Article 52 (right of establishment). The Commission also asked the Court as a matter of urgency to make an interim order under Article 186 regarding suspension of the Act's nationality requirements.

Having considered the directly effective rights *claimed* by the 'Anglo-Spanish' operators and UK national interests under the Common Fisheries Policy, the President of the Court ruled that the Commission had made out a prima facie case.

As regards the need for urgency, the President held that 'for fishing vessels which until 31 March 1989 were flying the British flag and fishing under a British fishing licence the loss of the flag and the cessation of their activities entail serious damage. There is no ground for believing that, pending delivery of the judgment in the main proceedings, these vessels can be operated in the pursuit of alternative fishing activities. The aforesaid damage must also, should the application in the main proceedings be granted, be regarded as irreparable'.

The President therefore ordered that: 'Pending delivery of the judgment in the main proceedings, the United Kingdom shall suspend the application of the nationality requirements laid down in the Merchant Shipping Act 1988 as regards the nationals of other Member States and in respect of fishing vessels which, until 31 March 1989, were pursuing a fishing activity under the British flag and under a British fishing licence'.

It is important to stress that this case clearly illustrates that at Community level the Court of Justice may grant interim relief against *national* measures which are the subject of an Article 169 action and in relation to which a prima facie case that they are in breach of Community law has been established. (In the main proceedings, Case 246/89 *Commission v UK (Re Merchant Shipping Rules)*, the Court held that the stringent rules introduced by the 1988 Act, requiring British nationality for owners of British registered fishing vessels entitled to fish under the UK fishing quotas, infringed Articles 7 and 52 of the Treaty and the illegality of the national requirement was not affected by the EEC fishery quota system).

Interim relief, again at Community level but in relation to a *Community* act, is similarly available, as can be seen in the context of an Article 173(2) annulment action brought by an undertaking against an anti-dumping measure in Case 113/77R *NTN Toyo Bearing Co v Council*.

It is important to appreciate that the question of interim relief has now been examined in a number of different contexts: at Community level it may be granted by the Court of Justice against the application of a disputed *Community* act (*NTN Toyo Bearing*) or against the application of *national* law alleged to be in violation of Community rules (*Re Merchant Shipping Rules*). Also, the Court has held that the Commission has powers to adopt interim measures in the context of the competition rules: see *Camera Care* in Chapter Seventeen and *La Cinq* below. In similar circumstances, at national level, an interim injunction was granted in *Cutsforth* v *Mansfield Inns Ltd* (1986), also discussed in Chapter Seventeen.

At national level again, a court may grant interim relief against the application of a national measure based on a disputed Community Act (*Zuckerfabrik Süderdithmarschen*, see the previous chapter). In the next section, it will be seen that a *national* court also has the power to grant interim relief against the application of national law alleged to be in violation of Community rules: Case C-213/89 R v *Secretary of State for Transport, ex parte Factortame*. The aim of the Court of Justice is to achieve balance and coherence as regards enforcement and remedies.

SUPERVISION AT NATIONAL LEVEL

The 'quota hopping' litigation (generally known as *Factortame*) not only involved the Commission's actions under Articles 169 and 186 but claims at the national level as well. The compatibility of the Merchant Shipping Act 1988 with Community law was the subject of challenge by Factortame Ltd and other members of the 'Anglo-Spanish' fishing fleet in the English courts. This challenge was similarly double-edged.

Factortame claimed that the Act's new registration requirements were in violation of their directly enforceable Community right not to be discriminated against on grounds of nationality under Article 7, in conjunction with their similar rights of establishment under Articles 52 and 58 of the Treaty. These claims became the subject of an Article 177 reference from the Divisional Court of the QBD for a interpretive ruling. However before examining this claim, or the second aspect of the case, Factortame's application for the relevant parts of the 1988 Act to be suspended by the *national* court pending a determination of their validity by the Court of Justice, it is important to recall the relationship between the first, substantive issue (concerning directly effective rights) and an enforcement action brought by the Commission under Article 169.

As we have seen on numerous occasions, on the basis of the twin principles of direct effect and the supremacy of Community law, an infringement of Community law by a Member State may be challenged by private parties at national level. Returning to the Court's landmark decision in Case 26/62 *Van Gend en Loos* regarding the standstill on customs duties in Article 12, following a reference from the Dutch customs court under Article 177, the Court stated in clear terms that:

> A restriction of the guarantees against an infringement of Article 12 by Member States to the procedures under Article 169 and 170 would remove all direct legal protection of the individual rights of their nationals ... The vigilance of individuals concerned to protect their rights amounts to an effective supervision in addition to the supervision entrusted by Articles 169 and 170 to the diligence of the Commission and of the Member States.

In this case the company's claim against the State was for the reimbursement of the excess customs duty levied on it in breach of Community law. In another important decision, in the case of *Defrenne* v *Sabena (No. 2)*, the effect of the Court's ruling was that compensation must be paid by any employer who discriminates against his employees in terms of pay. The equal treatment cases of *Marshall* and *Van Colson* each in their different ways established the plaintiff's right to compensation. In the latter, we have seen how national law was interpreted so as to provide damages beyond the merely nominal.

All these Article 177 rulings of the Court of Justice (and many others of course) were remitted to the originating national court or tribunal to be applied. An inquiry into the eventual outcome raises the important general question of the effectiveness of Community rights in national courts or tribunals in terms of the remedies available. For example, upon what terms did English law provide for compensation for Miss Marshall? What remedies were available for Factortame and the other member of the 'Anglo–Spanish' fishing fleet should their claims in the national courts succeed?

Community Rights in National Courts: National Procedural Rules and Remedies

Although Community law has increasingly established substantive rights for individuals, as regards their vindication it has as yet tended to leave the questions of the appropriate court, the *procedural rules* which apply and the *remedies* available to the national law of the Member States. As Steiner has explained:

> The growing acceptance by national courts of the principle of directly effective Community law has brought in its wake a second problem. If EEC law may be invoked by individuals before their national courts, what remedies are available for its breach? It has long been clear that EEC law may be invoked as a shield, whether in civil or criminal proceedings, or to provide the basis for an action in restitution, for example, for money paid in breach of Community law. It is less clear to what extent, and in what action, it may be invoked by an individual in order to prevent damage from occurring, or to seek compensation for damage already suffered. When, if at all, will a breach of EEC law give rise to a remedy in damages? When will an injunction be more appropriate? When a declaration? Where the defendant is a public body, should the plaintiff proceed by writ or by way of judicial review?

Guidance concerning the impact of *national procedural rules* on claims in national courts in respect of directly effective Community rights was given by the Court of Justice in Case 45/76 *Comet* v *Produktschap*:

> A levy had been paid on exports which was found to be a charge equivalent to a customs duty contrary to Article 16 of the Treaty. C's claim for reimbursement was met by the argument that it had been lodged after the expiry of the limitation period for such claims under Dutch law. C in return argued that this was an independent right of action unaffected by limitations provided for under national law, which were liable to weaken the impact of directly effective Community law.

Following an Article 177 reference, the Court of Justice endorsed the rights of Member States to apply national limitation periods in cases in national courts based on directly effective provisions of Community law, subject to what have been termed the principles of *effectiveness* and *non-discrimination*:

> Thus, in the application of the principle of co-operation laid down in Article 5 of the Treaty, the national courts are entrusted with ensuring the legal protection conferred on individuals by the direct effect of the provisions of Community law.

> Consequently, in the absence of any relevant Community rules, it is for the national legal order of each Member State to designate the competent courts and to lay down the procedural rules for proceedings

designed to ensure the protection of the rights which individuals acquire through the direct effect of Community law, provided that such rules are not less favourable than those governing the same right of action on an internal matter.

Articles 100 to 102 and 235 of the Treaty enable the appropriate steps to be taken as necessary, to eliminate differences between the provisions laid down in such matters by law, regulation or administrative action in Member States if these differences are found to be such as to cause distortion or to affect the functioning of the common market.

In default of such harmonisation measures, the rights conferred by Community law must be exercised before the national courts in accordance with the rules of procedure laid down by national law.

The position would be different only if those rules and time–limits made it impossible in practice to exercise rights which the national courts have a duty to protect.

This does not apply to the fixing of a reasonable period of limitation within which an action must be brought.

The fixing, as regards fiscal proceedings, of such a period is in fact an application of a fundamental principle of legal certainty which protects both the authority concerned and the party from whom payment is claimed.

The answer must therefore be that, in the case of a litigant who is challenging before the national courts a decision of a national body for incompatibility with Community law, that law, in its present state, does not prevent the expiry of the period within which proceedings must be brought under national law from being raised against him, provided that the procedural rules applicable to his case are not less favourable than those governing the same right of action on an internal matter.

Thus, 'in the absence of any relevant Community rules' on the subject, national procedures apply. Further, until such national rules are harmonised, the availability of remedies for private parties may well vary from one Member State to another. However, it is clear that in no event may national rules exclude or discriminate against the exercise of directly effective rights.

A more difficult question concerning time limits, within the context of Directives and the failure of Member States to implement them, arose in Case C-208/90 *Emmott* v *Minister for Social Welfare*. As regards the time limits within which proceedings must be brought before a national court by persons wishing to rely on a Directive against a defaulting Member State, the Court ruled that time begins to run, not from the date of the expiry of the implementation period, but from the later date when national implementing legislation is correctly adopted:

> Council Directive 79/7, which prohibits discrimination on grounds of sex in matters of social security, should have been implemented by the Irish authorities by December 1984. The complainant, Mrs Emmott, received less benefit than a man would have done in equivalent circumstances between that date and the properly effective entry into force of the national equalising legislation in 1988.

> Mrs Emmott initiated proceedings in 1987 on the basis of the vertical direct effect of the relevant article of Directive 79/7. It was at that time that she had first learnt of her rights, as established in another Irish case, Case 286/85 *Cotter and McDermott v Minister for Social Welfare*. The authorities denied her claim and argued that in any event she was statute-barred from presenting it.

> The Rules of the Superior Courts in Ireland provide that a claim for judicial review (for the purpose of recovering her benefits) must, except in exceptional circumstances, be brought within three months from the date when grounds for the application first arose – in Mrs Emmott's case, the date in December 1984 when Directive 79/7 came into force.

> Under Article 177 the High Court asked the Court of Justice whether it was 'contrary to the general principles of Community law for the relevant authorities of a Member State to rely upon national procedural rules, in particular rules relating to time limits', in order to refuse compensation for Mrs Emmott.

The Court ruled that:

> So long as a Directive has not been properly transposed into national law, individuals are unable to ascertain the full extent of their rights. That state of uncertainty for individuals subsists even after the Court has delivered a judgment finding that the Member State in question has not fulfilled its obligations under the Directive and even if the Court has held that a particular provision or provisions of the Directive are sufficiently precise and unconditional to be relied upon before a national court.

Only the proper transposition of the Directive will bring that state of uncertainty to an end and it is only upon that transposition that the legal certainty which must exist if individuals are to be required to assert their rights is created.

It follows that until such time as a Directive has been properly transposed a defaulting Member State may not rely on an individual's delay in initiating proceedings against it in order to protect rights conferred upon him by the provisions of the Directive and that a period laid down by national law within which proceedings must be initiated cannot begin to run before that time.

The answer to the question referred to the Court must therefore be that Community law precludes the competent authorities of a Member State from relying, in proceedings brought against them by an individual before the national courts in order to protect rights directly conferred upon him by Article 4(1) of Directive 79/7/EEC, on national procedural rules relating to time limits for bringing proceedings so long as that Member State has not properly transposed that Directive into its domestic legal system.

Turning to the availability of *remedies* in national courts necessary for the effective implementation of Community law, the Court of Justice has again provided guidelines. In Case 158/80 *Rewe v HZA Kiel*, the facts of which were similar to those in *Comet* above, the Court stated that:

... it must be possible for every type of action provided for by national law to be available for the purpose of ensuring observance of Community provisions having direct effect, on the same conditions as would apply were it a question of observing national law.

In Case 60/75 *Russo v AIMA*, a Member State introduced national measures in contravention of a CAP Regulation. Here the Court laid down that:

If an individual producer has suffered damage as a result of the intervention of a Member State in violation of Community law it will be for the State, as regards the injured party, to take the consequences upon itself in the context of the provisions of national law relating to the liability of the State.

In Case 222/84 *Johnston* v *CC of the RUC* (see Chapter Thirteen), the Court of Justice stressed that the existence of effective judicial protection was a general principle of Community law to be found in the constitutional traditions of the Member States. Sanctions provided by national law must have a 'real deterrent effect', being 'such as to guarantee full and effective legal protection': see Case 79/83 *Harz* v *Deutsche Tradax*. Thus, in this and the joined Case 14/83 *Von Colson*, although, as we have seen, the obligation under the Equal Treatment Directive to provide judicial remedies did not *require* any specific sanction such as damages, it was held that if a Member State's national law provided for damages to be awarded for breach of the equal treatment provisions, then such compensation should be adequate and not merely nominal (see Chapter Eight, and on the question of the measure — adequacy — of damages in the second *Marshall* case, see below).

As recently as 1990, Collins has said that:

> Some very difficult questions have been raised in England on the availability of the damages remedy, and the relationship between the right to damages and the possibility of obtaining interim relief pending the determination of cases in which directly effective rights are claimed [but have] not yet been definitely established.

In the case which follows (to which attention was drawn in Chapter Seventeen), interlocutory proceedings reached the House of Lords where difficult questions concerning injunctions and damages were considered by their Lordships but were not regarded as 'apt for decision' at that stage. The case involved a private law action brought against an undertaking in which Article 86 was used as a 'sword':

> *Garden Cottage Foods Ltd* v. *Milk Marketing Board* (1984)
> The plaintiffs regularly bought bulk butter from the Board for sale in the UK and abroad. As a result of a change of policy the Board reduced the number of its sales outlets and cut off supplies to the plaintiffs, who alleged that the Board had acted in breach of Article 86 by abusing its dominant position.

> At first instance, GCF's application for an interim injunction to compel the Board to resume supplies was refused principally on the ground that damages would be an adequate remedy. The Court of Appeal granted the injunction mainly because it was doubtful whether there was a cause of action in damages for breach of Article 86.

> By a 4-1 majority the House of Lords restored the decision at first instance. In the course of his speech Lord Diplock stated that:

The rights which the article confers on citizens in the United Kingdom accordingly fall within Section 2(1) of the 1972 Act. They are without further enactment to be given legal effect in the United Kingdom and enforced accordingly. A breach of the duty imposed by Article 86 not to abuse a dominant position in the Common Market or in a substantial part of it can thus be categorised in English law as a breach of statutory duty that is imposed not only for the purpose of promoting the general economic prosperity of the Common Market but also for the benefit of private individuals to whom loss or damage is caused by a breach of that duty. If this categorisation be correct, and I can see none other that would be capable of giving rise to a civil cause of action in English private law on the part of a private individual who sustained loss or damage by reason of a breach of a directly applicable provision of the EEC Treaty, the nature of the cause of action cannot, in my view, be affected by the fact that the legislative provision by which the duty is imposed takes the negative form of a prohibition of particular kinds of conduct rather than the positive form of an obligation to do particular acts.

Therefore, although only an interlocutory decision, this case supports the view that in principle a right of action for damages is available in English law under Article 86 on the basis of the tort of breach of statutory duty. It is not an authority for saying that an injunction will never be granted in cases involving Articles 85 and 86. An interim injunction was granted in *Cutsforth v Mansfield Inns Ltd* (1986) involving Article 85 (see Chapter Seventeen) and also in the *Factortame* case (see below), in which a preliminary ruling of the Court of Justice led to a position where, in the circumstances of the case, the House of Lords was obliged to grant an injunction, no remedy in damages being available.

The difficult and controversial question of the availability of damages against the Crown arose in the case of *Bourgoin v Ministry of Agriculture, Fisheries and Food* (1986). Following the decision in *Garden Cottage Foods*, the French plaintiff (and others) brought an action against the Ministry in tort for damages to compensate for substantial economic loss allegedly caused by the defendant. The basis of the claim was the Ministry's contravention of Article 30 when placing an embargo on imports of the plaintiff's goods: as decided by the Court of Justice in Case 40/82 *Commission v UK (Re Imports of Poultry Meat)*, see Chapter Twelve. However, the fact that the defendant was a public body was taken to raise new questions not encountered in the *Garden Cottage Foods* case. (Article 30 imposes obligations on Member States; Article 86 imposes them on undertakings). Did Bourgoin have a remedy in damages against the national authorities?

The legal background to a case such as this is to be found in English administrative law. The position has been summarised as follows in the

Report of the Committee of the JUSTICE – All Souls Review of Administrative Law in the United Kingdom (1988):

COMPENSATION: FINANCIAL LOSS CAUSED BY ADMINISTRATIVE ACTION

SUMMARY OF ARGUMENT. Special provisions apart, the existing law in the United Kingdom stops short of providing for compensation for economic loss caused by invalid administrative action or by excessive delay in arriving at an administrative decision, or by the giving of wrong advice by a public official. It has been suggested that liability for damages is inappropriate in such cases on the principle that it is always open to the person affected to ignore an invalid administrative decision; but we consider that unrealistic. The administration is liable for such of its wrongful conduct as fits into one of the recognised common-law categories such as trespass, nuisance, negligence, or breach of statutory duty. A particular difficulty occurs in the case of allegations of negligence in the exercise of statutory powers by a public body because such powers must necessarily often contain a large element of policy and that is a matter for the public body, not for the courts. But, generally speaking, the law of negligence is capable of dealing satisfactorily with cases of injury caused by negligence of the administration and in our view it should be allowed to develop on a case by case basis.

For the many types of wrongful administrative conduct that do not fit into the recognised common-law categories the court has no power to award damages. 'Wrongful' includes those cases of action or omission by a public authority where a court would find that the conduct or any resulting decision should be declared illegal or be quashed or held void or voidable. For the present, the law takes no account of the fact that the administration is capable of inflicting damage in ways in which a private person cannot.

Reform is clearly needed to provide a remedy for the person injured by wrongful administrative action not involving negligence. In French law there is a principle of general liability for injury caused by malfunctioning of the public service. There is no real likelihood that the common law will develop in that direction and we therefore suggest legislation to provide generally for compensation for material injury caused either by wrongful acts or omissions or by unreasonable or excessive delay of a public body. Decisions of courts and tribunals would be excluded.

Bourgoin v *Ministry of Agriculture, Fisheries and Food* (1986)

In September 1981 the Ministry effectively prohibited imports of turkeys from France purportedly on health grounds. Having failed to justify the ban under Article 36 (see Case 40/82 above), the Ministry later complied with the judgment of the Court by allowing imports to recommence. However the effect was that the French producers missed not only the 1981 Christmas season but that of 1982 as well.

Calculating their losses at £19 million, they alleged that the Minister's action in imposing the embargo amounted to the torts of (a) breach of statutory duty and (b) misfeasance in public office. On the hearing of a preliminary issue as to whether the statement of claim disclosed a cause of action, Mann J at first instance and a unanimous Court of Appeal were prepared to find an arguable cause of action in misfeasance (if the Minister, although not acting maliciously, knew that his act was *ultra vires*, being in breach of the directly effective Article 30, and that it would injure the plaintiff).

Mann J was also of the opinion that an action for breach of statutory duty would lie. He reasoned that Article 30, like Article 86 (in *Garden Cottage Foods*), was directly effective and its breach must give rise to rights which national courts must protect in an *effective* manner. Although the rights under Article 86 were to be seen as rights in *private* law (enforceable against another individual, the Milk Marketing Board), Mann J felt unable to differentiate between the two Articles, and accordingly held that a statutory duty claim could similarly lie against the Ministry.

This latter ruling was reversed by a majority of the Court of Appeal who felt that in this respect, since no remedy other than the public law remedy of judicial review would be available for a breach of a similar domestic legal right, judicial review was a sufficient remedy, together with a declaration as to the invalidity of the national measure which introduced the embargo. (By way of analogy, both judges drew attention to the restrictive conditions under which the Community might incur liability for damages under Article 215(2), see Chapter Nineteen). Oliver LJ (dissenting) agreed with Mann J particularly as regards the need for effective protection: 'in principle the 'protection' of the individual rights under Community law involves, subject to the procedural requirements of the national forum, the payment of compensation in respect of the period between the commission of the wrong and its rectification'.

In view of the later decision concerning interim relief in the *Factortame* case (see below), it is noteworthy that Oliver LJ added that 'the fact remains that in the absence of a remedy in damages or immediate interim relief, breaches of the EEC Treaty occurring prior to the decision in those proceedings will remain uncompensated'.

As with *Garden Cottage Foods*, this case only dealt with preliminary issues and can hardly be said to be conclusive on the question of the appropriateness of breach of statutory duty as a basis for damages following a breach of directly effective Community law. In *Bourgoin* leave to appeal to the House of Lords was granted but the case was settled before the appeal was heard. The Government paid Bourgoin £3.5 million in respect of damages, interest and costs, presumably either because they feared that the misfeasance claim would succeed or because they felt that the House of Lords would agree with Mann J and Oliver LJ on the breach of statutory duty point.

Academic opinion on these two cases varies (see particularly Steiner and Oliver in the list of further reading). For example, with reference to *Bourgoin*, Oliver suggests that:

> A far more satisfactory course would be for the courts to recognise a form of negligence action, in which the negligent act would consist in the infringement by the authorities of Article 30 when not acting reasonably and in good faith. This action would be *sui generis* in that it would not be beset with certain major difficulties which appear to be inherent in the action for negligence when brought against public authorities [*Anns* v *Merton LBC*, etc]. Thus, if such an action were to lie, a duty of care would have to be owed to the importers'.

On the other hand it has been argued, in line with the majority ruling in *Bourgoin*, that Article 30 was concerned with the act of a public officer possessing discretionary powers and duties within the field of economic policy making. Additionally, if the duty in question (regarding public health) was imposed by statute, as was the case, no action in damages can arise. The Treaty, this argument continues, confers private rights in the sense that it confers *locus standi* upon a person affected by a breach of Article 30 to seek judicial review – but it does not require any radical departure from the established pattern of English remedies for *ultra vires* acts. (Nevertheless, the question remains: Is judicial review an *effective* remedy?)

It might be asked why, as regards the pursuit of effective remedies, Bourgoin did not seek interim relief as soon as the embargo took effect in late 1981. The answer must be that it was accepted at that time that, despite a requirement that effective protection be afforded Community rights, interim relief was not available against the Crown: see section 21 of the Crown Proceedings Act 1947 in relation to civil proceedings, and see also *M* v *Home Office and Another* (1993).

Such non-availability (as a matter of domestic law) of an interlocutory injunction against the Crown or an officer of the Crown, together with serious doubts, following *Bourgoin*, as to any other than limited avenues to damages in tort against public authorities is the background against which to examine the claims at *national* level in the *Factortame* 'quota-hopping' affair, discussed earlier in this chapter in the section on the supervision of Member States at Community level: see Case C-246/89R *Commission* v *UK (Re Merchant Shipping Rules)*.

In the Divisional Court of the QBD, Factortame and the other members of the 'Anglo-Spanish' fishing fleet brought judicial review proceedings challenging the nationality (and other residence and domicile) requirements of the Merchant Shipping Act 1988 on the ground that, as in the case at Community level, they were in contravention of their directly effective Treaty rights, particularly their right of establishment under Article 52. This question was referred to the Court of Justice by the Divisional Court for a preliminary interpretive ruling under Article 177. As it would take perhaps two years for that ruling to be given and as in the meantime Factortame, not being able to fish against UK fishing quotas (or Spanish quotas either), claimed to be incurring heavy and irreparable financial loss, an application for interim relief pending final determination of the substantive issue was made to the court.

This application required the relevant section of the 1988 Act to be suspended to enable Factortame and the others to continue to operate their vessels as if duly registered as British ships. (It was also considered on the facts that in the light of *Bourgoin* no remedy in damages would be available.) On the basis of recent case law, the Divisional Court felt that it possessed the power in these circumstances to grant the application. This decision was reversed by the Court of Appeal, at which stage the Commission's application for interim relief under Article 186 with respect to the Act's nationality requirements was made and, as we have seen, was granted by the Court of Justice. Compliance was achieved by means of the Merchant Shipping Act 1988 (Amendment) Order 1989.

In the national courts, following a further appeal, the House of Lords held that, under *national* law, the English courts had no power to grant interim relief by way of an order suspending the operation of a statute pending a determination of its validity by the Court of Justice, nor had they the power to grant an interim injunction restraining the Secretary of State from enforcing the Act. Their Lordships, however, asked the Court for a preliminary ruling as to whether there was an overriding principle of Community law that a national court was under an obligation or had the power to provide an effective interlocutory remedy to protect directly effective rights where a seriously arguable claim to such rights had been advanced and irremediable loss was at stake.

Just over a year later, in June 1990, in response to this Article 177 reference, the Court, having drawn attention to the *Simmenthal* principle of the primacy of Community law and to the principle of co-operation in Article 5 EEC, designed to ensure the legal protection which persons derived from the direct effect of Community law, ruled that: Community law was to be interpreted as meaning that a national court which, in a case before it concerning Community law, considers that the sole obstacle precluding it from granting interim relief is a rule of national law, must set aside that rule: Case C-213/89 *R v Secretary of State for Transport, ex parte Factortame*.

Amid considerable controversy regarding what was perceived by some in the UK as an unacceptable intrusion on UK sovereignty, the House of Lords just a month later applied the Court's ruling. This was on the basis of the facts before it and pending final judgment by the Court of Justice on the validity of the 1988 Act in the face of Factortame's putative rights under the Treaty:

> *R v. Secretary of State for Transport, ex parte Factortame (No 2)* (1991)
> In July 1990, the House of Lords, using the powers established by the ruling of the Court of Justice, allowed Factortame's appeal and granted an interim injunction restraining the Government from withholding or withdrawing registration under the 1988 Act to named fishing vessels on grounds of residence or domicile abroad. (It will be recalled that the Act's nationality requirements had previously been suspended by an amendment to the Act following a ruling by the President of the Court of Justice, see above). The position was summed up by Lord Bridge as follows:

> 'If the supremacy within the European Community of Community law over the national law of Member States was not always inherent in the EEC Treaty it was certainly well-established in the jurisprudence of the European Court of Justice long before the UK joined the Community. Thus, whatever limitation of its sovereignty Parliament accepted when it enacted the European Communities Act 1972 it was entirely voluntary. Under the terms of the Act of 1972 it has always been clear that it was the duty of a UK court, when delivering final judgment, to override any rule of national law found to be in conflict with any directly enforceable rule of Community law'.

When considering its decision, the House of Lords had available to it unsworn evidence indicating that many of the owners of the 95 vessels involved (the 'Anglo-Spanish' fleet) had already suffered losses well in excess of £100,000 and that some feared imminent bankruptcy.

In reaching their unanimous decision, their Lordships took account of the two-stage guidelines for the exercise of the court's discretionary jurisdiction to grant interim injunctions as laid down by the House in *American Cyanamid* v *Ethicon* in 1975. Such jurisdiction concerns the power to grant an injunction where it is just or convenient on such terms and conditions as the court thinks fit: section 37 of the Supreme Court Act 1981. Their Lordships also considered that on the basis of the decision in *Bourgoin*, the applicants would be unable to recover damages from the Crown if the Act were ultimately found to be contrary to the Treaty (their being unable to establish wrongful conduct on the part of the Secretary of State). It was therefore agreed that an application for an interim injunction against the Crown should go directly to the second stage of consideration, regarding the balance of convenience, and need not pass through the first stage, regarding whether damages were an adequate remedy.

On the question of the balance of convenience (the balance of interests in Community law), it was stressed that matters of considerable weight had to be put in the balance to outweigh the desirability of enforcing, in the public interest, what was on its face the law of the land. Each case was to be considered in the light of the circumstances. There was no rule that it was necessary to show a prima facie case that the law was invalid; it was enough if the applicant could show that there was a serious case to be tried.

In this respect, it is noteworthy that in Case T-44/90 *La Cinq* v *Commission* the CFI annulled a Commission refusal to order interim measures (see also Case 792/79R *Camera Care* in Chapter Seventeen), stating that the complainant company need not show a clear and flagrant breach of the competition rules by another party, merely a prima facie case. On the question of damage to La Cinq if the interim measures were not ordered and the company had to await the outcome of the Commission's final decision, the Court stated that all the company's circumstances must be taken into account. Although the Court of Justice had held in Case 229/88R *Cargill* v *Commission* that damage is not serious and irreparable (a necessary requirement for the ordering of interim measures) if it is purely financial and can, if the complainant is successful in the main action, be fully recovered, La Cinq's position was that it ran the risk of going out of business altogether in the interim (cf. the position of Factortame and the others) and suffering serious and irreparable damage whatever the outcome of the final decision.

That the applicant in *Factortame* had a serious case to be tried was later confirmed by the Court of Justice in response to the original Article 177 reference from the Divisional Court of the QBD. The Court ruled that the nationality, residence and domicile requirements of the 1988 Act were contrary to Community law, in particular Article 52 concerning the applicant's directly effective right of establishment: Case C-221/89 *R* v *Secretary of State for Transport, ex parte Factortame*. As in the case brought by the Commission, the Court stated that the system of national quotas under the Common Fisheries Policy did not affect the decision. However, although introduced on sound, conservational grounds, the national quota system does appear to lie at the heart of this problem. Nonetheless, as Lord Bridge had stated earlier in these proceedings:

> ... it is common ground, that in so far as the applicants succeed before the ECJ in obtaining a ruling in support of the Community rights which they claim, those rights will prevail over the restrictions imposed on registration of British fishing vessels by Part II of the Act of 1988 and the Divisional Court will, in the final determination of the application for judicial review be obliged to make appropriate declarations to give effect to those rights.

As regards a further action for damages brought by Factortame and the other members of the 'Anglo-Spanish' fishing fleet against the British government, see the final part of this chapter.

Further difficulties have arisen in the UK regarding remedies despite the fact that the situation in question involved loss suffered as the result of a breach of an individual's directly effective rights and that damages to compensate for losses of the type in question were provided for under the relevant provisions of national law.

In Case 152/84 *Marshall* (see Chapters Eight and Thirteen), directly enforceable rights regarding equality in retirement ages were established on the basis of Article 5 of the Equal Treatment Directive. Miss Marshall's case then returned to the national industrial tribunal where the issue was solely that of the amount of compensation to be recovered from her employers. The problem which she faced was that section 65(2) of the Sex Discrimination Act 1975 laid down at that time a maximum award of £6,250. Seeing its duty as that of providing an *effective* remedy, Miss Marshall's claim having arisen some eight years earlier, the tribunal held that the limit laid down by Section 65(2) rendered the compensation (the only appropriate remedy) inadequate and in breach of Article 6 of the Directive (see below). It also awarded M £7,710 by way of interest, arguing that even if the 1975 Act did not allow it to do so (the relevant provisions may be said to be ambiguous), such a power existed under the Supreme Court Act 1981. The full award was £19,405. The AHA had already paid M £6,250 and paid her a further £5,445 but appealed against the award of interest.

Article 6 of the Equal Treatment Directive requires all Member States to introduce into their national legal systems 'such measures as are necessary to enable all persons who consider themselves wronged ... to pursue their claims by judicial process'. The tribunal had taken the view that such judicial process, as construed in *Von Colson* (see Chapter Thirteen), must include an adequate remedy, and that Miss Marshall, as an employee of the State, was entitled to rely on Article 6. The Employment Appeal Tribunal upheld the employer's appeal on the ground that Article 6 of the Directive had been held in *Von Colson* not to have direct effect. The case then proceeded to the Court of Appeal:

> *Marshall v. Southampton and S W Hampshire AHA (No. 2) (1990)*
> All three judges acknowledged the obligation based on Article 5 of the Treaty which, as developed by the Court of Justice in Von Colson, falls on national courts to interpret domestic law so as to ensure that the objectives of a Directive are fulfilled. (In *Von Colson* this meant that the German Court was required to interpret German law in such a way as to secure an effective remedy as required by Article 6 of the Equal Treatment Directive: the indirect effect solution).
>
> However, the appeal judges stressed that, while the statutory level of compensation did not provide an adequate and effective remedy as required by Article 6, the limitation imposed in Von Colson that a national court should interpret national law so as to comply with Community obligations only in so far as it is given a discretion to do so under national law applied in this case. The Court was not in a position to disregard the statutory ceiling on damages and the word 'damages' could not be construed to include interest.

A further appeal was made in *Marshall (No. 2)* to the House of Lords, where the case was made the subject of another reference to the Court of Justice under Article 177:

> Case C-271/91 *Marshall v Southampton and SW Hampshire AHA*
> *(No. 2)*
> The Court ruled that where financial compensation was the remedy adopted by a Member State in order to achieve the objective in Article 6 of the Directive (the restoration of equality of treatment when it had not been observed), such compensation had to be effective, as implied by Article 6. As such, the compensation had to enable the loss and damage actually sustained as the result of a discriminatory dismissal to be made good in full in accordance with the applicable national rules.

The fixing of an upper limit to compensation could not constitute proper implementation of Article 6, since it limited the amount of compensation *a priori* to a level which was not necessarily consistent with the requirement of ensuring real equality through adequate reparation. Neither could full compensation leave out of account factors, such as the effluxion of time, which might reduce its value. The award of interest, in accordance with the applicable national rules, was therefore to be regarded as an essential element of the compensation.

The importance of Article 6 in attaining the fundamental objective of the Directive was such that, combined with the basic right to equal treatment in Article 5, it gave rise, on the part of a person injured as a result of discriminatory dismissal, to rights which that person could rely upon in national courts against the State or an emanation thereof.

An individual could not be prevented from relying on Article 6 in a situation such as that in the main proceedings (ie in Case 152/84) where the State had no degree of discretion in applying *the chosen remedy.*

The Court's overriding consideration in this case was therefore to secure a compensatory remedy which guaranteed real and effective judicial protection and which had a real deterrent effect on employers. Miss Marshall's right to interest on the capital sum will have to be secured by a re-appraisal of the appropriate English law.

The Court of Justice also pointed out, by reference to its judgment in *Francovich*, that the right of a State to choose among several possible means of achieving the objectives of a Directive did not exclude the possibility for individuals of enforcing before national courts *rights whose content can be determined sufficiently precisely on the basis of the provisions of the Directive alone.* As seen in Chapter Eight, a Member State's liability under the *Francovich* principle, at least as regards its failure to take the steps necessary to achieve the result required by a Directive depends on the following conditions: (i) the result required by the Directive includes the conferring of rights for the benefit of individuals, (ii) the content of those rights is identifiable by reference to the Directive and (iii) a causal link exists between the breach of the State's obligations and the damage suffered by persons affected.

It will also be recalled that the *Francovich* principle does not only apply where, as in that case, due to its lack of precision, the Directive is *not* directly effective. The Court in *Francovich* stated that it was necessary to provide full protection of the rights of individuals, *in particular*, where those rights were conditional on the Member States taking certain action and where, as a result of a Member State's breach of Community law, such individuals were unable to rely on their Community rights. In other words, although the direct effect of Article 6 lay at the heart of Miss Marshall's success, it would appear that her case *also* met the three conditions necessary to establish a basis for the State's liability for damages under the *Francovich* principle.

However, the State's failure in *Marshall (No. 2)* was not the complete failure of the Italian State in *Francovich*. It was what Steiner (see Chapter Eight) characterised as 'a partial failure, where implementation measures have been adopted, but they are faulty or inadequate'. Her general conclusion was that 'States should not, in this context, be liable in the absence of fault'.

By placing a limit on the amount of compensation recoverable by a person discriminated against contrary to the terms of the Equal Treatment Directive, did the UK authorities bring themselves fully within the scope of the *Francovich* principle? Could liability on this basis have been established to render the Ministry of Agriculture, Fisheries and Food liable on the facts in *Bourgoin*? Or the Secretary of State for Transport in *Factortame*? Can inadequate implementation of a Directive be equated with the introduction of measures found to be in breach of Article 30 or with the amendment of a statute with the declared purpose of safeguarding national rights under the Common Fisheries Policy?

The rules regarding these issues vary considerably from one Member State to another. Further guidelines from the Court of Justice will no doubt be forthcoming. Harmonisation of such rules is not to be expected in the short term. In any event, national remedies will perforce continue to undergo a process of modification in order to meet the demands of Community law. Factortame and the other members of the 'Anglo–Spanish' fishing fleet are presently seeking damages against the British Government for breach of their directly effective rights. The High Court has referred questions on the scope and meaning of the *Francovich* decision to the Court of Justice.

Similarly, in *Brasserie du Pêcheur* v. *Germany* (1993), an action brought by a French company against the Federal Republic, the German Federal Court of Justice has referred a number of questions to the Court of Justice under Article 177 regarding its *Francovich* decision; in particular:

1. Does the principle of Community law according to which Member States are obliged to pay compensation for damage suffered by an individual as a result of infringements of Community law attributable to those States also apply where such an infringement consists of a failure to adapt a national parliamentary statute to the higher-ranking rules of Community law [this case concerning a failure to amend certain paragraphs of the German Law on Beer Duty to Article 30 EEC following the decision of the Court of Justice in Case 178/84 *Commission* v. *Germany (Re Beer Purity Laws)*, see Chapter Twelve.]

...

3. May the national legal system provide that any entitlement to compensation is to be conditional on fault (intent or negligence) on the part of the State officials responsible for the failure to adapt the legislation?

The answers to the questions referred in the 1993 *Factortame* and *Brasserie du Pêcheur* cases will take us further along the road towards defining the nature and scope of the Community law rights of individuals as the Court of Justice remodels the relationship between the individual and the State within the expanding sphere of Community competence.

Barav, A., 'Damages Against the State for Failure to Implement EC Directives', NLJ, 22 November 1991 (*Francovich*).

Barav, A., 'Enforcement of Community Rights in the National Courts: the Case for Jurisdiction to Grant an Interim Relief' (1989) 26 CML Rev. 369. (*Factortame*).

Barav, A., and Green, N., 'Damages in the National Courts for Breach of Community Law' (1986) 6 YEL 55.

Bebr, G., Case note on *Francovich* (1992) 29 CML Rev. 557.

Borchardt, G., 'The Award of Interim Measures by the European Court of Justice' (1985) 22 CML Rev. 203.

Bridge, J., 'Procedural Aspects of the Enforcement of European Community Law through the Legal Systems of the Member States' (1984) 9 EL Rev. 28.

Churchill, R.R., Case note on Factortame (1992) 29 CML Rev. 405.

Collins, L., *European Community Law in the United Kingdom*.

Craig, P., 'Supremacy of the UK Parliament after Factortame' (1991) 11 YEL 221.

Cripps, Y., 'European Rights, Invalid Actions and Denial of Damages' (1986) CLJ 165.

Curtin, D., 'Directives: The Effectiveness of Judicial Protection of Individual Rights' (1990) 27 CML Rev. 709.

Dashwood, A. and White, R., 'Enforcement Actions under Articles 169 and 170 EEC' (1989) 14 EL Rev. 388.

EC Commission's Sixth Report on the Monitoring and Application of Community Law (1989) OJ C 330.

Everling, U., 'The Member States of the European Community Before Their Court of Justice' (1984) 9 EL Rev. 215.

Gravells, N., 'Disapplying an Act of Parliament; Constitutional Enormity or Community Law Right?' (1989) PL 568 (*Factortame*).

Lewis, C. and Moore, S., 'Duties, Directives and Damages in European Community Law' (1993) PL 151.

Magliveras, K., 'Fishing in Troubled Waters: the Merchant Shipping Act 1988 and the EC' (1990) 39 ICLQ 899.

Oliver, P., 'Enforcing Community Rights in English Courts' (1987) 50 MLR 881.

Oliver, P., 'Interim Measures: Some Recent Developments' (1992) 29 CML Rev. 7.

Report of the Committee of the JUSTICE – All Souls Review of Administrative Law in the United Kingdom, Administrative Justice: Some Necessary Reforms (1988), particularly Chapter 11.

Steiner, J., 'How to Make the Action Fit the Case: Domestic Remedies for Breach of EEC Law' (1987) 12 EL Rev. 103.

Toth, A., Case note on *Factortame* (1990) 27 CML Rev. 573.

Wade, H.W.R., 'What Has Happened to the Sovereignty of Parliament?' (1991) 107 LQR 1.

Weatherill, S., 'National Remedies and Equal Access to Public Procurement' (1990) 10 YEL 243.

HOW TO FIND COMMUNITY LAW

THE TREATIES AND RELATED INSTRUMENTS

The Official Journal of the European Communities (OJ), published daily in all the official Community languages in Luxembourg by the Office for Official Publications of the European Communities (OOPEC), is the authoritative source of the texts of:

1. The three founding Treaties;
2. Amending Treaties such as the Merger Treaty 1965, the Single European Act 1986 (and the Maastricht Treaty on European Union, signed in 1992 but not yet in effect);
3. Documents concerning the accession of new Member States;
4. Agreements with non–Member States and international organisations.

For example:

The Accession of Spain and Portugal, OJ 1985 L302/1 (entire issue) 15.11.85.

The Single European Act, OJ 1987 L169/1 (entire issue) 29.6.87.

The Fourth ACP–EEC (Lomé) Convention, OJ 1991 L229/1 (entire issue) 17.8.91.

The Treaty on European Union (Maastricht), OJ 1992 C191/1 (entire issue) 29.7.92. A consolidated text of the EC Treaty as amended by the TEU is to be found at OJ 1992 C224/6.

N.B. 'L' denotes the Official Journal's *Legislation* series and 'C' the *Information and Notices* series (see below).

Consolidated editions are also published by OOPEC. The latest edition was published in 1987-88: *Treaties establishing the European Communities*. Volume I contains items 1 and 2 above (but not the Maastricht Treaty, which has been published *separately* by OOPEC); Volume II covers item 3. A shortened version, omitting many of the associated annexes and protocols, is also published. The latest edition, *Treaties establishing the European Communities: Abridged Edition*, was published in 1987.

All agreements between the EC and non-EC countries are to be found in a series called *Collection of the agreements concluded by the European Communities*, five volumes to 1975 plus annual supplements.

HM Stationery Office Editions of the Treaties are also available: ECSC Treaty 1951 (Amended text: Cmnd. 7461), EEC and Euratom Treaties 1957 (Amended text: Cmnd. 7460), the various Treaties concerning the accession of new Member States, the Single European Act 1986 (Cmnd. 9758), and the Maastricht Treaty on European Union 1992 (Cmnd. 1934).

All these publications are available in the UK from:

HMSO Books (PC 16)

HMSO Publications Centre

51 Nine Elms Lane

London SW8 5DR.

Tel. (071) 873 9090

Fax. GP3 873 8463

or in direct contact with:

Office for Official Publications of the European Communities

2, rue Mercier

L-2985 Luxembourg.

Tel. 499281

Fax 488573

Also legal and other bookshops.

Of particular value for students is Rudden and Wyatt's *Basic Community Laws*. The 1992 edition contains the following: Part I – the ECSC Treaty (extracts) and the EEC Treaty (neither as amended by the TEU) plus the Rules of Procedure of the Court of Justice, etc. Part II – a wide range of secondary legislation; Part III – UK Sources including the European Communities Act. Blackstone's *EEC Legislation* (ed. Nigel Foster), 1992, provides similar source material: the EEC Treaty and related documents, a selection of important secondary legislation, the Maastricht Treaty with various protocols, etc.)

Duffy and de Cara's *European Union: The Lawyers' Guide* (Longman, Student Edition, 1992) contains the full text of the Treaty on European Union, together with protocols and declarations. For Title II, Provisions amending the Treaty establishing the European Economic Community with a view to establishing the European Community, the Maastricht amendments are placed throughout below the Treaty of Rome provisions (as previously amended).

Annotated texts of the Treaties and of related Community instruments are to be found in *Halsbury's Statutes of England* (4th edn), 1989, Volume 50, with Supplements, and in Sweet and Maxwell's *Encyclopaedia of European Community Law*, 1992, Volumes B I – B IV, again with Supplements.

COMMUNITY ACTS

The official text of EC secondary legislation (EEC Regulations, Directives and Decisions and ESCS and Euratom measures) is contained in the 'L' series of the *Official Journal*.

The OJ is published every working day in each of the official languages of the Community. An English edition has appeared since 9 October 1972 and English texts of pre-accession secondary legislation is to be found in *Special Editions of the Official Journal of the European Communities* 1952-72.

The formal citation of an EC legislative act is made up as follows:

1. Institutional origin (Council or Commission);
2. The form of the act (Regulation, Directive, Decision, etc);
3. The act's number;
4. Year of enactment;
5. The treaty basis;
6. The date the act was passed.

However, the sequence of these elements may vary. For example:

Council Regulation (EEC) 4064/89 of 21 December 1989 on the control of concentrations between undertakings: see OJ 1990 L257/14.

91/250/EEC Council Directive of 14 May 1991 on the legal protection of computer programs: see OJ 1991 L122/42.

89/469/EEC Commission Decision of 28 July 1989 concerning protection measures relating to bovine spongiform encephalopathy in the United Kingdom: see OJ 1989 L 225/51.

In each issue of the 'L' series of the OJ, the texts of enacted legislation are divided into two categories:

1. Acts whose publication is obligatory (eg EEC Regulations).
2. Acts whose publication is not obligatory (eg EEC Directives and Decisions, Opinions and Recommendations).

In practice the text of all secondary (and primary) legislation appears in the OJ. A great many EC legislative acts deal with day-to-day agricultural and customs union matters and are valid only for a limited period of time.

The *Index to the Official Journal* is published monthly with an annual cumulation. It has two parts:

1. *Methodological tables* which list, with their OJ reference, all the legislative acts for the period in numerical order (plus the cases brought and the judgments of the Court of Justice).

2. *Alphabetical index* of which it can be said that, bearing in mind the immense scope of Community legislation, it is now relatively user-friendly. The index is subject-led.

The *Directory of Community legislation in force and other acts of Community institutions* dates from 1980 and has since 1987 been published twice a year, stating the position as on 1 June and 1 December. Volume 1 of the *Directory* (the Analytical Register) consists of seventeen chapters broken down into policy areas, further subdivided according to listed legislative acts. Volume 2 contains a chronological and alphabetical index. (Read the introductory 'Information for Readers' for help in using the Directory).

Annotated texts of Community secondary legislation can be found in Sweet and Maxwell's *Encyclopaedia of European Community Law*, 1992, Volumes C I – C IV.

OTHER OFFICIAL JOURNAL INFORMATION

Apart from the 'L' series, the *Official Journal* also contains a `C' series (*Information and Notices*), an `S' series (*Supplement*) and an *Annex* (containing the full text of debates held in the European Parliament and oral questions submitted).

The `C' series consists of a wide range of institutional information, in particular from:

1. *Commission*: the text of proposed legislation, details of EC funded research projects, membership of EC organisations and committees, etc.

2. *Council*: miscellaneous Decisions, Assents and Resolutions, etc.

3. *European Parliament*: minutes of plenary sessions, texts of EP resolutions, written questions to the EP, etc.

4. *Economic and Social Committee*: its Opinions, etc.

5. *Court of Justice*: lists of new actions brought, orders and judgments delivered (in brief).

6. *Court of Auditors*: annual report and replies of the institutions; other special reports.

The contents of each issue are listed on the front cover – in two parts: (1) Information (by institution), (2) Preparatory acts. Employment opportunities are also to be found in the 'C' series.

The 'S' series of the OJ contains details of supply and works contracts placed by public authorities within the Community. (Directives require notice to be given to all potential tenderers for such contracts and they also require Member States not to discriminate in favour of 'home' contractors as regards their public procurement requirements.)

COM DOCS

COM documents are issued by the Commission and primarily provide the texts of legislative proposals and explanatory memoranda. (The texts can also be found in the OJ 'C' series, see above.) They also contain a variety of Commission reports and communications. For example:

COM(87)203 final (Brussels, 11 May 1987) Second Report from the Commission to the Council and the European Parliament on the Implementation of the Commission's White Paper on completing the internal market.

COM(89)411 final (Brussels, 21 December 1989) Sixth Annual Report to the European Parliament on Commission Monitoring of the Application of Community Law 1988.

COM(91)530 FINAL (Brussels, 5 December 1991) Amended proposal for a COUNCIL DIRECTIVE on the adoption of standards for satellite broadcasting of television signals.

COMMUNITY CASE LAW

The judgments and opinions of the Court of Justice (together with the opinions of the Advocates General) are published in periodical parts by the Court in each of the official languages of the Community. The version in the procedural language of the case in question is the only authentic version.

The English version, the *European Court Reports* (ECR), has been published since 1973. Pre-accession reports (1953-72) are available in French or in English translation. Decisions of the Court of First Instance are reported from 1990. These decisions are prefixed by the letter 'T'; Court of Justice decisions now being prefixed by the letter 'C'. For example:

Case C-208/88 *Commission* v. *Denmark* [1990] ECR I-4445.

(The suffix 'P' (pourvoi) after the number of a case denotes a decision of the Court of Justice on appeal from the CFI.)

Case T-116/89 *Prodiforma* v. *Commission* [1990] ECR II – 843.

The *Common Market Law Reports* have been published by the European Law Centre at Sweet and Maxwell's since 1962. They contain translations of judgments of the Court of Justice, Commission decisions on restrictive practices and decisions of courts and tribunals of the Member States on points of Community Law. An *Antitrust Supplement* has been produced since 1988, reporting competition cases and related matters.

Cases in the United Kingdom courts with a Community dimension (and which may or may not have given rise to a reference to the Court of Justice) may also have been reported in the Law Reports, the All England Reports or, for example, the Industrial Court Reports.

OOPEC publishes at regular intervals an unofficial synopsis of the work of the Court of Justice, eg *Synopsis of the Work of the Court of Justice and the Court of First Instance of the European Communities in 1988 and 1989 and record of formal sittings in 1988 and 1989.*

SUBSIDIARY SOURCES

Out of the mass of material emanating from the Community institutions, the following are particularly important:

Commission: General Report of the Activities of the European Communities (annual).

Commission: Bulletin of the European Communities (monthly).

Commission: Report on Competition Policy (annual) with Special Supplements.

Commission: The Courier (ACP-EC) (6 times a year).

Council: Review of the Council's Work (annual).

JOURNALS, ETC.

The three English language journals devoted to Community law matters generally and containing articles and case notes, etc, across the spectrum are:

Common Market Law Review (1963/1964 – date).

European Law Review (1975/1976 – date).

Legal Issues of European Integration (1974 – date).

Specialist journals include:

European Competition Law Review.

European Intellectual Property Law Review.

European Taxation.

The *Yearbook of European Law* (1980 – date) is devoted mainly to Community law matters. Articles on Community law topics can also be found in the *British Yearbook of International Law*, the *International and Comparative Law Quarterly* and other leading law journals (*Law Quarterly Review, Cambridge Law Journal, Modern Law Review, Public Law, Journal of Business Law*, etc.)

Attention should also be drawn to the valuable *Journal of Common Market Studies* (1962–date) which covers political, economic and legal matters, and the bimonthly *European Access* which provides a first-class updating service.

Short, topical articles and case notes are to be found in the European Community Law section of the *Student Law Review* (published three times a year by Cavendish Publishing; free to students).

Regular coverage of Community affairs appears in the 'quality' press in the UK. The most comprehensive range can be found in the *Financial Times*. *The Times* contains *European Law Reports* of important decisions of the Court of Justice in addition to its feature articles and news reports.

All these materials (and many others) are, or should be, available in University libraries in their European Documentation Centre (EDC) or European Reference Centre (ERC) sections.

INFORMATION AVAILABLE IN ELECTRONIC MEDIA

Community law information is available direct to a computer terminal via modem link or CD-ROM. Enquire in your EDC or ERC for precise details.

The main sources are:

Celex – the main database on Community law, covering the original establishing treaties, legislation, case histories from the Court of Justice, proposals and Parliamentary questions. The system is subject led, providing quick reference to specific topics.

Abel – a daily reference and order service for the L Series of the Official Journal; consultation by on-line system enables the user to identify the information of interest and to order the relevant pages of the Official Journal, which are then despatched by telefax or mail.

Scad – a broad source of information on Community law and other information relating to the activities of the Community. Compiled both from official sources and external publications.

INFO 92 – a structured guide to the completion of the internal market, covering recent developments and previewing action in the near future; this guide is constructed to allow rapid progress through menus to reach the required information in any subject area.

Directory of EEC Information Sources (Euroconfidential, published annually).

Hitzler, Gerhard (ed), *Directory of European Institutions* (1991).

Martens, Hans, *EC Direct: A Comprehensive Directory of EC Contacts* (1992).

Recent Publications on the European Communities (OOPEC, monthly).

Thomson, Ian, *The Documentation of the European Communities: A Guide* (1989).

Yearbook of the European Communities and of other European Institutions (Editions Delta, published annually).

INDEX

INDEX

INDEX

INDEX

INDEX

INDEX